Database Programming
with C#

CARSTEN THOMSEN

Database Programming with C#

ISBN (pbk): 1-59059-010-4

Printed and bound in the United States of America 12345678910

Technical Reviewer: Douglas Milnes

Editorial Directors: Dan Appleman, Peter Blackburn, Gary Cornell, Jason Gilmore, Karen Watterson, John Zukowski

Managing Editor: Grace Wong

Copy Editors: Nicole LeClerc, Ami Knox

Production Editor: Tory McLearn

Compositor: Impressions Book and Journal Services, Inc.

Indexer: Valerie Haynes Perry

Cover Designer: Tom Debolski

Marketing Manager: Stephanie Rodriguez

Distributed to the book trade in the United States by Springer-Verlag New York, Inc., 175 Fifth Avenue, New York, NY, 10010 and outside the United States by Springer-Verlag GmbH & Co. KG, Tiergartenstr. 17, 69112 Heidelberg, Germany.

In the United States, phone 1-800-SPRINGER, email orders@springer-ny.com, or visit http://www.springer-ny.com.

Outside the United States, fax +49 6221 345229, email orders@springer.de, or visit http://www.springer.de.

For information on translations, please contact Apress directly at 2560 9th Street, Suite 219, Berkeley, CA 94710.

Email info@apress.com or visit http://www.apress.com.

The source code for this book is available to readers at http://www.apress.com in the Downloads section.

You will need to answer questions pertaining to this book in order to successfully download the code.

Contents at a Glance

Contents

Foreword

No matter what application you're building, there's no escape from dealing with data and, subsequently, with databases. While new technologies can make our lives easier, they're built with one thing in mind: to keep data at our fingertips.

The same goes for .NET, the new generation of Microsoft technology that promises to make data interchange easier and more flexible, even across disparate systems. .NET comes with a whole set of data-handling tools that will give developers more choices when they build applications.

Carsten's book is a wonderful introduction to all these choices, some of which even I did not give a second thought to before reading the book. Because problems in real-life applications demand different solutions, it is important for every developer to understand these different solutions. Not only will this make developers more productive, but it will also make them more marketable.

Moreover, I believe, by covering topics such as hierarchical databases, Message Queuing, and SQLXML, Carsten shows his expertise in the area of data handling within the .NET Framework, which goes beyond the ADO.NET coverage you see in most other books. Being a Microsoft MVP, Carsten often interacts with people to solve their day-to-day problems, and the same conduct continues in his book. So, when I was asked to review this book and write the foreword, I was more than happy to oblige.

I hope this book opens your mind to the new possibilities within .NET. I'm sure you'll appreciate Carsten's efforts to make learning data access with .NET easy.

Manohar Kamath
Microsoft MVP and .netBooks Editor, (http://www.dotnetbooks.com)
March 2002

About the Author

 **Carsten Thomsen** is a Microsoft MVP, recognition he received in August 1999. He lives in his native Denmark and currently holds the MCSE and MCSD certifications. Carsten has been programming in Visual Basic for almost 10 years, and he specializes in data access. With the advent of VB .NET and, more important, VS .NET, Carsten now focuses on data access using C# and VB .NET.

Carsten and his girlfriend Mia live in Esbjerg, Denmark. They have a 2-year-old daughter, Caroline, and are currently expecting a second child. Nicole, 7, is Carsten's oldest daughter and she lives with her mother in Dublin, Ireland. Carsten enjoys traveling to Dublin several times a year to spend time with Nicole.

About the Technical Reviewer

 **Douglas Milnes** is a freelance computer consultant who has been running his own consultancy and application development business since 1984. He lives in the heart of the United Kingdom's "Silicon Valley" near Reading, Berkshire, England. He has consulted for major companies such as IBM and Oracle and is a lead consultant with both DeeSoft (http://www.deesoft.net) and Boost Data (http://www.boost.net/Douglas).

Douglas started with computing at the beginning of the microcomputer boom and opened a pioneering retail business in the days before the IBM PC was launched. After disposing of that business, he worked for a range of companies implementing PC and UNIX systems. His specialty was accounting applications, which led him into stock control applications and his first "real" database exposure.

Douglas owns up to a wide experience in the computing world, admitting to being one of those programmers who carries a screwdriver with him. He has worked with DGE, DEC, IBM, and ICL minis and mainframes, but he's spent most of the last few years around PCs, linking to larger machines where necessary. Like any programmer who's been around for a time, he works on desktop computers these days that vastly outpower the multiuser minicomputers he learned about databases on.

Douglas has extensive experience with several programming languages, including Assembler, RPG, Visual Basic and, of course, C#. Tending to keep up with the times and being at the leading edge of technology, he has been involved with .NET since the beta pre-releases were available.

With his two children, Daniel, 12, and Rebecca, 15, and his beautiful wife, Douglas counts his blessings and enjoys a varied life. Douglas can be contacted by e-mail at Douglas@DeeSoft.net.

Acknowledgments

This book, which is based on my first book *Database Programming with VB .NET*, was somewhat easier for me to write than the first one. Having been through all the processes once before, I knew what to expect and how to plan accordingly. Obviously, a lot of the material in this book is taken from the first book, but a number of changes have been made, especially to correct the typos and more grave errors, and I've managed to add a lot more content to the book.

I couldn't have written this without Technical Reviewer Douglas Milnes, who proved to be extremely valuable for content of this book. Douglas found some of the mistakes that I made, but he also brought a number of excellent ideas to my attention, on how to arrange the book and on "sticking in" extra or just missing sections. My editor this time around was Peter Blackburn. I can't really say that we started off on the right foot (which was also the case with Douglas) but we sure as h*** made up for it along the way. Peter has an "annoying" habit of contacting me day and night on MSN Messenger, so we were always in close contact about the book, the whole process, and just about everything else. What I am getting at here, is that it truly has been an excellent partnership, not just with Peter and Douglas, but also with the rest of the crew: Grace, Nicole, Alexa, Ami, and Tory.

Carsten, carstent@dotnetservices.biz
Esbjerg, Denmark
March 2002

Introduction

THIS BOOK IS ALL ABOUT ACCESSING DATABASES of various kinds, such as Active Directory, SQL Server 2000, Exchange Server 2000, and Message Queuing. My intention with this book is to give you insight into how ADO.NET works and how you can use the classes from ADO.NET to access a database; use stored procedures, views, and triggers; get information from Active Directory and Exchange Server; and use Message Queuing in your applications. Having said that, my goal was to make the book as easy to read as possible, and although there are passages that aren't quite as easy to read as I'd like them to be, I think I've managed to accomplish what I set out to do.

Who This Book Is For

This book is targeted at intermediate users, meaning users who already know a little about Visual Studio .NET and perhaps previous versions of Visual Basic. Basic knowledge of Object Oriented Programming (OOP), ADO, and database design is also assumed. Parts of the book are at a beginner level and other parts are at a more advanced level. The beginner-level material appears where I feel it is appropriate to make sure you really understand what is being explained. The many listings and tables make this a good reference book, but it's also a book intended for reading cover to cover. It will take you through all the data access aspects of Visual Studio .NET with example code in C#. This includes how to create the various database items, such as databases, tables, constraints, database projects, stored procedures, views, triggers and so on. For the most part, I show you how to do this from within the VS .NET IDE as well as programmatically where possible. You'll build on the same example code from the beginning of the book until you wrap it up in the very last chapter. The example application, UserMan, is a complete user management system that includes SQL Server, Active Directory, and Message Queuing.

How This Book Is Organized

This book is organized in four parts:

Part One is a general introduction to Visual Studio .NET and the .NET Framework.

Part Two is the juicy part, where you take a look at how to connect to relational and hierarchical databases. You will also learn how to wrap your database access in classes and how to master exception handling. Part Two starts with a look at how to design a relational database, and you gradually learn the building blocks for the UserMan example application.

Part Three is where you finish the UserMan example application.

Appendix A covers how to use the SQLXML plug-in for manipulating SQL Server 2000 data using XML from managed code or using HTTP.

Technology Requirements

From the example code you can connect to SQL Server using any of these three .NET Data Providers: SQL Server .NET Data Provider, OLE DB .NET Data Provider, or ODBC .NET Data Provider. The example code also includes how to connect to and manipulate data in MySQL 3.23.45 or later, Oracle 8i or later, Microsoft Access 2000 or later, and SQL Server. For connecting to SQL Server 2000, you can find coverage of the SQLXML plug-in for manipulating SQL Server data using XML from managed code or using HTTP. Exchange Server 2000 connection and data manipulation is also covered.

Because I'm using some of the Enterprise functionality of Visual Studio .NET, you'll need either of the two Enterprise editions to follow all the exercises. However, the Professional edition will do for most of the example code, and it will certainly do if you just want to see how everything is done while you learn ADO.NET. This means that the only thing extra you get from the Enterprise editions in terms of database access is an extra set of database tools to be used from within the IDE.

Example Code

All the example code for this book can be found on the Apress Web site (http://www.apress.com) in the Downloads section, or on the UserMan Web site (http://www.userman.dk).

Data Source

The data source for the example code in this book is running on SQL Server 2000. However, the example code also includes how to connect to and manipulate data in MySQL 3.23.45 or later, Oracle 8i or later, Microsoft Access 2000 or later, and SQL Server.

Feedback

I can be reached at carstent@dotnetservices.biz and I'll gladly answer any e-mail concerning this book. Now, I don't need any unnecessary grief, but I'll try to respond to any queries you might have regarding this book.

I have set up a Web site for the UserMan example application, where you can post and retrieve ideas on how to take it further. The Web site address is http://www.userman.dk. Please check it out.

Part One

Getting Started

CHAPTER 1

A Lightning-Quick Introduction to C#

THE .NET FRAMEWORK IS AN ENVIRONMENT for building, deploying, and running services and other applications. This environment is all about code reuse and specialization, multilanguage development, deployment, administration, and security. The .NET Framework will lead to a new generation of software that melds computing and communication in a way that allows the developer to create truly distributed applications that integrate and collaborate with other complementary services. In other words, you now have the opportunity to create Web services, such as search engines and mortgage calculators, that will help transform the Internet as we know it today. No longer will it be about individual Web sites or connected devices; it's now a question of computers and devices, such as handheld computers, wristwatches, and mobile phones, collaborating with each other and thus creating rich services. As an example, imagine calling a search engine to run a search and then displaying and manipulating the results of the search in your own application.

There are rumors that the .NET Framework is solely for building Web sites, but this is not true. You can just as easily create your good old-fashioned Windows applications with the .NET Framework. The .NET Framework is actually more or less what would have been called COM+ 2.0 if Microsoft had not changed its naming conventions. Granted, the .NET Framework is now a far cry from COM+, but initially the development did start from the basis of COM+. I guess not naming it COM+ 2.0 was the right move after all.

This book is based on the assumption that you already know about the .NET Framework. However, this chapter provides a quick run-through of .NET concepts and terms. Although the terms are not specific to C#, but rather are relevant to all .NET programming languages, you'll need to know them if you're serious about using C# for all your enterprise programming.

Reviewing Programming Concepts

The .NET environment introduces some programming concepts that will be new even to those who are familiar with a previous version of a Windows programming language, such as Visual Basic or Visual C++. In fact, these concepts will be new to most Windows developers because the .NET programming tools, such as C#, are geared toward enterprise development in the context of Web-centric applications. This does not mean the days of Windows platform–only development is gone, but .NET requires you to change the way you think about Windows programming. The good old Registry is "gone"—that is, it's no longer used for registering your type libraries in the form of ActiveX/COM servers. Components of .NET Framework are self-describing; all information about referenced components, and so on, are part of the component in the form of metadata.

Visual Studio .NET is based on the Microsoft .NET Framework, which obviously means that the C# programming language is as well. C# is part of the Visual Studio .NET package and it's just one of the programming languages that Microsoft ships for the .NET platform.

At first some of these new terms and concepts seem a bit daunting, but they really aren't that difficult. If you need to refresh your memory regarding .NET programming concepts and the .NET Framework, simply keep reading, because this chapter is indeed a very quick review of these basics.

A Quick Look at Components of the .NET Framework

The .NET Framework adheres to the common type system (CTS) for data exchange and the Common Language Specification (CLS) for language interoperability. In short, three main parts make up the .NET Framework:

- Active Server Pages.NET (ASP.NET)

- Common language runtime (CLR)

- .NET Framework class library (the base classes)

The .NET Framework consists of these additional components:

- Assemblies

- Namespaces

- Managed components

- Common type system (CTS)

- Microsoft intermediate language (MSIL)

- Just-In-Time (JIT)

I discuss all of these components in the following sections.

Active Server Pages.NET

Active Server Pages.NET is an evolution of Active Server Pages (ASP) into so-called managed space, or rather managed code execution (see the sections "Common Language Runtime" and "Managed Data" later in this chapter). ASP.NET is a framework for building server-based Web applications. ASP.NET pages generally separate the presentation (HTML) from the logic/code. This means that the HTML is placed in a text file with an .aspx extension and the code is placed in a text file with a .cs extension (when you implement your application logic/code in C#, that is).

ASP.NET is largely syntax compatible with ASP, which allows you to port most of your existing ASP code to the .NET Framework and then upgrade the ASP files one by one. ASP.NET has different programming models that you can mix in any way. The programming models are as follows:

- *Web Forms* allow you to build Web pages using a forms-based UI. These forms are quite similar to the forms used in previous versions of Visual Basic. This also means that you have proper event and exception handling, unlike in ASP, where event and especially exception handling is a difficult task to manage.

- *XML Web services* are a clever way of exposing and accessing functionality on remote servers. XML Web services are based on the Simple Object Access Protocol (SOAP), which is a firewall-friendly protocol based on XML. SOAP uses the HTTP protocol to work across the Internet. XML Web services can also be invoked using the HTTP GET method simply by browsing to the Web service and the HTTP POST method.

- *Standard HTML* allows you to create your pages as standard HTML version 3.2 or 4.0.

Common Type System

The .NET environment is based on the common type system (CTS), which means that all .NET languages share the same data types. This truly makes it easy to exchange data between different programming languages. It doesn't matter if you exchange data directly in your source code (for example, inheriting classes created in a different programming language) or use Web services or COM+ components. CTS is built into the common language runtime (CLR). Have you ever had a problem exchanging dates with other applications? If so, I'm sure you know how valuable it is to have the CTS to establish the correct format. You don't have to worry about the format being, say, DD-MM-YYYY; you simply need to pass a **DateTime** data type.

Common Language Specification

The Common Language Specification (CLS) is a set of conventions used for promoting language interoperability. This means that the various programming languages developed for the .NET platform must conform to the CLS in order to make sure that objects developed in different programming languages can actually talk to each other. This includes exposing only those features and data types that are CLS compliant. Internally, your objects, data types, and features can be different from the ones in the CLS, as long as the exported methods, procedures, and data types are CLS compliant. So in other words, the CLS is really nothing more than a standard for language interoperability used in the .NET Framework.

Common Language Runtime

The common language runtime (CLR) is the runtime environment provided by the .NET Framework. The CLR's job is to manage code execution, hence the term *managed code*. The compilers for C# and Visual Basic .NET both produce managed code, whereas the Visual C++ compiler by default produces unmanaged code. By *unmanaged code*, I mean code for the Windows platform like that produced by the compilers for the previous versions of Visual C++. You can, however, use the managed code extensions for Visual C++ for creating managed code from within Visual C++.

Implications for JScript

Does the appearance of .NET and the CLR mean the end of JScript? Well, not quite. If you are referring to server-side development in the new compiled JScript language, I guess it's up to the developer. JScript as it is known today (i.e., client-side code execution) will continue to exist, largely because of its all-browser adoption. But if the CLR is ported to enough platforms and supported by enough software vendors, it might well stand a good chance of competing with the Virtual Machine for executing Java applets. Microsoft now also has a programming language called J#, which comes with upgrade tools for Visual J++ 6.0. You're reading this book because you like C#, Microsoft's Java-killer, but you might want to also check out J#, especially if you've crossed over from the Java camp (at least just to make sure you've made the right choice).

VBScript, VBA, and VSA

Okay, what about VBScript and Visual Basic for Applications (VBA)? This is obviously another issue that relates to the introduction of VB .NET, the other major .NET programming language. A new version of VBA, Visual Studio for Applications (VSA), is available for customizing and extending the functionality of your Web-based applications. VSA is built with a language-neutral architecture, but the first version only comes with support for one programming language, Visual Basic .NET. However, later versions will support other .NET languages such as C#.

Built-in CLR Tasks

The CLR performs the following built-in tasks:

- Managing data

- Performing automatic garbage collection

- Sharing a common base for source code

- Compiling code to the Microsoft intermediate language (MSIL)

I discuss these features in the next few sections.

Managed Data

The .NET Framework compilers mainly produce managed code, which is managed by the CLR. Managed code means managed data, which in turn means data with lifetimes managed by the CLR. This is also referred to as *garbage collection,* which you can read about in the next section. Managed data will definitely help eliminate memory leaks, but at the same time it also means you have less control over your data, because you no longer have deterministic finalization, which is arguably one of the strengths of COM(+).

Automatic Garbage Collection

When objects are managed (allocated and released) by the CLR, you don't have full control over them. The CLR handles the object layout and the references to the objects, disposing of the objects when they're no longer being used. This process is called *automatic garbage collection*. This process is very different from the one for handling objects in previous versions of Visual Basic or Visual C++ known as *deterministic finalization*. These programming languages used COM as their component model and, as such, they used the COM model for referencing and counting objects. As a result, whenever your application instantiated an object, a counter for this object reference was incremented by one, and when your application destroyed the object reference or when it went out of scope, the counter was decremented. When the counter hit zero, the object would be released automatically from memory. This is something you have to be very aware of now, because you no longer have full control over your object references. If you're a Java programmer, you probably already know about this.

Source Code Shares Common Base

Because all the CLR-compliant compilers produce managed code, the source code shares the same base—that is, the type system (CTS) and to some extent the language specification (CLS). This means you can inherit classes written in a language other than the one you're using, a concept known as *cross-language inheritance*. This is a great benefit to larger development teams, where the developers' skill sets are likely rather different. Another major benefit is when you need to debug—you can now safely debug within the same environment source code across various programming languages.

Intermediate Language Compilation

When you compile your code, it's compiled to what is called Microsoft intermediate language (MSIL) and stored in a portable executable (PE) file along with metadata that describes the types (classes, interfaces, and value types) used in the code. Because the compiled code is in an "intermediate state," the code is platform independent. This means the MSIL code can be executed on any platform that has the CLR installed. The metadata that exists in the PE file along with the MSIL enables your code to describe itself, which means there is no need for type libraries or Interface Definition Language (IDL) files. The CLR locates the metadata in the PE file and extracts it from there as necessary when the file is executed.

At runtime, the CLR's JIT compilers convert the MSIL code to machine code, which is then executed. This machine code is obviously appropriate for the platform on which the CLR is installed. The JIT compilers and the CLR are made by various vendors, and I suppose the most notable one is Microsoft's Windows CLR (surprise, eh?).

JIT: Another Word for Virtual Machine?

I believe we've all heard about the virtual machine used by Java applets. In short, the CLR's JIT compiler is the same as a virtual machine in the sense that it executes intermediate code and as such is platform independent. However, there is more to the way the CLR's JIT compiler handles the code execution than the way the so-called virtual machine does. The JIT compiler is dynamic, meaning that although it's made for a specific OS, it will detect and act upon the hardware layer at execution time.

The JIT compiler can optimize the code for the specific processor that's used on the system where the code is being executed. This means that once the JIT compiler detects the CPU, it can optimize the code for that particular CPU. For instance, instead of just optimizing code for the Pentium processor, the compiler can also optimize for a particular version of the Pentium processor, such as the Pentium IV. This is good, and although the current execution of managed code is somewhat slower than unmanaged code, we're probably not far from the point in time when managed code will execute faster than unmanaged code.

Another major difference between the Java Virtual Machine and the CLR is that whereas the former is invoked for every new process/application, this is not true for the latter.

Assemblies and Namespaces

The .NET Framework uses assemblies and namespaces for grouping related functionality, and you have to know what an assembly and a namespace really are. You could certainly develop some simple .NET applications without really understanding assemblies and namespaces, but you wouldn't get too far.

Assemblies

An *assembly* is the primary building block for a .NET Framework application, and it's a fundamental part of the runtime. All applications that use the CLR must consist of one or more assemblies. Each assembly provides the CLR with all the necessary information for an application to run. Please note that an application can be and often is made up of more than one assembly—that is, an assembly is not a unit of application deployment. You can think of an assembly in terms of classes in a DLL.

Although I refer to an assembly as a single entity, it might in fact be composed of several files. It is a logical collection of functionality that's deployed as a single unit (even if it's more than one file). This has to do with the way an assembly is put together. Think of an assembly in terms of a type library and the information you find in one. However, an assembly also contains information about everything else that makes up your application and is therefore said to be self-describing.

Because an assembly is self-describing by means of an assembly manifest, you won't have to deal anymore with shared DLLs in your application and the problems they have created over the years since Windows came of age. However, because you no longer use shared DLLs, your code will take up more memory and disk space, as the same functionality can now be easily duplicated on your hard disk and in memory. It is possible to share assemblies to get around this.

Actually, you can still use COM+ services (DLLs and EXEs) from within the .NET Framework, and you can even add .NET Framework components to a COM+ application. However, this book concentrates on using .NET Framework components.

As I touched upon previously, an assembly contains a *manifest,* which is little more than an index of all the files that make up the assembly. The assembly manifest is also called the assembly's metadata. (As mentioned earlier, *metadata* is data used to describe the main data.) Within the manifest, you have the components listed in Table 1-1.

Table 1-1. Assembly Manifest Components

ITEM	DESCRIPTION
Identity	Name, version, shared name, and digital signature
Culture, Processor, OS	The various cultures, processors, and OSs supported
File Table	Hash and relative path of all other files that are part of the assembly
Referenced Assemblies	A list of all external dependencies (i.e., other assemblies statically referenced)
Type Reference	Information on how to map a type reference to a file containing the declaration and implementation
Permissions	The permissions your assembly requests from the runtime environment in order to run effectively

Besides the assembly manifest components, a developer can also add custom assembly attributes. These information-only attributes can include the title and description of the assembly. The assembly manifest can be edited through the AssemblyInfo.cs file that is automatically created when you create a new project on the VS .NET IDE, as shown in Figure 1-1.

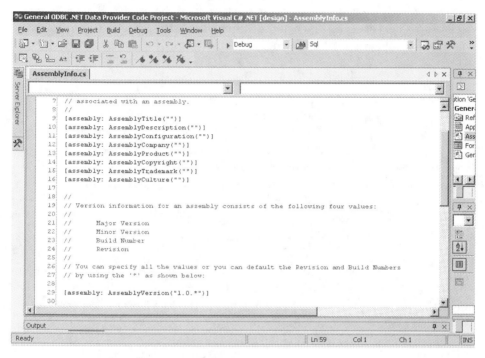

Figure 1-1. The AssemblyInfo.cs manifest file

In Figure 1-1, you can see the parts of the AssemblyInfo.cs manifest file that concern title, description, configuration, version information, and so on.

Namespaces

A *namespace* is a logical way to group or organize related types (classes, interfaces, or value types). A .NET namespace is a design-time convenience only, which is used for logical naming/grouping. At runtime it's the assembly that establishes the name scope.

The various .NET Framework types are named according to a hierarchical naming scheme with a dot syntax. Because the naming scheme is hierarchical, there is also a root namespace. The .NET root namespace is called **System**. To illustrate the naming scheme, for the second-level namespace **Timers** in the **System** namespace, the full name is **System.Timers**. In code, you would include the following to use types within the **System.Timers** namespace:

```
using System.Timers;
```

This would give you easy access to the types within that namespace. So to declare an object as an instance of the **Timer** class in the **System.Timers** namespace, you would enter the following:

```
Timer tmrTest = new Timer();
```

When the compiler encounters this declaration statement, it looks for the **Timer** class within your assembly, but when that fails, it appends **System.Timers.** to the **Timer** class to see if it can find the **Timer** class in that namespace. However, you can also directly prefix the class with the namespace. So, to declare an object as an instance of the **Timer** class in the **System.Timer** namespace, you would enter the following:

```
System.Timers.Timer tmrTest = new System.Timers.Timer();
```

As you can see, using the **using** statement can save you a fair bit of typing. I believe it will also make your code easier to read and maintain if you have all your **using** statements at the top of your class or module file. One look and you know what namespaces are being used.

A namespace is created using the following syntax:

```
namespace <NsName> {
}
```

where *<NsName>* is the name you want to give to your namespace. All types that are to be part of the namespace must be placed within the namespace block {}.

You need namespaces to help prevent ambiguity, which is also known as *namespace pollution*. This happens when two different libraries contain the same names, causing a conflict. Namespaces help you eliminate this problem.

If two namespaces actually do have the same class, and you reference this class, the compiler simply won't compile your code, because the class definition is ambiguous and the compiler won't know which one to choose. Say that you have two namespaces, Test1 and Test2, which both implement the class Show. You need to reference the Show class of the Test2 namespace and other classes within both the two namespaces, so you use the **using** statement:

```
using Test1;
using Test2;
```

Now, what happens when you create an object as an instance of the Show class within the same class or code file as the **using** statements, as follows:

```
Show Test = new Show;
```

Well, as I stated before, the compiler simply won't compile your code, because the Show class is ambiguous. It's only a warning and you can choose to continue to build your application, but any references to Show will be left out and will *not* be part of the compiled application. What you need to do in this case is this:

```
Test2.Show Test = new Test2.Show;
```

Namespaces can span more than one assembly, making it possible for two or more developers to work on different assemblies but create classes within the same namespace. Namespaces within the current assembly are accessible at all times; you do not have to import them.

> **NOTE** *Namespaces are explicitly public, and you cannot change that by using an access modifier such as **private**. However, you have full control over the accessibility of the types within the namespace. As stated, the visibility of a namespace is public, but the assembly in which you place it determines the accessibility of a namespace. This means the namespace is publicly available to all projects that reference the assembly into which it's placed.*

The runtime environment does not actually know anything about namespaces, so when you access a type, the CLR needs the full name of the type and the assembly that contains the type definition. With this information, the CLR can load the assembly and access the type.

The .NET Framework Class Library

The .NET Framework class library includes base classes and classes derived from the base classes. These classes have a lot of functionality, such as server controls, exception handling, and data access, of course, which is the subject of this book. The .NET Framework classes give you a head start when building your applications, because you don't have to design them from the ground up. The class library is actually a hierarchical set of unified, object-oriented, extensible class libraries, also called application programming interfaces (APIs). This differs from previous versions of various Windows programming languages, such as

Visual Basic and Visual C++, in which a lot of system and OS functionality could only be accessed through Windows API calls.

Getting Cozy with the VS .NET Integrated Development Environment

The Integrated Development Environment (IDE) hosts a slew of new, fantastic features, and I will mention the following ones very briefly:

- IDE shared by all .NET programming languages

- Two interface modes

- Built-in Web browser functionality

- Command Window

- Built-in Object Browser

- Integrated debugger

- Integrated Help system

- Macros

- Upgraded deployment tools

- Text editors

- IDE and tools modification

- Server Explorer

- Data connections

- Toolbox

- Task List

All Languages Share the IDE

VS .NET provides an IDE for all .NET languages to share (see Figure 1-2), giving developers the benefit of the same tools across the various programming languages. Basically, by "share" I mean that whether you open a C# or VB .NET project, the VS .NET IDE generally looks and feels the same. This is true for whatever language .NET language you are developing in.[1] However, you can use other IDEs, such as the Antechinus C# Programming Editor (http://www.c-point.com/csharp.htm), if you dislike the Microsoft IDE.

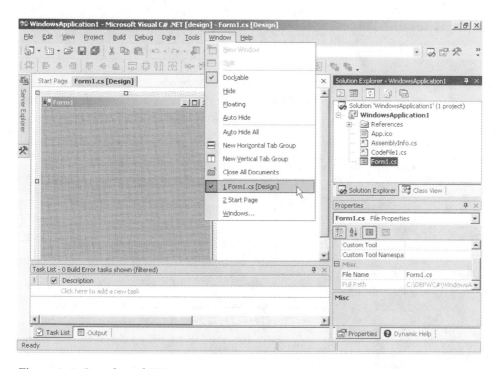

Figure 1-2. One shared IDE

---

1. Actually, it's up to the vendor of the .NET language to integrate it with the VS .NET IDE, and some languages come with their own IDE.

Two Interface Modes

The IDE supports two *interface modes,* which arrange windows and panes:

- *Multiple document interface (MDI) mode:* In this mode, the MDI parent window hosts a number of MDI children within the MDI parent window context. In Figure 1-3, you can see the two open windows, Start Page and Form1.cs [Design], overlap as MDI children windows.

- *Tabbed documents mode:* This is the default mode, and I personally prefer this mode, as it seems easier to arrange all your windows and panes than MDI mode. Either of the two open windows in Figure 1-2 can be displayed by clicking the appropriate tab, Start Page or Form1.cs [Design].

You can switch between the two interface modes using the Options dialog box. See the section "IDE Tools and Modification" later in this chapter.

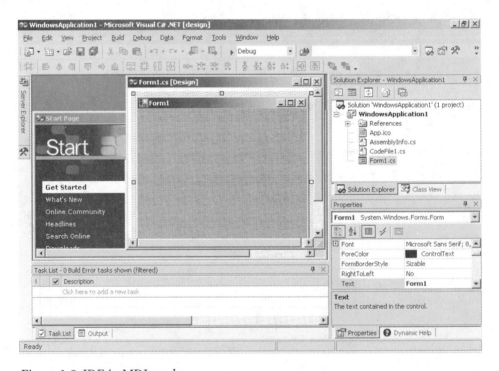

Figure 1-3. IDE in MDI mode

Built-in Web Browser Functionality

The IDE has built-in Web browser capabilities, so you do not need to have a separate browser installed on your development machine. However, I do recommend installing at least one separate Web browser for testing purposes. The built-in Web browser is great for viewing Web pages without having to compile and run the whole project. See the Browse – Under Construction window in Figure 1-4, which displays an HTML page within the built-in Web browser.

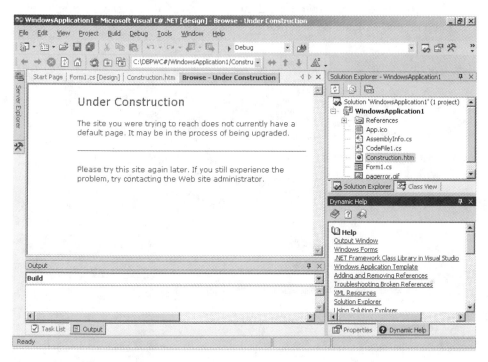

Figure 1-4. Built-in Web browser

In Figure 1-4 you see an HTML page that is part of the open project in the built-in browser, but you can also view any other HTML page, be it online or not. To browse to a specific URL, you need to make sure the Web toolbar is shown in the IDE. You can show it by checking the Web menu command in the View ➤ Toolbars menu. In Figure 1-4, this is the bottommost toolbar, and the address box contains the text "C:/DBPWC#/WindowsApplication1/Constru". In the text box, you can type in any URL (or filename, for that matter) to browse to a Web site or open a file. The built-in Web browser is just like your ordinary browser, which is in fact what it is.

Command Window

The Command Window has two modes:

- *Command mode*, which you can access by pressing Ctrl+Alt+A, allows you to type your IDE commands and create short name aliases for often-used commands (see Figure 1-5).

- *Immediate mode*, which you can access by pressing Ctrl+Alt+I, lets you evaluate expressions, set or read the value of variables, assign object references, and execute code statements (see Figure 1-6).

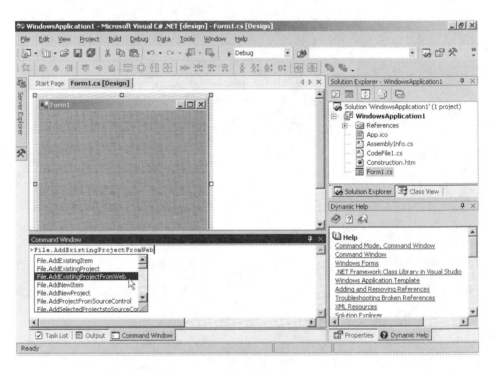

Figure 1-5. Command Window in command mode

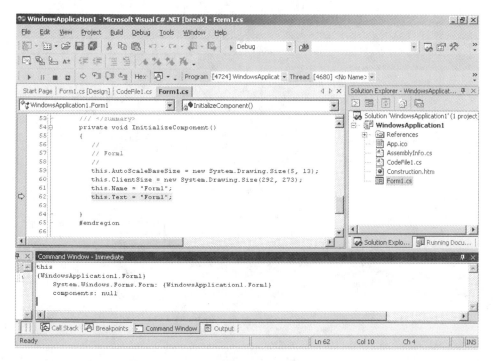

Figure 1-6. Command Window in immediate mode

You can find more information about the Command Window at this address:
`http://www.vb-joker.com/?doc=Books/CommandWindow.pdf`.

Built-in Object Browser

The built-in Object Browser, which you can open by pressing Ctrl+Alt+J, lets you examine objects and their methods and properties. The objects you can examine (also called the Object Browser's *browsing scope*) can be part of external or referenced components, or components in the form of projects in the current solution. The components in the browsing scope include COM components and .NET Framework components (obviously). Figure 1-7 shows the Object Browser.

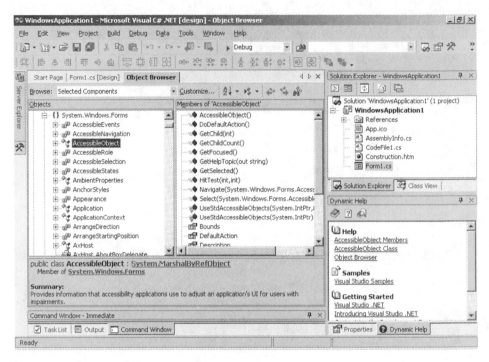

Figure 1-7. Object Browser

Integrated Debugger

The integrated debugger now supports cross-language debugging from within the IDE. You can also debug multiple programs at the same time, either by launching the various programs from within the IDE or by attaching the debugger to already running programs or processes (see Figure 1-8). One thing you must notice, especially if you've worked with an earlier version of Visual Basic, is that it's no longer possible to edit your code when you've hit a breakpoint and then continue code execution with the modified code. Last I heard, Microsoft was working on this for the next release.

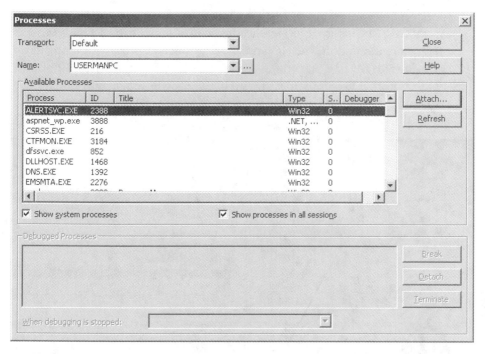

Figure 1-8. Debugger Processes window

Integrated Help System

The Help system in VS .NET is somewhat advanced and consists of the following:

- *Dynamic Help*: The Dynamic Help is great because the content of the Dynamic Help window is based on the current context and selection. This means that the Dynamic Help window, which is located in the lower-right corner of the IDE by default, changes its content to reflect the current selection when you move around in the code editor. This works not only when you are in the code editor, but also when you edit HTML code, use the XML Designer, design reports, edit Cascading Style Sheets (CSS), and so on.

  When you want to view one of the topics displayed in the Dynamic Help window, as shown in Figure 1-9, you simply click the topic and the help text pops up, either in the MSDN Library application or within the IDE as a document. This depends on whether your Help settings indicate external or internal display.

- *Microsoft Visual Studio .NET documentation*: The complete Help system for VS .NET is included, as is the Platform SDK and the .NET Framework SDK documentation. The Help browser has been improved from previous versions (as the one that comes with previous versions of Microsoft programming languages), and it's now a browser-style application with links to appropriate information on the various Microsoft Web sites.

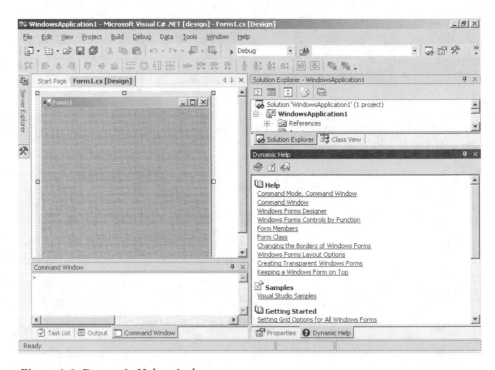

Figure 1-9. Dynamic Help window

Macros

You know that you must do some tasks or series of tasks repeatedly when developing. The VS .NET IDE gives you the opportunity to automate these repetitive tasks through the use of macros. Macros can be created and/or edited using either the Recorder or the Macros IDE. The Macros IDE is actually a rather familiar friend if you ever did any VBA programming, as it's quite similar. So too is the language, which looks like VBA. In fact, it's now called Visual Studio for Applications (VSA), as discussed earlier, and the macro language is in the first version based on Visual Basic .NET. However, newer versions will support other .NET languages as well, including C#. Figure 1-10 shows you the Macros IDE, which you can access from the VS .NET IDE by pressing Alt+F11 or by selecting the Macros IDE command in the Tools ➢ Macros submenu.

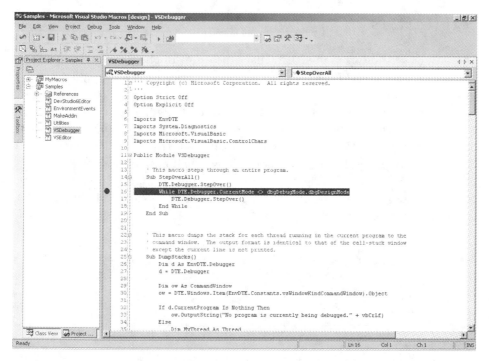

Figure 1-10. Visual Studio .NET Macro IDE

In Figure 1-10, you can see one of the accompanying sample macros, the VSDebugger macro, displayed in the Macros IDE. The source code is VB .NET and I have placed a breakpoint on Line 16 just to show you that the Macros IDE works pretty much the same as the VS .NET IDE.

Upgraded Deployment Tools

The deployment tools in VS .NET have been heavily upgraded since the previous version of VS. In VS .NET you can perform the following tasks, among others:

- Deploy application tiers to different test servers for remote debugging

- Deploy Web applications

- Distribute applications using the Microsoft Windows Installer

Text Editors

The various text editors in the IDE all have the same functionality that you've come to expect from a Windows editor. The shortcuts are the same, and most of the accelerator keys are well known.

However, something that may be new to you is the inclusion of line numbers, which are displayed at the left side of the editor. These optional line numbers are not part of the code or text, but are merely displayed for your convenience (see Figure 1-11). Actually, the default is not to show line numbers, but you can turn them on for one programming language or all of them using the Text Editor category from the Options dialog box. See the section "IDE Tools and Modification" later in this chapter.

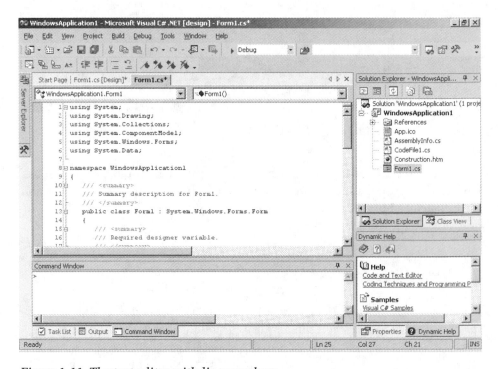

Figure 1-11. The text editor with line numbers

IDE and Tools Modification

By default, the IDE and all the tools within it have a certain look and feel, but you can modify most of the functionality from the Option dialog box, which you can access by selecting Tools ➤ Options (see Figure 1-12).

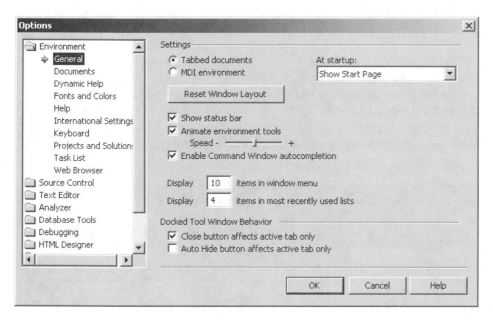

Figure 1-12. The IDE Options dialog box

In the Options dialog box, you can change the default behavior and look of the IDE and related tools. On the left, you have the tree view with all the categories you can change options for. In Figure 1-12, the Environment category or node is selected, which means you can change such options as whether you want the status bar shown in the IDE, or if you want to use tabbed documents or MDI mode within the IDE.

The various programming languages have slightly different settings, so if you need certain settings, such as tab size and font, to be the same in all the programming languages you use, you need to explicitly set these.

Server Explorer

You can use the Server Explorer window, which is located on the bar on the left side of the IDE by default, for manipulating resources on any server you can access. The resources you can manipulate include the following:

- Database objects

- Performance counters*

- Message queues*

- Services*

- Event logs*

Most of these resources are new (denoted by an asterisk), and you can drag them onto a Web form or Windows form and then manipulate them from within your code (see Figure 1-13). Please note that the accessibility of these resources from Server Explorer depends on the version of Visual Studio you buy.

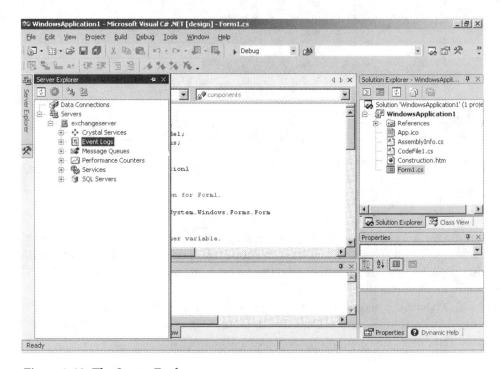

Figure 1-13. The Server Explorer

Data Connections

You can set up connections to a database and manipulate the database objects in a number of ways. Hey, wait a minute—I go into greater detail on this subject from Chapter 3 on, so don't get me started here!

Toolbox

The Toolbox window, which is located on the bar on the left side of the IDE by default, contains all the intrinsic tools you can use in the various design and editor modes, such as HTML design, Windows Form design, Web Form design, Code Editor, and UML Diagram design. When you have a window open, the content of the Toolbox changes according to what is available to work with in the current window (see Figure 1-14).

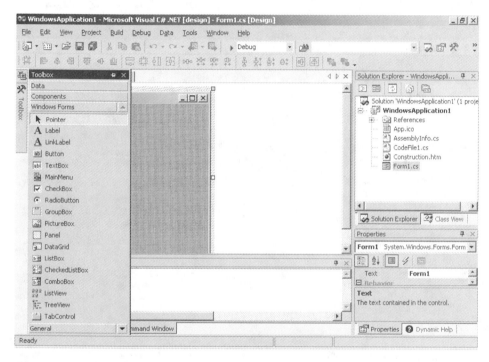

Figure 1-14. The Toolbox

Task List

The Task List window, which is docked at the bottom of the IDE by default, helps you organize and manage the various tasks you need to complete in order to build your solution. If the Task List window isn't shown, you can access it by pressing Ctrl+Alt+K. The developer and the CLR both use the Task List. This means that the developer can add tasks manually, but the CLR also adds a task if an error occurs when compiling. When a task is added to the list, it can contain a filename and line number. This way, you can double-click the task name and go straight to the problem or unfinished task.

Once you finish a certain task, you can select the appropriate check box to indicate the task has been completed (see Figure 1-15).

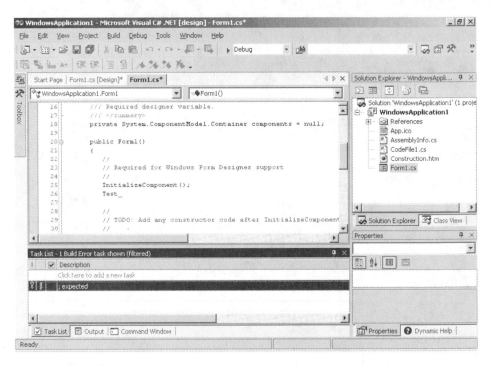

Figure 1-15. The Task List

Summary

This chapter provided a quick rundown of the concepts and terms in C#. I discussed assemblies and namespaces, and how they fit in the .NET Framework; the common language runtime (CLR), which unifies the .NET programming languages with a common base; the Common Language Specification (CLS), which is the standard all .NET languages must adhere to; the common type system (CTS), which dictates the base types used for data exchange; server-based Active Server Pages programming; and the .NET Framework class library. Finally, I presented a quick look at some of the new features of the shared IDE, such as line numbering in the text editors and the integrated debugger.

The next chapter is a short side trip from C#. It's a general chapter on how to design and talk to databases. Among other concepts, it covers how to normalize a database.

Part Two

Database Programming

CHAPTER 2

Using Databases

A Short Introduction
to General Database Terms and Concepts

IN THIS CHAPTER, I INTRODUCE YOU to the terms and concepts that I'll be using throughout the rest of the book. Consider this chapter a reference for the following chapters. I'll be looking at what a database really is, why you should use a database, and how to design a relational database. Although this chapter is not intended to teach you everything there is to know about designing a relational database, you'll get the basics. Please note that if you already know about database design, referential integrity, indexes, keys, and so on, this chapter will serve as a refresher. For additional information, you'll find a good article on database design and a link for database normalization at the following address on the Microsoft Product Services site: http://support.microsoft.com/support/kb/articles/Q234/2/08.ASP.

The hands-on exercise in the "UserMan Database Schema" section at the end of this chapter will reinforce the database concepts I present to you here.

What Is a Database?

I'm sure you know what a *database* is, but why not keep reading? You might just find something new or different to add to what you already know. Anyway, there are probably as many definitions of the term "database" as there are different software implementations of electronic databases. So for that reason, I'll try to keep it simple. A database is a collection of *data*, which can be information about anything really. A phone number is data, a name is data, a book contains data, and so on. What the data is about is not really important in the context of defining data.

A database is usually organized in some way. A phone book is a database, usually organized (sorted) alphabetically by surname. The main objective of a phone book is for the reader to be able to locate a phone number. With any given phone number you generally associate a name, consisting of a first name and surname, an address, and perhaps the title of the person who "owns" the phone number. Here I'm actually in the process of taking the phone book apart, or perhaps I should call it figuring out how the phone book is organized.

As you can see, a database doesn't have to be an electronic collection of data (a phone book isn't), and it doesn't have to be organized in any particular way. However, this book deals with electronic databases exclusively.

Why Use a Database?

When thinking of reasons for using databases, some words immediately spring to mind: storage, accessibility, organization, and manipulation.

- *Storage:* For a database to exist elsewhere other than in your head, you need to store it in some form. You can store it electronically on a disk and bring it with you, if that's what you want to do, or hand it to someone else. Your database could be in the form of a Microsoft Excel spreadsheet or a Microsoft Access database.

- *Accessibility:* Well, if you can't access your data within the database, the database is of no use to anyone. When using an electronic database, such as one created in Microsoft Access, you generally have a lot of options for accessing it. You can access a Microsoft Access database using the Microsoft Access front-end, or indeed any application capable of communicating with a driver that can talk to the Microsoft Access database. Now, accessibility depends on the format the database is saved in, but for argument's sake let's just say that it's a standard format, such as dBase or Microsoft Access, which means it's easy to get hold of a driver and/or application that can access and read the data in the database.

- *Organization:* The most logical way to organize a phone book is alphabetically. However, the phone book has a lot of duplicated data, which can take up twice as much space as you would expect nonduplicated data to take. The data is duplicated to allow you to use more than one way to look up data. In most countries, you can look up a listing under the surname, you can look up a listing using the address, and so on. Duplication is not a problem when speaking of an electronic database, if it has been properly implemented. You can use indexes to give your clients a variety of ways to access the data without duplicating it. Keys serve as pointers to the data, which means they're valuable tools for avoiding duplicated data.

- *Manipulation:* Editing a phone book is certainly not an easy task. You can strike over the text in case a phone number no longer exists, but what about changing the owner of a phone number or adding a new phone number? In how many places will you have to edit and/or add data? This just won't work, unless you're willing to redo the whole phone book! When it comes to your electronic database, if it has been properly implemented, it's simply a matter of locating the information you want to edit or delete, entering the data, and off you go. The data is now added and changed in all the right places.

Okay, so to quickly summarize, here are the benefits of using a database:

- Locating and manipulating the data is much easier when your data is in one place.

- Organization of the data is easier when it's in one place and it's stored electronically.

- You can access the data from a variety of applications and locations when your data is put in one place, your database.

From this point on, all references to databases are to electronic databases.

Relational vs. Hierarchical

Today there are two types of databases widely deployed, *relational* and *hierarchical.* The relational database is by far the most popular of these and it's probably the one you already know about. Mind you, you've probably been using a hierarchical database without knowing it! The Windows Registry and Active Directory in Windows 2000 are both hierarchical databases.

Hierarchical Databases

A *hierarchical database* has a treelike structure with a root element at the top (see Figure 2-1). The root element has one or more nodes, and the nodes themselves have nodes. It's just like a tree with branches and leaves. You've probably been using the Windows Explorer file manager, which relies on a treelike structure for representing your disk and files. Windows Explorer is more like a hierarchical DBMS (see the "What Is a Database Management System?" section later in this chapter) with multiple databases—that is, My Computer is a database, drive C on your local computer is a node of the root element My Computer, the folders on drive C are nodes of drive C, and so on.

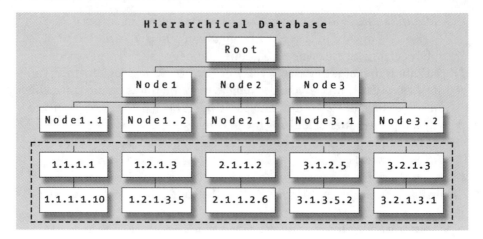

Figure 2-1. Hierarchical database

Hierarchical databases are usually very fast, because the data structures are directly linked, but they are not good for modeling complex relations such as the ones you have in a warehouse system with raw materials, products, boxed products, shelves, rows of shelves, and so on. All these items are somewhat related, and it's difficult to represent these relations in a hierarchical database without duplicating data and loss of performance.

These are some good candidates for hierarchical databases:

- File and directory systems

- Management/organization rankings

I'm sure you can think of a few more yourself.

Hierarchical databases are generally hard to implement, set up, and maintain, and they usually require a systems programmer to do so. However, IBM produces a hierarchical database system called the Information Management System (IMS), which you can find at `http://www-4.ibm.com/software/data/ims/`. IMS has tools similar to those in relational database systems (discussed next) for setting up and implementing your hierarchical database. I won't implement a hierarchical database in this book, but I'll show you how to access one, Active Directory. See Chapter 7 for more information on Active Directory and hierarchical databases in general.

Relational Databases

A *relational database* consists of tables (see the "What Are Tables?" section later in this chapter) that are related to each other in some way, either directly or indirectly. If you think in terms of objects, tables represent the objects, and these objects/tables are connected using relationships. One example might be an order system, where you have products, customers, orders, and so on. In a rather simple order system, you'll have separate objects or tables for holding information pertaining to orders, customers, and products. A customer has zero or more orders, and an order consists of one or more products, which means you have relationships between the objects, or rather tables. Please see the "What Is Relational Database Design?" section, later in this chapter, for more information on how a relational database should be designed.

What C# Programmers Need to Know About Relational Databases

In this section, you'll be introduced to a number of Frequently Asked Questions (FAQs) and answers to these questions. All the FAQs are related to what you really need to know if you design your own databases as a C# programmer. Although the rest of this section is in typical FAQ style, I recommend that you follow along from the beginning, because it might answer some of the questions you may raise in later chapters.

Q: What Is a Database Management System?

A: The term *database management system* (DBMS) is used in variety of contexts, some more correct than others. A complete DBMS consists of hardware, software, data, and users. However, in the context of this book, a DBMS is a software package through which you can administrate one or more databases, manipulate the data within a database, and export to/import from different data formats. A DBMS is not necessarily a database server system such as Microsoft SQL Server or Oracle; it can also be a desktop database such as Microsoft Access or Lotus Approach. A desktop database doesn't require a server; it's simply a file (or a set of related files) that you can access using the right software driver from within your own application or using accompanying front-end software.

Throughout this book, I'll use the terms *database* and *DBMS* interchangeably, for the sake of discussing the connection to and manipulation of data in a database.

Q: What Are Tables?

A: A (database) *table* is a structure for holding a collection of related information, such as a table of orders in an order system. The structure of a table is made up of columns and the content of a table is grouped in rows.

Q: What Are Rows and Records?

A: *Rows* are entities in a table, which means that a single row contains information about a single instance of the objects that the table holds, such as an order in an order system. *Rows* and *records* are the exact same thing. Remember that when you come across the two terms in the same context.

Q: What Are Columns and Fields?

A: A *column* is the building block of the table structure, and each column in a table structure holds a specific piece of information relating to the object that the table assembles, such as a column in an order table that holds the Order ID in an order system. Like rows and records, the terms *column* and *field* are synonymous.

Q: What Are Null Values?

A: The special value *null* refers to an empty or nonassigned value. When I say empty value, that's not to be compared to an empty string, because an empty string is an actual value ("").

Q: What Is the Relational Database Model?

A: The *Relational Database Model*, which was "created" by E. F. Codd, has become the de facto standard for relational database design today. The idea behind this model is not very complex, although it can be hard to grasp at first. Please see the next FAQ, "What Is Relational Database Design," for more information.

Q: What Is Relational Database Design?

A: *Relational database design* is the way in which you design your relational database. Okay, I know this is pretty obvious, but basically that's what it is. It's all about identifying the objects you need to store in your database and finding the relationships between these objects.

It's very important that you design your database properly the first time around, because it's so much harder to make structural changes after you've deployed it. Other reasons for implementing a good database design are performance and maintainability. Sometimes after you've been working on your database design for a while, you end up redesigning it simply because you find out that the current design doesn't facilitate what you're trying to achieve. Design your first database, go over the design, and change it according to your findings. You should keep doing this until you no longer find any problems with it.

There are many excellent tools for modeling a relational database, but even though these tools are good, you still need to know how to construct a relational database to fully exploit one of these tools. Here's a list of some of the tools available:

- ICT Database Designer Tool (http://www.ict-computing.com/prod01.htm)

- ER/Studio (http://www.embarcadero.com/products/erstudio/index.asp)

- ER*win* (http://www.cai.com/products/alm/erwin.htm)

- Visible Analyst DB Engineer
  (http://www.visible.com/Products/Analyst/vadbengineer.html)

Q: How Do You Identify Objects for Your Database?

A: When you set out to design your relational database, the first thing you need to do is sit down and find out what objects your database should hold. By "objects," I mean items in an order system, for instance, that represent customers (Customer objects), orders (Order objects), and products (Product objects), which you would find in a typical order system. It can be difficult to identify these objects, especially if you're new to relational database design. If this is so, I'm quite sure that the first object you identify, and perhaps the only object you can identify, is the Order object. The important thing to remember here is that while the Order object is a perfectly legitimate object, there is more to it than that. You need to keep breaking the objects apart until you're at the very lowest level. In the example order system, an order is made up of one or more OrderItem objects, a Customer object, and so on. The OrderItem object itself can be broken into more objects. An order item consists of product type and the number of products. The Price object can be derived from the Product object. Here's a list of typical objects for this order system:

- Order

- Customer

- Product

- OrderItem

- Price

Something's wrong with this list, however. When you split your objects into smaller ones, the criterion for doing so should be whether the derived object actually has a life of its own. Take a look at the Price object. Should it be an object, or is it simply a property of the Product object? By "property," I mean something that describes the object. The Price object will probably correspond to more than one Product object, and as such it will be duplicated. The price could be a separate object, but it would make more sense to have it be a property of the Product object. Consider the following questions and answers:

- **Q:** Does one price correspond to more than one product, or will the price be duplicated within the Product object?

  A: The price probably will correspond to more than one product, and as such it will be duplicated. You could treat the price as a separate object, but it would make more sense to have it be a property of the Product object. Although the price will be duplicated, you also have to think about maintainability. If you need to change the price of one product, what happens when you change the Price object and more than one product is linked to it? You change the price for all related products!

- **Q:** Does a price describe a product, or is it generic?

  A: The price relates to one product and one product only.

- **Q:** Is the price calculated (or will it be) when invoicing?

  A: The price is fixed so you'll have to store it somewhere.

It's necessary to identify these objects so you can start creating tables; the objects I have identified so far are indeed tables. The properties that I've come across, such as the price, are columns in the table.

Q: What Are Relationships?

A: When you've identified objects for your database, you need to tell the DBMS how the various objects or tables are related by defining *relationships*. There are three kinds of relationships:

- One-to-one

- One-to-many

- Many-to-many

Relationships are established between a *parent table* and *child tables.* The parent table is the primary object and the child tables are the related objects, meaning that data in the child tables relates to data in the parent table in such a way that the data in the child tables can only exist if it has related data in the parent table.

Q: What Is a One-to-One Relationship?

A: You use a *one-to-one relationship* when you want to create a direct relationship between two objects, a parent table and a child table. Basically, one-to-one relationships require that the related columns in the two tables are unique. Normally, information that makes up a one-to-one relationship would be put in one table, but sometimes it's necessary to keep some information in a separate table, effectively establishing a direct link or a one-to-one relationship between the two new tables. You can see reasons for such a relationship in Table 2-1.

Table 2-1. One-to-One Relationships

SPLIT REASON	DESCRIPTION
The table structure is large	If you have a large table structure (many columns), quite often only some of the columns are accessed and, in such cases, it can be advantageous to split the table into two, moving the least accessed columns into a new table.
Security concerns	Some columns are considered a security risk and are therefore moved to a new table, creating a one-to-one relationship. However, there are often other ways of getting around this, such as creating views. See Chapter 6 for more information about views.

Table 2-1 explains why you would split up an existing table into two tables, which is mostly the reason for having a one-to-one relationship, and provides a description of the reason you should split the table. In general, reference or lookup tables have a one-to-one relationship with a parent table.

Q: What Is a One-to-Many Relationship?

A: A *one-to-many relationship* is the most common database relationship, and you will implement it many times over the years as a database designer. This type of relationship exists between a parent table and a child table in cases where the parent row can have zero or more child rows. Table 2-2 provides examples of such a relationship.

Table 2-2. One-to-Many Relationships

PARENT TABLE	CHILD TABLE
Orders	OrderItems
Customers	Orders
Products	OrderItems

You interpret Table 2-2 as follows: One order can have one or more order items, one customer can have one or more orders, and one product may belong to one or more order items.

Q: What Is a Many-to-Many Relationship?

A: A *many-to-many relationship* exists in cases where a row in the parent table has many related rows in the child table and vice versa. Table 2-3 displays one example of such a relationship.

Table 2-3. Many-to-Many Relationship

PARENT TABLE	LINK TABLE	CHILD TABLE
Products	ProductParts	Parts

Many-to-many relationships can't be modeled directly between a parent table and a child table. Instead, you define two one-to-many relationships using a third table, called a *link table.* This table holds a unique ID of the row in the parent row as well as a unique ID of the row in the child table as one row (see Figure 2-2). So, in order to find a particular row in the link table, you need the unique IDs of both the parent and child rows. The two IDs are very good candidates for a composite primary key (see the next FAQ, "What Are Keys?"). Figure 2-2 should be read like this:

- One product contains one or more parts.

- One part belongs to zero or more products.

- A product part belongs to one product only and consists of one part only. The ProductParts table is the link table in this case.

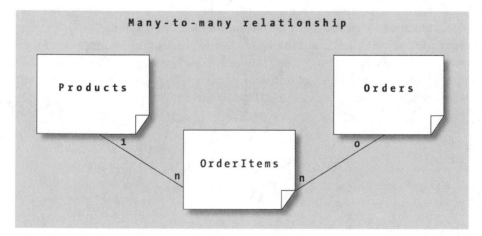

Figure 2-2. Many-to-many relationship

Q: What Are Keys?

A: *Keys* are important in relational database design, because they're used as row identifiers and for sorting query output. There are two types of keys: primary keys and foreign keys. Please note that any key is really just an index, meaning that a key is based on an index. See the "What Is an Index?" FAQ later in this chapter for more information on indexes.

Q: What Is a Primary Key?

A: The *primary key* of a table is always unique; that is, no two rows in the table hold the same value in the column(s) designated as the primary key. This means the primary key uniquely identifies each row in the table. This also means that a column that makes up or is part of a primary key can't contain a null value. The primary key index also functions as a *lookup key,* which helps you locate a specific row when you search for a value in the primary key index. In terms of relationships, the primary key of the parent table is always used in combination with a foreign key (discussed next) in the child table. In Figure 2-3, the primary key in the (parent) Orders table is marked PK. One row in the Orders table relates to zero or more rows in the OrderItems table.

Q: What Is a Foreign Key?

A: A *foreign key* is used in relationships as the lookup value in the child table. This means it directly corresponds to the value of the primary key in the parent table, so that you can use the value of the primary key to look up a related row in the child table. In a one-to-one relationship, the foreign key must be unique. In Figure 2-3, the foreign key in the OrderItems table is marked FK. There can be many rows in the OrderItems table that relate to a row in the Orders table. Please note that the Salesman column in the Orders table is a foreign key candidate for looking up orders belonging to a certain salesman. This obviously requires a separate Salesman table with a unique ID column as the primary key.

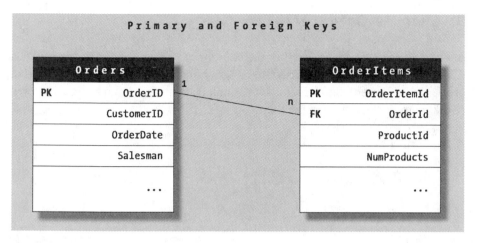

Figure 2-3. Primary and foreign keys

Q: What Is a Composite Key?

A: A key consisting of more than one column is called a *composite key*, simply because it is made up of more than one column. So you either have a composite key (more than one column) or a single-column key.

Q: What Is an Index?

A: You create an *index* to specify lookup columns. With many DBMSs you don't have to create an index for primary or foreign keys, because primary and foreign keys are automatically created as indexes to your tables. When you create an index, it's much faster to search for a value in the column(s) that makes up the index. There is some overhead when you create an index, but if you're careful when selecting the columns you want to use in indexes, the advantages outweigh the disadvantages.

The overhead results in extra disk space consumption and a slight performance penalty when adding or editing rows. Sometimes you need to try out an index and do some performance testing to see if you'll gain or lose performance by implementing it. One candidate for an index is the Name column in a Customer table. You can't use it as a primary key column as it more than likely will be duplicated, because many people have the same names. However, you'll probably need to look up a customer using his or her name, as he or she might not remember his or her customer ID (which could be the primary key) if the customer gives you a call.

Q: What Is Data Integrity?

A: *Data integrity* relates to whether the content of a database can be "trusted" or if it's up-to-date. In other words, data integrity means that no data is outdated or orphaned because of updates to related data. Data integrity can be ensured by checking for one or more of the following:

- Entity integrity

- Referential integrity

- Domain integrity

Q: What Is Entity Integrity?

A: *Entity integrity* states that no value in a primary key can be null. This goes for composite primary keys as well as single-column primary keys. Since primary keys must be unique, they must not be allowed to contain null values, and hence you should apply entity integrity when designing your database. Mind you, most DBMSs won't allow you to create primary keys that allow null values.

Q: What Is Referential Integrity?

A: *Referential integrity* has to do with relationships. Referential integrity ensures that no row in a child table has a foreign key that doesn't exist as a primary key in the parent table. This means that when you enforce referential integrity, you can't add a row to the child table with a foreign key that doesn't match a primary key in the parent table.

Depending on whether you specify restrictions or cascades when you set up referential integrity, the behavior in Table 2-4 is applied. A *cascade* refers to the process whereby related tables are updated when you update or delete a row in a parent table.

Table 2-4. Referential Integrity Behavior

TASK	CASCADE	RESTRICTION
Delete a row in a parent table for which there are related rows in a child table.	The related rows in the child table are also deleted.	The deletion is disallowed.
Update/change the primary key of a row in a parent table for which there are related rows in a child table.	The related rows in the child table are also updated.	The update/change is disallowed.

Referential integrity ensures that no row in a child table is *orphaned*, that is, has no related record in the parent table. There are two kinds of referential integrity: declarative integrity and procedural integrity.

Q: *What Is Declarative Referential Integrity?*

A: *Declarative referential integrity* (DRI) is the easiest to implement, because it simply means that you define what action to take at the time of creating your relationships. This means that you tell the DBMS to either restrict or cascade an update or deletion to tables that have a relationship. SQL Server 2000 was the first version of Microsoft SQL Server to support DRI.

Q: *What Is Procedural Referential Integrity?*

A: *Procedural referential integrity* (PRI) is when you create procedures in your database, or even in components handling your database access, that manage your referential integrity. This is normally handled by triggers that are invoked either before or after an update to a table in your database. See Chapter 6 for more information about triggers.

Procedural referential integrity gives you more control over how updates and deletions to your tables are handled, because you can specify just about any action in your triggers. However, using procedural referential integrity also means more work for you, because you need to program these triggers yourself, whereas DRI is handled by the DBMS.

Q: What Is Domain Integrity?

A: *Domain integrity* ensures that values in a particular column conform to the domain description in place, meaning that values in the column must match a particular format and/or data type. Domain integrity is ensured through physical and logical constraints applied to a specific column. When you try to add an invalid value to a column with domain constraints, the value will be disallowed. Such a domain constraint could be applied to a Phone Number column in the Customers table, as follows:

- Physical constraint: data type: string, length: 13

- Logical constraint: input format: (999) 9999999

Q: What Is Normalization?

A: Normalization is very much a process that can be applied to relational database design. *Normalization* is a method of data analysis you can use when you're designing your database. The normalization process, which is a series of progressive sets of rules, can be referred to as *normal forms*. A "progressive set of rules" means that one rule builds upon the previous rule and adds new restrictions. Think of it like this: The first rule states that a value must be of type integer. The second rule enforces the first rule, but it also adds another restriction: The value must be 5 or higher. The third rule enforces first and second rules and adds the restriction that the maximum value is 1500, and so on. (I'm sure you get the idea.)

Anyway, the purpose of normalization is to define tables, which you can modify with predictable results, and thus ensure data integrity with minimal maintenance. A "predictable result" means that no data inconsistency and/or redundancy occur when you modify the data. Inconsistency is when, for example, you update a value in one place and that value isn't updated in another place where it's referenced. Redundancy is, generally speaking, when you have some data that's duplicated. The normal forms were defined in the 1970s to overcome problems with table relations. These problems are also called *anomalies*.

Q: What Are the Normal Forms?

A: The *normal forms* are a progressive set of rules that should be applied to your database design beginning with the First Normal Form, then the Second Normal Form, and so on. (The various form levels are discussed later in this section.) Mind you, not all of the normal forms have to be applied to your database design. I would think that a lot of databases out there that have been normalized only adhere to the first three normal forms. I believe it's up to you as a database designer to pull the plug on the process, once you feel you've achieved your goal.

> **NOTE** *I had a hard time understanding the normal forms when I first came across them some years ago. These days I hardly think about them when I design my databases. I just design them and they generally conform to the first three to four normal forms. Actually, if you're going to design a number of databases in your career, I can only suggest you get to know these normal forms by heart. The hard work will pay off, believe me. If you already know about normalization and generally apply it to your database design, your job for the rest of this book is to catch my mistakes!*

Q: How Do You Achieve the First Normal Form?

A: You can achieve the *First Normal Form* (1NF) by putting all repeating groups of data (duplicated data) into separate tables and connecting these tables using one-to-many relationships. One example of this might be if the Orders table had columns for four OrderItems, as shown in Figure 2-4.

Figure 2-4. 1NF violation

Don't tell me you never made the mistake displayed in Figure 2-4. Think back to when you were first designing databases that were effectively flat file databases—that is, databases where all data is placed in the same table or file. If you want to conform to 1NF, your table design should instead look like Figure 2-5.

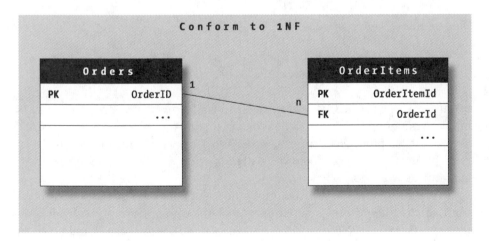

Figure 2-5. 1NF conformance

Q: What Is the Second Normal Form?

A: To conform to the *Second Normal Form* (2NF) you must first conform to 1NF. Actually, 2NF only applies to tables in 1NF with composite primary keys (see the "What Is a Composite Key" FAQ earlier in this chapter). So if your database conforms to 1NF and your tables only have primary keys made up of a single column, your database automatically conforms to 2NF. However, if your table does have a composite primary key, you need to eliminate the functional dependencies on a partial key. You can achieve this by putting the violating columns into a separate table.

Functional dependencies, you say? Okay, try this: If you have an OrderItems table and it contains the columns shown in Figure 2-6, the ProductDescription column violates 2NF. 2NF is violated because the ProductDescription column only relates to the ProductId column and not the OrderId column. This means that to conform to 2NF, you will have to move the ProductDescription column to the Products table. You can use the ProductId as a lookup value to retrieve the product description.

Figure 2-6. 2NF violation

Q: What Is the Third Normal Form?

A: You can achieve *Third Normal Form* (3NF) conformance by conforming to 2NF and by eliminating functional dependencies on nonkey columns. As is the case with 2NF, if you put the violating columns into a separate table, this condition is met. This means all nonkey columns will then be dependent on the whole key and only the whole key.

In Figure 2-7, the Location column is not dependent on the ProductId column, which is the primary key, but instead on the Warehouse column, which is not a key. Therefore, 3NF is violated, and you should create a new Warehouse table with the Warehouse and Location columns to conform to 3NF. You can then use the Warehouse column as a lookup value to retrieve the Warehouse location.

Figure 2-7. 3NF violation

Q: What Is the Fourth Normal Form?

A: If you want your database to conform to the *Fourth Normal Form* (4NF), the rows in your tables must conform to 3NF and they must have no multivalued dependencies. You can think of *multivalued dependencies* like this: A row may not contain two or more independent multivalued facts about an entity.

4NF only concerns relations that have three or more attributes, so if you don't have relations, or primary keys for that matter, with three or more attributes, your database automatically conforms to 4NF. If, however, your database does have relations with three or more attributes, you need to make sure that the primary key doesn't contain two or more independent multivalued facts about an entity. Confusing, eh? Okay, think about this:

- A customer can speak one or more languages.

- A customer can have one or more payment options.

In the example shown in Figure 2-8, you have the option of storing a payment option and a language for each customer. The only problem is that the language and the payment option are multivalued; that is, there is more than one language and more than one payment option, and the language and payment attributes are mutually independent attributes. This effectively means a single customer who speaks the languages English and Danish and has the payment options Cash On Delivery (COD) and Credit will require more than one customer row. Actually, this customer will require four rows if you need to hold all combinations (two languages × two payment options). Can you imagine the nightmare of updating all these rows once you change, say, a payment option? Another problem with this relation is that if only one row contains the value Danish in the Language column and you delete this row, what happens then? The Danish language would be lost from the database.

Figure 2-8. 4NF violation

To avoid violating 4NF as shown in Figure 2-8, you need to decompose the relation (Customers) into two separate relations (CustomerPayments and CustomerLanguages), as in Figure 2-9.

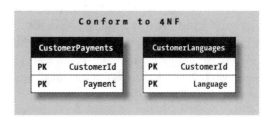

Figure 2-9. 4NF conformance

You need to conform to 4NF to make sure you don't have data redundancy and to make data updates easy.

Q: What Is the Fifth Normal Form?

A: The first four normal forms all relate to functional dependence, but the *Fifth Normal Form* (5NF) relates to join dependence. *Join dependence* means that when a table has been decomposed into three or more smaller tables, these smaller tables can be joined to form the original table.

Rows in your tables conform to 5NF when the information contained in the rows can't be reconstructed from several smaller rows (each row has fewer columns than the original row). This means that the information in a table can't be decomposed into smaller tables without them having the same key.

5NF is not much different from 4NF, and many experts believe that tables that conform to 4NF also conform to 5NF in most cases.

Q: What Is Denormalization?

A: *Denormalization* is the process of reversing normalization, usually because of a performance loss as a result of the normalization process. However, there are no hard-and-fast rules for when you need to start the denormalization process. Before you start doing any normalization, you can benchmark your current system and establish a baseline. When you're done with the normalization, you can again benchmark your system to see if any performance has been gained or lost. If the performance loss is too great, you start the denormalization process, where you reverse one or more of the changes you made in the normalization process. It's important that you only make one such change at a time in order to test for possible performance gains after every change.

Denormalization is also an important aspect to keep in mind when your database matures, because performance is most often degraded when you start adding data to your database.

UserMan Database Schema

The UserMan sample application that I build on throughout this book will feature a database, of course. The schema for this SQL Server database is shown in Figure 2-10.

UserMan Database Schema

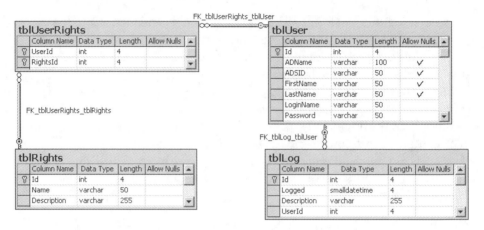

Figure 2-10. UserMan database schema

As you can see in Figure 2-10, the database includes four tables:

- *tblUser:* This is the main table that holds all standard information about a user, such as first name, last name, and so on.

- *tblUserRights:* This is a link table that holds many-to-many relationships between the tblUser and tblRights tables.

- *tblRights:* This table holds the various rights a user can be assigned in the system, which could allow a user to create a new user, delete an existing user, and so on.

- *tblLog:* The log table holds information on when a user did what. Let's keep those users under tight control!

EXERCISE

Examine the UserMan database schema and see if you can find a way to improve the design according to the various design tools that I've covered in this chapter.

As stated before, I'll be working on this database throughout this book, and in the final chapter, I'll give you ideas on how to extend the current schema and the sample application.

UserMan Database Conforms to 5NF

The UserMan database conforms to 5NF, but how can you tell? Figure 2-10 shows you the database schema with the four tables. Let's check the normal forms one by one and see if the UserMan database really does conform to 5NF.

- *1NF:* All repeating groups of data have been put into separate tables.

- *2NF:* Only the tblUserRights table has a composite primary key, but this table is a link table and therefore doesn't hold any "real" data. Basically, the absence of nonkey columns means that you don't have any functional dependencies on a partial key.

- *3NF:* All nonkey fields in the tables relate to the primary key.

- *4NF:* The UserMan database has doesn't have any relations or primary keys with three or more attributes; thus, no multivalued dependencies exist.

- *5NF:* None of tables can be further decomposed without using the same key—or can they?

Summary

This chapter explained databases, why you should use them, and how you should design them. I briefly outlined the differences between a relational database and a hierarchical database. Then, I discussed designing a relational database, and I showed you most of the concepts involved in building a relational database, such as the normal forms, keys (primary and foreign), the various types of relationships between tables and how to implement them logically, and indexes. I also covered data integrity in the form of entity, referential, and domain integrity.

The last section of this chapter detailed the database schema for the UserMan sample application. I'll be working with this database throughout the book.

The following two chapters take you on a journey through most of the classes in ADO.NET and explains how to use them.

Presenting ADO.NET: The Connected Layer

THIS CHAPTER AND ITS TWIN, Chapter 3B, cover ADO.NET. The classes in ADO.NET can be categorized into two groups: the connected layer and the disconnected layer. This chapter covers the connected layer.

The connected layer is provider specific, meaning you need to use a .NET Data Provider that supports your database, whereas the disconnected layer can be used with all of the .NET Data Providers. See the "Data Providers and Drivers" section later in this chapter for more information on providers. Simply put, you can use the disconnected layer if you don't need to access any data source and really just want to work with temporary data, or data that is being read and written to XML streams or files. If you need to retrieve data from, insert data into, update data in, or delete data from a data source, you need to use the connected layer. However, most often you'll be using classes from both layers, as you'll see in this chapter and the following ones, and the corresponding example code.

For some years now, Active Data Objects (ADO) has been the preferred interface for accessing various data sources. This is especially true for Visual Basic programmers. Think of ADO as the middle layer in your application, the layer between your front-end and the data source. ADO 2.7 is the latest version of this product.

Now, with the advent of ADO.NET and VS .NET, it's not just Visual Basic programmers, but also many other programmers using programming languages like C#, who can finally use it extensively as well. Active Data Objects.NET (ADO.NET) is the all-new singing-and-dancing version of ADO. ADO.NET has been designed to be a disconnected and distributed data access technology based on XML. This fits very well into the new, "hidden" Microsoft strategy of making it run on every platform that supports XML. It also means that you can easily pass ADO.NET data sets from one location to another over the Internet, because ADO.NET can penetrate firewalls. Actually, it's fair to say that ADO.NET is a revolution and not an evolution.

ADO vs. ADO.NET

This book refers to both of these data access technologies. Here is how you can distinguish one from the other:

- *ADO* will be used to describe the ADO technology that has been with us for some years now. This technology is COM based and can only be used through COM Interop.

- *ADO.NET* is a new version based entirely on the .NET Framework, and the underlying technology is very different from that of the COM-based ADO. Although the name ADO is still there, these are different technologies.

However, as you probably know, ADO is still here, although it requires COM Interop (interoperability) if you want to use it from within the .NET Framework. You'll get a chance to look at COM Interop in Chapter 3B, but you can also refer to the following book, which covers COM Interop:

- *Moving to Visual Basic.NET: Strategies, Concepts, and Code,* by Dan Appleman. Published by Apress, June 2001. ISBN 1893115976.

ADO.NET is what you'll be using in most of your .NET applications, because of its disconnected architecture. However, you should keep in mind that ADO.NET is firmly targeted at n-tier Web applications, or applications that are distributed over a number of different servers. This doesn't mean that you can't use it to build n-tier or client-server solutions for the Windows platform only, but it does mean that you should look into using good old ADO as well, before you make a decision on what data access technology you want to use. Please note that it's possible and perfectly legit to use both technologies in your applications, if you so desire or even need to; one technology doesn't rule out the other.

You'll get a look at ADO as well as ADO.NET here, but I won't be covering ADO in the same detail as ADO.NET. If you need more information on ADO, try these books:

- *Serious ADO: Universal Data Access with Visual Basic,* by Rob Macdonald. Published by Apress, August 2000. ISBN 1893115194.

- *ADO Examples and Best Practices,* by William R. Vaughn. Published by Apress, May 2000. ISBN 189311516X.

Also, if you need more information on ADO.NET from a VB .NET programmer's viewpoint, then you should take a look at this title:

- *Database Programming with Visual Basic.NET,* by Carsten Thomsen. Published by Apress, August 2001. ISBN 1893115291.

The overall object model looks the same for ADO and ADO.NET. In order to access a data source, you need a data provider. A *data provider* is really another word for driver, and it's simply a library that can access the data source in binary form. (See the "Data Providers and Drivers" section later in this chapter for details.) Once you have the data provider, you need to set up a connection from your application that uses the data provider to gain access to the data source. See Figure 3A-1 for a simplified picture. Now that the connection is set up and opened, you can execute queries and retrieve, delete, manipulate, and update data from the data source.

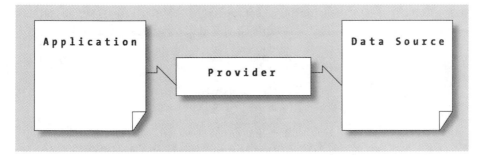

Figure 3A-1. How a data provider works

You need data objects in order to manipulate data. I'll explain these in the following sections.

> **NOTE** *Most of the code listings in this chapter and Chapter 3B are based on the SQL Server .NET Data Provider. However, the example code that can be downloaded from Apress (http://www.apress.com) or from the UserMan site (http://www.userman.dk) also shows you how to do it using the OLE DB .NET Data Provider and the ODBC .NET Data Provider. Basically, this means that you can use the example code to access the following data sources and more: SQL Server, Microsoft Access, Oracle version 7.0 and later, MySQL 3.23.45 and later, plus many more. Examples for the mentioned DBMSs can be found in the example code.*

Data-Related Namespaces

There are a number of namespaces in the .NET Framework that are of interest when dealing with data (see Table 3A-1). These namespaces hold the various data classes that you must import into your code in order to use the classes. Actually, you can prefix these classes with the namespace when you declare and instantiate your objects, but you still need to know where to find the classes in the first place.

> **CROSS-REFERENCE**   *If you are uncertain about what a namespace really is, see Chapter 1.*

Table 3A-1. Data-Related Namespaces

NAMESPACE	DESCRIPTION
System.Data	Holds the disconnected ADO.NET classes, like the **DataSet** and **DataTable** classes, and other miscellaneous generic classes, or classes that are subclassed in the .NET Data Providers.
System.Data.SqlClient	Holds the classes specific to Microsoft SQL Server 7.0 or later. This is the SQL Server.NET Data Provider.
System.Data.OleDb	Holds the collection of classes that are used for accessing an OLE DB data source. This is the OLE DB .NET Data Provider.
Microsoft.Data.Odbc	Holds the collection of classes that are used for accessing an Open Database Connectivity (ODBC) data source. This is the ODBC .NET Data Provider.[1]

You can import namespaces into a class in your code with the **using** statement, like this:

```
using System.Data;
```

---

1. The ODBC .NET Data Provider is a separate download, and it's not included in the VS .NET package. Well, at least not at the time of writing this (March 2002). For the latest version of the download, please look here: http://www.microsoft.com/data.

Instead of importing the namespaces, you can prefix the classes when declaring and/or instantiating your objects, like this:

```
System.Data.SqlClient.SqlConnection cnnUserMan; // Declare new connection
cnnUserMan = new System.Data.SqlClient.SqlConnection(); // Instantiate connection
```

Data Providers and Drivers

A *data provider* is simply just another phrase for driver, meaning it's a binary library that exposes an API that can be called from within your application. The library is a DLL file, and sometimes this DLL is dependent on other DLLs, so in fact a data provider can be made up of several files. The data providers and drivers discussed here are called *OLE DB providers* and *ODBC drivers*, and they can be accessed directly. However, when you use C#, you won't be accessing the OLE DB providers or ODBC drivers directly, but instead you'll be using the ADO.NET classes that wrap the API exposed by the provider or driver library. So, you don't have to worry about this low-level kind of programming. All you need to do is specify the name of the provider when you set up or open a connection.

OLE DB is really a specification that is used by OLE DB providers, and the primary purpose of an OLE DB provider is to translate OLE DB instructions into the language of the data source and vice versa. The same can be said about ODBC; it's a specification used by the native ODBC drivers for translating ODBC instructions into the language of the data source and vice versa.

There's one important distinction between ADO and ADO.NET: ADO calls the OLE DB provider through COM Interop, whereas ADO.NET uses the DataAdapter class, which then calls the OLE DB provider or the ODBC driver, also through COM Interop; Figure 3A-2 highlights the latter. Actually, sometimes the DataAdapter object directly accesses the API exposed by the DBMS, as can be the case with Microsoft SQL Server 7.0 or later (see Figure 3A-3). The .NET Data Provider for SQL Server uses a private protocol named tabular data stream (TDS) to talk to SQL Server. This means that if you're using ADO.NET and the OLE DB .NET Data Provider, the connected layer is using COM to access the OLE DB provider. However, you should note that the disconnected layer, which is discussed in Chapter 3B, doesn't use COM at all, even if COM Interop is used for talking to the OLE DB provider.

> **NOTE** *In ADO you can also access ODBC data sources, but this is done through the OLE DB ODBC provider, which means you have in effect three layers (ADO, OLE DB, ODBC) to go through in order to access your ODBC data source.*

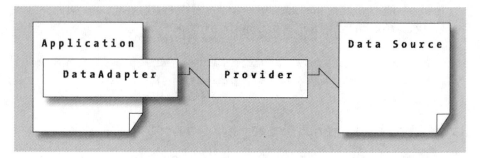

Figure 3A-2. DataAdapter using an OLE DB provider to access the data source

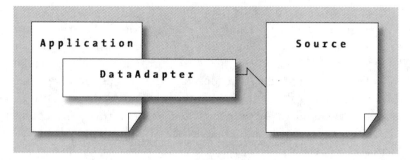

Figure 3A-3. DataAdapter accessing the data source directly

If you know at compile time that you have a .NET Data Provider for one of the data sources you need to connect to, then use that provider, because it has been optimized for that specific data source. If on the other hand you are creating a generic data wrapper to be used when you don't know the data sources you'll be connecting to at runtime, go with the generic OLE DB .NET Data Provider. The ODBC .NET Data Provider is for accessing ODBC data sources exclusively and can only be used in cases where you have the appropriate ODBC driver.

The OLE DB providers listed in Table 3A-2 work with the OLE DB .NET Data Provider. See the ".NET Data Providers" section later in this chapter for details. This list is far from exhaustive, but it does show you which current Microsoft OLE DB providers are compatible with the OLE DB .NET Data Provider.

Table 3A-2. OLE DB Providers Compatible with the OLE DB .NET Data Provider

PROVIDER NAME	DESCRIPTION
SQLOLEDB	Use with Microsoft SQL Server 6.5 or earlier
MSDAORA	Use with Oracle version 7.0 and later
Microsoft.Jet.OLEDB.4.0	Use with JET databases (Microsoft Access)

In Table 3A-2, the SQLOLEDB data provider is listed as good for connecting to Microsoft SQL Server 6.5 or earlier. However, it can also connect to SQL Server 7.0 or later, but because the SQL Server .NET Data Provider is an optimized data provider for these RDBMSs, I highly recommend you use that one instead.

The OLE DB .NET Data Provider doesn't support OLE DB version 2.5 interfaces or earlier, which also means that you need to install Microsoft Data Access Components (MDAC) 2.6 or later on your system. However, MDAC 2.7 is distributed and installed along with VS .NET.

Specifying a Provider or Driver When Connecting

There are several ways to open or set up a connection, but here is one way of specifying what provider or driver you want to use:

```
cnnUserMan.ConnectionString = "Provider=SQLOLEDB;Data Source=USERMANPC;" +
   "User ID=UserMan;Password=userman;Initial Catalog=UserMan;";
```

In the **ConnectionString** property of the connection cnnUserMan (declared and instantiated elsewhere, obviously), specify that you want to use the SQL Server provider (Provider=SQLOLEDB). See the section "ConnectionString Property" later in this chapter. Here you can see how to set up an ODBC connection string:

```
cnnUserMan.ConnectionString = "DRIVER={SQL Server};SERVER=USERMANPC;" +
   "UID=UserMan;PWD=userman;DATABASE=UserMan;";
```

The two connection strings are used for connecting to the same data source, the SQL Server by the name of USERMANPC, using the UserMan user credentials (userman as password) to the UserMan database.

.NET Data Providers

.NET Data Providers are a core part of the new ADO.NET programming model. Although a .NET Data Provider loosely maps to an OLE DB provider, it's in fact a lot closer to the ADO object model. This is because the OLE DB and ADO layers have been merged in the .NET Framework, giving the .NET Data Providers higher performance. The higher performance results from the fact that when using ADO.NET, you are effectively using only one layer as compared to using the ADO layer connected to the OLE DB layer. Nearly the same can be said about the ODBC .NET Data Provider, but this is even more of a "merger," because with ADO you also have the OLE DB provider and the ODBC driver to pass through when connecting to an ODBC data source.

Here's another way of looking at this. Previously you would tinker directly with the low-level OLE DB or ODBC API only if you really knew what you were doing. The reason for doing so was you wanted higher performance. No more, my friend! Now you have ADO.NET with its high-level programming interface, exposed by the ADO.NET object model, and yet you get the same performance as using OLE DB or ODBC directly. Isn't that great? Okay, before you start celebrating too much, let me make one final point: OLE DB and ODBC as specifications expose a data source in a rich way—that is, they expose all the functionality of all the various types of data sources out there, whereas .NET Data Providers expose minimal functionality. So OLE DB, or ODBC for that matter, isn't likely to disappear anytime soon, and as such will only be replaced by .NET Data Providers in the context of disconnected and distributed data access.

A .NET Data Provider actually consists of the following four data classes:

- Connection

- DataAdapter

- Command

- DataReader

These classes are discussed in detail in the following paragraphs. The .NET Data Provider is the first of two layers that compose the ADO.NET object model. This first layer is also called the *connected layer,* and the other layer is surprisingly called the *disconnected layer.* The disconnected layer is the **DataSet** object. See the "Using the DataSet Class" section in Chapter 3B for more information.

The Connection Class

The Connection class is part of the .NET Data Provider. You need a connection when you want to access a data source, but if you just want to save some related data in a table, you don't actually need one. I'll cover this topic in the section "Building Your Own DataTable" in Chapter 3B. I won't be discussing the ADO connection in this section, just the ADO.NET connection. From a source code point of view, the ADO connection has the same look and feel as the ADO.NET connection anyway. If you need specific information on the ADO Connection class, you may want to read one of the books mentioned at the beginning of this chapter.

Three of the managed connections that Microsoft provides with the .NET Framework are **OdbcConnection**, **OleDbConnection**, and **SqlConnection**. *Managed* means executed by and in the context of the common language runtime (CLR).

> **CROSS-REFERENCE** *See "Common Language Runtime" in Chapter 1 for details.*

Although the **OdbcConnection** and **OleDbConnection** classes can be used with SQL Server data sources, you should use **SqlConnection** for SQL Server 7.0 or later, because it has been optimized for connecting to this specific data source. Use **OleDbConnection** or **OdbcConnection** for all other data sources, unless you can get a hold of a third-party .NET Data Provider (and thus the specific Connection class) for your specific data source.

> **NOTE** *The **OdbcConnection** class, which uses the Platform Invoke feature, is roughly twice as fast for standard applications than the **OleDbConnection**. The latter uses COM, which is chatty, and hence has more server round-trips. So unless your application is shipping large amounts of data (hundreds of thousands of rows or more) per data request, you should at least consider using the **OdbcConnection** class. **SqlConnection** is roughly 20 percent faster than **OdbcConnection**.*

OdbcConnection

You should use the managed **OleDbConnection** class to connect with all your .NET-enabled applications when you have an ODBC driver for your data source.

OleDbConnection

Use the managed **OleDbConnection** class to connect with all your .NET-enabled applications. **OleDbConnection** is especially useful for creating a generic data wrapper to use when you need to connect to various data sources. **OleDbConnection** is for establishing a connection through an OLE DB provider.

SqlConnection

The **SqlConnection** class is only for use with Microsoft SQL Server 7.0 or later. It has been specifically optimized for connecting to this particular data source, and unless you are building a generic data wrapper, I recommend always using this managed connection with your .NET-enabled applications.

ConnectionString Property

The **ConnectionString** property, which is similar to an OLE DB or ODBC connection string, is used for specifying the values for connecting to a data source. The connection string that is returned is the same as the user-supplied **ConnectionString**, but it doesn't hold any security information unless the **Persist Security Info** value is set to **true**. This is also true for the password. Please note that the **Persist Security Info** value name can't be used with ODBC, which means that the security information, such as password and user id, is returned in the connection string.

> **NOTE** *You can set the DSN value in the connection string, if you need to keep the security information safe. See Table 3A-3 for more information on DSN values.*

You can set and get this property, the default value of which is an empty string, only when the connection is closed. You can specify all values by enclosing them in single quotes or double quotes, but this is optional. All value pairs (*valuename=value*) must be separated with a semicolon (;).

> **NOTE** *The separator used in the **ConnectionString** property is the same at all times. Even if you are an international user who relies on different character sets, separators, and so on, you still need to use the semicolon (ANSI character 0059) as the list separator for this property!*

The value names in a connection string are case-insensitive, whereas some of the values, such as the value for the **Password** or **PWD** value name, may be case sensitive. Table 3A-3 lists the **ConnectionString** property values. Note that only the most commonly used ODBC value names (all UPPERCASE) are listed, so please check the documentation for your specific ODBC driver.

Table 3A-3. **ConnectionString** *Property Values*

VALUE NAME	DEFAULT VALUE	REQUIRED
Addr or *Address*	The name of the .NET Data Provider	Yes
Application Name		No
AttachDBFilename		No
Database		Yes
DATABASE	"" (empty string)	Yes (when used with DBMS-based data sources)
Data Source		Yes
DBQ	"" (empty string)	Yes (when used with file-based data sources)
DRIVER		Yes

DESCRIPTION	EXAMPLE	PROVIDER SPECIFIC
The name or network address (like an IP address) of a SQL Server to which you want to connect.	Addr='USERMANPC' Address='10.0.0.1'	Yes (works with the **SqlConnection** class and the SQLOLEDB provider with the **OleDbConnection** class)
The name of your application.	Application Name='UserMan'	Yes (works with the **SqlConnection** class and the SQLOLEDB provider with the **OleDbConnection** class)
The name of the primary database file to attach. The name of the attachable database includes the full path. This value is typically used with file-based databases such as Microsoft Access.	AttachDBFileName='C:\\Program Files\\UserMan\\Data\\UserMan.mdb'	No
The name of your database.	Database='UserMan'	Yes (works with the **SqlConnection** class and the SQLOLEDB provider with the **OleDbConnection** class)
The name of your database. This value name is used with DBMS-based databases like SQL Server and Oracle.	DATABASE=UserMan	Yes (works with the **OdbcConnection** class)
Basically the same as **Addr** or **Address**, but it also works with a Microsoft Access JET database.	Data Source='C:\\Program Files\\UserMan\\Data\\UserMan.mdb' Data Source='USERMANPC'	No
The database filename, including the full file system path. This value name is used with file-based databases like dBase and Microsoft Access.	DBQ=C:\\UserMan.mdb	Yes (works with the **OdbcConnection** class)
The name of the ODBC driver enclosed in curly brackets {}.	Driver={SQL Server}	Yes (works with the **OdbcConnection** class)

(continued)

Table 3A-3. **ConnectionString** Property Values (continued)

VALUE NAME	DEFAULT VALUE	REQUIRED
DSN	"" (empty string)	No
Connect Timeout or Connection Timeout	15	No
Connection Lifetime	0	No

DESCRIPTION	EXAMPLE	PROVIDER SPECIFIC
You can use the Data Source Name (DSN), which exists on the local machine, to specify the name of an ODBC data source. You can use a DSN instead of specifying **DRIVER**, **UID**, **PWD** and other value names. A DSN can be user, system, or file based, which means that it's available to the current user, all users on the local machine, or anyone who can access the file that contains the DSN information. The file-based DSN is obviously a good option if you want to distribute it to other machines. You can see more in the ODBC Data Source Administrator that is installed on your machine (usually located under Programs ➤ Administrative Tools in the Start menu, but can often be accessed from the Control Panel as well). This application is used for creating, modifying, and deleting DSNs.	`DSN=UserMan`	Yes (works with the **OdbcConnection** class)
The number of seconds to wait when connecting to a database before terminating the connection attempt. An exception is thrown if a time-out occurs.	`Connection Timeout=15` `Connect Timeout=15`	Yes (works with the **SqlConnection** class only)
You can use this value to specify when the connection should be destroyed. This value is only relevant with regards to connection pooling, and as such the value (in seconds) specifies the acceptable time span compared to the time created and the time the connection is returned to the connection pool. In other words, this means the total number of seconds the connection has been alive (time of returning to pool minus time of creation) is compared to this value. If the **Connection Lifetime** value is less than the number of seconds the connection has been alive, then the connection is destroyed. This value is very useful in load-balancing situations, because if you set the **Connection Lifetime** to a low value, then it's more often the than not destroyed upon returning to the connection pool. This means that when the connection is re-created, it might be created on a different server, depending on the load on the servers.	`Connection Lifetime=10`	Yes (works with the **SqlConnection** class and the SQLOLEDB provider with the **OleDbConnection** class)

(continued)

Table 3A-3. **ConnectionString** *Property Values (continued)*

VALUE NAME	DEFAULT VALUE	REQUIRED
Connection Reset	'true'	No
Current Language		No
Enlist	'true'	No
FIL	"" (empty string)	Yes (when used with file-based data sources)
File Name		No
Initial Catalog (the same as *Database*)		
Initial File Name (the same as *AttachDBFilename*)		
Integrated Security	'false'	No
Max Pool Size	100	No

DESCRIPTION	EXAMPLE	PROVIDER SPECIFIC
This value determines if the connection is reset when it's destroyed, or rather removed from the connection pool. If you set this value to 'false', you can avoid an extra round-trip to the server when you require the connection. You should be aware that the connection has not been reset, so the connection will keep whatever values you've set before it was returned to the connection pool.	Connection Reset='false'	Yes (works with the **SqlConnection** class and the SQLOLEDB provider with the **OleDbConnection** class)
This is the SQL Server Language record name. Check your SQL Server documentation for a list of supported names. An exception is thrown if a nonsupported language is specified.	Current Language='English'	Yes (works with the **SqlConnection** class and the SQLOLEDB provider with the **OleDbConnection** class)
Enlists the connection in the thread's current transaction, when set to 'true'.	Enlist='false'	Yes (works with the **SqlConnection** class only)
This value name is used for specifying the file type when accessing a file-based data source, such as Microsoft Excel and Microsoft Access.	FIL=Excel 7.0	Yes (works with the **OdbcConnection** class)
For use with a Microsoft Data Link File (UDL).	File Name='Test.udl'	Yes (works with the **OleDbConnection** only)
Specifies if the connection should be secure. The possible values are 'true', 'yes', and 'sspi', which all specify a secure connection, and the default value 'false' and 'no', which obviously specify a non-secure connection.	Integrated Security='true'	Yes (works with the **SqlConnection** class)
Specifies the maximum number of connections in the connection pool.	Max Pool Size=200	Yes (works with the **SqlConnection** class and the SQLOLEDB provider with the **OleDbConnection** class)

(continued)

Table 3A-3. **ConnectionString** *Property Values (continued)*

VALUE NAME	DEFAULT VALUE	REQUIRED
Min Pool Size	0	No
Net or *Network Library*	'dbmssocn'	No
Network Address (the same as **Addr** or **Address**)		
Packet Size	8192	No
Password or *Pwd*		Yes, if your database has been secured
PWD	"" (empty string)	Yes
Persist Security Info	'false'	No

DESCRIPTION	EXAMPLE	PROVIDER SPECIFIC
Specifies the minimum number of connections in the connection pool. This number must be less than or equal to **Max Pool Size**, or an exception is thrown. Please be aware of the default value for **Max Pool Size**, meaning that if you don't specify **Max Pool Size**, which has a default value of 100, and you set the **Min Pool Size** to 101, an exception will be thrown.	`Min Pool Size=10`	Yes (works with the **SqlConnection** class and the SQLOLEDB provider with the **OleDbConnection** class)
The network library used for connecting to SQL Server. Possible values are 'dbmssocn' (TCP/IP), 'dbnmpntw' (Named Pipes), 'dbmsrpcn' (Multi-protocol), 'dbmsvinn' (Banyan Vines), 'dbmsadsn' (Apple Talk), 'dbmsgnet' (VIA), 'dbmsipcn' (Shared Memory), and 'dbmsspxn' (IPX/SPX). Please note that the corresponding library file (DLL) must be installed on both the system you connect to and the system from which you connect.	`Net='dbnmpntw'`	Yes (works with **SqlConnection** class and the SQLOLEDB provider with the **OleDbConnection** class)
The packet size specified in bytes for communicating with your data source across the network. This value must be in the range 512 to 32767. An exception is thrown if not.	`Packet Size='512'`	Yes (works with the **SqlConnection** class and the SQLOLEDB provider with the **OleDbConnection** class)
The password that corresponds to the User ID.	`Password='userman'` `Pwd='userman'`	No
The password that corresponds to the specified UID.	`PWD='userman'.`	Yes (works with the **OdbcConnection** class)
Helps you keep sensitive information like passwords safe. The possible values are 'true' and 'yes', which don't keep your sensitive information safe, and 'false' and 'no', which obviously do keep it safe.	`Persist Security Info='true'`	No

(continued)

Table 3A-3. **ConnectionString** *Property Values (continued)*

VALUE NAME	DEFAULT VALUE	REQUIRED
Pooling	'true'	No
Provider		Yes
Server (the same as **Addr** or **Address**)		
SERVER	"" (empty string)	Yes (when used with DBMS-based data sources)
Trusted_Connection (the same as **Integrated Security**)		
UID	"" (empty string)	Yes
User ID		Yes, if your database has been secured
Workstation ID	The name of the client computer or the computer from which you are connecting	No

DESCRIPTION	EXAMPLE	PROVIDER SPECIFIC
The connection object is taken from the appropriate pool, if the value is set to 'true'. If there are no available connection objects in the pool, a new one is created and added to the pool.	Pooling='false'	Yes (works with the **SqlConnection** class only)
Specifies the name of the OLE DB provider you want to use for accessing your data source.	Provider=SQLOLEDB	Yes (works with the **OleDbConnection** class only)
The server you want to connect to.	SERVER=USERMAN	Yes (works with the **OdbcConnection** class)
The user id you wish to connect with.	UID=UserMan	Yes (works with the **OdbcConnection** class)
The User ID you wish to connect with.	User ID='UserMan'	No
The name of the client computer or the computer from which you are connecting.	Workstation ID='USERMANPC'	No

Many of these values have corresponding properties, such as the **ConnectionTimeout** property, that can be set separately (see "Connection Class Properties" for more details). Mind you, you can only set these properties when the connection is closed! So if you have an open connection, you need to close it before you try to set any of these properties. The corresponding properties are set when you set the **ConnectionString** property.

When you set the connection string, it will be parsed immediately, which means that any syntax errors will be caught straight away and an exception thrown (a trappable error occurs). Syntax errors alone are caught at this time, because other errors are found only when you try to open the connection.

Once you open the connection, the validated connection string is returned as part of the connection object, with properties updated. Mind you, if you don't set the **Persist Security Info** value (which can't be used with ODBC) or if you set it to 'false', then sensitive information will NOT be returned in **ConnectionString**. The same goes for value names with default values; they aren't returned in the connection string. This is important to know, if you want to examine the **ConnectionString** property after it has been set.

If you set a value more than once in the **ConnectionString** property, only the last occurrence of the *valuename=value* pair counts. Actually, the exact opposite is true for ODBC connection strings, where it's the first occurrence that counts. Also, if you use one of the synonyms, like **Pwd** instead of **Password**, the "official" value name will be returned (**Password** in this case).

Finally, white space is stripped from values and from between value names, unless you use single quotes or double quotes to delimit the values, in which case the white space counts!

Connection Class Properties

Instead of using the **ConnectionString** property, you can actually set the various values individually by using their corresponding properties. Tables 3A-4, 3A-5, and 3A-6 list the public noninherited connection properties in alphabetical order.

Table 3A-4. **SqlConnection** *Class Properties*

PROPERTY NAME	CONNECTIONSTRING EQUIVALENT	DESCRIPTION	READ	WRITE
ConnectionTimeout	**Connection Timeout**		Yes	No
Database	**Database** or **Initial Catalog**		Yes	No
DataSource	**Addr** or **Address**		Yes	No
PacketSize	**Packet Size**		Yes	No
ServerVersion	There's no equivalent **ConnectionString** value.	This property receives a string from SQL Server containing the version of the current SQL Server. If the **State** property equals **Closed,** when you read this property, the **InvalidOperationException** exception is thrown.	Yes	No
State	There's no equivalent **ConnectionString** value.	This property gets the current state of the connection; possible values are **Open** and **Closed**. These values are taken from the **ConnectionState** enum, which is part of the **System.Data** namespace.	Yes	No
WorkstationId	**Workstation ID**	This property returns a string identifying the database client.	Yes	No

*Table 3A-5. **OleDbConnection** Class Properties*

PROPERTY NAME	CONNECTIONSTRING EQUIVALENT	DESCRIPTION	READ	WRITE
ConnectionTimeout	**Connection Timeout**		Yes	No
Database	**Database** or **Initial Catalog**		Yes	No
DataSource	**Addr** or **Address**		Yes	No
Provider	**Provider**		Yes	No
ServerVersion	There's no equivalent **ConnectionString** value.	This property receives a string from the DBMS containing the version number. If the **State** property equals **Closed,** when you read this property, the **InvalidOperationException** exception is thrown. An empty **string** is returned if the OLE DB provider doesn't support this property.	Yes	No
State	There's no equivalent **ConnectionString** value.	This property gets the current state of the connection; possible values are **Closed** and **Open**. These values are taken from the **ConnectionState** enum, which is part of the **System.Data** namespace.	Yes	No

Table 3A-6. **OdbcConnection** *Class Properties*

PROPERTY NAME	DEFAULT VALUE	CONNECTIONSTRING EQUIVALENT	DESCRIPTION	READ	WRITE
ConnectionTimeout	15	There's no equivalent **ConnectionString** value.	The number of seconds to wait when connecting to a database before terminating the connection attempt. An exception is thrown if a time-out occurs.	Yes	Yes
Database	"" (empty string)	**DATABASE**		Yes	No
DataSource	"" (empty string)	There's no equivalent **ConnectionString** value.	This property retrieves the filename and location of the data source.	Yes	No
Driver		There's no equivalent **ConnectionString** value.	Returns the name of the ODBC driver, which is usually the name of the driver DLL.	Yes	No
ServerVersion		There's no equivalent **ConnectionString** value.	This property receives a string from the DBMS containing the version number. If the **State** property equals **Closed,** when you read this property, the **InvalidOperationException** exception is thrown. An empty **string** is returned if the ODBC driver doesn't support this property.	Yes	No
State		There's no equivalent **ConnectionString** value.	This property gets the current state of the connection; possible values are **Closed** and **Open**. These values are taken from the **ConnectionState** enum, which is part of the **System.Data** namespace.	Yes	No

Connection Class Methods

Tables 3A-7, 3A-8, and 3A-9 list the public methods of the Connection class. Methods inherited from classes other than the base classes, like **object**, aren't shown. The tables are only reference lists, so if you need information on how to use these methods, such as how to open a connection, then read the explanations following the tables. The same goes if you need to see all the various overloaded functions, which are marked Overloaded. See "Handling Connection Class Exceptions" later in this chapter for details.

*Table 3A-7. **SqlConnection** Class Methods*

METHOD NAME	DESCRIPTION	RETURN VALUE	OVERLOADED
BeginTransaction()	Begins a transaction on the connection object. This method is overloaded, so see "Transactions" later in this chapter for more information.	The instantiated **SqlTransaction** object	Yes
ChangeDatabase(string strDatabase)	This method, which can't be overridden, changes the database for the connection to the database passed in the strDatabase argument. The connection must be open or else an **InvalidOperationException** exception is thrown.		No
Close()	This method takes no arguments, and it simply closes an open connection. Any pending transactions are rolled back when you call this method.		No
CreateCommand()	This method creates a **SqlCommand**. The **SqlCommand** object is associated with the connection object.	The instantiated **SqlCommand** object	No
Equals()	This method, which is inherited from the **object** class, can be used to determine if two connections are the same.	Data type **bool**	Yes
GetHashCode()	This method, which is inherited from the **object** class, returns the hash code for the connection.	Data type **Integer**	No
GetType()	This method, which is inherited from the **object** class, returns the object type, or rather the metadata associated with the class from which an object is inherited. If you need the class name, you can get it using cnnUserMan.GetType.ToString();.	Data type **Type**	No

(continued)

Table 3A-7. **SqlConnection** *Class Methods (continued)*

METHOD NAME	DESCRIPTION	RETURN VALUE	OVERLOADED
Open()	This method, which can't be overridden, is used for opening the connection to the data source with the current property settings. Different exceptions can be thrown under various circumstances (see "Handling Connection Class Exceptions" later in this chapter).		No
ToString()	This method, which is inherited from the **object** class, returns a string representation of the connection. If you call the method using `MessageBox.Show(cnnUserMan.ToString());`, the message box displayed should contain the text "System.Data.SqlClient.SqlConnection". This is the name of the object (**SqlConnection**) including the namespace in which it's contained (**System.Data.SqlClient**).	Data type **string**	No

Table 3A-8. **OleDbConnection** *Class Methods*

METHOD NAME	DESCRIPTION	RETURN VALUE	OVERLOADED
BeginTransaction()	Begins a transaction on the connection object. This method is overloaded, so see "Transactions" later in this chapter for more information.	The instantiated **OleDbTransaction** object	Yes
ChangeDatabase(string strDatabase)	This method, which can't be overridden, changes the database for the connection to the database passed in the strDatabase variable. The connection must be open or else an **InvalidOperationException** exception is thrown.		No
Close()	This method takes no arguments, and it simply closes an open connection. Any pending transactions are rolled back when you call this method.		No
CreateCommand()	This method creates an **OleDbCommand**. The **OleDbCommand** object is associated with the connection object.	The instantiated **OleDbCommand** object	No

(continued)

*Table 3A-8. **OleDbConnection** Class Methods (continued)*

METHOD NAME	DESCRIPTION	RETURN VALUE	OVERLOADED
Equals()	This method, which is inherited from the **object** class, can be used to determine if two connections are the same.	Data type **bool**	Yes
GetOleDbSchemaTable (Guid guiSchema, object[] objRestrictions)	This method is used for retrieving the schema table for the guiSchema after applying objRestrictions. You can use this method to return a list of tables in the current database and other schema information.	Data type **DataTable**	No
GetType()	This method, which is inherited from the **object** class, returns the object type, or rather the metadata associated with the class that an object is inherited from. If you need the class name, you can get it using cnnUserMan.GetType.ToString();.	Data type **Type**	No
Open()	This method, which can't be overridden, is used for opening the connection to the data source with the current property settings. Different exceptions can be thrown under various circumstances (see "Handling Connection Class Exceptions" later in this chapter for details.		No
ReleaseObjectPool()	This method is used for indicating that the connection pool can be cleared when the last underlying OLE DB provider is released.		No
ToString()	This method, which is inherited from the **object** class, returns a string representation of the connection. If you call the method using MessageBox.Show(cnnUserMan.ToString());, the message box displayed should contain the text "System.Data.OleDb.OleDbConnection". This is the name of the object (**OleDbConnection**) including the namespace in which it's contained (**System.Data.OleDb**).	Data type **string**	No

*Table 3A-9. **OdbcConnection** Class Methods*

METHOD NAME	DESCRIPTION	RETURN VALUE	OVERLOADED
BeginTransaction()	Begins a transaction on the connection object. This method is overloaded, so see "Transactions" later in this chapter for more information.	The instantiated **OdbcTransaction** object	Yes
ChangeDatabase(string strDatabase)	This method, which can't be overridden, changes the database for the connection to the database passed in the `strDatabase` variable. The connection must be open or else an **InvalidOperationException** exception is thrown.		No
Close()	This method takes no arguments, and it simply closes an open connection. Any pending transactions are rolled back when you call this method.		No
CreateCommand()	This method creates an **OdbcCommand**. The **OdbcCommand** object is associated with the connection object.	The instantiated **OdbcCommand** object	No
Equals()	This method, which is inherited from the **object** class, can be used to determine if two connections are the same.	Data type **bool**	Yes
GetHashCode()	This method, which is inherited from the **object** class, returns the hash code for the connection. The hash code is a number that corresponds to the value of the connection.	Data type **int**	No
GetType()	This method, which is inherited from the **object** class, returns the object type, or rather the metadata associated with the class that an object is inherited from. If you need the class name, you can get it using `cnnUserMan.GetType.ToString();`.	Data type **Type**	No
Open()	This method, which can't be overridden, is used for opening the connection to the data source with the current property settings. Different exceptions can be thrown under various circumstances (see "Handling Connection Class Exceptions" later in this chapter for details).		No

(continued)

83

Table 3A-9. **OdbcConnection** Class Methods (continued)

METHOD NAME	DESCRIPTION	RETURN VALUE	OVERLOADED
ReleaseObjectPool()	This method is used for indicating that the connection pool can be cleared when the last underlying ODBC driver is released.		No
ToString()	This method, which is inherited from the **object** class, returns a string representation of the connection. If you call the method using `MessageBox.Show(cnnUserMan.ToString());`, the message box displayed should contain the text "System.Data.OleDb.OdbcConnection". This is the name of the object (**OdbcConnection**) including the namespace in which it's contained (**Microsoft.Data.Odbc**).	Data type **string**	No

Connection Class Events

All three Connection classes covered in this chapter, **SqlConnection**, **OleDbConnection**, and **OdbcConnection**, expose the same events, and the noninherited events are shown in Table 3A-10.

Table 3A-10. Connection Class Events

EVENT NAME	DESCRIPTION
InfoMessage	This event is triggered when the provider, driver, or data source sends a warning or an informational message. Basically, this event is triggered if the provider, driver, or data source needs to inform the connecting application about any nonserious event, or anything else besides errors. See the "Handling Provider, Driver, and Data Source Messages" section later in this chapter for some example code that handles this event. In the case of SQL Server, this event is triggered when SQL server raises a message with a severity of 10 or less. Serious problems at your data source, provider, or driver trigger an exception that you must catch in an exception handler (see Chapter 5 for more information about exception handling). In the case of SQL Server, exceptions are thrown when messages with a severity between 11 and 20 (both inclusive) are raised. So, to catch all kinds of messages from the provider, driver, and data source, you really need to handle the **InfoMessage** event, as well as set up an exception handler. In the case of SQL Server, when a message with a severity of 21 is raised, the connection is closed. However, this doesn't trigger the InfoMessage event, nor does it throw an exception, but you can catch this error in the StateChange event.
StateChange	This event is triggered immediately, when the state of your connection changes—that is, when your connection goes from open to closed and vice versa. The procedure that handles the event is passed an argument of type **StateChangeEventArgs**, which holds two properties that can tell you the current state and the original state. This means that you know whether the connection was being closed or opened. See the "Handling Connection State Changes" section later in this chapter to see how to handle state change events.

Opening a Connection

Once you've set the properties required to open a connection, it's time to actually open it. This is quite simple if you've set the connection properties correctly. See Listing 3A-1 for an example.

Listing 3A-1. Opening a Connection

```
 1 public void OpenConnection(string strConnectionString) {
 2     // Declare connection object
 3     SqlConnection cnnUserMan;
 4
 5     // Instantiate the connection object
 6     cnnUserMan = new SqlConnection();
 7     // Set up connection string
 8     cnnUserMan.ConnectionString = strConnectionString;
 9
10     // Open the connection
11     cnnUserMan.Open();
12 }
```

Note that the **Open** method doesn't take any arguments, so you need to be sure that you've set the properties necessary to connect to your data source. If you haven't set all the required properties or the connection is already open, an exception is thrown. See "ConnectionString Property Exceptions" later in this chapter for details. When you open a connection, the **StateChange** event is triggered.

Closing a Connection

Close a connection whenever you don't need to use it so it doesn't consume any more memory than needed. Closing a connection also returns it to the connection pool, which is the default behavior, if it belongs to one. You close a connection like this:

```
cnnUserMan.Close();
```

When you call the **Close** method, it tries to wait for all transactions to finish before closing the connection. If a transaction isn't finished up after a period of time, an exception is thrown. When you close a connection, the **StateChange** event is triggered.

Disposing of a Connection

You can dispose of your connection by calling the **Dispose** method, like this:

```
cnnUserMan.Dispose();
```

The **Dispose** method destroys the reference to the connection and tells the Garbage Collector that it can do its job and destroy the connection itself, assuming of course that this is the only reference to the connection. The **Dispose** method also closes the connection if it's open.

Comparing Two Connection Objects

If you've been copying a connection object or setting one connection variable equal to another, it can be hard to know if two instances of a Connection class in fact are the same connection, or if they point to the same location in memory. Mind you, it isn't too difficult to find out programmatically. You can perform a comparison using the following:

- The **==** operator

- The **Equals** method

- The **static ReferenceEquals** method of the **object** class

Comparing Using the == Operator

Using the == operator is perhaps the easiest way of comparing two connection objects:

```
blnEqual = cnnUserMan1 == cnnUserMan2;
```

The **bool** variable blnEqual will be set to **true** if cnnUserMan1 and cnnUserMan2 refer to the same location in memory; otherwise it's set to **false**.

Comparing Using the Equals Method

The **Equals** method, which is inherited from the **object** class, is actually intended for you to use for comparing values and not references. When two connection variables hold a reference to the same location in memory, however, they actually hold the same "value." As such you can use the **Equals** method for connection object comparison. The **Equals** method comes in two flavors. One checks if the passed connection object is equal to the connection object that performs the method:

```
blnEqual = cnnUserMan1.Equals(cnnUserMan2);
```

The **bool** variable blnEqual will be set to **true** if cnnUserMan1 and cnnUserMan2 refer to the same connection; otherwise it's set to **false**. The second, overloaded version of the method takes two connection objects as arguments and checks if these are equal:

```
blnEqual = object.Equals(cnnUserMan1, cnnUserMan2);
```

The **bool** variable blnEqual will be set to **true** if cnnUserMan1 and cnnUserMan2 refer to the same connection; otherwise it's set to **false**. With this overloaded version of the method you can actually compare two connection objects separate from the connection object performing the method. Please note that the second overloaded version of the **Equals** method is static and as such it must be called using the type identifier (**object** in this case).

Comparing Using the ReferenceEquals Method

The static **ReferenceEquals** method of the **object** class is for comparing references and as such it should be preferred over the **Equals** method, which is for comparing values. Here is how you use the **ReferenceEquals** method:

```
blnEqual = object.ReferenceEquals(cnnUserMan1, cnnUserMan2);
```

The **bool** variable blnEqual will be set to **true** if cnnUserMan1 and cnnUserMan2 refer to the same connection; otherwise it's set to **false**.

> **NOTE** *The **Equals** and the **ReferenceEquals** methods use arguments of data type **object**. This means the comparison can be done using any data type inherited from the base type **object**.*

Manipulating the Connection State

When dealing with connections, it's often a good idea to check their states before attempting to get or set one of the properties or execute one of the methods. You can use the Connection class's **State** property to determine the current state. (See "Connection Class Properties" earlier in this chapter for details.) You check the **State** property against the **ConnectionState** enum. See Table 3A-11 for a list of the members in the **ConnectionState** enum.

*Table 3A-11. Members of the **ConnectionState** Enum*

NAME	DESCRIPTION
Closed	The connection is closed.
Open	The connection is open.
Connecting	The connection is currently connecting to the data source.
Executing	The connection is executing a command.
Fetching	The connection is retrieving data from the data source.
Broken	The connection can't be used as the connection is in error. This usually occurs if the network fails. The only valid method in this state is **Close**, and all properties are read-only.

Table 3A-11 shows you all the members of the **ConnectionState** enum, but currently only the **Closed** and **Open** members are supported.

Comparing State to ConnectionState

You can compare the **State** property with the **ConnectionState** enum using the following statement:

```
if (cnnUserMan.State == ConnectionState.Open) { }
```

I use the == operator to perform a bitwise comparison between the two enum values. In this case, I am checking if the connection is open. If you want to check if the connection is closed, you can do it like this:

```
if (cnnUserMan.State == ConnectionState.Closed) { }
```

Handling Connection State Changes

If you want to handle changes to the connection state, you need to set up an event handler that can receive and process these changes. Listing 3A-2 shows you how to do this.

Listing 3A-2. Handling Connection State Changes

```
1 public class CGeneral {
2     // Declare and instantiate connection
3     private SqlConnection prcnnUserMan =
4         new SqlConnection(STR_CONNECTION_STRING);
5     public CGeneral() {
6         // Set up event handler
7         prcnnUserMan.StateChange  +=
8             new StateChangeEventHandler(OnStateChange);
9     }
10    protected static void OnStateChange(object sender,
11        StateChangeEventArgs args) {
12        // Display the original and the current state
13        MessageBox.Show("The original connection state was: " +
14            args.OriginalState.ToString() +
15            "\nThe current connection state is: " +
16            args.CurrentState.ToString());
17    }
18    public void TriggerStateChangeEvent() {
19        // Open the connection
20        prcnnUserMan.Open();
21        // Close the connection
22        prcnnUserMan.Close();
23    }
24 }
```

In Listing 3A-2, you can see how you can capture connection state changes. On Line 3, I declare and instantiate the connection, and in the class constructor I set up the event handler (Lines 7 and 8). Lines 10 through 17 are the actual event handler procedure, which shows the two properties of the **StateChangeEventArgs** argument, **OriginalState** and **CurrentState**. Finally, Lines 18 through 23 are the procedure that triggers the state change event. The event is actually triggered twice—when you open the connection and when you close it again.

Pooling Connections

Connection pooling, or connection sharing and reuse between applications and components, is automatically applied to the OLE DB .NET Data Provider and the ODBC .NET Data Provider. This is important, because connection pooling will reserve resources, as the connections are being reused. However, the SQL Server .NET Data Provider uses an implicit pooling model by default, and you can use the **ConnectionString** property to control the implicit pooling behavior of a **SqlConnection** object.

A connection pool is distinct on one count only, the **ConnectionString** property. This means that all connections in any given pool have the exact same connection string. You must know that white space in the connection string will lead to two otherwise identical connections being added to different connection pools. The two instances of **SqlConnection** in Listing 3A-3 will NOT be added to the same pool, because of the white space in the connection string for the cnnUserMan2 connection. There's an extra space character after the separator (semicolon) that separates the **Password** and **Data Source** value names.

*Listing 3A-3. White Space in **ConnectionString** Property*

```
1 public void CheckConnectionStringWhiteSpace() {
2     SqlConnection cnnUserMan1 = new SqlConnection();
3     SqlConnection cnnUserMan2 = new SqlConnection();
4
5     // Set the connection string for the connections
6     cnnUserMan1.ConnectionString = "User Id=UserMan;Password=userman;" +
7         "Data Source='USERMANPC';Initial Catalog='UserMan';" +
8         "Max Pool Size=1;Connection Timeout=5"
9     cnnUserMan2.ConnectionString = "User Id=UserMan;Password=userman; " +
10        "Data Source='usermanpc';Initial Catalog='UserMan';" +
11        "Max Pool Size=1;Connection Timeout=5";
12
13    // cnnUserMan1 and cnnUserMan2 will NOT be added to the same pool
14    // because cnnUserMan2 contains an extra space char right after
15    // Password=userman;
16    try {
17        // Open the cnnUserMan1 connection
18        cnnUserMan1.Open();
19        // Open the cnnUserMan2 connection
20        cnnUserMan2.Open();
21    }
22    catch (Exception objE) {
23        // This message will be displayed if the connection strings are equal,
24        // because then the connection pool will have reached its max size (1)
25        // If you don't see the message, the connections are drawn from
26        //  different pools
27        MessageBox.Show(objE.Message);
28    }
29 }
```

Testing for the Same Pool

One way to test if your connections go in the same pool or not is to set up two connections with identical connection strings and make sure the **Max Pool Size** value is set to 1. When you open the first connection, a new pool will be created for this specific connection string, and the connection will be added. When you try to open the second connection, the object pooler will try and add it to the existing pool. Because the existing pool doesn't allow any more connections (the maximum pool size has been reached), the request is queued. If the first connection isn't returned to the pool (by closing the connection), a time-out will occur for the second connection, when the **ConnectionTimeout** period elapses. Once you've set up this scenario, you can change the connection strings, and if a time-out occurs at runtime, then your connections do go in the same pool.

Pooling Connections of Data Type SqlConnection

When you set up the **SqlConnection** class's **ConnectionString** property, you must set the **Pooling** value name to the value 'true' or leave out the value pair, because 'true' is the default value for **Pooling**. So by default, a **SqlConnection** object is taken from a connection pool when the connection is opened, and if no pool exists, one is created to hold the connection being opened.

The **Min Pool Size** and **Max Pool Size** value names of the **ConnectionString** property determine how many connections a pool can hold. Connections will be added to a pool until the maximum pool size is reached. Requests will then be queued by the object pooler, and a time-out will occur if no connections are returned to the pool before the time-out period elapses. Connections are only returned to the pool when they are closed using the **Close** method or if you explicitly destroy your connections with a call to the **Dispose** method. This is also true even if the connections are broken. Once a broken or invalid connection is returned to the pool, the object pooler removes the connection from the pool. This is done at regular intervals, when the object pooler scans for broken connections.

Another way to remove connections from the pool is to specify a value for the **Connection Lifetime** value name of the **ConnectionString** property. This value is 0 by default, which means that the connection will never automatically be removed from the pool. If you specify a different value (in seconds), this value will be compared to the connection's time of creation and the current time once the connection is returned to the pool. If the lifetime exceeds the value indicated in the **Connection Lifetime** value name, the connection will be removed from the pool.

Resetting Connections in the Connection Pool

The **Connection Reset** value name is used for determining if the connection should be reset when it's returned to the pool. The default value is 'true', indicating the connection is reset upon returning to the pool. This is quite meaningful, if you've tampered with the properties when the connection was open. If you know that your connections stay the same whenever open, you can set the value to 'false' and thus avoid the extra round-trip to the server, sparing network load and saving time.

Pooling Connections of Data Type OleDbConnection

Although the OLE DB .NET Data Provider supplies automatic pooling, you can still manually override or even disable it programmatically.

Disabling OLE DB Connection Pooling

It's possible to disable the automatic connection pooling if you specify the **OLE DB Services** value in your connection string. The following connection will NOT have automatic connection pooling:

```
string strConnectionString = "Provider=SQLOLEDB;OLE DB Services=-4;";
strConnectionString += "Data Source=USERMANPC;User ID=UserMan;";
strConnectionString += "Password=userman;Initial Catalog=UserMan;";
cnnUserMan.Open(strConnectionString);
```

You can learn more about the **OLE DB Services** value by reading the document "OLE DB Programmer's Reference" at this address: http://msdn.microsoft.com/library/default.asp?url=/library/en-us/oledb/htm/oledbabout_the_ole_db_documentation.asp.

Clearing OLE DB Object Pooling

Because the connection pool is being cached when a provider is created, it's important to call the connection's **ReleaseObjectPool** method when you are done using your connection.

Using the ReleaseObjectPool Method

The **ReleaseObjectPool** method tells the connection pooler that the connection pool can be cleared when the last provider is released. You should call this method when you've closed your connection and you know you won't need the connection within the time frame the OLE DB Services normally keeps pooled connections alive (see Listing 3A-4).

*Listing 3A-4. When to Call the **ReleaseObjectPool** Method*

```
// Open the connection
cnnUserMan.Open();
// Do your stuff
... ...
// Close the connection and release pool
cnnUserMan.Close();
OleDbConnection.ReleaseObjectPool();
```

Pooling Connections of Data Type OdbcConnection

Although the ODBC .NET Data Provider supplies automatic pooling, you can still manually override or even disable it. Actually, the ODBC Driver Manager utility manages this, but as stated; it's applied automatically.

Disabling ODBC Connection Pooling

It's not possible to disable the automatic connection pooling from the connection string, and in fact it's not possible through using methods or properties from the **Microsoft.Data.Odbc** namespace. However, you can manually disable it from the ODBC Data Source Administrator,[2] which is usually located under Programs ➤ Administrative Tools in the Start menu, but sometimes it can also be accessed from the Control Panel as well (see Figure 3A-4).

---

2. The name of this utility seems to change with every version of Windows, but you can run it from the command prompt by entering its filename, which is ODBCAD32.EXE.

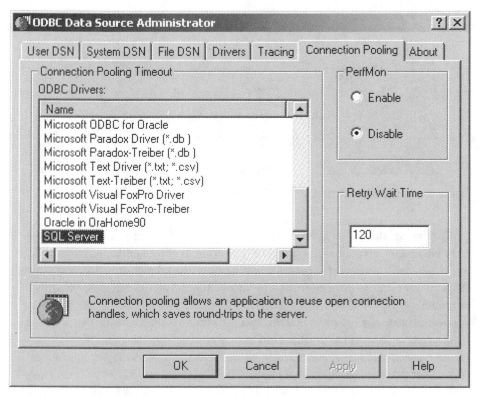

Figure 3A-4. The ODBC Data Source Administrator application

You need to enable or disable connection pooling from the Connection Pooling tab. On the ODBC Drivers list, double-click the driver for which you want to change the connection pooling options. This brings up the Set Connection Pooling Attributes dialog box as shown in Figure 3A-5.

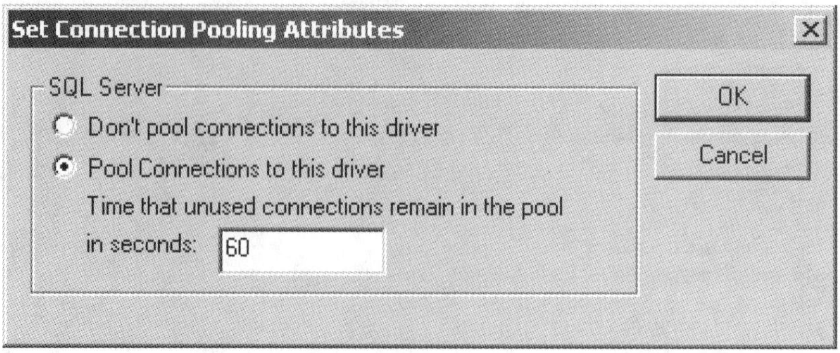

Figure 3A-5. The Set Connection Pooling Attributes dialog box

In this dialog box, you can disable or enable the connection pooling for the selected driver. If you enable connection pooling, you must also make sure you've set the connection lifetime, meaning how long the connection remains in the pool after being released from your application. The default is 60 seconds as shown.

You can learn more about ODBC by reading the document "ODBC Programmer's Reference" at this address: http://msdn.microsoft.com/library/default.asp?url=/library/en-us/odbc/htm/odbcabout_this_manual.asp?frame=true.

Clearing ODBC Object Pooling

Because the connection pool is being cached when a provider is created, it's important to call the connection's **ReleaseObjectPool** method when you are done using your connection.

Using the ReleaseObjectPool Method

The **ReleaseObjectPool** method tells the connection pooler that the connection pool can be cleared when the last driver is released. You should call this method when you've closed your connection and you know you won't need the connection within the time frame the ODBC Driver Manager keeps pooled connections alive (see Listing 3A-5).

*Listing 3A-5. When to Call the **ReleaseObjectPool** Method*

```
// Open the connection
cnnUserMan.Open();
// Do your stuff
... ...
// Close the connection and release pool
cnnUserMan.Close();
OdbcConnection.ReleaseObjectPool();
```

Handling Provider, Driver, and Data Source Messages

If you want to handle warnings and messages from the provider, driver, or data source, you need to set up an event handler that can receive and process these warnings and messages. Listing 3A-6 shows you how to do this.

Listing 3A-6. Handling Connection State Messages

```
1 public class CGeneral {
2    // Declare and instantiate connection
3    private SqlConnection prcnnUserMan =
4       new SqlConnection(STR_CONNECTION_STRING);
5    public CGeneral() {
6       // Set up event handler
7       prcnnUserMan.InfoMessage +=
8          SqlInfoMessageEventHandler(OnInfoMessage);
9    }
10   protected static void OnInfoMessage(object sender,
11      SqlInfoMessageEventArgs args) {
12      // Loop through all the error messages
13      foreach (SqlError objError in args.Errors) {
14         // Display the error properties
15         MessageBox.Show("The " + objError.Source +
16            " has raised a warning on the " +
17            objError.Server + " server. These are the properties :\n\n"  +
18            "Severity: " + objError.Class + "\nNumber: " +
19            objError.Number + "\nState: " + objError.State +
20            "\nLine: " + objError.LineNumber + "\n" +
21            "Procedure: " + objError.Procedure + "\nMessage: " +
22            objError.Message);
23      }
24
25      // Display the message and the source
26      MessageBox.Show("Info Message: " + args.Message +
27         "\nInfo Source: " + args.Source);
28   }
29   public void TriggerInfoMessageEvent() {
30      SqlCommand cmmUserMan =
31         new SqlCommand("RAISERROR('This is an info message event.', 10, 1)",
32         prcnnUserMan);
33      // Open the connection
```

```
34          prcnnUserMan.Open();
35          // Execute the T-SQL command
36          cmmUserMan.ExecuteNonQuery();
37     }
38 }
```

In Listing 3A-6, you can see how to capture warnings and messages from the provider, driver, and data source. On Line 3, I declare and instantiate the connection, and in the class constructor, I set up the event handler (Lines 7 and 8). Lines 10 through 28 are the actual event handler procedure, which displays all properties of the error objects in the Errors collection of the **SqlInfoMessageEventArgs** argument. Then the two properties of the **SqlInfoMessageEventArgs** argument, **Message** and **Source**, are displayed. Finally, Lines 29 through 37 show the procedure that triggers the state info message event. This is done by calling the T-SQL function RAISERROR through the cmmUserMan **SqlCommand** object with a severity of 10 and a state of 1.

Transactions

Transactions are a way of grouping related database operations so that if one fails, they all fail. Likewise, if they all succeed, the changes will be applied permanently to the data source. So transactions are a safety net, ensuring that your data stays in sync.

One classic example of a transaction is a banking system. Suppose you are moving money from your current account to your savings account. This is an operation that requires two updates: credit the amount to the current account and debit the amount to the savings account. Let us assume that this operation is under way, and the amount has been credited to the current account. Now, for whatever reason, the system crashes, and the amount is never debited to the savings account. This is no good and will certainly make someone unhappy. If this operation had been performed within a single transaction, the amount credited to the current account would have been rolled back once the system was back up and running. Although I've simplified the whole process, it should be clear why you want to use transactions!

ADO.NET offers you two ways of handling transactions within your application: manual and automatic.

Defining Transaction Boundaries

All transactions have a *boundary*, which is the scope or the "surrounding border" for all the resources within a transaction. Resources within the boundary share the same transaction identifier. This means internally all the resources, such as a database server, are assigned this identifier, which is unique to the transaction boundary. A transaction boundary is abstract, meaning that it's like an invisible frame. The boundary can also be extended and reduced. How this is done all depends on whether you are using automatic (implicit) or manual (explicit) transactions.

Manual Transactions

The .NET Data Providers that come with ADO.NET support manual transactions through methods of the Connection class. When dealing with manual transactions, it's a good idea to check the state of the connection before attempting to perform one of the transaction methods. See "Manipulating the Connection State" earlier in this chapter for details.

Starting a Manual Transaction

To start a transaction, you need to call the **BeginTransaction** method of the Connection class. You must call this method before performing any of the database operations that are to take part in the transaction. The call in its simplest form is performed as shown in Listing 3A-7.

Listing 3A-7. Begin Transaction with Default Values
```
traUserMan = cnnUserMan.BeginTransaction();
```

The connection object (cnnUserMan) must be a valid and open connection, or the **InvalidOperationException** is thrown. See "BeginTransaction Method Exceptions" for more details. traUserMan now holds a reference to the transaction object created by the **BeginTransaction** method. The **BeginTransaction** method is overloaded, and Tables 3A-12, 3A-13, and 3A-14 show you the various versions of the method.

*Table 3A-12. The **BeginTransaction** Method of the **SqlConnection** Class*

CALL	DESCRIPTION
BeginTransaction()	This version takes no arguments, and you should use it when you aren't nesting your transactions and you include the default isolation level (see Listing 3A-7).
BeginTransaction(IsolationLevel enuIsolationLevel)	Takes the transaction's isolation level as the only argument. You should use this version of the method when you want to specify the isolation level (see Listing 3A-8).
BeginTransaction(string strName)	Takes the name of the transaction as the only argument. You should use this version of the method when you want to nest your transactions and thus name those for easier identification (see Listing 3A-9). Please note that strName can't contain spaces and has to start with a letter or one of the following characters: # (pound sign), _ (underscore). Subsequent characters may also be numeric (0–9).
BeginTransaction(IsolationLevel enuIsolationLevel string strName)	Takes the transaction's isolation level and the name of the transaction as arguments. You should use this version of the method when you want to specify the isolation level and you want to nest your transactions and thus name those for easier identification (see Listing 3A-10). Please note that strName can't contain spaces and has to start with a letter or one of the following characters: # (pound sign), _ (underscore). Subsequent characters may also be numeric (0–9).

*Table 3A-13. The **BeginTransaction** Method of the **OleDbConnection** Class*

CALL	DESCRIPTION
BeginTransaction()	This version takes no arguments, and you should use it when you aren't nesting your transactions and you include the default isolation level (see Listing 3A-7).
BeginTransaction(IsolationLevel enuIsolationLevel)	Takes the transaction's isolation level as the only argument. You should use this version of the method when you want to specify the isolation level. Refer to Listing 3A-8, but replace **SqlConnection** and **SqlTransaction** in the example with **OleDbConnection** and **OleDbTransaction**.

*Table 3A-14. The **BeginTransaction** Method of the **OdbcConnection** Class*

CALL	DESCRIPTION
BeginTransaction()	This version takes no arguments, and you should use it when you aren't nesting your transactions and you include the default isolation level (see Listing 3A-7).
BeginTransaction(IsolationLevel enuIsolationLevel)	Takes the transaction's isolation level as the only argument. You should use this version of the method when you want to specify the isolation level. Refer to Listing 3A-8, but replace **SqlConnection** and **SqlTransaction** in the example with **OdbcConnection** and **OdbcTransaction**.

All the overloaded versions of the **BeginTransaction** method return an instance of the Transaction class inherited from the **SqlTransaction**, **OleDbTransaction**, or **OdbcTransaction** class. The **IsolationLevel** enum, which belongs to the **System.Data** namespace, specifies the local transaction locking behavior for the connection. If the isolation level is changed during a transaction, the server is expected to apply the new locking level to all the remaining statements. See Table 3A-15 for an overview of the **IsolationLevel** enum.

*Table 3A-15. Members of the **IsolationLevel** Enum*

NAME	DESCRIPTION
Chaos	You can't overwrite pending changes from more highly isolated transactions.
ReadCommitted	Although the shared locks will be held until the end of the read, thus avoiding dirty reads, the data can be changed before the transaction ends. This can result in phantom data or nonrepeatable reads. This means the data you read isn't guaranteed to be the same the next time you perform the same read request.
ReadUncommitted	Dirty reads are possible, because no shared locks are in effect and any exclusive locks won't be honored.
RepeatableRead	All data that is part of the query will be locked so that other users can't update the data. This will prevent nonrepeatable reads, but phantom rows are still possible.
Serializable	The **DataSet** is locked using a range lock, and this prevents other users from updating or inserting rows in the **DataSet** until the transaction ends (see "Using the DataSet Class" in Chapter 3B).
Unspecified	The isolation level can't be determined, because a different isolation level than the one specified is being used.

In Listings 3A-8 through 3A-10, the transaction is named using a constant, which obviously makes it easier later on to recognize the transaction you want to deal with. See the following section, "Nesting Transactions and Using Transaction Save Points with SqlTransaction," for details.

Listing 3A-8. Beginning a Transaction with a Nondefault Isolation Level

```
 1 public void BeginNonDefaultIsolationLevelTransaction() {
 2    SqlConnection cnnUserMan;
 3    SqlTransaction traUserMan;
 4
 5    // Instantiate the connection
 6    cnnUserMan = new SqlConnection(STR_CONNECTION_STRING);
 7    // Open the connection
 8    cnnUserMan.Open();
 9    // Begin transaction
10    traUserMan = cnnUserMan.BeginTransaction(IsolationLevel.ReadCommitted);
11 }
```

Listing 3A-9. Beginning a Named SQL Transaction

```
1  public void BeginNamedTransaction() {
2      const string STR_MAIN_TRANSACTION_NAME = "MainTransaction";
3
4      SqlConnection cnnUserMan;
5      SqlTransaction traUserMan;
6
7      // Instantiate the connection
8      cnnUserMan = new SqlConnection(STR_CONNECTION_STRING);
9      // Open the connection
10     cnnUserMan.Open();
11     // Begin transaction
12     traUserMan = cnnUserMan.BeginTransaction(STR_MAIN_TRANSACTION_NAME);
13 }
```

*Listing 3A-10. Beginning a Named SQL Transaction
with a Nondefault Isolation Level*

```
1  public void BeginNamedNonDefaultIsolationLevelTransaction() {
2      const string STR_MAIN_TRANSACTION_NAME = "MainTransaction";
3
4      SqlConnection cnnUserMan;
5      SqlTransaction traUserMan;
6
7      // Instantiate the connection
8      cnnUserMan = new SqlConnection(STR_CONNECTION_STRING);
9      // Open the connection
10     cnnUserMan.Open();
11     // Begin transaction
12     traUserMan = cnnUserMan.BeginTransaction(IsolationLevel.ReadCommitted,
13         STR_MAIN_TRANSACTION_NAME);
14 }
```

> **NOTE** *It's actually not necessary to save the returned transaction object, which means that you can leave out the* `traUserMan` = *bit in Listings 3A-7, 3A-8, 3A-9, and 3A-10. Mind you, there's no point in doing so, because you probably will want to commit or roll back the pending changes at a later stage. This is only possible if you save the reference to the transaction object. This differs from ADO, where the rollback and commit functionality were methods of the Connection class. In ADO.NET, this functionality is now part of the Transaction class.*

Nesting Transactions and Using Transaction Save Points with SqlTransaction

This topic is only valid for the **SqlConnection** and **SqlTransaction** classes. If you are nesting your transactions, it's good idea to give each transaction a name that is readily identifiable, making it easier for yourself later on to tell the transactions apart. Well, I say transactions, but in ADO.NET you can't have more than one transaction on a single connection. Unlike ADO, where you can start several transactions on a connection by calling the **BeginTransaction** method a number of times and specifying a name for each transaction, you only have the one transaction, also starting with the **BeginTransaction** method. However, the transaction object that is returned from the **BeginTransaction** method has a **Save** method that can be used for the very same purpose. Actually, I think it has become somewhat easier to nest transactions in ADO.NET, but you be the judge of that.

So, let's have a look at this new way of nesting transactions. It's actually not nesting as such, but a way of saving specific points in a transaction that you can roll back to. The **SqlTransaction** class's **Save** method is used for saving a reference point in the transaction, as shown in Listing 3A-11.

Listing 3A-11. Saving a Reference Point in a Transaction

```
1 public void UseTransactionSavePoints() {
2     const string STR_MAIN_TRANSACTION_NAME = "MainTransaction";
3     const string STR_FAMILY_TRANSACTION_NAME = "FamilyUpdates";
4     const string STR_ADDRESS_TRANSACTION_NAME = "AddressUpdates";
5
6     SqlConnection cnnUserMan;
7     SqlTransaction traUserMan;
8
9     // Instantiate the connection
10    cnnUserMan = new SqlConnection(STR_CONNECTION_STRING);
11    // Open the connection
12    cnnUserMan.Open();
13
14    // Start named transaction
15    traUserMan = cnnUserMan.BeginTransaction(STR_MAIN_TRANSACTION_NAME);
16    // Update family tables
17    // ...
18
19    // Save transaction reference point
20    traUserMan.Save(STR_FAMILY_TRANSACTION_NAME);
21    // Update address tables
22    // ...
23    // Save transaction reference point
```

```
24    traUserMan.Save(STR_ADDRESS_TRANSACTION_NAME);
25    // Roll back address table updates
26    traUserMan.Rollback(STR_FAMILY_TRANSACTION_NAME);
27 }
```

In Listing 3A-11, the connection is opened, the transaction started, and the family tables updated. After this a reference point is saved before another update of the database. This time the address table is updated and again a reference point is saved. Finally you come to the real trick: a rollback to a named reference in the transaction occurs, namely the point after the family tables were updated. (For more information on the **Rollback** method of the Transaction class, please see "Aborting a Manual Transaction.") When the rollback operation is performed, the updates to the address tables will be undone, whereas the changes to the family tables are still there. When I say still there, I am referring to the fact that the transaction hasn't been committed yet, but if the **Commit** method of the Transaction class were executed, using `traUserMan.Commit();`, then the family table updates would be applied permanently.

Nesting Transactions with OleDbTransaction

This topic is only valid for the **OleDbConnection** class. Unlike ADO, where you can start several transactions on a connection by calling the **BeginTransaction** method a number of times, you only have the one transaction, also starting with the **BeginTransaction** method. However, the transaction object that is returned from the **BeginTransaction** method has a **Begin** method that can be used for nesting purposes. An example of using the **OleDbTransaction** class's **Begin** method is shown in Listing 3A-12.

Listing 3A-12. Beginning a Nested OleDb Transaction

```
1 public void NestTransactions() {
2     OleDbConnection cnnUserMan;
3     OleDbTransaction traUserManMain;
4     OleDbTransaction traUserManFamily;
5     OleDbTransaction traUserManAddress;
6
7     // Instantiate the connection
8     cnnUserMan = new OleDbConnection(STR_CONNECTION_STRING);
9     // Open the connection
10    cnnUserMan.Open();
11
12    // Start main transaction
13    traUserManMain = cnnUserMan.BeginTransaction();
14    // Update family tables
```

```
15    // ...
16    // Begin nested transaction
17    traUserManFamily = traUserManMain.Begin();
18    // Update address tables
19    // ...
20    // Begin nested transaction
21    traUserManAddress = traUserManFamily.Begin();
22    // Roll back address table updates
23    traUserManAddress.Rollback();
24  }
```

Please note that the SQLOLEDB OLE DB provider doesn't support nesting. So, if you run Listing 3A-12 using this provider, an **InvalidOperationException** exception is thrown.

Nesting Transactions with OdbcTransaction

Unlike the **SqlTransaction** and **OleDbTransaction** classes, the **OdbcTransaction** class doesn't support nested transactions, which basically means that you can have only one transaction per connection object.

Aborting a Manual Transaction

If for some reason you want to abort the transaction—that is, roll back all the changes since you started the transaction—you need to call the Transaction class's **Rollback** method. This will ensure that no changes are applied to the data source, or rather the data source is rolled back to its original state. The call is performed like this:

```
traUserMan.Rollback();
```

You can also use the overloaded version of the **Rollback** method with which you specify the name of the transaction, as was done in Listing 3A-11. The **Rollback** method can't be used before the **BeginTransaction** method of the Connection class has been called, and it must be called before the Transaction class's **Commit** method is called. An exception is thrown if you don't do as prescribed.

Always Use Named Transactions

Although you can call the **Rollback** method without passing the name of
a transaction, it's advisable that you do include a transaction name if you are
using the **SqlTransaction** class (the **OleDbTransaction** and **OdbcConnection**
classes don't have this feature). When you start the transaction, use one of the
overloaded **BeginTransaction** methods that let you pass the name of a transaction as an argument as demonstrated in Listings 3A-9, 3A-10, and 3A-11. This
way, you can always use the overloaded **Rollback** method of the Transaction
class and pass the name of the transaction. When you use the standard version
of the **Rollback** method, all pending changes will be rolled back. Personally,
I think it makes the code more readable if you always supply the transaction
name when you begin the transaction, save a reference point, and roll back
a transaction.

Committing a Manual Transaction

When you are done manipulating your data, it's time to commit the changes
to the data source. Calling the Transaction class's **Commit** method does this.
All the changes you've made to the data since you started the transaction
with a call to the **BeginTransaction** method will be applied to the data source.
Actually, this is only fully true for the **OleDbTransaction** class. If you are using the
SqlTransaction class, you might save some reference points and use the
Rollback method to roll back to one or more of these reference points. In such
a case, the operations that have been rolled back obviously won't be committed.

Determining the Isolation Level of a Running Transaction

If you are uncertain of the isolation level of a running transaction, you can use
the **IsolationLevel** property of the Transaction class, as shown in Listing 3A-13.

Listing 3A-13. Determining the Isolation Level of a Running Transaction

```
1 public void DetermineTransactionIsolationLevel() {
2    SqlConnection cnnUserMan;
3    SqlTransaction traUserMan;
4
5    // Instantiate the connection
6    cnnUserMan = new SqlConnection(STR_CONNECTION_STRING);
7    // Open the connection
8    cnnUserMan.Open();
9
```

```
10    // Start transaction with nondefault isolation level
11    traUserMan = cnnUserMan.BeginTransaction(IsolationLevel.ReadCommitted);
12
13    // Return the isolation level as text
14    MessageBox.Show(traUserMan.IsolationLevel.ToString());
15 }
```

Examining the Transaction Class

The Transaction class, which can only be instantiated by the Connection class's **BeginTransaction** method, can't be inherited. Once a transaction has been started using **BeginTransaction**, all further transaction operations are performed on the transaction object returned by **BeginTransaction**. In Table 3A-16, you can see the properties of the Transaction classes.

Table 3A-16. **Transaction** *Class Properties*

PROPERTY NAME	DESCRIPTION	READ	WRITE
Connection	Retrieves the Connection object that is associated with the transaction. **null** is returned if the transaction is invalid.	Yes	No
IsolationLevel	Specifies the level of isolation for the transaction. See "Determining the Isolation Level of a Running Transaction" and "Examining the Isolation Level" earlier in this chapter for more details.	Yes	No

In Table 3A-17, you can see the methods of the Transaction classes. Inherited and overridden methods aren't shown.

*Table 3A-17. **Transaction** Class Methods*

METHOD NAME	DESCRIPTION	RETURN VALUE	OVERLOADED
Begin() (**OleDbTransaction** only)	Begins a new transaction, nested within the current transaction. See "Nesting Transactions with OleDbTransaction" earlier in this chapter.	**OleDbTransaction** object	Yes
Commit()	This method commits the current database transaction. See "Committing a Manual Transaction" earlier in this chapter.		No
Rollback()	Rolls back the pending changes, so they aren't applied to the database. See "Aborting a Manual Transaction" earlier in this chapter.		Yes
Save() (**SqlTransaction** only)	Saves a reference point, which you can roll back to using the **Rollback** method		No

Manual Transaction Summary

Handling transactions manually isn't really that big a deal. Here are the few steps you need to remember:

- Start a transaction by using the **BeginTransaction** method of the Connection class. You can only execute **BeginTransaction** once per connection, or rather you can't have parallel transactions. You need to commit a running transaction before you can use the **BeginTransaction** method again on the same connection. **BeginTransaction** returns the transaction object needed for rolling back or committing the changes to the data source.

- Roll back a transaction by using the **Rollback** method of the Transaction class.

- Commit a transaction by using the **Commit** method of the Transaction class.

Automatic Transactions

Automatic transactions are a little different from manual transactions in the sense that they aren't necessarily applied. When I say not necessarily, I mean the following: if the object in which you are using the .NET Data Provider data classes isn't enlisted in a transaction, your data source won't be either. So to cut it short, if you're using transactions for your application, then the data source will be enlisted automatically.

The .NET Data Providers OLE DB .NET Data Provider, ODBC .NET Data Provider, and SQL Server .NET Data Provider automatically enlist in a transaction and obtain the details of the transaction from the Windows Component Services context.

Handling Connection Class Exceptions

This section describes how you deal with exceptions when you work with connections. An exception, which is more or less the same as what used to be called a trappable error, can be caught using the **try {} . . . catch {}** statement construct. If you are using the **SqlConnection** class, please look up the property or method in the section that follows, "SqlConnection Exceptions," for the correct exception. Please note that only exceptions to noninherited properties and methods are mentioned. So, exceptions caused by the **Equals** method, which is inherited from the **object** class, aren't shown. The list is also not exhaustive, but merely shows the more common exceptions you'll encounter. **OleDbConnection** exceptions are discussed under "OleDbConnection Exceptions" and **OdbcConnection** exceptions are discussed under "OdbcConnection Exceptions" later in this chapter.

SqlConnection Exceptions

Here I'll show you how to deal with some of the most common exceptions thrown when working with the **SqlConnection** class, but some of these exceptions are also thrown when working with the **OleDbConnection** and **OdbcConnection** classes. Please see the individual sections for more information on what Connection class throws the listed exception.

Why Did You Get an Exception?

For each exception, I show you a piece of code that can help you determine why an exception occurred. This is useful when the code in the **try** section of a **try** {} **...catch** {} construct contains multiple procedure calls that can throw an exception. Be aware that this is simple code, and it's only there to help you get an idea of how to proceed with your exception handling. In the examples provided, I show you how to find out what method, property, and so on threw the exception. However, some methods and properties can throw more than one type of exception, and this is when you need to set up multiple catch blocks, like this:

```
try {
...}
catch (InvalidOperationException objInvalid) {
...}
catch (ArgumentException objArgument) {
...}
catch (Exception objE) {
...}
```

One of the most common mistakes is to provide a "faulty" connection string. It often happens that a user needs to type in a user ID and password, which is then passed as part of the connection string, without first being validated. If the user has typed in any special characters, such as a semicolon, an exception is thrown. For more information on exception handling, please refer to Chapter 5.

BeginTransaction Method Exceptions

The **InvalidOperationException** exception is thrown when you call the **BeginTransaction** method on an invalid or closed connection. You can check if the connection is closed, like this:

```
// Check if the connection is open
if ((bool) cnnUserMan.State == ConnectionState.Open) {}
```

The **InvalidOperationException** exception is also thrown if you try to start parallel transactions by calling the **BeginTransaction** method twice, before committing or rolling back the first transaction.

Listing 3A-14 shows you how you can check if the exception was thrown because of the **BeginTransaction** method. This only works with the **SqlConnection** class.

*Listing 3A-14. Checking If **BeginTransaction** Caused the Exception*

```
1 public void CheckBeginTransactionMethodException() {
2    SqlConnection cnnUserMan;
3    SqlTransaction traUserMan;
4
5    // Instantiate the connection
6    cnnUserMan = new SqlConnection(STR_CONNECTION_STRING);
7    // Open the connection
8    // If the following line is commented out, the BeginTransaction exception
9    // will be thrown.
10   cnnUserMan.Open();
11
12   try {
13      // Start transaction with nondefault isolation level
14      traUserMan = cnnUserMan.BeginTransaction(IsolationLevel.ReadCommitted);
15   }
16   catch (Exception objException) {
17      // Check if a BeginTransaction method threw the exception
18      if (objException.TargetSite.Name.ToString() == "BeginTransaction") {
19         MessageBox.Show("The BeginTransaction method threw the exception!");
20      }
21   }
22 }
```

ConnectionString Property Exceptions

The **InvalidOperationException** exception is thrown when the connection is open or broken and you try to set the property. Listing 3A-15 shows you how you can check if the **InvalidOperationException** exception was thrown because of the **ConnectionString** property.

*Listing 3A-15. Checking If **ConnectionString** Caused the Exception*

```
1 public void CheckConnectionStringPropertyException() {
2    SqlConnection cnnUserMan;
3
4    // Instantiate the connection
5    cnnUserMan = new SqlConnection(STR_CONNECTION_STRING);
6    // Open the connection
7    cnnUserMan.Open();
```

```
8
9    try {
10       // Set the connection string
11       cnnUserMan.ConnectionString = STR_CONNECTION_STRING;
12    }
13    catch (Exception objException) {
14       // Check if setting the ConnectionString threw the exception
15       if (objException.TargetSite.Name == "set_ConnectionString") {
16          MessageBox.Show(
17             "The ConnectionString property threw the exception!");
18       }
19    }
20 }
```

ConnectionTimeout Property Exceptions

The **ArgumentException** exception is thrown when you try to set the property
to a value less than 0. Actually, the **ConnectionTimeout** property is read-only,
so you can't set it directly. However, you can set this property through the
Connection Timeout value name in the **ConnectionString** property.
Listing 3A-16 shows you how you can check if the **ArgumentException**
exception was thrown because of the **ConnectionTimeout** property. This
only works with the **SqlConnection** class.

Listing 3A-16. Checking If ***ConnectionTimeout*** *Caused the Exception*

```
1 public void CheckConnectionTimeoutPropertyException() {
2    SqlConnection cnnUserMan;
3
4    try {
5       // Instantiate the connection
6       cnnUserMan = new SqlConnection(STR_CONNECTION_STRING +
7          ";Connection Timeout=-1");
8       // Open the connection
9       cnnUserMan.Open();
10    }
11    catch (Exception objException) {
12       // Check if setting the Connection Timeout to an invalid value threw
13       // the exception
14       if (objException.TargetSite.Name == "SetConnectTimeout") {
15          MessageBox.Show(
16             "The Connection Timeout value threw the exception!");
17       }
18    }
19 }
```

Database Property and ChangeDatabase Method Exceptions

The **InvalidOperationException** exception is thrown if the connection isn't open. Actually, the **Database** property is read-only, so you can't set it directly. However, you can set this property through the **ChangeDatabase** method or using a Transact-SQL statement. You can in fact change from the current database to the master database by executing the simple SQL statement USE master using the **ExecuteNonQuery** method of the **SqlCommand** class. The **Database** property is then dynamically updated, and it's after this that an exception can be thrown.

> **NOTE** *Transact-SQL (T-SQL), which is used in SQL Server, is Microsoft's dialect of the ANSI SQL standard. T-SQL is fully ANSI compliant, but it also features many enhancements. You can find an excellent explanation of T-SQL at Garth Wells' site, SQLBOOK.COM, at* http://www.sqlbook.com/code_centric—sample_chapters.html. *Check out sample Chapter 1.*

Listing 3A-17 shows you how you can check if the **InvalidOperationException** exception was thrown because of the **Database** property. This only works with the **SqlConnection** class.

*Listing 3A-17. Checking If **Database** Caused the Exception*

```
1 public void CheckChangeDatabaseMethodException() {
2    SqlConnection cnnUserMan;
3
4    try {
5       // Instantiate the connection
6       cnnUserMan = new SqlConnection(STR_CONNECTION_STRING);
7       // Open the connection
8       // If the following line is commented out,
9       // the ChangeDatabase exception will be thrown
10      //cnnUserMan.Open();
11      // Change database
12      cnnUserMan.ChangeDatabase("master");
13   }
14   catch (Exception objException) {
15      // Check if we tried to change database on an invalid connection
16      if (objException.TargetSite.Name == "ChangeDatabase") {
17         MessageBox.Show("The ChangeDatabase method threw the exception!");
18      }
19   }
20 }
```

Open Method Exceptions

The **InvalidOperationException** exception is thrown when you try to open an already open or broken connection. When this exception is thrown, simply close the connection and open it again. Listing 3A-18 shows you how you can check if the **InvalidOperationException** exception was thrown because of the **Open** method.

*Listing 3A-18. Checking If **Open** Caused the Exception*

```
1 public void CheckOpenMethodException() {
2     SqlConnection cnnUserMan;
3
4     try {
5         // Instantiate the connection
6         cnnUserMan = new SqlConnection(STR_CONNECTION_STRING);
7         // Open the connection
8         cnnUserMan.Open();
9         // Open the connection
10        cnnUserMan.Open();
11    }
12    catch (Exception objException) {
13        // Check if we tried to open an already open connection
14        if (objException.TargetSite.Name == "Open") {
15            MessageBox.Show("The Open method threw the exception!");
16        }
17    }
18 }
```

OleDbConnection Exceptions

Whenever an error occurs when you are working with an OLE DB .NET Data Provider that **OleDbDataAdapter** can't handle (see the "The DataAdapter Explained" section later in this chapter), an **OleDbException** is thrown. This exception class, which can't be inherited, is derived from the **ExternalException** class. The **OleDbException** class holds at least one instance of the **OleDbError** class. It's up to you to traverse through all the instances of **OleDbError** classes contained in the **OleDbException** class, in order to check what errors occurred. Listing 3A-19 shows how you can do it. The example catches exceptions that occur when you try to open a connection, but the code in the catch section can be used for any OLE DB exceptions encountered.

*Listing 3A-19 Traversing Through an **OleDbException** Class*

```
1 public void TraversingAllOleDbErrors() {
2     OleDbConnection cnnUserMan;
3
4     try {
5         // Instantiate the connection
6         cnnUserMan = new OleDbConnection(STR_CONNECTION_STRING);
7         // Open the connection
8         cnnUserMan.Open();
9         // Do your stuff...
10        //...
11    }
12    catch (OleDbException objException) {
13        // This catch block will handle all exceptions that
14        // the OleDbAdapter can't handle
15        foreach (OleDbError objError in objException.Errors) {
16            MessageBox.Show(objError.Message);
17        }
18    }
19    catch (Exception objException) {
20        // This catch block will catch all exceptions that
21        // the OleDbAdapter can handle
22        MessageBox.Show(objException.Message);
23    }
24 }
```

Listing 3A-19 shows you how to extract all instances of the **OleDbError** class from the **Errors** property collection of the **OleDbException** class.

Examining the OleDbError Class

In Listing 3A-19, I've only specified to display the error message, but there are actually a few more properties in the **OleDbError** class that are of interest. See Table 3A-18 for a list of all these properties. Incidentally, the **OleDbError** class, which is noninheritable, is inherited directly from the **object** class.

Table 3A-18. **OleDbError** *Class Properties*

PROPERTY NAME	DESCRIPTION
Message	Returns a description of the error as a variable of data type **string**.
NativeError	Returns the database-specific error information as a variable of data type **int**.
Source	Returns the name of the provider in which the exception occurred or was generated from as a variable of data type **string**.
SQLState	Returns the ANSI SQL standard error code as a variable of data type **string**. This error code is always five characters long.

All the properties in Table 3A-18 are read-only. They don't look all that different from the ones in the ADO errors collection, do they?

Examining the OleDbException Class

Besides the **Errors** collection, the **OleDbException** class has a few other properties and methods of interest as you can see in Tables 3A-19 and 3A-20. Both tables are in alphabetical order.

Table 3A-19. **OleDbException** *Class Properties*

PROPERTY NAME	ACCESSIBILITY	DESCRIPTION	RETURN VALUE	READ	WRITE
ErrorCode	**public**	This property returns the error identification number for the error. The identification number is either an HRESULT or a Win32 error code.	Data type **int**	Yes	No
Errors	**public**	This is actually a collection of the **OleDbError** class. See the preceding section, "Examining the OleDbError Class".	Data type **OleDbErrorCollection**	Yes	No
HelpLink	**public**	This property, which is inherited from the **Exception** class, returns or sets the URN or URL that points to an HTML help file.	Data type **string**	Yes	Yes

(continued)

Table 3A-19. **OleDbException** *Class Properties (continued)*

PROPERTY NAME	ACCESSIBILITY	DESCRIPTION	RETURN VALUE	READ	WRITE
HResult	**protected**	This property, which is inherited from the **Exception** class, returns or sets the HRESULT for an exception.	Data type **int**	Yes	Yes
InnerException	**public**	This property, which is inherited from the **Exception** class, returns a reference to the inner exception. This property generally holds the previously occurring exception or the exception that caused the current exception.	Data type **Exception**	Yes	No
Message	**public**	This property is overridden, so check out the **Message** property of the **OleDbError** class.		Yes	No
Source	**public**	This property is overridden, so check out the **Source** property of the **OleDbError** class.		Yes	No
StackTrace	**public**	This property, which is inherited from the **Exception** class, returns the stack trace. You can use the stack trace to identify the location in your code where the error occurred.	Data type **string**	Yes	No
TargetSite	**public**	This property, which is inherited from the **Exception** class, returns the method that threw the exception. Check out general error handling in Chapter 5, for more information about the **MethodBase** object.	Data type **MethodBase**	Yes	No

Table 3A-20. **OleDbException** *Class Methods*

METHOD NAME	ACCESSIBILITY	DESCRIPTION	RETURN VALUE
GetBaseException()	**public**	This method, which is inherited from the **Exception** class, returns the original exception thrown. It's useful in cases where one exception has triggered another and so forth. The reference returned will point to the current exception, if this is the only exception thrown.	Data type **Exception**
ToString()	**public**	This method, which is inherited from the **object** class, can be used on the **OleDbException** class, where it returns the fully qualified exception name. The error message (**Message** property), the inner exception name (**InnerException** property), and the stack trace (**StackTrace** property) might also be returned.	Data type **string**

OdbcConnection Exceptions

When you're working with the ODBC .NET Data Provider and an exception is thrown that the **OdbcDataAdapter** can't handle (see the "The DataAdapter Explained" section later in this chapter), an **OdbcException** is thrown. This exception class, which can't be inherited, is derived from the **SystemException** class. The **OdbcException** class holds at least one instance of the **OdbcError** class. It's up to you to traverse through all the instances of **OdbcError** classes contained in the **OdbcException** class, in order to check what errors occurred. Listing 3A-20 shows how you can do it. The example catches exceptions that occur when you try to open a connection, but the code in the catch section can be used for any ODBC exceptions encountered.

*Listing 3A-20 Traversing Through an **OdbcException** Class*

```
1 public void TraversingAllOdbcErrors() {
2     OdbcConnection cnnUserMan;
3
4     try {
5         // Instantiate the connection
6         cnnUserMan = new OdbcConnection(STR_CONNECTION_STRING);
7         // Open the connection
8         cnnUserMan.Open();
9         // Do your stuff...
10        //...
11    }
12    catch (OdbcException objException) {
13        // This catch block will handle all exceptions that
14        // the OdbcAdapter can't handle
15        foreach (OdbcError objError in objException.Errors) {
16            MessageBox.Show(objError.Message);
17        }
18    }
19    catch (Exception objException) {
20        // This catch block will catch all exceptions that
21        // the OdbcAdapter can handle
22        MessageBox.Show(objException.Message);
23    }
24 }
```

Listing 3A-20 shows you how to extract all instances of the **OdbcError** class from the **Errors** property collection of the **OdbcException** class.

Examining the OdbcError Class

In Listing 3A-20, all I've specified is to display the error message, but there are actually a few more properties in the **OdbcError** class that are of interest. See Table 3A-21 for a list of all these properties. Incidentally, the **OdbcError** class, which is noninheritable, is inherited directly from the **object** class.

Table 3A-21. **OdbcError** *Class Properties*

PROPERTY NAME	DESCRIPTION
Message	Returns a description of the error as a variable of data type **string**.
NativeError	Returns the database-specific error information as a variable of data type **int**.
Source	Returns the name of the driver in which the exception occurred or was generated from as a variable of data type **string**.
SQLState	Returns the ANSI SQL standard error code as a variable of data type **string**. This error code is always five characters long.

All the properties in Table 3A-21 are read-only. As is the case with the **OleDbError** class properties, they don't look all that different from the ones in the ADO errors collection, do they?

Examining the OdbcException Class

Besides the **Errors** collection, the **OdbcException** class has a few other properties and methods of interest as you can see in Tables 3A-22 and 3A-23. Both tables are in alphabetical order.

Table 3A-22. **OdbcException** *Class Properties*

PROPERTY NAME	ACCESSIBILITY	DESCRIPTION	RETURN VALUE	READ	WRITE
Errors	**public**	This is actually a collection of the **OdbcError** class. See the preceding section, "Examining the OdbcError Class".	Data type **OdbcErrorCollection**	Yes	No
HelpLink	**public**	This property, which is inherited from the **Exception** class, returns or sets the URN or URL that points to a HTML help file.	Data type **string**	Yes	Yes
HResult	**protected**	This property, which is inherited from the **Exception** class, returns or sets the HRESULT for an exception.		Yes	Yes

(continued)

Table 3A-22. **OdbcException** *Class Properties (continued)*

PROPERTY NAME	ACCESSIBILITY	DESCRIPTION	RETURN VALUE	READ	WRITE
InnerException	**public**	This property, which is inherited from the **Exception** class, returns a reference to the inner exception. This property generally holds the previously occurring exception or the exception that caused the current exception.	Data type **Exception**	Yes	No
Message	**public**	This property is overridden, so check out the **Message** property of the **OdbcError** class.		Yes	No
Source	**public**	This property is overridden, so check out the **Source** property of the **OdbcError** class.		Yes	No
StackTrace	**public**	This property, which is inherited from the **Exception** class, returns the stack trace. You can use the stack trace to identify the location in your code where the error occurred.	Data type **string**	Yes	No
TargetSite	**public**	This property, which is inherited from the **Exception** class, returns the method that threw the exception. Check out general error handling in Chapter 5, for more information about the **MethodBase** object.	Data type **MethodBase**	Yes	No

Table 3A-23. **OdbcException** *Class Methods*

METHOD NAME	ACCESSIBILITY	DESCRIPTION	RETURN VALUE
GetBaseException()	**public**	This method, which is inherited from the **Exception** class, returns the original exception thrown. It's useful in cases where one exception has triggered another and so forth. The reference returned will point to the current exception, if this is the only exception thrown.	Data type **Exception**
ToString()	**public**	This method, which is inherited from the **object** class, has already been described in Table 3A-7. When used on the **OleDbException** class, it returns the fully qualified exception name. The error message (**Message** property), the inner exception name (**InnerException** property), and the stack trace (**StackTrace** property) might also be returned.	Data type **string**

Using Command Objects

A *command object* is used when you need to execute a query against your database. The command object is the simplest and easiest way of doing this. The three Command classes in ADO.NET that are of interest to you are **OleDbCommand**, **OdbcCommand**, and **SqlCommand**. The **OleDbCommand** class is part of the **System.Data.OleDb** namespace, the **OdbcCommand** class is part of the **Microsoft.Data.Odbc** namespace, and the **SqlCommand** class is part of the **System.Data.SqlClient** namespace.

> **TIP** *If you are uncertain about which namespace a certain class in your code belongs to, then simply move the cursor over the class, and the namespace will be displayed in the little tool tip that pops up.*

OleDbCommand, OdbcCommand, and SqlCommand

As with the providers and Connection classes, you should make up your mind if you are going to connect to a Microsoft SQL Server 7.0 or later data source or a different data source. The **SqlCommand** should be used with SQL Server, the **OdbcCommand** with any other ODBC data source, and the **OleDbCommand** with any other OLE DB data source. Because the **SqlCommand** class has been optimized for use with SQL Server, it outperforms the **OleDbCommand** and **OdbcCommand** classes. However, if you want you can use **OleDbCommand** or **OdbcCommand** instead of **SqlCommand** in much the same way. In Listing 3A-21, you can see how to declare and instantiate a **SqlCommand**.

*Listing 3A-21. Instantiating a **SqlCommand***

```
 1 public void InstantiateCommandObject() {
 2     SqlConnection cnnUserMan;
 3     SqlCommand cmmUserMan;
 4     string strSQL;
 5
 6     // Instantiate the connection
 7     cnnUserMan = new SqlConnection(STR_CONNECTION_STRING);
 8     // Open the connection
 9     cnnUserMan.Open();
10     // Build query string
11     strSQL = "SELECT * FROM tblUser";
12     // Instantiate the command
13     cmmUserMan = new SqlCommand(strSQL, cnnUserMan);
14 }
```

In Listing 3A-21, I reuse the same connection code shown previously. In addition, I declare the command object cmmUserMan and the query string strSQL. Once the connection has been opened, the query string is built and the command instantiated using the query string and the open connection. The way the command object is instantiated here is one of four different instantiation procedures available, because the method is overloaded.

Instantiating the OleDbCommand Object

Here are the four different ways you can instantiate an **OleDbCommand** object (the command object, the query string, and the connection string have all been declared elsewhere):

- `cmmUserMan = new OleDbCommand ();` instantiates `cmmUserMan` with no arguments. If you use this way to instantiate your command, you need to set some of the properties, such as **Connection**, before you execute or otherwise use the command. The following properties are set to initial values when you instantiate:

  `CommandText = ""`

  `CommandTimeout = 30`

  `CommandType = CommandType.Text`

  `Connection = null`

- `cmmUserMan = new OleDbCommand(string strSQL);` instantiates `cmmUserMan` with the query command text (`strSQL`). You also need to supply a valid and open connection by setting the **Connection** property. The following properties are set to initial values when you instantiate:

  `CommandText = strSQL`

  `CommandTimeout = 30`

  `CommandType = CommandType.Text`

  `Connection = null`

- `cmmUserMan = new OleDbCommand(string strSQL, OleDbConnection cnnUserMan);` instantiates `cmmUserMan` with the query command text (`strSQL`) and a valid and open connection, `cnnUserMan`. The following properties are set to initial values when you instantiate:

  `CommandText = strSQL`

  `CommandTimeout = 30`

  `CommandType = CommandType.Text`

  `Connection = cnnUserMan`

- cmmUserMan = new OleDbCommand(string strSQL, OleDbConnection cnnUserMan, OleDbTransaction traUserMan); instantiates cmmUserMan with the query command text and a connection object. cnnUserMan must be a valid and open connection and traUserMan must be a valid and open transaction that has been opened on cnnUserMan. This version should be used when you've started a transaction with the **BeginTransaction** method of the Connection class. The following properties are set to initial values when you instantiate:

CommandText = strSQL

CommandTimeout = 30

CommandType = CommandType.Text

Connection = cnnUserMan

Instantiating the OdbcCommand Object

Here are the four different ways you can instantiate an **OdbcCommand** object (the command object, the query string, and the connection string have all been declared elsewhere):

- cmmUserMan = new OdbcCommand(); instantiates cmmUserMan with no arguments. If you use this way to instantiate your command, you need to set some of the properties, such as **Connection**, before you execute or otherwise use the command. The following properties are set to initial values when you instantiate:

CommandText = ""

CommandTimeout = 30

CommandType = CommandType.Text

Connection = null

- cmmUserMan = new OdbcCommand(string strSQL); instantiates cmmUserMan with the query command text (strSQL). You also need to supply a valid and open connection by setting the **Connection** property. The following properties are set to initial values when you instantiate:

```
CommandText = strSQL

CommandTimeout = 30

CommandType = CommandType.Text

Connection = null
```

- cmmUserMan = new OdbcCommand(string strSQL, OdbcConnection cnnUserMan); instantiates cmmUserMan with the query command text (strSQL) and a valid and open connection, cnnUserMan. The following properties are set to initial values when you instantiate:

```
CommandText = strSQL

CommandTimeout = 30

CommandType = CommandType.Text

Connection = cnnUserMan
```

- cmmUserMan = new OdbcCommand(string strSQL, OdbcConnection cnnUserMan, OdbcTransaction traUserMan); instantiates cmmUserMan with the query command text and a connection object. cnnUserMan must be a valid and open connection and traUserMan must be a valid and open transaction that has been opened on cnnUserMan. This version should be used when you've started a transaction with the **BeginTransaction** method of the Connection class. The following properties are set to initial values when you instantiate:

```
CommandText = strSQL

CommandTimeout = 30

CommandType = CommandType.Text

Connection = cnnUserMan
```

Instantiating the SqlCommand Object

There are the four different ways you can instantiate a **SqlCommand** object (the command object, the query string, and the connection string have all been declared elsewhere):

- `cmmUserMan = new SqlCommand();` instantiates `cmmUserMan` with no arguments. If you use this way to instantiate your command, you need to set some of the properties, such as **Connection**, before you execute or otherwise use the command. The following properties are set to initial values when you instantiate:

  `CommandText = ""`

  `CommandTimeout = 30`

  `CommandType = CommandType.Text`

  `Connection = null`

- `cmmUserMan = new SqlCommand(string strSQL);` instantiates `cmmUserMan` with the query command text (`strSQL`). You also need to supply a valid and open connection by setting the **Connection** property. The following properties are set to initial values when you instantiate:

  `CommandText = strSQL`

  `CommandTimeout = 30`

  `CommandType = CommandType.Text`

  `Connection = null`

- `cmmUserMan = new SqlCommand(string strSQL, SqlConnection cnnUserMan);` instantiates `cmmUserMan` with the query command text (`strSQL`) and a valid and open connection, `cnnUserMan`. The following properties are set to initial values when you instantiate:

  `CommandText = strSQL`

  `CommandTimeout = 30`

  `CommandType = CommandType.Text`

  `Connection = cnnUserMan`

- cmmUserMan = new SqlCommand(string strSQL, SqlConnection cnnUserMan, SqlTransaction traUserMan); instantiates cmmUserMan with the query command text and a connection object. The cnnUserMan must be a valid and open connection and traUserMan must be a valid and open transaction that has been opened on cnnUserMan. This version should be used when you've started a transaction using the **BeginTransaction** method of the Connection class. The following properties are set to initial values when you instantiate:

  CommandText = strSQL

  CommandTimeout = 30

  CommandType = CommandType.Text

  Connection = cnnUserMan

Which of the ways to instantiate your command object (**SqlCommand, OleDbCommand**, or **OdbcCommand**) you should choose really depends on the context and what you are trying to achieve. However, you must always use cmmUserMan = new SqlCommand(string strSQL, ????Connection cnnUserMan, ????Transaction traUserMan); when a transaction has been started on the connection object and you want your command to be part of the transaction.

Command Class Properties

Tables 3A-24, 3A-25, and 3A-26 list all the public, noninherited Command class properties in alphabetical order and shows the equivalent Command class constructor argument (see the preceding sections "Instantiating the SqlCommand Object," "Instantiating the OleDbCommand Object," and "Instantiating the OdbcCommand Object"). Please note that in most cases the properties are only checked for syntax when you set them. The real validation takes place when you perform one of the **Execute** . . . methods.

*Table 3A-24. **SqlCommand** Class Properties*

PROPERTY NAME	DESCRIPTION	COMMAND CONSTRUCTOR EQUIVALENT	DEFAULT VALUE	READ	WRITE
CommandText	The Transact-SQL query text or the name of a stored procedure to execute. When you set this property to the same value as the current one, the assignment is left out. You need to set this property to the name of a stored procedure, when the **CommandType** property is set to **CommandType.StoredProcedure**.	strSQL	"" (empty string)	Yes	Yes
CommandTimeout	This is the number of seconds to wait for the command to execute. If the command has not been executed within this period, an exception is thrown.		30	Yes	Yes
CommandType	This property determines how the **CommandText** property is interpreted. The following **CommandType** enum values are valid: **StoredProcedure**: The **CommandText** property must hold the name of a stored procedure. **Text**: The **CommandText** property is interpreted as a query like a SELECT statement, and so on.		**Text**	Yes	Yes
Connection	This is the connection to the data source.	cnnUserMan	**null**	Yes	Yes
DesignTimeVisible	Used to indicate whether the command object should be visible in a Windows Forms Designer control.		**false**	Yes	Yes
Parameters	Retrieves the **SqlParameterCollection**, which holds the parameters of the Transact-SQL statement.		Empty collection	Yes	No

(continued)

Table 3A-24. **SqlCommand** *Class Properties*

PROPERTY NAME	DESCRIPTION	COMMAND CONSTRUCTOR EQUIVALENT	DEFAULT VALUE	READ	WRITE
Transaction	This property is used for retrieving or setting the transaction the command is executing in, if any. Please note that the transaction object must be connected to the same connection object as the command object.	traUserMan	**null**	Yes	Yes
UpdatedRowSource	Retrieves or sets if and how the command results are applied to the row source after the command has been executed. This property needs to be set to one the following **UpdateRowSource** enum values: **Both**: the sum of the **FirstReturnedRecord** and **OutputParameters** values. **FirstReturnedRecord**: only data in the first returned record is mapped to the changed row in the data set. **None**: returned parameters and/or rows will be ignored. **OutputParameters**: only the output parameters are mapped to the changed row in the Dataset.		**Both** (**None**, if the command is automatically generated)	Yes	Yes

Table 3A-25. **OleDbCommand** *Class Properties*

PROPERTY NAME	DESCRIPTION	COMMAND CONSTRUCTOR EQUIVALENT	DEFAULT VALUE	READ	WRITE
CommandText	The query text or the name of a stored procedure to execute. When you set this property to the same value as the current value, the assignment is left out. You need to set this property to the name of a stored procedure when the **CommandType** property is set to **CommandType.StoredProcedure**. You can only set this property when the connection is open and available, which means that the connection can't be fetching rows when you set this property.	strSQL	"" (empty string)	Yes	Yes
CommandTimeout	This is the number of seconds to wait for the command to execute. If the command has not been executed within this period, an exception is thrown.		30	Yes	Yes
CommandType	This property determines how the **CommandText** property is interpreted. The following values are valid: **StoredProcedure**: the **CommandText** property must hold the name of a stored procedure. **TableDirect**: the **CommandText** property must hold name of a table. All columns for this table will be returned. This is instead of using a query such as "SELECT * FROM TableName".		**Text**	Yes	Yes

(continued)

Table 3A-25. **OleDbCommand** *Class Properties (continued)*

PROPERTY NAME	DESCRIPTION	COMMAND CONSTRUCTOR EQUIVALENT	DEFAULT VALUE	READ	WRITE
CommandType (continued)	**Text**: the **CommandText** property is interpreted as a query like a SELECT statement, and so on. Please note that the OLE DB .NET Data Provider doesn't support named parameters, which means that you must specify arguments using the question mark, "?". You can only set this property when the connection is open and available, which means that the connection can't be executing or fetching rows when you set the property.		**Text**	Yes	Yes
Connection	This is the connection to the data source.	cnnUserMan	**null**	Yes	Yes
DesignTimeVisible	Used to indicate whether the command object should be visible in a Windows Forms Designer control.		**false**	Yes	Yes
Parameters	Retrieves the **OleDbParameterCollection**, which holds the parameters of the **CommandText** property.		Empty collection	Yes	No
Transaction	This property is used for retrieving or setting the transaction the command is executing in, if any. Please note that the transaction object must be connected to the same connection object as the command object.	traUserMan	**null**	Yes	Yes

(continued)

Table 3A-25. **OleDbCommand** *Class Properties (continued)*

PROPERTY NAME	DESCRIPTION	COMMAND CONSTRUCTOR EQUIVALENT	DEFAULT VALUE	READ	WRITE
UpdatedRowSource	Gets or sets if and how the command results are applied to the row source after the command has been executed. This property needs to be set to one the following **UpdateRowSource** enum values: **Both**: the sum of the **FirstReturnedRecord** and **OutputParameters** values. **FirstReturnedRecord**: only data in the first returned record is mapped to the changed row in the data set. **None**: returned parameters and/ rows will be ignored. **OutputParameters**: only the output parameters are mapped to the changed row in the Dataset.		**Both** (**None**, if the command is automatically generated)	Yes	Yes

Table 3A-26. **OdbcCommand** *Class Properties*

PROPERTY NAME	DESCRIPTION	COMMAND CONSTRUCTOR EQUIVALENT	DEFAULT VALUE	READ	WRITE
CommandText	This is the query text or the name of a stored procedure to execute. You need to set this property to the name of a stored procedure when the **CommandType** property is set to **CommandType.StoredProcedure**. However, the property must be set using standard ODBC escape sequences for stored procedures (see the note later in this section for more information). You can only set this property when the connection is open and available, which means that the connection can't be executing or fetching rows when you set the property.	strSQL	"" (empty string)	Yes	Yes
CommandTimeout	This is the number of seconds (0 if no limit) to wait for the command to execute. If the command has not been executed within this period, an exception is thrown.		30	Yes	Yes
CommandType	This property determines how the **CommandText** property is interpreted. The following values are valid: **StoredProcedure**: the **CommandText** property must hold the name of a stored procedure specified using standard ODBC escape sequences.				

(continued)

135

*Table 3A-26. **OdbcCommand** Class Properties (continued)*

PROPERTY NAME	DESCRIPTION	COMMAND CONSTRUCTOR EQUIVALENT	DEFAULT VALUE	READ	WRITE
CommandType (continued)	**Text**: the **CommandText** property is interpreted as a query like a SELECT statement, and so on. Please note that the ODBC .NET Data Provider doesn't support named parameters, which means that you must specify arguments using the question mark, "?". You can only set this property when the connection is open and available, which means that the connection can't be executing or fetching rows when you set the property.		**Text**	Yes	Yes
Connection	This is the connection to the data source. You can only set this property when the connection is open and available, which means that the connection can't be executing or fetching rows when you set the property.	cnnUserMan	**null**	Yes	Yes
DesignTimeVisible	Used to indicate whether the command object should be visible in a Windows Forms Designer control.		**false**	Yes	Yes
Parameters	Retrieves the **OdbcParameterCollection**, which holds the parameters of the **CommandText** property.		empty collection	Yes	No
Transaction	This property is used for retrieving or setting the transaction the command is executing in, if any. Please note that the transaction object must be connected to the same connection object as the command object. This property can only be set if it hasn't been set previously.	traUserMan	**null**	Yes	Yes

(continued)

Table 3A-26. **OdbcCommand** *Class Properties (continued)*

PROPERTY NAME	DESCRIPTION	COMMAND CONSTRUCTOR EQUIVALENT	DEFAULT VALUE	READ	WRITE
UpdatedRowSource	Gets or sets if and how the command results are applied to the row source after the command has been executed. This property needs to be set to one the following **UpdateRowSource** enum values: **Both**: the sum of the **FirstReturnedRecord** and **OutputParameters** values. **FirstReturnedRecord**: only data in the first returned record is mapped to the changed row in the data set. **None**: returned parameters and/ rows will be ignored. **OutputParameters**: only the output parameters are mapped to the changed row in the Dataset.		**Both** (**None**, if the command is automatically generated by a command builder)	Yes	Yes

---

NOTE *Information for ODBC standard escape sequences can be found in the documentation for your ODBC driver or at these addresses:* http://msdn.microsoft.com/library/default.asp?url=/library/ en-us/odbc/htm/odbcescape_sequences_in_odbc.asp *and* http://msdn.microsoft.com/library/default.asp?url=/library/ en-us/odbc/htm/odbcodbc_escape_sequences.asp.

Command Class Methods

Table 3A-27 lists all the public, noninherited Command class (**SqlCommand**, **OdbcCommand**, and **OleDbCommand**) methods in alphabetical order.

Table 3A-27. Command Class Methods

METHOD NAME	DESCRIPTION
Cancel()	Cancels the executing command, if there is one. Otherwise nothing happens.
CreateParameter()	This method can be used to create and instantiate an **SqlParameter**, **OdbcParameter**, or **OleDbParameter** object. This is the equivalent of instantiating an **SqlParameter** object using prmTest = new SqlParameter();, an **OdbcParameter** object using prmTest = new OdbcParameter();, or an **OleDbParameter** using prmTest = new OleDbParameter();. Mind you, there's actually one not-so-small difference between these two ways of instantiating the parameter object: The **CreateParameter** method adds the instantiated parameter object to the parameters collection and thus saves you the extra line of code. The parameters collection can be retrieved using the **Parameters** property.
ExecuteNonQuery()	Executes the query specified in the **CommandText** property. The number of rows affected is returned. Even if the **CommandText** property contains a row-returning statement, no rows will be returned. The value –1 is returned if you specify a row-returning statement as command text. This is also true if you specify any other statement that doesn't affect the rows in the data source.
ExecuteReader()	Executes the query specified in the **CommandText** property. The returned object is a forward-only, read-only data object of type **SqlDataReader**, **OdbcDataReader**, or **OleDbDataReader**. This method is used when you execute a row-returning command, such as an SQL SELECT statement. Although it's possible to execute a non–row-returning command using this method, it's recommended that you use the **ExecuteNonQuery** method for that purpose. The reason for this is that even though the query doesn't return rows, the method still tries to build and return a forward-only data object. This method is overloaded (see "Executing a Command").
ExecuteScalar()	This method is for retrieving a single value, such as an aggregate value like COUNT(*). There's less overhead and coding involved in using this method than in using the **ExecuteReader** method (see "Executing a Command"). Basically, only the first column of the first row is returned. This means that if the query returns several rows and columns, they will be ignored.

(continued)

Table 3A-27. Command Class Methods (continued)

METHOD NAME	DESCRIPTION
ExecuteXmlReader()	This method is for retrieving a result set as XML (see "Executing a Command"). This is an **SqlCommand** class method only.
Prepare()	This method is used for compiling (preparing) the command. You can use this method when the **CommandType** property is set to **Text** or **StoredProcedure**. If, however, the **CommandType** property is set to **TableDirect**, nothing happens. The method takes no arguments, and it's simply called like this: `cmmUserMan.Prepare();`.
ResetCommandTimeout()	Resets the **CommandTimeout** property to the default value. The method takes no arguments, and it's called like this: `cmmUserMan.ResetCommandTimeout();`.

Executing a Command

Now you know how to set up and instantiate a command object, but you really need to execute it as well in order to fully exploit a command object's potential. As you can see from the various methods of the Command class, the **ExecuteNonQuery**, **ExecuteReader**, **ExecuteScalar,** and **ExecuteXmlReader** methods are the ones you need for this purpose. Actually, this is fairly simple, and if you carefully read the names of the methods, you should have no doubt about which one to use (see Table 3A-28).

Table 3A-28. Executing a Command

METHOD NAME	WHEN TO USE	EXAMPLE
ExecuteNonQuery	Use this method when you want to execute a non–row-returning command, such as a DELETE statement. Although you can use this method with row-returning statements, it doesn't make much sense, as the result set is discarded.	See Listing 3A-22, which shows how to insert a new user (User99) into the tblUser table.
ExecuteReader	This method should be used when you want to execute a row-returning command, such as a SELECT statement. The rows are returned in an **SqlDataReader**, an **OdbcDataReader**, or an **OleDbDataReader**, depending on which .NET Data Provider you are using. Please note that the DataReader class is a read-only, forward-only data class, which means that it should only be used for retrieving data to display or similar purposes. You can't update data in a DataReader!	See Listing 3A-23, which shows how to retrieve all users from the tblUser table.
ExecuteScalar	You should use this method when you only want the first column of the first row of the result set returned. If there's more than one row in the result set, they are ignored by this method. This method is faster and has substantially less overhead than the **ExecuteReader** method. So use it when you know you'll only have one row returned, or when you are using an aggregate function such as COUNT.	See Listing 3A-24, which shows how the number of rows in the tblUser table is returned.
ExecuteXmlReader (**SqlCommand** class only)	This method is similar to the **ExecuteReader** method, but the returned rows must be expressed using XML.	See Listing 3A-25, which shows how all the rows in the tblUser table are returned as XML.

Listings 3A-22 to 3A-25 all use the SQL Server .NET Data Provider, but you can simply replace it with the OLE DB .NET Data Provider or the ODBC .NET Data Provider, if you want to use a different data source. Mind you, **ExecuteXmlReader** only works with the **SqlCommand** class! Don't forget to change the **ConnectionString** property according to the data source you want to use.

*Listing 3A-22. Using the **ExecuteNonQuery** Method*

```
1 public void ExecuteNonQueryCommand() {
2     SqlConnection cnnUserMan;
3     SqlCommand cmmUserMan;
4     string strSQL;
5
6     // Instantiate the connection
7     cnnUserMan = new SqlConnection(STR_CONNECTION_STRING);
8     // Open the connection
9     cnnUserMan.Open();
10    // Build delete query string
11    strSQL = "DELETE FROM tblUser WHERE LoginName='User99'";
12    // Instantiate and execute the delete command
13    cmmUserMan = new SqlCommand(strSQL, cnnUserMan);
14    cmmUserMan.ExecuteNonQuery();
15    // Build insert query string
16    strSQL = "INSERT INTO tblUser (LoginName) VALUES('User99')";
17    // Instantiate and execute the insert command
18    cmmUserMan = new SqlCommand(strSQL, cnnUserMan);
19    cmmUserMan.ExecuteNonQuery();
20 }
```

*Listing 3A-23. Using the **ExecuteReader** Method*

```
1 public void ExecuteReaderCommand() {
2     SqlConnection cnnUserMan;
3     SqlCommand cmmUserMan;
4     SqlDataReader drdTest;
5     string strSQL;
6
7     // Instantiate the connection
8     cnnUserMan = new SqlConnection(STR_CONNECTION_STRING);
9     // Open the connection
10    cnnUserMan.Open();
11    // Build query string
12    strSQL = "SELECT * FROM tblUser";
13    // Instantiate and execute the command
14    cmmUserMan = new SqlCommand(strSQL, cnnUserMan);
15    drdTest = cmmUserMan.ExecuteReader();
16 }
```

*Listing 3A-24. Using the **ExecuteScalar** Method*

```
1 public void ExecuteScalarCommand() {
2     SqlConnection cnnUserMan;
3     SqlCommand cmmUserMan;
4     int intNumRows;
5     string strSQL;
6
7     // Instantiate the connection
8     cnnUserMan = new SqlConnection(STR_CONNECTION_STRING);
9     // Open the connection
10    cnnUserMan.Open();
11    // Build query string
12    strSQL = "SELECT COUNT(*) FROM tblUser";
13    // Instantiate the command
14    cmmUserMan = new SqlCommand(strSQL, cnnUserMan);
15    // Save the number of rows in the table
16    intNumRows = (int) cmmUserMan.ExecuteScalar();
17 }
```

*Listing 3A-25. Using the **ExecuteXmlReader** Method*

```
1 public void ExecuteXmlReaderCommand() {
2     SqlConnection cnnUserMan;
3     SqlCommand cmmUserMan;
4     XmlReader drdTest;
5     string strSQL;
6
7     // Instantiate the connection
8     cnnUserMan = new SqlConnection(STR_CONNECTION_STRING);
9     // Open the connection
10    cnnUserMan.Open();
11    // Build query string to return result set as XML
12    strSQL = "SELECT * FROM tblUser FOR XML AUTO";
13    // Instantiate the command
14    cmmUserMan = new SqlCommand(strSQL, cnnUserMan);
15    // Retrieve the rows as XML
16    drdTest = cmmUserMan.ExecuteXmlReader();
17 }
```

In Listing 3A-25, the result set is retrieved as XML, because the FOR XML AUTO clause appears at the end of the query. This instructs SQL Server 2000 to return the result set as XML.

Handling Command Class Exceptions

There are a number of exceptions that can be thrown when you work with the properties and methods of the Command class. The following sections discuss the most common ones and how to deal with them.

CommandTimeout Property

The **ArgumentException** exception is thrown when you try to set the **CommandTimeout** property to a negative value. Listing 3A-26 shows you how you can check if the **ArgumentException** exception was thrown when the command time-out was changed.

Listing 3A-26. Checking If the Exception Was Caused When Setting Command Time-Out

```
 1 public void CheckCommandTimeoutPropertyException() {
 2     SqlConnection cnnUserMan;
 3     SqlCommand cmmUserMan;
 4     string strSQL;
 5
 6     try {
 7         // Instantiate the connection
 8         cnnUserMan = new SqlConnection(STR_CONNECTION_STRING);
 9         // Open the connection
10         cnnUserMan.Open();
11         // Build query string
12         strSQL = "SELECT * FROM tblUser";
13         // Instantiate the command
14         cmmUserMan = new SqlCommand(strSQL, cnnUserMan);
15         // Change command timeout
16         cmmUserMan.CommandTimeout = -1;
17     }
18     catch (ArgumentException objException) {
19         // Check if we tried to set command timeout to an invalid value
20         if (objException.TargetSite.Name == "set_CommandTimeout") {
21             MessageBox.Show("The CommandTimeout property threw the exception.");
22         }
23     }
24 }
```

CommandType Property

The **ArgumentException** exception is thrown if you try to set the property to an invalid command type. Listing 3A-27 shows you how you can check if the **ArgumentException** exception was thrown when the command type was changed.

Listing 3A-27. Checking If the Exception Was Caused When Setting Command Type

```
1 public void CheckCommandTypePropertyException() {
2     SqlConnection cnnUserMan;
3     SqlCommand cmmUserMan;
4     string strSQL;
5
6     try {
7         // Instantiate the connection
8         cnnUserMan = new SqlConnection(STR_CONNECTION_STRING);
9         // Open the connection
10        cnnUserMan.Open();
11        // Build query string
12        strSQL = "SELECT * FROM tblUser";
13        // Instantiate the command
14        cmmUserMan = new SqlCommand(strSQL, cnnUserMan);
15        // Change command type
16        cmmUserMan.CommandType = CommandType.TableDirect;
17    }
18    catch (ArgumentException objException) {
19        // Check if we tried to set command type to an invalid value
20        if (objException.TargetSite.Name == "set_CommandType") {
21            MessageBox.Show("The CommandType property threw the exception.");
22        }
23    }
24 }
```

Prepare Method

The **InvalidOperationException** exception is thrown if the connection variable is set to a null value or if the connection isn't open. Listing 3A-28 shows you how you can check if the **InvalidOperationException** exception was thrown when preparing the command.

Listing 3A-28. Checking If Exception Was Thrown When Trying to Prepare the Command

```
1  public void CheckPrepareMethodException() {
2      SqlConnection cnnUserMan;
3      SqlCommand cmmUserMan;
4      string strSQL;
5
6      try {
7          // Instantiate the connection
8          cnnUserMan = new SqlConnection(STR_CONNECTION_STRING);
9          // Open the connection
10         // If the following line is commented out, the ValidateCommand
11         // exception will be thrown
12         //cnnUserMan.Open()
13         // Build query string
14         strSQL = "SELECT * FROM tblUser";
15         // Instantiate the command
16         cmmUserMan = new SqlCommand(strSQL, cnnUserMan);
17         // Prepare command
18         cmmUserMan.Prepare();
19     }
20     catch (InvalidOperationException objException) {
21         // Check if we tried to prepare the command on an invalid connection
22         if (objException.TargetSite.Name == "ValidateCommand") {
23             MessageBox.Show("The Prepare method threw the exception.");
24         }
25     }
26 }
```

UpdatedRowSource Property

The **ArgumentException** exception is thrown if the row source update property was set to a value other than an **UpdateRowSource** enum value. Listing 3A-29 shows you how to check if the **ArgumentException** exception was thrown.

Listing 3A-29. Checking If Exception Was Thrown When Trying to Change Row Source Update

```
1  public void CheckUpdateRowSourcePropertyException() {
2      SqlConnection cnnUserMan;
3      SqlCommand cmmUserMan;
4      string strSQL;
5
```

```
 6    try {
 7        // Instantiate the connection
 8        cnnUserMan = new SqlConnection(STR_CONNECTION_STRING);
 9        // Open the connection
10        cnnUserMan.Open();
11        // Build query string
12        strSQL = "SELECT * FROM tblUser";
13        // Instantiate the command
14        cmmUserMan = new SqlCommand(strSQL, cnnUserMan);
15        // Change Row source Update
16        cmmUserMan.UpdatedRowSource = UpdateRowSource.OutputParameters + 3;
17    }
18    catch (ArgumentException objException) {
19    // Check if we tried to set the row source update to an invalid value
20        if (objException.TargetSite.Name == "set_UpdatedRowSource") {
21            MessageBox.Show(
22                "The UpdatedRowSource property threw the exception.");
23        }
24    }
25 }
```

Using the DataReader Class

The DataReader class is a read-only, forward-only data class, and it's very efficient when it comes to memory usage, because only one row is ever in memory
at a time. This is in contrast to the **DataTable** class (discussed in Chapter 3B),
which allocates memory for all rows retrieved.

You can only instantiate an object of type DataReader by using the
ExecuteReader method of the Command class (see "Executing a Command" earlier in this chapter for details). When you use the DataReader, the associated
connection can't perform any other operations. This is because the connection as
such is serving the DataReader, and you need to close the DataReader before the
connection is ready for other operations. Another thing you definitely need to
know is that the DataReader class seems to be jamming communications at the
server and locking rows,[3] leaving queries from other connections hanging and
eventually leading to time-outs. The DataReader class is one of the ADO.NET
classes that resemble the ADO **Recordset** class the most. Well, it is, if you think
Recordset with a read-only, forward-only cursor. One of the differences is how
you get the next row (see "Reading Rows in a DataReader" later in this chapter).

---

3. This is NOT part of the DataReader description, and I can't really give you a reason as to why
    and when it happens. Only one thing is sure: don't overdo the use of the DataReader, and if
    you happen to run into the mentioned problems, redesign your application, because you'll
    have little if no luck solving it.

SqlDataReader, OdbcDataReader, and OleDbDataReader

As with the Connection and Command classes, there are also three general DataReader classes of interest[4]: **SqlDataReader** is for use with Microsoft SQL Server 7.0 or later, **OdbcDataReader** is for use with any other ODBC data source, and **OleDbDataReader** is for use with any other OLE DB 2.5–compliant data source. Please note that if you are using an **SqlConnection** object, then you can't use **OleDbCommand** and/or an **OdbcDataReader** class with the connection. The same goes the other way around. In other words, you can't mix Odbc, OleDb, and Sql data classes; they can't work together!

Declaring and Instantiating a DataReader Object

The DataReader class can't be inherited, which effectively means that you can't create your own data class based on the DataReader class.

The following sample code is wrong:

```
SqlDataReader drdTest = new SqlDataReader();
```

It's wrong because it tries to instantiate drdTest using the **new** keyword, but that doesn't work, because the DataReader class doesn't have a constructor. Listing 3A-30 shows you what you need to do to declare and instantiate an **SqlDataReader** object.

*Listing 3A-30. Instantiating an **SqlDataReader** Object*

```
 1 public void InstantiateDataReader() {
 2     SqlConnection cnnUserMan;
 3     SqlCommand cmmUserMan;
 4     SqlDataReader drdUserMan;
 5     string strSQL;
 6
 7     // Instantiate the connection
 8     cnnUserMan = new SqlConnection(STR_CONNECTION_STRING);
 9     // Open the connection
10     cnnUserMan.Open();
11     // Build query string
12     strSQL = "SELECT * FROM tblUser";
13     // Instantiate the command
14     cmmUserMan = new SqlCommand(strSQL, cnnUserMan);
```

---

4. Well, there's actually one more, the **XmlReader** discussed in the "XmlReader" section later in this chapter.

```
15    // Instantiate data reader using the ExecuteReader method
16    // of the Command class
17    drdUserMan = cmmUserMan.ExecuteReader();
18 }
```

Reading Rows in a DataReader

Since the DataReader class is a forward-only data class, you need to read the rows sequentially from start to finish if you need to read all the returned rows. In Listing 3A-31, you can see how to loop through a populated data reader.

Listing 3A-31. Looping Through All Rows in a DataReader

```
 1 public void ReadRowsFromDataReader() {
 2     SqlConnection cnnUserMan;
 3     SqlCommand cmmUserMan;
 4     SqlDataReader drdUser;
 5     string strSQL;
 6     long lngCounter = 0;
 7
 8     // Instantiate the connection
 9     cnnUserMan = new SqlConnection(STR_CONNECTION_STRING);
10     // Open the connection
11     cnnUserMan.Open();
12     // Build query string
13     strSQL = "SELECT * FROM tblUser";
14     // Instantiate the command
15     cmmUserMan = new SqlCommand(strSQL, cnnUserMan);
16     // Execute command and return rows in data reader
17     drdUser = cmmUserMan.ExecuteReader();
18     // Loop through all the returned rows
19     while (drdUser.Read()) {
20         ++lngCounter;
21     }
22
23     // Display the number of rows returned
24     MessageBox.Show(lngCounter.ToString());
25 }
```

Listing 3A-31 loops through the rows in the data reader and counts the number of rows. This is obviously just an example of how to sequentially go through all the rows returned by the **ExecuteReader** method of the Command class.

Closing a DataReader

Because the DataReader object keeps the connection busy while it's open, it's good practice to close the DataReader once you are done with it. The DataReader is closed using the **Close** method, like this:

```
drdTest.Close();
```

You can use the **IsClosed** property to check if the data reader is closed, as follows:

```
if (! drdTest.IsClosed) {}
```

This little piece of example code will execute the code in the curly brackets if the DataReader is NOT (!) closed!

Checking for Null Values in Columns

Null values can be a burden to deal with, because they can crash your application, if you haven't set up your code to appropriately handle them. Null values are empty references or nothing at all, meaning an unknown value. A null value is unlike an empty string, because an empty string is something: a string, albeit empty.

> **NOTE** *One thing you should be aware of when dealing with null values in your database is whether the ANSI SQL-92 standard is being used by your DBMS. If it's being used, you can't compare a column value to NULL, because SQL-92 dictates that a comparison made in a SELECT statement always returns false, when you compare a column value with NULL. In SQL Server, you can turn this option on and off using the SET ANSI_NULLS statement. See your DBMS documentation for more information.*

When you've instantiated your data reader and positioned it in a valid row using the **Read** method, you can check if a particular column contains a null value. This is done by using the **IsDBNull** method, which compares the content of a specific column in the current row with the **DBNull** class. If the column contains a null value, the **IsDBNull** method returns **true**. Otherwise **false** is returned. Listing 3A-32 shows how you can perform the check.

Listing 3A-32. Checking for Null Value in Column

```
1  public void CheckForNullValueInColumn(int intColumn) {
2      SqlConnection cnnUserMan;
3      SqlCommand cmmUserMan;
4      SqlDataReader drdUser;
5      string strSQL;
6
7      // Instantiate the connection
8      cnnUserMan = new SqlConnection(STR_CONNECTION_STRING);
9      // Open the connection
10     cnnUserMan.Open();
11     // Build query string
12     strSQL = "SELECT * FROM tblUser";
13     // Instantiate the command
14     cmmUserMan = new SqlCommand(strSQL, cnnUserMan);
15     // Execute command and return rows in data reader
16     drdUser = cmmUserMan.ExecuteReader();
17     // Advance reader to first row
18     drdUser.Read();
19     // Check if the column contains a NULL value
20     if (drdUser.IsDBNull(intColumn)) {
21         MessageBox.Show(
22             "Column " + intColumn.ToString() + " contains a NULL value!");
23     }
24     else {
25         MessageBox.Show("Column " +
26             intColumn.ToString() + " does not contain a NULL value!");
27     }
28  }
```

Handling Multiple Results

The DataReader class can handle multiple results returned by the Command class. This is one advantage the DataReader class has over the ADO "equivalent," a forward-only, read-only **RecordSet**. If the Command class returned multiple results by specifying a batch of SQL statements separated by a semicolon, you can use the **NextResult** method to advance to the next result. Please note that you can only move forward, so as much as it would be nice to have a **PreviousResult** method, it isn't possible. I guess it might just have something to do with the fact that the DataReader class is forward-only.

DataReader Properties

The DataReader class has the properties shown in ascending order in Table 3A-29.

Table 3A-29. DataReader Class Properties

NAME	DESCRIPTION
Depth	This read-only property is used with hierarchical result sets, such as XML data. The return value indicates how far down a node you currently are or the depth of the current element in the stack of XML elements. This isn't supported by the SQL Server .NET Data Provider, which means it will always return 0, because this is the depth value for the outermost table.
FieldCount	This read-only property returns the number of columns in the current row and 0 if the data reader isn't positioned at a valid row, like when the data reader has been instantiated and you haven't called the **Read** method yet. The **NotSupportedException** is thrown, if the DataReader isn't connected to a data source.
IsClosed	This property, which is read-only, indicates whether the data reader is closed. **true** is returned if the data reader is closed, and **false** if not.
RecordsAffected	This read-only property retrieves the number of records that was affected (inserted, updated, or deleted) by the command. This property won't be set until you've read all the rows and closed the data reader.

DataReader Methods

Table 3A-30 lists the noninherited and public methods of the DataReader class in alphabetical order. Please note that all the methods marked with an asterisk (*) require that the data contained in the specified column be of the same type as the method indicates. This is because no conversion is performed on the content of the specified column. If you try to use any of the methods on a column containing content of a different data type, the **InvalidCastException** is thrown. Also, these methods can't be overridden in an inherited class. In the case of the **OdbcDataReader** class, conversions are performed by your ODBC driver. This means that the method will fail, if the conversion is not supported by the driver.

Table 3A-30. DataReader Class Methods

NAME	DESCRIPTION	EXAMPLE
Close()	Closes the data reader. You must call this method before you can use the connection for any other purpose. This is because the data reader keeps the connection busy as long as it's open.	`drdTest.Close();`
GetBoolean(int intOrdinal)	Returns the **bool** value of the specified column intOrdinal. The corresponding SQL Server data type is **bit**.	`bool blnTest =` `drdTest.GetBoolean(0);`
GetByte(int intOrdinal)	Returns the value of the specified column intOrdinal as a **byte**. The corresponding SQL Server data type is **tinyint**.	`byte bytTest = drdTest.GetByte(0);`

GetBytes(int intOrdinal, long lngDataIndex, byte[] arrbytBuffer, int intBufferIndex, int intLength)	Returns the value of the specified column intOrdinal as an array of **byte**s in the arrbytBuffer argument. The length of the specified column is returned as the result of the method call. intLength specifies the maximum number of bytes to copy into the byte array. intBufferIndex is the starting point in the buffer. When the bytes are copied into the buffer, they are placed starting from the intBufferIndex point. The bytes are copied from the data source starting from the lngDataIndex point. You can use this method when you need to read large images from the database and the method largely corresponds to the **GetChunk** method in ADO. The corresponding SQL Server data types are **binary**, **image**, and **varbinary**.	`lngNumBytes = drdSql.GetBytes(1,`
		`0, null, 0, int.MaxValue);`
		`byte[] arrbytImage =`
		`new byte[lngNumBytes];`
		`drdSql.GetBytes(1, 0, arrbytImage,`
		`0, (int) lngNumBytes);`
		This example reads an image from column 1 in the current row of the data reader. The image is saved in the arrbytImage byte array. The first line retrieves the size of the image, which is then used for sizing the array on the second line, and finally the third line retrieves the image.

(continued)

Table 3A-30. DataReader Class Methods (continued)

NAME	DESCRIPTION	EXAMPLE
GetChar(int intOrdinal)	Returns the value of the specified column (`intOrdinal`) as a **char**. The corresponding SQL Server data type is **char**.	`chrTest = drdTest.GetChar(0);`

GetChars(int intOrdinal, long lngDataIndex, char[] arrchrBuffer, int intBufferIndex, int intLength)	Returns the value of the specified column (`intOrdinal`) as an array of **char**s in the `arrchrBuffer` argument. The length of the specified column is returned as the result of the method call. `intLength` specifies the maximum number of characters to copy into the character array. `intBufferIndex` is the starting point in the buffer. When the characters are copied into the buffer, they are placed starting from the `intBufferIndex` point. The characters are copied from the data source starting from the `lngDataIndex` point. The corresponding SQL Server data types are **char**, **nchar**, **ntext**, **nvarchar**, **text,** and **varchar**.	`lngNumChars = drdSql.GetChars(1, 0, null, 0, int.MaxValue);`
		`char[] arrchrTest = new char[lngNumChars];`
		`drdSql.GetChars(1, 0, arrchrTest, 0, (int) lngNumChars);`

GetData(int intOrdinal)	Not currently supported.	
GetDataTypeName(int intOrdinal)	Returns the name of the data type used by the data source for the specified column.	`strDataType = drdTest.GetDataTypeName(0);`
GetDateTime(int intOrdinal)	Returns the **DateTime** value stored in the column specified by `intOrdinal`. The corresponding SQL Server data types are **datetime** and **smalldatetime**.	`dtmTest = drdTest.GetDateTime(0);`
GetDecimal(int intOrdinal)	Returns the **decimal** value stored in the column specified by `intOrdinal`. The corresponding SQL Server data types are **decimal**, **money**, **numeric,** and **smallmoney**.	`decTest = drdTest.GetDecimal(0);`

(continued)

153

Table 3A-30. DataReader Class Methods (continued)

NAME	DESCRIPTION	EXAMPLE
GetDouble(int intOrdinal)	Returns the **double** value stored in the column specified by intOrdinal. The corresponding SQL Server data type is **float**.	`dblTest = drdTest.GetDouble(0);`
GetFieldType(int intOrdinal)	Returns the data type of the column specified by intOrdinal. The returned object is of type **Type**.	`typTest = drdTest.GetFieldType(0);`
GetFloat(int intOrdinal)	Returns the single precision floating-point number stored in the column specified by intOrdinal. The returned object is of data type **float**. The corresponding SQL Server data type is **real**.	`fltTest = drdTest.GetFloat(0);`
GetGuid(int intOrdinal)	Returns the globally unique identifier stored in the column specified by intOrdinal. The returned object is of data type **Guid**. The corresponding SQL Server data type is **uniqueidentifier**.	`guiTest = drdTest.GetGuid(0);`
GetInt16(int intOrdinal)	Returns the 16-bit signed integer stored in the column specified by intOrdinal. The returned object is of data type **short**. The corresponding SQL Server data type is **smallint**.	`shrTest = drdTest.GetInt16(0);`
GetInt32(int intOrdinal)	Returns the 32-bit signed integer stored in the column specified by intOrdinal. The returned object is of data type **int**. The corresponding SQL Server data type is **int**.	`intTest = drdTest.GetInt32(0);`

(continued)

Table 3A-30. DataReader Class Methods (continued)

NAME	DESCRIPTION	EXAMPLE
*GetInt64(int intOrdinal)	Returns the 64-bit signed integer stored in the column specified by intOrdinal. The returned object is of data type **long**. The corresponding SQL Server data type is **bigint**.	lngTest = drdTest.GetInt64(0);
GetName(int intOrdinal)	Returns the name of the column specified by intOrdinal. The returned object is of data type **string**. This method is the reverse of **GetOrdinal**.	strTest = drdTest.GetName(0);
GetOrdinal(string strName)	Returns the ordinal for the column specified by strName. The returned object is of data type **int**. This method is the reverse of **GetName**.	intTest = drdTest.GetOrdinal(0);
GetSchemaTable()	This method returns a **DataTable** object that describes the metadata for the columns in the DataReader. The metadata includes column name, size, ordinal, and key information.	dtbSchema = drdTest.GetSchemaTable();
*GetSqlBinary(int intOrdinal) (**SqlDataReader** only)	Returns the variable-length binary data stream stored in the column specified by intOrdinal. The returned object is of data type **SqlBinary**. The corresponding SQL Server data types are **binary** and **image**.	sbnTest = drdTest.GetSqlBinary(0);

(continued)

Table 3A-30. DataReader Class Methods (continued)

NAME	DESCRIPTION	EXAMPLE
GetSqlBoolean(int intOrdinal) (**SqlDataReader** only)	Returns the value stored in the column specified by intOrdinal. The returned object is of data type **SqlBoolean** and can only be one of the values **true, false,** or **null**. The corresponding SQL Server data type is **bit**. Although this method works with the same SQL Server data type as the **GetBoolean** method, the return value is different.	sbtTest = drdTest.GetSqlBit(0);
GetSqlByte(int intOrdinal) (**SqlDataReader** only)	Returns the 8-bit unsigned integer stored in the column specified by intOrdinal. The returned object is of data type **SqlByte**. The corresponding SQL Server data type is **tinyint**.	sbyTest = drdTest.GetSqlByte(0);
GetSqlDateTime(int intOrdinal) (**SqlDataReader** only)	Returns the date and time value stored in the column specified by intOrdinal. The returned object is of data type **SqlDateTime**. The corresponding SQL Server data types are **datetime** and **smalldatetime**.	sdtTest = drdTest.GetSqlDateTime(0);
GetSqlDecimal(int intOrdinal) (**SqlDataReader** only)	Returns the **SqlDecimal** value stored in the column specified by intOrdinal.	sdbTest = drdTest.GetSqlDouble(0);
GetSqlDouble(int intOrdinal) (**SqlDataReader** only)	Returns the **SqlDouble** value stored in the column specified by intOrdinal. The corresponding SQL Server data type is **float**.	sdbTest = drdTest.GetSqlDouble(0);
GetSqlGuid(int intOrdinal) (**SqlDataReader** only)	Returns the globally unique identifier stored in the column specified by intOrdinal. The returned object is of data type **SqlGuid**. The corresponding SQL Server data type is **uniqueidentifier**.	sguTest = drdTest.GetSqlGuid(0);

(continued)

Table 3A-30. DataReader Class Methods (continued)

NAME	DESCRIPTION	EXAMPLE
GetSqlInt16(int intOrdinal) (**SqlDataReader** only)	Returns the 16-bit signed integer stored in the column specified by intOrdinal. The returned object is of data type **SqlInt16**. The corresponding SQL Server data type is **smallint**.	s16Test = drdTest.GetSqlInt16(0);
GetSqlInt32(int intOrdinal) (**SqlDataReader** only)	Returns the 32-bit signed integer stored in the column specified by intOrdinal. The returned object is of data type **SqlInt32**. The corresponding SQL Server data type is **int**.	s32Test = drdTest.GetSqlInt32(0);
GetSqlInt64(int intOrdinal) (**SqlDataReader** only)	Returns the 64-bit signed integer stored in the column specified by intOrdinal. The returned object is of data type **SqlInt64**. The corresponding SQL Server data type is **bigint**.	s64Test = drdTest.GetSqlInt64(0);
GetSqlMoney(int intOrdinal) (**SqlDataReader** only)	Returns the **SqlMoney** value stored in the column specified by intOrdinal. The corresponding SQL Server data types are **money** and **smallmoney**.	smoTest = drdTest.GetSqlMoney(0);
GetSqlSingle(int intOrdinal) (**SqlDataReader** only)	Returns the **SqlSingle** value stored in the column specified by intOrdinal. The corresponding SQL Server data type is **real**.	ssgTest = drdTest.GetSqlSingle(0);
GetSqlString(int intOrdinal) (**SqlDataReader** only)	Returns the **SqlString** value stored in the column specified by intOrdinal. The corresponding SQL Server data types are **char**, **nchar**, **ntext**, **nvarchar**, **text**, and **varchar**.	sstTest = drdTest.GetSqlString(0);

(continued)

Table 3A-30. DataReader Class Methods (continued)

NAME	DESCRIPTION	EXAMPLE
GetSqlValue(int intOrdinal) (**SqlDataReader** only)	Returns an object that represents the underlying data type and value stored in the column specified by intOrdinal. The returned object is of data type **object**. You can use **GetType**, **ToString**, and other methods on the returned object to get the information wanted.	`objTest = drdTest.GetSqlValue(0);`
GetSqlValues(object[] arrobjValues) (**SqlDataReader** only)	Returns all the attribute fields for the column in the current row in the arrobjValues array. The array supplied can have fewer or more elements than there are columns in the current row. Only the number of elements in the array is copied from the current row, if there are fewer elements in the array. The returned **int** is the number of objects in the array.	`object[] arrobjValues = new object[int.MaxValue];` `intNumFields =` `drdTest.GetSqlValues` `(arrobjValues);`
*GetString(int intOrdinal)	Returns the **string** value stored in the column specified by intOrdinal. The corresponding SQL Server data types are **char**, **nchar**, **ntext**, **nvarchar**, **text**, and **varchar**.	`strTest = drdTest.GetString(0);`
*GetTimeSpan(int intOrdinal) (**OleDbDataReader** class only)	Returns the **TimeSpan** value stored in the column specified by intOrdinal.	`tmsTest = drdTest.GetTimeSpan(0);`
GetValue(int intOrdinal)	Returns the value stored in the column specified by intOrdinal as a variable of data type **object**. The value returned is in native .NET format.	`objTest = drdTest.GetValue(0);`

(continued)

Table 3A-30. DataReader Class Methods (continued)

NAME	DESCRIPTION	EXAMPLE
GetValues(object[] arrobjValues)	Returns all the attribute column values for the current row in the arrobjValues array. The array supplied can have fewer or more elements than there are columns in the current row. Only the number of elements in the array is copied from the current row, if there are fewer elements in the array. The returned **int** is the number of objects in the array.	`object[] arrobjValues = new object[int.MaxValue]; intNumFields = drdTest.GetValues(arrobjValues);`
IsDBNull(int intOrdinal)	This method returns **true** if the column specified by `intOrdinal` is equal to **DBNull**; otherwise it returns **false**. **DBNull** means that the column does not hold a known value or a null value.	`if (drdTest.IsDBNull(0)) {}`
NextResult()	This method positions the data reader at the next result in the result set returned by the command. This method has no effect if the command query does not contain a batch of row-returning SQL statements or if the current result is the last in the result set. **true** is returned if there are more results and **false** otherwise. The data reader is positioned at the first result by default when instantiated.	`if (drdTest.NextResult()) {}`
Read()	This method positions the data reader at the next row. Please note that you must call this method after the data reader has been instantiated before you can access any of the data in the data reader. This is because the data reader, unlike the **Recordset** object in ADO, isn't positioned at the first row by default. **true** is returned if the data reader is positioned at the next row and **false** if not.	`if (drdTest.Read()) {}`

All the **GetSql . . .** methods such as **GetSqlBinary**, which are relevant to the **SqlDataReader** class only, belong to the **System.Data.SqlTypes** namespace. Most of these methods have corresponding methods that work with all the data reader classes. They work with the same data types in the data source (SQL Server), but the data type returned is different. So which method you should pick when working with SQL Server as your data source really depends on the data types you want to work with in your application: do you want native SQL Server data types or do you want .NET Framework data types?

Handling DataReader Exceptions

The properties and methods of the DataReader class can throw the exceptions shown in Table 3A-31.

Table 3A-31. DataReader Class Exceptions

NAME	DESCRIPTION	THROWN BY PROPERTY/METHOD
ArgumentException	This exception is thrown when an argument is out of range.	
InvalidCastException	If you try to implicitly cast or convert a database value using one the **Get*** methods, then this exception is thrown.	All the methods marked by an asterisk (*)
InvalidOperationException	When you try to perform an operation (property or method) that isn't valid in the object's current state, this exception is thrown.	
NotSupportedException	This exception is thrown when you try to use an I/O property or method on a DataReader object that is closed or otherwise not connected.	

When to Use the DataReader Class

The DataReader class should be used in cases where you want a minimal overhead in terms of memory usage. Now obviously you don't want to use a DataReader object if you are expecting hundreds of thousands of rows returned, because it could take forever to sequentially loop through all these rows.

If you are looking at only one or even a few rows returned, in which you just need to read one or two fields or columns, then the DataReader is definitely a good choice. The DataReader class is read-only, so if you need to update your data, then the DataReader class is obviously NOT a good choice! Another point to make is that the DataReader is a forward-only scrolling data-aware class. So there's no moving backwards in the returned rows or jumping to the first or last row.[5]

XmlReader

The **XmlReader** class, which is similar to the other three DataReader classes I discussed in the previous section, is quite obviously for handling data formatted as XML. Actually, the **XmlReader** class, which is part of the **System.Xml** namespace, must be overridden, and this has already been done in the .NET Framework. You can still choose to override the **XmlReader** class yourself, but there are already three classes that all implement the **XmlReader** class, and they are **XmlTextReader**, **XmlValidatingReader**, and **XmlNodeReader**.

- *XmlTextReader:* This class is for fast, noncached, forward-only stream access. The class checks for well-formed XML, but if you need data validation, you must use the **XmlValidatingReader** class.

- *XmlValidatingReader:* This class provides XDR, XSD, and DTD schema validation of the XML data.

- *XmlNodeReader:* The **XmlNodeReader** class reads XML data from an **XmlNavigator** class, which means it can read data stored in an **XmlDocument** or **XmlDataDocument**.

I won't go into more detail on these three derived XML readers, but I'll take a closer look at the parent class **XmlReader**.

XmlReader Properties

The **XmlReader** class has the properties, shown in alphabetical order, in Table 3A-32.

---

5. Well, you can close the DataReader and reopen it, effectively making it move to the first row again.

*Table 3A-32. **XmlReader** Class Properties*

NAME	DESCRIPTION
AttributeCount	Returns the number of attributes, including default attributes, on the current node. Only the **Element**, **DocumentType,** and **XmlDeclaration** type nodes have attributes, which means that this property is only relevant to these types of nodes. If you've used the **ExecuteXmlReader** method of a Command class, then the **AttributeCount** property will return the number of nonnull values in the current row. This property is abstract and read-only.
BaseURI	Returns the base URI of the current node. An empty string is returned if there's no base URI. This property is abstract and read-only, and it has no real meaning if your **XmlReader** has been returned by the **ExecuteXmlReader** method of a Command class.
CanResolveEntity	This property is virtual and read-only, and it returns a value that indicates whether the reader can parse and resolve entities. **false** is always returned for instances of the **XmlReader** class that don't support DTD information.
Depth	The return value indicates how far down a node you currently are or the depth of the current node in the stack of XML elements. This property is abstract and read-only.
EOF	This property, which is abstract and read-only, returns a **bool** value that indicates whether the **XmlReader** is positioned at the end of the stream.
HasAttributes	This property, which is virtual and read-only, returns a **bool** value that indicates whether the current node has any attributes.
HasValue	This abstract and read-only property returns a **bool** value that indicates whether the current node can hold a value. The value is of property type **Value**.
IsDefault	This property, which is abstract and read-only, returns a **bool** value that indicates whether the current node is an attribute generated from a default value, which is defined in a schema or DTD.
IsEmptyElement	This property, which is abstract and read-only, returns a **bool** value that indicates whether the current node is an empty element. An empty element can be defined like this: `<DataElement/>`.
LocalName	This property, which is abstract and read-only, returns the name of the current node without the namespace prefix. An empty **string** is returned for node types that don't have a name. If you've used the **ExecuteXmlReader** method of a Command class, then the **LocalName** property will return the name of the table.
Name	This property, which is abstract and read-only, returns the qualified name of the current node or the name with the namespace prefix.

(continued)

*Table 3A-32. **XmlReader** Class Properties (continued)*

NAME	DESCRIPTION
NameSpaceURI	This property, which is abstract and read-only, returns the namespace URI for the current node. Note that this property is only relevant to Element and Attribute nodes.
NameTable	This property, which is abstract and read-only, returns the **XmlNameTable** that is associated with the implementation.
NodeType	This abstract and read-only property returns the type for the current node. The data type returned is **XmlNodeType**.
Prefix	This property returns the namespace prefix for the current node. This property is abstract and read-only.
QuoteChar	This property returns the quotation mark used for enclosing values of attribute nodes. This property is abstract and read-only and it returns either a single quotation mark (') or a double quotation mark ("). The property only applies to attribute nodes and the return value is of data type **char**.
ReadState	This property returns the read state of the stream. This property is abstract and read-only and it returns a member of the **ReadState** enum. The following members can be returned: **Closed**: the Close method has been executed on the **XmlReader**. **EndOfFile:** end of stream has been reached (successfully). **Error:** an error has occurred. This means that **XmlReader** can't continue reading the stream. **Initial:** you haven't called the **Read** method yet, so the reader is at its initial position. **Interactive:** a read operation is currently in progress, but you can still call other methods on the reader.
Value	This abstract and read-only property returns the text value of the current node. If the current node does not have a value to return, an empty string is returned.
XmlLang	This abstract and read-only property returns the xml:lang scope currently being used. Please note that this property value is also part of the **XmlNameTable** returned from the **NameTable** property.
XmlSpace	This abstract and read-only property returns the xml:space scope currently being used as a member of the **XmlSpace** enum. The **XmlSpace** enum has the following members: **Default:** the xml:space scope is "default". **None:** there's no xml:space scope. **Preserve:** the xml:space scope is "preserve".

XmlReader Methods

Table 3A-33 lists the noninherited and public methods of the **XmlReader** class in alphabetical order. Please note that all the methods marked with an asterisk (*) require the data contained in the specified column to be of the same type as the method indicates. This is because no conversion is performed on the content of the specified column. If you try to use any of the methods on a column containing content of a different data type, the **InvalidCastException** is thrown.

*Table 3A-33. **XmlReader** Class Methods*

NAME	DESCRIPTION	EXAMPLE
Close()	This abstract method resets all properties, releases any resources held, and changes the **ReadState** property to **Closed**.	`xrdTest.Close();`
GetAttribute()	This abstract and overloaded method returns the value of an attribute. See the example code, which returns the LoginName for the current node or row in the tblUser table. The reader has been instantiated elsewhere with the **ExecuteXmlReader** method of the Command class.	`xrdTest.GetAttribute(3);` `xrdTest.GetAttribute (` `"LoginName");`
IsName(string strName)	This static method returns a **bool** value indicating whether strName is a valid XML name.	`blnValidName =` `xrdTest.IsName("XML Name");`
IsNameToken(string strNameToken)	The **IsNameToken** method is static and returns a **bool** value indicating whether strNameToken is a valid XML name token.	`blnValidNameToken =` `xrdTest.IsNameToken("XML Name` `Token");`
IsStartElement()	This virtual and overloaded method returns a **bool** value indicating whether the current content node is a start tag or an empty element tag.	`if (xrdTest.IsStartElement()) {}`
LookupNamespace(string strPrefix)	This abstract method resolves strPrefix in the current elements scope and returns the namespace URI for the strPrefix.	`xrdTest.LookupNamespace` `("MyNameSpace");`

(continued)

*Table 3A-33. **XmlReader** Class Methods (continued)*

NAME	DESCRIPTION	EXAMPLE
MoveToAttribute()	This abstract and overloaded method moves to the attribute matching the passed argument. If your **XmlReader** has been returned by the **ExecuteXmlReader** method of a Command class, this method can be used to move between the columns in the current row.	`xrdTest.MoveToAttribute(0); or` `xrdTest.MoveToAttribute (` `"LoginName");`
MoveToContent()	This virtual method checks if the current node is a content node, and skips to the next content node, or EOF, if no content node is found. If the current node is an attribute node, then the reader's position is moved back to the element that owns the attribute node.	`xrdTest.MoveToContent();`
MoveToElement()	This abstract method moves to the element in which the current attribute node exists. A **bool** value is returned based on whether the current attribute is owned by an element. If your **XmlReader** has been returned by the **ExecuteXmlReader** method of a Command class, this method can be used in conjunction with the **MoveToAttribute** method to move to a specific attribute/column and then back to the element or row that owns the attribute or column. A **bool** value is returned indicating whether the move was successful.	`blnAttributePos =` `xrdTest.MoveToElement();`
MoveToFirstAttribute()	This abstract method moves to the first attribute in an element. If your **XmlReader** has been returned by the **ExecuteXmlReader** method of a Command class, this method can be used to move to the first column in the current row. A **bool** value is returned indicating whether the move was successful.	`blnMoved =` `xrdTest.MoveToFirstAttribute();`

(continued)

Table 3A-33. **XmlReader** *Class Methods (continued)*

NAME	DESCRIPTION	EXAMPLE
MoveToNextAttribute()	This abstract method moves to the next attribute in an element. If your **XmlReader** has been returned by the **ExecuteXmlReader** method of a Command class, this method can be used to move to the next column in the current row. A **bool** value is returned indicating whether there is a next node and thus the move succeeded.	blnMoved = xrdTest.MoveToNextAttribute();
Read()	Reads the next node in the stream. This abstract method must be called before any other properties or methods can be called. Actually, this isn't quite true, as the initial value can be returned from some properties if the reader has not yet been positioned at the first row or element.	blnRead = xrdTest.Read();
ReadAttributeValue()	This abstract method parses the attribute value into **Text**, **EndEntity,** or **EntityReference** nodes. A **bool** value is returned indicating whether there are any nodes to return.	blnRead = xrdTest.ReadAttributeValue();
ReadElementString()	This virtual, overloaded method is used for reading simple text elements.	xrdTest.ReadElementString(); xrdTest.ReadElementString ("ElementName");
ReadEndElement()	This virtual method is for checking if the current node is an end tag. If the current node is an end tag, the reader position is advanced to the next node.	xrdTest.ReadEndElement();
ReadInnerXml()	The abstract **ReadInnerXml** method returns all the content of the current node as a string. The returned string includes markup text.	strContent = xrdTest.ReadInnerXml();

(continued)

*Table 3A-33. **XmlReader** Class Methods (continued)*

NAME	DESCRIPTION	EXAMPLE
ReadOuterXml()	The abstract **ReadOuterXml** method returns all the content of the current node and all the children nodes as a string. The returned string includes markup text. If your **XmlReader** has been returned by the **ExecuteXmlReader** method of a Command class, this method will return the current row as an XML node. Please note that only nonnull columns will be returned as attributes.	`strContent = xrdTest.ReadOuterXml();`
ReadStartElement()	This virtual and overloaded method is for checking if the current node is an element. If the current node is an element, the reader position is advanced to the next node.	`xrdTest.ReadStartElement();`
ReadString()	This abstract method is for reading the contents of an element or text node and returning it as a **string**.	`strElement = xrdTest.ReadString();`
ResolveEntity()	This abstract method is for use with **EntityReferences** nodes. It resolves the entity reference for this type of node.	`xrdTest.ResolveEntity();`
Skip()	Skips the current element or moves to the next element. Depending on where the reader is positioned, the **Skip** method can perform the same function as the **Read** method. This happens when the reader is positioned on a leaf node. Please note that this method checks for well-formed XML.	`xrdTest.Skip();`

Declaring and Instantiating an XmlReader Object

The **XmlReader** class must be overridden, which means that you can't create an instance of the **XmlReader** class.

The following sample code is wrong:

```
XmlReader xrdTest = new XmlReader();
```

It's wrong because it tries to instantiate xrdTest using the **new** keyword. Listing 3A-33 shows you how to perform the instantiation correctly.

*Listing 3A-33. Instantiating an **XmlReader** Object*

```
1 public void InstantiateXmlReader() {
2     SqlConnection cnnUserMan;
3     SqlCommand cmmUserMan;
4     XmlReader xrdUserMan;
5     string strSQL;
6
7     // Instantiate the connection
8     cnnUserMan = new SqlConnection(STR_CONNECTION_STRING);
9     // Open the connection
10    cnnUserMan.Open();
11    // Build query string
12    strSQL = "SELECT * FROM tblUser FOR XML AUTO";
13    // Instantiate the command
14    cmmUserMan = new SqlCommand(strSQL, cnnUserMan);
15    // Instantiate data reader using the ExecuteXmlReader method
16    // of the Command class
17    xrdUserMan = cmmUserMan.ExecuteXmlReader();
18 }
```

Reading Rows in an XmlReader

Since the **XmlReader** is a forward-only data class, you need to read the rows sequentially from start to finish if you need to read all the returned rows. In Listing 3A-34, you can see how you loop through a populated XML reader.

Listing 3A-34. Looping Through All Rows in an XmlReader

```
 1 public void ReadRowsFromXmlReader() {
 2     SqlConnection cnnUserMan;
 3     SqlCommand cmmUserMan;
 4     XmlReader xrdUserMan;
 5     string strSQL;
 6     long lngCounter = 0;
 7
 8     // Instantiate the connection
 9     cnnUserMan = new SqlConnection(STR_CONNECTION_STRING);
10     // Open the connection
11     cnnUserMan.Open();
12     // Build query string
13     strSQL = "SELECT * FROM tblUser FOR XML AUTO";
14     // Instantiate the command
15     cmmUserMan = new SqlCommand(strSQL, cnnUserMan);
16     // Execute command and return rows in data reader
17     xrdUserMan = cmmUserMan.ExecuteXmlReader();
18     // Loop through all the returned rows
19     while (xrdUserMan.Read()) {
20         ++lngCounter;
21     }
22
23     // Display the number of rows returned
24     MessageBox.Show(lngCounter.ToString());
25 }
```

The code in Listing 3A-34 loops through the rows in the data reader and counts the number of rows. This is obviously just an example on how to sequentially go through all the rows returned by the **ExecuteXmlReader** method of the Command class.

Closing an XmlReader

Because the **XmlReader** object keeps the connection busy while it's open, it's good practice to close the XML reader once you are done with it. The XML reader is closed using the **Close** method, as follows:

```
xrdTest.Close();
```

Handling XmlReader Exceptions

The methods of the **XmlReader** class typically throw the exceptions shown in
Table 3A-34.

*Table 3A-34. **XmlReader** Exceptions*

NAME	DESCRIPTION	THROWN BY PROPERTY/METHOD
ArgumentOutOfRangeException	This exception is thrown when an argument is out of range.	**GetAttribute** and **MoveToAttribute** methods
InvalidOperationException	This exception is thrown when you try to perform an operation that isn't valid in the object's current state.	**ResolveEntity** method
XmlException	This exception is thrown if the **XmlReader** object encounters invalid or incorrect XML in the input stream.	**IsStartElement**, **MoveToContent**, **ReadElementString**, **ReadEndElement**, and **ReadStartElement** methods

The DataAdapter Explained

The DataAdapter class is used for retrieving data from your data source and populating your **DataSet** and related classes such as the **DataTable**; see Chapter 3B
for more information on these disconnected data classes. The DataAdapter class
is also responsible for propagating your changes back to the data source. In other
words, the data adapter is the "connector" class that sits between the disconnected and the connected parts of ADO.NET. It would indeed be very appropriate
to say that the DataAdapter class is your toolbox when you want to manipulate
data in your data source!

The data adapter connects to a data source using a Connection object and then it uses Command objects to retrieve data from the data source and to send data back to the data source. With the exception of the DataReader class, all data access in ADO.NET goes through the data adapter. Actually, this can be put differently: all disconnected data access works through the data adapter. The data adapter is the bridge between the data source and the data set!

When the data adapter needs to retrieve or send data to and from the data source, it uses Command objects. You must specify these command objects. Now, this is very different from what happens in ADO, where you have little control over the way queries are executed. You specify the command objects for selecting, updating, and deleting rows in the data source. This is done by creating your command objects, and then assigning them to the appropriate data adapter property: **SelectCommand**, **InsertCommand**, **UpdateCommand,** or **DeleteCommand**. Please note that in some cases these properties can be automatically generated using the **CommandBuilder** class. See the "Using the CommandBuilder Class" section later in this chapter.

The DataAdapter class comes in three flavors, the **OleDbDataAdapter** class, the **OdbcDataAdapter** class, and the **SqlDataAdapter** class.

DataAdapter Properties

The DataAdapter class has the properties shown in Table 3A-35, in alphabetical order. Please note that only the public, noninherited properties are shown. Actually, this isn't entirely true, because only properties that are inherited from base classes like **object** are left out. This means that properties inherited from the DataAdapter class are shown. The properties listed are the same for the three data adapter classes: **SqlDataAdapter**, **OdbcDataAdapter**, and **OleDbDataAdapter**.

Table 3A-35. DataAdapter Class Properties

NAME	DESCRIPTION
AcceptChangesDuringFill	This read-write property returns or sets a **bool** value indicating whether the **AcceptChanges** method is called on the **DataRow** class after it has been added to a **DataTable**. The default value is **true**.
ContinueUpdateOnError	This property returns or sets a **bool** value that indicates whether the update should continue if an error is encountered during a row update. Otherwise, an exception is thrown. The default is **false**.
DeleteCommand	This read-write property returns or sets the SQL statement that will be used when rows are deleted from the data source. The corresponding deleted rows in the **DataSet** are deleted from the data source when the **Update** command is called on the DataAdapter.
InsertCommand	This read-write property returns or sets the SQL statement that will be used when rows are inserted into the data source. The corresponding inserted rows in the **DataSet** are inserted into the data source when the **Update** command is called on the DataAdapter.
MissingMappingAction	This read-write property returns or sets a value that indicates whether unmapped source tables or source columns should be parsed with their source names, or if an exception should be thrown. This means that this property decides which action to take when there's no mapping for a source table or source column. The valid values are all the members of the **MissingMappingAction** enum and the default value is **Passthrough**.
MissingSchemaAction	This read-write property returns or sets a value that indicates whether missing source tables, source columns, and relationships should be added to the schema in the data set, if they should be ignored, or if an exception should be thrown. This means that this property decides which action to take when a table, column, and/or relationship in the data source is missing from the data set. The valid values are all the members of the **MissingSchemaAction** enum and the default value is **Add**.
SelectCommand	This read-write property returns or sets the SQL statement that will be used when rows are selected/retrieved from the data source using the **Fill** command of the DataAdapter.
TableMappings	This read-only property returns a value that indicates how a table in the data source should be mapped to a table in the data set. The returned value is a collection of **DataTableMapping** objects. The default value is an empty collection.
UpdateCommand	This read-write property returns or sets the SQL statement that will be used when rows are updated in the data source. The corresponding updated rows in the **DataSet** are updated in the data source when the **Update** command is called on the DataAdapter.

DataAdapter Methods

Table 3A-36 lists the noninherited and public methods of the DataAdapter class in ascending order. The methods listed are the same for the three data adapter classes: **SqlDataAdapter**, **OdbcDataAdapter**, and **OleDbDataAdapter**, unless otherwise stated.

Table 3A-36. DataAdapter Class Methods

NAME	DESCRIPTION	EXAMPLE
Fill() (**SqlDataAdapter** and **OdbcDataAdapter** only)	The **Fill** method is overloaded and inherited from the **DbDataAdapter** class. The method is used for adding and/or updating rows in the data set. This means you'll have a copy of the requested data in the data source in your data set.	See "Populating Your DataSet Using the DataAdapter" in Chapter 3B for examples.
Fill() (**OleDbDataAdapter** only)	The **Fill** method is overloaded and some of the overloaded versions of the method are inherited from the **DbDataAdapter** class. The method is used for adding and/or updating rows in the data set based on the rows in an ADO **Recordset** or ADO **Record** object, or from your data source.	See "Populating Your DataSet Using the DataAdapter" in Chapter 3B for examples.
FillSchema()	The **FillSchema** method is overloaded and inherited from the **DbDataAdapter** class. The method is used for adding a **DataTable** object to the data set. This **DataTable** object is configured according to the arguments passed.	See "Using the DataTable Class" in Chapter 3B for some examples.

(continued)

Table 3A-36. DataAdapter Class Methods (continued)

NAME	DESCRIPTION	EXAMPLE
GetFillParameters()	The **GetFillParameters** method is inherited from the **DbDataAdapter** class. The method retrieves all the parameters that are used when the SELECT statement is executed. The returned value should be stored in an array of data type **IDataParameter**.	`arrprmSelect = dadUser.GetFillParameters()`
Update()	The **Update** method is overloaded and inherited from the **DbDataAdapter** class. The method is used for updating the data source with the changes from the data set. This means the command object associated with the **InsertCommand**, **UpdateCommand**, and **DeleteCommand** properties will be executed for each inserted, modified, and deleted row respectively.	See "Updating Your Data Source Using the Data Adapter" in Chapter 3B for some examples.

DataAdapter Events

Table 3A-37 lists the noninherited and public events of the DataAdapter class in alphabetical order. The events listed are the same for the three data adapter classes: **SqlDataAdapter**, **OdbcDataAdapter**, and **OleDbDataAdapter**.

Table 3A-37. DataAdapter Class Events

NAME	DESCRIPTION	EXAMPLE
FillError	The **FillError** event is inherited from the **DbDataAdapter** class. It's triggered whenever an error occurs during a fill operation, meaning when you populate or refresh your **DataSet** or **DataTable** with the **Fill** method. Basically, you can use this event to respond to errors during a fill operation and decide whether the operation should continue.	See the "Handling Fill Operation Errors" section later in this chapter for examples.
RowUpdated	This event is triggered after a command has been executed against your data source. You can use this event to inspect possible errors that don't throw an exception, the status of the update command, the **DataRow** with the values that have been used for updating the data source, and other properties. This event is called for every row you change in your **DataSet** or **DataTable**, when you call the **Update** method, and you can use it in conjunction with the **RowUpdating** event to "supervise" an update operation.	See the "Handling Row Updates" section later in this chapter.
RowUpdating	This event is triggered before a command is executed against your data source. You can use this event to inspect possible errors that don't throw an exception, the status of the update command, the **DataRow** with the values that will be used for updating the data source, and other properties. This event is called for every row you change in your **DataSet** or **DataTable**, when you call the **Update** method, and you can use it in conjunction with the **RowUpdated** event to "supervise" an update operation.	See the "Handling Row Updates" section later in this chapter.

Instantiating a DataAdapter

As with all other objects, the DataAdapter must be instantiated before you can use it. The DataAdapter class is instantiated using the constructor, which is overloaded. Listings 3A-35, 3A-36, and 3A-37 show you some examples.

*Listing 3A-35. Instantiating an **SqlDataAdapter***

```
1 public void InstantiateAndInitializeDataAdapter() {
2    const string STR_SQL_USER = "SELECT * FROM tblUser";
3
4    SqlConnection cnnUserMan;
5    SqlCommand cmmUser;
6    SqlDataAdapter dadDefaultConstructor;
7    SqlDataAdapter dadSqlCommandArgument;
8    SqlDataAdapter dadSqlConnectionArgument;
9    SqlDataAdapter dadStringArguments;
10
11   // Instantiate and open the connection
12   cnnUserMan = new SqlConnection(STR_CONNECTION_STRING);
13   cnnUserMan.Open();
14   // Instantiate the command
15   cmmUser = new SqlCommand(STR_SQL_USER);
16
17   // Instantiate data adapters
18   dadDefaultConstructor = new SqlDataAdapter();
19   dadSqlCommandArgument = new SqlDataAdapter(cmmUser);
20   dadSqlConnectionArgument = new SqlDataAdapter(STR_SQL_USER, cnnUserMan);
21   dadStringArguments = new SqlDataAdapter(STR_SQL_USER,
22     STR_CONNECTION_STRING);
23   // Initialize data adapters
24   dadDefaultConstructor.SelectCommand = cmmUser;
25   dadDefaultConstructor.SelectCommand.Connection = cnnUserMan;
26 }
```

*Listing 3A-36. Instantiating an **OleDbDataAdapter***

```
1 public void InstantiateAndInitializeDataAdapter() {
2    const string STR_SQL_USER = "SELECT * FROM tblUser";
3
4    OleDbConnection cnnUserMan;
5    OleDbCommand cmmUser;
6    OleDbDataAdapter dadDefaultConstructor;
7    OleDbDataAdapter dadOleDbCommandArgument;
8    OleDbDataAdapter dadOleDbConnectionArgument;
```

```
 9     OleDbDataAdapter dadStringArguments;
10
11     // Instantiate and open the connection
12     cnnUserMan = new OleDbConnection(STR_CONNECTION_STRING);
13     cnnUserMan.Open();
14     // Instantiate the command
15     cmmUser = new OleDbCommand(STR_SQL_USER);
16
17     // Instantiate data adapters
18     dadDefaultConstructor = new OleDbDataAdapter();
19     dadOleDbCommandArgument = new OleDbDataAdapter(cmmUser);
20     dadOleDbConnectionArgument = new OleDbDataAdapter(STR_SQL_USER,
21         cnnUserMan);
22     dadStringArguments = new OleDbDataAdapter(STR_SQL_USER,
23         STR_CONNECTION_STRING);
24     // Initialize data adapters
25     dadDefaultConstructor.SelectCommand = cmmUser;
26     dadDefaultConstructor.SelectCommand.Connection = cnnUserMan;
27 }
```

Listing 3A-37. Instantiating an **OdbcDataAdapter**

```
 1 public void InstantiateAndInitializeDataAdapter() {
 2     const string STR_SQL_USER = "SELECT * FROM tblUser";
 3
 4     OdbcConnection cnnUserMan;
 5     OdbcCommand cmmUser;
 6     OdbcDataAdapter dadDefaultConstructor;
 7     OdbcDataAdapter dadOdbcCommandArgument;
 8     OdbcDataAdapter dadOdbcConnectionArgument;
 9     OdbcDataAdapter dadStringArguments;
10
11     // Instantiate and open the connection
12     cnnUserMan = new OdbcConnection(STR_CONNECTION_STRING);
13     cnnUserMan.Open();
14     // Instantiate the command
15     cmmUser = new OdbcCommand(STR_SQL_USER);
16
17     // Instantiate data adapters
18     dadDefaultConstructor = new OdbcDataAdapter();
19     dadOdbcCommandArgument = new OdbcDataAdapter(cmmUser);
20     dadOdbcConnectionArgument = new OdbcDataAdapter(STR_SQL_USER,
21         cnnUserMan);
22     dadStringArguments = new OdbcDataAdapter(STR_SQL_USER,
```

```
23        STR_CONNECTION_STRING);
24    // Initialize data adapters
25    dadDefaultConstructor.SelectCommand = cmmUser;
26    dadDefaultConstructor.SelectCommand.Connection = cnnUserMan;
27 }
```

If you use the default constructor for the data adapter (Lines 6, 18, 24, 25, and 26), you have to specify the command object for the actions you'll perform. This means that if you want to retrieve rows from the data source, you'll at least have to set the **SelectCommand** property. (See the next section, "Setting the Command Properties," for more information on how to set command properties.) On Lines 24 and 25, I've set the command property to a valid command object. However, this isn't necessary, as I could have instead specified a string be selected (STR_SQL_USER).

The other three constructors don't need any further initialization for retrieving rows from your data source. However, if you want to insert, delete, and update your data source, you must specify the corresponding command properties. (See the next section, "Setting the Command Properties," for more information on how to do this.)

Which method you want to use is really up to you, but if you are using the same connection with all your command objects, why not specify it when you instantiate the data adapter?

As you can see from Listings 3A-33, 3A-34, and 3A-35, there's no real difference between instantiating an **OleDbDataAdapter**, an **OdbcDataAdapter**, and an **SqlDataAdapter** object. The real difference between these three classes appears when you want to populate your data set. See "Populating Your DataSet Using the DataAdapter" in Chapter 3B for more information on how to do this.

Setting the Command Properties

If you only use the data adapter to retrieve data from your data source, you don't have to set the command properties of your data adapter, if you've already specified the **SelectCommand** property using the data adapter constructor (see "Instantiating a DataAdapter" earlier). However, if you need to insert, update, or delete rows from your data source, or if you haven't set the **SelectCommand** property when instantiating the data adapter, you'll have to set these properties before you start using the data adapter. The **SelectCommand** is for retrieving rows from the data source, whereas the other three command properties are for updating the data source when the **Update** method is called.

Here are the four command properties:

- **SelectCommand**

- **InsertCommand**

- **DeleteCommand**

- **UpdateCommand**

ADO doesn't give you these choices, which provide you full control over how data is passed to and from the data source. If you assign command objects to these properties, you'll also be able to control what these objects do through events like errors. Yes, there's a little more coding involved, but you definitely get to be in the driver's seat when it comes to data source flow control.

With regards to setting the properties, it's actually quite simple. If you've created command objects, you only have to assign them to the corresponding property, as shown in Listings 3A-38, 3A-39, and 3A-40.

*Listing 3A-38. Setting the Command Properties of an **SqlDataAdapter***

```
1  public void SetDataAdapterCommandProperties() {
2     const string STR_SQL_USER_SELECT = "SELECT * FROM tblUser";
3     const string STR_SQL_USER_DELETE  = "DELETE FROM tblUser WHERE Id=@Id";
4     const string STR_SQL_USER_INSERT = "INSERT INTO tblUser(FirstName, " +
5        "LastName, LoginName, Password) VALUES(@FirstName, @LastName, " +
6        "@LoginName, @Password)";
7     const string STR_SQL_USER_UPDATE = "UPDATE tblUser SET FirstName=" +
8        "@FirstName, LastName=@LastName, LoginName=@LoginName, " +
9        "Password=@Password WHERE Id=@Id";
10
11    SqlConnection cnnUserMan;
12    SqlCommand cmmUserSelect;
13    SqlCommand cmmUserDelete;
14    SqlCommand cmmUserInsert;
15    SqlCommand cmmUserUpdate;
16    SqlDataAdapter dadUserMan;
17    SqlParameter prmSQLDelete, prmSQLUpdate;
18
19    // Instantiate and open the connection
20    cnnUserMan = new SqlConnection(STR_CONNECTION_STRING);
21    cnnUserMan.Open();
22    // Instantiate the commands
23    cmmUserSelect = new SqlCommand(STR_SQL_USER_SELECT, cnnUserMan);
```

```
24   cmmUserDelete = new SqlCommand(STR_SQL_USER_DELETE, cnnUserMan);
25   cmmUserInsert = new SqlCommand(STR_SQL_USER_INSERT, cnnUserMan);
26   cmmUserUpdate = new SqlCommand(STR_SQL_USER_UPDATE, cnnUserMan);
27
28   // Instantiate data adapter
29   dadUserMan = new SqlDataAdapter(STR_SQL_USER_SELECT, cnnUserMan);
30   // Set data adapter command properties
31   dadUserMan.SelectCommand = cmmUserSelect;
32   dadUserMan.InsertCommand = cmmUserInsert;
33   dadUserMan.DeleteCommand = cmmUserDelete;
34   dadUserMan.UpdateCommand = cmmUserUpdate;
35
36   // Add Delete command parameters
37   prmSQLDelete = dadUserMan.DeleteCommand.Parameters.Add("@Id",
38      SqlDbType.Int, 4, "Id");
39   prmSQLDelete.Direction = ParameterDirection.Input;
40   prmSQLDelete.SourceVersion = DataRowVersion.Original;
41
42   // Add Update command parameters
43   cmmUserUpdate.Parameters.Add("@FirstName", SqlDbType.VarChar, 50,
44      "FirstName");
45   cmmUserUpdate.Parameters.Add("@LastName", SqlDbType.VarChar, 50,
46      "LastName");
47   cmmUserUpdate.Parameters.Add("@LoginName", SqlDbType.VarChar, 50,
48      "LoginName");
49   cmmUserUpdate.Parameters.Add("@Password", SqlDbType.VarChar, 50,
50      "Password");
51
52   prmSQLUpdate = dadUserMan.UpdateCommand.Parameters.Add("@Id",
53      SqlDbType.Int, 4, "Id");
54   prmSQLUpdate.Direction = ParameterDirection.Input;
55   prmSQLUpdate.SourceVersion = DataRowVersion.Original;
56
57   // Add insert command parameters
58   cmmUserInsert.Parameters.Add("@FirstName", SqlDbType.VarChar, 50,
59      "FirstName");
60   cmmUserInsert.Parameters.Add("@LastName", SqlDbType.VarChar, 50,
61      "LastName");
62   cmmUserInsert.Parameters.Add("@LoginName", SqlDbType.VarChar, 50,
63      "LoginName");
64   cmmUserInsert.Parameters.Add("@Password", SqlDbType.VarChar, 50,
65      "Password");
66 }
```

Listing 3A-39. Setting the Command Properties of an ***OleDbDataAdapter***

```
1  public void SetDataAdapterCommandProperties() {
2     const string STR_SQL_USER_SELECT = "SELECT * FROM tblUser";
3     const string STR_SQL_USER_DELETE  = "DELETE FROM tblUser WHERE Id=?";
4     const string STR_SQL_USER_INSERT = "INSERT INTO tblUser(FirstName, " +
5        "LastName, LoginName, Password) VALUES(?, ?, ?, ?)";
6     const string STR_SQL_USER_UPDATE = "UPDATE tblUser SET FirstName=?, " +
7        "LastName=?, LoginName=?, Password=? WHERE Id=?";
8
9     OleDbConnection cnnUserMan;
10    OleDbCommand cmmUserSelect;
11    OleDbCommand cmmUserDelete;
12    OleDbCommand cmmUserInsert;
13    OleDbCommand cmmUserUpdate;
14    OleDbDataAdapter dadUserMan;
15    OleDbParameter prmSQLDelete, prmSQLUpdate;
16
17    // Instantiate and open the connection
18    cnnUserMan = new OleDbConnection(STR_CONNECTION_STRING);
19    cnnUserMan.Open();
20    // Instantiate the commands
21    cmmUserSelect = new OleDbCommand(STR_SQL_USER_SELECT, cnnUserMan);
22    cmmUserDelete = new OleDbCommand(STR_SQL_USER_DELETE, cnnUserMan);
23    cmmUserInsert = new OleDbCommand(STR_SQL_USER_INSERT, cnnUserMan);
24    cmmUserUpdate = new OleDbCommand(STR_SQL_USER_UPDATE, cnnUserMan);
25
26    // Instantiate data adapter
27    dadUserMan = new OleDbDataAdapter(STR_SQL_USER_SELECT, cnnUserMan);
28    // Set data adapter command properties
29    dadUserMan.SelectCommand = cmmUserSelect;
30    dadUserMan.InsertCommand = cmmUserInsert;
31    dadUserMan.DeleteCommand = cmmUserDelete;
32    dadUserMan.UpdateCommand = cmmUserUpdate;
33
34    // Add Delete command parameters
35    prmSQLDelete = dadUserMan.DeleteCommand.Parameters.Add("@Id",
36       OleDbType.Integer, 4, "Id");
37    prmSQLDelete.Direction = ParameterDirection.Input;
38    prmSQLDelete.SourceVersion = DataRowVersion.Original;
39
40    // Add Update command parameters
41    cmmUserUpdate.Parameters.Add("@FirstName", OleDbType.VarChar, 50,
42       "FirstName");
```

```
43    cmmUserUpdate.Parameters.Add("@LastName", OleDbType.VarChar, 50,
44        "LastName");
45    cmmUserUpdate.Parameters.Add("@LoginName", OleDbType.VarChar, 50,
46        "LoginName");
47    cmmUserUpdate.Parameters.Add("@Password", OleDbType.VarChar, 50,
48        "Password");
49
50    prmSQLUpdate = dadUserMan.UpdateCommand.Parameters.Add("@Id",
51        OleDbType.Integer, 4, "Id");
52    prmSQLUpdate.Direction = ParameterDirection.Input;
53    prmSQLUpdate.SourceVersion = DataRowVersion.Original;
54
55    // Add insert command parameters
56    cmmUserInsert.Parameters.Add("@FirstName", OleDbType.VarChar, 50,
57        "FirstName");
58    cmmUserInsert.Parameters.Add("@LastName", OleDbType.VarChar, 50,
59        "LastName");
60    cmmUserInsert.Parameters.Add("@LoginName", OleDbType.VarChar, 50,
61        "LoginName");
62    cmmUserInsert.Parameters.Add("@Password", OleDbType.VarChar, 50,
63        "Password");
64 }
```

*Listing 3A-40. Setting the Command Properties of an **OdbcDataAdapter***

```
1 public void SetDataAdapterCommandProperties() {
2    const string STR_SQL_USER_SELECT = "SELECT * FROM tblUser";
3    const string STR_SQL_USER_DELETE  = "DELETE FROM tblUser WHERE Id=?";
4    const string STR_SQL_USER_INSERT = "INSERT INTO tblUser(FirstName, " +
5        "LastName, LoginName, Password) VALUES(?, ?, ?, ?)";
6    const string STR_SQL_USER_UPDATE = "UPDATE tblUser SET FirstName=?, " +
7        "LastName=?, LoginName=?, Password=? WHERE Id=?";
8
9    OdbcConnection cnnUserMan;
10    OdbcCommand cmmUserSelect;
11    OdbcCommand cmmUserDelete;
12    OdbcCommand cmmUserInsert;
13    OdbcCommand cmmUserUpdate;
14    OdbcDataAdapter dadUserMan;
15    OdbcParameter prmSQLDelete, prmSQLUpdate;
16
17    // Instantiate and open the connection
18    cnnUserMan = new OdbcConnection(STR_CONNECTION_STRING);
19    cnnUserMan.Open();
20    // Instantiate the commands
```

```
21      cmmUserSelect = new OdbcCommand(STR_SQL_USER_SELECT, cnnUserMan);
22      cmmUserDelete = new OdbcCommand(STR_SQL_USER_DELETE, cnnUserMan);
23      cmmUserInsert = new OdbcCommand(STR_SQL_USER_INSERT, cnnUserMan);
24      cmmUserUpdate = new OdbcCommand(STR_SQL_USER_UPDATE, cnnUserMan);
25
26      // Instantiate data adapter
27      dadUserMan = new OdbcDataAdapter(STR_SQL_USER_SELECT, cnnUserMan);
28      // Set data adapter command properties
29      dadUserMan.SelectCommand = cmmUserSelect;
30      dadUserMan.InsertCommand = cmmUserInsert;
31      dadUserMan.DeleteCommand = cmmUserDelete;
32      dadUserMan.UpdateCommand = cmmUserUpdate;
33
34      // Add Delete command parameters
35      prmSQLDelete = dadUserMan.DeleteCommand.Parameters.Add("@Id",
36          OdbcType.Integer, 4, "Id");
37      prmSQLDelete.Direction = ParameterDirection.Input;
38      prmSQLDelete.SourceVersion = DataRowVersion.Original;
39
40      // Add Update command parameters
41      cmmUserUpdate.Parameters.Add("@FirstName", OdbcType.VarChar, 50,
42          "FirstName");
43      cmmUserUpdate.Parameters.Add("@LastName", OdbcType.VarChar, 50,
44          "LastName");
45      cmmUserUpdate.Parameters.Add("@LoginName", OdbcType.VarChar, 50,
46          "LoginName");
47      cmmUserUpdate.Parameters.Add("@Password", OdbcType.VarChar, 50,
48          "Password");
49
50      prmSQLUpdate = dadUserMan.UpdateCommand.Parameters.Add("@Id",
51          OdbcType.Integer, 4, "Id");
52      prmSQLUpdate.Direction = ParameterDirection.Input;
53      prmSQLUpdate.SourceVersion = DataRowVersion.Original;
54
55      // Add insert command parameters
56      cmmUserInsert.Parameters.Add("@FirstName", OdbcType.VarChar, 50,
57          "FirstName");
58      cmmUserInsert.Parameters.Add("@LastName", OdbcType.VarChar, 50,
59          "LastName");
60      cmmUserInsert.Parameters.Add("@LoginName", OdbcType.VarChar, 50,
61          "LoginName");
62      cmmUserInsert.Parameters.Add("@Password", OdbcType.VarChar, 50,
63          "Password");
64  }
```

There are only minor differences between Listings 3A-38, 3A-39, and 3A-40, and they are all due to what .NET Data Provider you are using, the SQL Server .NET Data Provider, the OLE DB .NET Data Provider, or the ODBC .NET Data Provider. Besides setting the command properties of the data adapter, the parameters of the command objects are also configured to work with the tblUser table in the UserMan database. I've used named parameters exclusively, because I do believe it makes code easier to read.

Handling Fill Operation Errors

When you execute the **Fill** method of the DataAdapter class, one or more errors can occur. If the errors occur at the client side, meaning they are generated at the data source, but the data retrieved from the data source is being inserted into the **DataSet** or **DataTable**, the **FillError** event is triggered. You can handle these events by setting up an event handler to intercept the event. If you don't set up an event handler for this event, and an error occurs, an **InvalidCastException** is thrown. Listing 3A-41 shows you how to set up the event handler.

Listing 3A-41. Handling Fill Operation Errors

```
 1 protected static void OnFillError(object sender, FillErrorEventArgs args) {
 2     // Display a message indicating what table an error occurred in and
 3     // let the user decide whether to continue populating the dataset
 4     args.Continue = (bool) (MessageBox.Show(
 5         "There were errors filling the Data Table: " + args.DataTable +
 6         ". Do you want to continue?", "Continue Updating",
 7         MessageBoxButtons.YesNo, MessageBoxIcon.Question) == DialogResult.Yes);
 8 }
 9
10 public void TriggerFillErrorEvent() {
11     DataSet dstUser = new DataSet("Users");
12     // Declare and instantiate connection
13     SqlConnection cnnUserMan = new SqlConnection(STR_CONNECTION_STRING);
14     // Declare and instantiate data adapter
15     SqlDataAdapter prdadUserMan = new SqlDataAdapter("SELECT * FROM tblUser",
16         cnnUserMan);
17     // Set up event handler
18     prdadUserMan.FillError  += new FillErrorEventHandler(OnFillError);
19
20     // Open the connection
22     cnnUserMan.Open();
23     // Populate the dataset
24     prdadUserMan.Fill(dstUser, "tblUser");
25 }
```

In Listing 3A-41, I've created a procedure to handle the **FillError** event (Lines 1 through 8), and on Lines 10 through 25, I've created the `TriggerFillErrorEvent` standard procedure for filling the `dstUser` **DataSet**. In this procedure, I set up the event handler on Line 18, which means that if any errors occur when populating `dstUser` on Line 24, the `OnFillError` procedure is invoked. In the `OnFillError` procedure, I display a message and leave it up to the user to decide if I should continue populating `dstUser`. This is done by setting the `args.Continue` property to true or false, depending on whether the user clicks the Yes or No button in the message box. Although there are other uses for the **FillError** event, its main purpose is to decide if the filling should continue if an error occurs.

The `TriggerFillErrorEvent` procedure doesn't necessarily trigger the **FillError** event; it only happens when an error occurs.

Handling Row Updates

When you update your data source using the **Update** method of the DataAdapter, two events are triggered that you can respond to: **RowUpdating**, which occurs before the data source is updated, and **RowUpdated**, which occurs after the update of the data source.

> **NOTE** *The **RowUpdating** and **RowUpdated** events are triggered once for every row that is being sent to the data source for updating.*

Listing 3A-42 shows you how you can set up and use the two events.

Listing 3A-42. Handling Row Updates

```
1 protected static void OnRowUpdating(object sender,
2     SqlRowUpdatingEventArgs e) {
3     // Display a message showing all the Command properties
4     // if a command exists
5     if (! (e.Command == null)) {
6         MessageBox.Show("Command Properties:\n\n" +
7             "CommandText: " + e.Command.CommandText + "\n" +
8             "CommandTimeout: " + e.Command.CommandTimeout.ToString() + "\n"  +
9             "CommandType: " + e.Command.CommandType.ToString(),
10            "RowUpdating", MessageBoxButtons.OK,
11            MessageBoxIcon.Information);
12    }
13    // Display a message showing all the Errors properties,
14    // if an error exists
```

```
15    if (! (e.Errors == null)) {
16       MessageBox.Show("Errors Properties:\n\n" +
17          "HelpLink: " + e.Errors.HelpLink + "\n"  +
18          "Message: " + e.Errors.Message + "\n"  +
19          "Source: " + e.Errors.Source + "\n" +
20          "StackTrace: " + e.Errors.StackTrace  + "\n" +
21          "TargetSite: " + e.Errors.TargetSite  + "\n",
22          "RowUpdating", MessageBoxButtons.OK,
23          MessageBoxIcon.Information);
24    }
25    // Display a message showing all the Errors properties
26    MessageBox.Show("Misc. Properties:\n\n" +
27       "StatementType: " + e.StatementType.ToString() + "\n"   +
28       "Status: " + e.Status.ToString(),
29       "RowUpdating", MessageBoxButtons.OK,
30       MessageBoxIcon.Information);
31 }
32
33 protected static void OnRowUpdated(object sender, SqlRowUpdatedEventArgs e) {
34    // Display a message showing all the Command properties
35    // if a command exists
36    if (! (e.Command == null)) {
37       MessageBox.Show("Command Properties:\n\n" +
38          "CommandText: " + e.Command.CommandText + "\n" +
39          "CommandTimeout: " + e.Command.CommandTimeout.ToString() + "\n"   +
40          "CommandType: " + e.Command.CommandType.ToString(),
41          "RowUpdating", MessageBoxButtons.OK,
42          MessageBoxIcon.Information);
43    }
44    // Display a message showing all the Errors properties,
45    // if an error exists
46    if (! (e.Errors == null)) {
47       MessageBox.Show("Errors Properties:\n\n" +
48          "HelpLink: " + e.Errors.HelpLink + "\n"  +
49          "Message: " + e.Errors.Message + "\n"  +
50          "Source: " + e.Errors.Source + "\n" +
51          "StackTrace: " + e.Errors.StackTrace  + "\n" +
52          "TargetSite: " + e.Errors.TargetSite  + "\n",
53          "RowUpdating", MessageBoxButtons.OK,
54          MessageBoxIcon.Information);
55    }
56    // Display a message showing all the Errors properties
57    MessageBox.Show("Misc. Properties:\n\n" +
```

```
58        "StatementType: " + e.StatementType.ToString() + "\n"  +
59        "Status: " + e.Status.ToString(),
60        "RowUpdating", MessageBoxButtons.OK,
61        MessageBoxIcon.Information);
62 }
63
64 public void TriggerRowUpdateEvents() {
65     DataSet dstUser = new DataSet("Users");
66     // Declare and instantiate connection
67     SqlConnection cnnUserMan = new SqlConnection(STR_CONNECTION_STRING);
68     // Declare and instantiate data adapter
69     SqlDataAdapter dadUserMan = new SqlDataAdapter("SELECT * FROM tblUser",
70         cnnUserMan);
71     // Declare and instantiate command builder
72     SqlCommandBuilder cmbUser = new SqlCommandBuilder(dadUserMan);
73     // Set up event handlers
74     dadUserMan.RowUpdating  += new SqlRowUpdatingEventHandler(OnRowUpdating);
75     dadUserMan.RowUpdated   += new SqlRowUpdatedEventHandler(OnRowUpdated);
76
77     // Open the connection
78     cnnUserMan.Open();
79     // Populate the dataset
80     dadUserMan.Fill(dstUser, "tblUser");
81     // Modify second row
82     dstUser.Tables["tblUser"].Rows[1]["FirstName"] = "Tom";
83     // Populate the data source
84     dadUserMan.Update(dstUser, "tblUser");
85 }
```

In Listing 3A-42, you can see how I've set up event handlers for the **RowUpdating** and **RowUpdated** events. Both of the two procedures that handle the events, OnRowUpdating and OnRowUpdated, display the same properties. I am using a command builder to generate the **UpdateCommand** property of the DataAdapter, and if you want more information on the CommandBuilder class, please see the next section "Using the CommandBuilder Class."

I trigger the two events by modifying the second row of the tblUser data table (Line 82) and then I use the **Update** method of the DataAdapter class. This will always trigger a **RowUpdating** event, but not necessarily the **RowUpdated** event. Why is that? Well, if you run the example code in Listing 3A-42 twice, and look at some of the properties being displayed in the message box, you'll notice that the second time around, the **Status** property being displayed in the OnRowUpdating procedure has a value of **SkipCurrentRow**. This means that the row won't be updated, because you're not really making any modifications to the row. The original values and the current values are the same. These two events are valuable tools when searching for bugs, if nothing else.

On Lines 5, 15, 36, and 46, I check to see if the **Errors** or Command objects have been set before trying to access them. I need to do this, because they aren't necessarily set. Basically, the **Errors** object is set if there are any errors, otherwise it holds a **null** value. The same can be said about the Command object; if the **Status** property is set to **SkipCurrentRow**, the Command object holds a **null** value, because no commands will be executed.

Using the CommandBuilder Class

The CommandBuilder class is used for generating the following properties of the DataAdapter class automatically:

- **InsertCommand**

- **UpdateCommand**

- **DeleteCommand**

Before moving on, I would like to add that there is no CommandBuilder class per se, but instead you use the **SqlCommandBuilder**, **OleDbCommandBuilder**, or the **OdbcCommandBuilder** class, depending on the data adapter you use (**SqlDataAdapter**, **OleDbDataAdapter**, or **OdbcDataAdapter**). The example shown uses the **SqlCommandBuilder** class and related data classes.

When to Use the CommandBuilder Class

The CommandBuilder class can only be used when your **DataTable**[6] maps to a single database table. This means that if your database query is a join of two or more tables, you cannot use CommandBuilder, but you'll have to write the code yourself. This is the whole secret to the CommandBuilder class; it will let you write less code. Nothing more, nothing less! So there is need for despair if your **DataTable**s are generated from more than one database table. The "Setting the Command Properties" section earlier in this chapter describes how to set up the properties needed for performing the INSERT, UPDATE, and DELETE SQL operations.

---

6. The **DataTable** class, which is discussed in Chapter 3B, is used to represent a single table. However, the schema and the values in your **DataTable** can be made up of columns from several tables in your data source, by using a join in your SELECT query.

In addition to the restriction that a **DataTable** must be based on a single database table, the following restrictions apply:

- The CommandBuilder won't work, or rather the automatic generation will fail, if the table and/or column names contain any special characters. These special characters include a period (.), any of the quotation marks (", "), a space, or any nonalphanumeric character. This is also true if the table or column name containing the special character(s) is enclosed in brackets ([]). However, fully qualified names are supported. Here's an example of a fully qualified name, taken from the UserMan database in SQL Server: UserMan.dbo.tblUser.

- The CommandBuilder only works with **DataTable**s that aren't related to any other **DataTable**s in your **DataSet**. The CommandBuilder ignores any relationships in your data source, or rather isn't aware of them, which means that if you try to update a table in your data source that has a relationship with another table in your data source, the update might fail. This can happen because you might be trying to update a foreign key value. Basically, you should use the CommandBuilder with single, nonrelated database tables, or write the code for the DataAdapter properties yourself.

Preparing the DataAdapter

You need to set up the DataAdapter properly before you can use the CommandBuilder. This includes setting the **SelectCommand** property, because the schema retrieved by this property is used for determining the syntax for the automatic generation.

Not only do you need to set up the **SelectCommand** property, you also need to make sure that at least one primary key or unique column is returned as part of the SELECT statement. Obviously a SELECT * . . . statement will return the required column, if the table holds a unique column, but you need to be aware of this requirement when you specify the columns to retrieve as part of the SELECT statement.

If you use the tblUser table from the UserMan database, the following statement will make the CommandBuilder generate the mentioned properties:

```
SELECT Id, FirstName, LastName, Password FROM tblUser
```

However, if you remove the Id column from the SELECT statement, like this:

```
SELECT FirstName, LastName, Password FROM tblUser
```

the CommandBuilder class can't be used to generate the mentioned properties. Okay, so the first statement will work with the CommandBuilder, because the ID column, which is the primary key and thus unique, is one of the columns retrieved. The second statement will cause the CommandBuilder to fail (that is, that an **InvalidOperationException** exception is thrown), because none of the retrieved columns are unique.

Another thing you need to be aware of when using the CommandBuilder class is that when it's executed, only properties that haven't been set, or rather properties that are equal to **null**, will be automatically generated. However, this can be exploited if you, for whatever reason, want to set the **UpdateCommand** property yourself and have the CommandBuilder generate the **InsertCommand** and **DeleteCommand** properties for you.

Listing 3A-43 does the same as Listing 3A-38, but it uses the **SqlCommandBuilder** class instead of setting the properties manually.

Listing 3A-43. Using the SqlCommandBuilder Class

```
1 public void SetDataAdapterCommandPropertiesUsingCommandBuilder() {
2    const string STR_SQL_USER_SELECT = "SELECT * FROM tblUser";
3
4    SqlConnection cnnUserMan = new SqlConnection(STR_CONNECTION_STRING);
5    SqlCommand cmmUserSelect = new SqlCommand(STR_SQL_USER_SELECT,
6        cnnUserMan);
7    SqlDataAdapter dadUserMan = new SqlDataAdapter(cmmUserSelect);
8    SqlCommandBuilder cmbUser = new SqlCommandBuilder(dadUserMan);
9    DataSet dstDummy = new DataSet("DummyDataSet");
10
11   // Open the connection
12   cnnUserMan.Open();
13
14   // Fill dummy data set, update row in table and update dataset
15   dadUserMan.Fill(dstDummy, "tblUser");
16   dstDummy.Tables["tblUser"].Rows.Add(new object[7] {null, null, null,
17       "1st Name", "LastName", DateTime.Now.ToString().Replace(" ", ""), ""});
18   dadUserMan.Update(dstDummy, "tblUser");
19 }
```

If you compare Listing 3A-43 with Listing 3A-38, you'll see how much work the CommandBuilder class does for you; you save more than 50 lines of code!

> **NOTE** *The CommandBuilder class uses the **CommandTimeout**, **Connection**, and **Transaction** properties referenced by the **SelectCommand** property of the DataAdapter class. This means you need to call the **RefreshSchema** method of the CommandBuilder class, if you change any of these properties or change the **SelectCommand** itself. No exception will be thrown if you don't call the method, but the original values will be used, meaning the changes you've made won't be reflected in the automatically generated commands.*

Summary

This chapter introduced you to the two different data access technologies, ADO and ADO.NET. ADO.NET is for building distributed n-tier Web applications, whereas ADO is your best bet for traditional Windows client-server/n-tier applications programming in a heterogeneous networking environment, where you are connected at all times on a LAN link. The object model for the connected layer of ADO.NET was introduced and comparisons were made to the ADO object model wherever needed. As well as being an introduction to the connected layer of ADO.NET and to some extent ADO, this chapter serves as a reference to the various connected classes, methods, events, and properties of this data access technology.

This chapter covered the following ground:

- *Connection, Command, DataReader, and DataAdapter data classes:* The ADO.NET classes were compared to their equivalents in ADO and suggestions were offered about when to use which data class.

- *Transactions, automatic and manual:* I showed you transaction boundaries and how to use them with the Connection and Transaction classes.

- *The CommandBuilder class, in the form of the **SqlCommandBuilder**, **OleDbCommandBuilder**, or the **OdbcCommandBuilder** class:* This class, in its various forms, is used for automatically generating the DataAdapter properties used for updating the data source. There are restrictions to when it can be used, but if you set up the DataAdapter correctly and your **DataTable** and table in the database conform to the restrictions applied by the CommandBuilder, you'll save many lines of coding. Use it whenever you have a trivial database table you want to update using a **DataSet** or **DataTable** class.

- *Three .NET Data Providers that come with the .NET Framework, the OLE DB .NET Data Provider, the ODBC .NET Data Provider, and the SQL Server .NET Data Provider:* They all have their own set of related, but not interchangeable, data classes. In other words, you can't mix connections from the OLE DB .NET Data Provider with Command classes from the SQL Server .NET Data Provider and vice versa.

- *The SQL Server .Net Data Provider versus the OLE DB .NET Data Provider and the ODBC .NET Data Provider:* I discussed the use the SQL Server .NET Data Provider whenever you access an SQL Server 7.0 or later, the OLE DB .NET Data Provider for all other data sources for which you have an OLE DB provider, and the ODBC .NET Data Provider for all other data sources for which you have an ODBC driver.

The following chapter covers the classes in the disconnected layer of ADO.NET.

CHAPTER 3B

Presenting ADO.NET: The Disconnected Layer

THIS CHAPTER AND ITS TWIN, Chapter 3A, cover ADO.NET. The classes in ADO.NET can be categorized into two groups: the connected layer and the disconnected layer. This chapter exclusively covers the disconnected layer. Simply put, you can use the disconnected layer if you don't need to access any data source and really just want to work with temporary data, or data that is being read and written to XML streams or files. If you need to retrieve data from, insert data into, update data in, or delete data from a data source, you need to use the connected layer. However, most often you'll be using classes from both layers, as you'll see from this chapter and the following ones, and the corresponding example code.

I suggest you read Chapter 3A first, if you're new to ADO.NET, before continuing with this chapter. However, this chapter will serve you very well as a reference on its own. One thing to point out, if you're familiar with ADO, is that whereas ADO is based on a connected model, ADO.NET is based on a disconnected model.

Using the DataSet Class

The **DataSet** class can be a fairly complex one to deal with and understand. Well, at least until you have had a closer look at it and realize that you don't really need to know everything there is to know about it. I'll go through all aspects of the **DataSet** class, so you can see for yourself how you can use it. The **DataSet** class is part of the **System.Data** namespace.

First things first: A data set is rather closely related to a relational database in structure. When I say that it resembles a relational database, I mean that the **DataSet** class actually exposes a hierarchical object model (which has nothing to do with hierarchical databases). This object model consists of tables, rows, and columns, and it also contains relations and constraints. In fact, the **DataSet** and **DataTable**[1] classes hold collections containing the following objects:

---

1. The **DataTable** class is a disconnected class that resembles a database table in structure.

- **DataSet** class holds the **Tables** collection, which contains objects of data type **DataTable**, and the **Relations** collection, which contains objects of data type **DataRelation**.

- **DataTable** class holds the **Rows** collection, which contains objects of data type **DataRow,** and the **Columns** collection, which contains objects of data type **DataColumn**. The **Rows** collection holds all the rows in the table and the **Columns** collection is the actual schema for the table.

In order to exploit the full potential of the **DataSet** class, you need to use it in conjunction with at least the **DataTable** class.

If nothing else, the **DataSet** class is a local container or in-memory cache for the data you retrieve from the database. You can call it a virtual data store, because all the data retrieved from the database, including the schema for the data, is stored in the disconnected cache, known as the data set. The real trick of the **DataSet** is that although you are disconnected from the data source, you can work with the data in it in much the same way you would with the data in the database. If you are thinking, "Ah, so the data in the **DataSet** is really a copy of the real data," you would be correct, my friend! Now you may be wondering if updating the real data is difficult. Well, yes and no. Yes, because it requires more than just using the good old ADO **Recordset** class, but no, because you have several options available for this purpose. I'll get to this in a moment.

So how do you get the data from the database and into the **DataSet**? This is a job for the DataAdapter class, the connected part of ADO.NET. The DataAdapter is the class that either works directly with the data source, as is the case with SQL Server 7.0 or later, or uses the underlying OLE DB provider to talk to the database. The DataAdapter class is explained in Chapter 3A.

One more thing to notice about the **DataSet** class is that it's NOT subclassed, or rather this is the class that will work with whatever provider you are dealing with. There are no SqlDataSet, OdbcDataSet, and OleDbDataSet classes!

Recordset vs. DataSet

If you are familiar with ADO, then you probably know the **Recordset** object and how it can be used with various cursors and so on. Although the **Recordset** class doesn't have a direct equivalent in ADO.NET, I'll show you some of the things that make the **DataSet** class and its associated data class, **DataTable**, behave in similar ways to the **Recordset** object. When ADO.NET was on the drawing board, one of the major obstacles was to find a way of making the connected ADO **Recordset** class a disconnected class. The result is that the ADO **Recordset** class has been mapped to a few different classes in ADO.NET. This includes the disconnected **DataSet** class, which uses the connected DataAdapter class for retrieving data.

Even though ADO has introduced the concept of a disconnected recordset through Remote Data Services (RDS), the connected part of the setup is still evident behind the scenes.

Simply put, the **DataSet** class is really a collection of disconnected **Recordset** objects, which are exposed using the **DataTable** class. So if you like using the ADO **Recordset** object, but want to use ADO.NET at the same time, you do have the option, and this option is called the **DataTable** class. The **DataTable** class works much the same way as an ADO recordset. See the "Using the DataTable Class" section later in this chapter for details.

Data Source Independence

One of the strengths of a **DataSet** is the fact that it is completely independent of the data source. It is in other words a container, or cache, of data that is copied from the data source. The fact that a **DataSet** is disconnected and thereby independent of the data source makes it ideal for containing data from multiple data sources, such as tables from various databases. The data source independence also makes it ideal for temporary storage of especially relational data, because you can create a data set from scratch and use it without ever being connected to a data source.

XML Is the Format

When data is moved from a data source, such as a database, to the data set (or the other way around), the format used to facilitate this is XML. This is one of the key concepts of ADO.NET; everything is XML based! Because the format is XML, not only can you transfer data sets across process and machine boundaries, but you can also transfer data sets across networks that use a firewall! That's right, XML makes this possible! Now you truly have a way of manipulating data coming across the Internet from any data source that understands XML.

Okay, so the format used for transferring the data is XML, but this isn't the only place ADO.NET uses XML. XML is the underlying format for all data in ADO.NET, and if you need to persist or serialize your data to a file, the format used is once again XML. This means that you can read the persisted file using any XML-capable reader.

One point should be made very clear before you continue: although the underlying or fundamental data format in ADO.NET is XML, the data in a data set is NOT expressed using XML. The ADO.NET data APIs automatically handle the creation of XML data when you exchange data between data sets and data sources, but the data inside the data set is in a format that is much more efficient to work with. So you don't actually have to know anything about XML in order to use ADO.NET. However, I would recommend that you do learn at least the basics of XML, because it's such an integral part of Visual Studio .NET. You can learn a great deal from this book:

- *XML Programming Using the Microsoft XML Parser,* by Soo Mee Foo and Wei Meng Lee. Published by Apress, February 2002. ISBN: 1893115429.

Typed vs. Untyped Data Sets

A data set can be *typed* or *untyped.* The difference is that the typed data set has a schema and the untyped data set doesn't. You can choose to use either kind of data set in your application, but you need to know that there's more support for the typed data sets in Visual Studio, and as such there are more tools for your convenience.

A typed data set gives you easier access to the content of table fields through strongly typed programming. Strongly typed programming uses information from the underlying data scheme. This means you're programming directly against your declared objects and not the tables you're really trying to manipulate. A typed data set has a reference to an XML schema file. This schema file (*.xsd) describes the structure of all the tables contained within the data set. A typed data set is based on a class file that is derived from the **DataSet** class.

> **CROSS-REFERENCE**   *See Chapter 4 for more information on how to create a typed data set.*

In Listing 3B-1, you can see how strong typing changes the way you would normally access the content of a column in a table.

Listing 3B-1. Strong Typing vs. Weak Typing

```
1 // Display value from ADO Recordset
2 MessageBox.Show(rstUser.Fields["FirstName"].Value.ToString());
3 // Display value from ADO.NET DataSet using strong typing
4 MessageBox.Show(dstUser.tblUser[0].FirstName.ToString());
5 // Display value from ADO.NET DataSet using weak typing
6 MessageBox.Show(dstUser.Tables["tblUser"].Columns[3].ToString())
```

As Listing 3B-1 shows, the syntax is much simpler when you use strong typing. Simply reference the table and field by using the table name and field name directly (see Line 4). The rstUser recordset and the dstUser data set have been declared, instantiated, and opened or populated elsewhere.

DataSet Properties

The **DataSet** class has the properties shown in Table 3B-1 in alphabetical order. Please note that only the public, noninherited properties are shown.

Table 3B-1. **DataSet** *Class Properties*

NAME	DESCRIPTION	EXAMPLE
CaseSensitive	This read-write property determines if string comparisons in the **DataTable** objects, contained in the **Tables** collection, are case sensitive. The default value is **false**. This property also affects how filter, sort, and search operations are performed. When you set this property, you also by default set the same property of all the **DataTable** objects in the **Tables** collection. This doesn't mean that it's forced upon the **DataTable** objects, because if you explicitly set this property of a **DataTable** in the **Tables** collection, either before or after you set the property on the **DataSet**, the value for the property in the **DataTable** won't be changed.	
DataSetName	Returns or sets the name of the **DataSet**. The name is for the developers use only; it's not used by the **DataSet**, meaning that it's there for you to use, if you want an easy way of telling **DataSet** objects apart. This property can also be set when instantiating the **DataSet**, by supplying the name as the only argument.	See Listing 3B-20.
DefaultViewManager	Returns a view of the data in the data set. This view can be filtered or sorted, and you can search and navigate through it. The returned value is of data type **DataViewManager**.	
EnforceConstraints	This property value determines if the constraint rules are enforced when an update operation is executed. The default value is **true**. The **ConstraintException** exception is thrown if one or more constraints can't be enforced.	

ExtendedProperties	Returns the collection of custom properties or custom user information. The returned data type is a **PropertyCollection** class. You can add information to the property collection by using the **Add** method of the collection as shown in the Example column.	`dstUserMan`
		`.ExtendedProperties`
		`.Add("New`
		`Property", "New`
		`Property Value");`

(continued)

Table 3B-1. **DataSet** *Class Properties (continued)*

NAME	DESCRIPTION	EXAMPLE
HasErrors	Returns a **bool** value indicating if there are any errors in the rows in the **DataTable** objects contained in the **Tables** collection of the **DataSet**. You can use this property before checking any of the individual tables that also have a **HasErrors** property, meaning if the **HasErrors** property of the **DataSet** object returns **false**, there's no need to check the individual **DataTable** objects contained in the **Tables** collection of the **DataSet**.	See Listing 3B-4
Locale	This read-write property holds the locale information that is used for comparing strings in a table. The value is of data type **CultureInfo**. The default is **null**. When you set this property you also set the same property of all **DataTable** objects in the **Tables** collection. This doesn't mean that it's forced upon the **DataTable** objects, because if you explicitly set this property of a **DataTable** in the **Tables** collection, either before or after you set the property on the **DataSet**, the value for the property in the **DataTable** won't be changed.	See Listing 3B-20
Namespace	This read-write property holds the namespace for the data set. It's employed when you read an XML document into the data set or when you write an XML document from the data set, using either of these methods: **ReadXml**, **ReadXmlSchema**, **WriteXml**, or **WriteXmlSchema**. The namespace is used for scoping the XML elements and attributes in the **DataSet**. When you set this property, you also set the same property of all **DataTable** objects in the **Tables** collection. This doesn't mean that it's forced upon the **DataTable** objects, because if you explicitly set this property of a **DataTable** in the **Tables** collection, either before or after you set the property on the **DataSet**, the value for the property in the **DataTable** won't be changed.	See Listing 3B-20
Prefix	This read-write property holds the namespace prefix for the data set. The prefix is used in an XML document for identifying which elements belong to the namespace of the data set object. The namespace is set with the **Namespace** property. When you set the **Prefix** property, you also set the same property of all **DataTable** objects in the **Tables** collection. This doesn't mean that it's forced upon the **DataTable** objects, because if you explicitly set this property of a **DataTable** in the **Tables** collection, either before or after you set the property on the **DataSet**, the value for the property in the **DataTable** won't be changed.	See Listing 3B-20

(continued)

Table 3B-1. **DataSet** *Class Properties (continued)*

NAME	DESCRIPTION	EXAMPLE
Relations	Returns the collection of relations from the **DataSet**. The returned value is of data type **DataRelationCollection**, and it holds objects of data type **DataRelation**. **null** is returned if no data relations exist. The **DataRelationCollection** allows you to navigate between related parent and child **DataTable** objects.	
Tables	Returns the collection of **DataTable** objects contained in the data set. The returned value is of data type **DataTableCollection**, which holds objects of data type **DataTable**. **null** is returned if no data tables exist.	

DataSet Methods

Table 3B-2 lists the noninherited and public methods of the **DataSet** class in alphabetical order.

Table 3B-2. **DataSet** *Class Methods*

NAME	DESCRIPTION	EXAMPLE
AcceptChanges()	This method accepts or commits all the changes that have been made to the data set since the last time the method was called or since the data set was loaded. Be aware that this method will call the **AcceptChanges** method on ALL tables in the **Tables** collection, which in turn calls the **AcceptChanges** method on all **DataRow** objects in the **Rows** collection of each **DataTable**. So if you need to only accept changes to a specific table, then call the **AcceptChanges** method on that particular table.	See Listing 3B-10
Clear()	This method clears the data set for data, which means that all rows are being removed from all tables. This method does NOT clear the data structure, only the data itself.	dstUser.Clear();
Clone()	The **Clone** method is for cloning or copying the data structure of the data set. This does NOT include the data itself, but only the tables, schemas, relations, and constraints. If you need to copy the data as well, you need to use the **Copy** method.	dstClone = dstUser.Clone();

(continued)

Table 3B-2. **DataSet** *Class Methods (continued)*

NAME	DESCRIPTION	EXAMPLE
Copy()	The **Copy** method is for cloning the data structure of the data set and copying the data from the data set into the new data structure. If you only need to clone the data structure, you need to use the **Clone** method.	`dstCopy = dstUser.Copy();`
GetChanges()	This overloaded method is used for retrieving a copy of the data set that contains all the changes that have been made since the last time the **AcceptChanges** method was called or since the data set was loaded. You can use the method without an argument, or you can indicate what kind of changes you want returned in the data set by specifying a member of the **DataRowState** enum.	See Listing 3B-8
GetXml()	The **GetXml** method returns the data in the data set as XML data in a **string** variable.	`strXMLData = dstUser.GetXml();`
GetXmlSchema()	The **GetXmlSchema** method returns the XSD schema for data in the data set in a **string** variable.	`strXMLSchema = dstUser .GetXmlSchema();`
HasChanges()	This method can be used to detect if there are any changes to the data in the data set. The method is overloaded, and one version takes a member of the **DataRowState** enum as an argument. This way you can specify whether you only want to detect a specific change, such as added rows. A **bool** value indicating if there are any changes is returned.	See Listing 3B-9
InferXmlSchema()	This overloaded method infers or copies the XML schema from an **XmlReader**, a **Stream**, a **TextReader**, or a file into the data set.	`dstUser .InferXmlSchema (xrdUser, arrstrURIExclude);`
Merge()	The **Merge** method is overloaded and is used for merging the data set with other data, in the form of an array of **DataRow** objects, into another **DataSet** or with a **DataTable**.	See Listings 3B-5, 3B-6, and 3B-7
ReadXml()	This overloaded method is for reading XML schema and data into the data set. The XML schema and data is read from a **Stream,** a file, a **TextReader**, or an **XmlReader**. If you only want to read the XML schema, you can use the **ReadXmlSchema** method.	`dstUser .ReadXml(stmUser); dstUser.ReadXml (strXMLFile); dstUser .ReadXml(trdUser); dstUser .ReadXml(xrdUser);`

(continued)

*Table 3B-2. **DataSet** Class Methods (continued)*

NAME	DESCRIPTION	EXAMPLE
ReadXmlSchema()	This overloaded method is for reading XML schema into the data set. The XML schema is read from an **XmlReader**, a **Stream**, a file, or a **TextReader**. If you want to read the XML schema and the data, you can use the **ReadXml** method.	`dstUser.ReadXmlSchema (xrdUser);` `dstUser.ReadXmlSchema (stmUser);` `dstUser.ReadXmlSchema (strXMLFile);` `dstUser.ReadXmlSchema (trdUser);`
RejectChanges()	This method rejects or rolls back the changes made to the data set since the last time the **AcceptChanges** method was called or since the **DataSet** was loaded. Be aware that this method will call the **RejectChanges** method on ALL tables in the **Tables** collection, which in turn calls the **RejectChanges** method on all **DataRow** objects in the **Rows** collection of each **DataTable**. So if you need to reject changes only to a specific table, then call the **RejectChanges** method on this table.	See Listing 3B-10
Reset()	This overridable method resets the data set to its original state, meaning the state it had after instantiation.	`dstUser.Reset();`
WriteXml()	This overloaded method is for writing XML schema and data from the data set. The XML schema and data is written to an **XmlWriter**, a **Stream**, a file, or a **TextWriter**. If you want to write only the XML schema, you can use the **WriteXmlSchema** method.	`dstUser .WriteXml(xwrUser);` `dstUser .WriteXml(stmUser);` `dstUser.WriteXml (strXMLFile);` `dstUser.WriteXml (twrUser);`
WriteXmlSchema()	This overloaded method is for writing the XML schema from the data set. The XML schema is written to an **XmlWriter**, a **Stream**, a file, or a **TextWriter**. If you want to write the XML schema and the data, you can use the **WriteXml** method.	`dstUser.WriteXmlSchema (xrdUser);` `dstUser.WriteXmlSchema (stmUser);` `dstUser.WriteXmlSchema (strXMLFile);` `dstUser.WriteXmlSchema (trdUser);`

DataSet Events

The **DataSet** class only has one noninherited event, the **MergeFailed** event. This event can be used when you merge a data set with an array of **DataRow** objects, another **DataSet**, or a **DataTable**, and you want to handle possible merge failures. The event is triggered when the schema of the data classes being merged are conflicting and the **EnforceConstraints** property has been set to **true**. One such conflict can be when two tables in the data set have different primary keys. Listing 3B-2 shows you how to set up and handle this event.

Listing 3B-2. Handling Merge Failures

```
1  private static void OnMergeFailed(object sender, MergeFailedEventArgs args) {
2      // Display a message detailing the merge conflict
3      MessageBox.Show("There were errors when merging the datasets:\n\n" +
4          args.Conflict + " The conflict happened in table " + args.Table + ".");
5  }
6
7  public void TriggerMergeFailureEvent() {
8      // Declare and instantiate data sets
9      DataSet dstUser1 = new DataSet("Users1");
10     DataSet dstUser2 = new DataSet("Users2");
11
12     // Declare and instantiate connections
13     SqlConnection cnnUserMan1 = new SqlConnection(STR_CONNECTION_STRING);
14     SqlConnection cnnUserMan2 = new SqlConnection("Data Source=DBSERVER;" +
15         "User Id=UserMan;Password=userman;Initial Catalog=UserMan");
16     // Declare and instantiate data adapters
17     SqlDataAdapter prdadUserMan1 = new SqlDataAdapter("SELECT * FROM tblUser",
18         cnnUserMan1);
19     SqlDataAdapter prdadUserMan2 = new SqlDataAdapter("SELECT * FROM tblUser",
20         cnnUserMan2);
21     // Set up event handler
22     dstUser1.MergeFailed += new MergeFailedEventHandler(OnMergeFailed);
23
24     // Open the connections
25     cnnUserMan1.Open();
26     cnnUserMan2.Open();
27     // Populate the datasets
28     prdadUserMan1.Fill(dstUser1, "tblUser");
29     prdadUserMan2.Fill(dstUser2, "tblUser");
30     // Close the connections
31     cnnUserMan1.Close();
```

```
32     cnnUserMan2.Close();
33
34     // Merge the data sets
35     dstUser1.Merge(dstUser2);
36 }
```

In Listing 3B-2, I populate two data sets with the tblUser table from two different data sources (Lines 28 through 29). I then merge the two data sets on Line 35. If any conflicts arise when the data sets are merged, the OnMergeFailed procedure is called, because I've set up this procedure as the event handler for the **MergeFailed** event of the **DataSet** class on Line 22.

Instantiating a DataSet

There isn't much fuss to instantiating a **DataSet** object. It can be done when declaring it, as demonstrated here:

```
DataSet dstUnnamed = new DataSet();
DataSet dstNamed = new DataSet("UserManDataSet");
```

As you can see from the two lines of code, the only difference is the name I've given to the dstNamed data set. Giving a data set a name like this is especially useful when it's persisted as XML, because the XML document element is then given a name you can recognize. You can also declare the variable first and then instantiate like this:

```
DataSet dstUnnamed;
DataSet dstNamed;

dstUnnamed = new DataSet();
dstNamed = new DataSet("UserManDataSet");
```

Populating Your DataSet Using the DataAdapter

Once you've set up the data adapter and the data set, you need to populate the data set. The **Fill** method of the DataAdapter class is used for populating and refreshing the **DataSet** object. The **Fill** method is overloaded, and there are more method versions for the **OleDbDataAdapter** class than the **OdbcDataAdapter** and **SqlDataAdapter** classes. This is because the **OleDbDataAdapter** class supports populating a data set from an ADO **Recordset** object or an ADO **Record** object. Yes, that's right—you can mess about with the good old ADO **Recordset** object and the somewhat newer ADO **Record** object. In Table 3B-3, I show you the various public versions of the **Fill** method. The example code here assumes that you've instantiated and initialized the various objects. You can see in the previous listings how it's done, because I am essentially building on the same code.

*Table 3B-3. The Various Versions of the Overloaded **Fill** Method (DataAdapter)*

EXAMPLE CODE	DESCRIPTION
`intNumRows = dadUserMan.Fill(dstUser);`	This version of the method populates the `dstUser` data set and saves the number of rows returned in `intNumRows`. Because you haven't specified the table name anywhere, the new data table in the **Tables** collection is called "Table". You can check the table name using a statement similar to the following: `MessageBox.Show(dstUserMan.Tables[0].TableName.ToString());`.
`intNumRows = dadUserMan.Fill(dstUser, "tblUser");`	This version of the method populates the `dstUser` data set and returns the number of rows returned in `intNumRows`. Because you've specified the source table name, the new data table in the **Tables** collection in the data set is called "tblUser" (like in the UserMan data source). You can check the table name using a statement similar to the following: `MessageBox.Show(dstUserMan.Tables[0].TableName.ToString());`
`intNumRows = dadUserMan.Fill(dstUser, 0, 2, "tblUser");`	This version of the method populates the `dstUser` data set and returns the number of rows returned in `intNumRows`. Because you've specified the source table name, the new data table in the **Tables** collection in the data set is called "tblUser", like in the data source. The 0 indicates that the population should start at the row with index 0, which is the first row. The 2 forces a maximum of two rows to be returned. This method should be used if you don't want all rows returned. You can check the number of rows returned in the `intNumRows` variable.
`intNumRows = dadUserMan.Fill(dtbUser);`	This version of the method doesn't actually populate a data set, but a **DataTable** object instead. The number of rows returned is saved in `intNumRows`. Because you haven't specified the source table name, the data table doesn't have a name. You can prevent this by giving the **DataTable** a name when you instantiate it, using a statement like `dtbUser = new DataTable("tblUser");`, or you can do it after you instantiate the data table. This is done by setting the **TableName** property.
`intNumRows = dadUserMan.Fill(dtbUser, rstADO);` (**OleDbDataAdapter** only)	This version of the method doesn't actually populate a data set, but a **DataTable** object instead. The number of rows returned is saved in `intNumRows`. The rows from the ADO **Recordset** object are copied to the data table. You can also specify an ADO **Record** object in case of the rstADO **Recordset** object.

(continued)

*Table 3B-3. The Various Versions of the Overloaded **Fill** Method (DataAdapter) (continued)*

EXAMPLE CODE	DESCRIPTION
intNumRows = dadUserMan.Fill(dstUser, rstADO, "tblUser"); (**OleDbDataAdapter** only)	This version of the method populates the dstUser data set and returns the number of rows returned in intNumRows. The number of rows returned is saved in intNumRows. Because you've specified the source table name, the new data table in the **Tables** collection in the data set is called "tblUser". The rows from the ADO **Recordset** object are copied to the data table. You can also specify an ADO **Record** object in case of the rstADO **Recordset** object.

Since I won't be going over how to use ADO **Recordset** and ADO classes in general, perhaps this is a good time to show you a complete code example that opens an ADO **Recordset** and uses this **Recordset** to fill a **DataSet**. Listing 3B-3 shows you how to do this.

*Listing 3B-3. Populating a **DataSet** from an ADO **Recordset***

```
1  public void FillDataSetFromRecordset() {
2      const string STR_SQL_USER_SELECT = "SELECT * FROM tblUser";
3
4      OleDbConnection cnnUserMan;
5      OleDbDataAdapter dadUserMan;
6      DataSet dstUserMan;
7
8      ADODB.Recordset rstUser;
9      ADODB.Connection cnnADOUserMan;
10
11     int intNumRows;
12
13     // Instantiate and open the connections
14     cnnUserMan = new OleDbConnection(STR_CONNECTION_STRING);
15     cnnUserMan.Open();
16     cnnADOUserMan = new ADODB.Connection();
17     cnnADOUserMan.Open(STR_CONNECTION_STRING, "UserMan", "userman", 0);
18
19     // Instantiate data adapter
20     dadUserMan = new OleDbDataAdapter(STR_SQL_USER_SELECT, cnnUserMan);
21
22     // Instantiate dataset
23     dstUserMan = new DataSet();
24     // Instantiate recordset
25     rstUser = new ADODB.Recordset();
26
```

```
27    // Populate recordset
28    rstUser.Open(STR_SQL_USER_SELECT, cnnADOUserMan,
29        ADODB.CursorTypeEnum.adOpenStatic, ADODB.LockTypeEnum.adLockReadOnly,
30        0);
31    // Fill dataset
32    intNumRows = dadUserMan.Fill(dstUserMan, rstUser, "tblUser");
33 }
```

In Listing 3B-3, I make use of some ADO classes, and in order to do this, you must add a reference to the ADO COM libraries from your project. See "COM Interop" later in this chapter for information on how to this. There isn't much wizardry to the code in Listing 3B-3; I open two connections, one ADO.NET connection and one ADO connection. I then instantiate the data adapter and the record set, populate the record set, and then use the record set to populate the data set. You can use an ADO **Record** object instead of the **Recordset** object and/or you can populate a **DataTable** instead of a **DataSet**. See Table 3B-3 for more information on how you can do this using the **Fill** method of the DataAdapter.

Updating Your Data Source Using the DataAdapter

When you are finished manipulating the data in your data set, it's time to update the data source. This is done using the **Update** method of the DataAdapter class. This method is responsible for examining the **RowState** property of each of the **DataRow** objects in the **DataRowsCollection**, which can be accessed using the **Rows** property. The **Rows** property is a member of each of the **DataTable** objects contained in the **Tables** collection of the data set. So the data adapter starts by looping through all the tables in the **Tables** collection in the data set, and for each table it loops through the **DataRowsCollection** collection to examine the **RowState** property. If a row has been inserted, updated, or deleted, the DataAdapter uses one of the command properties to handle the update. This means that the **InsertCommand** property is used if you are inserting a new row, the **UpdateCommand** property is used if you are updating an existing row, and the **DeleteCommand** is used if you are deleting an existing row.

In Listing 3B-4, I set up a data adapter, a data set, and some command objects to manipulate the tblUser table in the UserMan database. Next I add, modify, and delete a row from the table. I then use the **HasChanges** method to check if there are any changes to the data in the data set. If so, I specify that all the changed rows be loaded into the dstChanges data set using the **GetChanges** method. The changes are rejected if there are any errors; otherwise the data source is updated using the **Update** method. The code in Listing 3B-4 doesn't handle exceptions when I try to update the data source, but check out Chapter 5 for example code and recommendations on how to handle exceptions.

Listing 3B-4. Propagating Changes Back to the Data Source

```
1  public void UpdateDataSet() {
2      const string STR_SQL_USER_SELECT = "SELECT * FROM tblUser";
3      const string STR_SQL_USER_DELETE = "DELETE FROM tblUser WHERE Id=@Id";
4      const string STR_SQL_USER_INSERT = "INSERT INTO tblUser(FirstName" +
5          ", LastName, LoginName, Password) VALUES(@FirstName, @LastName, " +
6          "@LoginName, @Password)";
7      const string STR_SQL_USER_UPDATE = "UPDATE tblUser SET FirstName=" +
8          "@FirstName, LastName=@LastName, LoginName=@LoginName, " +
9          "Password=@Password WHERE Id=@Id";
10
11     SqlConnection cnnUserMan;
12     SqlCommand cmmUserSelect;
13     SqlCommand cmmUserDelete;
14     SqlCommand cmmUserInsert;
15     SqlCommand cmmUserUpdate;
16     SqlDataAdapter dadUserMan;
17     DataSet dstUserMan, dstChanges;
18     DataRow drwUser;
19     SqlParameter prmSQLDelete, prmSQLUpdate;
20
21     // Instantiate and open the connection
22     cnnUserMan = new SqlConnection(STR_CONNECTION_STRING);
23     cnnUserMan.Open();
24
25     // Instantiate the commands
26     cmmUserSelect = new SqlCommand(STR_SQL_USER_SELECT, cnnUserMan);
27     cmmUserDelete = new SqlCommand(STR_SQL_USER_DELETE, cnnUserMan);
28     cmmUserInsert = new SqlCommand(STR_SQL_USER_INSERT, cnnUserMan);
29     cmmUserUpdate = new SqlCommand(STR_SQL_USER_UPDATE, cnnUserMan);
30
31     // Instantiate data adapter
32     dadUserMan = new SqlDataAdapter(STR_SQL_USER_SELECT, cnnUserMan);
33     // Set data adapter command properties
34     dadUserMan.SelectCommand = cmmUserSelect;
35     dadUserMan.InsertCommand = cmmUserInsert;
36     dadUserMan.DeleteCommand = cmmUserDelete;
37     dadUserMan.UpdateCommand = cmmUserUpdate;
38
39     // Add Delete command parameters
40     prmSQLDelete = dadUserMan.DeleteCommand.Parameters.Add("@Id",
41         SqlDbType.Int, 0, "Id");
42     prmSQLDelete.Direction = ParameterDirection.Input;
```

```
43    prmSQLDelete.SourceVersion = DataRowVersion.Original;
44
45    // Add Update command parameters
46    cmmUserUpdate.Parameters.Add("@FirstName", SqlDbType.VarChar, 50,
47        "FirstName");
48    cmmUserUpdate.Parameters.Add("@LastName", SqlDbType.VarChar, 50,
49        "LastName");
50    cmmUserUpdate.Parameters.Add("@LoginName", SqlDbType.VarChar, 50,
51        "LoginName");
52    cmmUserUpdate.Parameters.Add("@Password", SqlDbType.VarChar, 50,
53        "Password");
54
55    prmSQLUpdate = dadUserMan.UpdateCommand.Parameters.Add("@Id",
56        SqlDbType.Int, 0, "Id");
57    prmSQLUpdate.Direction = ParameterDirection.Input;
58    prmSQLUpdate.SourceVersion = DataRowVersion.Original;
59
60    // Add insert command parameters
61    cmmUserInsert.Parameters.Add("@FirstName", SqlDbType.VarChar, 50,
62        "FirstName");
63    cmmUserInsert.Parameters.Add("@LastName", SqlDbType.VarChar, 50,
64        "LastName");
65    cmmUserInsert.Parameters.Add("@LoginName", SqlDbType.VarChar, 50,
66        "LoginName");
67    cmmUserInsert.Parameters.Add("@Password", SqlDbType.VarChar, 50,
68        "Password");
69
70    // Instantiate dataset
71    dstUserMan = new DataSet();
72    // Populate the data set
73    dadUserMan.Fill(dstUserMan, "tblUser");
74
75    // Add new row
76    drwUser = dstUserMan.Tables["tblUser"].NewRow();
77    drwUser["FirstName"] = "New User";
78    drwUser["LastName"] = "New User LastName";
79    drwUser["LoginName"] = "NewUser";
80    drwUser["Password"] = "password";
81    dstUserMan.Tables["tblUser"].Rows.Add(drwUser);
82
83    // Update an existing row (with index 3)
84    dstUserMan.Tables["tblUser"].Rows[3]["FirstName"] = "FirstName";
85    dstUserMan.Tables["tblUser"].Rows[3]["LastName"] = "LastName";
```

```
86    dstUserMan.Tables["tblUser"].Rows[3]["LoginName"] = "User3";
87
88    // Delete row with index 4
89    dstUserMan.Tables["tblUser"].Rows[4].Delete();
90
91    // Check if any data has changed in the data set
92    if (dstUserMan.HasChanges()) {
93       // Save all changed rows in a new data set
94       dstChanges = dstUserMan.GetChanges();
95       // Check if the changed rows contains any errors
96       if (dstChanges.HasErrors) {
97          // Reject the changes
98          dstUserMan.RejectChanges();
99       }
100      else {
101         // Update the data source
102         dadUserMan.Update(dstChanges, "tblUser");
103      }
104   }
105 }
```

Clearing Data from a DataSet

When you've added tables, relations, constraints, and so on to a data set, or what makes up the structure in your data set, you frequently need a way of clearing all the data from the data set. This can easily be accomplished using the **Clear** method, as shown in the following example:

```
dstUser.Clear();
```

Copying a DataSet

Sometimes it's necessary to copy a data set for various reasons. If you need to manipulate some data for testing purposes, copying a data set is a good way of leaving the original data intact. Depending on what you actually need to do, there are two ways you can approach this: copy just the data structure, or copy the data structure and the data within it. The next sections describe each of these methods.

Copying the Data Structure of a DataSet

Do you need to copy, or rather clone, the structure of a data set? If that's the case, there is a method of the data set called **Clone** that does exactly this, as shown in the following code line:

```
dstClone = dstUser.Clone();
```

Copying the Data and Structure of a DataSet

When you need a complete copy of the data structure and the data contained therein from a data set, you can use the **Copy** method for this purpose, as shown here:

```
dstCopy = dstUser.Copy();
```

Merging Data in a DataSet with Other Data

From time to time you'll probably want to combine data from a data set and data that exist in another form. For example, say you have a **DataSet** that you filled with data structure and data using the **Fill** method of the DataAdapter, and you want to combine this with a **DataSet** or **DataTable** that you've created programmatically. Once you are done manipulating the data, you want to merge the data in the two objects. You can achieve this by merging the data into the data set. Data in the form of an array of **DataRow** objects, a **DataTable** object, or a **DataSet** object can be merged using the **Merge** method of the **DataSet**. The resulting merged data set replaces the data in the data set, which executes the **Merge** method. See Listings 3B-5, 3B-6, and 3B-7 for some examples using the **Merge** method.

*Listing 3B-5. Merging a **DataSet** Object with an Array of **DataRow** Objects*

```
 1 public void MergeDataSetWithDataRows() {
 2     SqlConnection cnnUserMan;
 3     SqlCommand cmmUser;
 4     SqlDataAdapter dadUser;
 5     DataSet dstUser;
 6     DataTable dtbUser;
 7     DataRow[] arrdrwUser = new DataRow[1];
 8     DataRow drwUser;
 9
10     // Instantiate and open the connection
11     cnnUserMan = new SqlConnection(STR_CONNECTION_STRING);
12     cnnUserMan.Open();
```

```
13      // Instantiate the command, data set and data table
14      cmmUser = new SqlCommand("SELECT * FROM tblUser", cnnUserMan);
15      dstUser = new DataSet();
16      dtbUser = new DataTable();
17      // Instantiate and initialize the data adapter
18      dadUser = new SqlDataAdapter("SELECT * FROM tblUser", cnnUserMan);
19      dadUser.SelectCommand = cmmUser;
20      // Fill the data set
21      dadUser.Fill(dstUser, "tblUser");
22      // Create new row and fill with data
23      drwUser = dstUser.Tables["tblUser"].NewRow();
24      drwUser["LoginName"] = "NewUser1";
25      drwUser["FirstName"] = "New";
26      drwUser["LastName"] = "User";
27      arrdrwUser.SetValue(drwUser, 0);
28      // Merge the data set with the data row array
29      dstUser.Merge(arrdrwUser);
30 }
```

*Listing 3B-6. Merging Two **DataSet** Objects*

```
1 public void MergeDataSets() {
2      SqlConnection cnnUserMan;
3      SqlCommand cmmUser;
4      SqlDataAdapter dadUser;
5      DataSet dstUser;
6      DataSet dstCopy;
7
8      // Instantiate and open the connection
9      cnnUserMan = new SqlConnection(STR_CONNECTION_STRING);
10     cnnUserMan.Open();
11     // Instantiate the command and data set
12     cmmUser = new SqlCommand("SELECT * FROM tblUser", cnnUserMan);
13     dstUser = new DataSet();
14     // Instantiate and initialize the data adapter
15     dadUser = new SqlDataAdapter("SELECT * FROM tblUser", cnnUserMan);
16     dadUser.SelectCommand = cmmUser;
17     // Fill the data set
18     dadUser.Fill(dstUser, "tblUser");
19     // Copy the data set
20     dstCopy = dstUser.Copy();
21     // Do your stuff with the data sets
22     // ...
23     // Merge the two data sets
24     dstUser.Merge(dstCopy);
25 }
```

*Listing 3B-7. Merging a **DataSet** Object with a **DataTable** Object*

```
 1 public void MergeDataSetWithDataTable() {
 2     SqlConnection cnnUserMan;
 3     SqlCommand cmmUser;
 4     SqlDataAdapter dadUser;
 5     DataSet dstUser;
 6     DataTable dtbUser;
 7
 8     // Instantiate and open the connection
 9     cnnUserMan = new SqlConnection(STR_CONNECTION_STRING);
10     cnnUserMan.Open();
11     // Instantiate the command, data set and data table
12     cmmUser = new SqlCommand("SELECT * FROM tblUser", cnnUserMan);
13     dstUser = new DataSet();
14     dtbUser = new DataTable();
15     // Instantiate and initialize the data adapter
16     dadUser = new SqlDataAdapter("SELECT * FROM tblUser", cnnUserMan);
17     dadUser.SelectCommand = cmmUser;
18     // Fill the data set and data table
19     dadUser.Fill(dstUser, "tblUser");
20     dadUser.Fill(dtbUser);
21     // Do your stuff with the data set and the data table
22     // . . .
23     // Merge the data set with the data table
24     dstUser.Merge(dtbUser);
25 }
```

Please note that in Listings 3B-5 through 3B-7, I've chosen to create the data structure and fill the data table using the data adapter's **Fill** method. You can obviously create the data structure yourself and fill it with data from a variety of sources before you merge it with the data set. See "Using the DataTable Class" later in this chapter for more information on how to do this.

Detecting and Handling Changes to Data in a DataSet

Sometimes it's necessary to know if the data in your data set has been changed. Changes in this context include new rows and deleted rows as well as modified rows. The **DataSet** class has the **HasChanges** method that can be used for this purpose. This method actually exists for the individual **DataTable** objects in the **Tables** collection, but if you just want to know if any of the data in the data set has changed, you need to use the data set's method.

The **HasChanges** method is overloaded, and you can see how to use the various versions in Listings 3B-8 and 3B-9.

*Listing 3B-8. Detecting All Data Changes in a **DataSet** Object*

```
 1 public void DetectAllDataSetChanges() {
 2    SqlConnection cnnUserMan;
 3    SqlCommand cmmUser;
 4    SqlDataAdapter dadUser;
 5    DataSet dstUser;
 6    DataSet dstChanges;
 7
 8    // Instantiate and open the connection
 9    cnnUserMan = new SqlConnection(STR_CONNECTION_STRING);
10    cnnUserMan.Open();
11    // Instantiate the command and data set
12    cmmUser = new SqlCommand("SELECT * FROM tblUser", cnnUserMan);
13    dstUser = new DataSet();
14    // Instantiate and initialize the data adapter
15    dadUser = new SqlDataAdapter("SELECT * FROM tblUser", cnnUserMan);
16    dadUser.SelectCommand = cmmUser;
17    // Fill the data set
18    dadUser.Fill(dstUser, "tblUser");
19    // Do your stuff with the data set
20    // ...
21    // Check if any data has changed in the data set
22    if (dstUser.HasChanges()) {
23       // Save all changes in a new data set
24       dstChanges = dstUser.GetChanges();
25    }
26 }
```

In Listing 3B-8, all the data changes are simply saved to a new data set. Obviously this doesn't do anything to the data, but once you have changes isolated you can manipulate the data and check for errors. This is particularly useful when you want to update the data source. Don't forget that the **DataSet** is disconnected from the data source and any changes won't be propagated back to the data source until you explicitly update the data source! Before checking for changes to the **DataSet** on Line 22, you might want to check if there are any errors in the **DataSet**, using the **HasErrors** method. It's good programming practice, and it does prevent a possible exception being thrown when manipulating the data in the **DataSet**.

Listing 3B-9 is basically the same code as in Listing 3B-8, but it shows how to filter the different changes into different data sets.

*Listing 3B-9. Detecting the Different Data Changes in a **DataSet** Object*

```
1  public void DetectDifferentDataSetChanges() {
2      SqlConnection cnnUserMan;
3      SqlCommand cmmUser;
4      SqlDataAdapter dadUser;
5      DataSet dstUser;
6      DataSet dstChanges;
7      DataSet dstAdditions;
8      DataSet dstDeletions;
9
10     // Instantiate and open the connection
11     cnnUserMan = new SqlConnection(STR_CONNECTION_STRING);
12     cnnUserMan.Open();
13     // Instantiate the command and data set
14     cmmUser = new SqlCommand("SELECT * FROM tblUser", cnnUserMan);
15     dstUser = new DataSet();
16     // Instantiate and initialize the data adapter
17     dadUser = new SqlDataAdapter("SELECT * FROM tblUser", cnnUserMan);
18     dadUser.SelectCommand = cmmUser;
19     // Fill the data set
20     dadUser.Fill(dstUser, "tblUser");
21     // Do your stuff with the data set
22     // ...
23     // Check if any data has changed in the data set
24     if (dstUser.HasChanges()) {
25         // Save all modified rows in a new data set
26         dstChanges = dstUser.GetChanges(DataRowState.Modified);
27         // Save all added rows in a new data set
28         dstAdditions = dstUser.GetChanges(DataRowState.Added);
29         // Save all deleted rows in a new data set
30         dstDeletions = dstUser.GetChanges(DataRowState.Deleted);
31     }
32 }
```

Accepting or Rejecting Changes to Data in a DataSet

When changes have been made to data in the data set, you can choose to reject or accept them. The **DataSet** class has two methods for doing this: the **AcceptChanges** and **RejectChanges** methods. One thing you have to note about these methods is that they work on the data in the data set and NOT in the data source itself. This goes back to the fact that the data set is disconnected and as such doesn't interact with the data source.

One reason for rejecting changes to the data in the **DataSet** can be that you have user feedback on the updates and perhaps the user wants to reject the changes he or she has been making. (See "RejectChanges Method" later in this chapter for more on this topic.) A reason for accepting changes in the **DataSet** can be that the **DataSet** is used as a temporary data store that has been built from scratch, like in Listing 3B-11. In this kind of situation, you might have made a number of changes, and now you need to make another batch of changes, but you want to ensure you can distinguish the new changes from all nonchanged rows. You can do this by calling the **AcceptChanges** method before making the second batch of changes. See the upcoming section for more on this method.

> **NOTE** *If you call either of the **AcceptChanges** or **RejectChanges** methods, you also "reset" the **HasChanges** method, meaning it will return **false**.*

The AcceptChanges Method

When using this method, any changes to a row in a data table in the **Tables** collection will be accepted. This is done by calling the **AcceptChanges** method on each of the **DataTable** objects in the table collection. When the **AcceptChanges** method is called on a data table, the data table invokes the **AcceptChanges** method on each **DataRow** object in the **Rows** collection. What happens then is the **RowState** property of each data row is examined. If the row state is **Added** or **Modified**, then the **RowState** property is changed to **Unchanged**. Rows with the **Deleted** row state are removed from the respective data table. If a **DataRow** is being edited when the **AcceptChanges** method is called, the row in question will successfully exit edit mode. See Listing 3B-10 in the next section for an example of how **AcceptChanges** can be used and how it affects a **DataSet**. If you call **AcceptChanges** just before calling the **Update** method of the data adapter, no changes will be written back to the data source because you've just accepted the changes and they are now marked **Unchanged**!

> **NOTE** *If a data set contains any **ForeignKeyConstraint** objects, the **AcceptRejectRule** property is enforced once the **AcceptChanges** method is called. The **AcceptRejectRule** property is used to determine if the changes or deletions should be cascaded across a relationship. Please see the "What Is a Foreign Key?" section in Chapter 2 for more information on foreign keys.*

The RejectChanges Method

When using the **RejectChanges** method, any changes to a row in a data table in the **Tables** collection will be rejected. This is done by calling **RejectChanges** on each of the **DataTable** objects in the table collection. When the **RejectChanges** method is called on a data table, the data table invokes the **AcceptChanges** method on each **DataRow** object in the **Rows** collection. What happens then is the **RowState** property of each data row is examined. If the row state is **Added**, then the row is removed from the respective data table. The **RowState** property for rows with **Modified** and **Deleted** row states is changed to **Unchanged** and the original content of the rows restored. If a **DataRow** is being edited when the **RejectChanges** method is called, the row in question will cancel edit mode. See Listing 3B-10 for an example of how **RejectChanges** can be used and how it affects a **DataSet** object.

*Listing 3B-10. Accepting or Rejecting Changes to the Data in a **DataSet** Object*

```
1 public void AcceptOrRejectDataSetChanges() {
2      SqlConnection cnnUserMan;
3      SqlCommand cmmUser;
4      SqlDataAdapter dadUser;
5      DataSet dstUser, dstChanges;
6      DataRow drwUser;
7
8      // Instantiate and open the connection
9      cnnUserMan = new SqlConnection(STR_CONNECTION_STRING);
10     cnnUserMan.Open();
11     // Instantiate the command and the data set
12     cmmUser = new SqlCommand("SELECT * FROM tblUser", cnnUserMan);
13     dstUser = new DataSet();
14     // Instantiate and initialize the data adapter
15     dadUser = new SqlDataAdapter("SELECT * FROM tblUser", cnnUserMan);
16     dadUser.SelectCommand = cmmUser;
17     // Fill the data set
18     dadUser.Fill(dstUser, "tblUser");
19     // Create a new data row with the schema from the user table
20     drwUser = dstUser.Tables["tblUser"].NewRow();
21     // Enter values in the data row columns
22     drwUser["LoginName"] = "NewUser1";
23     drwUser["FirstName"] = "New";
24     drwUser["LastName"] = "User";
25     // Add the data row to the user table
26     dstUser.Tables["tblUser"].Rows.Add(drwUser);
27     // Check if any data has changed in the data set
```

```
28    if (dstUser.HasChanges()) {
29       // Save all changed rows in a new data set
30       dstChanges = dstUser.GetChanges();
31       // Check if the changed rows contains any errors
32       if (dstChanges.HasErrors) {
33          // Display the row state of all rows before rejecting changes
34          for (int intCounter = 0;
35             intCounter <= dstUser.Tables[0].Rows.Count - 1; intCounter++) {
36             MessageBox.Show("HasErrors=True, Before RejectChanges, "
37                "RowState=" +
38                dstUser.Tables[0].Rows[intCounter].RowState.ToString() +
39                ", LoginName=" +
40                dstUser.Tables[0].Rows[intCounter]["LoginName"].ToString());
41          }
42
43          // Reject the changes to the data set
44          dstUser.RejectChanges();
45          // Display the row state of all rows after rejecting changes
46          for (int intCounter = 0;
47             intCounter <= dstUser.Tables[0].Rows.Count - 1; intCounter++) {
48             MessageBox.Show("HasErrors=True, After RejectChanges, "
49                "RowState=" +
50                dstUser.Tables[0].Rows[intCounter].RowState.ToString() +
51                ", LoginName=" +
52                dstUser.Tables[0].Rows[intCounter]["LoginName"].ToString());
53          }
54       }
55    }
56    else {
57       // Display the row state of all rows before accepting changes
58       for (int intCounter = 0;
59          intCounter <= dstUser.Tables[0].Rows.Count - 1; intCounter++) {
60          MessageBox.Show("HasErrors=false, Before AcceptChanges, "
61             "RowState=" +
62             dstUser.Tables[0].Rows[intCounter].RowState.ToString() +
63             ", LoginName=" +
64             dstUser.Tables[0].Rows[intCounter]["LoginName"].ToString());
65       }
66       // Accept the changes to the data set
67       dstUser.AcceptChanges();
68       // Display the row state of all rows after accepting changes
69       for (int intCounter = 0; intCounter <= dstUser.Tables[0].Rows.Count - 1;
70          intCounter++) {
```

```
71              MessageBox.Show("HasErrors=false, After AcceptChanges, RowState=" +
72                  dstUser.Tables[0].Rows[intCounter].RowState.ToString() +
73                  ", LoginName=" +
74                  dstUser.Tables[0].Rows[intCounter]["LoginName"].ToString());
75          }
76      }
77 }
```

Listing 3B-10 shows how to use the **AcceptChanges** and **RejectChanges** methods of the **DataSet** class. It also shows you how to check for changes and errors in the changed rows. As the example stands, the **HasErrors** method returns **false**, which means that the changes are accepted. You can manipulate the example code so that the changes are rejected and the **RejectChanges** method will be used instead.

Using the DataTable Class

The **DataTable** class is used for manipulating the content of a table contained in the **Tables** collection of the **DataSet** class. The **DataTable** class is part of the **System.Data** namespace. The **DataTable** is an in-memory cache of the data from exactly one table. One last thing to notice about the **DataTable** class is that, like the **DataSet** class, it's NOT subclassed—in other words, this class will work with whatever provider you are dealing with.

> **NOTE**   *There are no SqlDataTable, OdbcDataTable, and OleDbDataTable classes.*

DataTable Properties

The **DataTable** class has the properties shown in alphabetical order in Table 3B-4. Please note that only the public, noninherited properties are shown.

*Table 3B-4. **DataTable** Class Properties*

NAME	DESCRIPTION
CaseSensitive	This property indicates if a string comparison in the table is case sensitive. A **bool** value is set or returned. If the **DataTable** is part of a data set, this property is set to the value of the data set's **CaseSensitive** property. However, if the **DataTable** has been created programmatically, this property is set to **false** by default.
ChildRelations	The **ChildRelations** property returns a collection of child relations for the data table. This property is read-only and the data type returned is **DataRelationCollection**. If no relations exist, **null** is returned.
Columns	This property returns the **DataColumnCollection** collection of columns that makes up the data table. This property is read-only. **null** is returned if no columns exist.
Constraints	The **Constraints** property returns the collection of constraints belonging to the data table. This property is read-only and the data type returned is **ConstraintCollection**. If no constraints exist, **null** is returned.
DataSet	This read-only property returns the data set the table belongs to. This means the returned object is of data type **DataSet**.
DefaultView	This read-only property returns a **DataView** object that is a customized view of the table. The returned data view can be used for filtering, sorting, and searching a data table. See "Using the DataView Class" later in this chapter for more information on the **DataView** class.
DisplayExpression	The **DisplayExpression** property returns or sets an expression, which returns a value that is used to represent the table in the UI. This property can be used to dynamically create text based on the current data.
ExtendedProperties	This read-only property returns a **PropertyCollection** collection of customized user information. You can use the **Add** method of this property to add custom information to a data table, like this: `dtbUser.ExtendedProperties.Add("New Property", "New Property Value");`.
HasErrors	This read-only property returns a **bool** value indicating if any errors occurred in any of the rows in the data table.
Locale	The **Locale** property returns or sets the **CultureInfo** object. This object provides the locale information that is used for comparing strings in the data table. This means you can specify the locale that matches the data contained in the data table and thus make sure specific characters are sorted correctly and string comparisons are performed according to the rules of the locale. By default this property is set to the value of the data set's **Locale** property. However, if the data table doesn't belong to a data set, this property is set to the culture of the current system.

(continued)

Table 3B-4. **DataTable** *Class Properties (continued)*

NAME	DESCRIPTION
MinimumCapacity	This property returns or sets the initial starting size for the data table. The property is of data type **int** and the default value is 25. The value specifies the number of rows that the data table will be able to hold initially before creating extra resources to accommodate more rows. You should set this property when performance is critical, because it's faster to allocate the resources before you start populating the data table. So set the property to the smallest value appropriate for the number of rows returned when performance is critical.
Namespace	The **Namespace** property returns or sets the namespace used for XML representation of the data in the data table.
ParentRelations	The **ParentRelations** property returns a collection of parent relations for the data table as a **DataRelationCollection** object. This property is read-only. **null** is returned if no parent relations exist.
Prefix	This read-write property holds the namespace prefix for the data table. The namespace prefix is used when the data table is represented as XML. The data type for this property is **string**.
PrimaryKey	The **PrimaryKey** property is read-write enabled, and it returns or sets an array of **DataColumn** objects that are the primary keys for the data table. A **DataException** exception is thrown if you try to set a column that is already a foreign key.
Rows	This read-only property returns the **DataRowCollection** object that holds all the **DataRow** objects that make up the data in this data table. **null** is returned if there are no rows in the table.
TableName	This read-write property holds the name for the data table. The name property is used when the table is looked up in the **Tables** collection of the data set. The data type for this property is **string**.

DataTable Methods

Table 3B-5 lists the noninherited and public methods of the **DataTable** class in alphabetical order.

*Table 3B-5 **DataTable** Class Methods*

NAME	DESCRIPTION	EXAMPLE
AcceptChanges()	This method accepts or commits all the changes that have been made to the data table since the last time the method was called or since the data table was loaded. Because this method changes the row state of all changed rows in the data table, you should not call this method until after you attempt to call the **Update** method on the data adapter. If **AcceptChanges** is called before you update the data set, no changes will be propagated back to the data set because the **RowState** property of the changed rows will revert to **Unchanged**, meaning they won't appear to have been changed.	`dtbUser.AcceptChanges();`
BeginLoadData()	The **BeginLoadData** method is used in conjunction with the **EndLoadData** method. This method turns off index maintenance, constraints, and notifications while loading the data with the **LoadDataRow** method.	`dtbUser.BeginLoadData();`
Clear()	This method clears all rows from the data table. If any of the rows has child rows in other data tables with which the current data table has an enforced relationship,[2] an exception is thrown, unless the relationship specifies a cascading delete.	`dtbUser.Clear();`
Clone()	The **Clone** method is for cloning or copying the data structure of the data table. This does NOT include the data itself, but only the schemas, relations, and constraints. If you need to copy the data as well, you have to use the **Copy** method.	`dtbClone = dtbUser.Clone();`
Compute(string strExpression, string strFilter)	The **Compute** method computes `strExpression` on the current rows that pass the `strFilter` criteria. Please note that the `strExpression` expression must contain an aggregate function, such as SUM or COUNT.	`objCompute = dtbUser.Compute ("COUNT(FirstName)", "LastName IS NOT NULL");`

(continued)

---

2. Constraints, such as foreign keys, are enforced when the **EnforceConstraints** property is set to **true**, which is the default.

*Table 3B-5 **DataTable** Class Methods (continued)*

NAME	DESCRIPTION	EXAMPLE
Copy()	The **Copy** method is for cloning the data structure of the data table and copying the data from the data table into the new data table. If you only need to clone the data structure, you should use the **Clone** method.	```dtbCopy = dtbUser.Copy();```
EndLoadData()	The **EndLoadData** method turns back on index maintenance, constraints, and notifications after it has been turned off with the **BeginLoadData** method. Use the **EndLoadData** and **BeginLoadData** methods when loading the data with the **LoadDataRow** method.	```dtbUser.EndLoadData();```
GetChanges()	This overloaded method is used for retrieving a copy of the data table that contains all the changes that have been made since the last time the **AcceptChanges** method was called or since the data table was loaded. You can use the method without arguments or you can indicate what kind of changes you want returned in the data table by specifying a member of the **DataRowState** enum.	```dtbChanges = dtbUser.GetChanges(); dtbAdded = dtbUser.GetChanges (DataRowState.Added);```
GetErrors()	The **GetErrors** method returns an array of **DataRow** objects. The array includes all rows in the **DataTable** that contain errors.	```arrdrwErrors = dtbUser.GetErrors();```
ImportRow(DataRow drwImport)	The **ImportRow** method copies a **DataRow** object into a **DataTable**. The copy includes original and current values, errors, and **DataRowState** values. In short, everything from the **DataRow** object is copied across.	```dtbUser.ImportRow (drwImport);```
LoadDataRow(object[] arrobjValues, bool blnAcceptChanges)	The **LoadDataRow** method finds a specific row using the values in the **arrobjValues** array. The values in the array are used to match with primary key column(s). If a matching row is found, it's updated. Otherwise a new row is created using the **arrobjValues** values.	```drwLoad = dtbUser.LoadDataRow (arrobjValues, false);```
NewRow()	The **NewRow** method creates a new **DataRow** object with the same schema as the data table.	```drwNew = dtbUser.NewRow();```

(continued)

*Table 3B-5 **DataTable** Class Methods (continued)*

NAME	DESCRIPTION	EXAMPLE
RejectChanges()	This method rejects or rolls back the changes made to the data table since the last time the **AcceptChanges** method was called or since the **DataTable** was loaded.	`dtbUser.RejectChanges();`
Reset()	This overridable method resets the data set to its original state.	`dtbUser.Reset();`

Select()	The **Select** method is overloaded and is used for retrieving an array of **DataRow** objects. The returned data rows are ordered after the primary key. If no primary key exists, the rows are returned ordered the way they were originally added to the data table. Actually, this is only true if you use one of the overloaded versions that don't take the sort order as an argument.	`arrdrwAllDataRows = dtbUser.Select();`
		`arrdrwFirstNameUnsortedDataRows = dtbUser.Select("FirstName = 'John'");`
		`arrdrwFirstNameSortedDataRows = dtbUser.Select("FirstName = 'John'", "LastName ASC");`
		`arrdrwFirstNameSortedOriginal DataRows = dtbUser.Select("FirstName = 'John'", "LastName ASC", DataViewRowState.OriginalRows);`

DataTable Events

Table 3B-6 lists the noninherited and public events of the **DataTable** class in alphabetical order.

*Table 3B-6 **DataTable** Class Events*

NAME	DESCRIPTION	EXAMPLE
ColumnChanged	This event occurs after a **DataColumn** value has been changed.	See the "Handling Column Changes" section later in this chapter.
ColumnChanging	The **ColumnChanging** event occurs before a **DataColumn** value is changed.	See the "Handling Column Changes" section later in this chapter, including Listing 3B-16.
RowChanged	This event occurs after a **DataRow** in the **DataTable** has been changed.	See the "Handling Row Changes" section later in this chapter.
RowChanging	The **RowChanging** event occurs before a **DataRow** in the **DataTable** is changed.	See the "Handling Row Changes" section later in this chapter, including Listing 3B-17.
RowDeleted	This event occurs after a **DataRow** in the **DataTable** has been deleted.	See the "Handling Row Deletions" section later in this chapter, including Listing 3B-18.
RowDeleting	The **RowDeleting** event occurs before a **DataRow** in the **DataTable** is deleted.	See the "Handling Row Deletions" section later in this chapter.

As you can see from the various events in Table 3B-6, it's possible to programmatically intercept and react to changes to the values in your **DataTable** objects in a number of ways. Please see the sections listed in the Example column for example code and more information about a specific event.

Declaring and Instantiating a DataTable

There are various ways to instantiate a **DataTable** object. You can use the overloaded class constructors or you can reference a specific table in the **Tables** collection of a data set. Here is how you instantiate a data table when you declare it:

```
DataTable dtbNoArguments = new DataTable();
DataTable dtbTableNameArgument = new DataTable("TableName");
```

You can also declare it and then instantiate it when you need to, as follows:

```
DataTable dtbNoArguments;
DataTable dtbTableNameArgument;

dtbNoArguments = new DataTable();
dtbTableNameArgument = new DataTable("TableName");
```

I've used two different constructors, one with no arguments and one that takes the table name as the only argument. Your other option is to first declare the **DataTable** object, and then have it reference a table in the **Tables** collection of a populated data set, like this:

```
DataTable dtbUser;

dtbUser = dstUser.Tables("tblUser");
```

Building Your Own DataTable

Sometimes you need storage for temporary data that has a table-like structure, meaning several groups of data sequences with the same structure. Because of the table-like structure, a **DataTable** is an obvious choice for storage, although not your only one. Listing 3B-11 demonstrates how to create a data structure from scratch like the one in the tblUser table in the UserMan database.

*Listing 3B-11. Building Your Own **DataTable***

```
1 public void BuildDataTable() {
2     DataTable dtbUser;
3     DataColumn dclUser;
4     DataColumn[] arrdclPrimaryKey = new DataColumn[1];
5
6     dtbUser = new DataTable("tblUser");
7
8     // Create table structure
9     dclUser = new DataColumn();
10    dclUser.ColumnName = "Id";
11    dclUser.DataType = Type.GetType("System.Int32");
12    dclUser.AutoIncrement = true;
13    dclUser.AutoIncrementSeed = 1;
14    dclUser.AutoIncrementStep = 1;
15    dclUser.AllowDBNull = false;
16    // Add column to data table structure
17    dtbUser.Columns.Add(dclUser);
18    // Add column to PK array
19    arrdclPrimaryKey[0] = dclUser;
20    // Set primary key
21    dtbUser.PrimaryKey = arrdclPrimaryKey;
22
23    dclUser = new DataColumn();
24    dclUser.ColumnName = "ADName";
```

```
25    dclUser.DataType = Type.GetType("System.String");
26    dclUser.MaxLength = 100;
27    // Add column to data table structure
28    dtbUser.Columns.Add(dclUser);
29
30    dclUser = new DataColumn();
31    dclUser.ColumnName = "ADSID";
32    dclUser.DataType = Type.GetType("System.String");
33    // Add column to data table structure
34    dtbUser.Columns.Add(dclUser);
35
36    dclUser = new DataColumn();
37    dclUser.ColumnName = "FirstName";
38    dclUser.DataType = Type.GetType("System.String");
39    dclUser.MaxLength = 50;
40    // Add column to data table structure
41    dtbUser.Columns.Add(dclUser);
42
43    dclUser = new DataColumn();
44    dclUser.ColumnName = "LastName";
45    dclUser.DataType = Type.GetType("System.String");
46    dclUser.MaxLength = 50;
47    // Add column to data table structure
48    dtbUser.Columns.Add(dclUser);
49
50    dclUser = new DataColumn();
51    dclUser.ColumnName = "LoginName";
52    dclUser.DataType = Type.GetType("System.String");
53    dclUser.MaxLength = 50;
54    dclUser.AllowDBNull = false;
55    dclUser.Unique = true;
56    // Add column to data table structure
57    dtbUser.Columns.Add(dclUser);
58    dclUser = new DataColumn();
59    dclUser.ColumnName = "Password";
60    dclUser.DataType = Type.GetType("System.String");
61    dclUser.MaxLength = 50;
62    dclUser.AllowDBNull = false;
63    // Add column to data table structure
64    dtbUser.Columns.Add(dclUser);
65 }
```

The example code in Listing 3B-11 uses the **DataColumn** and **DataRow** classes as well as the **DataTable** class. The **DataRow** class is covered later in this chapter. The data table created in the listing can now be used for storage using the **Add** method of the **Rows** collection of the **DataTable** and/or you can add the data table to a **DataSet**. This is the "manual" way of doing it, but you can also do it the "normal" way, as shown in the following section.

Populating a DataTable

Populating a **DataTable** can be done in various ways. You can manually add rows to the data table by creating a **DataRow** object, set the column values, and then add it to the data table using the **Add** method of the **Rows** property. There is an example of how to create your own **DataTable** in Listing 3B-11.

Otherwise you can use the **Fill** method of the DataAdapter class for this purpose, as demonstrated in the next section.

Clearing Data from a DataTable

When you've added relations, constraints, and so on to a data table, or what makes up the structure in your data table, you frequently need a way of clearing all the data from the data table. This is quite easy and it can be accomplished using the **Clear** method, as shown in the following example:

```
dtbUser.Clear();
```

Copying a DataTable

It is sometimes necessary to copy a data table. If you need to manipulate some data for testing purposes, work on a copy of a data table in order to leave the original data intact. Depending on what you actually need to do, there are two ways you can approach this: you can copy just the data structure (similar to working with a data set), or you can copy the data structure and the data within it. See the example code for both techniques in the next two sections.

Copying the Data Structure of a DataTable

If you need to copy the data structure of a **DataTable**, without also copying the data in it, you can use the **Clone** method. See Listing 3B-12 for an example of copying the data structure of a **DataTable**.

*Listing 3B-12. Cloning the Data Structure from a **DataTable***

```
1 public void CloneDataTableStructure() {
2      SqlConnection cnnUserMan;
3      SqlCommand cmmUser;
4      SqlDataAdapter dadUser;
5      DataTable dtbUser;
6      DataTable dtbClone;
7
8      // Instantiate and open the connection
9      cnnUserMan = new SqlConnection(STR_CONNECTION_STRING);
10     cnnUserMan.Open();
11     // Instantiate the command and data table
12     cmmUser = new SqlCommand("SELECT * FROM tblUser", cnnUserMan);
13     dtbUser = new DataTable();
14     // Instantiate and initialize the data adapter
15     dadUser = new SqlDataAdapter("SELECT * FROM tblUser", cnnUserMan);
16     dadUser.SelectCommand = cmmUser;
17     // Fill the data table
18     dadUser.Fill(dtbUser);
19     // Clone the data table
20     dtbClone = dtbUser.Clone();
21 }
```

Copying the Data and Structure of a DataTable

When you need a complete copy of the data structure and data contained therein from a data table, you can use the **Copy** method for this purpose, as shown in Listing 3B-13.

*Listing 3B-13. Copying the Data Structure and Data from a **DataTable***

```
1 public void CopyDataTable() {
2      SqlConnection cnnUserMan;
3      SqlCommand cmmUser;
4      SqlDataAdapter dadUser;
5      DataTable dtbUser;
6      DataTable dtbCopy;
7
8      // Instantiate and open the connection
9      cnnUserMan = new SqlConnection(STR_CONNECTION_STRING);
10     cnnUserMan.Open();
11     // Instantiate the command and data tables
12     cmmUser = new SqlCommand("SELECT * FROM tblUser", cnnUserMan);
```

```
13    dtbUser = new DataTable();
14    // Instantiate and initialize the data adapter
15    dadUser = new SqlDataAdapter("SELECT * FROM tblUser", cnnUserMan);
16    dadUser.SelectCommand = cmmUser;
17    // Fill the data table
18    dadUser.Fill(dtbUser);
19    // Copy the data table
20    dtbCopy = dtbUser.Copy();
21 }
```

Searching a DataTable and Retrieving a Filtered Data View

The only direct method for finding a specific row in the **DataTable** class is the **Select** method. However, this method is only useful when you want to retrieve specific rows and manipulate them in a separate array of **DataRow** objects. So, if you were to retrieve all users with the last name Doe, as in Listing 3B-14, but you wanted these rows in an array of **DataRow** objects, you would do it this way:

```
DataRow[]arrdrwFilter;

arrdrwFilter = dtbUser.Select("LastName = 'Doe'");
```

Please note that the **Select** method can also be used for other purposes, such as retrieving all rows that haven't been changed. You can specify the **RowState** of the rows you want to return. Check out the **Select** method in Table 3B-5 earlier in this chapter.

Instead of looking at the **DataTable** class for direct properties or methods to help you locate a specific row, you can achieve this with the help of the **DefaultView** property. This property—or should I say class, as the property returns or sets a **DataView** object—has a **RowFilter** property that works pretty much the same as the **Filter** property of an ADO **Recordset** object. See Listing 3B-14 for some example code that filters all the users in the tblUser table with the last name of Doe.

*Listing 3B-14. Searching in a **DataTable** Class*

```
 1 public void SearchDataTable() {
 2     SqlConnection cnnUserMan;
 3     SqlCommand cmmUser;
 4     SqlDataAdapter dadUser;
 5     DataTable dtbUser;
 6
 7     // Instantiate and open the connection
 8     cnnUserMan = new SqlConnection(STR_CONNECTION_STRING);
 9     cnnUserMan.Open();
10     // Instantiate the command and data table
11     cmmUser = new SqlCommand("SELECT * FROM tblUser", cnnUserMan);
12     dtbUser = new DataTable();
13     // Instantiate and initialize the data adapter
14     dadUser = new SqlDataAdapter("SELECT * FROM tblUser", cnnUserMan);
15     dadUser.SelectCommand = cmmUser;
16     // Fill the data table
17     dadUser.Fill(dtbUser);
18     // Filter the data table view
19     dtbUser.DefaultView.RowFilter = "LastName = 'Doe'";
20
21     // Loop through all the rows in the data table view
22     for (int intCounter = 0; intCounter <= dtbUser.DefaultView.Count - 1;
23         intCounter++) {
24         MessageBox.Show(
25             dtbUser.DefaultView[0].Row["LastName"].ToString());
26     }
27 }
```

Please note that the number of visible rows in the data table itself does NOT change when you filter the data table view as in the preceding listing. If you were to check the number of rows in the data table (using dtbUser.Rows.Count()) before and after the filtering, the number would be the same.

Copying Rows in a DataTable

Sometimes you need to copy one or more rows from one table to another, or even duplicate one or more rows in the same table. This is indeed possible and can even be done using different methods of the **DataTable** class. See Listing 3B-15 for an example of how to copy rows in a **DataTable**.

*Listing 3B-15. Copying Rows in a **DataTable***

```
 1 public void CopyRowsInDataTable() {
 2     SqlConnection cnnUserMan;
 3     SqlCommand cmmUser;
 4     SqlDataAdapter dadUser;
 5     DataTable dtbUser;
 6     SqlCommandBuilder cmbUser;
 7
 8     // Instantiate and open the connection
 9     cnnUserMan = new SqlConnection(STR_CONNECTION_STRING);
10     cnnUserMan.Open();
11     // Instantiate the command and data table
12     cmmUser = new SqlCommand("SELECT * FROM tblUser", cnnUserMan);
13     dtbUser = new DataTable();
14     // Instantiate and initialize the data adapter
15     dadUser = new SqlDataAdapter("SELECT * FROM tblUser", cnnUserMan);
16     dadUser.SelectCommand = cmmUser;
17     cmbUser = new SqlCommandBuilder(dadUser);
18     // Fill the data table
19     dadUser.Fill(dtbUser);
20
21     // Copy a row from the same table using ImportRow method
22     dtbUser.ImportRow(dtbUser.Rows[0]);
23     // Make sure the Update method detects the new row
24     dtbUser.Rows[dtbUser.Rows.Count - 1]["LoginName"] = "NewLogin1";
25
26     // Copy the first row from the same table using the LoadDataRow
27     // If you change the last argument of this method to true, the
28     // RowState property will be set to Unchanged
29     dtbUser.LoadDataRow(new Object[7] {null, dtbUser.Rows[0]["ADName"],
30         dtbUser.Rows[0]["ADSID"], dtbUser.Rows[0]["FirstName"],
31         dtbUser.Rows[0]["LastName"], "NewLogin2",
32         dtbUser.Rows[0]["Password"]}, false);
33
34     // Loop through all the rows in the data table,
35     // displaying the Id and RowState value
36     for (int intCounter = 0; intCounter <= dtbUser.Rows.Count - 1;
37         intCounter++) {
38         MessageBox.Show(dtbUser.Rows[intCounter]["Id"].ToString() + " " +
39             dtbUser.Rows[intCounter].RowState.ToString());
40     }
41
42     // Update the data source
43     dadUser.Update(dtbUser);
44 }
```

In Listing 3B-15, you can see how to copy one or more rows in a **DataTable**. I am using the **ImportRow** method on Line 22 to import a row from the same table, but you can just as well import a row from a different table, as long as the schema is compatible with the **DataTable** you're trying to import the row into. There is, however, one problem with the **ImportRow** method or one thing you should be aware of: the **ImportRow** method copies everything as it is, it doesn't change anything. This means that if the row's **RowState** property is set to **Unchanged**, the **Update** method of the DataAdapter class (Line 43) won't detect the new row, even if you just added it. Basically, you'll have to change a value in the row after importing it as is done on Line 24. Now the **RowState** property value changes to **Modified**. The **Update** method on Line 43 will then detect a change, but will it add the new row? No, it will update the original row, because the ID of the new row is still the same and the **RowState** is **Modified**. You can see that from the message boxes, if you run the example code. What I'm trying to say here is that you shouldn't be using the **ImportRow** method to copy a row. It's too much hassle, if you're going to propagate the changes back to the data source. The method is just fine for temporary data storage or even for output to a different data source.

You can use the **LoadDataRow** method instead as I've done on Lines 29 through 32, where I simply copy the content of the first row into the new row. I pass a **null** value in the case of the ID, because this is automatically generated by the data source.

Examining the Order of Column and Row Change Events

Both the **DataRow** and **DataColumn** classes expose change events that you can respond to before and after the change takes place. You'll find a detailed description of these events in the following sections, but in general it's useful to know in which order the events are triggered, so I'll list that order here:

1. **DataRow.Changing**
2. **DataRow.Changed**
3. **DataColumn.Changing**
4. **DataColumn.Changed**
5. **DataRow.Changing**
6. **DataRow.Changed**

Although this is the order in which the change events occur, it doesn't indicate there's a one-to-one correspondence. This means that the various events don't happen one at a time in the shown order, because the **DataRow.Changing** and **DataRow.Changed** events happen multiple times for each column changed in the **DataTable**. Please read on and follow/run the example code in the following sections carefully. You might be in for a surprise.

Handling Column Changes

Sometimes it's desirable to be able to control the process of updating the values in the columns in the rows of your **DataTable**. Unlike ADO, ADO.NET gives you very good control over the process. Basically, there are two events that are tied to the column value change process; **ColumnChanging** and **ColumnChanged**. As you've probably guessed from the event names, you can use the former for controlling the process before the column value is changed and the latter for controlling the process after the column value has been changed. Both events give you access to the following properties: the **DataColumn** in which a value is being or has been changed (**Column** property), the new value for the **DataColumn** (**ProposedValue** property), and the **DataRow** in which the **DataColumn** is located (**Row** property). See Listing 3B-16 for an example of how to set up and handle the column changes.

*Listing 3B-16. Handling Column Changes in a **DataTable***

```
1 private static void OnColumnChanging(object sender,
2    DataColumnChangeEventArgs e) {
3    // Display a message showing some of the Column properties
4    MessageBox.Show("Column Properties:\n\n" +
5       "ColumnName: " + e.Column.ColumnName + "\n" +
6       "DataType: " + e.Column.DataType.ToString() + "\n"  +
7       "CommandType: " + e.Column.Table.ToString() + "\n"  +
8       "Original Value: " + e.Row[e.Column.ColumnName,
9       DataRowVersion.Original].ToString() + "\n"  +
10      "Proposed Value: " + e.ProposedValue.ToString(),
11      "ColumnChanging", MessageBoxButtons.OK,
12      MessageBoxIcon.Information);
13 }
14
15 private static void OnColumnChanged(object sender,
16    DataColumnChangeEventArgs e) {
17    // Display a message showing some of the Column properties
18    MessageBox.Show("Column Properties:\n\n" +
19       "ColumnName: " + e.Column.ColumnName + "\n" +
```

```
20        "DataType: " + e.Column.DataType.ToString() + "\n"   +
21        "CommandType: " + e.Column.Table.ToString() + "\n"   +
22        "Original Value: " + e.Row[e.Column.ColumnName,
23        DataRowVersion.Original].ToString() + "\n"   +
24        "Proposed Value: " + e.ProposedValue.ToString(),
25        "ColumnChanged", MessageBoxButtons.OK,
26        MessageBoxIcon.Information);
27 }
28
29 public void TriggerColumnChangeEvents() {
30     DataTable dtbUser = new DataTable("tblUser");
31     // Declare and instantiate connection
32     SqlConnection cnnUserMan = new SqlConnection(STR_CONNECTION_STRING);
33     // Declare and instantiate data adapter
34     SqlDataAdapter dadUserMan = new SqlDataAdapter("SELECT * FROM tblUser",
35         cnnUserMan);
36     // Set up event handlers
37     dtbUser.ColumnChanging += new
38         DataColumnChangeEventHandler(OnColumnChanging);
39     dtbUser.ColumnChanged += new
40         DataColumnChangeEventHandler(OnColumnChanged);
41
42     // Open the connection
43     cnnUserMan.Open();
44     // Populate the data table
45     dadUserMan.Fill(dtbUser);
46     // Modify second row, this triggers the Column Change events
47     dtbUser.Rows[1]["FirstName"] = "Tom";
48 }
```

In Listing 3B-16, I have the **TriggerColumnChangeEvents** procedure (Lines 29 through 48) that sets up the event handlers for the **ColumnChanging** and **ColumnChanged** events (Lines 37 through 40). On Line 47, I trigger these events by setting the FirstName column of the second row to a new value, "Tom". This invokes the **OnColumnChanging** and **OnColumnChanged** procedures in that order. These procedures (Lines 1 through 27) display the properties that are accessible from the **DataColumnChangeEventArgs** argument. Basically, you have the opportunity to inspect all the properties of the column, which is having its value changed, and even change it should you want to do that. See the "Using the DataColumn Class" section later in this chapter for more information on the **DataColumn** class. You can also access the **DataRow** that the column belongs to, through the **Row** property. Finally, because you have access to all these properties before and after the change, you're in full control of the change, and you can apply any logic to the change procedures.

Handling Row Changes

As is the case with changes to the value in a particular column, it certainly can
be desirable to be able to control the process of updating the rows of your
DataTable. Basically, there are two events that are tied to the row change process:
RowChanging and **RowChanged**. As you can gather from the event names, you
can use the former for controlling the process before the row is changed and the
latter for controlling the process after the row has been changed. Both events give
you access to the following properties: the **DataRow** in which the change occurs
(**Row** property), and a **DataRowAction** enum member that indicates what action
is being processed (**Action** property). See Listing 3B-17 for an example of how to
set up and handle the row changes.

*Listing 3B-17. Handling Row Changes in a **DataTable***

```
1 private static void OnRowChanging(object sender, DataRowChangeEventArgs e) {
2     // Display a message showing some of the Row properties
3     MessageBox.Show("Row Properties:\n\n" +
4         "RowState: " + e.Row.RowState.ToString() + "\n" +
5         "Table: " + e.Row.Table.ToString() + "\n" +
6         "Action: " + e.Action.ToString(),
7         "RowChanging", MessageBoxButtons.OK,
8         MessageBoxIcon.Information);
9 }
10
11 private static void OnRowChanged(object sender, DataRowChangeEventArgs e) {
12     // Display a message showing some of the Row properties
13     MessageBox.Show("Row Properties:\n\n" +
14         "RowState: " + e.Row.RowState.ToString() + "\n" +
15         "Table: " + e.Row.Table.ToString() + "\n" +
16         "Action: " + e.Action.ToString(),
17         "RowChanged", MessageBoxButtons.OK,
18         MessageBoxIcon.Information);
19 }
20
21 public void TriggerRowChangeEvents() {
22     DataTable dtbUser = new DataTable("tblUser");
23     // Declare and instantiate connection
24     SqlConnection cnnUserMan = new SqlConnection(STR_CONNECTION_STRING);
25     // Declare and instantiate data adapter
26     SqlDataAdapter dadUserMan = new SqlDataAdapter("SELECT * FROM tblUser",
27         cnnUserMan);
28     // Set up event handlers
29     dtbUser.RowChanging += new DataRowChangeEventHandler(OnRowChanging);
```

```
30      dtbUser.RowChanged += new DataRowChangeEventHandler(OnRowChanged);

31

32      // Open the connection
33      cnnUserMan.Open();
34      // Populate the data table
35      dadUserMan.Fill(dtbUser);
36      // Modify second row, this triggers the row Change events
37      dtbUser.Rows[1]["FirstName"] = "Tom";
38 }
```

In Listing 3B-17, I have the **TriggerRowChangeEvents** procedure (Lines 21 through 38) that sets up the event handlers for the **RowChanging** and **RowChanged** events (Lines 29 through 30). On Lines 37, I trigger these events by setting the FirstName column of the second row to a new value, "Tom". This invokes the **OnRowChanging** and **OnRowChanged** procedures in that order, just like what happens with the column change events in Listing 3B-16. These procedures (Lines 1 through 19) display the properties that are accessible from the **DataRowChangeEventArgs** argument. Basically, you have the opportunity to inspect all the properties of the row, which is being changed, and even change it should you want to do that. See the "Using the DataRow Class" section later in this chapter for more information on the **DataRow** class. Finally, because you have access to all these properties before and after the change, you're in full control of the change, and you can apply any logic to the change procedures.

One thing that is different for the row change events compared to the column change events is the number of times they're being called. Try out the example code and notice how the **Action** and **RowState** property changes for every call. It's interesting.

Handling Row Deletions

As with the column changes and row changes, you can control the process of deleting the rows of your **DataTable**. Basically, two events are tied to the row delete process: **RowDeleting** and **RowDeleted**. You can use the former for controlling the process before the row is deleted and the latter for controlling the process after the row has been deleted. Both events give you access to the following properties: the **DataRow** in which the change occurs (**Row** property), and a **DataRowAction** enum member that indicates what action is being processed (**Action** property). See Listing 3B-18 for an example of how to set up and handle the row changes.

*Listing 3B-18. Handling Row Deletions in a **DataTable***

```
 1 private static void OnRowDeleting(object sender, DataRowChangeEventArgs e) {
 2     // Display a message showing some of the Row properties
 3     MessageBox.Show("Row Properties:\n\n" +
 4         "RowState: " + e.Row.RowState.ToString() + "\n" +
 5         "Table: " + e.Row.Table.ToString() + "\n" +
 6         "Action: " + e.Action.ToString(),
 7         "RowChanging", MessageBoxButtons.OK,
 8         MessageBoxIcon.Information);
 9 }
10
11 private static void OnRowDeleted(object sender, DataRowChangeEventArgs e) {
12     // Display a message showing some of the Row properties
13     MessageBox.Show("Row Properties:\n\n" +
14         "RowState: " + e.Row.RowState.ToString() + "\n" +
15         "Table: " + e.Row.Table.ToString() + "\n" +
16         "Action: " + e.Action.ToString(),
17         "RowChanged", MessageBoxButtons.OK,
18         MessageBoxIcon.Information);
19 }
20
21 public void TriggerRowDeleteEvents() {
22     DataTable dtbUser = new DataTable("tblUser");
23     // Declare and instantiate connection
24     SqlConnection cnnUserMan = new SqlConnection(STR_CONNECTION_STRING);
25     // Declare and instantiate data adapter
26     SqlDataAdapter dadUserMan = new SqlDataAdapter("SELECT * FROM tblUser",
27         cnnUserMan);
28     // Set up event handlers
29     dtbUser.RowDeleting += new DataRowChangeEventHandler(OnRowDeleting);
30     dtbUser.RowDeleted += new DataRowChangeEventHandler(OnRowDeleted);
31
32     // Open the connection
33     cnnUserMan.Open();
34     // Populate the data table
35     dadUserMan.Fill(dtbUser);
36     // Delete second row, this triggers the row delete events
37     dtbUser.Rows[1].Delete();
38 }
```

In Listing 3B-18, I have the **TriggerRowDeleteEvents** procedure (Lines 21 through 38) that sets up the event handlers for the **RowDeleting** and **RowDeleted** events (Lines 29 through 30). On Line 37, I trigger these events by setting deleting the second row. This invokes the **OnRowDeleting** and **OnRowDeleted** procedures in that order, just like it happens with the column change events in Listing 3B-16 and the row change events in Listing 3B-17. These procedures (Lines 1 through 19) display the properties that are accessible from the **DataRowChangeEventArgs** argument. Basically, you have the opportunity to inspect all the properties of the row, which is being deleted, and even change it should you want to do that. See the "Using the DataRow Class" section later in this chapter for more information on the **DataRow** class. Finally, because you have access to all these properties before and after the change, you're in full control of the change, and you can apply any logic to the change procedures.

Using the DataView Class

The **DataView** class is used for having more than just one view, the default view (**DataTable.DefaultView**), of your **DataTable** objects. The **DataView** class is part of the **System.Data** namespace, and as stated, this class is for creating a different view of your **DataTable** than your default view. You can use this class for filtering, sorting/alphabetizing, searching and navigating and even editing the rows in your **DataTable**, and you can create as many **DataView** objects on a **DataTable** as you like. A **DataView** is excellent for creating partial views of a **DataTable** based on what user you're presenting the data for. Some users may see all of the columns in a **DataTable**, whereas others are only allowed to see some of the columns.

Like the **DataSet** and the **DataTable** class, the **DataView** is NOT subclassed, or rather this class will work with whatever provider you are dealing with.

> **NOTE**   *There are no SqlDataView, OdbcDataView, and OleDbDataView classes!*

DataView Properties

The **DataView** class has the properties shown in Table 3B-7 in alphabetical order.
Please note that only the public, noninherited properties are shown.

*Table 3B-7. **DataView** Class Properties*

NAME	DESCRIPTION
AllowDelete	The **AllowDelete** property returns or sets a **bool** value that indicates if deletions in the data view, or rather the underlying **DataTable**, are allowed.
AllowEdit	The **AllowEdit** property returns or sets a **bool** value that indicates if editing of the rows in the data view, or rather the underlying **DataTable**, is allowed.
AllowNew	The **AllowNew** property returns or sets a **bool** value that indicates if you can add new rows to the data view, or rather the underlying **DataTable**, with the **AddNew** method.
ApplyDefaultSort	This property returns or sets a **bool** value that indicates if the default sort should be used.
Count	This read-only property returns the number of visible rows in the view. By visible I mean rows that aren't affected by the settings of the **RowFilter** and **RowStateFilter** properties.
DataViewManager	The **DataViewManager** property is read-only and it returns the **DataViewManager** that is associated with this data view, or rather the data view manager that owns the data set and hence created this data view. **null** is returned if no **DataViewManager** exists.
RowFilter	The **RowFilter** property is a **string** property that retrieves or sets the expression that is used to filter which rows are visible in the **DataView**. See Listing 3B-13 for an example of how to use this property.
RowStateFilter	This property retrieves or sets the row state filter that is used in the **DataView**. This means that you can filter the rows based on their row state, such as **Unchanged**, **Added**, or **Deleted**. The value must be a member of the **DataViewRowState** enum.
Sort	The **Sort** property retrieves or sets the sort column(s) and the sort order for the table. Some people refer to this as alphabetizing. The data type for the **Sort** property is **string**. You specify the columns separated by a comma and then followed by the sort order, **ASC** (default) or **DESC** for ascending or descending, like this: dvwUser.Sort = "LastName DESC, FirstName ASC";.
Table	This property returns or sets the source **DataTable**, meaning the data table that supplies the data view with data. This property can be set only if the current value is **null**.

DataView Methods

Table 3B-8 lists the noninherited and public methods of the **DataView** class in ascending order.

*Table 3B-8. **DataView** Class Methods*

NAME	DESCRIPTION	EXAMPLE
AddNew()	The **AddNew** method adds a new row to the **DataView**. The return value is of data type **DataRowView**. Please note that the **AllowNew** property must be set to **true**, or a **DataException** exception is thrown when you call this method.	drvNew = dvwUser.AddNew();
CopyTo(object[] arrobjCopy, int intStart)	The **CopyTo** method is used for copying the rows from the **DataView** into the **arrobjCopy** array, starting at the **intStart** index. Please note that the array must hold at least one element and that the **intStart** index must be at least one less than the number of elements in the arrobjCopy array.	object[] arrobjCopy = new object[1]; dvwUser.CopyTo(arrobjCopy, 0);
Delete(int intIndex)	This method deletes a row at the specified index, **intIndex**. If you regret deleting a row, you can undo it by calling the **RejectChanges** method on the **DataTable**. You can use the **Find** method to locate the index for a specific row.	dvwUser.Delete(5);
Find()	This overloaded method is used for locating a row in the **DataView** by looking up one or more primary key values.	intIndex = dvwUser.Find(objValue); intIndex = dvwUser.Find(arrobjValues);
FindRows()	This overloaded method is used for returning an array of **DataRowView** objects from the **DataView**, where the column values matches the values in the **object** argument or array of **object**'s argument.	arrdrvMatch = dvwUser.FindRows(objValue); arrdrvMatch = dvwUser.FindRows (arrobjValues);
GetEnumerator()	This method, which can't be overridden, returns an enumerator for navigating through the list. The return value is of data type **IEnumerator**.	enmDataView = dvwUser.GetEnumerator();

DataView Events

The **DataView** class only has one noninherited event; the **ListChanged** event. This event is triggered when the list that the **DataView** manages changes. Changes include additions, deletions, and updates to items in the list. The **ListChanged** event gives you access to the following properties: the type of change that has taken place, indicated by a member of the **ListChangedType** enum (**ListChangedType** property), and the old and new list index, indicated by the two **int OldIndex** and **NewIndex** properties. See Listing 3B-19 for an example of how to set up the **DataView** list changes.

*Listing 3B-19. Handling **DataView** List Changes*

```
 1 protected void OnListChanged(object sender,
 2    System.ComponentModel.ListChangedEventArgs args) {
 3    // Display a message showing some of the List properties
 4    MessageBox.Show("List Properties:\n\n" +
 5        "ListChangedType: " + args.ListChangedType.ToString() + "\n" +
 6        "OldIndex: " + args.OldIndex.ToString() + "\n" +
 7        "NewIndex: " + args.NewIndex.ToString(),
 8        "ListChanged", MessageBoxButtons.OK,
 9        MessageBoxIcon.Information);
10 }
11
12 public void TriggerListChangeEvent() {
13    DataTable dtbUser = new DataTable("tblUser");
14    // Declare and instantiate connection
15    SqlConnection cnnUserMan = new SqlConnection(STR_CONNECTION_STRING);
16    // Declare and instantiate data adapter
17    SqlDataAdapter dadUserMan = new SqlDataAdapter("SELECT * FROM tblUser",
18        cnnUserMan);
19
20    // Open the connection
21    cnnUserMan.Open();
22    // Populate the data table
23    dadUserMan.Fill(dtbUser);
24    // Declare and instantiate data view
25    DataView dvwUser = new DataView(dtbUser);
26    // Set up event handler
27    dvwUser.ListChanged  += new
28        System.ComponentModel.ListChangedEventHandler(OnListChanged);
29    // Trigger list change event by adding new item/row
30    dvwUser.AddNew();
31 }
```

In Listing 3B-19, I have the **TriggerListChangeEvent** procedure (Lines 12 through 31) that sets up the event handler for the **ListChanged** event (Lines 27 through 28). On Line 30, I trigger the event by adding a new row to the **DataView**. This invokes the **OnListChanged** procedure (Lines 1 through 10), which display the properties that are accessible from the **ListChangedEventArgs** argument. You're probably wondering why the underlying **DataTable** is referred to as a list, but my guess is that, besides being a list in an abstract kind of way, the .NET Framework tends to "reuse" a lot of classes and enums. This is also the case here, where the argument **ListChangedEventArgs** comes from the **System.ComponentModel** namespace. If you have a better explanation, do let me know.

Declaring and Instantiating a DataView

There are various ways to instantiate a **DataView** object. You can use the over-loaded class constructors, or you can reference the **DefaultView** property of the **DataTable** object. Here is how you instantiate a data view when you declare it:

```
DataView dvwNoArguments = new DataView();
DataView dvwTableArgument = new DataView(dstUser.Tables("tblUser"));
```

You can also declare it and then instantiate it when you need to, like this:

```
DataView dvwNoArguments;
DataView dvwTableArgument;

dvwNoArguments = new DataView();
dvwTableArgument = new DataView(dstUser.Tables("tblUser"));
```

I've used two different constructors, one with no arguments and one that takes the data table as the only argument. The other option is to first declare the **DataView** object and then have it reference the **DefaultView** property of the **DataTable** object, as shown here:

```
DataView dvwUser;

dvwUser = dstUser.DefaultView();
```

Searching a DataView

You can use the **Find** method for finding a specific row. This method, which is overloaded, takes an object or an array of objects as the only argument. See Listing 3B-20 for some example code that finds the user with an ID of 1 in the tblUser table in the UserMan database.

*Listing 3B-20. Searching in a **DataView** Class*

```
1 public void SearchDataView() {
2      SqlConnection cnnUserMan;
3      SqlCommand cmmUser;
4      SqlDataAdapter dadUser;
5      DataTable dtbUser;
6      DataView dvwUser;
7      Object objPKValue;
8      int intIndex;
9
10     // Instantiate and open the connection
11     cnnUserMan = new SqlConnection(STR_CONNECTION_STRING);
12     cnnUserMan.Open();
13     // Instantiate the command and data table
14     cmmUser = new SqlCommand("SELECT * FROM tblUser", cnnUserMan);
15     dtbUser = new DataTable();
16     // Instantiate and initialize the data adapter
17     dadUser = new SqlDataAdapter("SELECT * FROM tblUser", cnnUserMan);
18     dadUser.SelectCommand = cmmUser;
19     // Fill the data table
20     dadUser.Fill(dtbUser);
21     // Filter the data table view
22     dtbUser.DefaultView.RowFilter = "LastName = 'Doe'";
23     // Create the new data view
24     dvwUser = dtbUser.DefaultView;
25     // Specify a sort order
26     dvwUser.Sort = "Id ASC";
27     // Find the user with an id of 1
28     objPKValue = 1;
29     intIndex = dvwUser.Find(objPKValue);
30 }
```

Even if you can specify as many values as you like in the form of objects in the object array, the values in the array are only intended to be matched with the primary key columns in the **DataView**. It is no good specifying more than one value if your data view only has one primary key column.

Sorting a DataView

If you access the rows in a **DataTable**, they are sorted as they were retrieved from your data source. However, using the **DefaultView** property of the **DataTable**, you can change the way it's sorted. Actually, you don't change the way the **DataTable** is sorted, only the way the rows are accessed using the **DefaultView** property.

See Listing 3B-21 for example code that sorts the rows by **LastName** in ascending order.

*Listing 3B-21. Sorting Rows in a **DataTable/DataView***

```
 1 public void SortDataView() {
 2     SqlConnection cnnUserMan;
 3     SqlCommand cmmUser;
 4     SqlDataAdapter dadUser;
 5     DataTable dtbUser;
 6
 7     // Instantiate and open the connection
 8     cnnUserMan = new SqlConnection(STR_CONNECTION_STRING);
 9     cnnUserMan.Open();
10     // Instantiate the command and data table
11     cmmUser = new SqlCommand("SELECT * FROM tblUser", cnnUserMan);
12     dtbUser = new DataTable();
13     // Instantiate and initialize the data adapter
14     dadUser = new SqlDataAdapter("SELECT * FROM tblUser", cnnUserMan);
15     dadUser.SelectCommand = cmmUser;
16     // Fill the data table
17     dadUser.Fill(dtbUser);
18     // Sort the data table view after LastName in ascending order
19     dtbUser.DefaultView.Sort = "LastName ASC";
20
21     // Loop through all the rows in the data table,
22     // displaying the LastName
23     for (int intCounter = 0; intCounter <= dtbUser.DefaultView.Count - 1;
24         intCounter++) {
25         MessageBox.Show(
26             dtbUser.DefaultView[intCounter]["LastName"].ToString());
27     }
28 }
```

In Listing 3B-21, you can see how you can use the **DefaultView** property of a **DataTable** to sort the rows by **LastName** in ascending order. If you want to sort in descending order, you simply change the ASC on Line 19 to DESC.

Using the DataRow Class

The **DataRow** class is used for representing a single row in the **DataTable** class. The **DataRow** together with the **DataColumn** class are in fact the primary building blocks of the **DataTable** class. This makes sense really, because when you have a table in a database it also consists of rows and columns. So why make this object model any different?

Okay, let's take a look at the properties and methods of this class. Table 3B-9 shows you all the noninherited, public properties of the **DataRow** class.

*Table 3B-9. The **DataRow** Class Properties*

PROPERTY NAME	DESCRIPTION
HasErrors	The **HasErrors** property returns a **bool** value that indicates whether there are any errors in the row or rather columns collection. This property is read-only, but you can use it in conjunction with the **GetColumnsInError** method.
ItemArray	The **ItemArray** property returns or sets the values for all the columns in this **DataRow** object using an array of **object**s.
RowError	This property returns or sets a custom error description for a **DataRow**.
RowState	The **RowState** property, which is read-only, returns the current state of the **DataRow**. The returned value is one of the **DataRowState** enum values. The state of a row is used by the **GetChanges** and **HasChanges** methods.
Table	This read-only property returns the **DataTable** to which the row belongs.

Table 3B-10 shows you all the noninherited, public methods of the **DataRow** class.

Table 3B-10. **DataRow** *Class Methods*

METHOD NAME	DESCRIPTION	EXAMPLE
AcceptChanges()	This method commits all changes made to the **DataRow** since the last time **AcceptChanges** was called or since the row was loaded. The **EndEdit** method is automatically called for any edits in progress.	`drwUser.AcceptChanges();`
BeginEdit()	The **BeginEdit** method starts an edit operation on the **DataRow**. When the row is in edit mode, all events are disabled. This means that you can make changes to the contents of the row, without any events firing or validation rules triggering. Use this method in conjunction with the **EndEdit** method and/or the **CancelEdit** method.	`drwUser.BeginEdit();`
CancelEdit()	This method cancels the current row editing. Use this method in conjunction with the **BeginEdit** method.	`drwUser.CancelEdit();`
ClearErrors()	Use this method to clear all errors for the **DataRow**. This includes the **RowError** property and also errors that have been set with the **SetColumnError** method.	`drwUser.ClearErrors();`
Delete()	This method deletes the **DataRow**. Actually, this isn't entirely true. If the **RowState** of the row is **added**, the row is deleted, but if not, the **RowState** is changed to **Deleted**. This means the row won't actually be deleted until you call the **AcceptChanges** method or the **Update** method on the **DataSet**. This also means that you can undo the deletion of the row by calling the **RejectChanges** method. If you try to delete a row that has already been marked **Deleted**, a **DeletedRowInaccessibleException** exception is thrown.	`drwUser.Delete();`
EndEdit()	This method ends the current editing of the row. Use this method in conjunction with the **BeginEdit** method.	`drwUser.EndEdit();`

(continued)

Table 3B-10. **DataRow** Class Methods (continued)

METHOD NAME	DESCRIPTION	EXAMPLE
GetChildRows()	This overloaded method is used for retrieving the child rows of the **DataRow**. This is done using a **DataRelation** object; the name of a **DataRelation** object; a **DataRelation** object and a **DataRowVersion** object; or the name of a **DataRelation** object and a **DataRowVersion** object. The return value is an array of **DataRow** objects.	arrdrwChildRows = drwUser.GetChildRows (drlUser); arrdrwChildRows = drwUser.GetChildRows (strRelationName); arrdrwChildRows = drwUser.GetChildRows (drlUser, drvUser); arrdrwChildRows = drwUser.GetChildRows (strRelationName, drvUser);
GetColumnError()	This overloaded method returns the error description for the specified column using a **DataColumn** object, an **int**, or a **string**.	strError = drwUser.GetColumnError (dtcName); strError = drwUser.GetColumnError (intColumn); strError = drwUser.GetColumnError (strColumn);
GetColumnsInError()	The **GetColumnsInError** method returns an array of **DataColumn** objects that all have errors. You should use the **HasErrors** method of the **DataRow** object to determine if any errors exist in the row before calling this method.	arrdtcError = drwUser .GetColumnsInError();
GetParentRow()	This overloaded method is used for retrieving the parent row of the **DataRow**. This is done using a **DataRelation** object; the name of a **DataRelation** object; a **DataRelation** object and a **DataRowVersion** object; or the name of a **DataRelation** object and a **DataRowVersion** object.	drwParent = drwUser.GetParentRow (drlUser); drwParent = drwUser.GetParentRow (strRelationName); drwParent = drwUser.GetParentRow (drlUser, drvUser); drwParent = drwUser.GetParentRow (strRelationName, drvUser);

(continued)

Table 3B-10. **DataRow** *Class Methods (continued)*

METHOD NAME	DESCRIPTION	EXAMPLE

GetParentRows()	This overloaded method is used for retrieving the parent rows of the **DataRow**. This is done using a **DataRelation** object; the name of a **DataRelation** object; a **DataRelation** object and a **DataRowVersion** object; or the name of a **DataRelation** object and a **DataRowVersion** object.	`arrdrwParent = drwUser`
		`.GetParentRows(drlUser);`
		`arrdrwParent = drwUser`
		`.GetParentRows`
		`(strRelationName);`
		`arrdrwParent = drwUser`
		`.GetParentRows (drlUser,`
		`drvUser);`
		`arrdrwParent =`
		`drwUser.GetParentRows`
		`(strRelationName, drvUser);`

HasVersion (DataRowVersion drvVersion)	This method returns a **bool** value that indicates if the specified version (**drvVersion**) exists. The argument (**drvVersion**) must be one of the members of the **DataRowVersion** enum.	`blnExist =`
		`drwUser.HasVersion`
		`(DataRowVersion.Default);`

IsNull()	This overloaded method returns a **bool** value that indicates if the specified column contains a null value.	`blnNull =`
		`drwUser.IsNull(dtcNull);`
		`blnNull = drwUser.IsNull`
		`(intColumn);`
		`blnNull =`
		`drwUser.IsNull(strColumn);`
		`blnNull =`
		`drwUser.IsNull(dtcNull,`
		`drwVersion);`

RejectChanges()	Rejects all changes made to the row since **AcceptChanges** was last called or since the **DataRow** was loaded.	`drwUser.RejectChanges();`

SetColumnError()	The **SetColumnError** method, which is overloaded, sets the error description for the specified column.	`drwUser.SetColumnError`
		`(dtcError, strError);`
		`drwUser.SetColumnError`
		`(intColumn, strError);`
		`or drwUser.SetColumnError`
		`(strColumn, strError);`

SetParentRow()	This overloaded method is used for setting the parent row of the **DataRow**. This is done using a **DataRow** object or using a **DataRow** object and a **DataRelation** object.	`drwUser.SetParentRow`
		`(drwParent)`
		`drwUser.GetParentRow`
		`(drwParent, drlParent);`

Declaring and Instantiating a DataRow

There is only one way to instantiate a **DataRow** object. The **DataRow** object doesn't have a constructor, which means you rely on the **DataTable** to help you out. The **NewRow** method of the **DataTable** is what you need:

```
DataRow drwUser;

drwUser = dtbUser.NewRow();
```

Building Your Own DataRow

In Listing 3B-11, you can see how to create your own **DataRow**. This listing also shows you how to create a **DataTable** that looks like the tblUser table in the UserMan database.

Using the DataColumn Class

The **DataColumn** class is used for representing the schema of a single column in the **DataRow** class. The **DataColumn** class is also said to be the fundamental building block for creating a **DataTable**. Well, you really need to use the **DataColumn** class in conjunction with the **DataRow** class.

The schema of a column consists of information about the data type, if the column can contain **null** values, if it's unique or read-only, and if there are other restrictions on what can be inserted as a value than those placed by the data type and so on.

Let's take a look at the properties of this class (there are no public, noninherited methods). Table 3B-11 shows you all the noninherited, public properties of the **DataColumn** class.

*Table 3B-11. The **DataColumn** Class Properties*

PROPERTY NAME	DESCRIPTION
AllowDBNull	This property retrieves or sets a value that indicates if **null** values are allowed in the column. The data type for the property is **bool** and the default value is **true**.
AutoIncrement	The **AutoIncrement** property retrieves or sets a value that indicates if the column automatically increments the value of the column when a new row is added to the table. The data type for the property is **bool** and the default value is **false**.
AutoIncrementSeed	The **AutoIncrementSeed** property retrieves or sets the starting value or seed for a column where the **AutoIncrement** property is set to **true**. The default value is 1.
AutoIncrementStep	The **AutoIncrementStep** property retrieves or sets the increment that is used by the column when the **AutoIncrement** property is set to **true**. This means the value added to the column value in the column of the row that was added to the table. For example, if the value of the column of the row that was last added is 5 and the increment is 1, then the value of the new column will be 6 (5 + 1).
Caption	This property sets or retrieves the caption for the column. This caption is used by controls that support the display of a column caption. One such control is the Windows **DataGrid** control (**System.Windows.Forms.DataGrid**). This means that instead of displaying the name of the column (**ColumnName**), the caption will be displayed instead. The default value of this property is that of the **ColumnName** property.
ColumnMapping	This property sets or retrieves the **MappingType** of the column. This property is for when the data set, in which the column resides, is saved in XML format.
ColumnName	The **ColumnName** property sets or retrieves the name of the column used in the **DataColumnCollection**. The default is an empty **string**, but once the column is added to a **DataColumnCollection**, the column is automatically assigned a name. This is obviously only true if you haven't already set this property. The name assigned depends on the location in the collection, meaning the first column is given the name "Column1" and the next column the name "Column2", and so on.
DataType	This property is used for setting or retrieving the data type that can be stored in the column. The data type of the column is **Type** and it must be set to one of these .NET Frameworks base data types: **Boolean (bool), Byte (byte), Char (char), DateTime, Decimal (decimal), Double (double), Int16 (short), Int32 (int), Int64 (long), SByte (sbyte), Single (float), String (string), TimeSpan, UInt16 (ushort), UInt32 (uint),** or **UInt64 (ulong)**. You can't set this property if the column is already storing data. One way of setting the property is using the **GetType** method of the **Type** class, like this: `dclUser.DataType = Type.GetType("System.String");`.
DefaultValue	The **DefaultValue** property is obviously for setting or retrieving the default value for the column. This value is used when a new row is created.

(continued)

*Table 3B-11. The **DataColumn** Class Properties (continued)*

PROPERTY NAME	DESCRIPTION
Expression	This property is for retrieving or setting an expression that is used for filtering the rows, creating an aggregate column, or calculating the values in the column.
ExtendedProperties	This property returns the collection of custom properties or custom user information. The returned data type is a **PropertyCollection** class. You can add information to the property collection by using the **Add** method of the collection as follows: `dclUser.ExtendedProperties.Add("New Property", "New Property Value");`.
MaxLength	The **MaxLength** property is for setting or retrieving the maximum length of a text column, meaning the maximum number of characters allowed in the column. This property is ignored for columns that don't hold text values. The default value is -1, which is also the value of this property, if there's no maximum length or if it's unknown.
Namespace	This read-write property holds the namespace for the data column. It is used when you read an XML document into the data set or when you write an XML document from the data set, using either of these methods: **ReadXml**, **ReadXmlSchema**, **WriteXml**, or **WriteXmlSchema**. The namespace is used for scoping the XML elements and attributes in the **DataSet**.
Ordinal	This property returns the position of the column in the **DataColumnCollection** collection. If the column isn't contained in a collection, –1 is returned.
Prefix	This read-write property holds the namespace prefix for the data set. The prefix is used in an XML document for identifying which elements belong to the namespace of the data set object. The namespace is set with the **Namespace** property.
ReadOnly	This property is used for indicating whether the column is to allow changes to the column value, once the row, which the column is part of, has been added to the table. The data type for this property is **bool**, and the default value is **false**.
Table	This property returns the **DataTable** that the column is part of.
Unique	This property is used for indicating if the column values must be unique. This means that no two values in the columns of the rows that make up the table can be the same. The data type for this property is **bool**, and the default value is **false**. A unique constraint is created on the column when this property is set to **true**.

Declaring and Instantiating a DataColumn

There are four ways to instantiate a **DataColumn** object using the column constructor, and they are shown in Listing 3B-22.

*Listing 3B-22. Declaring and Instantiating a **DataColumn***

```
1 public void InstantiateDataColumn() {
2    DataColumn dtcDefaultValues = new DataColumn();
3    DataColumn dtcColumnName = new DataColumn("ColumnName");
4    DataColumn dtcColumnNameAndDataType = new DataColumn("ColumnName",
5        Type.GetType("System.String"));
6    DataColumn dtcColumnNameAndDataTypeAndExpression = new
7        DataColumn("ColumnName", Type.GetType("System.String"),
8        "ColumnName + 'Extra Text'");
9    DataColumn dtcColumnNameAndDataTypeAndExpressionAndMappingType = new
10       DataColumn("ColumnName", Type.GetType("System.Int32"),
11       "ColumName + 10", MappingType.Attribute);
12 }
```

Which constructor you choose to use is really a matter of preference, because you can set the properties, which you specify in the constructor, after you've instantiated the column object. The constructor used on Line 2 is the simplest and in most cases you'll need to specify the properties afterwards. The constructor used on Lines 9 through 11 is for specifying the mapping type, which is used when the data set is saved as an XML document.

Using the DataRelation Class

The **DataRelation** class is used for representing a parent/child relationship between two **DataTable**s. This is done through "linking" one or more matching[3] **DataColumn** objects from each of the **DataTable** objects. The relationships can be cascading, meaning that changes to the parent table, such as deletions, can be cascaded to the child table, effectively making sure no child rows are ever orphaned.

---

3. Matching in this case means that the data type of the columns must be the same in both **DataTable** objects.

The **DataRelation** objects of a **DataTable** are contained in the **DataRelationCollection**, which you can access through a **DataTable**'s **ParentRelations** or **ChildRelations** property. In a **DataSet**, you can access all **DataRelation**s through the **Relations** property.

DataRelation Exceptions

When you create and set up a **DataRelation** object, the data in the linking columns in both the parent and child **DataTable**s are verified, making sure that the relation can be made between the two **DataTable**s. If there are data in any of the columns that violate the constraints that the relation enforces, an exception is thrown. The exception is one of the following:

- **ArgumentNullException**, thrown when one or both of the related columns contains a **null** value.

- **InvalidConstraintException**, thrown if the two related **DataTable**s aren't located in the same **DataSet**, or if the data types of the related columns are different.

Table 3B-12 shows you all the noninherited, public properties of the **DataRelation** class.

*Table 3B-12. The **DataRelation** Class Properties*

PROPERTY NAME	DESCRIPTION
ChildColumns	The **ChildColumns** property, which is read-only, retrieves the child columns for the relationship. The child columns are returned as an array of **DataColumn** objects.
ChildKeyConstraint	This read-only property retrieves the foreign key constraints for the relationship. The return value is of data type **ForeignKeyConstraint**.
ChildTable	The read-only **ChildTable** property retrieves the relationships' child table. The child table is returned as an object of data type **DataTable**.
DataSet	This read-only property retrieves the **DataSet** to which the relationship belongs.
ExtendedProperties	The **ExtendedProperties** property, which is read-only, retrieves the customized properties. The customized properties are returned as a **PropertyCollection** object.
Nested	This property sets or retrieves a **bool** value that indicates if the **DataRelation** object is nested. Nesting can be in connection with hierarchical data, such as XML documents.
ParentColumns	The **ParentColumns** property, which is read-only, retrieves the parent columns for the relationship. The parent columns are returned as an array of **DataColumn** objects.
ParentKeyConstraint	This read-only property retrieves the unique key constraints for the relationship. The return value is of data type **UniqueConstraint**.
ParentTable	The read-only **ParentTable** property retrieves the relationships' parent table. The parent table is returned as an object of data type **DataTable**.
RelationName	This property sets or retrieves the name that is used for retrieving a **DataRelation** from the **DataRelationCollection** (see the **Relations** property of the **DataSet** class).

Declaring and Instantiating a DataRelation

There are five ways to instantiate a **DataRelation** object using the column constructor, and they are shown in Listing 3B-23.

*Listing 3B-23. Declaring and Instantiating a **DataRelation***

```
1 public void InstantiateDataRelation() {
2    // Declare parent and child columns for use in relationship
3    DataColumn dtcParentColumn = new DataColumn("ParentColumn");
```

```
 4    DataColumn dtcChildColumn = new DataColumn("ChildColumn");
 5    // Declare and initialize array of parent and child
 6    // columns for use in relationship
 7    DataColumn[] arrdtcParentColumn = new DataColumn[2];
 8    DataColumn[] arrdtcChildColumn = new DataColumn[2];
 9    arrdtcParentColumn[0] = new DataColumn("ParentColumn1");
10    arrdtcParentColumn[1] = new DataColumn("ParentColumn2");
11    arrdtcChildColumn[0] = new DataColumn("ChildColumn1");
12    arrdtcChildColumn[1] = new DataColumn("ChildColumn2");
13
14    // This constructor will fail, unless you add the
15    // specified parent and child columns to a table
16    DataRelation dtrParentColumnAndChildColumn =
17        new DataRelation("RelationName", dtcParentColumn,
18        dtcChildColumn);
19    // This constructor will fail, unless you add the
20    // specified parent and child columns to a table
21    DataRelation dtrParentColumnAndChildColumnAndConstraints =
22        new DataRelation("RelationName", dtcParentColumn,
23        dtcChildColumn, false);
24
25    // This constructor will fail, unless you add the
26    // specified arrays of parent and child columns to a table
27    DataRelation dtrParentColumnsAndChildColumns =
28        new DataRelation("RelationName", arrdtcParentColumn,
29        arrdtcChildColumn, false);
30    // This constructor will fail, unless you add the
31    // specified arrays of parent and child columns to a table
32    DataRelation dtrParentColumnsAndChildColumnsAndConstraints =
33        new DataRelation("RelationName", arrdtcParentColumn,
34        arrdtcChildColumn, false);
35
36    // This constructor takes string values for all arguments
37    // except for the last argument, Nested. This argument is
38    // used for indicating if this relation is used in connection
39    // with hierarchical data, like an XML document
40    DataRelation dtrStringsAndNested =
41        new DataRelation("RelationName", "ParentTableName",
42        "ChildTableName", new string[1] {"PrimaryKeyColumn1"},
43        new string[1] {"ForeignKeyColumn1"}, false);
44 }
```

In Listing 3B-23, you can see the five different constructors for the
DataRelation class. Lines 2 through 12 are simply used for declaring and instan-
tiating columns and arrays of columns used when instantiating the relationships.
All five constructors take the name of the relationship as the first argument, but
this is really the only thing they all have in common. Please note that it's possible
to pass an empty **string** ("") as the first argument, in which case the
DataRelation object is given a default name when it's added to the
DataRelationCollection of the **DataSet**.

The constructor used on Lines 16 through 18 for the
dtrParentColumnAndChildColumn **DataRelation** object takes a single parent and
child column as arguments. You should use this constructor when you are creating a relationship between two tables, where you have single column primary
and foreign keys. Please see the "What Are Keys?" section in Chapter 2, if you
need more information on primary and foreign keys.

Now, you want an example of how to create relationships, don't you? That's
a rhetorical question, so in Listing 3B-24, I've created the UserMan example database from scratch, using a **DataSet** object, four **DataTable** objects, and **DataRow**,
DataColumn, and **DataRelation** objects.

*Listing 3B-24. Building the UserMan Database as **DataSet***

```
1 public void BuildUserManDatabase() {
2     // Declare and instantiate data set
3     DataSet dstUserMan = new DataSet("UserMan");
4     // Declare and instantiate tables in data set
5     DataTable dtbUser = new DataTable("tblUser");
6     DataTable dtbRights = new DataTable("tblRights");
7     DataTable dtbUserRights = new DataTable("tblUserRights");
8     DataTable dtbLog = new DataTable("tblLog");
9     // Declare table elements
10    DataColumn dclUser, dclRights, dclUserRights, dclLog;
11    DataColumn[] arrdclUserPrimaryKey, arrdclRightsPrimaryKey,
12        arrdclUserRightsPrimaryKey, arrdclLogPrimaryKey;
13    // Declare table relations
14    DataRelation dtrUser2Log, dtrUser2UserRights, dtrRights2UserRights;
15
16    // Set data set namespace for saving to XML
17
18    dstUserMan.Namespace = "UserMan";
19    // Create user table structure
20    // Create Id column
21    dclUser = new DataColumn("Id", Type.GetType("System.Int32"),"",
22        MappingType.Element);
23    // Make the Id column an auto increment column, incrementing by 1
```

```
24    // every time a new row is added to the table, with a seed of 1
25    dclUser.AutoIncrement = true;
26    dclUser.AutoIncrementSeed = 1;
27    dclUser.AutoIncrementStep = 1;
28    // Disallow null values in column
29    dclUser.AllowDBNull = false;
30    // Add Id column to user table structure
31    dtbUser.Columns.Add(dclUser);
32    // Create single-column primary key
33    arrdclUserPrimaryKey = new DataColumn[1];
34    // Add Id column to PK array
35    arrdclUserPrimaryKey[0] = dclUser;
36    // Set primary key
37    dtbUser.PrimaryKey = arrdclUserPrimaryKey;
38
39    // Create ADName column
40    dclUser = new DataColumn("ADName", Type.GetType("System.String"));
41    dclUser.MaxLength = 100;
42    // Add column to user table structure
43    dtbUser.Columns.Add(dclUser);
44
45    // Create ADSID column
46    dclUser = new DataColumn("ADSID", Type.GetType("System.String"));
47    // Add column to user table structure
48    dtbUser.Columns.Add(dclUser);
49
50    // Create FirstName column
51    dclUser = new DataColumn("FirstName", Type.GetType("System.String"));
52    dclUser.MaxLength = 50;
53    // Add column to user table structure
54    dtbUser.Columns.Add(dclUser);
55
56    // Create LastName column
57    dclUser = new DataColumn("LastName", Type.GetType("System.String"));
58    dclUser.MaxLength = 50;
59    // Add column to user table structure
60    dtbUser.Columns.Add(dclUser);
61
62    // Create LoginName column
63    dclUser = new DataColumn("LoginName", Type.GetType("System.String"));
64    // Disallow null values in column
65    dclUser.AllowDBNull = false;
66    // Disallow duplicate values in column
```

```
67      dclUser.Unique = true;
68      dclUser.MaxLength = 50;
69      // Add column to user table structure
70      dtbUser.Columns.Add(dclUser);
71
72      // Create Password column
73      dclUser = new DataColumn("Password", Type.GetType("System.String"));
74      // Disallow null values in column
75      dclUser.AllowDBNull = false;
76      dclUser.MaxLength = 50;
77      // Add column to user table structure
78      dtbUser.Columns.Add(dclUser);
79
80      // Add User table to dataset
81      dstUserMan.Tables.Add(dtbUser);
82
83      // Create Rights table structure
84      // Create Id column
85      dclRights = new DataColumn("Id", Type.GetType("System.Int32"),"",
86          MappingType.Element);
87      // Make the Id column an auto increment column, incrementing by 1
88      // every time a new row is added to the table, with a seed of 1
89      dclRights.AutoIncrement = true;
90      dclRights.AutoIncrementSeed = 1;
91      dclRights.AutoIncrementStep = 1;
92      // Disallow null values in column
93      dclRights.AllowDBNull = false;
94      // Add Id column to Rights table structure
95      dtbRights.Columns.Add(dclRights);
96      // Create single-column primary key
97      arrdclRightsPrimaryKey = new DataColumn[1];
98      // Add Id column to PK array
99      arrdclRightsPrimaryKey[0] = dclRights;
100     // Set primary key
101     dtbRights.PrimaryKey = arrdclRightsPrimaryKey;
102
103     // Create Name column
104     dclRights = new DataColumn("Name", Type.GetType("System.String"));
105     dclUser.MaxLength = 50;
106     // Add column to Rights table structure
107     dtbRights.Columns.Add(dclRights);
108
109     // Create Description column
```

```
110    dclRights = new DataColumn("Description", Type.GetType("System.String"));
111    dclUser.MaxLength = 255;
112    // Add column to Rights table structure
113    dtbRights.Columns.Add(dclRights);
114
115    // Add Rights table to dataset
116    dstUserMan.Tables.Add(dtbRights);
117
118    // Create Log table structure
119    // Create Id column
120    dclLog = new DataColumn("Id", Type.GetType("System.Int32"),"",
121       MappingType.Element);
122    // Make the Id column an auto increment column, incrementing by 1
123    // every time a new row is added to the table, with a seed of 1
124    dclLog.AutoIncrement = true;
125    dclLog.AutoIncrementSeed = 1;
126    dclLog.AutoIncrementStep = 1;
127    // Disallow null values in column
128    dclLog.AllowDBNull = false;
129    // Add Id column to Log table structure
130    dtbLog.Columns.Add(dclLog);
131    // Create single-column primary key
132    arrdclLogPrimaryKey = new DataColumn[1];
133    // Add Id column to PK array
134    arrdclLogPrimaryKey[0] = dclLog;
135    // Set primary key
136    dtbLog.PrimaryKey = arrdclLogPrimaryKey;
137
138    // Create Logged column
139    dclLog = new DataColumn("Logged", Type.GetType("System.DateTime"));
140    // Add column to Log table structure
141    dtbLog.Columns.Add(dclLog);
142
143    // Create Description column
144    dclLog = new DataColumn("Description", Type.GetType("System.String"));
145    dclUser.MaxLength = 255;
146    // Add column to Log table structure
147    dtbLog.Columns.Add(dclLog);
148
149    // Create UserId column
150    dclLog = new DataColumn("UserId", Type.GetType("System.Int32"),"",
151       MappingType.Element);
152    // Disallow null values in column
```

```
153    dclLog.AllowDBNull = false;
154    // Add UserId column to Log table structure
155    dtbLog.Columns.Add(dclLog);
156
157    // Add Log table to dataset
158    dstUserMan.Tables.Add(dtbLog);
159
160    // Create UserRights table structure
161    // Create UserId column
162    dclUserRights = new DataColumn("UserId", Type.GetType("System.Int32"),"",
163        MappingType.Element);
164    // Disallow null values in column
165    dclUserRights.AllowDBNull = false;
166    // Disallow duplicate values in column
167    dclUserRights.Unique = true;
168    // Add Id column to UserRights table structure
169    dtbUserRights.Columns.Add(dclUserRights);
170
171    // Create composite primary key
172    arrdclUserRightsPrimaryKey = new DataColumn[2];
173    // Add UserId column to PK array
174    arrdclUserRightsPrimaryKey[0] = dclUserRights;
175
176    // Create RightsId column
177    dclUserRights = new DataColumn("RightsId",
178    Type.GetType("System.Int32"),"", MappingType.Element);
179    // Disallow null values in column
180    dclUserRights.AllowDBNull = false;
181    // Disallow duplicate values in column
182    dclUserRights.Unique = true;
183    // Add RightsId column to UserRights table structure
184    dtbUserRights.Columns.Add(dclUserRights);
185
186    // Add RightsId column to PK array
187    arrdclUserRightsPrimaryKey[1] = dclUserRights;
188    // Set primary key
189    dtbUserRights.PrimaryKey = arrdclUserRightsPrimaryKey;
190
191    // Add UserRights table to dataset
192    dstUserMan.Tables.Add(dtbUserRights);
193
194    // Create table relations
195    dtrUser2Log = new DataRelation("User2Log", "tblUser",
```

```
196          "tblLog", new string[1] {"Id"},
197          new string[1] {"UserId"}, false);
198    dtrUser2UserRights = new DataRelation("User2UserRights", "tblUser",
199          "tblUserRights", new string[1] {"Id"},
200          new string[1] {"UserId"}, false);
201    dtrRights2UserRights = new DataRelation("Rights2UserRight", "tblRights",
202          "tblUserRights", new string[1] {"Id"},
203          new string[1] {"RightsId"}, false);
204 }
```

In Listing 3B-24, you can see how I gradually build the entire UserMan database, table-by-table, column-by-column. I set up the primary and foreign keys and add the tables to the dstUserMan **DataSet**. Finally, I create the relations between the tables.

Now, even if the preceding code actually runs, it can be quite hard to "see" what happens, but don't despair: you simply add this line of code to the example code in Listing 3B-24 to write the data set schema to a text file in XML format:

```
dstUserMan.WriteXmlSchema("C:\\UserManDatabase.xml");
```

You can open the file in Internet Explorer to see the XML document with color coding of the nodes, elements, and attributes. You can then compare it to an XML document created the same way, but where the **DataSet** is generated using the DataAdapter class's **Fill** method. See "Populating Your DataSet Using the DataAdapter" earlier in this chapter for more information on how to populate a **DataSet**.

Looking at Cursors

A *cursor* is for use with databases, and it's merely a pointer to a specific row in a result set. This means you have a means of navigating through a result set and working with a specific row, the row the cursor is pointing at. However, a cursor doesn't order the rows in a result set in any way; your query statement does this. Depending on the data class used, the cursor is generally positioned at the first row or just before the first row (see Figure 3B-1) in the result set, when you open it.

In ADO and ADO.NET, a result set is usually represented as a data class such as the ADO **Recordset** object or the ADO.NET DataReader or **DataTable** classes. In ADO, you have a lot of choices for how to deal and work with cursors, whereas your options in ADO.NET are quite limited, meaning you don't have support for server-side cursors (see the "Server-side Cursors" section later in this chapter).

This is because of the disconnected architecture of ADO.NET and its data source independence, but I suspect you'll see some improvement in later versions.

Having unintentionally implied that ADO is better than ADO.NET when it comes to cursors, I also have to add to the equation that any row in the **DataTable** class in ADO.NET can be accessed using an indexer. This means that you can access any row, without moving the cursor to that specific row; you simply specify the zero-based index for the wanted row, and you then have access to the data contained in that particular row.

Many professional developers using Microsoft SQL Server generally don't work with cursors, even if the tools they use give them the option to do so. It's considered bad programming practice to use cursors by many, but personally I can see it both ways.

Anyway, cursors are generally categorized by their characteristics: location and type.

Cursor Location

In regard to location, cursors come in two different flavors: client-side cursors and server-side cursors. As the names imply, they refer to pointers to data on either the client side or server side. There are advantages and disadvantages to both types, as discussed in the following sections.

Client-Side Cursors

Client-side cursors, or local cursors, are used for navigating in a result set located locally, or on the client.[4] This means that all the rows you select in your query and so forth will have to be transferred to the client in one form or another. Depending on the number of rows, this can be costly in terms of network traffic and storage space on the client. Storage space can be memory as well as disk space, depending on the cursor type and/or available memory on the client.

Server-Side Cursors

Server-side cursors, or remote cursors, are used for navigating in a result set located remotely, or on the server. ADO.NET doesn't currently have intrinsic support for the use of server-side cursors, except for the DataReader class (see the

---

4. Please note that even though I specifically state "on the client," I'm really referring to any-where but the database server. This also goes for client-side cursors used at the middle tier, where you might have your data and/or business logic running.

next paragraph), so your only choice here is ADO. The reason may be that the various data sources differ a lot in the way they are implemented. This means it's extremely difficult to expose server-side cursors (and other server-side functionality) in a way that hides the complexity that goes into dealing with many different data sources. What you want is for the server-side cursor to behave and operate the same way, whatever data source you are accessing!

I am sure there will be some server-side functionality in later versions, however. Having said that, note that the DataReader class uses a server-side cursor. Mind you, you can't really control the DataReader class—you can only move forward one row at a time—so what you would normally expect from server-side cursor functionality isn't exactly what you get from the DataReader class.

ADO.NET only uses client-side cursors (except for the DataReader class), whereas you can specify your cursor location preference with ADO. So to cut a long story short, if you need the functionality of server-side cursors, ADO is currently your only choice! Actually, if you are after server-side processing, then look into using stored procedures and triggers, which is discussed in Chapter 6.

Cursor Types

There are numerous cursor types. The following sections briefly describe the ones you can use in ADO and ADO.NET, which are listed here:

- Forward-only cursors

- Static cursors

- Dynamic cursors

- Keyset cursors

Forward-Only Cursors

This cursor type requires the least amount of overhead. As the name suggests, you can only move forward one row at a time in a result set with this kind of cursor. Well, this isn't entirely true—you can close the data class holding the result set and then reopen it to move the cursor to the first row or BOF (Beginning-Of-File), which is just before the first row (see Figure 3B-1).

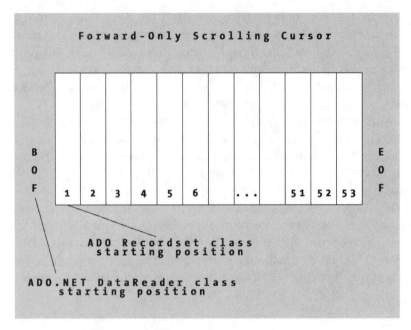

Figure 3B-1. BOF (Beginning-Of-File)

A forward-only cursor is dynamic by default, meaning that when a row is accessed it's read from the data source, so that changes that have been committed to the row after the result set was generated will be seen. This, however, is NOT the case with the ADO.NET DataReader class. Changes to the underlying rows in an open DataReader object can't be seen!

This cursor type is the only one used by the ADO.NET DataReader class, and it's one of four cursor types used by the ADO **Recordset** class.

Static Cursors

A static cursor is exactly what the name says, static! Well, let's get one thing straight: it's the data set that is static, not the cursor, which means that the content of a result set is static, or that the content of the result set won't change after you've opened it. Changes made to the result set after it's opened won't be detected, although changes made by the static cursor itself generally are detected and reflected in the result set, depending on the implementation.

Unlike a forward-only cursor, the static cursor has the ability to scroll both forward and backward. This cursor is one of four cursor types used by the ADO **Recordset** class.

Dynamic Cursors

The dynamic cursor is very good for dealing with concurrency issues, because it detects all changes made to the result set after the cursor is open. The dynamic cursor can of course scroll both forward and backward. The dynamic cursor has the most overhead of the four cursor types described and as such it can prove costly to use, especially in situations where one of the other cursor types can be used instead.

This cursor is one of four cursor types used by the ADO **Recordset** class.

Keyset Cursors

The keyset cursor can be thought of as a cross between a static cursor and a dynamic cursor, because it has functionality that is unique to one or the other. Changes to values in data columns are detected. Insertions made by the cursor will be appended to the result set, whereas insertions made by others will only be visible if the cursor is closed and opened again. Deletions are a completely different ball game when you have a keyset cursor. Deletions made by other cursors can be detected, but deletions made by the keyset cursor itself can't be detected.

This cursor is one of four cursor types used by the ADO **Recordset** class.

Examining Data Source Locking

When you update the data source with changes from your **DataSet** and **DataTable** objects, it's important to know what happens at the data source. It's important because the data you have in your **DataSet** or **DataTable** might not be up to date, meaning that someone else may have changed the data after you retrieved it from the data source. This can be a problem, especially with a disconnected architecture like ADO.NET's, because there's no standard way of locking the rows at the data source that you're manipulating in your **DataSet**. In classic ADO, all depending on your data source, you can specify various types and levels of locking, because ADO has a connected architecture. This isn't the case with ADO.NET, which means that ADO.NET uses what is referred to as *optimistic locking*.

Two kinds of general locking are available, pessimistic locking and optimistic locking, and both of them are described in the coming sections. However, it's always a good idea to minimize the extent of the locking at the data source, because it will cause problems when more than one client or a server process wants to update the data at the same time. On the other hand, it can also be a problem if no locking is applied and one client updates some data, which is later overwritten by another client (typical optimistic locking scenario).

There are no hard and fast rules for how and when you should apply locking at the data source, because it really depends on the application architecture, the number of clients, the update frequency, and so on. So, it's generally up to you as a developer to make the most of what your DBMS and database administrator presents you with in terms of access and locking capabilities, and to provide your users with a minimum of problems in terms of performance, lost or overwritten data, and denied data access caused by locked rows.

Pessimistic Locking

Pessimistic locking, or pessimistic concurrency[5], is a locking type that locks a section of the table at the data source when you request the data[6], effectively denying changes from all other clients, until you've released the locking. The lock is generally put in place when you retrieve the data and released when you disconnect from the data source or release the data you've retrieved. Pessimistic locking can be a good option in environments with a high contention for the data, meaning the data is manipulated frequently and by a large number of clients. However, if a client locks data for more than just a short period, it will most certainly cause problems for other clients that need to access and update the same data.

Although pessimistic locking can't be achieved directly with ADO.NET, you can apply it to your application using transactions. I won't be going into how to use transactions here, as it's covered in Chapter 3A, but what you need to do is to look at how you can use the **IsolationLevel** enum with transactions to achieve some kind of locking at the data source. See Listing 3B-25 for an example on how to do this.

Listing 3B-25. Using Transactions to Lock Data at Data Source

```
1 public void LockDataSourceRowsUsingTransactions() {
2     const string STR_SQL_USER_SELECT = "SELECT * FROM tblUser";
3
4     SqlConnection cnnLocked, cnnUnlocked;
5     SqlDataAdapter dadLocked, dadUnlocked;
6     SqlTransaction traUserMan;
7     SqlCommand cmdSelectUsers;
8     DataSet dstLocked = new DataSet("Locked DataSet");
9     DataSet dstUnlocked = new DataSet("Unlocked DataSet");
```

---

5. Locking really isn't the same as concurrency, but we all have different ideas about concepts such as concurrency. Anyway, although locking is related to concurrency, concurrency is really the requirement for access to data for any reason, meaning it refers as much to reads as to writes.

6. With most kinds of pessimistic concurrency, you have the option of specifying that you only want read-only data returned, which means no locks will be applied at the data source.

```
10
11    // Instantiate and open the connections
12    cnnLocked = new SqlConnection(STR_CONNECTION_STRING);
13    cnnLocked.Open();
14    cnnUnlocked = new SqlConnection(STR_CONNECTION_STRING);
15    cnnUnlocked.Open();
16    // Begin transaction
17    traUserMan = cnnLocked.BeginTransaction(IsolationLevel.Serializable);
18    // Set up select command
19    cmdSelectUsers = new SqlCommand(STR_SQL_USER_SELECT, cnnLocked,
20        traUserMan);
21
22    // Instantiate and initialize data adapters
23    dadLocked = new SqlDataAdapter(STR_SQL_USER_SELECT, cnnLocked);
24    dadLocked.SelectCommand = cmdSelectUsers;
25    dadUnlocked = new SqlDataAdapter(STR_SQL_USER_SELECT, cnnUnlocked);
26    // Declare and instantiate command builders
27    SqlCommandBuilder cmbUser1 = new SqlCommandBuilder(dadLocked);
28    SqlCommandBuilder cmbUser2 = new SqlCommandBuilder(dadUnlocked);
29
30    // Populate the data sets
31    dadLocked.Fill(dstLocked, "tblUser");
32    dadUnlocked.Fill(dstUnlocked, "tblUser");
33
34    // Update an existing row in unlocked data set
35    dstUnlocked.Tables["tblUser"].Rows[2]["FirstName"] = "FirstName";
36
37    try {
38        // Update the unlocked data source
39        dadUnlocked.Update(dstUnlocked, "tblUser");
40        // Commit transaction
41        traUserMan.Commit();
42    }
43    catch (SqlException objE) {
44        // Roll back transaction
45        traUserMan.Rollback();
46        MessageBox.Show(objE.Message);
47    }
48    finally {
49        // Close connections
50        cnnLocked.Close();
51        cnnUnlocked.Close();
52    }
53 }
```

In Listing 3B-25, I set up and use two **SqlDataAdapter** objects, two
SqlConnection objects, two **DataSet** objects, two **SqlCommandBuilder** objects,
one **SqlCommand** object, and one **SqlTransaction** object. Except for
the traUserMan transaction, which is instantiated and started by calling the
BeginTransaction method of the cnnLocked connection object on Line 17, the
two data adapters do the same. However, the transaction object makes the difference by specifying the **Serializable** isolation level enum member, which means
that all rows in the dadLocked **DataSet** will be locked at the data source. Because
the two data adapters work on the same data (they're populated on Lines 31 and
32), the update of the data source with changes made to the dstUnlocked
DataSet, which occurs on Line 39, will fail. The lock placed at the data source
results in a time-out exception when you call the **Update** method on the
dadUnlocked data adapter. The lock doesn't prevent any other client from reading
the same data, only updating and deleting them. See Chapter 3A for more information on the **Transaction** class and the **IsolationLevel** enum.

> **NOTE** *This method works with all three .NET Data Providers described in
> this book (SQL Server .NET Data Provider, OLE DB .NET Data Provider,
> and ODBC .NET Data Provider), provided the underlying data source sup-
> ports transactions and row locking! This effectively rules out Microsoft
> Access and MySQL 3.23.45.*

Optimistic Locking

Optimistic locking, or optimistic concurrency, isn't really a locking concept,
because no locking is applied. When you extract the data from the data source
and into your **DataSet**, any other client with the right permissions can modify
that same data at the data source. If this happens and you later update the same
data, you're effectively overwriting the changes made to the data between the
time you retrieved the data and the time you update it; *last in wins.* Optimistic
locking can help you prevent this and should generally be used when your application has a disconnected architecture, like when accessing data over the
Internet or any other WAN, and when you want a scalable solution that doesn't
lock data at the data source.

ADO.NET uses or rather can use optimistic concurrency, meaning that it's up
to you as a programmer to apply optimistic locking, to avoid the last-in-wins
problem. ADO.NET gives you the "tools" to write your application logic to handle
problems that optimistic locking can cause. Let's say that you retrieve data from
your data source and save it in your **DataSet**, and then you change the data in the
DataSet, while someone else changes the original data at the data source. If you

then try to update the data source with the changes from your **DataSet**, a concurrency violation occurs and the **DBConcurrencyException** is thrown.

> **NOTE** *A concurrency violation only occurs if changes are made to the same row, meaning that you can have two clients update different rows without a **DBConcurrencyException** being thrown. However, the **DBConcurrencyException** is thrown if you update different columns in the same row.*

Listing 3B-26 shows you how to trigger and catch a concurrency violation.

Listing 3B-26. Trigger and Catch Concurrency Violation

```
1 public void TriggerConcurrencyViolation() {
2    const string STR_SQL_USER_SELECT = "SELECT * FROM tblUser";
3
4    SqlConnection cnnUser1, cnnUser2;
5    SqlDataAdapter dadUser1, dadUser2;
6    DataSet dstUser1 = new DataSet("User1 DataSet");
7    DataSet dstUser2 = new DataSet("User2 DataSet");
8
9    // Instantiate and open the connections
10   cnnUser1 = new SqlConnection(STR_CONNECTION_STRING);
11   cnnUser1.Open();
12   cnnUser2 = new SqlConnection(STR_CONNECTION_STRING);
13   cnnUser2.Open();
14
15   // Instantiate and initialize data adapters
16   dadUser1 = new SqlDataAdapter(STR_SQL_USER_SELECT, cnnUser1);
17   dadUser2 = new SqlDataAdapter(STR_SQL_USER_SELECT, cnnUser2);
18   SqlCommandBuilder cmbUser1 = new SqlCommandBuilder(dadUser1);
19   SqlCommandBuilder cmbUser2 = new SqlCommandBuilder(dadUser2);
20
21   // Populate the data sets
22   dadUser1.Fill(dstUser1, "tblUser");
23   dadUser2.Fill(dstUser2, "tblUser");
24
25   // Update an existing row in first data set
26   dstUser1.Tables["tblUser"].Rows[2]["FirstName"] = "FirstName";
27   // Update the data source with changes to the first data set
28   dadUser1.Update(dstUser1, "tblUser");
29   // Update an existing row in second data set
30   dstUser2.Tables["tblUser"].Rows[2]["FirstName"] = "FName";
```

```
31
32    try {
33        // Update the data source with changes to the second data set
34        dadUser2.Update(dstUser2, "tblUser");
35    }
36    catch (DBConcurrencyException objE) {
37        MessageBox.Show(objE.Message);
38    }
39    finally {
40        // Close connections
41        cnnUser1.Close();
42        cnnUser2.Close();
43    }
44 }
```

In Listing 3B-26, I set up two data adapters (Lines 16 through 19) that populate two **DataSet**s (Lines 22 through 23) with the same data from the very same data source. Then, I change the FirstName column of the third row of the tblUser table in the first **DataSet** (Line 26), and propagate the change back to the data source (Line 28). Then, I make a similar change to the second **DataSet** and try to update the data source. Because there has been a change to the original data that you're now trying to update, a concurrency violation occurs. What happens is that the data adapter looks at the original column values in a row (**DataRowVersion.Original**) and compares it with the row that it tries to update at the data source. If any of the column values at the data source are different from the original column values in the **DataSet**, the concurrency violation occurs. Now, as you can see from Listing 3B-26, I'm using two **SqlCommandBuilder** objects (Lines 18 and 19) to automatically generate the INSERT, UPDATE, and DELETE statements. It's actually these statements that take care of generating a **DBConcurrencyException** exception. If you look at the auto generated code for the UPDATE statement, which is the only one needed in the example, you can see how much the CommandBuilder class does for you (the listing has been edited to make it appear nicer, meaning extra spaces have been taken out, etc.):

```
UPDATE tblUser SET ADName=@p1, ADSID=@p2, FirstName=@p3, LastName=@p4,
LoginName=@p5, Password=@p6 WHERE ((Id=@p7) AND ((ADName IS NULL AND @p8 IS
NULL) OR (ADName=@p9)) AND ((ADSID IS NULL AND @p10 IS NULL) OR (ADSID=@p11))
AND ((FirstName IS NULL AND @p12 IS NULL) OR (FirstName=@p13)) AND ((LastName IS
NULL AND @p14 IS NULL) OR (LastName=@p15)) AND ((LoginName IS NULL AND @p16 IS
NULL) OR (LoginName=@p17)) AND ((Password IS NULL AND @p18 IS NULL) OR
(Password=@p19)))
```

As you can see, the UPDATE statement tries to update all the columns, if new values have been set in the row, using the SET clause, but it's the WHERE clause that's the important one here. Basically, the WHERE clause makes sure that you only update the row in the data source, if it hasn't been deleted (the NULL check, like ADName IS NULL AND @p8 IS NULL) and if *all* original values are present. The current values in the data source are matched with the original values in the row (ADName=@p9), which means that the **SqlDataAdapter** uses the **DataRowVersion.Original** column values as the parameter (@p9) for the matching. You need to keep this in mind, if you construct your own SQL statements, instead of using the CommandBuilder class, which you definitely will be doing when the **DataTable**s in your **DataSet** are made up of two or more joined tables from the data source.[7]

If you don't want to handle concurrency violations, you can apply the last-in-wins way of working with your application, like in Listing 3B-27.

Listing 3B-27. Ignoring Concurrency Violations

```
 1 public void IgnoreConcurrencyViolations() {
 2     const string STR_SQL_USER_SELECT = "SELECT * FROM tblUser";
 3     const string STR_SQL_USER_UPDATE = "UPDATE tblUser SET ADName=@ADName, "
 4         "ADSID=@ADSID, FirstName=@FirstName, LastName=@LastName, "
 5         "LoginName=@LoginName, Password=@Password WHERE Id=@Id";
 6
 7     SqlCommand cmmUserUpdate1, cmmUserUpdate2;
 8     SqlParameter prmSQLUpdate;
 9
10     SqlConnection cnnUser1;
11     SqlDataAdapter dadUser1, dadUser2;
12     DataSet dstUser1 = new DataSet("User DataSet1");
13     DataSet dstUser2 = new DataSet("User DataSet2");
14
15     // Instantiate and open the connection
16     cnnUser1 = new SqlConnection(STR_CONNECTION_STRING);
17     cnnUser1.Open();
18
19     // Instantiate the update commands
20     cmmUserUpdate1 = new SqlCommand(STR_SQL_USER_UPDATE, cnnUser1);
21     cmmUserUpdate2 = new SqlCommand(STR_SQL_USER_UPDATE, cnnUser1);
22
```

---

7. The CommandBuilder class can only be used when dealing with **DataTable** objects that are based on single tables in the data source. See Chapter 3A for more information on the CommandBuilder class.

```
23    // Instantiate and initialize data adapters
24    dadUser1 = new SqlDataAdapter(STR_SQL_USER_SELECT, cnnUser1);
25    dadUser2 = new SqlDataAdapter(STR_SQL_USER_SELECT, cnnUser1);
26
27    // Set data adapters update command property
28    dadUser1.UpdateCommand = cmmUserUpdate1;
29    dadUser2.UpdateCommand = cmmUserUpdate2;
30
31    // Add Update command parameters
32    cmmUserUpdate1.Parameters.Add("@ADName", SqlDbType.VarChar, 100,
33       "ADName");
34    cmmUserUpdate1.Parameters.Add("@ADSID", SqlDbType.VarChar, 50, "ADSID");
35    cmmUserUpdate1.Parameters.Add("@FirstName", SqlDbType.VarChar, 50,
36       "FirstName");
37    cmmUserUpdate1.Parameters.Add("@LastName", SqlDbType.VarChar, 50,
38       "LastName");
39    cmmUserUpdate1.Parameters.Add("@LoginName", SqlDbType.VarChar, 50,
40       "LoginName");
41    cmmUserUpdate1.Parameters.Add("@Password", SqlDbType.VarChar, 50,
42       "Password");
43
44    prmSQLUpdate = dadUser1.UpdateCommand.Parameters.Add("@Id", SqlDbType.Int,
45       4, "Id");
46   prmSQLUpdate.Direction = ParameterDirection.Input;
47    prmSQLUpdate.SourceVersion = DataRowVersion.Original;
48
49    cmmUserUpdate2.Parameters.Add("@ADName", SqlDbType.VarChar, 100,
50       "ADName");
51    cmmUserUpdate2.Parameters.Add("@ADSID", SqlDbType.VarChar, 50, "ADSID");
52    cmmUserUpdate2.Parameters.Add("@FirstName", SqlDbType.VarChar, 50,
53       "FirstName");
54    cmmUserUpdate2.Parameters.Add("@LastName", SqlDbType.VarChar, 50,
55       "LastName");
56    cmmUserUpdate2.Parameters.Add("@LoginName", SqlDbType.VarChar, 50,
57       "LoginName");
58    cmmUserUpdate2.Parameters.Add("@Password", SqlDbType.VarChar, 50,
59       "Password");
60
61    prmSQLUpdate = dadUser2.UpdateCommand.Parameters.Add("@Id", SqlDbType.Int,
62       4, "Id");
63    prmSQLUpdate.Direction = ParameterDirection.Input;
64    prmSQLUpdate.SourceVersion = DataRowVersion.Original;
65
```

```
66    // Populate the data sets
67    dadUser1.Fill(dstUser1, "tblUser");
68    dadUser2.Fill(dstUser2, "tblUser");
69
70    // Update an existing row in first data set
71    dstUser1.Tables["tblUser"].Rows[2]["FirstName"] = "FirstName";
72    // Update the data source with changes to the first data set
73    dadUser1.Update(dstUser1, "tblUser");
74    // Update an existing row in second data set
75    dstUser2.Tables["tblUser"].Rows[2]["FirstName"] = "FName";
76    // Update the data source with changes to the second data set
77    dadUser2.Update(dstUser2, "tblUser");
78 }
```

In Listing 3B-27, I build the UPDATE statement manually on Lines 3 through 5, and it's quite different from the one created by the CommandBuilder class in Listing 3-30. I'm not creating the INSERT and UPDATE statements, as they're not needed by the example code, because it only updates a row. Anyway, the real difference between Listings 3B-26 and 3B-27 is Lines 27 through 64, which is the manual setup of the UPDATE statement, including instantiation of the Command classes and parameters needed for the update. If you run the example code in Listing 3B-27, no exceptions will be thrown and the value of the FirstName column will be "FName", because as far as the second DataAdapter (dadUser2) is concerned, the row in the data source hasn't been changed since the rows were retrieved on Line 68. When dadUser2 matches the rows in the dstUser2 **DataSet**, it only compares the ID column, which will always be the same, because this is the primary key. Well, if some donkey has deleted the row before you get to call the **Update** method on Line 77, a **SqlException** exception is thrown. You can add an exception handler to catch this kind of exceptions, should you want to use the last-in-wins method in your application.

However, should you choose to handle concurrency violations, rather than ignoring them, you can do this using an exception handler, as shown in Listing 3B-28.

Listing 3B-28. Handling Concurrency Violations

```
1 public void HandleConcurrencyViolations() {
2    const string STR_SQL_USER_SELECT = "SELECT * FROM tblUser";
3
4    SqlConnection cnnUser1;
5    SqlDataAdapter dadUser1, dadUser2;
6    DataSet dstUser1 = new DataSet("User DataSet1");
7    DataSet dstUser2 = new DataSet("User DataSet2");
8
```

```
 9     // Instantiate and open the connection
10     cnnUser1 = new SqlConnection(STR_CONNECTION_STRING);
11     cnnUser1.Open();
12
13     // Instantiate and initialize data adapters
14     dadUser1 = new SqlDataAdapter(STR_SQL_USER_SELECT, cnnUser1);
15     dadUser2 = new SqlDataAdapter(STR_SQL_USER_SELECT, cnnUser1);
16     // Declare and instantiate command builder
17     SqlCommandBuilder cmbUser1 = new SqlCommandBuilder(dadUser1);
18     SqlCommandBuilder cmbUser2 = new SqlCommandBuilder(dadUser2);
19
20     // Populate the data sets
21     dadUser1.Fill(dstUser1, "tblUser");
22     dadUser2.Fill(dstUser2, "tblUser");
23
24     // Update an existing row in first data set
25     dstUser1.Tables["tblUser"].Rows[2]["FirstName"] = "FirstName";
26     // Update the data source with changes to the first data set
27     dadUser1.Update(dstUser1, "tblUser");
28     // Update an existing row in second data set
29     dstUser2.Tables["tblUser"].Rows[2]["FirstName"] = "FName";
30
31     try {
32        // Update the data source with changes to the second data set
33        dadUser2.Update(dstUser2, "tblUser");
34     }
35     catch (DBConcurrencyException objE) {
36        DialogResult objResult;
37        string strCurrentDataSourceFirstName;
38        // Instantiate command to find the current data source value
39        SqlCommand cmdCurrentDataSourceValue =
40           new SqlCommand("SELECT FirstName FROM tblUser WHERE Id=" +
41           objE.Row["Id", DataRowVersion.Original].ToString(), cnnUser1);
42
43        // Find current value in data source
44        strCurrentDataSourceFirstName = (string)
45           cmdCurrentDataSourceValue.ExecuteScalar();
46
47        // Prompt the user about which value to save
48        objResult = MessageBox.Show(
49           "A concurrency violation exception was thrown when updating the " +
50           "source. These are the values for the column in error:\n\n" +
51           "Original DataSet Value: " + objE.Row["FirstName",
```

```
52            DataRowVersion.Original].ToString()  + "\n"  +
53        "Current Data Source Value: " + strCurrentDataSourceFirstName  +
54        "\nCurrent DataSet Value: " + objE.Row["FirstName",
55            DataRowVersion.Current].ToString()  + "\n"  +
56        "Do you want to overwrite the current data source value?",
57        "Concurrency Violation",
58        MessageBoxButtons.YesNo, MessageBoxIcon.Question);
59      // Does the user want to overwrite the current data source value?
60      if (objResult == DialogResult.Yes) {
61        // Merge the content of the data source with the dataset in error
62        dstUser2.Merge(dstUser1, true);
63        dadUser2.Update(dstUser2, "tblUser");
64      }
65    }
66  finally {
67      // Close connection
68      cnnUser1.Close();
69    }
70 }
```

Now, the example code in Listing 3B-28 takes care of concurrency violations and leaves it up to the user, if the new value should be overwritten. The trick to overwriting the current values in the data source with the current values in the **DataSet**, despite the fact that the original values in the **DataSet** don't match the current data source values, can be found on Line 62; I merge the values from the first **DataSet** into the second **DataSet**, preserving the changes I've made. In this case, it means that the original value of the changed FirstName column in the second **DataSet** is set to the current value of the same column in the equivalent row in the first **DataSet**, which is in fact the same as the current value in the data source, unless another user has changed it again.

The example code in Listing 3B-28 isn't fully finished as it only looks at the one column I know has been tampered with, but I'm sure you now know how to create code that handles concurrency on a more general level, meaning violations in all columns are handled.

Anyway, this isn't the only way to deal with concurrency violations. Many other ways are available, an example of which is to make use of unique values across your database. The unique values, one column per table row, are then updated automatically every time a row is changed. The value can be a date and time, but as long as it's unique and changes can be detected, it doesn't matter what kind of a value it is. What you do then is to match the current value of this column at the data source with the original value in your row in the **DataSet**, before you update the row in the data source. SQL Server has a data type that automatically implements this for you, the **timestamp** data type. The unique value approach is really much the same technique as Listing 3B-28 uses, but to some extent it's simpler and yet not quite as flexible. In Listing 3B-28, you're in charge of how many columns you want to check for changes[8] before the concurrency violation is thrown, whereas the timestamp method is based on the entire row.

In Listing 3B-28, I've used the automatic approach with the DataAdapters with regard to building the INSERT, UPDATE, and DELETE statements. However, if you want to do it the manual way, like in Listing 3B-27, all you need to do is change the STR_SQL_USER_UPDATE constant to this:

```
const string STR_SQL_USER_UPDATE = "UPDATE tblUser SET ADName=@ADName, " +
    "ADSID=@ADSID, FirstName=@FirstName, LastName=@LastName, " +
    "LoginName=@LoginName, Password=@Password WHERE ((Id=@Id) AND " +
    "((ADName IS NULL AND @ADName IS NULL) OR (ADName=@ADName)) AND ((ADSID IS" +
    " NULL AND @ADSID IS NULL) OR (ADSID=@ADSID)) AND ((FirstName IS NULL AND " +
    "@FirstName IS NULL) OR (FirstName=@FirstName)) AND ((LastName IS NULL AND" +
    " @LastName IS NULL) OR (LastName=@LastName)) AND ((LoginName IS NULL " +
    "AND @LoginName IS NULL) OR (LoginName=@LoginName)) AND ((Password IS NULL" +
    " AND @Password IS NULL) OR (Password=@Password)))";
```

Using "Classic" ADO and COM Interop

Because previous versions of ADO are built as COM components, you also need to use COM Interop for this purpose. COM Interop provides a way of interfacing with COM components in order to use them and vice versa for that matter. I'll only be discussing the COM-to-.NET usage in this section.

You need to use COM Interop whenever you want to access a COM component. There is much more to COM Interop than I am going to cover in this section, so if you need some more information, I suggest you check out this book:

- *Moving to Visual Basic .NET: Strategies, Concepts and Code,* by Dan Appleman. Published by Apress, June 2001. ISBN 1893115976.

There are several ways of using COM components from within the .NET Framework. They all involve exposing a COM component to the world of managed code. The CLR expects all types to be defined as metadata in an assembly. This goes for COM types as well. So the job at hand is to convert your COM types

---

8. You can edit the example code to ignore changes to one or more columns when matching the original row values with the current data source values—for instance, changes to the ADSID and ADName columns might be unimportant to you.

to metadata, or rather generate metadata for your COM types. This metadata is really an assembly called the *Runtime Callable Wrapper* (RCW). The .NET application uses the RCW, which exposes the COM classes, method, and properties contained in the COM DLL to the .NET application. The RCW takes care of the communication between the .NET application and the COM DLL.

I'll show you the two easy ways of generating the metadata, and I suggest that you pick either method for use with previous versions of ADO. The first involves running the command-line Type Library Importer, TlbImp.exe, on the COM component to generate metadata in an assembly. Please note that the component must contain a type library. If it doesn't, then there's probably a separate type library file for importing (*.tlb). Any client that writes managed code can use the resulting assembly. Say you want to import the ADO 2.7 library, which is usually located in the Program Files\Common Files\System\Ado folder. This is one way to make sure that you can run the example code in Listing 3B-3. To do so, you would open a command prompt, go to the Ado folder, and then execute the following command: `\Program Files\Microsoft Visual Studio .NET\FrameworkSDK\Bin\TlbImp.tlb`. Replace the path to match your setup. I know the file name looks as if it's ado version 2.6, but Microsoft has chosen to name the file like this. It's probably because version 2.7 is really only a minor upgrade, which was originally intended to be a service pack. Anyway, the output from running the TlbImp.exe file is the ADODB.DLL assembly, which holds the ADODB namespace. Surely this must look familiar to you. Adding a reference to your project can reference this assembly. See the next option for generating metadata. If you need to see all the command options available to you, just run TlbImp.exe with no arguments from the command line. The options will then be displayed.

The second way to generate the metadata involves adding a reference to the COM components in your project, as shown in Figure 3B-2. This way the IDE generates the metadata for you. You can access the Add Reference dialog box by clicking the Add Reference command in the Project menu.

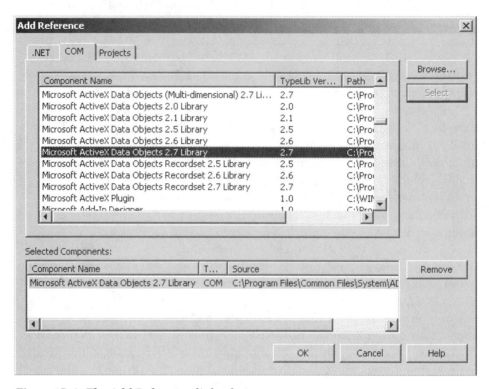

Figure 3B-2: The Add Reference dialog box

You can use either of these two methods to access any COM types, and as such all of your COM components can still be part of your applications. Mind you, it's advisable to port all of these components to .NET classes, because there's overhead when using COM Interop. Once you've added a reference to a COM component in your project, you can use the Object Browser to see all the types.

Okay, now that I've suggested you do all this, I might as well reveal that it isn't really necessary. It's not necessary because Microsoft has decided to include some Primary Interop Assemblies with VS .NET. Guess what, ADO is one of them. This means a .NET Framework wrapper already exists for the ADO COM libraries. So all you really have to do is add a reference to this wrapper. You can access the Add Reference dialog box by clicking the Add Reference command in the Project menu. In the Add Reference dialog box the wrapper assembly can be found on the .NET tab with the component name adodb. Select it from the list, click Select, and then click OK. Now the RCW has been added to your project.

The Primary Interop Assemblies can be found in the \Program Files\Microsoft.NET\Primary Interop Assemblies folder. If you place your RCWs in this folder, they are automatically added to the .NET tab in the Add Reference dialog box.

Summary

This chapter, together with the preceding chapter, introduced you to the two different data access technologies ADO and ADO.NET. ADO.NET is generally for building distributed n-tier Web applications, whereas ADO can be your best bet for traditional Windows client-server/n-tier applications programming in a heterogeneous networking environment, in which you are connected at all times on a LAN link. The object model for the disconnected layer of ADO.NET was introduced and a comparison was made with the ADO object model wherever needed. As well as being an introduction to the disconnected layer of ADO.NET and to some extent ADO, this chapter is a reference to the various classes, methods, and properties of this data access technology.

This chapter also covered the following ground:

- **DataSet**, **DataTable**, **DataView**, **DataRow**, **DataColumn**, and **DataRelation** data classes were discussed. The ADO.NET classes were compared to their equivalents in ADO and suggestions were offered about when to use which data class.

- Cursors, including location and type.

- Data source locking, including pessimistic and optimistic concurrency.

- COM Interop, which is required in order to use ADO 2.7 or earlier.

The following chapter takes you through the various data-related features of the IDE, such as how to create database projects.

CHAPTER 4

Presenting the IDE from a Database Viewpoint

THIS CHAPTER INTRODUCES YOU to the Integrated Development Environment (IDE), and more specifically how IDEs relate to databases. I'll be discussing how you create database projects and how you let the various designers do the hard work for you—in other words, how you perform tasks from the IDE that you would otherwise do through code or using other external tools.

In this chapter, I've included several hands-on exercises that will take you through creating a database project and adding scripts, queries, and command files. Just look for the Exercise items that appear throughout this text.

Using the Server Explorer

The Server Explorer is located on the left-hand side of the IDE, and it's displayed if you move the mouse cursor over the Server Explorer tab or if you press Ctrl+Alt+S. The Server Explorer is hidden again if you click any other part of the IDE, such as the Code Editor. The Server Explorer window contains a tree view of the data connections that have been created and the servers to which you've connected.

> **NOTE** *The resources shown in the Server Explorer window are NOT specific to the project that is currently open.*

When you open up the Visual Studio .NET IDE for the first time, the Server Explorer doesn't display any data connections or servers, and it looks like the example shown in Figure 4-1.

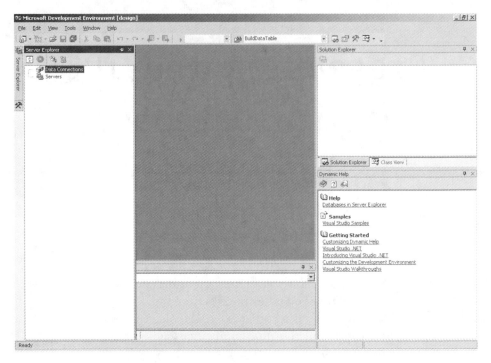

Figure 4-1. Empty Server Explorer window

Handling Data Connections

If you need to manipulate a database or create a strongly typed data set, you have to create a data connection first. Depending on your access privileges, you can perform most database tasks from the Server Explorer.

Adding a Data Connection

You can add a data connection by right-clicking the Data Connections node and selecting Add Connection from the pop-up menu. This brings up the Data Link Properties dialog box. You might need to click the Provider tab to see the dialog box shown in Figure 4-2.

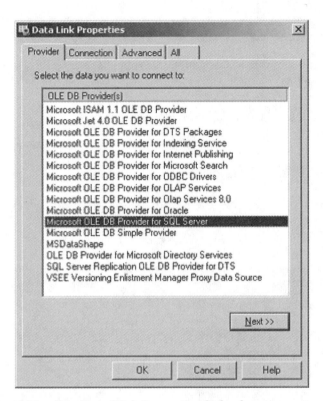

Figure 4-2. Provider tab in Data Link Properties dialog box

On the Provider tab of the Data Link Properties dialog box, you must select the appropriate provider for the data source you are going to connect to, and click Next. This brings the Connection tab to the front.

EXERCISE

On the Provider tab of the Data Link Properties dialog box, select Microsoft OLE DB Provider for SQL Server.

On the Connection tab, you must enter the appropriate details concerning the database to which you are connecting, that is, the user name and password for a user that has access rights to the database. See the following exercise for an example.

EXERCISE

1) On the Connection tab of the Data Link Properties dialog box, you must enter the following text:

   USERMANPC (or the name of your SQL Server)

   See Figure 4-3. The password is *userman* and you must replace *USERMANPC* with the name of your SQL Server.

2) Click OK, or try clicking the Test button first to see if there are any problems connecting to the data source.

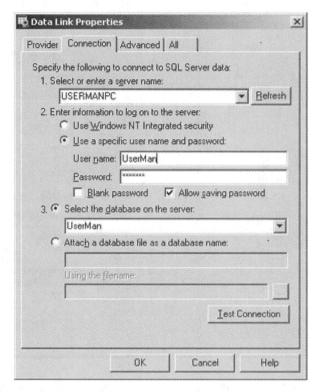

Figure 4-3. SQL Server setup on the Connection tab in Data Link Properties dialog box

Deleting a Data Connection

When a data connection is no longer relevant to you, you should delete it from the Server Explorer, because it can quickly become "overcrowded." There are three ways in which you can delete a data connection from the Server Explorer. First you must select the appropriate data connection node in the tree view and then do one of the following:

- Press the Delete key.

- Right-click the tree-view node and select the Remove command from the pop-up menu.

- Select the Remove command from the Edit menu.

Please note that this procedure only deletes the connection, and not the database to which you are connecting! If you need to delete a SQL Server database, please see "Deleting/Dropping a SQL Server Database" later in this chapter.

Creating Database Objects

If you want to create database objects such as tables, diagrams, views, stored procedures, or functions, you can do this by first selecting the corresponding tree-view node. In this case, corresponding tree-view node means the Tables node or the Stored Procedures node in the database you want to create a table in, and so on. Next, right-click the node, and select the New Table command, or the New Stored Procedure command, and so on from the pop-up menu. Check out Chapter 6 for more information on how to create database objects. Chapter 2 holds information on how to design a relational database the "right" way.

Handling Servers

Under the Servers node in the Server Explorer, you can add any server to which you have access. You should add at least all the servers that the current project will be accessing, because it's easier to control and manipulate the servers once they are shown with their resources in the Server Explorer window.

Adding a Server

You can add a server by right-clicking the Servers node and selecting Add Server from the pop-up menu. The Add Server dialog box, shown in Figure 4-4, appears.

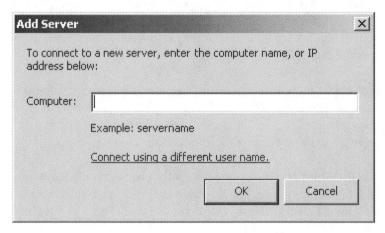

Figure 4-4. Add Server dialog box

In the Add Server dialog box, you can add a server by typing the name of the server in the Computer text box. The name can be specified in two different ways:

- Using the name (URL or UNC file path) if the server is on a local network— for example, USERMANPC

- Using the IP address of the server—for example, 192.129.192.15

Type the name of your server in the Name text box of the Add Server dialog box and click OK.

If you want to connect to the server as a different user, you must click the link Connect using a different user name. This brings up the Connect As dialog box as shown in Figure 4-5.

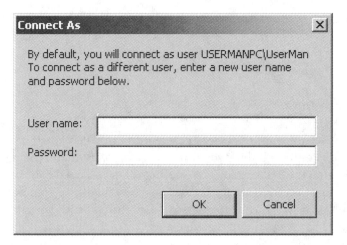

Figure 4-5. Connect As dialog box

The Connect As dialog box has two text boxes you must fill in:

- *User Name:* Type the name of the user you want to connect as. If this user is in a different domain, you must also specify the domain name; use the format *DomainName\UserName*.

- *Password:* Type the password that corresponds to the user name entered. Leave this text box empty if the user doesn't have a password.

Once you've added a server to the Server Explorer, you can view all the resources this server has to offer by expanding the tree node (click the + icon next to the node if it isn't already expanded).

There are a number of different resources on a server, but I'll only cover the ones that are database related, including message queues and SQL Servers.

Using Server Resources

The following sections describe how to use the database-related resources on the server of your choice.

Using Message Queues

Chapter 8 covers message queues extensively, so I won't go into too many details here. Having said this, I'll show you how to create, manipulate, and delete a message queue from the Server Explorer. Another thing you need to be aware of is that you can only access message queues on a server with a dependent message queue. This means workgroup message queue setup isn't supported. A workgroup setup is an independent message queue, which means that it's not dependent on a server for storage of messages.

Three types of message queues can be seen in the Server Explorer, although which message you can actually see depends on your permissions:

- *Private queue:* This is a queue registered on the local computer and isn't part of a directory service. Generally this kind of queue cannot be located by other applications. See Chapter 8 for more information.

- *Public queue:* This is a queue registered in the directory service. This queue can be located by any other message queuing application. See Chapter 8 for more information.

- *System queue:* This kind of queue is generally used by the OS for internal messaging. See Chapter 8 for more information.

Figure 4-6 shows you the expanded Message Queue node in the Server Explorer.

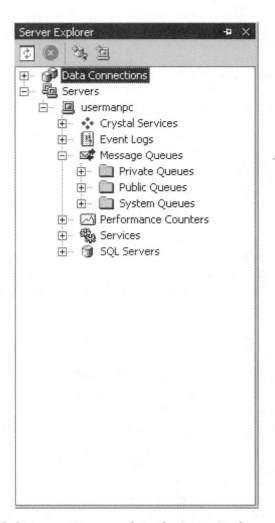

Figure 4-6. Expanded Message Queue node in the Server Explorer

Creating a Message Queue

Right-click the queue node where you want to create the new queue and select Create Queue from the pop-up menu. This brings up the Create Message Queue dialog box as shown in Figure 4-7.

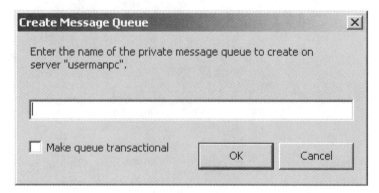

Figure 4-7. Create Message Queue dialog box

You give the message queue a name by typing it in the text box. Select the Make queue transactional check box to accept only those messages that are part of a transaction. Note that you need permissions to create a message queue on the server to which you are connected. Click OK to create the queue.

Deleting a Message Queue

If a message queue is no longer of use to you, you can delete it. This is done by right-clicking the message queue and selecting Remove from the pop-up menu, or by selecting it and pressing the Delete key. A confirmation of the deletion is required. All messages in the queue will be deleted permanently.

Deleting Messages from a Message Queue

If you need to clear one or more messages from a queue, there are two ways of doing so from the Server Explorer. You can delete one at a time or you can delete all messages from a queue. Clearing all messages from a queue is done by expanding the queue node and right-clicking the Queue messages node. Select Clear Messages from the pop-up menu and then confirm the deletion. A single message is cleared from the queue by selecting it, right-clicking it, and selecting Remove from the pop-up menu.

Using SQL Server Databases

You can use the SQL Server resources to see if a specific server actually hosts a SQL Server. Click the + icon to expand the SQL Servers node. If you click a SQL Server, the SQL Server Login dialog box pops up if the service isn't already running. This is in contrast to using Data Connections, where the service must be started for you to add a connection! Please see the next section for information on how to add a SQL Server instance to a server.

Registering a SQL Server Instance

If you haven't registered an instance of SQL Server on the server you've expanded under the Servers node in the Server Explorer, you can do so by right-clicking the SQL Servers node and selecting Register SQL Server Instance from the pop-up menu. This brings up the Register SQL Server Instance dialog box as shown in Figure 4-8.

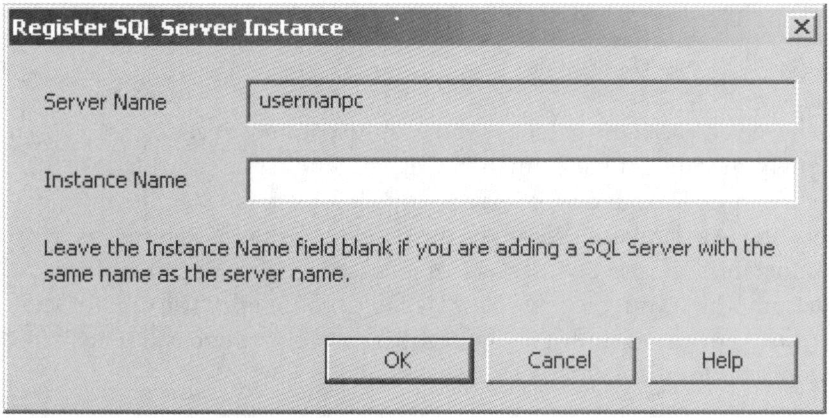

Figure 4-8. Register SQL Server Instance dialog box

In Figure 4-8, you can see the Register SQL Server Instance dialog box, which is used for registering an instance of SQL Server on the selected server. If your SQL Server instance is named the same as your server,[1] all you have to do is click the OK button. However, if you've given it a different name from that of your server, you need to type it in the Instance Name text box and click OK. This adds the specified SQL Server instance to the SQL Servers node in the Server Explorer.

> **NOTE** *Although the registering and unregistering of SQL Server instances looks and feels like the same process in the Enterprise Manager, the two have nothing to do with each other, meaning the actions you perform in the Server Explorer don't show in Enterprise Manager and vice versa.*

---

1. For SQL Servers prior to version 2000, the instance name is always the same as the server name.

Unregistering a SQL Server Instance

If you've registered an instance of SQL Server that you no longer need, or if for any other reason you don't want the SQL Server instance to show up under the SQL Servers node in the Server Explorer, you can unregister it by right-clicking the SQL Servers node and selecting Register SQL Server Instance from the pop-up menu. Please be aware that you're not required to confirm this action—as soon as you've selected the command from the pop-up menu, the instance is unregistered.

Creating a SQL Server Database

If you haven't created the database you want to connect to yet, here's a way of doing it. In the Server Explorer window, expand the server on which the SQL Server is running, expand SQL Servers, and right-click the SQL Server where you want to create a database. Please see the previous section, "Registering a SQL Server Instance," if your SQL Server instance isn't shown. This brings up a pop-up menu from which you select the New Database command. The Create Database dialog box appears, as shown in Figure 4-9, and this is where you specify the initial properties for the database.

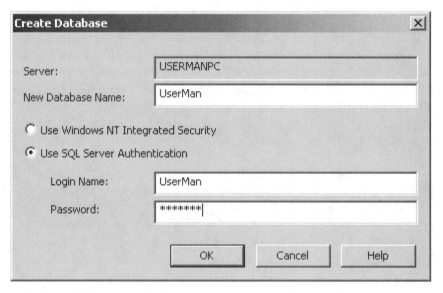

Figure 4-9. Create Database dialog box

If you've ever used the Server Explorer in SQL Server 7.0 or later, you'll probably recognize the content of this dialog box.

- *Server:* This is the name of the server that hosts the SQL Server. If you need to change this, you have to cancel this dialog box and bring up the same dialog box on the required server.

- *New Database Name:* This is the name you want to give your new database. The name must conform to the limitations imposed by the target file system.

- *Use Windows NT Authentication:* Select this option if you want to use Windows NT authentication for connecting to the SQL Server. Whatever user you are connected as will be used for authentication on the server that hosts the SQL Server. (I won't be demonstrating the use of this option in this book.)

- *Use SQL Server Authentication:* Select this option if you want to use SQL Server's own authentication. With this option, you have to create a login to use if you aren't going to use the system administrator account, sa.

- *Login Name:* This is where you must indicate the name of the login you want to use. This text box isn't enabled if you use Windows NT authentication.

- *Password:* Type the password that corresponds to the login name. This text box isn't enabled if you use Windows NT authentication.

---

sa

sa is the system administrator login for Microsoft SQL Server. It's generally the only account on SQL Servers used for development purposes. If you log in as sa, you have the rights to perform any valid task, such as creating and deleting databases and users. However, when you test your application, you should always test the database access using the user credentials that your application will be using. It's worth noting that when you install SQL Server, the sa user account has a blank password by default. sa or any other SQL Server login can only be used if your SQL Server setup employs mixed mode authentication, meaning Windows and SQL Server authentication. See your SQL Server documentation for information on user authentication.

EXERCISE

You might already have created a UserMan database on your SQL Server. However, if you'd like to create a new database, simply follow these instructions on how to fill in the Create Database dialog box:

1) Type or select the name of your server in the Server combo box.

2) Type **Test** in the New Database Name text box.

3) Select the Use SQL Server Authentication option.

4) Type a login name that has create database privileges in the Login Name text box.

5) Type the corresponding password for the login account used in Step 4.

6) Click OK to create the new database and refresh the display so that it includes the new database.

I cover connecting to SQL Server databases earlier in this chapter in the section "Handling Data Connections." When you create a database this way, it has one disadvantage worth noting: if you need to re-create the database, you don't have a script to do it; you need to do it manually again.

> **NOTE** *When you create a SQL Server database this way, all the default values for a new database will be used. These values are set on the server. If you want to create a database with nondefault values or properties, you must either do so in code using a CREATE DATABASE SQL statement or from the SQL Server Enterprise Manager Microsoft Management Console (MMC) snap-in. Alternatively you can create your database as shown and then change some of the default values, like where the database and/or log files are located, through code using an ALTER DATABASE SQL statement.*

You cannot create a file-based database, like a Microsoft Access JET database, using the Server Explorer. For this purpose you need to use the corresponding front-end tool (Microsoft Access in this case). You can also execute a CREATE DATABASE SQL statement from code using the appropriate provider or driver.

Deleting/Dropping a SQL Server Database

You cannot delete or drop a SQL Server database automatically from the Server Explorer window. You need to do this from the SQL Server Enterprise Manager or through code using a DROP DATABASE SQL statement.

EXERCISE

If you created the Test database in the previous exercise, and you want to delete or drop it again, work through the instructions that follow.

TIP *Actually, it's possible to delete or drop a SQL Server database from the Server Explorer window, if you have the rights to access the master database and the permissions to drop a database. If you have these access rights, you can do the following:*

1) *Open a database other than the master database on the server in question. This has to be a database in which you have a login name that has the right permissions, as just described.*
2) *Expand the Tables node and right-click a table.*
3) *Select the Retrieve Data from Table command from the pop-up menu.*
4) *Click the Show SQL Pane button on the Query Toolbar (check the Tool Tip).*
5) *Delete the SELECT * . . . SQL statement from the SQL Pane.*
6) *Type **USE master** and click the Run Query button on the Query toolbar.*
7) *Click OK in the resulting dialog box.*
8) *Delete the content of the SQL Pane and type **DROP DATABASE** database-basename (where databasename is the actual name of the database you want to delete or drop) and click Run Query.*
9) *Click OK.*

Deleting a Server

If a server becomes obsolete to you, you should delete it from the Server Explorer. There are three ways in which you can delete a server from the current project. First, you must select the appropriate node in the tree view, and then do one of the following:

- Press the Delete key.

- Right-click the tree-view node and select the Remove command from the pop-up menu.

- Select the Remove command from the Edit menu.

Looking at Database Projects

A database project is used for storing connections, SQL scripts, and command files (such as those for batching scripts and/or scheduled script execution). Besides this, through a database project you can also use Visual SourceSafe for handling the various versions of your database objects. In other words, a database project is for manipulating your database objects directly!

You can create a database project by following these steps:

1. Select the File/New/Project menu command or press Ctrl+Shift+N. This brings up the New Project dialog box, as shown in Figure 4-10.

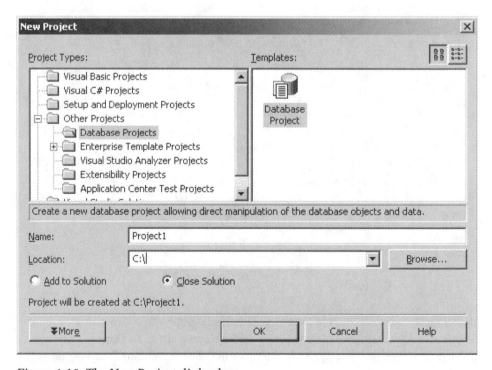

Figure 4-10. The New Project dialog box

2. In the New Project dialog box, expand the Other Projects node and select Database Projects.

3. Give the project a name by typing the name in the Name text box, and specify the location in the Location text box.

4. Finally you need to specify if the new project should be added to the current solution or if the current solution should be closed and a new one created. Select the Add to Solution option or the Close Solution option to specify which you want. Please note that the Add to Solution option and the Close Solution option are only available if you currently have a project open.

EXERCISE

In the New Project dialog box, type **UserMan DB Project** in the Name text box. Save the project to your hard disk.

---

5. Click OK. Now the Add Database Reference dialog box appears. This dialog box is shown in Figure 4-11.

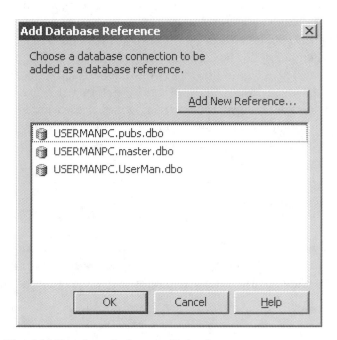

Figure 4-11. The Add Database Reference dialog box

The Add Database Reference dialog box has a list of all the data connections from the Server Explorer; see "Handling Data Connections" earlier in this chapter for details. Select the desired data connection. If the database connection you want to reference isn't shown on the list, you can add it by clicking Add New Reference. This will bring up the Data Link Properties dialog box, which is described under "Adding a Data Connection" earlier in this chapter. Click OK and the new project will now appear in the Solution Explorer.

6. If you need to add more database references to your project, right-click the Database References node in the Solution Explorer and select New Database Reference from the pop-up menu.

> **NOTE** *When you add a database reference that doesn't exist under Data Connections in the Server Explorer to a database project, it's automatically added to the Data Connections node.*

If you have more than one database reference in your project, you can set one of them to be the default reference. As a result of specifying a default reference, when you create for example a script, the list of tables to add to the script will consist of tables from the default database. In addition, the default database reference is the one used when you run scripts and queries within your project. You can set the default database reference by right-clicking the root project folder and selecting Set Default Reference from the pop-up menu. This brings up the Set Default Reference dialog box, which looks very similar to the Add Database Reference dialog box in Figure 4-11. Select the database you want as your default, and click OK. After you do so, you'll notice the Database References node in the Solution Explorer has changed. You can also right-click the wanted database reference in the Solution Explorer, and select Set as Project Default from the pop-up menu. The default database reference has a new icon, indicating that it's the default reference.

Creating a Database Project Folder

If you look in the Solution Explorer for a database project (make sure the database project is expanded), you can see that three subfolders have already been created. These folders are used for grouping your database objects as described here:

- The Change Scripts folder is for holding delete and update scripts, and so on.

- The Create Scripts is for creation scripts (tough one to guess, eh?), such as those for creating a database or a table.

- The Queries folder is for scripts that return rows or single/scalar values and the like.

If you need more folders or just want to create your own set of folders for grouping your database objects, then feel free to do so. All you need to do is right-click a database project node in the Solution Explorer and select New Folder from the pop-up menu. The new folder is automatically added to the Solution Explorer. You can give the new folder a meaningful name and create subfolders as you would in any normal file system. Please also note that you can create a default database reference to every folder you have in your project, which means you can make more than one folder for create scripts or change scripts or any other kind of folder. The point is that you can then have a folder for each of these categories for each of the different database connections in your project.

> **TIP** *Although you can group your database objects any way you want, following a commonsense folder-naming scheme, like the one used for the default folders, and making sure that the database objects are placed in the appropriate folders is the best approach. This will make it a lot easier to find a specific database object, and obviously it will also make it easier to create command files that only contain scripts from one folder.*

Deleting a Database Project Folder

You can delete folders as well as you can create them for your database objects. You do this by right-clicking the folder you want to delete, selecting Remove from the pop-up menu, and confirming the deletion of the folder. Actually, you can choose to just remove the folder from the project or to delete the folder from your hard disk as well as remove it from the project.

> **CAUTION** *You have to be careful when you delete a folder, because all database objects in the folder will be deleted as well.*

Adding Database Objects to a Database Project

You can add both new and existing database objects to your database project. See the following sections for information on how to do either task.

Adding New Database Objects

If you want to add a new database object to any of the folders in a project, including the project root folder, right-click the desired folder and select Add New Item from the pop-up menu. Actually, there are other options for this purpose on the pop-up menu, but the Add New Item command covers both the Add SQL Script and Add Query commands. After you make the selection, the Add New Item dialog box pops up (see Figure 4-12).

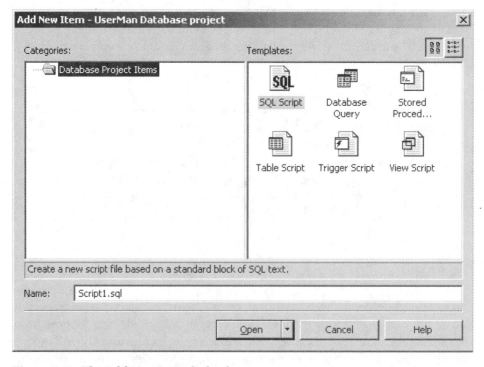

Figure 4-12. The Add New Item dialog box

As you can see from Figure 4-12, there are a few different database objects that can be added to your database project. When you add a new database object to your project, it must be based on a template. Available templates are shown in the right-hand pane of the Add New Item dialog box. Except for the Database Query template, they all open up the SQL Editor for editing once you click Open.

(See the "Script Editing Using the SQL Editor" section later in this chapter for more information on how to use this feature.) If you create a new database object based on the Database Query template, the Query Designer is opened once you click Open. (See "Designing Queries with the Query Designer" later in this chapter for more information on how to use the Query Designer.)

The Query Designer and the SQL Editor overlap in a few areas when it comes to creating scripts or queries. What I mean is that some things can be achieved by using either of the two, and which one you choose is simply a matter of preference. The Query Designer, with its drag-and-drop features, is easier to use, whereas you can perform more complex tasks using the SQL Editor. Table 4-1 lists the templates available and describes which template is best for creating certain database objects as well as which tool to use.

Table 4-1. Database Object Templates

TEMPLATE NAME	DEFAULT TOOL	DESCRIPTION
Database Query	Query Designer	Use a database query for creating row-returning queries, delete and update queries, make/create table queries, and insert queries. You can use the SQL Editor for this purpose as well, but the Query Designer is perfectly designed for this task. It's much simpler because of its query grid and the drag-and-drop features.
SQL Script	SQL Editor	You should use the SQL Script template when you want to create a script that isn't covered by any of the other templates.
Stored Procedure Script	SQL Editor	Use the Stored Procedure template to create stored procedures for fast server-side processing of repeating queries or functions. See Chapter 6 for more information on stored procedures.
Table Script	SQL Editor	Use the Table Script template to make CREATE TABLE SQL scripts. Personally, I think it's easier to use the Query Designer for this purpose, but sometimes you might add an existing create table script and then you can use the SQL Editor to edit it. It's your call.
Trigger Script	SQL Editor	The Trigger Script template should be used to create triggers for server-side processing or validation of data manipulation. See Chapter 6 for more information on triggers.
View Script	SQL Editor	The View Script template should be used for creating views that make row-returning queries faster. See Chapter 6 for more information on views.

Running Scripts in the IDE

Once you have a created a script, like the Create UserMan database script from the UserMan database project, you can actually test it in the IDE. Right-click the script in the Solution Explorer and select Run from the pop-up menu. This will execute the script on the default database. If you want to execute the script on a different database, select Run On from the aforementioned pop-up menu. This brings up the Run On dialog box, as shown in Figure 4-13.

Figure 4-13. The Run On dialog box

The Run On dialog box is quite similar to the Add Database Reference dialog box in Figure 4-11, but with one exception, the temporary reference (represented by <temporary reference>). You can use this temporary reference to create a temporary database connection, which is only created for running the script and is destroyed as soon as the script ends. This is ideal for dial-up connections, which you don't want the IDE to keep open after running the script.

Once you've selected the reference you require, click OK to run the script on the selected reference.

Adding a Command File

If you want to execute several scripts at a time, it's a good idea to put them all in a single command file. This way you can execute a batch of scripts at any time by executing the command file. Actually, since a command file can be executed at the command line, it's also a good candidate for scheduled execution. This means that it even makes sense to put one script in a command file. The command file is a Windows command file with the *.cmd extension.

You create a command file by right-clicking the folder in the Solution Explorer in which you want the command file to be placed. The Create Command File dialog box appears after you select Create Command File from the pop-up menu (see Figure 4-14).

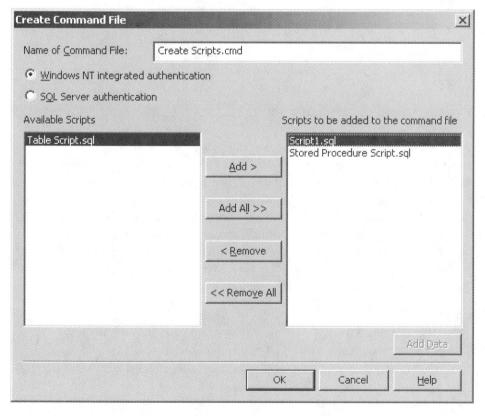

Figure 4-14. The Create Command File dialog box

In the Create Command File dialog box, you can give the command file a name and choose which scripts should be part of the command file. The scripts listed under Available Scripts are taken from the folder in which you are creating the command file. You cannot select scripts from folders other than subfolders. This is why it's so important to organize your scripts in the correct folders. (This goes for queries as well!)

The last thing you need to do is to choose if you want to use Windows NT authentication or SQL Server authentication. If you choose Windows NT authentication, the scripts will be executed with the permissions of the logged-in user or the user account assigned to the scheduler service. However, if you choose SQL Server authentication, you must provide the login name and password at the command prompt when you execute the script. Click OK when you're done, and the command file will be placed in the folder you right-clicked when you first began creating the file.

When you execute the command file, you need to supply the name of the server and the name of the database, like this:

```
CommandFileName.cmd ServerName DatabaseName
```

Adding Existing Database Objects

If you've already created one or more of the database objects that you want to add to your project, all you have to do is add them using the pop-up menu. Right-click the folder that you want to add the object to and select Add Existing Item from the pop-up menu. This brings up the Add Existing Item dialog box, in which you can browse and select the database objects. You can select more than one database object from the same folder at one time by holding down the Ctrl key when clicking the objects you want. Click Open once you've selected the desired object(s). The selected objects are added to your project immediately and shown in the updated Solution Explorer window.

> **NOTE** *There's no validation of the existing items you add to your project, so it's up to you to add the correct types of database objects.*

Designing Databases with Visio for Enterprise Architect

The Enterprise Architect edition of VS .NET comes with Visio for VS .NET. This tool can be used for modeling and documenting your application and database using the Unified Modeling Language (UML). Figure 4-15 shows you a reverse-engineered Visio database model diagram of the UserMan database. Visio can be used for creating and documenting your databases, but also for reverse-engineering an existing database and updating it from a Visio document.

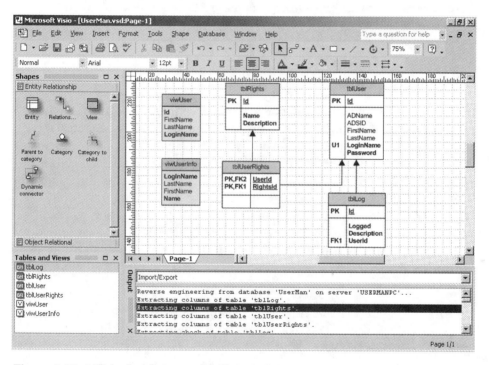

Figure 4-15. A Visio database model diagram

However, database design using UML and Visio is really beyond the scope of an intermediate reader and as such isn't covered in this book, but do look for the following book to be published second quarter 2002, if you want to get involved with UML and Visio.

- *Enterprise Development with .NET and UML,* by John Hansen and Carsten Thomsen. Published by Apress (forthcoming). ISBN 1590590422.

Designing Databases with the Database Designer

The Database Designer is a visual tool for designing your SQL Server and Oracle databases. Unfortunately this tool can't be used to create databases in any databases other than the ones mentioned. You can use it for creating tables, including columns, keys, indexes, constraints, and relationships between tables. The Database Designer creates a diagram through which you can visualize your database objects as you add and manipulate them. The database diagram depicts the database graphically, showing the database structure. This means that a database diagram can only hold database objects from one database. In other words, you can have several diagrams in one database, but only one database in any diagram.

Creating a Database Diagram

The *database diagram* is a visual tool for creating your database. You can add or create tables, add relationships between tables, and perform just about all the tasks you normally would when you design your database. You can create a database diagram from the Server Explorer. Expand the Data Connections node and the database for which you want to create the diagram. Right-click the Database Diagrams node and select New Diagram from the pop-up menu. This brings up the Add Table dialog box, as shown in Figure 4-16. In this dialog box, you can select the tables from the database that you want on the diagram. Select the desired table(s) and click Add. Click Close to close the dialog box and continue with the diagram.

> **NOTE** *Database diagrams are NOT available for Microsoft Access (JET Engine) databases, only SQL Server and Oracle databases!*

EXERCISE

Create a new database diagram and add all the tables in the UserMan database that start with tbl.

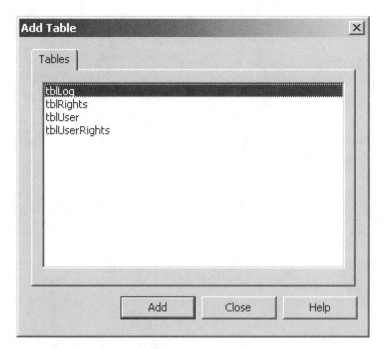

Figure 4-16. The Add Table dialog box

When the diagram opens, the tables you selected are automatically added to the diagram, and if you've set up relations between any of the tables, they are automatically shown as well (see Figure 4-17).

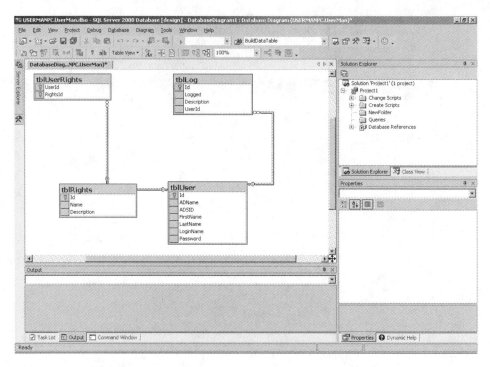

Figure 4-17. A database diagram

In Figure 4-17, you can see the diagram for the UserMan database. There are four tables, all named as indicated at the top of each table box:

- tblUser

- tblRights

- tblUserRights

- tblLog

The columns of each table are shown below the table name, meaning UserId and RightsId are the columns of the tblUserRights table. The tables are related, and you can see the relationships displayed in Figure 4-17 as the lines connecting the tables. These lines are solid, indicating that the DBMS enforces referential integrity. (See Chapter 2 for more information about referential integrity.) If a line is dotted, it means that referential integrity isn't enforced for that particular relationship. The parent table for the relationship is the table with the key as an endpoint, and the child table is the one with figure eight (∞) as an endpoint. All the relationships in the UserMan database are one-to-many relationships (key-∞). The primary key field(s) in each table is marked with a key in the left-hand column of each table.

Adding Tables

If you need to add more tables to the diagram, you can right-click any blank space in the diagram and select Add Table from the pop-up menu. This brings up the Add Table dialog box shown in Figure 4-16. Select the tables you want on the diagram and click Add. Click Close to close the dialog box and continue with the database diagram.

Deleting and Removing Tables

If you've added a table to the diagram that you don't really need, all you have to do is remove it. Well, there's more to it than that, because removing a table from the diagram is one thing, deleting a table from the database is a completely different story. Here is what you do to remove a table from a diagram:

1. Right-click the table in question.

2. Select Remove Table from Diagram from the pop-up menu.

Please note that no confirmation is required for this task! If on the other hand you actually want to delete the table from the database, then this is how you do it:

1. Right-click the table in question.

2. Select Delete Table from Database from the pop-up menu.

3. Click Yes in the confirmation dialog box.

Creating a New Table

If you haven't already created the table you want to add to the database diagram, you can create it from within the diagram. Right-click any blank space on the diagram and select New Table from the pop-up menu. This brings up the Choose Name dialog box in which you need to enter the name of the new table. Click OK when done entering the name. When you've entered the name and clicked OK, the new table is displayed on the database diagram.

For each field, or column, in the new table you can specify a column name, data type, and length, and indicate whether the column allows null values. So to add a new column, simply fill in these attributes as appropriate under Column Name, Data Type, Length, and Allows Nulls, and move to the next row (see Figure 4-18). I know this may seem a little weird and confusing, what with the columns that make up a table being represented as rows in this table design view, but just hang in there, and you'll get it eventually.

Fill in the column attributes as shown in Figure 4-18 and press Ctrl+S to save the table and diagram.

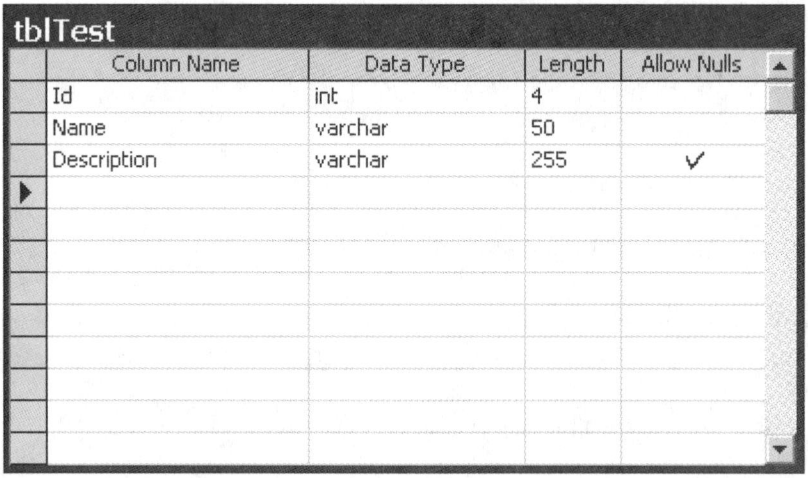

Figure 4-18. Column attributes

One of the first things you may notice is that the Data Type Column attribute is DBMS specific. This means the drop-down list of data types is filled with valid data types for the database the diagram is created in.

Once you are done entering the columns and the column attributes, press Ctrl+S to save the diagram and to create the new table. Although it's convenient to create and edit tables with the Database Designer database diagram, it can be of greater help to use the Table Designer. See the "Using the Table Designer" section later in this chapter for more information.

Adding Relationships

Relationships are used for indicating relations between data in different tables. Once you've created your tables, all you need to do is create relationships by dragging a field from a table to the related field in another table. This brings up the Create Relationship dialog box, where you can define your relationship. In Figure 4-17, you can see the relationships between the tables in the UserMan database as the lines or links connecting the tables on the database diagram.

> **CROSS-REFERENCE**   *See Chapter 2 for a more detailed description of relationships.*

Deleting Relationships

If a relationship has become obsolete for some reason, you can delete it by right-clicking the relationship and selecting Delete Relationship from Database from the resulting pop-up menu. You are required to confirm this deletion. As with all other changes you make to the database diagram, the deletion isn't saved to the database until you save the diagram.

Editing Database Properties

If you need to change the properties of the database, such as the keys of a table or the relationship between two tables, you simply right-click any table or relationship and select Property Pages from the pop-up menu. This brings up the Property Pages dialog box, where you can edit the owner, keys, indexes, and constraints of a table and the relationships between tables.

Database Diagram Overview

I am sure you've had the same problems as me in previous versions of Microsoft database tools: once you've added many tables to a diagram, it's nearly impossible to get the full overview of the diagram. Well, there are actually a few features available to help you:

- *Zoom in to view just one table or so, or zoom out to view the entire diagram*: You can zoom using the shortcut menu; right-click any blank space on the diagram, select Zoom from the pop-up menu, and specify the percentage you want to zoom to. The current zoom percentage is checked on the menu if you've previously changed the zoom percentage. One command on the Zoom submenu is of special interest: the To Fit command. This command will automatically choose the zoom percentage that will let you view the entire database diagram in the current view.

- *Move the view port, or rather change the viewable area of the diagram*: Locate the view port icon in the lower-right corner of the diagram (see Figure 4-19). If you click the view port icon, you can see the entire diagram in the overview window, as shown in Figure 4-20. If you hold down the left mouse button, you can move the view port around the diagram. The view port is the dotted rectangle you can see in the middle of the overview window when you first click on the view port icon.

EXERCISE

Zoom the database diagram to 200% and click the view port icon. Hold down the left mouse button and move the view port around the database diagram. Once you've selected the right area of the diagram, let go of the mouse button. Now the area of the database diagram you can see should be the same as the one you just selected using the overview window.

- *Arrange all tables so that related tables sit together nice and orderly*: Right-click any blank space on the diagram, and select Arrange Tables from the pop-up menu.

- *Show relationship names*: Right-click any blank space on the diagram and select Show Relationship Labels from the pop-up menu. This will display a name label next to the relationship.

- *Add descriptive free text labels to the diagram*: Right-click any blank space on the diagram and then, select New Text Annotation from the pop-up menu. This will open a text field where you right-clicked the diagram. When you've finished typing your text, you simply click any other part of the diagram to finish editing the text annotation. Use these text annotations to add descriptive text that makes your diagram easier to read. These text annotations are NOT part of the database in any way. If you need to edit an existing text annotation, just click the text on the diagram and the text field opens up for editing.

- *Change the table view:* If you want to see more or fewer table attributes than what is displayed, you can select the table(s) in question and right-click one of the selected tables. Next, select Table View from the pop-up menu and click the desired view in the submenu. Standard view is very useful when designing a database, whereas the Column Names view is good as an overview.

- *Automatically size the tables:* If the size of one or more tables doesn't fit the number of rows and/or columns, you can select the table(s) in question, right-click one of the selected tables and then click Autosize Selected Tables from the pop-up menu.

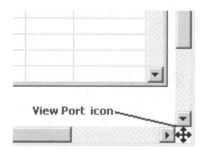

Figure 4-19. The database diagram view port icon

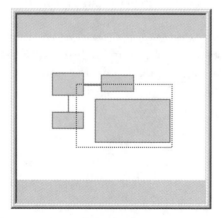

Figure 4-20. The database diagram overview window

Saving the Database Diagram

When you have the database diagram open, you can press Ctrl+S any time to save the diagram. The diagram is validated before it's saved to the database. If any existing data violates any new relationships and/or constraints, the diagram cannot be saved. A dialog box detailing the error will appear. You'll have to correct the error before you can save the diagram and thus save the changes to the database. Although the diagram can be seen under the Diagram node in the Server Explorer, it isn't actually an object on its own. The diagram is saved to the system table dtproperties in your database. This table doesn't show up under the Tables node in the Server Explorer, but you can see it using the Enterprise Manager that comes with SQL Server. Don't try to edit this table manually, only through the diagram itself. If you try to edit it manually, you might end up destroying other diagrams and objects in the database.

Using the Table Designer

The Table Designer is by far the most comprehensive tool for creating a new table in a database. Although you can use the Database Designer to add a new table to a diagram and thus the database, you have a much better overview of a table when you use the Table Designer. However, there's nothing stopping you from creating the initial database, including all the tables in a database diagram, and then editing the table design of each of the tables individually in the Table Designer afterwards.

To create a new table using the Table Designer, you must open up Server Explorer, expand the desired database, and right-click the Tables node in this database. Selecting New Table from the pop-up menu brings up the Table Designer, as shown in Figure 4-21.

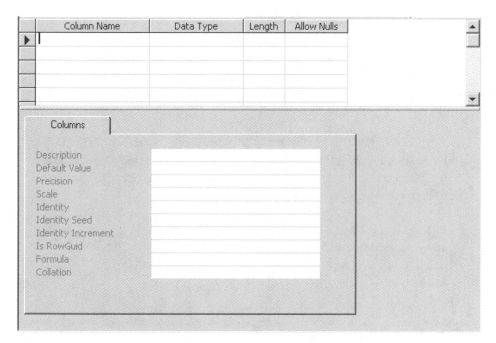

Figure 4-21. The Table Designer

At first, the Table Designer looks similar to the table view you see when you use the New Table feature of the Database Designer (see the "Adding Tables" section earlier in this chapter), but it's a little more sophisticated.

Adding Columns

To add a new column to your table, you simply type the name of the column in the Column Name column. The Data Type attribute must also be filled in with the desired data type for the column. Please note that the data types in the drop-down list box are DBMS specific, which means that the list only contains data types that are valid for the database you are connected to. The Length attribute is also required when you specify a data type that can have varying lengths such as the varchar data type of SQL Server. The Allow Nulls attribute is always checked by default when you create a new column (by typing in the name of the column). If a column allows null values, it cannot be a key field, so be sure you clear this attribute for your key field before you start adding data to a table, as it can be quite hard to change this attribute afterwards.

What I've described so far is pretty much the same as using the Database Designer to add a new table. Here is the big difference: the Columns attributes pane at the bottom of the Table Designer[2] (see Figure 4-21). The Columns attributes pane varies depending on the database to which you are connected. In the case of Figure 4-21, I am using SQL Server 2000. Some attributes are the same, however, as is the case with the following:

- *Description:* Use this attribute to add a description of the column, such as what kind of values it holds. This can be very valuable to someone taking over your database at a later stage in the life of the database or even valuable to yourself when working on a large project.

- *Default Value:* The Default value is used for specifying a value that will be saved with rows that don't contain a value for this particular column. This can be used in place of allowing Null values, which can be hard to handle from code.

Setting the Primary Key

You can set the primary key by right-clicking the grid next to the Column Name column for the column you want to have as the primary key. See the "What Is a Primary Key?" section in Chapter 2 for more information about primary keys. Next, click Set Primary Key to set the column as the primary key (see Figure 4-22). If you need to have a composite primary key, then you have to select all the columns that make up the primary key before you right-click the grid next to the Column Name column. You can select several columns the same way you would select multiple items on a list, that is, by holding down Ctrl when selecting the columns one by one. If the columns are contiguous, you can select the first column and then hold the Shift key and select the last column before you right-click the grid next to the Column Name column.

---

2. The Columns attributes pane can be accessed from within a database diagram, however, if you open the Properties dialog box for a table on the diagram.

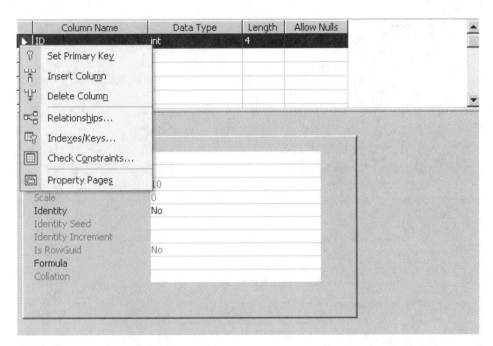

Figure 4-22. Setting the primary key

Adding Indexes and Keys

It's often a good idea to create an index on a column that is used for searching a table. See the "What Is an Index?" section in Chapter 2 for more information about indexes. You can create an index by right-clicking anywhere on the table grid in the Table Designer and selecting Indexes/Keys from the pop-up menu. This brings up the Property Pages dialog box with the Indexes/Keys tab shown (see Figure 4-23). Please note that the tab looks different if you've already created an index and/or primary key. The Selected Index list box in this case is then populated and one of the existing indexes is selected. Another thing to observe is that the content of this tab is also DBMS specific so it changes depending on the database you are connected to. The Indexes/Keys tab in Figure 4-23 shows a connection to a SQL Server database.

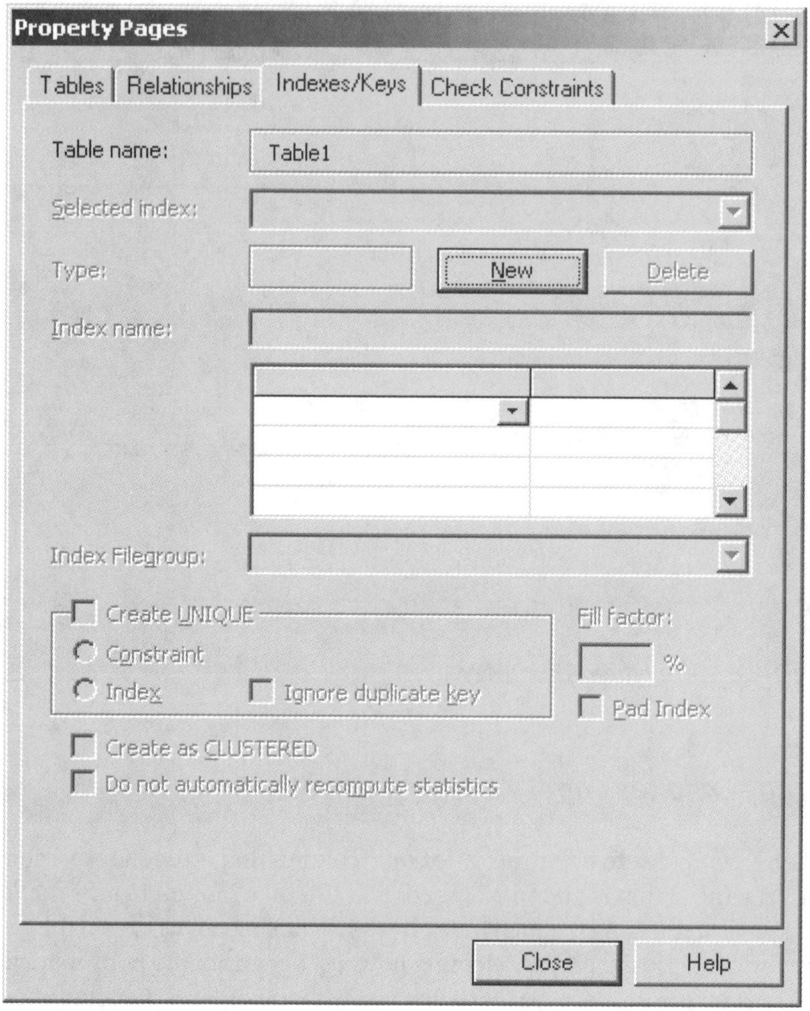

Figure 4-23. The Indexes/Keys tab of the Property Pages dialog box

To create a new index, you click the New button. This will enable some of the text boxes and check boxes on the tab. Start out by giving your index a name in the Index name text box and then, add the columns that make up the index in the grid below the Index name text box. For each column you add to the grid, you must specify if the sorting order is ascending or descending. This obviously depends on the data in the index and how it will be searched. The other options shown in Figure 4-23 are SQL Server specific, and I recommend you read the help files for SQL Server, if you are in doubt about these options. Once you click Close, the index is saved. Well, this isn't quite true, as it's only saved to memory. This means the index won't be saved to the database until you save the diagram. Just to avoid confusion any more than necessary, only the primary key is designated as a key. So if you want to add a foreign key to use in a relationship, you just add an index to the column(s) in question.

Adding Constraints

Sometimes the values in a particular column in your table must be in a particular range. If so, it's a good idea to create a constraint that will enforce your rules or ensure that the values are indeed within the required range. You can create a constraint by right-clicking anywhere on the table grid in the Table Designer and selecting Check Constraints from the pop-up menu. This brings up the Property Pages dialog box with the Check Constraints tab shown (see Figure 4-24).

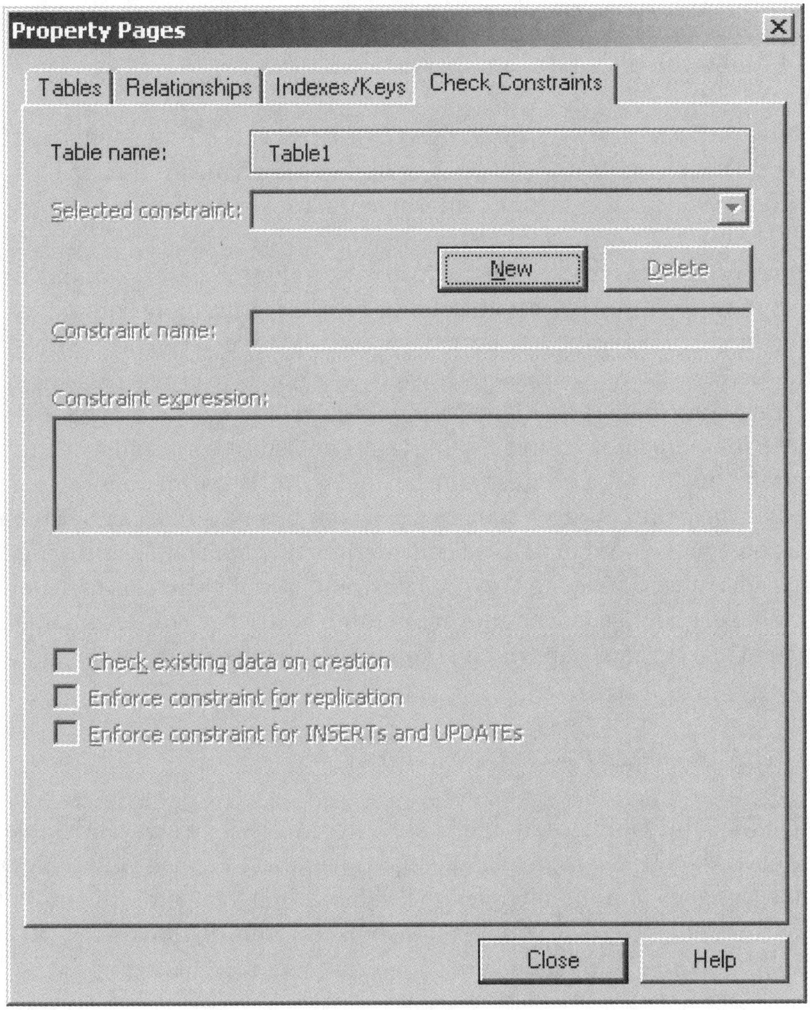

Figure 4-24. The Check Constraints tab of the Property Pages dialog box

To create a new constraint, click the New button. This will enable some of the text boxes and check boxes on the tab. Start out by giving your constraint a name in the Constraint name text box, and then type the constraint expression in the Constraint expression text box. Here's an example of a constraint:

```
Test <> ''
```

This means the field Test cannot hold an empty string. Following is a description of the check box options on the tab:

- *Check existing data on creation:* When the table is saved, any existing data is validated to see if it conflicts with the constraint. Unlike an index, it's possible to have values in a table that don't conform to a column constraint.

- *Enforce constraint for replication:* This option enforces the constraint when the table is replicated to another database.

- *Enforce constraint for INSERTs and UPDATEs:* This is option enforces the constraint when data is inserted or updated. This means that an insert or update will fail if it doesn't conform to the constraint.

The constraint is saved to memory when you click Close. Constraints are a good option when you work with column-level integrity, more commonly known as domain integrity. However, business rules, which can be enforced by constraints, can also be enforced by triggers. A *trigger* is really a special kind of stored procedure that is automatically invoked, just like a constraint. See Chapter 6 for more information about triggers and stored procedures. A trigger can perform any task that a constraint can and more. However, there is more overhead in invoking a trigger, so basically if your business rule can be enforced using a constraint, you should use a constraint. If not, look into using a trigger.

One advantage a trigger has over a constraint is that it can compare or validate a value in a row against a value in a column located in a different table. It's fair to state that a trigger can contain more complex logic than a constraint.

Creating a Relationship

Although the Table Designer should be the preferred tool for creating a table, it's not the easiest way to create a relationship. Once you've created your tables using the Table Designer, you should open up a database diagram and use the Database Designer to create your relationships. For information on how to accomplish this, see "Adding Relationships" earlier in this chapter.

Designing Queries with the Query Designer

The Query Designer is to queries what the Table Designer is to tables, a visual tool that makes it easy to create your queries. This should be your preferred tool for creating even the simplest of queries, because it has drag-and-drop features as well as a text pane in which you can type in your query manually. Here is how you create a simple select query in the UserMan example database (if you are uncertain on how to perform the following tasks, please see the "Adding New Database Objects" section earlier in this chapter):

1. Open up the UserMan database project if it isn't already open in the IDE.

2. Add a new query named Select Users.

3. Add the tblUser table to the query.

The Query Designer should now look like Figure 4-25. The top part where the table is placed is called the Diagram pane. The part beneath this is called the Grid pane, followed by a pane displaying free text, which is called the SQL pane. The Results pane resides in the bottom part of the designer.

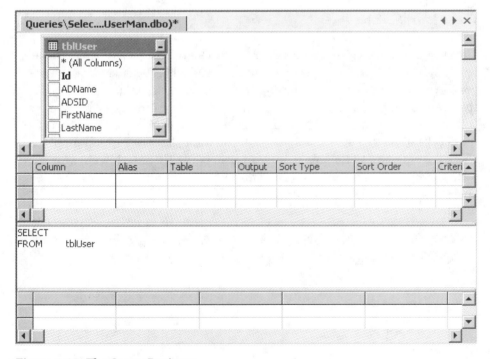

Figure 4-25. The Query Designer

Taking a Closer Look at the Query Designer Panes

As mentioned in the preceding section, there are four panes in the Query Designer:

- Diagram pane

- Grid pane

- SQL pane

- Results pane

These panes all have a function to perform, but with the exception of the Results pane, they overlap in functionality. The Diagram, Grid, and SQL panes allow successively greater complexity in the query, though they overlap in functionality for very simple queries, and if you look at the other two panes when you edit one pane, you'll find that these three panes stay synchronized. I guess it's really a matter of preference which pane you use. See the following sections on what each of the panes can do for you.

The Diagram Pane

The Diagram pane, which is the top part of the Query Designer, is where you add and show the tables used in the query. You can add tables by dragging them from the Server Explorer or by right-clicking anywhere in the Diagram pane and selecting Add Table from the pop-up menu. For each table in the Diagram pane, you can select which columns are included in the query. You do this by checking the check box next to the column name. If you want all rows output, simply check the option * (All Columns). You can also right-click the table, click Select All Columns on the pop-up menu, and toggle the check marks by pressing the Space key.

> **CAUTION**   *If you check all the columns in a table as well as the option * (All Columns), you'll get all the rows as output of your query twice.*

Removing Tables

Right-click a table and select Remove from the pop-up menu to remove the table from the Diagram pane. The number of tables allowed in the Diagram pane depends on the query type. A SELECT, Make Table, and INSERT Results query can hold any number of tables, whereas the UPDATE, DELETE, and INSERT VALUES queries can only hold one table. If the tables in the Diagram pane are related or if there are relationships between any two of the tables, they are shown on the diagram. However, you can't change or delete the relationships in the Query Designer. Actually this isn't quite true. If any two tables have an inner or outer join, and you remove this join from the Diagram pane, the join is changed to a cross-join. A cross-join outputs all selected columns from the tables in question in all possible combinations. In other words, you cannot delete a join/relationship between two tables using the Diagram pane. You only change the join in the Diagram pane to affect how the query will behave and not the database itself. You need to use the Table Designer or the Database Designer if you want to change a relationship between two tables.

Changing the Join Type

You can also change the join type by right-clicking the join and selecting Property Pages from the pop-up menu. In the Property Pages dialog box, you can change the join to include all rows from one or both of the joined tables or simply just the selected columns in the tables. (In SQL, these are called a LEFT OUTER JOIN or RIGHT OUTER JOIN, FULL OUTER JOIN or INNER JOIN.) In addition, you can change the way the tables are joined by changing the column comparison symbol to one of the following: = (equal to), <> (not equal to), < (less than), <= (less than or equal to), > (greater than), or >= (greater than or equal to). I am, of course, talking about the column in each table that is used for joining the tables. When the Property Pages dialog box isn't shown, you can see from the join itself how the tables are joined. In the middle, you can see the comparison sign, and if the join is an OUTER JOIN, a box is added to the diamond shape. See Figure 4-26 for examples of the various combinations of diamond and rectangle shapes that represent joins.

Figure 4-26. Various join types depicted in the Diagram pane

The four join shapes in Figure 4-26 depict the following, from left to right:

- Full Outer Join, joining columns not equal

- Full Outer Join, joining columns equal

- Left Outer Join, joining columns equal

- Inner Join, joining columns equal

Besides the joins mentioned, there is also the cross-join, which is when you have every single row in the left table combined with all rows in the right table. Basically this means that the result of a cross-join, also called the Cartesian product, is the number of rows in the left table multiplied by the number of rows in the right table.

If you have many tables in the Diagram pane, then you can choose to show only the name of a table and thus save some real estate onscreen for more tables. This is done by right-clicking the table and selecting Name Only from the pop-up menu. Right-click the table and click Column Names to show the full table again.

Grouping and Sorting the Output

The output can be sorted (ordered) and grouped as in any normal SQL statement using the Diagram pane. You can sort the columns by right-clicking the column in a table and selecting Sort Ascending or Sort Descending. A sort symbol is placed next to the column name when you want output sorted by a specific column. You can cancel the sorting by right-clicking the column in the table and clicking the checked sort order.

Grouping is done nearly the same way as sorting, except you need to click the Group By button on the Query toolbar first. In Figure 4-27, the Group By button is the second from the right. Once the Group By button is pressed, you can select the columns you want to group by. When a column is part of the output grouping, a grouping symbol like the one the Group By button displays is placed to the far right of the column name. You can remove a grouping by pressing the Group By button again. Please note that the grouping is done in the order you select the columns. As in any SQL query, at least all output columns must be part of the grouping.

Figure 4-27. The query toolbar

If you are in doubt about how to create a SQL statement in the SQL pane, then using the Diagram pane is a good way to learn, because you can see what effect a change in the Diagram pane has on the corresponding SQL statement in the SQL pane.

The Grid Pane

Recall that the Grid pane allows you to make the same changes as in the Diagram pane and the SQL pane. However, there is one difference to the Grid pane: you cannot add tables to it. So in order to add tables to the query, you must use the functionality of the Diagram pane or the SQL pane. Okay, when I say the functionality isn't there, I mean there is no pop-up menu with an Add Table command for the Grid pane, but you can actually use the Add Table command on the Query menu to add a table.

> **NOTE** *When you enter data in the various columns, the data is validated, or verified, as soon as you move to another row or column.*

The Grid pane holds a number of named columns (what a surprise, eh?), and in Table 4-2, you can see a description of each these named columns. Please note that not all columns are visible for all the different query types. Check the Valid Query Types column to see if the column is valid for a particular query.

Table 4-2. Grid Pane Columns Explained

COLUMN NAME	VALID QUERY TYPES	DESCRIPTION
Column	All query types	This is the name of the column in the table referenced in the Table column.
Alias	SELECT, INSERT Results, and Make Table	If you give a column an alias, the alias is what the output column will be named. Use the Alias column to give your output a more descriptive name. Aliases are also used for computed columns, or when including the same column twice for whatever reason. This is the same as the AS SQL clause in the SQL pane.
Table	SELECT, INSERT Results, UPDATE, DELETE, and Make Table	This is where you select the name of the table into which your column is placed. You can only select tables from the drop-down list. If you need to add more tables, use the Add Table command on the Query menu. If the column is computed, this column should be left blank.
Output	SELECT, INSERT Results, and Make Table	This column indicates if the column is to be output as part of the result.
Sort Type	SELECT, INSERT Results, and Make Table	If you leave this column empty, the output isn't sorted. To specify a sort order, choose Ascending or Descending from the drop-down list. This is the same as the ORDER BY clause in the SQL pane: ASC for ascending or DESC for descending.
Sort Order	SELECT, INSERT Results, and Make Table	This is where you specify in which order the columns are sorted, if you want to sort by more than one column. The columns will be sorted first by the column starting with 1, and then by the column with number 2, and so on. This is the same as the list of columns following the ORDER BY clause in the SQL pane.
Group By	SELECT, INSERT Results, and Make Table	This is the same as the GROUP BY clause in the SQL pane.
Criteria	SELECT, INSERT Results, UPDATE, DELETE, and Make Table	You don't specify the column name, because you add the criteria to the row with the correct table column. If you need to add more than one criteria using the Or operator, you put each criteria in a separate Or . . . column. If you need to add criteria using the And operator, you do it in the same column, like this: > 1 AND < 5. This means that the result set will hold rows where the column (indicated in the Column Name column) is greater than 1 and less than 5.

(continued)

Table 4-2. Grid Pane Columns Explained (continued)

COLUMN NAME	VALID QUERY TYPES	DESCRIPTION
Or . . .	SELECT, INSERT Results, UPDATE, DELETE, and Make Table	This is for adding more than one criterion. You just keep adding one criterion in each of the Or . . . columns until you've added all your criteria for that table.
Append	INSERT Results	This is for appending the results of a row-returning query to an existing table. The result value in Column column is appended to the column named in the Append column in the destination table. Normally this column is filled out by the Query Designer, if it's able to figure out what destination column matches the source column (Column).
New Value	UPDATE and INSERT VALUES	This dictates the new value for the column specified in the Column column. The new value can be an expression that will be evaluated or a literal value.

If you are in doubt about how to create a SQL statement in the SQL pane, then the grid pane is a good way to learn, because you can see what effect a change in the Grid pane has on the corresponding SQL statement in the SQL pane. Live and learn.

The SQL Pane

The SQL pane is for entering your queries in free text based on the SQL standard for the database to which you are connected. Most relational databases these days rely on the ANSI SQL standard as the base with added functionality. I am not going to go into detail about the SQL standards, as that is a subject for a whole book on its own. If you need specifics on one dialect of a SQL standard, I can only recommend you read the help files and/or documentation that come with your database, or alternatively buy yourself a copy of a book that covers the subject. However, there are also a number of online tutorials on the subject, and here are the URLs to a few of them:

- http://ioc.unesco.org/oceanteacher/resourcekit/Module2/Database/DBMS/Sql/sql.html

- http://spectral.mscs.mu.edu/javadev/databases/sqltut.html

- http://www.sqlcourse.com/

You can do anything in the SQL pane that you can do in the Grid and Diagram panes. One major difference though is that you need to verify the SQL syntax before these other two panes are updated based on the contents of the SQL pane. (See "Verifying the SQL Syntax" later in this chapter for details.) Actually, you can also move to either the Diagram or Grid pane in order to accomplish an update of these panes, but it's not verified as such. You can type the name of an invalid column in a SELECT statement, and this will be shown in the Grid pane. So use the Verify SQL Syntax facility frequently when you are editing your queries using the SQL pane. It will save you a lot of hassle.

The Results Pane

The Results pane is quite different from the other three panes in the Query Designer, because it's not intended for editing your query. As the name implies, it's simply an output window. The Results pane is only for row-returning queries, such as SELECT queries and scalar queries with aggregate functions like SELECT COUNT(*) FROM TableName.

In the case of a row-returning query, other than a GROUP BY query, if such a query has returned rows from a single table, it's actually possible to use the Results pane to add new rows to the source table. If you are familiar with Microsoft Access or SQL Server's Query Analyzer, then you probably recognize the grid in the Results pane, and you also know that you can add a new row by typing the column values in the last row in the grid (the one marked with an asterisk). If you want to edit the values returned by the query, you can do so by typing the new value in the desired column. Once you've typed in the column values, you simply move to another row, and the Query Designer will try to update the database immediately. If an error occurs when updating, a message box will be displayed, detailing the error. Once you click OK, the cursor is placed in the row in the grid where the error occurred.

Hiding and Showing the Various Panes

All the panes can be hidden, but at least one of the panes has to be visible when the Query Designer is shown. You can hide a pane by right-clicking the pane and selecting Hide Pane from the pop-up menu. Actually, you can also hide the panes using the Query toolbar shown in Figure 4-27, which appears by default when you open the Query Designer. If the toolbar isn't showing, you can use one of the menu commands in the View ➤ Panes menu. The first four buttons from the left on the toolbar are for hiding and showing the Query Designer panes. The tool tips help you figure out which button does what; to view a tool tip, position the mouse pointer over a button and keep it there for a little while. These buttons are the only way you can show a pane once it's hidden—you cannot use a command on a pop-up menu to show a pane as you can to hide it.

Verifying the SQL Syntax

If you want to make sure that your query is valid, you can use the Verify SQL Syntax facility. This is only necessary if you are using the SQL pane to edit your query, as the other panes automatically verify your changes. You can perform the task by clicking the Verify SQL Syntax button on the Query toolbar or by clicking Verify SQL Syntax on the Query menu. Alternatively, you can right-click the SQL pane and select Verify SQL Syntax from the pop-up menu. A message box appears when the query has been validated. It simply tells you that your query is valid or that your query needs to be changed according to the explanation shown in the message box.

Typical errors are typos, like in Figure 4-28. If your query is invalid, you may get more information by clicking the Help button in the message box displayed in Figure 4-29.

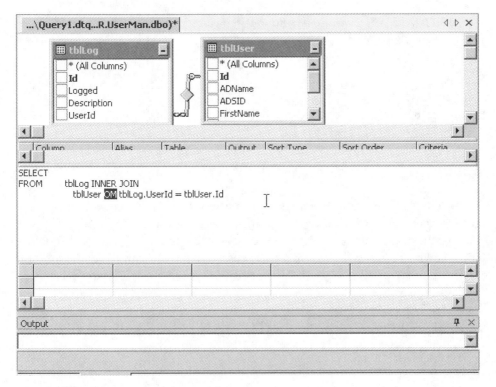

Figure 4-28. A typo makes this invalid SQL script.

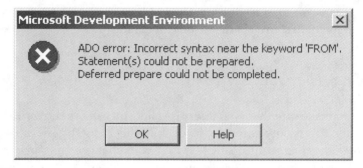

Figure 4-29. Error Message dialog box with help button

Executing a Query

When you've finished building your query, you might want to execute it. You can execute, or run, your query by clicking the Run Query button on the Query toolbar, by clicking the Run command on the Query menu, or by right-clicking a blank space in the Diagram pane and selecting Run from the pop-up menu.

> **CAUTION** *Queries cannot be undone, so if you are deleting rows from one or more tables, make sure they are expendable!*

The query won't execute if the SQL syntax in the SQL pane is invalid. If you are uncertain if your query is correct, then try verifying the syntax before you run the query. See "Verifying the SQL Syntax" earlier in this chapter for details.

Examining the Various Query Types

By default the query created is a SELECT query, but you can change the query type by clicking the Change Type button on the Query toolbar. You can also change the query type using the Change Type command on the Query menu. In the following sections, you'll find a short description and example (in the form of SQL statement queries) of all the query types offered by the IDE. Here's a list of them:

- SELECT

- INSERT

- UPDATE

- DELETE

- Make Table

SELECT Query

The SELECT query is always used for returning rows from one or more tables in the database. Sometimes the SELECT statement is combined with or part of an INSERT query to append the result to an existing table (INSERT Results query) or add the result to a new table (Make Table query, covered shortly).

This is the SELECT query in its very simplest form: `SELECT * FROM tblUser`. This query returns all rows in the tblUser table. All columns (*) are output. Please note that unless you have a specific reason for always wanting all columns, you should avoid the asterisk for good programming practice: you only have to ask "Do I want all the additional fields that a developer at a later stage might add to this table, rather than specific fields I need for the current task?"

UPDATE Query

The UPDATE query is for updating column values in specific rows in the destination table. The query `UPDATE tblUser SET FirstName='Peter'` updates all rows in the tblUser table and sets the FirstName column to "Peter". If you only want to update specific rows, you need to include the WHERE clause, like this:

```
UPDATE tblUser SET FirstName='Peter' WHERE FirstName='John'
```

This will only update the rows where the FirstName column holds the value "John". If you need to update more than one column in each row that matches the criteria in the WHERE clause, you can separate the columns with a comma, like this:

```
UPDATE tblUser SET FirstName='Peter', LastName='Johnson' WHERE FirstName='John'
```

You can only update rows in one table at a time.

DELETE Query

If you want to delete certain rows from a table, this is your best choice. The DELETE query is quite simple and here is an example: `DELETE FROM tblUser`. This will delete all rows in the tblUser table. As with the update query, you can select which rows to delete using the WHERE clause, like this:

```
DELETE tblUser WHERE FirstName='John'
```

This will delete all rows where the FirstName column holds the value "John". You can only delete rows from one table at a time.

Make Table Query

The Make Table query is actually a little more complex than the name implies. Although a table is created when you use this query, it also selects some rows that are inserted into the new table. The INTO keyword in the following example is what makes the difference; it creates a new table and copies all the rows from the tblUser into the new table (tblTest).

```
SELECT * INTO tblTest FROM tblUser
```

As you can see from the example, the SELECT statement is used for retrieving the rows from the tblUser table that are inserted into the new tblTest table. An error occurs if tblTest already exists in the database. If you need to append the result to an existing table, you need to use an INSERT Results query.

The Make Table query is very good for copying certain rows and/or columns from a source database into a temporary table, where you can manipulate it without messing up the "real" data. It can also be used for backing up data from one or more tables and then restoring it later on. If you wish to only create a copy of the table schema, you can do so with a statement like this:

```
SELECT * INTO tblTest FROM tblUser WHERE 1=2
```

This little trick won't be copying any data, because 1 never equals 2. However, you can only create one table at a time with a Make Table query.

> **NOTE** *Copying a table in this manner doesn't copy the extended column attributes, such as default values or descriptions.*

INSERT Queries

There are actually two INSERT queries, one for inserting the result of a row-returning query into another table and one for inserting values into a table.

INSERT Results Query

The INSERT Results query is for appending rows to an existing table. If you need to add rows to a new table, then you must use the Make Table query. The INSERT Results query is structured like this:

```
INSERT INTO tblUser (LoginName, FirstName, LastName, Password) _
 SELECT LoginName, FirstName, LastName, Password FROM tblTest
```

In this query, I retrieve the columns LoginName, FirstName, and LastName from the table tblTest, and I append it to the tblUser table. The column names in the source table tblTest do NOT have to be same as in the destination table tblUser, but the order in which the columns appear obviously matters.

You can retrieve rows from as many tables as you like, as long as the number of columns match the number of columns in the destination table. There is always only one destination table.

INSERT VALUES Query

The INSERT VALUES query is quite similar to the UPDATE query in the way the SQL statement is constructed:

```
INSERT INTO tblUser (LoginName,FirstName, LastName, Password) _
 VALUES('peterj', 'Peter', 'Johnson', 'password')
```

This query will insert a row into the tblUser table with the values "peterj", "Peter", "Johnson", "password" for the columns LoginName, FirstName, LastName, and Password. The order of the values (VALUES) must match how the columns, specified in the first set of parentheses, are ordered. You can leave out the field names and the parentheses after the table name, if you specify values for all the columns in the order in which they appear in the database. It's not recommended to use this kind of query while developing your application, because the table design will more than likely be altered at least a few times.

> **NOTE** *You can only insert one row into the destination table at a time.*

Script Editing Using the SQL Editor

The SQL Editor is a text editor and it's the same editor that is used for writing
your C# code. This means it has the same facilities as the code editor, such as
color coding and line numbering. However, there is no IntelliSense! You can
change the default behavior of the editor by opening up the Options dialog box,
by clicking Options on the Tools menu. See Figure 4-30 for a view of the Options
dialog box with the Text Editor node expanded.

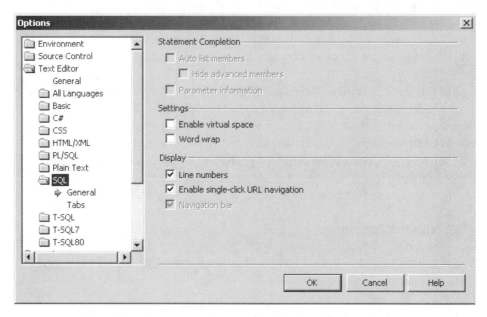

Figure 4-30. The Options dialog box with the Text Editor node expanded

As you can see from Figure 4-30, there are several options available for cus-
tomization for different SQL dialects such as PL/SQL (Oracle) and various
versions of T-SQL (Microsoft SQL Server). There are also some options under the
Database Tools node that are relevant to the SQL Editor.

EXERCISE

Add a Create Table Script in the Create Scripts folder named Create SQL Server
Table. See "Adding New Database Objects" for more information on how to add
new database objects to your database project. Once the script has been created,
it should look like Figure 4-31.

```
 1   IF EXISTS (SELECT * FROM sysobjects WHERE type = 'U' AND name = 'Table_Name')
 2      BEGIN
 3         PRINT 'Dropping Table Table_Name'
 4         DROP  Table Table_Name
 5      END
 6   GO
 7
 8   /********************************************************************************
 9   **      File:
10   **      Name: Table_Name
11   **      Desc:
12   **
13   **      This template can be customized:
14   **
15   **
16   **      Auth:
17   **      Date: |
18   ********************************************************************************
19   **      Change History
20   ********************************************************************************
21   **      Date:      Author:           Description:
```

Figure 4-31. The SQL Editor with the Create SQL Server Table script open

Use the Replace functionality (Ctrl+H) of the Text Editor to replace all occurrences of the string Table_Name with tblTest. After the starting parentheses, "(", below the CREATE TABLE statement, and before the closing parentheses, ")", type in the following text: **Id int PRIMARY KEY NOT NULL IDENTITY, Test varchar(50) DEFAULT('Test')**.

Using the Query Editor to Produce SQL Statements

If you are like me, you can't remember the syntax for all the various SQL statements there are, but instead of looking up syntax in the help files for your database, you can use the Query Editor for this purpose. You can access the Query Editor without leaving the SQL Editor by right-clicking anywhere in the SQL Editor and selecting Insert SQL from the pop-up menu. This brings up the Query Editor, or rather the Query Builder as it's called when invoked from within the SQL Editor.

Although you can right-click anywhere in the SQL Editor to bring up the Query Builder, perhaps I should point out that the text generated using the Query Builder is placed where you right-click in order to select the Insert SQL command. So, make sure that you place the mouse cursor where you want the SQL text inserted before you right-click. When you are done using the Query Builder, close the window and you'll be prompted to save the content. Click Yes if you want the generated text inserted into your script or click No if you don't want to save the text. If you click No, the generated text is discarded, and you cannot retrieve it again! See "Designing Queries with the Query Designer" earlier in this chapter for information on using the Query Editor/Query Builder.

Saving a Script

Once you are done editing your script, or even better, once you've done some work you don't want to lose due to unforeseen circumstances, you should save your script. This is as easy as pressing Ctrl+S. You can also access the save functionality using the menus. Select the Save Create Scripts ➤ Create SQL Server Table.sql command on the File menu. This menu command is obviously dynamically created, so if you called your script something different, then the menu command looks different. The script is saved to the folder that was selected in the Solution Explorer when you added the script to your project.

EXERCISE

Save your script.

Editing and Using Script Templates

I have chosen to create a script for Microsoft SQL Server simply because the default template is the SQL Server one. You can change the templates by editing them using any text editor that can save in plain text, such as NotePad. The templates are located in the \Program Files\Microsoft Visual Studio .NET\Common7\Tools\Templates\Database Project Items folder. If you placed Visual Studio .NET on a different drive and/or in a different folder when you ran Setup, you need to change the path to the templates accordingly.

Running SQL Scripts

When you've created your script, you can run the script by right-clicking it in the Solution Explorer and selecting Run On from the pop-up menu. Select the desired database connection or reference from the Run On dialog box and click OK. The script now runs against the selected database connection.

This is a nice little improvement over previous versions of Microsoft Visual Database Tools where you had to explicitly assign a connection to a script. Now you can assign a connection to a script before running it. Mind you, not all scripts are compatible with any database connection or reference.

However, this isn't the only way to run a script. If you have a script open in the SQL Editor, you can right-click anywhere in the editor and select Run from the pop-up menu. Mind you, if you haven't saved the changes to your script, you'll be prompted to do so before the script is run.

When the script is running, all output from the script is written to the output window, which is located just below the SQL Editor by default. It's always a good idea to examine the output to see if the script was executed correctly.

Creating Typed Data Sets

If you want to work with typed data sets, you have to create the typed data set manually or at least with the help of some tools. (See Chapter 3B for an explanation of typed versus untyped data sets.) You cannot create a typed data set from code!

There are a number of steps required in order to generate a typed data set:

1. Get or create the schema.

2. Generate the data set class.

3. Create an instance of the newly generated and derived data set class.

So, what you can glean from the preceding steps is that a typed data set is really nothing more than a class that wraps the data access and provides you with strong typing, or the IntelliSense feature and compile time syntax checking, and so on.

There are three tools (actually only two, because the DataSet Designer and the XML Designer are really the same) you can use to create a typed data set:

- Component Designer

- DataSet Designer

- XML Designer

I'll show you how to create a typed data set in the following sections.

Using the XML Designer to Create a Typed Data Set

Although you can use the XML Designer to create a schema, it's easier to use the DataSet Designer. The DataSet Designer is really the XML Designer with a little extra functionality added, so do yourself a favor and use the DataSet Designer. Because most of the functionality is duplicated in the XML Designer and the DataSet Designer, I'll only cover how to use the DataSet Designer to create your typed data sets.

Using the DataSet Designer to Create a Typed Data Set

You can actually use the DataSet Designer to create a new schema from scratch and thus also use it to create a new table or even a new database. I am not going to go through that particular task in this book, but instead I'll concentrate on creating a schema based on an existing table.

EXERCISE

Open up the Typed DataSet Project located in the Chapter 4 folder.

If you have a project open that is NOT a database project, you can add a new data set if you right-click the project in the Solution Explorer and select the Add New Item command from the Add submenu. In the Add New Item dialog box, select the DataSet template and give the data set a name before you click Open.

EXERCISE

Open the UserManDataSet.xsd schema and make sure you have it open in DataSet schema view and not XML view. You can change views by clicking the tabs at the bottom of the UserManDataSet.xsd window. See Figure 4-32.

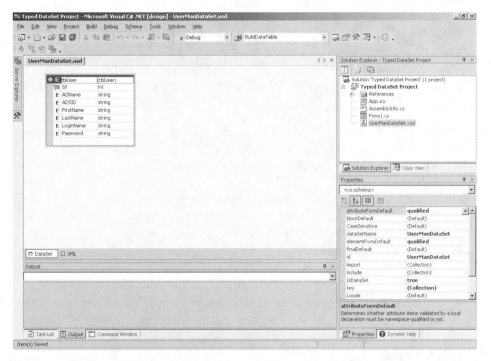

Figure 4-32. The UserManDataSet.xsd DataSet schema file

EXERCISE

Open the Server Explorer, expand the UserMan database node and the Tables node, and drag the tblUserRights table over to the DataSet Designer window and drop it. Now you have two tables in the DataSet Designer window. You need to give this new table a name, and I suggest you name it tblUserRights, as it's originally called. This is done by clicking the textbox next to the capital *E* in the header of the new table. Delete the current text and type in the new name. Click anywhere else on the DataSet Designer to save the name in memory. Press Ctrl+S to save the schema file to disk. Now you need to build the data set or rather the C# DataSet class file. You accomplish this by pressing Ctrl+Shift+B, or selecting the Build Solution menu command in the Build menu, which starts the build process. Now you've created a typed data set!

> **CAUTION**   The ***DataSet*** *class file isn't visible in the Solution Explorer, and you should not edit this file even though it's accessible in the same folder as the schema file. Any changes will be overwritten the next time you build your solution!*

The code in the Form1 Windows form class file needs to be modified in order to use the new typed table that I added. Take a quick look at Listing 4-1 to see how I use the strong typing in the button1_Click event.

Listing 4-1. Accessing a Typed DataSet Using Object Names

```
 1 private void button1_Click(object sender, System.EventArgs e) {
 2    UserManDataSet dstUserMan = new UserManDataSet();
 3    SqlDataAdapter dadUserMan;
 4    SqlConnection cnnUserMan;
 5
 6    // Instantiate and open connection
 7    cnnUserMan = new SqlConnection("Data Source=USERMANPC;" +
 8       "Initial Catalog=UserMan;User Id=UserMan;Password=userman");
 9    cnnUserMan.Open();
10    // Instatiate data adapter
11    dadUserMan = new SqlDataAdapter("SELECT * FROM tblUser", cnnUserMan);
12    // Fill data set
13    dadUserMan.Fill(dstUserMan, "tblUser");
14    // Display the login name for the first row in the user table
15    MessageBox.Show(dstUserMan.tblUser[0].LoginName.ToString());
16 }
```

Line 15 of Listing 4-1 shows how you can access a typed **DataSet** using the actual table and column names.

Summary

This chapter took you on a journey through all the features of the IDE that are database related. You had a look at the Server Explorer, which holds server resources. The data connections and message queues were the ones specifically discussed. The exercise for this chapter took you through all the steps required to create a database project using database references, scripts, queries, and command files.

You saw how to use the Database Designer to create database diagrams and the Table Designer for creating tables with keys and indexes, constraints, and relationships. I delved into using the SQL Editor for creating scripts and stored procedures. I then demonstrated how to create a typed data set.

The next chapter demonstrates how to handle exceptions in your applications.

CHAPTER 5

Exception Handling

ANY APPLICATION NEEDS TO HANDLE ERRORS that occur at runtime. Unfortunately it can be difficult to resolve all the possible errors that can occur. However, it's always a good idea to try to create code that can resolve or foresee most events and exceptions, so that the user doesn't have to worry about them. You should then attempt to catch the rest of them and display an error message with detailed information to the user about how to continue from this point. The overall purpose of exception handlers is to allow the application to gracefully recover from things going awry. This is especially important when dealing with relational databases. Because you are passing through multiple layers of technology, there are many places that an application can break. Although this chapter is about handling data-related exceptions, I'll cover the basics for handling all kinds of exceptions briefly.

Now, let's get one thing straight before moving on: for the discussions in this chapter, exceptions include errors, therefore from this point on, when I use the word *exception*, I'm referring to both.

One question that I often hear is this: "Do I need exception handling in all my procedures?" My answer is always a firm NO, because some procedures are so simple and they don't use variables that can overflow or something similar. These procedures might call a few other very simple procedures, and in such cases, you know that no application exceptions will occur. Don't put an exception handler in these types of procedures. It's a waste! Obviously knowing when to use an exception handler is a matter of experience and perhaps preference, but if you are in doubt, just stick one in there!

Unlike Visual Basic .NET, which has two programmatic ways of dealing with runtime exceptions, C# only has one: structured exception handling. Personally, I say thank the higher powers for that. Trust me: if you haven't experienced exception handling in previous versions of Visual Basic, well good for you!

Exception handling works like this: it marks blocks of code as *guarded*, which means that if any line of code within the block throws an exception, it will be caught by one of the associated exception handlers. The guarded block of code is marked using the **try . . . catch** statements, and as such the guarded code must be inserted between these statements. These statements are part of the **try . . . catch . . . finally** construct. This gives you a control structure that monitors the code in the guarded block, catches exceptions when they are thrown, and addresses these through a so-called filter handler. The control structure also separates the code that potentially throws exceptions from your "normal" code. I personally like this approach as I think it makes your code easy to read.

Listing 5-1 shows you how the **try . . . catch . . . finally** construct is put together.

*Listing 5-1. The **try . . . catch . . . finally** Construct*

```
// The try statement on the next line marks the beginning of guarded code
try {
 ... // This is the guarded block of code
}
catch [(Exception objException)]{
 ... // This is where you place your exception handling code. Code that can
    // resolve and recover from exceptions.
}
finally {
 ... // This block of code is always executed
}
```

The **try** statement, which doesn't take any arguments, is mandatory if you want to use exception handling. Besides this statement, you also need at least either a **catch** or **finally** statement. Here is what the different code blocks do:

- *try block:* This is where you place the lines of code you want to monitor, because they might throw an exception.

- *catch* block(s): The **catch** block is optional, and you can have as many **catch** blocks as you like, but the filter must be different. In Listing 5-1, I'm catching all exceptions in the one catch block, whether the optional filter is specified or not. I'll get to the exception filtering in the "Handling Exceptions in the Exception Handler" and "Filtering Exceptions" sections later in this chapter. In these blocks, you place your exception handling code—code that can possibly resolve the exceptions by examining the exception (Exception objException in Listing 5-1)—and let execution continue without notifying a possible user. The **catch** block is also called the *fault handler.*

- *finally block:* The **finally** block, which is optional, is where you put the lines of code that should run immediately after all exception processing has ended. You may be thinking, "Wait a minute; why not just place those lines of code after the end of the exception handler?" Well, my friend, you could do that, but it doesn't make your code easier to read does it? By plac- ing it in the **finally** block, you indicate that this code has something to do with the guarded code in the **try** block. Oh, I nearly forgot, if you place the code after the exception handler, it won't be executed if there is a **return** statement in the **catch** block that processes the exception. Place the code in the **finally** block, and it will run. So any code that really needs to run, whether or not an exception is thrown in the **try** block, goes here! The **finally** block is also called the *finally handler*.

> **NOTE** *There is NO performance penalty in placing code in the **try** block, even if no exception is thrown.*

When you deal with guarded blocks of code, there are three types of exception handlers:

- *Fault handler:* This is the same as the **catch** block when no filter has been specified.

- *Filter handler:* The filter handler is the same as the **catch** block when a filter has been specified. C# supports the *Type-filter handler*. This filter handler is used for handling exceptions of a specified class and any subclasses thereof.

- *Finally handler:* This is the same as the **finally** block.

Enabling Exception Handling

Well, perhaps the heading is inaccurate, because you don't really "enable" exception handling. Instead you place the code you believe might throw an exception in a guarded block, called the **try** block. All code placed in this block is monitored, and any exceptions thrown are passed to the fault handler in your **try...catch...finally** construct. Please see the beginning of the "Exception Handling" section earlier in this chapter for more information.

Using Two or More Exception Handlers in One Procedure

It's possible to have more than one exception handler in the same procedure. You simply encapsulate your code in the **try...catch...finally** construct wherever you feel the need. In many cases, this is probably overkill because it's possible to filter the various exceptions, determine the reason for an exception being thrown, and then recover from it, even if you have many lines of code in the **try** block. I guess it's a matter of preference and making your code readable. Listing 5-2 shows you how two exception handlers can coexist in the same procedure.

Listing 5-2. Two Exception Handlers in One Procedure

```
1 public void TwoExceptionHandlers() {
2     long lngResult;
3     long lngValue = 0;
4
5     try {     // First exception handler
6         lngResult = 8 / lngValue;
7     }
8     catch (Exception objFirst) {
9         MessageBox.Show(objFirst.Message);
10    }
11
12    try {     // Second exception handler
13        lngResult = 8 / lngValue;
14    }
15    catch (Exception objSecond) {
16        MessageBox.Show(objSecond.Source);
17    }
18 }
```

There is no hocus pocus to Listing 5-2; it's simply plain code that shows you it is indeed possible to have more than one exception handler in the same procedure.

Examining the Exception Class

The **Exception** class holds information about the last thrown exception. This is why it's usually a good idea to check the properties of this class when you catch an exception in your exception handler. Table 5-1 lists these properties.

Table 5-1. **Exception** *Class Properties*

NAME	DESCRIPTION
HelpLink	The **HelpLink** property returns or sets a link to the help file that is associated with the exception. The data type for this property is **string**, and it must be specified using a URL or a URN.
InnerException	This read-only property returns a reference to the inner exception. This property is often used when an exception handler catches a system exception and stores this information in the **InnerException** property in a new exception object. This new exception object is then used to throw a new exception, an exception that is user friendly. If the exception handler that catches the new exception wants to know the original exception, it can examine the **InnerException** property. If there's no inner exception, this property is **null**.
Message	This read-only property, which can be overridden in your own derived exception class, is of data type **string**. It returns the error message text that describes the exception in detail.
Source	The **Source** property returns or sets a **string** value that holds the name of the application or the object that threw the exception. If this property is not set, the returned value is a **string** holding the name of the assembly in which the exception was thrown.
StackTrace	This read-only property, which can be overridden, returns the stack trace. The stack trace pinpoints the location in your code where the exception was thrown, down to the exact line number. The returned value is data type **string**. The stack trace is captured immediately before an exception is thrown.
TargetSite	The **TargetSite** property is read-only and returns an object of data type **MethodBase**. The returned object contains the method that threw the exception. However, if the exception-throwing method is unavailable, the method is obtained from the stack trace. **null** is returned if the method is unavailable and the stack trace is **null**.

The **Exception** class also has the public, noninherited methods described in Table 5-2.

*Table 5-2. **Exception** Class Methods*

NAME	DESCRIPTION
GetBaseException()	This overridable method returns a reference to the original exception that was thrown. The returned object is of type **Exception**.
GetObjectData(SerializationInfo objInfo StreamingContext objContext)	The **GetObjectData** method sets objInfo with all the information about the thrown exception that must be serialized.

Handling Exceptions in the Exception Handler

When an exception is thrown, your code needs to handle it. If you can resolve or recover from the exception, you can continue execution, and if not, you have to let the user know and/or perhaps log the exception.

The **catch** block is where you deal with the thrown exceptions. In its simplest form, the **catch** block is also called the fault handler. The simplest form is not to specify any filter and simply catch all exceptions, as shown in Listing 5-3.

*Listing 5-3. The **catch** Block in Its Simplest Form (Fault Handler)*

```
1 public void SimpleCatchBlock() {
2     long lngResult;
3     long lngValue = 0;
4
5     try {
6         lngResult = 8 / lngValue;
7     }
8     catch {
9         MessageBox.Show("catch");
10    }
11 }
```

In Listing 5-3, there is only one **catch** block, and it will receive all exceptions that are thrown in the **try** block. The problem with this form is you haven't specified that you want a copy of the **Exception** object. This means you don't have any access to the exception that was thrown. However, if you do specify an **Exception** object as part of the **catch** statement, as in Listing 5-4, you have full access to the thrown exception.

*Listing 5-4. The **catch** Block with Exception Object*

```
1 public void CatchBlockWithExceptionObject() {
2     long lngResult;
3     long lngValue = 0;
4
5     try {
6         lngResult = 8 / lngValue;
7     }
8     catch (Exception objE) {
9         MessageBox.Show(objE.ToString());
10    }
11 }
```

Listing 5-4 specifies that you want all exceptions and that you want the property values from the thrown exception stored in the objE variable. The objE variable is instantiated as an object of type **Exception** and the values from the thrown exception are then stored in objE. If you want to specify exactly what kind of exception is handled by a particular **catch** block, you need to filter the exceptions. See "Filtering Exceptions" later in this chapter for more information on how to filter exceptions.

> **NOTE** *If you have more than one **catch** block in your exception handler, they will be tried one by one by the CLR when an exception is thrown from the code in the corresponding **try** block. When I say tried, I mean that the various **catch** statements will be examined in top-to-bottom fashion, as in a **switch** construct, and when a **catch** statement matches the exception, this **catch** block is executed. If none of the **catch** statements match the exception, the CLR will display a standard message to the user detailing the exception.*

Okay, once you've caught an exception, what do you do with it? In order to be able to recover from an exception, you need to know what kind of exception has been thrown. Table 5-3 shows a list of some of the standard exception types of interest that the CLR provides, in order of inheritance.

Table 5-3. Standard Exception Types

EXCEPTION TYPE	BASE TYPE	DESCRIPTION	EXAMPLE
Exception	**object**	This is the base class for all exceptions. See "Examining the Exception Class" for more information.	See one of the subclasses for more information.
SystemException	**Exception**	The **SystemException** class is the base class for all exceptions thrown by the CLR. It's thrown by the CLR for exceptions that are recoverable by the user application. This means nonfatal exceptions. This class adds no new functionality to the class it's derived from (**Exception**) and generally you shouldn't throw exceptions of this type.	See one of the subclasses for more information.
IndexOutOfRangeException	**SystemException**	This exception is thrown by the CLR, when you try to access a nonexistent element in an array, meaning an element with an index that is out-of-bounds. This class cannot be inherited.	See Listing 5-5.
NullReferenceException	**SystemException**	The **NullReferenceException** exception is thrown by the CLR if you try to reference an invalid object. An invalid object has the value **null**.	See Listing 5-6.

(continued)

Table 5-3. Standard Exception Types (continued)

EXCEPTION TYPE	BASE TYPE	DESCRIPTION	EXAMPLE
InvalidOperationException	**SystemException**	This exception is thrown by a method if the object that the method belongs to is in an invalid state.	See Listing 5-7.
ArgumentException	**SystemException**	This exception type is the base class for all argument exceptions. You should use one the subclassed exceptions when throwing an exception if one exists.	See one of the subclasses for more information.
ArgumentNullException	**ArgumentException**	This exception is thrown by methods of an object, when you supply a null value for an argument that doesn't allow the argument to be **null**.	See Listing 5-8.
ArgumentOutOfRangeException	**ArgumentException**	The **ArgumentOutOf RangeException** is thrown by a method when one or more of the arguments aren't within the valid range.	See Listing 5-9.

In Listing 5-5, I try to set the third element (Line 5) of the reference to the arrlngException array, but there are only two elements in the array (Line 2), so an **IndexOutOfRangeException** exception is thrown.

*Listing 5-5. Throwing an **IndexOutOfRangeException** Exception*

```
1 public void ThrowIndexOutOfRangeException() {
2     long[] arrlngException = new long[2];
3
4     try {
5         arrlngException[2] = 5;
6     }
7     catch (Exception objE) {
8         MessageBox.Show(objE.ToString());
9     }
10 }
```

In Listing 5-6, I try to reference the objException object, but this object has been destroyed, so a **NullReferenceException** exception is thrown.

*Listing 5-6. Throwing a **NullReferenceException** Exception*

```
1 public void ThrowNullreferenceException() {
2     Exception objException = new Exception();
3
4     try {
5         objException = null;
6       MessageBox.Show(objException.Message);
7     }
8     catch (Exception objE) {
9         MessageBox.Show(objE.ToString());
10     }
11 }
```

On Line 15 in Listing 5-7, I try to execute a non–row-returning query using the cmmUser command, but the command requires an open-and-ready connection. Because the connection (cnnUserMan) is busy serving the data reader while the data reader is open, an **InvalidOperationException** exception is thrown.

*Listing 5-7. Throwing an **InvalidOperationException** Exception*

```
1 public void ThrowInvalidOperationException() {
2     SqlConnection cnnUserMan;
3     SqlCommand cmmUser;
4     SqlDataReader drdUser;
5
6     try {
7         // Instantiate and open the connection
8         cnnUserMan = new SqlConnection(STR_CONNECTION_STRING);
9         cnnUserMan.Open();
```

```
10        // Instantiate command
11        cmmUser = new SqlCommand(STR_SQL_USER_SELECT, cnnUserMan);
12        // Instantiate and populate data reader
13        drdUser = cmmUser.ExecuteReader();
14        // Execute query while data reader is open
15        cmmUser.ExecuteNonQuery();
16     }
17   catch (Exception objE) {
18        MessageBox.Show(objE.ToString());
19     }
20 }
```

On Line 20 in Listing 5-8, I try to update the data source using the data adapter, but the data set supplied as the only argument has been destroyed on Line 15. Because the data set object is **null**, an **ArgumentNullException** exception is thrown.

*Listing 5-8. Throwing an **ArgumentNullException** Exception*

```
1 public void ThrowArgumentNullException() {
2     SqlConnection cnnUserMan;
3     SqlCommand cmmUser;
4     DataSet dstUser = new DataSet();
5     SqlDataAdapter dadUser;
6
7     try {
8         // Instantiate and open the connection
9         cnnUserMan = new SqlConnection(STR_CONNECTION_STRING);
10        cnnUserMan.Open();
11        // Instantiate command
12        cmmUser = new SqlCommand();
13        // Instatiate data adapter
14        dadUser = new SqlDataAdapter(cmmUser);
15        dstUser = null;
16        // Update data source
17        dadUser.Update(dstUser);
18     }
19   catch (Exception objE) {
20        MessageBox.Show(objE.ToString());
21     }
22 }
```

In Listing 5-9 on Line 7, I try to display the first 200 characters from the connection string, but there aren't that many characters in the connection string, which is why an **ArgumentOutOfRangeException** exception is thrown.

*Listing 5-9. Throwing an **ArgumentOutOfRangeException** Exception*

```
1 public void ThrowArgumentOutOfRangeException() {
2    try {
3        // Display the first 200 chars from the connection string
4        MessageBox.Show(STR_CONNECTION_STRING.Substring(1, 200));
5    }
6    catch (Exception objE) {
7        MessageBox.Show(objE.ToString());
8    }
9 }
```

Now you know what kind of standard exceptions you can expect to catch. How do you deal with them in the **catch** block? Well, it depends on what exception you're talking about and how you catch it. First of all you need to look at how you can filter the exceptions so that you make sure that the right **catch** block handles the right exception. See the next section for more information.

Filtering Exceptions

When you set up your exception handler, it's always good to know what kind of exceptions you can expect, although this isn't always possible. However, depending on the code you put in the **try** block, it can be quite easy to predict some of the possible exceptions that can be thrown. If you make a call to a method that takes one or more arguments, and the values you pass are variables, it's conceivable that one of the arguments is out of range or even set to **null**. This will throw a standard exception, which you can handily filter using a type filter. Type filtering works by filtering the exceptions by type or class to be technically correct. If you specify a class in a **catch** statement, the catch block will handle the class and all of its subclasses. See Listing 5-10 for some example code.

Listing 5-10. Type-Filtering Exceptions

```
 1 public void TypeFilterExceptions() {
 2     long[] arrlngException = new long[2];
 3     Exception objException = new Exception();
 4     long lngResult;
 5     long lngValue = 0;
 6
 7     try {
 8         arrlngException[2] = 5;
 9         objException = null;
10         MessageBox.Show(objException.Message);
11         lngResult = 8 / lngValue;
12     }
13     catch (NullReferenceException) {
14         MessageBox.Show("NullReferenceException");
15     }
16     catch (IndexOutOfRangeException) {
17         MessageBox.Show("IndexOutOfRangeException");
18     }
19     catch (Exception) {
20         MessageBox.Show("Exception");
21     }
22 }
```

In Listing 5-10, there are three potential exceptions in the **try** block. Only one of the lines of code will ever be executed, because the code will throw an exception and then you enter the exception handler. You need to comment out the lines of code you don't want to throw an exception and then run the code.

However, Listing 5-10 shows you how to include more than one **catch** block, and they each have a different task to do, or rather different types of exceptions to handle. When the first line of code (Line 8) in the **try** block is executed, an exception is thrown. This means the CLR looks at the available handlers for this block of code. It starts with Line 13, but seeing there is no match between the exception that Line 8 throws (**IndexOutOfRangeException**), it then looks at Line 16, which is a match. As a result, a message box will appear displaying the message "IndexOutOfRangeException".

Notice that I have created a "generic" exception handler at the bottom in Line 19 to catch any exceptions that haven't been caught by the other handlers. You don't have to do this, and it isn't always appropriate to have one, but in some cases where you are uncertain about the exceptions that are thrown, it can be a good idea to include this catch-all handler. When it catches an unhandled exception, you can display a message to the user, log the exception, or do whatever you fancy with it.

Creating Your Own Exception

Sometimes it's necessary to create your own custom exception. Perhaps you are creating a class or component from which you want to throw a custom exception. In such cases you need to create a class that inherits from the **ApplicationException** class. The **ApplicationException** class is the base exception class for exceptions thrown by user applications. Mind you, this is only true when a nonfatal exception is thrown (see Listing 5-11).

Listing 5-11. Creating Your Own Custom Exception Class

```
1 public class UserManException : ApplicationException {
2    private string prstrSource = "UserManException";
3
4    public override string Message {
5        get { return "This exception was thrown because you ... "; }
6    }
7
8    public override string Source {
9        get { return prstrSource; }
10
11       set { prstrSource = value; }
12    }
13 }
```

In Listing 5-11, you can see how to create your own custom exception classes. The sample code shown overrides two of the inherited properties; all other properties and methods are taken from the base class, the **ApplicationException** class. This is a very simple exception class, but it does show the basics for creating your own exception classes.

Throwing an Exception

If you need to throw an exception, you can use the **throw** statement for this very purpose. The **throw** statement is quite often used for testing your exception handler using this format:

```
throw expression;
```

The required argument *expression* is the exception you want to throw. The following code will raise a new **IndexOutOfRangeException** exception:

```
throw new IndexOutOfRangeException();
```

Now, throwing an exception is very easy, and as such it can be used for general communication. However, as the name suggests, exceptions are for exceptional circumstances. So, don't use it for general communication purposes. It's guaranteed to confuse the heck out of whoever looks at your code. If you are dealing with classes, then simply create events to handle the communication with the client or use callbacks.

Handling Data-Related Exceptions

Now that I've covered the basics of exception handling, it's time to look at how you can use it with data-related exceptions (see Listing 5-12). If you follow my earlier instructions on NOT putting too much code in the same guarded block, it's actually quite easy to figure out which data-related procedure or object throws the exception.

*Listing 5-12. Catch **SqlConnection** Class Exceptions*

```
1 public void CatchSqlConnectionClassExceptions() {
2     SqlConnection cnnUserMan;
3
4     try {
5         // Instantiate the connection
6         cnnUserMan = new SqlConnection(STR_CONNECTION_STRING +
7             ";Connection Timeout=-1");
8     }
9     catch (ArgumentException objException) {
10        if (objException.TargetSite.Name == "SetConnectTimeout") {
11            MessageBox.Show(objException.StackTrace);
12        }
13    }
14 }
```

In Listing 5-12, I try to instantiate the **SqlConnection** with an invalid **Connection Timeout** value. This obviously throws an **ArgumentException**, which I can catch. Because I know that this kind of exception is fairly common and I know that other lines of code can throw it, I also check to see if it was a **Connection Timeout** exception (Line 10). Okay, I know the example is rather short, but I am sure you can see where I am heading with this. All the information you need is in the **Exception** object or a subclassed object, so you have to just dig it out!

> **NOTE** *It's bad programming practice to rely on exception handling where you can easily avoid an exception by validating the input. This is the case with Listing 5-12, where you should be able to validate the value for the Connection Timeout value name. However, Listing 5-12 serves as an example of how to catch anticipated exceptions, in cases where there can be an overhead in validating input.*

It's all about filtering the exceptions, as I have shown earlier on in this chapter. I could go on in this chapter and show you how to catch and filter every method of every data-related class in ADO.NET, but why not just stick to a rule of thumb? What you do is look up a particular method and check what kind of exceptions it can throw. You set up your exception handler to type-filter those exceptions, and then if necessary perform an extra check on the **TargetSite.Name**. This will make sure you process an exception with the right exception handler!

Common Data-Related Exceptions

As with general application exceptions, some data-related exceptions are very common and you can avoid many of these, if only you look for them when developing your application. These common data-related exceptions include, but aren't limited to, the following:

- Connection exceptions, invalid connection string values

- Unexpected null values in columns

- Time-out exceptions, queries take too long, server is down, and so on

- Invalid characters in queries, not handling apostrophes in string comparisons

- Empty result sets, causes application logic to fail

Some of these exceptions are already explained in Chapters 3A and 3B with example code showing how to deal with them.

CLR Handling of Exceptions

If you've read the previous part of the chapter, I am sure you have a pretty good idea of how the CLR handles exceptions, but here is a quick run-through of how it works.

First of all, the CLR uses guarded blocks of code and exception objects to handle exceptions. If and when an exception is thrown, the CLR creates an exception object and fills it with information about the exception.

In every executable there is an information table for exceptions, and every method in the executable has an associated array in this information table. This array holds information about the exception handling, but it can be empty. Every element in this array has a description of a guarded code block, all the exception filters that are associated with the code, and all the exception handlers.

The exception table is very efficient, and therefore it sacrifices neither processor time, nor memory consumption. You obviously use more resources when an exception is thrown, but if no exception is thrown the overhead is the same as with "normal" code.

So when an exception is thrown, the CLR starts the exception process. This two-step process begins with the CLR searching through the array. The CLR looks for the first guarded block of code, which guards the currently executing line of code, and contains an exception handler and a filter that is associated with the exception.

The second step in this process depends on whether or not such a match is found. If a match is found, the CLR creates the exception object that describes the exception, and then executes all the finally and/or fault statements between the line of code where the exception was thrown and the statement that handles the exception. You must be aware that the order of the exception handlers is very important, because the innermost exception handler is always evaluated first.

If no match is found, all of the calling methods are searched, meaning that the caller of the current method is searched, whereby the calling method becomes the current method, and this goes on all the way up the stack. If after this search still no match is found, the CLR aborts the application after dumping the stack trace.

Using the Debug Class

The **Debug** class, which can be found in the **System.Diagnostics** namespace, can be used for debugging your code, while you're developing it. Any calls to methods or properties in the **Debug** class won't be compiled into the release version of your application. You're probably thinking, "Okay, so far so good, but what is the **Debug** class, what can it actually do for me?" Well, the **Debug** class has a number of properties and methods that can be used during development and debugging, such as making assertions. *Asserting* means that you test for a specific condition (such as if an object is **null**), and if the condition is **false**, a message is displayed. This message can be user supplied. It's a bit like all those **MessageBox.Show** method calls I've placed throughout the example code, after checking a certain condition with an **if** () {} statement. However, the difference is that the assertion, which is made with a call to the **Assert** method of the **Debug** class, isn't included in the release version of your software by default. With regards to exception handling, this makes it a perfect tool to include in your exception handlers, displaying potentially more information about thrown exceptions than you want the user of your software to see once it has been released.

Enabling Debugging

In order to use the **Debug** class, you must enable it before use. This can be done in various ways: you either enable it locally in a file, or you enable it globally for your project.

To enable it locally, you simply add the following line to the top of the file you want to use the **Debug** class in:

```
#define DEBUG
```

Globally, you can enable it in two different ways: by adding the /d:DEBUG flag to the command line compiler command or specifying it in the Project Property Pages dialog box, as shown in Figure 5-1.

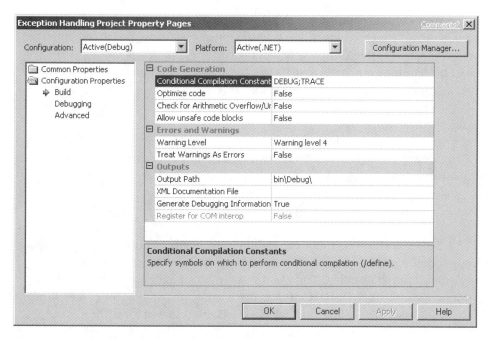

Figure 5-1. Project Property Pages dialog box

Figure 5-1 shows you the Project Property Pages dialog box, which can be opened by right-clicking your project in Solution Explorer and selecting Properties from the pop-up menu, or by selecting the Properties command from the Project menu. In Figure 5-1, you can see the Build node, with the Conditional Compilation Constant item selected under the Code Generation option. You can also see that I've added the DEBUG constant in the text box, which means that calls to the **Debug** class in your project code will be compiled.

> **NOTE** *Enabling calls to the **Debug** class as shown here has nothing to do with general debugging, which when enabled creates a pdb[1] file in addition to the standard executable. If you look at the Configuration list box in Figure 5-1, you can see that general debugging is enabled, but you can disable this and manually add the DEBUG constant to the Conditional Compilation Constant item text box.*

---

1. This is really called a Program Database file (PDB), and it contains symbols for debugging your code using a debugger.

You can actually add calls to the **Debug** class' properties and methods in your code, without enabling these calls as shown previously, but that means the calls won't be compiled with the rest of the code.

Another thing you need to do is to add the following statement to the top of the files in which you're using the **Debug** class:

```
using System.Diagnostics;
```

Strictly speaking you don't have to do this, but if you don't, you'll have to add the full namespace path to the class when using it, like this:

```
System.Diagnostics.Debug.Assert(blnAssertion)
```

Whether or not you enable the **Debug** class locally or project wide is really all your decision, but keep in mind that enabling the local use of the **Debug** class overrides the global setting. This means that you can have one or more files in your project, in which the **Debug** class use is enabled, whereas other files won't have it enabled, even if there are calls to the **Debug** class in these files.

Disabling Debugging

Well, there isn't really much to say about this, because all you have to do is to remove the /d:DEBUG flag from the command line when compiling or remove it from the project Property Pages dialog box, which you can see in Figure 5-1. However, if any of the files in your project has enabled the use of the **Debug** class locally, this will be compiled into your executable, regardless of the setting on the command line or in the Project Property Pages dialog box.

Using Debug Assertions

You can use the **Assert** method of the **Debug** class to check for certain conditions at runtime and have a message box displayed, if a condition evaluates to **false**. You need to keep this is mind, because this isn't an **if** () {} construct where you can choose to perform an action whether the condition evaluates to **true** or **false**. Assertions only act if the condition evaluates to **false**. Generally, this shouldn't be a problem, because you simply form your conditions to conform to this, but you need be aware of it.

The **Assert** method has three overloads, and you can see them in Table 5-4.

*Table 5-4. **Assert** Method Overloads*

DEFINITION	DESCRIPTION
Assert(blnCondition)	This overload, which is the simplest, only accepts the condition to test for. This also means you won't see a user-supplied message, only the call stack, which is supplied by the CLR.
Assert(blnCondition, strMessage)	This overload takes two arguments; the `blnCondition` condition and the message to display, if the condition evaluates to **false**. The CLR-supplied call stack is also shown in the message box, below the text in `strMessage`.
Assert(blnCondition, strMessage, strDetailedMessage)	This overload takes three arguments; the `blnCondition` condition, the message to display, and a detailed message. If the condition evaluates to **false**, the two messages are shown, with `strMessage` at the top, `strDetailedMessage` just below it on a new line, and finally the call stack supplied by the CLR.

The message box displayed has three buttons that lets you decide what to do: Abort, Retry, and Ignore. Abort allows you to quit the application; Retry lets you attempt once more to debug the application; and Ignore, well, means you want to ignore the assertion. Also, the message boxes referenced in Table 5-4 are only shown when you're running in user interface mode (default trace output), but you can have the trace output sent to a log file instead. You need to set this up in the configuration file for your application. I won't be covering this, but there are some good examples in the VS .NET documentation. Listing 5-13 shows you how to use debug assertions.

Listing 5-13. Using Debug Assertions

```
1 public void TestDebugAssert() {
2     DataSet dstUser = new DataSet();
3     DataSet dstLog = new DataSet();
4
5     try {
6         // Do your stuff
7         // ...
8         // Destroy Log dataset
9         dstLog.Dispose();
10        dstLog = null;
11        // This obviously throws the
```

```
12        // NullReferenceException exception
13        MessageBox.Show(dstLog.DataSetName);
14    }
15    catch (NullReferenceException objNullReference) {
16        // Check if both our object instances are null
17        Debug.Assert(((dstUser == null) & (dstLog == null)),
18            "Assert Message");
19    }
20    catch (Exception objE) {
21        // Handle all other exceptions here
22    }
23 }
```

In Listing 5-13, I instantiate two **DataSet** objects and then in the exception handler destroy the dstLog **DataSet** object on Line 10. This means that the reference to this object on Line 13 will throw a **NullReferenceException** exception. Now, my application logic is that if one of the **DataSet** objects is **null**, then the other must be too, so this is what I have as my condition in the call to the **Debug.Assert** method on Lines 17 and 18 in the **catch** block. If you run the example code in Listing 5-13 as it is, the assert message will appear. I know this is a very simple example, but it should give you an idea as to how the **Assert** method can be used from within your exception handler. However, you should take a look at the **Fail** method, presented later in this chapter, as well.

What to Watch Out For

Although the **Debug** class is great for finding problems in your code at development time, there is one thing you need to look out for. You need to make sure you don't place function calls as part of your condition, because this might change a variable here and there and finally end up having an impact on the execution of your application. This is all fine if you want it this way. You need to keep in mind, however, that unless you've locally enabled the use of the **Debug** class, the **Assert** method won't be compiled into your released software, making it all too possible that the behavior of your application is different from what you expect when running it in the IDE.

Using Debug Error Messages

The **Debug** class has one method that is well suited for exception handling and that's the **Fail** method. This method displays an error message and as such doesn't do anything that the **MessageBox** class can't do if you're running in the

IDE. However, the **Fail** method only displays a message during development, meaning it's a great tool for debugging when setting up exception handlers. Listing 5-14 illustrates what I'm trying to say.

Listing 5-14. Using Debug Error Messages

```
1 public void TestDebugFail() {
2    try {
3        // Do your stuff here
4        // ...
5        throw new Exception("I'm not really expected!");
6    }
7    catch (NullReferenceException objNullReference) {
8        // Handle the NullReferenceException here
9    }
10   catch (IndexOutOfRangeException objIndexOutOfRange) {
11       // Handle the IndexOutOfRangeException here
12   }
13   catch (Exception objE) {
14       Debug.Fail("Fail Message",
15           "An unexpected exception has been thrown.\n\n" + objE.Message);
16   }
17 }
```

In Listing 5-14, I've set up an exception handler that expects that the code in the **try** block can throw exceptions of types **NullReferenceException** and **IndexOutOfRangeException**. These two exception types have their own catch block that handles them, but what about other exception types? Well, they're caught by the **catch** block with the general **Exception** object. This means this **catch** block will handle all other exceptions thrown in the **try** block. However, in many cases this can be the kind of exception you really don't expect to see, and you certainly don't want your end users to see a message displayed here, so you basically have to put the call to the **Fail** method in there. This gives you one of two advantages:

- Your messages won't be displayed in the release version of your application.

- You can enable the **Debug** class in the release version of your application, but have it write to a log file instead of the screen. You can then use the log file later when bug fixing.

The **Fail** method has two overloads, and they look similar to the **Assert** method overloads. One takes one **string** argument, and the other accepts two

string arguments, **Message** and **Detailed Message**. If you log the output from the **Assert** methods, you might want to use the overload with the two strings, because then you can use the **Message** argument as the title of the exception you've caught to make it easier for the reviewer of the log file to scan it by means of the title. If the reviewer then comes across an unknown or unexpected title, he or she can read the detailed message. That's one possibility, anyway.

Debug Class Methods and Properties

The **Debug** class has other methods and a handful of properties, but none are as important as the **Assert** and **Fail** methods. I encourage you to have a look at the **Debug** class in the VS .NET documentation, especially if you need information on how to do the following:

- Save the output to a file instead of showing it onscreen.

- Format the output (**Indent** and **Unindent** methods, and **IndentSize** property).

> **NOTE** *The **Debug** class and all of its methods and properties are static, so you don't have to declare an instance of the **Debug** class in order to use it.*

Summary

This chapter has shown you how to use exception handling for catching exceptions in your data processing applications. You were also introduced to the **Debug** class from the **System.Diagnostics** namespace. This class can be used when developing and debugging your code; by default it won't be compiled into the release version of your software unless you specify otherwise.

The next chapter will tell you how to deal with stored procedures, triggers, and views on the server. In other words, you'll be shown how to process your data on the server, instead of letting the client do it. If you implement this correctly, it can lead to performance improvements.

CHAPTER 6

Using Stored Procedures, Views, and Triggers

How to Use Stored Procedures, Views, and Triggers

SERVER-SIDE PROCESSING, which is when you let a server process your queries and the like, is probably a concept you have heard of and it's the very topic of this chapter. Well, to some extent anyway. I discuss three specific ways of doing server-side processing: stored procedures, triggers, and views. The good thing about server-side processing is that you can use the power and resources of your server for doing purely data-related processing and thus leave your client free to do other stuff, and your network clearer of data that the client doesn't want. It's not always appropriate to do so, but in many cases you can benefit from it.

This chapter includes several hands-on exercises that will take you through creating stored procedures, views, and triggers. See the Exercise items that appear throughout the text.

Although this chapter primarily focuses on SQL Server 2000 features, some of the functionality can certainly be reproduced in the other DBMSs I cover in this book:

- *SQL Server 7.0:* All functionality shown in this chapter can be reproduced. However, SQL Server 7.0 doesn't support the INSTEAD OF triggers described in "Using Triggers."

- *Microsoft Access:* Microsoft Access doesn't support stored procedures or triggers. However, views can be reproduced as queries in Microsoft Access, but you can't do this from within the VS .NET IDE; you have to use other means, like the Microsoft Access front-end. If you are unfamiliar with

Microsoft Access, I can recommend you read the following book to get you up to speed: *From Access to SQL Server*, by Russell Sinclair. Published by Apress, September 2000. ISBN: 1893115-240.

- *Oracle:* Oracle supports all the server-side processing described in this chapter.

- *MySQL:* For the examples in this book, I have been using MySQL version 3.23.45, which doesn't support triggers, views, or stored procedures, meaning there is no example code for MySQL in this chapter. However, at the time of writing (March 2002), an alpha version (4.0) of MySQL is available for download from http://www.mysql.com. The final version 4.0 is supposed to support stored procedures, views, and triggers. Even when these server-side processing means are available in MySQL, it's still not possible to create any of these items from within the VS .NET IDE.

The code for this chapter has examples for all the listed DBMSs where appropriate.

Optimization Issues

When I talk about optimizing performance of an application, there are a number of things to consider, but let's just make one thing clear before I go on: I am only talking distributed applications and not stand-alone applications that sit nicely on a possibly disconnected single PC. These stand-alone applications are also called *single tier* or *monolithic applications*.[1] The applications I discuss here use a network of some sort to access data and business services.

Okay, now that the basics are out of the way, I can focus on the obstacles that can lead to decreasing performance and how you need to know these obstacles well when you start the optimization process. You should keep such obstacles in mind when you design your application. However, the various resources, such as network bandwidth, processor power, available RAM, and so on, most often change over time, and then you'll have to reconsider if your application needs changing.

Table 6-1 lists all the varying factors that can influence the performance of your application, which could be a topic for an entire book. However, although I only describe these factors briefly, I want you to be aware of the resources mentioned; they have great influence on what server-side processing resources you should choose when you design your application. In general, it's often the client queries and not the server itself that create the biggest performance problems.

---

1.   Stand-alone applications don't have to be single tier, but they generally are.

Table 6-1. Performance Resources Optimization

RESOURCE NAME	DESCRIPTION
Network resources	When speaking of network resources, I am referring to the actual bandwidth of the network. Consider your network setup—whether you are on a LAN or you are accessing resources over a WAN such as the Internet, and so on. If you have a low bandwidth, it's obvious that you want to transfer as little data across the network as possible. If on the other hand you have plenty of bandwidth, you might want to transfer large amounts of data across the network. However, best practices prescribe that you only transfer the data needed across your network, even when you have wide bandwidth.
Local processing resources	If you have the raw power available on your local box, it can be good to do most of the data processing there. Mind you, it all depends on the available bandwidth and the processing resources on the server.
Server processing resources	Server-side processing is desirable, if the server has resources to do so. Another thing you should consider is whether it has the resources to serve all your clients, if you let the server do some of the data processing.
Data distribution	Although strictly speaking this isn't a resource as such, it's definitely another issue you might need to consider. If your data comes from various different and even disparate data sources, it often doesn't make too much sense to have one server process data from all the data sources, just to send the result set to the client. In most cases, it makes sense to have all the data delivered directly to the client.

Table 6-1 just provides a quick overview. Table 6-2 shows you some different application scenarios.

Table 6-2. Different Application Scenarios

CLIENT MACHINE	SERVER	NETWORK	RECOMMENDATION
Limited processing resources	Plenty of processing resources	Limited bandwidth	Now, this one is obvious. You should use the raw processing power of the server to process the data and only return the requested data. This will save resources on the network and on the client.
Plenty of processing resources	Plenty of processing resources	Limited bandwidth	Hmm, processing could be done on either the client or the server, but it really depends on the amount of data you need to move across the network. If it's a limited amount of data, processing on either side will do, but if it's a lot of data, then let the server do the processing. Another solution could be to store the data locally and then use replication or batch processing to update the server.
Plenty of processing resources	Limited processing resources	Limited bandwidth	In this case, processing should be done on the client, but it really depends on the amount of data you need to move across the network. If it's a limited amount of data, the client should do the processing; but if it's a lot of data, you might consider letting the server do some of the processing, or even better; upgrade your server.
Plenty of processing resources	Limited processing resources	Plenty of bandwidth	Okay, don't think too hard about this one—processing should be done on the client.

I could add plenty more scenarios to the list, but I think you get the picture. You'll rarely encounter a situation that matches a straightforward scenario with a simple answer. It's your job to know about all the potential issues when you design your application and have to decide on where to process your data. Quite often different aspects of an application have different data processing needs, so the answer may vary even within a single application. One book that will help you with many common problems you may encounter with SQL Server is this one:

- *SQL Server: Common Problems, Tested Solutions,* by Neil Pike. Published by Apress, October 2000. ISBN: 189311581X.

Troubleshooting Performance Degradation

When you realize that you have performance problems or when you just want to optimize your server, you need one or more tools to help. SQL Server and Windows NT/2000 provides a number of tools you can use when troubleshooting and here are a few of them:

- Database Consistency Checker (DBCC) (SQL Server)

- Performance Monitor (Windows NT/2000)

- Query Analyzer (SQL Server)

- System Stored Procedures (SQL Server)

I'll briefly describe what you can use these tools for and give you links for obtaining more information.

Database Consistency Checker

The *Database Consistency Checker* (DBCC) is used for checking the logic as well as the consistency of your databases using T-SQL DBCC statements. Furthermore, many of the DBCC statements can also fix the problems detected when running. DBCC statements are T-SQL enhancements and as such must be run as SQL scripts. Here is one example of a DBCC statement:

```
DBCC CHECKDB
```

This DBCC statement is used for checking the structural integrity of the objects in the database you specify. It can also fix the problems found when running. There are many DBCC statements, and this isn't the place to go over these, but check SQL Server Books Online (included with SQL Server) for more information about DBCC.

Performance Monitor

The *Performance Monitor* (perfmon) is used for tracking and recording activity on your machine or rather any machine within your enterprise. perfmon comes with Windows NT/2000/XP and is located in the Administrative Tools menu, but you can also run it from a command prompt, or the Run facility of Windows Start Menu, by executing perfmon. Any of the Windows platforms mentioned produces counters that can be tracked or polled by perfmon at regular intervals if needed. SQL Server also comes with counters that can be tracked or polled by perfmon. Some of the more general counters are used for polling processor time, disk access, memory usage, and so on. Arguably the best of it all is the ability to save a session of all activity recorded or polled within any given time frame. You can then play back a saved session, whenever appropriate. This is especially important when you want to establish a baseline against which to compare future session recordings.

Check your Windows NT/2000/XP documentation for more information about perfmon.

Query Analyzer

The *Query Analyzer* is an external tool that comes with SQL Server for analyzing and optimizing your queries. You can find it in the menus created by SQL Server Setup.

Query Analyzer can be used for validating your queries in the form of script files and queries you type yourself in the query window. Besides validating a query, you can get Query Analyzer to analyze it by running. The analysis includes an execution plan, statistics, and a trace of the query being executed. Queries can get complicated, and many do when joining tables, and it isn't always obvious how much processing a particular query will take. There's normally more than one way to get to complex data, so the trace is invaluable in optimizing your data requests.

See SQL Server Books Online (included with SQL Server) for more information about Query Analyzer. You can actually invoke the Query Analyzer part of the SQL Server Books Online help text from within Query Analyzer by pressing F1.

System Stored Procedures

The *System Stored Procedures* is a set of stored procedures that comes with SQL Server for database administrators to use for maintaining and administering SQL Server. There are a number of System Stored Procedures, including two XML ones, and I certainly can't cover them here, but I can mention some of the functionality they cover: they let you see who's logged on to the system, administer registration with Active Directory, set up replication, set up full-text search, create and edit maintenance plans, and administer a database in general.

See SQL Server Books Online (comes with SQL Server) for more information about the System Stored Procedures.

Using Stored Procedures

A *stored procedure* is a precompiled batch[2] of SQL statement(s) that is stored on the database server. The SQL statements are always executed on the database server. Stored procedures have long been a good way of letting the server process your data. They can significantly reduce the workload on the client, and once you get to know them you'll wonder how you ever managed without them.

There is certainly more to a stored procedure than just mentioned, but I do think this is the most significant aspect of a stored procedure. Think about it: it's a way of grouping a batch of SQL statements, storing it on the database server, and executing it with a single call. The fact that the stored procedure is precompiled will save you time as well when executed. Furthermore, the stored procedure can be executed by any number of users, meaning you might save a lot of bandwidth just by calling the stored procedure instead of sending the whole SQL statement every time.

A stored procedure can contain any SQL statement that your database server can understand. This means you can use stored procedures for various tasks, such as executing queries—both so-called action queries, such as DELETE queries, and row-returning queries, such as SELECT statements.

Another task you can use a stored procedure for is database maintenance. Use it to run cleanup SQL statements when the server is least busy and thus save the time and effort of having to do this manually. I won't cover maintenance tasks in this chapter, but they are important, and you should be aware of the various tasks you can perform with stored procedures. If you're like me, you have been or are working for a small company that doesn't have a database administrator, in which case you're in charge of keeping the database server running. Granted, it's not an ideal situation, but you certainly get to know your DBMS in different ways than you would just being a programmer, and that's not bad at all.

To sum it up: a stored procedure is a precompiled SQL statement or batch of SQL statements that is stored on the database server. All processing takes place on the server, and any result requested by a client is then returned in a prepared format.

---

2.   Actually some stored procedures only hold one SQL statement.

Why Use a Stored Procedure?

You should use a stored procedure in the following cases (please note that other cases do apply, depending on your circumstances):

- Executing one or more related SQL statements on a regular basis

- Hiding complex table structures from client developers

- Returning the result of your SQL statements because you have a limited bandwidth on your network

- Delegating data processing to the server because you have limited processing resources on your client

- Ensuring processes are run, on a scheduled basis, without user intervention

Granted, there can be substantially more work in setting up a stored procedure than in just executing the SQL statement(s) straight from the client, but my experience has confirmed that the extra work saves you at least tenfold the time once you start coding and using you application. Even SQL Server itself and other major DBMSs use stored procedures for maintenance and other administrative tasks.

One last thing I want to mention is the fact that if you base a lot of your data calls on stored procedures, it can be much easier to change the data calls at a later date. You can simply change the stored procedure and not the application itself, meaning you don't have to recompile a business service or even your client application, depending on how you have designed your application. On the negative side, stored procedures are often written using database vendor–specific SQL extensions, which mean that they're hard to migrate to a different RDBMS. This of course is only a real concern if you're planning to move to another RDBMS.

Planning a Move to a Different RDBMS

If you're planning to move to another RDBMS from SQL Server, or just want to make it as easy as possible should management decide so in the future, it'll probably be a good idea to look up the following T-SQL statements in the SQL Server Books Online Help Documentation:

- **SET ANSI_DEFAULTS**: This statement sets the ANSI defaults on for the duration of the query session, trigger, or stored procedure.

- **SET FIPS_FLAGGER**: This statement can be used to check for compliance with the ANSI SQL-92 standard.

If you use these statements appropriately, they can certainly help ease the move from SQL Server to another ANSI SQL-92–compliant RDBMS.

Creating and Running a Stored Procedure

Creating a stored procedure is fairly easy, and you're probably used to working with the Enterprise Manager that comes with SQL Server or a different stored procedure editor for SQL Server or Oracle. If this is the case, you may want to check out the facilities in the Server Explorer in the VS .NET IDE. Among other things, it's much easier to run and test a stored procedure directly from the text editor. Anyway, here's how you would create a stored procedure for the example UserMan database:

1. Open up the Server Explorer window.

2. Expand the UserMan database on your database server.

3. Right-click the Stored Procedures node and select New Stored Procedure.

This brings up the Stored Procedure text editor, which incidentally looks a lot like your C# code editor. Except for syntax checking and other minor stuff, they are exactly the same (see Figure 6-1).

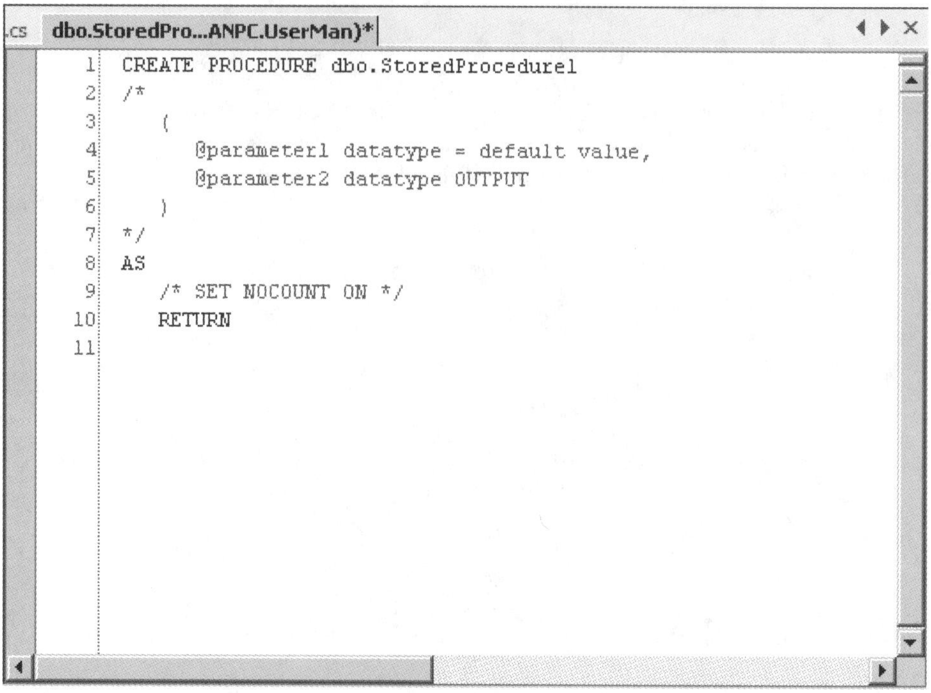

```
     dbo.StoredPro...ANPC.UserMan)*                           ◀ ▶ ✕
  1    CREATE PROCEDURE dbo.StoredProcedure1
  2    /*
  3        (
  4            @parameter1 datatype = default value,
  5            @parameter2 datatype OUTPUT
  6        )
  7    */
  8    AS
  9        /* SET NOCOUNT ON */
 10        RETURN
 11
```

Figure 6-1. Stored procedure editor with SQL Server default template

> **NOTE** *With SQL Server it's only possible to use T-SQL for your stored procedures. However, the upcoming version of SQL Server, code-named Yukon, will have support for the .NET programming languages. Knowing this, perhaps you'll want to create your stored procedures in C# or VB .NET.*

Creating a Simple Stored Procedure

Once you've created a stored procedure, you need to give it a name. As you can see from your stored procedure editor, the template automatically names it StoredProcedure1. If you're wondering about the dbo prefix, it simply means that the stored procedure is created for the dbo user. In SQL Server terms, dbo stands for *database owner*, and it indicates who owns the database object, which is a stored procedure in this case. If you've been working with SQL Server for a while, you probably know the term *broken ownership chain*. An ownership chain is the dependency of a stored procedure upon tables, views, or other stored procedures.

Generally, the objects that a view or stored procedure depend on are also owned by the owner of the view or stored procedure. In such a case there are no problems, because SQL Server doesn't check permissions in this situation. (It doesn't really have to, does it?) However, when one or more of the dependent database objects are owned by a different user than the one owning the view or stored procedure, the ownership chain is said to be broken. This means that SQL Server has to check the permissions of any dependent database object that has a different owner. This can be avoided, if the same user, such as dbo, owns all of your database objects. I am not telling you to do it this way, but it's one option available to you.

Okay, let's say you've deleted the `StoredProcedure1` name and replaced it with `SimpleStoredProcedure`. To save the stored procedure before continuing, press Ctrl+S. If you saved your stored procedure at this point, you would notice that you don't have to name it using a Save As dialog box, because you've already named it. The editor will make sure that the stored procedure is saved on the database server with the name you've entered, which in this case is `SimpleStoredProcedure`. You shouldn't save it until you've renamed it, because you'll end up having to remove unwanted stored procedures.

Although you can see your stored procedure in the Stored Procedure folder of the SQL Server Enterprise Manager and the Stored Procedure node in the Server Explorer, there isn't actually an area in your database designated for just stored procedures. The stored procedure is saved to the system tables as are most other objects in SQL Server.

As soon as you have saved it, the very first line of the stored procedure changes. The SQL statement CREATE PROCEDURE is changed so that the first line reads:

```
ALTER PROCEDURE dbo.SimpleStoredProcedure
```

Why? Well, you just saved the newly created stored procedure, which means that you can't create another with the same name. Changing CREATE to ALTER takes care of that. It's that simple. In case you're wondering what happens when you change the name of your stored procedure and the SQL statement still reads ALTER PROCEDURE . . . , I can tell you: the editor takes care of it for you and creates a new procedure. Try it and see for yourself! Basically, this means that CREATE PROCEDURE is never actually needed; one can simply use ALTER PROCEDURE, even on brand new procedures. However, this can be a dangerous practice, if you inadvertently change the name of your stored procedure to the name of an already existing one.

The `SimpleStoredProcedure` doesn't actually do a lot, does it? Okay, let me show you how to change that. In Figure 6-1, you can see two parts of the stored procedure: The first part is the header and then there is the actual stored procedure itself. The header consists of all text down to and including Line 7. Basically, the header declares how the stored procedure should be called, how many arguments to include and what type of arguments, and so on. Since this is a very simple procedure, I don't want any arguments, so I'll leave the commented-out text alone.

If you haven't changed the default editor settings, text that is commented out or any comments you have inserted yourself are printed in green. In a SQL Server stored procedure, comments are marked using start and end tags: /* for the comment start tag and */ for the comment end tag. This has one advantage over the way you insert comments in your C# code in that you don't have to have a comment start tag on every line you want to comment out. You only need to have both a start and end tag.

The second part of the stored procedure is the part that starts with the AS clause on Line 8. The AS clause indicates that the text that follows is the body of the stored procedure, the instructions on what to do when the stored procedure is called and executed.

EXERCISE

1) Create a stored procedure, name it **SimpleStoredProcedure**, and save it as described earlier.

2) Type the following text on Line 10 in the SimpleStoredProcedure in place of the RETURN statement:

SELECT COUNT(*) FROM tblUser

Now the stored procedure should look like the example in Figure 6-2. The stored procedure will return the number of rows in the tblUser table. Please note that it's generally good practice to keep the RETURN statement as part of your stored procedure, but I'm taking it out and leaving it for an explanation later, when I discuss return values and how they're handled in code.

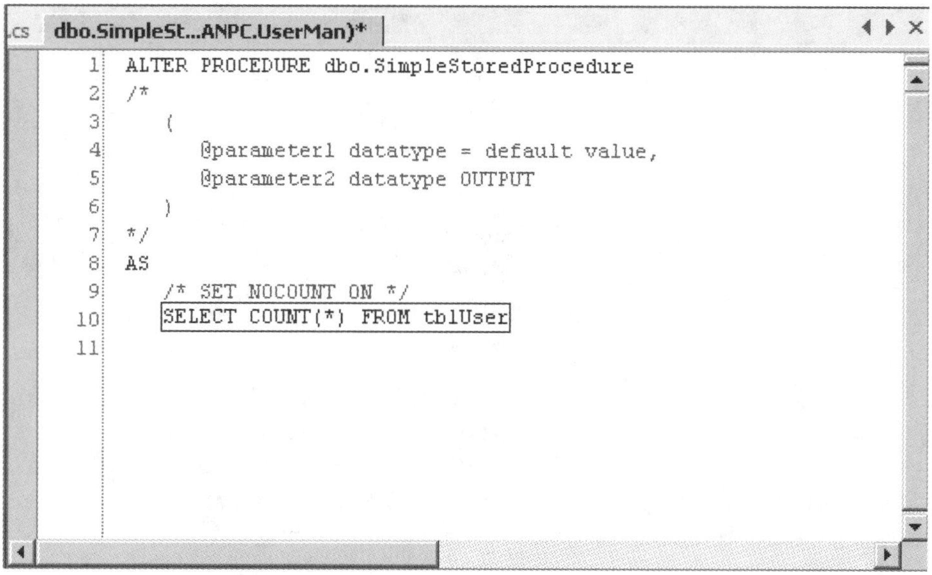

```
.cs   dbo.SimpleSt...ANPC.UserMan)*                          ◀ ▶ ✕
      1    ALTER PROCEDURE dbo.SimpleStoredProcedure
      2    /*
      3        (
      4            @parameter1 datatype = default value,
      5            @parameter2 datatype OUTPUT
      6        )
      7    */
      8    AS
      9        /* SET NOCOUNT ON */
     10    SELECT COUNT(*) FROM tblUser
     11
```

Figure 6-2. Stored procedure that returns the number of rows in the tblUser table

3) Don't forget to save the changes using Ctrl+S.

Running a Simple Stored Procedure from the IDE

Of course, there's no point in having a stored procedure that just sits there, so here's what you do to run it: if you have the stored procedure open in the stored procedure editor window, you can right-click anywhere in the editor window and select Run Stored Procedure from the pop-up menu. If you do this with the stored procedure you created in the exercise in the previous section, the Output window, located just below the editor window, should display the output from the stored procedure as shown in Figure 6-3.

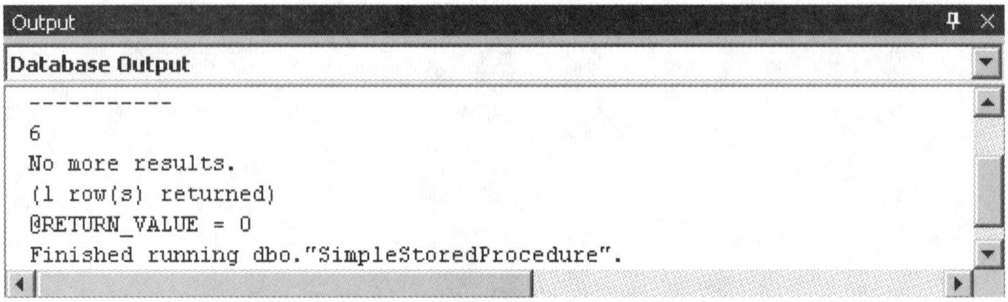

Figure 6-3. The Output window with output from SimpleStoredProcedure

If you have closed down the stored procedure editor window, you can run the stored procedure from the Server Explorer. Expand the database node, right-click the Stored Procedures node, and select Run Stored Procedure from the pop-up menu. This will execute the stored procedure the exact same way as if you were running it from the editor window.

Running a Simple Stored Procedure from Code

Okay, now that you have a fully functional stored procedure, you can try and run it from code. Listing 6-1 shows you some very simple code that will run the stored procedure. The example code in this listing uses data classes that were introduced in Chapters 3A and 3B.

Listing 6-1. Running a Simple Stored Procedure

```
 1 public void ExecuteSimpleSP() {
 2     SqlConnection cnnUserMan;
 3     SqlCommand cmmUser;
 4     object objNumUsers;
 5
 6     // Instantiate and open the connection
 7     cnnUserMan = new SqlConnection(STR_CONNECTION_STRING);
 8     cnnUserMan.Open();
 9
10     // Instantiate and initialize command
11     cmmUser = new SqlCommand("SimpleStoredProcedure", cnnUserMan);
12     cmmUser.CommandType = CommandType.StoredProcedure;
13
14     objNumUsers = cmmUser.ExecuteScalar();
15     MessageBox.Show(objNumUsers.ToString());
16 }
```

The code in Listing 6-1 retrieves the return value from the stored procedure. Now, this isn't usually all you want from a stored procedure, but it merely demonstrates what a simple stored procedure looks like. The stored procedure itself could just as well have had a `DELETE FROM tblUser WHERE LastName='Johnson'` SQL statement. If you want to execute this from code, you need to know if the stored procedure returns a value or not. It doesn't in this case, so you need to use the **ExecuteNonQuery** method of the **SqlCommand** class.

EXERCISE

1) Create a new stored procedure and save it with the name **uspGetUsers**.

2) Type in the following text on Line 10 in place of the RETURN statement:

SELECT * FROM tblUser

Now the stored procedure should look like the one in Figure 6-4. This stored procedure will return all rows in the tblUser table.

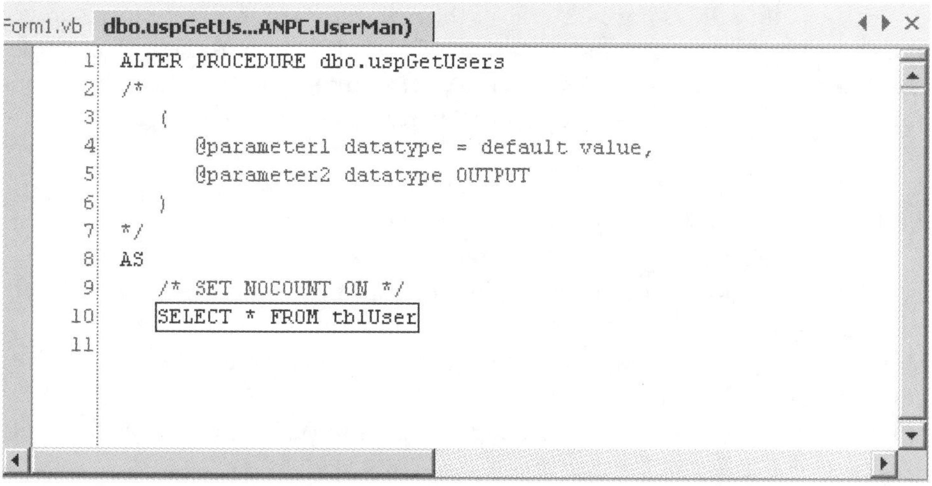

```
Form1.vb  dbo.uspGetUs...ANPC.UserMan)                    ◀ ▶ ✕
    1  ALTER PROCEDURE dbo.uspGetUsers
    2  /*
    3      (
    4          @parameter1 datatype = default value,
    5          @parameter2 datatype OUTPUT
    6      )
    7  */
    8  AS
    9      /* SET NOCOUNT ON */
   10      SELECT * FROM tblUser
   11
```

Figure 6-4. The uspGetUsers *stored procedure*

3) Don't forget to save the changes using Ctrl+S.

What you need now is some code to retrieve the rows from the stored procedure (see Listing 6-2).

Listing 6-2. Retrieving Rows from a Stored Procedure

```
1 public void ExecuteSimpleRowReturningSP() {
2     SqlConnection cnnUserMan;
3     SqlCommand cmmUser;
4     SqlDataReader drdUser;
5
6     // Instantiate and open the connection
7     cnnUserMan = new SqlConnection(STR_CONNECTION_STRING);
8     cnnUserMan.Open();
9
10    // Instantiate and initialize command
11    cmmUser = new SqlCommand("uspGetUsers", cnnUserMan);
12    cmmUser.CommandType = CommandType.StoredProcedure;
13
14    // Retrieve all user rows
15    drdUser = cmmUser.ExecuteReader();
16 }
```

The example in Listing 6-2 retrieves the rows returned from the stored procedure by using the **ExecuteReader** method of the **SqlCommand** class. Please note that this method and the related **ExecuteXmlReader** method are the only options for retrieving rows as the result of a function call with the Command class.

Creating a Stored Procedure with Arguments

Sometimes it's a good idea to create a stored procedure with arguments[3] instead of having more stored procedures essentially doing the same. It also gives you some flexibility with regards to making minor changes to your application without having to recompile one or more parts of it, because you can add to the number of arguments and keep existing applications running smoothly by specifying a default value for the new arguments.

Another reason for using arguments with stored procedures is to make the stored procedure behave differently, depending on the input from the arguments. One argument might hold the name of a table, view, or another stored procedure to extract data from.

---

3. I'm using the word *argument* here, but I might as well call it *parameter*, like T-SQL does. However, the two words are synonymous in this case.

TIP *In SQL Server you can use the* EXECUTE sp_executesql *statement and System Stored Procedure with arguments of type **ntext**, **nchar**, or **nvarchar** to execute parameterized queries. See the SQL Server Books Online Help Documentation for more information.*

EXERCISE

1) Create a new stored procedure and save it with the name **uspGetUsersByLastName**.

2) Type in the following text on Lines 10 and 11 in place of the RETURN statement:

SELECT * FROM tblUser
WHERE LastName = @strLastName

3) Uncomment Lines 2 to 7, and insert the following text instead of Lines 3 and 4:

@strLastName varchar(50)

The stored procedure should look like the one in Figure 6-5. This stored procedure will return all rows in the tblUser table where the LastName column matches the strLastName argument.

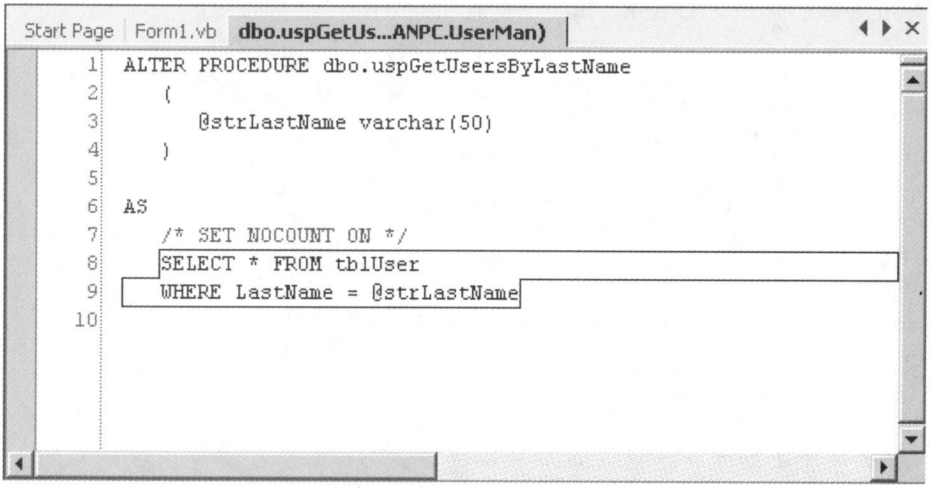

```
Start Page   Form1.vb   dbo.uspGetUs...ANPC.UserMan)                    ◄ ► ×
     1   ALTER PROCEDURE dbo.uspGetUsersByLastName
     2       (
     3           @strLastName varchar(50)
     4       )
     5
     6   AS
     7       /* SET NOCOUNT ON */
     8       SELECT * FROM tblUser
     9       WHERE LastName = @strLastName
    10
```

Figure 6-5. The uspGetUsersByLastName *stored procedure*

4) Don't forget to save your changes using Ctrl+S.

Arguments in stored procedures can be either input or output. If you include an input argument, you don't have to specify anything after the data type, but if you use an output argument, you need to specify the OUTPUT keyword after the data type.

> **NOTE**   *I only cover the absolute basics of how to create a stored procedure in this chapter. If you need more information, I suggest you look up the CREATE PROCEDURE statement in the Books Online help application that comes with SQL Server.*

Running a Stored Procedure with Arguments from the IDE

Try and run the stored procedure you created in the last exercise and see how the argument affects how it's run. You can try running the stored procedure from either the editor window or the Server Explorer window. The Run dialog box asks you for a value for the strLastName argument. Type **Doe** in the text box and click OK. Now all users with the last name of Doe are returned as the result of the stored procedure.

Using a Stored Procedure with Arguments

The uspGetUsersByLastName stored procedure seems to work, so try and run it from code. Listing 6-3 shows how you would do this.

Listing 6-3. Retrieving Rows from a Stored Procedure with an Input Argument

```
1 public void GetUsersByLastName() {
2     SqlConnection cnnUserMan;
3     SqlCommand cmmUser;
4     SqlDataReader drdUser;
5     SqlParameter prmLastName;
6
7     // Instantiate and open the connection
8     cnnUserMan = new SqlConnection(STR_CONNECTION_STRING);
9     cnnUserMan.Open();
10
11     // Instantiate and initialize command
12     cmmUser = new SqlCommand("uspGetUsersByLastName", cnnUserMan);
13     cmmUser.CommandType = CommandType.StoredProcedure;
14     // Instantiate, initialize and add parameter to command
15     prmLastName = cmmUser.Parameters.Add("@strLastName", SqlDbType.VarChar,
16         50);
```

```
17    // Indicate this is an input parameter
18    prmLastName.Direction = ParameterDirection.Input;
19    // Set the value of the parameter
20    prmLastName.Value = "Doe";
21
22    // Return all users with a last name of Doe
23    drdUser = cmmUser.ExecuteReader();
24 }
```

In Listing 6-3, a **SqlParameter** object specifies the input parameter of the stored procedure. On Lines 15 and 16, I ask the command object to create and associate a parameter with the @strLastName argument. The value of this parameter is set to "Doe", which effectively means that only rows containing a last name of Doe are returned.

As you can see, I have specified that the parameter is an input argument using the **ParameterDirection** enum, although you don't really have to, because this is the default. Don't worry too much about parameter and argument; they are essentially the same thing.

Creating a Stored Procedure with Arguments and Return Values

So far I have created stored procedures that return a single value or a result set (rows) and a stored procedure that takes an input argument. In many cases, this is all you want, but sometimes it's not enough. What if you want a value and a result set returned at the same time? Actually, you may want several values and a result set, but I'm sure you get the idea. In such instances, you can use output arguments.

Actually, you can return as many different values and result sets as you want by including multiple SELECT statements after the AS clause, but I personally think this approach looks messy. If I return rows and one or more values, I generally use OUTPUT arguments for the values. I guess to some extent this is a matter of preference. However, you should be aware that including an output parameter is a faster approach than having it returned in a **DataSet** object, but sometimes you might need the richer functionality of the **DataSet** class, once the values have been returned.

Instead of using the following example code to return a scalar value, two result sets, and another scalar value in that order:

```
...
AS
    SELECT 19
    SELECT * FROM tblUser
    SELECT * FROM tblUserRights
    SELECT 21
```

I would use something like this:

```
...
AS
    SELECT * FROM tblUser
    SELECT * FROM tblUserRights
```

The two return values should then be returned as OUTPUT arguments. But it's your call, my friend, as to which approach you prefer to use. Please note that OUTPUT arguments can also serve as INPUT arguments by default, meaning you can actually supply a value in the OUTPUT argument when calling the stored procedure, and get a different value back. Just like a value passed by reference from one procedure to another.

EXERCISE

Create a new stored procedure and save it with the name **uspGetUsersAndRights**. This stored procedure should return the value 55 for the OUTPUT argument lngNumRows, and then all rows in the tblUser table and all rows in the tblUserRights table.

The stored procedure should look like the one in Figure 6-6.

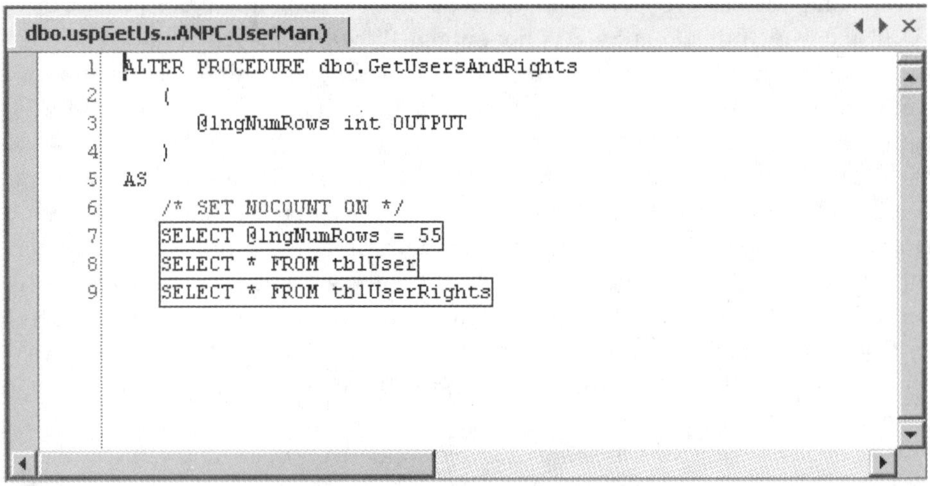

```
dbo.uspGetUs...ANPC.UserMan)                                    ◀ ▶ ✕

    1   ALTER PROCEDURE dbo.GetUsersAndRights
    2       (
    3            @lngNumRows int OUTPUT
    4       )
    5   AS
    6       /* SET NOCOUNT ON */
    7       SELECT @lngNumRows = 55
    8       SELECT * FROM tblUser
    9       SELECT * FROM tblUserRights
```

Figure 6-6. The uspGetUsersAndRights *stored procedure*

In the `uspGetUsersAndRights` stored procedure, shown in Figure 6-6, you can see that the `@lngNumRows int` argument is set to the value 55 on Line 7. However, using a default value for the argument you can achieve the same result, by changing Line 3 like this:

```
@lngNumRows int = 55 OUTPUT
```

This means that if for some reason you don't set the value of this parameter when calling the stored procedure or within the stored procedure itself, it'll return 55 as the output value. Default argument values also work for input arguments, and they're specified the same way, using the equal sign followed by the default value, right after the data type.

Running a Stored Procedure with Arguments and Return Values from the IDE

If you've created and saved the stored procedure in the previous exercise, test it by running it. You can try running the stored procedure from either the editor window or the Server Explorer window. The Output window, located just below the editor window, will display the output from the stored procedure, and it should look similar to the output in Figure 6-7.

> **NOTE** *Syntax testing of your stored procedure is done when you save it, and I have a feeling you have already encountered this. If not, just know that's how it is—syntax errors are caught when you try to save your stored procedure.*

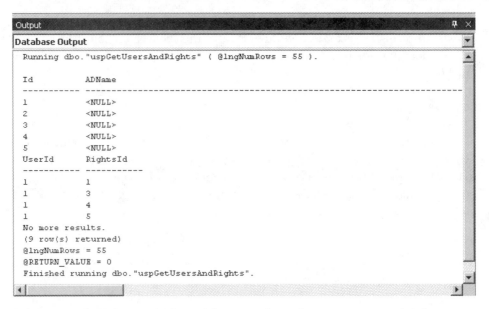

Figure 6-7. The Output window with output from the uspGetUsersAndRights
stored procedure

Using a Stored Procedure with Arguments and Return Values

Listing 6-4 shows the code to execute the uspGetUsersAndRights stored procedure
programmatically.

Listing 6-4. Retrieving Rows and Output Values from a Stored Procedure

```
1 public void GetUsersAndRights() {
2     SqlConnection cnnUserMan;
3     SqlCommand cmmUser;
4     SqlDataReader drdUser;
5     SqlParameter prmNumRows;
6
7     // Instantiate and open the connection
8     cnnUserMan = new SqlConnection(STR_CONNECTION_STRING);
9     cnnUserMan.Open();
10
11    // Instantiate and initialize command
12    cmmUser = new SqlCommand("uspGetUsersAndRights", cnnUserMan);
13    cmmUser.CommandType = CommandType.StoredProcedure;
14    // Instantiate, initialize and add parameter to command
15    prmNumRows = cmmUser.Parameters.Add("@lngNumRows", SqlDbType.Int);
16    // Indicate this is an output parameter
```

```
17      prmNumRows.Direction = ParameterDirection.Output;
18      // Get first batch of rows (users)
19      drdUser = cmmUser.ExecuteReader();
20
21      // Display the last name of all user rows
22      while (drdUser.Read()) {
23          MessageBox.Show(drdUser["LastName"].ToString());
24      }
25
26      // Get next batch of rows (user rights)
27      if (drdUser.NextResult()) {
28          // Display the id of all rights
29          while (drdUser.Read()) {
30              MessageBox.Show(drdUser["RightsId"].ToString());
31          }
32      }
33  }
```

In Listing 6-4, two result sets are returned, and therefore I use the **NextResult** method of the DataReader class to advance to the second result set on Line 27. Otherwise this stored procedure works pretty much the same as one with input parameters, although the parameter direction is specified as an output on Line 17.

Retrieving a Value Specified with RETURN

In a stored procedure, you can use the RETURN statement to return a scalar value. However, this value cannot be retrieved using the **ExecuteScalar** method of the Command class, as it would when you use the SELECT statement (refer back to Figure 6-2). Of course there is a way of retrieving this value, which I show you after the following exercise.

Create a new stored procedure and save it with the name
uspGetRETURN_VALUE. This stored procedure should return the value 55 as the
RETURN_VALUE. The stored procedure should look like the one in Figure 6-8.

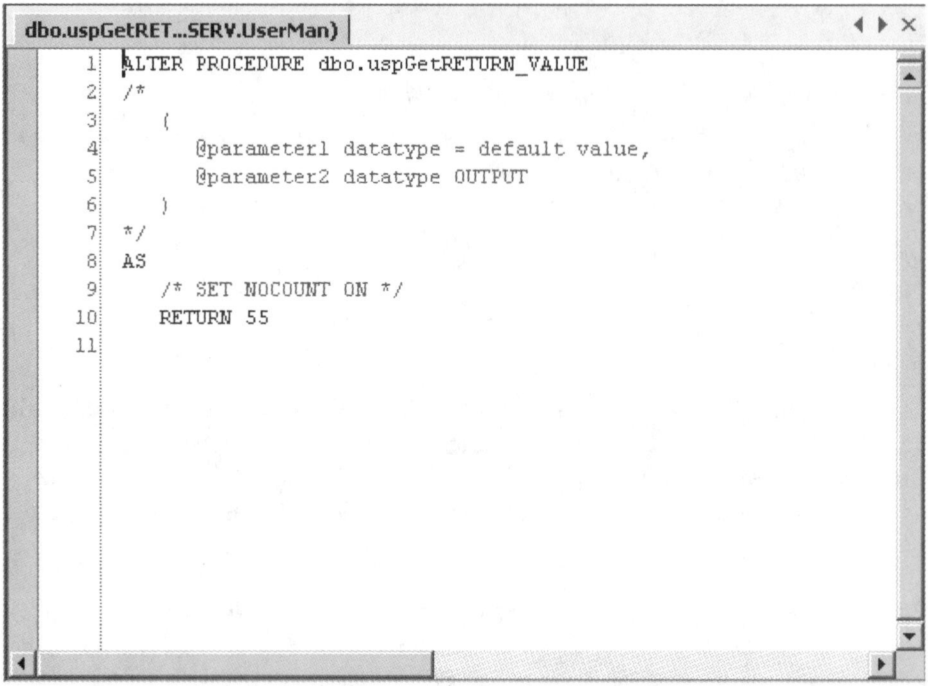

```
dbo.uspGetRET...SERV.UserMan)                              ◄ ► ✕
 1  ALTER PROCEDURE dbo.uspGetRETURN_VALUE
 2  /*
 3     (
 4        @parameter1 datatype = default value,
 5        @parameter2 datatype OUTPUT
 6     )
 7  */
 8  AS
 9     /* SET NOCOUNT ON */
10     RETURN 55
11
```

Figure 6-8. The uspGetRETURN_VALUE *stored procedure*

Listing 6-5 shows you how to retrieve the value from code.

Listing 6-5. Retrieving RETURN_VALUE from a Stored Procedure

```
1 public void GetRETURN_VALUE() {
2    SqlConnection cnnUserMan;
3    SqlCommand cmmUser;
4    SqlParameter prmNumRows;
5    object objResult;
6
7    // Instantiate and open the connection
8    cnnUserMan = new SqlConnection(STR_CONNECTION_STRING);
9    cnnUserMan.Open();
10
```

```
11    // Instantiate and initialize command
12    cmmUser = new SqlCommand("uspGetRETURN_VALUE", cnnUserMan);
13    cmmUser.CommandType = CommandType.StoredProcedure;
14    // Instantiate, initialize and add parameter to command
15    prmNumRows = cmmUser.Parameters.Add("@RETURN_VALUE", SqlDbType.Int);
16    // Indicate this is a return value parameter
17    prmNumRows.Direction = ParameterDirection.ReturnValue;
18    // Get RETURN_VALUE like this, . . .
19    objResult = cmmUser.ExecuteScalar();
20    // or like this
21    MessageBox.Show(prmNumRows.Value.ToString());
22 }
```

In Listing 6-5, the **ExecuteScalar** method gets the RETURN_VALUE from a stored procedure. Normally, you would use this method to return the value in the lngResult variable, but this variable will contain the default value, 0, in this case. However, because I have specified the **Direction** property of the prmNumRows parameter with the **ReturnValue** member of the **ParameterDirection** enum, I can simply look at the **Value** property of the parameter after executing the command.

Changing the Name of a Stored Procedure

If you change the name of your stored procedure in the editor window, the stored procedure is saved with the new name when you save (Ctrl+S). However, if you're not using this method to copy an existing stored procedure, you should be aware that the old stored procedure still exists. So you'll have to delete it if you don't want it.

Viewing Stored Procedure Dependencies

In SQL Server Enterprise Manager, you can see what tables and other objects your stored procedure uses or is dependent on. Open up Enterprise Manager, expand your SQL Server, expand databases and your database, select the Stored Procedures node, right-click the stored procedure you want to see the dependencies for, and select All Task Display Dependencies from the pop-up menu. This brings up the Dependencies dialog box, where you can see what database objects your stored procedure depends on and vice versa. This is also called the *ownership chain*.

Running Oracle Stored Procedures

Oracle stored procedures and stored functions are different from those of SQL
Server. That's why I've chosen to explain the Oracle stored procedures in a separate section. When discussing what you can do with stored procedures/functions
in Oracle compared to stored procedures in SQL Server, it's pretty much the
same, but the implementation is quite different.

SQL Server stored procedures can return a value, just like a function in C#,
whereas in Oracle you have stored procedures and stored functions. This means
that if you want a return value that isn't a parameter, you must use a stored
function. In this chapter, you won't see how to create stored procedures and
stored functions in Oracle, but you can use the Oracle Database Project located
in the example code, which you can download from the Apress Web site
(http://www.apress.com) or the UserMan site (http://www.userman.dk), to create
the tables, stored procedures, views, and triggers used by the Oracle example
code. Please consult your Oracle documentation if you need more information
on how to implement stored procedures and stored functions in Oracle.

When you use ADO.NET and ADO for that matter, you can't use the
ExecuteScalar method of the DataReader class to retrieve a return value, as
shown in Listings 6-1 and 6-5 and discussed in the "Retrieving a Value Specified
with RETURN" section. This is also true if you execute a stored function. You
need to return any return values in output parameters, just as I've demonstrated
in Listing 6-4. If you only need to return a value, as in Listing 6-1, which is what
the Oracle stored function in Listing 6-6 does, you can do as is shown in
Listing 6-7, which is really more or less the same code as in Listing 6-1.

Listing 6-6. A Simple Oracle Stored Function

```
1 CREATE OR REPLACE FUNCTION SIMPLESTOREDFUNCTION
2 RETURN NUMBER
3 AS
4     lngNumRows NUMBER;
5 BEGIN
6     SELECT COUNT(*) INTO lngNumRows FROM TBLUSER;
7     RETURN lngNumRows;
8 END SIMPLESTOREDFUNCTION;
```

In Listing 6-6, you can see an Oracle stored function that returns the number
of rows in the tblUser table. You can see in Listing 6-7 how you can access this
stored function and retrieve the return value.

Listing 6-7. Running a Simple Oracle Stored Function

```
1 public void ExecuteSimpleOracleSF() {
2     OleDbConnection cnnUserMan;
3     OleDbCommand cmmUser;
4     OleDbParameter prmNumRows;
5     object objReturnValue;
6
7     // Instantiate and open the connection
8     cnnUserMan = new OleDbConnection(STR_CONNECTION_STRING);
9     cnnUserMan.Open();
10
11    // Instantiate and initialize command
12    cmmUser = new OleDbCommand("SimpleStoredFunction", cnnUserMan);
13    cmmUser.CommandType = CommandType.StoredProcedure;
14    // Instantiate output parameter and add to parameter
15    // collection of command object
16    prmNumRows = cmmUser.CreateParameter();
17    prmNumRows.Direction = ParameterDirection.ReturnValue;
18    prmNumRows.DbType = DbType.Int64;
19    prmNumRows.Precision = 38;
20    prmNumRows.Size = 38;
21    cmmUser.Parameters.Add(prmNumRows);
22
23    // Retrieve and display value
24    objReturnValue = cmmUser.ExecuteScalar();
25    MessageBox.Show(cmmUser.Parameters[0].Value.ToString());
26 }
```

In Listing 6-7, I've actually used the **ExecuteScalar** method of the DataReader class on Line 24, but if you look carefully, you'll see that I don't use the value returned from the function call (objReturnValue) as in Listing 6-1. However, I do retrieve the return value in the prmNumRows parameter, which is instantiated, initialized, and set up as a return value on Lines 12 through 21, and display it after executing the command on Line 25. I use **ExecuteScalar** method, because it has the least overhead of any of the **Execute** methods of the DataReader class. So even if you don't use the return value from the **ExecuteScalar** method, which is always **null** when calling an Oracle stored function or stored procedure, you can still get the return value from the stored function. The trick is add a parameter to the command object and make sure you set the **Direction** property of the parameter object to the **ReturnValue** member of the **ParameterDirection** enum, as is shown on Line 13.

If you want to use an Oracle stored procedure instead of a stored function, like the one shown in Listing 6-8, to retrieve one or more simple data types using output parameters, you can use the example code shown in Listing 6-9.

Listing 6-8. A Simple Oracle Stored Procedure

```
1 CREATE OR REPLACE PROCEDURE  SIMPLESTOREDPROCEDURE
2 (lngNumRows OUT NUMBER)
3 AS
4 BEGIN
5   SELECT COUNT(*) INTO lngNumRows FROM TBLUSER;
6 END SIMPLESTOREDPROCEDURE;
```

The Oracle stored procedure in Listing 6-8 accepts one output parameter (lngNumRows) and sets this parameter to the number of rows in the tblUser table when executed. You can see how you can call this stored procedure from code, in Listing 6-9.

Listing 6-9. Running a Simple Oracle Stored Procedure

```
1 public void ExecuteSimpleOracleSP() {
2     OleDbConnection cnnUserMan;
3     OleDbCommand cmmUser;
4     OleDbParameter prmNumRows;
5     object objReturnValue;
6
7     // Instantiate and open the connection
8     cnnUserMan = new OleDbConnection(STR_CONNECTION_STRING);
9     cnnUserMan.Open();
10
11    // Instantiate and initialize command
12    cmmUser = new OleDbCommand("SimpleStoredProcedure", cnnUserMan);
13    cmmUser.CommandType = CommandType.StoredProcedure;
14    // Instantiate output parameter and add to parameter
15    // collection of command object
16    prmNumRows = cmmUser.CreateParameter();
17    prmNumRows.Direction = ParameterDirection.Output;
18    prmNumRows.DbType = DbType.Int64;
19    prmNumRows.Precision = 38;
20    prmNumRows.Size = 38;
21    cmmUser.Parameters.Add(prmNumRows);
22
23    // Retrieve and display value
24    objReturnValue = cmmUser.ExecuteScalar();
25    MessageBox.Show(cmmUser.Parameters[0].Value.ToString());
26 }
```

In Listing 6-9, I again use the **ExecuteScalar** method of the DataReader class on Line 24 for retrieving a value from a stored procedure. The example code on Listing 6-9 really isn't all that different from Listing 6-7, but it does show you how to call a stored procedure instead of a stored function.

The Oracle stored procedures and stored functions, and the example code to execute them shown so far, only deal with simple return values. If you need to return result sets, such as in Listings 6-2, 6-3, and 6-4, you need to use cursors in the stored procedures.[4] Listing 6-10 shows a stored procedure that returns a result set using cursors.

Listing 6-10. Oracle Stored Procedure Returning Result Set

```
1 CREATE OR REPLACE PACKAGE PKGTBLUSER
2 AS
3   TYPE CUR_TBLUSER IS REF CURSOR RETURN TBLUSER%ROWTYPE;
4 END PKGTBLUSER;
5
6 CREATE OR REPLACE PROCEDURE USPGETUSERSBYLASTNAME
7   (ROWS OUT PKGTBLUSER.CUR_TBLUSER, strLastName IN VARCHAR2)
8 IS
9 BEGIN
10 OPEN ROWS FOR SELECT * FROM TBLUSER
11 WHERE LASTNAME = strLastName;
12 END USPGETUSERSBYLASTNAME;
```

In Listing 6-10, you can see how I first create a package definition (Lines 1 through 4) in my Oracle database, and in this package I define the CUR_TBLUSER cursor type, which is of data type **REF CURSOR,**[5] that returns rows from the tblUser table. The package definition only holds the type declaration, which is used in the stored procedure. Please note that the notion of Oracle package definitions and package bodies are beyond the scope of this book, although you can certainly use a package body instead of the stored procedure shown on Lines 6 through 12. Please see your Oracle documentation for more information on packages.

You need to declare the cursor type in a package, because you're using it as the data type for one of the parameters in the USPGETUSERSBYLASTNAME stored procedure. You can't declare a data type in the parameters section of a stored

---

4. You can also use cursors with a stored function, but because I won't be using the function return value from this point on, I'll concentrate on using stored procedures.
5. This is short for REFERENCE CURSOR, and basically it's used as a pointer to the original data. Please see your Oracle documentation for more information.

procedure, which is why you need it declared elsewhere. If you look at the parameters declaration on Line 7, you can see that I need to use the full path to the data type, PKGTBLUSER.CUR_TBLUSER. Lines 10 and 11 of Listing 6-10 is where the rows that match the passed last name criterion, are retrieved with the CUR_TBLUSER cursor and saved in the ROWS OUT parameter. Listing 6-11 shows you how to retrieve the result set from the stored procedure.

Listing 6-11. Retrieving Result Set from Oracle Stored Procedure

```
1 public void OracleGetUsersByLastName() {
2     OleDbConnection cnnUserMan;
3     OleDbCommand cmmUser;
4     OleDbParameter prmLastName;
5     OleDbDataReader drdUser;
6
7     // Instantiate and open the connection
8     cnnUserMan = new OleDbConnection(STR_CONNECTION_STRING);
9     cnnUserMan.Open();
10
11    // Instantiate and initialize command
12    cmmUser = new OleDbCommand("USPGETUSERSBYLASTNAME", cnnUserMan);
13    cmmUser.CommandType = CommandType.StoredProcedure;
14    // Instantiate, initialize and add parameter to command
15    prmLastName = cmmUser.Parameters.Add("strLastName", OleDbType.VarChar,
16        50);
17    // Indicate this is an input parameter
18    prmLastName.Direction = ParameterDirection.Input;
19    // Set the type and value of the parameter
20    prmLastName.Value = "Doe";
21
22    // Retrieve rows
23    drdUser = cmmUser.ExecuteReader();
24    // Loop through the returned rows
25    while (drdUser.Read()) {
26        // Display the last name of all user rows
27        MessageBox.Show(drdUser["LastName"].ToString());
28    }
29 }
```

In Listing 6-11, you can see how I set up the command object on Lines 12 through 13, and then prepare the prmLastName input parameter with the value of "Doe". I then call the **ExecuteReader** method of the Command class, which returns the DataReader with all users with a last name of Doe. If you compare the stored procedure in Listing 6-10 and the example code in Listing 6-11, you'll see that there's a mismatch of the number of parameters. The stored procedure has two parameters, the last name input parameter and the result set output parameter. However, I only set up one parameter in Listing 6-11 and that's the last name input parameter. The command object takes care of returning the result set as the return value of the function call (**ExecuteReader**) instead of as an output parameter. It almost works the same as with the SQL Server example code in Listing 6-3.

> **NOTE**   *It doesn't matter where you place the* ROWS OUT *parameter in the stored procedure parameter declaration—that is, whether you place it first as is done in Listing 6-10, or last like this:*
> `(strLastName IN VARCHAR2, ROWS OUT PKGTBLUSER.CUR_TBLUSER)`

There are other ways of calling a stored procedure in your Oracle database, such as using the ODBC `{call storedprocedurename}` syntax, but I've chosen to show you the way that looks and feels as close to the one used for calling SQL Server procedures.

Using Views

A *view* is, as the word suggests, a display of data in your database. Perhaps it helps to think of a view as a virtual table. It can be a subset of a table or an entire table, or it can be a subset of several joined tables. Basically, a view can represent just about any subset of data in your database, and you can include other views in a view. Including a view in another view is called *nesting*, and it can be a valuable way of grouping display data. However, nesting too deeply can also result in performance problems and can certainly make it a real challenge to track down errors. There isn't really any magic to a view or any big secrets that I can let you in on; it's simply just a great tool for manipulating your data. In the rest of this section, I am going to look at why, when, where, and how you should use a view.

> **NOTE**   *The example code shown in this section is SQL Server only, but if you take a look at the accompanying example code, you'll see that it works exactly the same with Microsoft Access queries. Only the SQL Server .NET Data Provider has been changed to the OLE DB .NET Data Provider. The same goes for Oracle views. See the example code, which is almost identical to the Microsoft Access code. Views aren't supported in MySQL 3.23.45.*

View Restrictions

A view is almost identical to a row-returning query, with just a few exceptions. Some of the restrictions are detailed here:

- COMPUTE and COMPUTE BY clauses cannot be included in your view.

- ORDER BY clauses aren't allowed in a view, unless you specify the TOP clause as part of the SELECT statement. However, you can index a view with SQL Server 2000.

- The INTO keyword cannot be used to create a new table.

- Temporary tables cannot be referenced.

There are other restrictions, so please check with your SQL Server documentation and/or Help Files.

Why Use a View?

Like stored procedures, views are used for server-side processing of your data, but whereas stored procedures mainly are used for security and performance reasons, views are generally used to secure access to your data and to hide complexity of queries that contain many joins. You may want to use a view for a variety of reasons:

- *Security:* You don't want your users to access the tables directly, and with the help of a view you can restrict users to seeing only the parts of a table they are allowed to see. You can restrict access to specific columns and/or rows and thus make it easy for your users to use for their own queries.

- *Encryption:* You can encrypt a view so that no one can see where the underlying data comes from. Mind you, this is an irreversible action, meaning that the textual SQL statements that form the view can't be retrieved again!

- *Aggregated data:* Views are often used on large scale systems to provide aggregated data.

There are other reasons for creating a view, but the mentioned reasons are certainly two of the most common.

Creating a View

It's easy to create a view. If you are used to working with the SQL Server's **Server Manager**, you should check out what the **Server Explorer** has to offer you. Here's how you create a view using the UserMan database as an example:

1. Open up the Server Explorer window.

2. Expand the UserMan database on your database server.

3. Right-click the Views node and select New View.

This brings up the View Designer, which in fact is the same as the Query Designer.

> **NOTE** *The Query Designer is described in detail in Chapter 4. Although the View Designer and Query Designer have the same look and feel, you cannot create views that don't adhere to the view restrictions mentioned in the section, "View Restrictions."*

The Add Table dialog box is also shown when the View Designer is displayed. In this dialog box, simply select the tables you want to retrieve data from and click Add. Click Close when all the required tables have been added.

As you start selecting in the Diagram pane the columns that should be output when the view is run, the SQL pane and the Grid pane change accordingly. When you are done selecting the columns to output, you should save the view using Ctrl+S.

EXERCISE

1) Create a new view. This view should contain the following tables: tblUser, tblRights, and tblUserRights. The following fields should be output: tblUser.LoginName, tblUser.FirstName, tblUser.LastName, and tblRights.Name.

2) Save the view under the name **viwUserInfo**. The new view should look like the one in Figure 6-9.

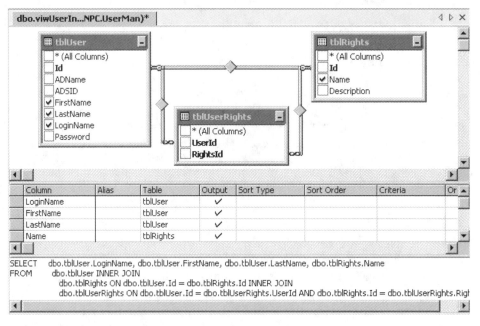

Figure 6-9. The viwUserInfo *view*

Running a View from the IDE

"Running a view" is perhaps not the most appropriate phrase when you think about it. On the other hand, the view does have to retrieve the data from all the tables referenced in the view, so I guess this phrase will have to do.

Anyway, you can run a view from the View Designer by right-clicking a blank area of the View Designer and selecting Run from the pop-up menu. The data retrieved by the view is then displayed in the Results pane of the View Designer.

EXERCISE

1) Run the `viwUserInfo` view from the View Designer. The Results pane now displays rows like the ones in Figure 6-10.

LoginName	FirstName	LastName	Name
▶ UserMan	John	Doe	AddUser
*			

Figure 6-10. The results of running the `viwUserInfo` view

2) Notice that the Name field of the tblRights table seems a bit confusing, because it doesn't really show what Name means. So in the Grid pane, you should add the text **RightsName** to the Alias column in the Name row.

3) Run the view again and notice how the new column name appears in the Results pane.

4) Save the view with Ctrl+S.

Using a View from Code

Actually, it's very easy to use a view in code, because a view is referenced like any standard table in your database, which means that you can retrieve data using a command object or a data adapter that fills a data set, and so on.

> **NOTE** *Please see Chapter 3B for specific information on how to manipulate data in a table.*

Retrieving Read-Only Data from a View in Code

The simplest use of a view is for display purposes, like when you just need to display some information from one or more related tables. Because in the example code I don't have to worry about updates, I don't have to set up anything particular. Listing 6-12 demonstrates how to return all rows from a view and populate a data reader.

Listing 6-12. Retrieving Rows in a View

```
1 public void RetrieveRowsFromView() {
2    SqlConnection cnnUserMan;
3    SqlCommand cmmUser;
4    SqlDataReader drdUser;
5
6    // Instantiate and open the connection
7    cnnUserMan = new SqlConnection(STR_CONNECTION_STRING);
8    cnnUserMan.Open();
9
10   // Instantiate and initialize command
11   cmmUser = new SqlCommand("SELECT * FROM viwUserInfo", cnnUserMan);
12   // Get rows
13   drdUser = cmmUser.ExecuteReader();
14 }
```

Listing 6-12 is just like any other row-returning query, except that a view is queried instead of a table.

Manipulating Data in a View from Code

Listing 6-12 shows you how to retrieve data from a view into a data reader, and this means the data cannot be updated, because the data reader doesn't allow updates. However, it's possible to update data in a view. The problem with this is that various versions of SQL Server support different levels of update support for views. If you only have one table in a view, this isn't a problem at all; however, if you have multiple tables in a view, only SQL Server 2000 supports updating rows in more than one of the source tables. Besides the mentioned problems, you'll certainly run into even bigger problems if you need to migrate to a different RDBMS. Generally, I would discourage updating data in views.

1) Create a new view. This view should contain the tblUser table. The following fields should be output: Id, FirstName, LastName, and LoginName.

2) Save the view under the name **viwUser**. The new view should look like the one in Figure 6-11.

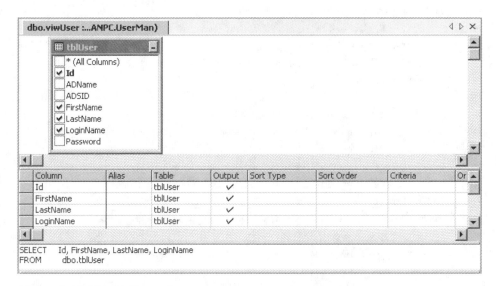

Figure 6-11. The viwUser *view*

This view, which can be located on SQL Server 7.0 as well as SQL Server 2000, can be manipulated using the code in Listing 6-13.

Listing 6-13. Manipulating Data in a View Based on a Single Table

```
1  public void ManipulatingDataInAViewBasedOnSingleTable() {
2      const string STR_SQL_USER_SELECT = "SELECT * FROM viwUser";
3      const string STR_SQL_USER_DELETE = "DELETE FROM viwUser WHERE Id=@Id";
4      const string STR_SQL_USER_INSERT = "INSERT INTO viwUser(FirstName, " +
5          "LastName, LoginName, Logged, Description) VALUES(@FirstName, " +
6          "@LastName, @LoginName)";
7      const string STR_SQL_USER_UPDATE = "UPDATE viwUser SET FirstName=" +
8          "@FirstName, LastName=@LastName, LoginName=@LoginName WHERE Id=@Id";
9
10     SqlConnection cnnUserMan;
11     SqlCommand cmmUser;
```

```
12   SqlDataAdapter dadUser;
13   DataSet dstUser;
14
15   SqlCommand cmmUserSelect;
16   SqlCommand cmmUserDelete;
17   SqlCommand cmmUserInsert;
18   SqlCommand cmmUserUpdate;
19
20   SqlParameter prmSQLDelete, prmSQLUpdate;
21
22    // Instantiate and open the connection
23   cnnUserMan = new SqlConnection(STR_CONNECTION_STRING);
24   cnnUserMan.Open();
25
26   // Instantiate and initialize command
27   cmmUser = new SqlCommand("SELECT * FROM viwUser", cnnUserMan);
28   // Instantiate the commands
29   cmmUserSelect = new SqlCommand(STR_SQL_USER_SELECT, cnnUserMan);
30   cmmUserDelete = new SqlCommand(STR_SQL_USER_DELETE, cnnUserMan);
31   cmmUserInsert = new SqlCommand(STR_SQL_USER_INSERT, cnnUserMan);
32   cmmUserUpdate = new SqlCommand(STR_SQL_USER_UPDATE, cnnUserMan);
33   // Instantiate command and data set
34   cmmUser = new SqlCommand(STR_SQL_USER_SELECT, cnnUserMan);
35   dstUser = new DataSet();
36
37   dadUser = new SqlDataAdapter();
38   dadUser.SelectCommand = cmmUserSelect;
39   dadUser.InsertCommand = cmmUserInsert;
40   dadUser.DeleteCommand = cmmUserDelete;
41   dadUser.UpdateCommand = cmmUserUpdate;
42
43   // Add parameters
44    prmSQLDelete = dadUser.DeleteCommand.Parameters.Add("@Id", SqlDbType.Int,
45      0, "Id");
46   prmSQLDelete.Direction = ParameterDirection.Input;
47   prmSQLDelete.SourceVersion = DataRowVersion.Original;
48
49   cmmUserUpdate.Parameters.Add("@FirstName", SqlDbType.VarChar, 50,
50      "FirstName");
51   cmmUserUpdate.Parameters.Add("@LastName", SqlDbType.VarChar, 50,
52      "LastName");
53   cmmUserUpdate.Parameters.Add("@LoginName", SqlDbType.VarChar, 50,
54      "LoginName");
```

```
55    prmSQLUpdate = dadUser.UpdateCommand.Parameters.Add("@Id", SqlDbType.Int,
56        0, "Id");
57    prmSQLUpdate.Direction = ParameterDirection.Input;
58    prmSQLUpdate.SourceVersion = DataRowVersion.Original;
59
60    cmmUserInsert.Parameters.Add("@FirstName", SqlDbType.VarChar, 50,
61        "FirstName");
62    cmmUserInsert.Parameters.Add("@LastName", SqlDbType.VarChar, 50,
63        "LastName");
64    cmmUserInsert.Parameters.Add("@LoginName", SqlDbType.VarChar, 50,
65        "LoginName");
66
67    // Populate the data set from the view
68    dadUser.Fill(dstUser, "viwUser");
69
70    // Change the last name of user in the second row
71    dstUser.Tables["viwUser"].Rows[1]["LastName"] = "Thomsen";
72    dstUser.Tables["viwUser"].Rows[1]["FirstName"] = "Carsten";
73    // Propagate changes back to the data source
74    dadUser.Update(dstUser, "viwUser");
75 }
```

In Listing 6-13, a data adapter and a data set were set up to retrieve and hold data from the viwUser view. The LastName column of row 2 is then updated as well as the data source with the changes in the data set. This simple demonstration was designed to show you how to work with views based on a single table.

Using Triggers

A *trigger* is actually a stored procedure that automatically invokes (triggers) when a certain change is applied to your data. Triggers are the final server-side processing functionality that I'll discuss in this chapter. Until SQL Server 2000 was released, triggers were a vital part of enforcing referential integrity, but with the release of SQL Server 2000, you now have that capability built in. In the rest of this section, I'll show you what a trigger is and when and how you can use it, but there is little C# programming involved with using triggers, because they operate entirely internally, only passing status or error indicators back to the client.

Triggers respond to data modifications using INSERT, UPDATE, and DELETE operations. Basically, you can say that a trigger helps you write less code; you can incorporate business rules as triggers and thus prevent the inclusion of data that is invalid because it violates your business rules.

SQL Server implements AFTER triggers, meaning that the trigger is invoked after the modification has occurred. However, this doesn't mean that a change can't be rolled back, because the trigger has direct access to the modified row and as such can roll back any modification. When SQL Server 2000 was released you also got support for the notion of BEFORE triggers, which you might know from the Oracle RDBMS. In SQL Server 2000, they are called INSTEAD OF triggers.

> **NOTE** *The example code shown in this section is SQL Server only, but if you take a look at the accompanying example code, you'll see that Oracle after triggers work almost the same as SQL Server triggers, although the syntax is different. Only the SQL Server .NET Data Provider has been changed to the OLE DB .NET Data Provider. Triggers aren't supported in Microsoft Access or MySQL 3.23.45.*

Why Use a Trigger?

Triggers are automatic, so you don't have to apply the business logic in your code. Here's a perfect situation for a business rule: you need to check if a member of an organization has paid his or her annual fee and therefore is allowed to order material from the organization's library. An INSERT trigger could perform the lookup in the members table when a member tries to order material and check if the member has paid the annual fee. This is exactly what makes a trigger more useful than a constraint in some situations, because a trigger can access columns in other tables, unlike a constraint, which can only access columns in the current table or row. If your code is to handle your business rule, this would mean that you need to look up the member's information in the members table before you can insert the order in the orders table. With the trigger, this lookup is done automatically, and an exception is thrown if you try to insert an order for library material if the member hasn't paid his or her annual fee. Furthermore, you don't have to rely on another front-end code developer to know what the business rules are.

In short, use a trigger for keeping all your data valid or to comply with your business rules. Think of triggers as an extra validation tool, while at the same time making sure you have set up referential integrity.

> **NOTE** *With SQL Server 2000, you shouldn't use triggers for referential integrity (see Chapter 2), because you can set that up with the Database Designer. See Chapter 4 for information on the Database Designer.*

Creating a Trigger

It's quite easy to create a trigger. This can be done using the Server Manager that comes with SQL Server, but I'll use the Server Explorer. Here's how you create a trigger for the example UserMan database:

1. Open up the Server Explorer window.

2. Expand the UserMan database on your database server.

3. Expand the Tables node.

4. Right-click the table for which you want to create a trigger and select New Trigger from the pop-up menu.

This brings up the trigger text editor, which is more or less the same editor you use for your C# code (see Figure 6-12).

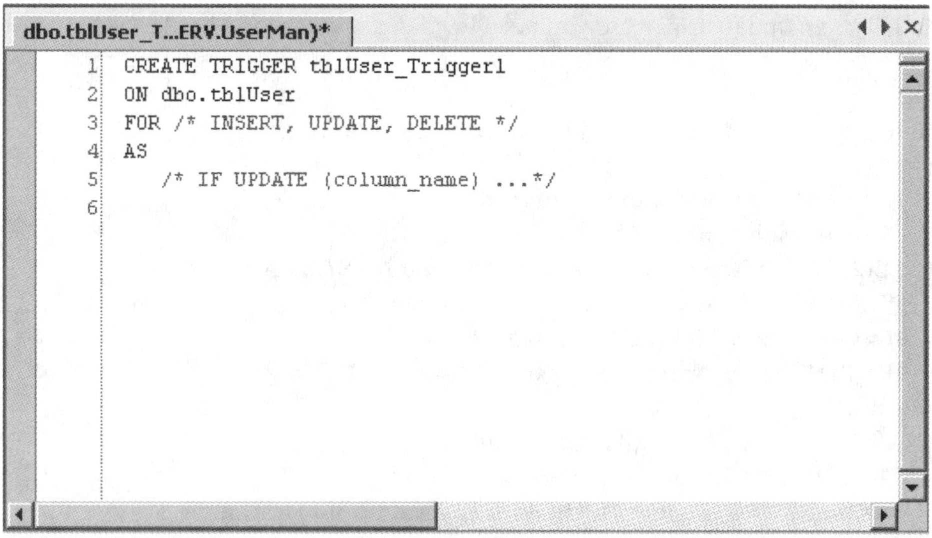

```
dbo.tblUser_T...ERV.UserMan)*

1   CREATE TRIGGER tblUser_Trigger1
2   ON dbo.tblUser
3   FOR /* INSERT, UPDATE, DELETE */
4   AS
5       /* IF UPDATE (column_name) ...*/
6
```

Figure 6-12. Trigger editor with default template

In the trigger editor, you can see that the template automatically names a new trigger Trigger1 prefixed with the name of the table. Actually, if another trigger with this name already exists, the new trigger is named Trigger2, and so on.

Once you are done editing your trigger, you need to save it by pressing Ctrl+S. As soon as you have saved it, the very first line of the stored procedure changes. The SQL statement CREATE TRIGGER is changed so that the first line reads as follows:

```
ALTER TRIGGER dbo. . . .
```

> **NOTE** *The trigger editor performs syntax checking when you save your trigger, meaning if the syntax of your trigger is invalid, you aren't allowed to save it to your database.*

EXERCISE

1) Create a new trigger for the tblUser table and save it with the name **tblUser_Update**.

2) This is an update trigger, so you need to change the text on Line 3 to **FOR UPDATE**.

3) Replace the text on Line 5 and down with the following:

> **DECLARE @strFirstName varchar(50)**
> **/* Get the value for the FirstName column */**
> **SELECT @strFirstName = (SELECT FirstName FROM inserted)**
> **/* Check if we're updating the LastName column.**
> **If so, make sure FirstName is not NULL */**
> **IF UPDATE (LastName) AND @strFirstName IS NULL**
> **BEGIN**
>   **/* Roll back update and raise exception */**
>   **ROLLBACK TRANSACTION**
>   **RAISERROR ('You must fill in both LastName and FirstName', 11, 1)**
> **END**

Now the stored procedure should look like the one in Figure 6-13.

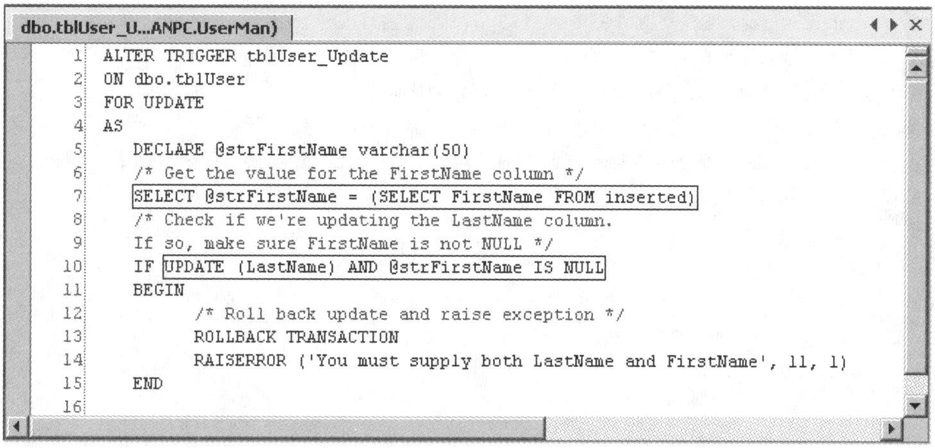

```
dbo.tblUser_U...ANPC.UserMan)                                      ◄ ► ✕
  1  ALTER TRIGGER tblUser_Update
  2  ON dbo.tblUser
  3  FOR UPDATE
  4  AS
  5     DECLARE @strFirstName varchar(50)
  6     /* Get the value for the FirstName column */
  7     SELECT @strFirstName = (SELECT FirstName FROM inserted)
  8     /* Check if we're updating the LastName column.
  9     If so, make sure FirstName is not NULL */
 10     IF UPDATE (LastName) AND @strFirstName IS NULL
 11     BEGIN
 12         /* Roll back update and raise exception */
 13         ROLLBACK TRANSACTION
 14         RAISERROR ('You must supply both LastName and FirstName', 11, 1)
 15     END
 16
```

Figure 6-13. The tblUser_Update *trigger*

4) Don't forget to save the changes using Ctrl+S.

When a trigger has been saved to the database, you can locate it under the table to which it belongs in the **Server Explorer**.

The tblUser_Update trigger is invoked when updating a row in the user table. The trigger first tests to see if the LastName column is updated. If it is, then the trigger checks to see if the FirstName column is empty, because if it is the update is rolled back and an exception is raised. Please note that this trigger is designed to work with only one updated or inserted row at a time. If more rows are inserted at the same time, the trigger will have to be redesigned to accommodate this. However, this trigger only serves as a demonstration. The functionality of this trigger can easily be implemented using constraints, because the check I perform is done in the same table. If I had looked up a value in a different table, then the trigger would be your only choice.

Please see your SQL Server documentation if you need more information on how to create triggers. Listing 6-14 shows you how to execute the new trigger, demonstrating how to raise an exception you can catch in code.

Listing 6-14. Invoking Trigger and Catching Exception Raised

```
1 public void TestUpdateTrigger() {
2     const string STR_SQL_USER_SELECT = "SELECT * FROM tblUser";
3     const string STR_SQL_USER_DELETE = "DELETE FROM tblUser WHERE Id=@Id";
4     const string STR_SQL_USER_INSERT = "INSERT INTO tblUser(FirstName, " +
5         "LastName, LoginName) VALUES(@FirstName, @LastName, @LoginName)";
6     const string STR_SQL_USER_UPDATE = "UPDATE tblUser SET " +
7         FirstName=@FirstName, LastName=@LastName, LoginName=@LoginName WHERE" +
8         " Id=@Id";
9
10    SqlConnection cnnUserMan;
11    SqlCommand cmmUser;
12    SqlDataAdapter dadUser;
13    DataSet dstUser;
14
15    SqlCommand cmmUserSelect;
16    SqlCommand cmmUserDelete;
17    SqlCommand cmmUserInsert;
18    SqlCommand cmmUserUpdate;
19
20    SqlParameter prmSQLDelete, prmSQLUpdate, prmSQLInsert;
21
22    // Instantiate and open the connection
23    cnnUserMan = new SqlConnection(STR_CONNECTION_STRING);
24    cnnUserMan.Open();
25
26    // Instantiate and initialize command
27    cmmUser = new SqlCommand("SELECT * FROM tblUser", cnnUserMan);
28    // Instantiate the commands
29    cmmUserSelect = new SqlCommand(STR_SQL_USER_SELECT, cnnUserMan);
30    cmmUserDelete = new SqlCommand(STR_SQL_USER_DELETE, cnnUserMan);
31    cmmUserInsert = new SqlCommand(STR_SQL_USER_INSERT, cnnUserMan);
32    cmmUserUpdate = new SqlCommand(STR_SQL_USER_UPDATE, cnnUserMan);
33    // Instantiate command and data set
34    cmmUser = new SqlCommand(STR_SQL_USER_SELECT, cnnUserMan);
35    dstUser = new DataSet();
36
37    dadUser = new SqlDataAdapter();
38    dadUser.SelectCommand = cmmUserSelect;
39    dadUser.InsertCommand = cmmUserInsert;
40    dadUser.DeleteCommand = cmmUserDelete;
41    dadUser.UpdateCommand = cmmUserUpdate;
42
```

```
43      // Add parameters
44      prmSQLDelete = dadUser.DeleteCommand.Parameters.Add("@Id", SqlDbType.Int,
45          0, "Id");
46      prmSQLDelete.Direction = ParameterDirection.Input;
47      prmSQLDelete.SourceVersion = DataRowVersion.Original;
48
49      cmmUserUpdate.Parameters.Add("@FirstName", SqlDbType.VarChar, 50,
50          "FirstName");
51      cmmUserUpdate.Parameters.Add("@LastName", SqlDbType.VarChar, 50,
52          "LastName");
53      cmmUserUpdate.Parameters.Add("@LoginName", SqlDbType.VarChar, 50,
54          "LoginName");
55      prmSQLUpdate = dadUser.UpdateCommand.Parameters.Add("@Id", SqlDbType.Int,
56          0, "Id");
57      prmSQLUpdate.Direction = ParameterDirection.Input;
58      prmSQLUpdate.SourceVersion = DataRowVersion.Original;
59
60      cmmUserInsert.Parameters.Add("@FirstName", SqlDbType.VarChar, 50,
61          "FirstName");
62      cmmUserInsert.Parameters.Add("@LastName", SqlDbType.VarChar, 50,
63          "LastName");
64      cmmUserInsert.Parameters.Add("@LoginName", SqlDbType.VarChar, 50,
65          "LoginName");
66
67      // Populate the data set from the view
68      dadUser.Fill(dstUser, "tblUser");
69
70      // Change the name of user in the second row
71      dstUser.Tables["tblUser"].Rows[1]["LastName"] = "Thomsen";
72      dstUser.Tables["tblUser"].Rows[1]["FirstName"] = null;
73
74      try {
75          // Propagate changes back to the data source
76          dadUser.Update(dstUser, "tblUser");
77      }
78      catch (Exception objE) {
79          MessageBox.Show(objE.Message);
80      }
81  }
```

In Listing 6-14, the second row is updated, and the LastName column is set to "Thomsen" and the FirstName to a **null** value. This will invoke the update trigger that throws an exception, which is caught in code and displays the error message.

This should give you a taste for using triggers, and they really aren't that hard to work with. Just make sure you have a well-designed database that doesn't use triggers for purposes that can easily be achieved by other means such as referential integrity.

Viewing Trigger Source

In SQL Server Enterprise Manager, you can see the source for your triggers. Open up Enterprise Manager, expand your SQL Server, and expand databases and your database. Next, select the Tables node, right-click the table you have created the trigger for, and select All Task Manage Triggers from the pop-up menu. This brings up the Triggers Properties dialog box, where you can see and edit the triggers for the selected table.

In the Server Explorer in the VS .NET IDE, you can also view the trigger source by expanding your database, expanding the Tables node, expanding the table with the trigger, and double-clicking the trigger.

Summary

In this chapter, I discussed how to create various server-side objects for server-side processing of your data. I demonstrated stored procedures, views, and triggers, and showed you how to create, run, and execute a stored procedure from code; how to create, run, and use a view from code, including updating the view; and finally how to create triggers.

I went into enough details about stored procedures, views, and triggers as to what a C# programmer needs to know, but if you are also responsible for coding the SQL Server database and you need more information and example code, I can certainly recommend you read this book:

- *Code Centric: T-SQL Programming with Stored Procedures and Triggers,* by Garth Wells. Published by Apress, February 2001. ISBN: 1893115836.

The next chapter is about hierarchical databases. I'll discuss how you use the LDAP protocol to access a network directory database like the Active Directory and you'll see how to access information stored on Exchange Server 2000.

CHAPTER 7

Hierarchical Databases

IN THIS CHAPTER, I WILL DISCUSS the Lightweight Directory Access Protocol (LDAP) directory service protocol and how it can be used for connecting to Active Directory, Microsoft's network directory service, and how you can access Microsoft Exchange Server 2000. Active Directory is a hierarchical database, and you can find a general description of such a database in Chapter 2.

Looking at LDAP

Since you will be accessing Active Directory in the example application, I believe providing some brief background on Active Directory and LDAP is in order. Active Directory is a network directory service, like the Domain Name System (DNS) and Novell Directory Services (NDS). A *network directory service* holds information on objects such as users, printers, clients, servers, and so on. In short, a network directory service holds information, which is used to manage or access a network. This chapter contains hands-on exercises that will take you through accessing Active Directory.

Active Directory was first introduced with the Microsoft Windows 2000 operating system. Active Directory is an X.500-compliant network directory based on open standards protocols such as LDAP. Because Active Directory is X.500 compliant, it is a hierarchical database with a treelike structure. When the specifications for the X.500 directory were under development, an access protocol for accessing a network directory based on the X.500 specification was needed, and thus the Directory Access Protocol (DAP) was created. However, the specification for DAP was too overwhelming and the overhead too big, which resulted in very few clients and/or applications being able to connect to DAP. If you need more information about the X.500 directory standard as it is defined by the International Organization for Standardization (ISO) and the International Telecommunication Union (ITU), you can visit http://www.nexor.com/x500frame.htm.

The challenge of the DAP specification being too overwhelming was met by a group of people at the University of Michigan who realized that reducing the DAP overhead could result in faster retrieval of the same directory information and much smaller clients. This group created a new protocol specification, the Lightweight Directory Access Protocol (LDAP).

> **NOTE**   *See Chapter 2 for information on how a hierarchical database is structured.*

LDAP runs directly over the TCP/IP stack. The network directory service needs to host an LDAP service if you want to use LDAP to access the directory, though, which means that LDAP is client-server based.

These days LDAP is becoming the de facto standard for clients to access directory information. This is true for clients working over both the Internet and intranets, with standard LAN directory access now also moving toward LDAP.

One of the most important aspects of the LDAP protocol standard is that it gives us an API that is common and, most notably, platform independent. As a result, applications that access a directory service such as Microsoft Active Directory or Novell Directory Services (NDS) will be a lot easier and less expensive to develop.

> **NOTE**   *The LDAP directory service protocol gives you access to an existing directory; it cannot create a new directory.*

Exploring Active Directory

The fact that Active Directory server is currently available only with Windows 2000 means you need at least a Windows 2000 Server, with Active Directory installed, in order to follow this discussion. However, Windows .NET Servers[1] should be available not long after you read this.

Not only is Active Directory accessible, it is also extendable, which is significant. If you have an object that you want to expose to a network, you can extend the schema of Active Directory and make it available to anyone who can access the Active Directory implementation in question. The schema in Active Directory defines all the object classes and attributes that can be stored in

---

1.   Windows .NET Servers are the next version of Windows 2000 or, to be more correct, they are the server version of Windows XP.

the directory. This doesn't mean that all the objects defined in the schema are actually present in Active Directory, but the schema allows them to be created, so to speak. For each object class, the schema also defines where the object can be created in the directory tree by specifying the class' valid or legal parents. Furthermore, the content of a class is defined by a list of attributes that the class must or may contain. This means that an Active Directory object is a named set of attributes. This set of attributes is distinct and is used to describe a user or printer, for instance. Anything on the network that is a physical entity can be specified as an object in Active Directory.

As I won't go into much more detail about Active Directory, check out `http://www.microsoft.com/windows2000/technologies/directory/default.asp` if you want more specifics about Active Directory.

So to sum up quickly: Active Directory is a network directory service, based on the X.500 specifications, that can be accessed using the client-server–based LDAP directory service protocol.

Accessing Active Directory Programmatically

Active Directory can, of course, be accessed programmatically from C#, as is the case with previous versions of Windows programming languages such as Visual Basic 6.0. However, unlike these previous versions of programming languages, C# has some built-in features that let you access Active Directory without having to go through the Windows API. The **System.DirectoryServices** namespace has everything you need for this purpose.

Examining the System.DirectoryServices Namespace

The **System.DirectoryServices** namespace holds a number of classes that let you access Active Directory. Table 7-1 lists some of the classes important to this namespace.

*Table 7-1. **System.DirectoryServices** Classes*

CLASS NAME	DESCRIPTION
DirectoryEntries	This collection class contains the child entries of an Active Directory entry (**DirectoryEntry.Children** property). Please note that the collection only contains immediate children.
DirectoryEntry	The **DirectoryEntry** class encapsulates an object or a node in the Active Directory database hierarchy.
DirectorySearcher	This class is used for performing queries against Active Directory using the LDAP protocol.
PropertyCollection	This collection holds all the properties of a single **DirectoryEntry** class (**DirectoryEntry.Properties** property).
PropertyValueCollection	The **PropertyValueCollection** collection holds values for a multivalued property (**DirectoryEntry.Properties.Values** property).
ResultPropertyCollection	This collection holds the properties of a **SearchResult** object (**SearchResultCollection[0].Properties** property).
ResultPropertyValueCollection	The **ResultPropertyValueCollection** collection holds values for a **SearchResult** object.
SchemaNameCollection	This collection holds a list of schema names that is used for the **DirectoryEntries** class' **SchemaFilter** property.
SearchResult	This class encapsulates a node in the Active Directory database hierarchy. This node is returned as the result of a search performed by an instance of the **DirectorySearcher** class. Use the **SearchResult** class with the **FindOne** method of the **DirectorySearcher** class.
SearchResultCollection	This collection contains the instances of the **SearchResult** class that are returned when querying the Active Directory hierarchy using the **DirectorySearcher.FindAll** method.
SortOption	The **SortOption** class specifies how a query should be sorted.

In order to use these classes, you need to be aware of the following restrictions:

- The Active Directory Services Interface Software Development Kit (ADSI SDK) or the ADSI runtime must be installed on your computer. If you're running Windows 2000, it's installed by default. If you're running an earlier version of Windows, you can install the SDK by downloading it from the Microsoft Web site: `http://www.microsoft.com/windows2000/techinfo/howitworks/activedirectory/adsilinks.asp`.

- A directory service provider, such as Active Directory or LDAP, must be installed on your computer.

I won't explain all the classes in the **System.DirectoryServices** namespace, but the **DirectoryEntry** class is quite important, so I discuss this class in the following section.

Studying the DirectoryEntry Class

Recall that the **DirectoryEntry** class encapsulates an object in the Active Directory database hierarchy. You can use this class for binding to objects in Active Directory or for manipulating object attributes. This class and the helper classes can be used with the following providers: **IIS**, **LDAP**, **NDS**, and **WinNT**. More providers will probably follow. As you may have guessed, I will only demonstrate the use of LDAP to access Active Directory in this chapter.

Table 7-2 shows you the noninherited, public properties of the **DirectoryEntry** class.

*Table 7-2. **DirectoryEntry** Class Properties*

PROPERTY NAME	DESCRIPTION
AuthenticationType	This property returns or sets the type of authentication to be used. The value must be a member of the **AuthenticationTypes** enum. The default value is **None**, and the following are the other values of the enum: **Anonymous**, **Delegation**, **Encryption**, **FastBind**, **ReadonlyServer**, **Sealing**, **Secure**, **SecureSocketsLayer**, **ServerBind**, and **Signing**.
Children	This read-only property returns a **DirectoryEntries** class (collection) that holds the child entries of the node in the Active Directory database hierarchy. Only immediate children are returned.
Guid	The **Guid** property returns the globally unique identifier of the **DirectoryEntry** class. If you're binding to an object in Active Directory, you should use the **NativeGuid** property instead. This property is read-only.

(continued)

Table 7-2. **DirectoryEntry** Class Properties (continued)

PROPERTY NAME	DESCRIPTION
Name	This read-only property returns the name of the object. The value returned is the name of the **DirectoryEntry** object as it appears in the underlying directory service. Note that the **SchemaClassName** property together with this property are what make the directory entry unique; in other words, these two names make it possible to tell one directory entry apart from its siblings.
NativeGuid	The **NativeGuid** property returns the globally unique identifier of the **DirectoryEntry** class as it is returned from the provider. This property is read-only.
NativeObject	This read-only property returns the native ADSI object. You can use this property when you want to work with a COM interface.
Parent	The **Parent** property returns the **DirectoryEntry** object's parent in the Active Directory database hierarchy. This property is read-only.
Password	This property returns or sets the password that is used when the client is authenticated. When the **Password** and **Username** properties are set, all other instances of the **DirectoryEntry** class that are retrieved from the current instance will automatically be created with the same values for these properties.
Path	The **Path** property returns or sets the path for the **DirectoryEntry** class. The default is an empty **string**. This property is used for uniquely identifying the object in a network.
Properties	This property returns a **PropertyCollection** class holding the properties that have been set on the **DirectoryEntry** object.
SchemaClassName	The **SchemaClassName** property returns the name of the schema that is used for the **DirectoryEntry** object.
SchemaEntry	This property returns the **DirectoryEntry** object that is holding the schema information for the current **DirectoryEntry** object. The **SchemaClassName** property of a **DirectoryEntry** class determines the properties that are valid, both mandatory and optional, for the **DirectoryEntry** instance.
UsePropertyCache	This property returns or sets a **bool** value that indicates if the cache should be committed after each operation or not. The default is **true**.
Username	The **Username** property returns or sets the user name that is used for authenticating the client. When the **Password** and **Username** properties are set, all other instances of the **DirectoryEntry** class that are retrieved from the current instance will automatically be created with the same values for these properties.

To sum up what the **DirectoryEntry** class contains, check out its methods. Table 7-3 shows you the noninherited, public methods of the **DirectoryEntry** class.

*Table 7-3. **DirectoryEntry** Class Methods*

METHOD NAME	DESCRIPTION	EXAMPLE
Close()	This method closes the **DirectoryEntry** object. This means that any system resources used by the **DirectoryEntry** object are released at this point.	`objAD.Close();`
CommitChanges()	The **CommitChanges** method saves any changes you have made to the **DirectoryEntry** object to the Active Directory database.	`objAD.CommitChanges();`
CopyTo() As DirectoryEntry	This overloaded method is used for creating a copy of the **DirectoryEntry** object as a child of `objADParent`, with or without a new name (`strNewName`).	`objADCopy = objAD.CopyTo(objADParent);` `objADCopy = objAD.CopyTo(objADParent, strNewName);`
DeleteTree()	The **DeleteTree** method does exactly what it says: it deletes the **DirectoryEntry** object and the entire subtree from the Active Directory database hierarchy.	`objAD.DeleteTree();`
Exists(string strPath)	This **static** method is used for searching at `strPath` to see if an entry exists. A **bool** value is returned, but because the method is **static**, you need to call this method from the type and not an instantiated object.	`DirectoryEntry.Exists (strPath);`
Invoke(string strMethodName, params object[] arrArgs args)	This method calls the `strMethodName` method on the native Active Directory with the `arrArgs` arguments.	
MoveTo()	This overloaded method is used for moving the **DirectoryEntry** object to the `objADParent` parent, with or without a new name (`strNewName`).	`objAD.MoveTo(objADParent);` `objAD.MoveTo(objADParent, strNewName);`
RefreshCache()	This overloaded method loads property values for the **DirectoryEntry** object into the property cache. Either all property values are loaded or just the ones specified with the `arrstrProperties` argument.	`objAD.RefreshCache();` `objAD.RefreshCache (arrstrProperties);`

(continued)

*Table 7-3. **DirectoryEntry** Class Methods (continued)*

METHOD NAME	DESCRIPTION	EXAMPLE
Rename(string strNewName)	The **Rename** method renames or changes the name of the **DirectoryEntry** object to strNewName.	objAD.Rename(strNewName);

Looking at the LDAP Syntax

In order to bind to or search Active Directory, you need to know about the LDAP syntax used for binding and querying, so let's take a closer look at it.

Each object in Active Directory is identified by two names when you use LDAP for access: the relative distinguished name (RDN) and the distinguished name (DN). The DN actually consists of both the RDN and all of its parents/ancestors. Here is an example:

- The RDN for the UserMan object is CN=UserMan.

- The DN for the UserMan object in my Active Directory can look like this: \C=DK\O=UserMan\OU=developers\CN=UserMan.

Each node in the hierarchy is separated by a backslash (\). The DN is unique across the directory service. This means that for each node the object name is unique. If you look at the DN, the common name (CN) UserMan must be unique in the developer's node. The organizational unit (OU) developers must be unique in the UserMan node, and so on. The O in O=UserMan represents an organization, and the C in C=DK represents a country, Denmark in this case. For the United States, you would use C=US. Sometimes, I use commas and sometimes a slash (forward or backward slash) as the separator. Actually, you can use both kinds, but you have to be aware that the order in which the DN is put together changes. For example, if you use a comma as the delimiter, the DN starts with the end object or the object that is lowest in the hierarchy, and then you traverse up the tree node until you have added the top-level node. On the other hand, if you use a slash as the delimiter, the reverse order is expected:

LDAP://DC=dk/DC=userman/CN=Users/CN=UserMan

I can't tell you which separator to use—in most cases it's simply a matter of preference.

These prefixes are called *monikers,* and they're used to identify the object category. CN (common name) is the most common moniker of them all. This moniker is used by most of the objects below an organizational unit (OU) node in the hierarchy. Table 7-4 shows some of the most common monikers.

Table 7-4. Common Monikers

MONIKER NAME	DESCRIPTION	EXAMPLE
Common name (CN)	The most common of all the monikers is logically called common name. It is used for most of the objects below the O or OU nodes or objects.	CN=UserMan
Country (C)	This moniker is used to describe the top-level node.	C=DK or C=US
Domain component (DC)	The DC moniker is used to describe a domain. Because you are not allowed to use periods in a relative distinguished name (RDN), you need to use two DC monikers to describe your domain.	DC=userman, DC=dk
Organization (O)	The O moniker is used for describing an organization, and usually this is the company name.	O=UserMan
Organizational unit (OU)	If your organization has more units, the OU moniker is used to describe these.	OU=developers

Here is an example of a complete LDAP path for the UserMan user on my system:

```
LDAP://CN=UserMan,CN=Users,DC=userman,DC=dk
```

Actually, I've changed the domain name, but I'm sure you get the picture. The example starts by indicating that LDAP is the protocol (LDAP://) I want to use followed by a comma-delimited list of RDNs to make up the DN. Translating the query into plain English, the path looks for the user UserMan belonging to the Users group in the userman.dk domain.

Binding to an Object in Active Directory

To do anything in Active Directory using a class from the **System.DirectoryServices** namespace, you must first bind to an object. Not that it's hard to do the binding, but if you're new to LDAP and specifically to LDAP syntax, you're in for a surprise. Make sure you read the "Looking at the LDAP Syntax" section before you start binding to Active Directory. Check out Listing 7-1 for a very simple example of how to bind to a specific user in Active Directory.

Listing 7-1. Binding to an Object in Active Directory

```
1 public void BindToUserManObjectInAD() {
2    DirectoryEntry objEntry;
3
4    objEntry = new DirectoryEntry(
5       "LDAP://CN=UserMan,CN=Users,DC=userman,DC=dk",
6       "Administrator", "adminpwd");
7 }
```

In Listing 7-1, I have instantiated the **DirectoryEntry** object and bound it to the **UserMan** user object in Active Directory. I have also specified the user Administrator and the password for this account. You will have to change these credentials to an account on your system with at least read access to Active Directory. As you can see, it is pretty simple once you know what object to bind to.

Searching for an Object in Active Directory

When you want to search for a specific object in Active Directory, you can use an instance of the **DirectorySearcher** class, as shown in Listing 7-2.

Listing 7-2. Searching for a Specific Object in Active Directory

```
1 public void SearchForSpecificObjectInAD() {
2    DirectoryEntry objEntry;
3    DirectorySearcher objSearcher;
4    SearchResult objSearchResult;
5
6    // Instantiate and bind to Users node in Active Directory
7    objEntry = new DirectoryEntry("LDAP://CN=Users,DC=userman,DC=dk",
8       "UserMan", "userman");
9
10   // Set up to search for UserMan on the Users node
11   objSearcher = new DirectorySearcher(objEntry, "(&(objectClass=user)" +
12      "(objectCategory=person)(userPrincipalName=userman@userman.dk))");
13
14   // Find the user
15   objSearchResult = objSearcher.FindOne();
16
17   // Check if the user was found
18   if (objSearchResult != null) {
19      // Display path for user
20      MessageBox.Show("Users Path: " + objSearchResult.Path);
21   }
```

```
22    else {
23        MessageBox.Show("User not found!");
24    }
25 }
```

In Listing 7-2, I include an instance of the **DirectorySearcher** object to locate the UserMan user on the Users node. I use the **FindOne** method to return exactly one result that matches the userPrincipalName. Please see Table 7-5 later in this chapter for more information on userPrincipalName. If more objects are found when searching, only the first object found is returned. If you want more objects returned, you need to use the **FindAll** method. See Listing 7-3 for some example code.

Listing 7-3. Searching for All Objects of a Specific Class in Active Directory

```
1 public void SearchForAllUserObjectsInAD() {
2     DirectoryEntry objEntry;
3     DirectorySearcher objSearcher;
4     SearchResultCollection objSearchResults;
5
6     // Instantiate and bind to root node in Active Directory
7     objEntry = new DirectoryEntry("LDAP://DC=userman,DC=dk", "UserMan",
8         "userman");
9
10    // Set up to search for all users
11    objSearcher = new DirectorySearcher(objEntry,
12        "(&(objectClass=user)(objectCategory=person))");
13
14    // Find all objects of class user
15    objSearchResults = objSearcher.FindAll();
16
17    // Check if any users were found
18    if (objSearchResults != null) {
19        // Loop through all users returned
20        foreach (SearchResult objSearchResult in objSearchResults) {
21            // Display path for user
22            MessageBox.Show("Users Path: " + objSearchResult.Path);
23        }
24    }
25    else {
26        MessageBox.Show("No users were found!");
27    }
28 }
```

In Listing 7-3, all objects in Active Directory of the class user and category person were returned. However, what you don't see from the example code is that not all properties of the objects were returned. By default, only the adsPath and Name properties are returned. If you want other properties returned, you have to specify them, as shown in Listing 7-4.

Listing 7-4. Returning Nondefault Properties from an Active Directory Node or Object

```
1 public void ReturnNonDefaultNodeProperties() {
2     DirectoryEntry objEntry;
3     DirectorySearcher objSearcher;
4     SearchResult objSearchResult;
5
6     // Instantiate and bind to Users node in Active Directory
7     objEntry = new DirectoryEntry("LDAP://CN=Users,DC=userman,DC=dk",
8         "UserMan", "userman");
9
10    // Set up to search for UserMan on the Users node
11    objSearcher = new DirectorySearcher(objEntry, "(&(objectClass=user)" +
12        "(objectCategory=person)(userPrincipalName=userman@userman.dk))",
13        new string[3] {"sn", "telephoneNumber", "givenName"});
14
15    try {
16        // Find the user
17        objSearchResult = objSearcher.FindOne();
18    }
19    catch (Exception objE) {
20        // Catch any mistakes made when setting up
21        // the DirectoryEntry object, like wrong domain
22        MessageBox.Show(objE.Message);
23        return;
24    }
25
26    // Check if the user was found
27    if (objSearchResult != null) {
28        // Display all returned user properties
29        // Loop through all the properties returned
30        foreach (string strName in objSearchResult.Properties.PropertyNames) {
31            // Loop through all the values for each property
32            foreach (object objValue in objSearchResult.Properties[strName]) {
33                // Display the property and value
34                MessageBox.Show("Property Name: " + strName.ToString() +
35                    " - Value: " + objValue.ToString());
```

```
36            }
37        }
38    }
39    else {
40        MessageBox.Show("User not found!");
41    }
42 }
```

If you need a list of LDAP display names that can represent a user in Active Directory, please visit http://msdn.microsoft.com/library/default.asp?url=/library/en-us/netdir/adschema/w2k2/DN_computer.asp?frame=true.

In Listing 7-4, I specify the extra properties I want returned with the object found. This is done on Line 13, where a **string** array consisting of three properties is added as an argument to the **DirectorySearcher** constructor. Please note that although you have specified these extra properties, they're only returned if they have a value. This means that the telephoneNumber property is only returned if a phone number has been entered for the user. Alternatively, you can add the objects by using the **Add** or **AddRange** methods of the **PropertiesToLoad** property, as follows:

```
1 // Add properties one by one
2 objSearcher.PropertiesToLoad.Add("sn");
3 objSearcher.PropertiesToLoad.Add("telephoneNumber");
4 objSearcher.PropertiesToLoad.Add("givenName");
5 // Add properties in one go
6 objSearcher.PropertiesToLoad.AddRange(new string[3]
7    {"sn", "telephoneNumber", "givenName"});
```

The following links provide more information on how to construct your LDAP query filter:

- http://msdn.microsoft.com/library/default.asp?url=/library/en-us/netdir/ad/creating_a_query_filter.asp

- http://msdn.microsoft.com/library/default.asp?url=/library/en-us/netdir/adsi/search_filter_syntax.asp

- http://msdn.microsoft.com/library/default.asp?url=/library/en-us/netdir/adsi/ldap_dialect.asp

Manipulating Object Property Values

Often, it's okay to just read the data returned from the Active Directory. However, sometimes you may want to manipulate the data as well. Once you have bound to an object, you can actually edit, delete, or add the object's property values.

Checking for the Existence of a Property

One of the first things you need to learn is to check whether a certain property has been returned with the object. For this purpose you would use the **Contains** method of the **Properties** collection. This method and collection are part of the **DirectoryEntry** and the **SearchResult** classes. Here is how you check to see if the **telephoneNumber** property was returned:

```
if (objEntry.Properties.Contains("telephoneNumber")) {}
if (objSearchResult.Properties.Contains("telephoneNumber")) {}
```

If you don't check whether a property is in the **Properties** collection before accessing it, you risk throwing an exception!

Using a Local Cache for the Properties

When you work with instances of the **DirectoryEntry** class, the properties and the property values are by default cached locally. This means access to the **DirectoryEntry** object is faster, because any change will only be applied to the local cache and not committed to the Active Directory database. The properties are cached when you first read a property.

The default behavior can, however, be changed using the **UsePropertyCache** property. The default value is **true**, which means properties are cached locally. If you set this property to **false**, all changes to the cache will be committed to the Active Directory database after each operation.

If there has been a change to the Active Directory database, you can update the cache by calling the **RefreshCache** method. If you have made changes to the content of the cache, you should call the **CommitChanges** method before you call **RefreshCache**. Otherwise, you will overwrite the noncommitted changes in the cache.

Editing an Existing Property

Editing an existing property of an object in the Active Directory is quite easy. See Listing 7-5 for an example.

Listing 7-5. Editing an Existing User Property

```
1 public void EditUserProperty() {
2     DirectoryEntry objEntry;
3
4     // Bind to UserMan user object
5     objEntry = new DirectoryEntry("LDAP://CN=UserMan,CN=Users," +
6         "DC=userman,DC=dk", "Administrator", "adminpwd");
7
8     // Check if the user already had an e-mail address
9     if (objEntry.Properties.Contains("mail")) {
10        // Change the e-mail address for the user
11        objEntry.Properties["mail"][0] = "userman@userman.dk";
12        // Commit the changes to the Active Directory database
13        objEntry.CommitChanges();
14    }
15 }
```

The example code in Listing 7-5 binds to the UserMan Active Directory object on Lines 5 and 6, and on Line 11, I change the e-mail address of the user. The changes are committed on Line 13. Please note that on Line 9, I check to see if the property already exists in the property collection before I try to edit it.

Adding a New Property

If you want to add a new property to an existing object in Active Directory, you can use the **Add** method of the **DirectoryEntry** class. See Listing 7-6 for some example code.

Listing 7-6. Adding a New User Property

```
1  public void AddNewUserProperty() {
2      DirectoryEntry objEntry;
3
4      // Bind to UserMan user object
5      objEntry = new DirectoryEntry("LDAP://CN=UserMan,CN=Users," +
6          "DC=userman,DC=dk", "Administrator", "adminpwd");
7
8      // Check if the user already had an e-mail address
9      if (objEntry.Properties.Contains("mail") != true) {
10         // Add new e-mail address
11         objEntry.Properties["mail"].Add("userman@userman.dk");
12         // Commit the changes to the Active Directory database
13         objEntry.CommitChanges();
14     }
15 }
```

In Listing 7-6, I add an e-mail address to the UserMan user by including the **Add** method of the objEntry object. This happens on Line 11, but before I can do that I have to bind to the UserMan user object in Active Directory, and this is done on Lines 5 and 6. Finally, I use the **CommitChanges** method on Line 13 to propagate the changes back to the Active Directory database.

Listings 7-5 and 7-6 are obvious candidates for a single piece of code, as shown in Listing 7-7.

Listing 7-7. Manipulating a User Property

```
1  public void ManipulateUserProperty() {
2      DirectoryEntry objEntry;
3
4      // Bind to UserMan user object
5      objEntry = new DirectoryEntry("LDAP://CN=UserMan,CN=Users,DC=userman," +
6          "DC=dk", "Administrator", "adminpwd");
7
8      // Check if the user already had an e-mail address
9      if (objEntry.Properties.Contains("mail")) {
10         // Change the e-mail address for the user
11         objEntry.Properties["mail"][0] = "userman@userman.dk";
12     }
13     else {
14         // Add new e-mail address
15         objEntry.Properties["mail"].Add("userman@userman.dk");
16     }
```

```
17
18     // Commit the changes to the Active Directory database
19     objEntry.CommitChanges();
20 }
```

Listing 7-7 is simply a piece of example code where I have made one function out of Listings 7-5 and 7-6. Basically it checks if the UserMan user already has an e-mail address. If the user already has an e-mail address, it is edited, and if not, it is added.

Updating the Active Directory Database

If the **UsePropertyCache** property of a **DirectoryEntry** object is set to **false**, you don't have to worry about committing your changes to the Active Directory database, as on Line 19 in Listing 7-7, because it's done automatically. However, if the **UsePropertyCache** property is set to **true**, which is the default, you must manually commit the changes. You can do this by calling the **CommitChanges** method of the **DirectoryEntry** class.

> **NOTE** *If you've changed any information that resides in your cache, because the **UsePropertyCache** property is set to **true**, you can abort these changes by calling the **RefreshCache** method of the **DirectoryEntry** class, which will overwrite any information in the cache.*

Accessing Active Directory Using the OLE DB .NET Data Provider

Although you can achieve just about anything in relation to Active Directory with the classes in the **System.DirectoryServices** namespace, it can be a lot easier to use the OLE DB .NET Data Provider instead, because it allows you to implement standard SQL syntax to extract the wanted data. See Listing 7-8 for an example.

Listing 7-8. Using OLE DB .NET to Access Active Directory

```
1 public void AccessADWithOleDb() {
2    OleDbConnection cnnAD;
3    OleDbCommand cmmAD;
4    OleDbDataReader drdAD;
5
6    // Instantiate and open connection
7    cnnAD = new OleDbConnection("Provider=ADsDSOObject;User Id=UserMan;" +
8       "Password=userman");
9    cnnAD.Open();
10   // Instantiate command
11   cmmAD = new OleDbCommand("SELECT cn, AdsPath FROM 'LDAP://userman.dk' " +
12      "WHERE objectCategory='person' AND objectClass='user' AND " +
13      "cn='UserMan'", cnnAD);
14
15   // Retrieve rows in data reader
16   drdAD = cmmAD.ExecuteReader();
17 }
```

Listing 7-8 shows you how to retrieve all rows from Active Directory for the userman.dk domain with the user name UserMan. You need to change the user ID and password on Lines 7 and 8 to match a user with read access to your Active Directory. On Line 11, you will need to change the domain name to match the name of the domain to which you are connecting.

The objectCategory and objectClass references on Line 12 are standard LDAP-style query calls, and they ensure that only user objects are searched.

Specifying an OLE DB Provider for the Connection

There is only one provider to use with the OLE DB .NET Data Provider for accessing Active Directory, **ADsDSOObject**, which you can see in Line 7 in Listing 7-8.

Basically, you can use the following code to open a connection to Active Directory:

```
OleDbConnection cnnAD = new OleDbConnection("Provider=ADsDSOObject");
cnnAD.Open();
```

Obviously, you need to be logged onto a system that uses Active Directory with an account that has permission to read from Active Directory, but it's really that simple! If you aren't logged on or you don't have read access to Active Directory, you can always use the syntax specified in Lines 7 and 8 in Listing 7-8.

Specifying What Domain to Access with the LDAP Protocol

When you try to access Active Directory after opening an **OleDbConnection**, you need to specify the protocol and the domain name of the Active Directory to access. This is done where you would normally specify the table name in a SELECT statement, like this:

```
FROM 'LDAP://userman.dk'
```

As you can see, I have put the protocol name and domain name in single quotes. This is a must—if you don't do this, an exception will be thrown. Specifying the protocol is the same as it is when you use your browser: you specify either HTTP or FTP followed by a colon and two slashes (://).

See Listing 7-8 for a complete example of how to construct a SELECT statement that retrieves rows from Active Directory.

Specifying What Information to Retrieve from Active Directory

As in any other SELECT statement, you can tell the command which "columns" you want returned.

Table 7-5 shows a list of some of the information you can retrieve from Active Directory. Please note that this list is not exhaustive, but merely a starting point for how to get user information. The User Properties Dialog Box Equivalent column refers to the information you can find using the Active Directory Users and Computers MMC snap-in. You then double-click the user you want to see information for and the user dialog box pops up. Figures 7-1 and 7-2 show you the General and Account tabs of the user properties dialog box in the Active Directory Users and Computers MMC snap-in.

Table 7-5. User Information "Columns"

NAME	DESCRIPTION	USER PROPERTIES DIALOG BOX EQUIVALENT
adsPath	This is the full path to the object, including the protocol header.	None.
mail	This is the user's e-mail account. Please note that this has nothing to do with any e-mail accounts created in Exchange Server.	General tab, E-mail text box. See Figure 7-1.
objectSid	This represents the user's security identifier (SID). Please note that this is returned as an array of bytes. You need to convert the SID if you want to display it in a human readable format (S-1-5-21- . . .). You can learn more about SIDs at this address: `http://msdn.microsoft.com/library/default.asp?url=/library/en-us/security/accctrl_5lyq.asp`.	None.
samAccountName	This is the name used by the Security Account Manager (SAM).	Account tab, User logon name (pre–Windows 2000) text box. See Figure 7-2.
userPrincipalName	The user principal name (UPN) is an Internet-style login name for a user. The UPN is based on the Internet standard RFC 822, and is most often the same as **mail**.	Account tab, User logon name text box and drop-down list. This is most often the same as the user's e-mail address as it comes from the concept of one logon name to access all services.

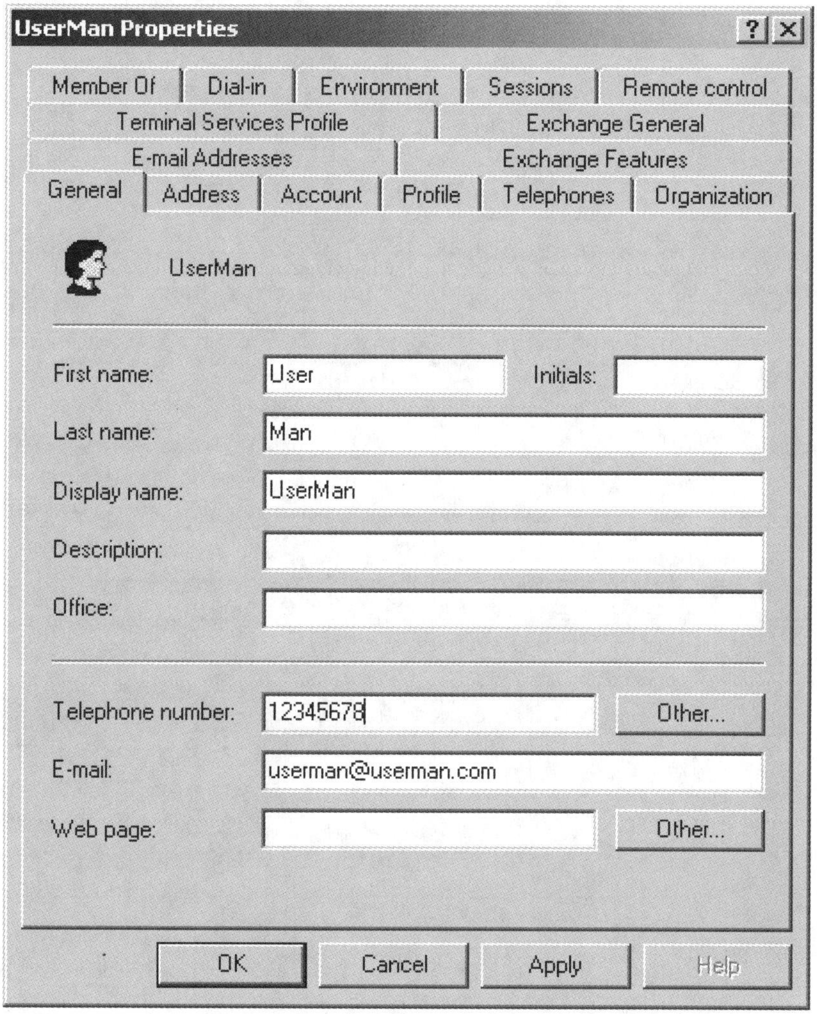

Figure 7-1. General tab of the user properties dialog box

Figure 7-1 shows you the General tab of the user properties dialog box in the Active Directory Users and Computers MMC snap-in.

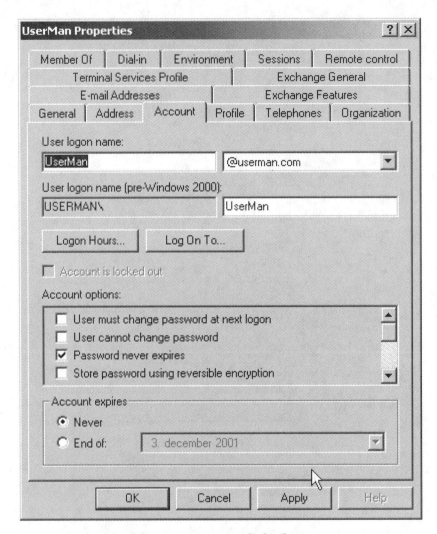

Figure 7-2. Account tab of the user properties dialog box

Figure 7-2 shows you the Account tab of the user properties dialog box in the Active Directory Users and Computers MMC snap-in.

Please note that you cannot specify the asterisks (*) to retrieve all "columns" as you would in a standard SQL statement. If you do, the query will only return **adsPath**. Refer to the SQL Dialect at this address:

```
http://msdn.microsoft.com/library/default.asp?url=/library/
en-us/netdir/adsi/sql_dialect.asp.
```

If you want more information about the Active Directory schema, its objects, the objects' attributes, and so on, visit this address:

```
http://msdn.microsoft.com/library/default.asp?url=/library/
en-us/netdir/ad/about_the_active_directory_schema.asp.
```

Updating an Active Directory Object

The current OLE DB provider for ADSI, the one that comes with MDAC 2.6 and 2.7, is read-only, meaning you cannot issue an UPDATE statement. Microsoft says this will change, but I haven't found any information detailing if this is to change with ADSI in Windows .NET or if ADSI with Windows 2000 is also part of these plans. Stay alert, my friend!

Retrieving the SID for a User

You've probably noticed that the tblUser table in the UserMan database holds two columns that are named ADName and ADSID. They are there to hold the SID (objectSid) and the SAM account name (samAccountName) for the user (see Table 7-5 for a description of objectSid and samAccountName). Take a look at Listing 7-9 to see how to retrieve these two values for the UserMan user. You obviously need to have added the UserMan user to Active Directory on your network for this to work.

Listing 7-9. Retrieving the SAM Account Name and SID from Active Directory

```
 1 public void GetSIDAndSAMAccountNameFromAD() {
 2     OleDbConnection cnnAD;
 3     OleDbCommand cmmAD;
 4     OleDbDataReader drdAD;
 5     string strSAMAccountName;
 6     string strSID;
 7
 8     // Instantiate and open connection
 9     cnnAD = new OleDbConnection("Provider=ADsDSOObject;User Id=UserMan;" +
10         "Password=userman");
11     cnnAD.Open();
12     // Instantiate command
13     cmmAD = new OleDbCommand("SELECT objectSid, samAccountName FROM " +
14         "'LDAP://userman.dk' WHERE objectCategory='person' AND " +
15         "objectClass='user' AND cn='UserMan'", cnnAD);
16
17     // Retrieve rows in data reader
18     drdAD = cmmAD.ExecuteReader();
19     // Go to first row
20     drdAD.Read();
21     // Get SAM Account name
22     strSAMAccountName = drdAD["samAccountName"].ToString();
23     // Get SID
24     strSID = drdAD["objectSid"].ToString();
25 }
```

In Listing 7-9, the SID and SAM account name are retrieved from Active Directory using the OLE DB provider for Microsoft Directory Services. Once returned, I save the values in local variables. In Chapter 11, I will expand on this example and show you how to save the values to your UserMan database.

Accessing Microsoft Exchange Server

Microsoft Exchange Server 2000 is classified as a hierarchical database. One very simple reason for this is its treelike folder structure. Exchange Server 2000 uses Active Directory for storing setup and other non–mail-related information. This means that you can access Exchange Server information using the techniques described earlier in this chapter, but this is *not* recommended. Microsoft warns about doing it this way, and it's understandable, because you can damage not only your Exchange Server setup, but also accidentally your Active Directory setup. Trust me, I know. The Microsoft Exchange Server coverage here is by no means exhaustive, but it should serve as an overview with example code and references to more information. One book I can recommend is this one:

- *Programming Microsoft Outlook and Microsoft Exchange*, by Thomas Rizzo. Published by Microsoft Press, June 2000. ISBN: 0735610193.

Anyway, there are other means of accessing your Exchange Server data besides using Active Directory, such as the following:

- Microsoft OLE DB Exchange Server Provider (ExOLEDB)

- Microsoft OLE DB Provider for Internet Publishing (MSDAIPP)

- Accessing Exchange Server as a linked server from SQL Server

You can find descriptions of and example code for using these protocols in the sections that follow. Please note that this is by no means a thorough walk-through of these access methods, but merely a teaser on how to do them. If you're used to using the Microsoft Collaboration Data Objects (CDO) for formatting and sending messages, I can only recommend that you look into using the classes in the **System.Web.Mail** namespace instead. The classes in this namespace use the CDO for Windows 2000 (CDOSYS) messaging component. Listing 7-10 shows you a very simple example of sending a message.

Listing 7-10. Sending a Mail Message Using SMTP

```
 1 public void SendMessageUsingCDOSYS() {
 2     MailMessage msgMail = new MailMessage();
 3
 4     // Prepare message
 5     msgMail.From = "UserMan <userman@userman.dk>";
 6     msgMail.To = "Carsten Thomsen <carstent@userman.dk>";
 7     msgMail.Body = "This is the e-mail body";
 8     msgMail.Subject = "This is the e-mail subject";
 9
10     // Set the SMTP server (you can use an IP address,
11     // NETBIOS name or a FQDN)
12     SmtpMail.SmtpServer = "10.8.1.19";
13     SmtpMail.SmtpServer = "EXCHANGESERVER";
14     SmtpMail.SmtpServer = "exchangeserver.userman.dk";
15
16     // Send the prepared message using the
17     // specified SMTP server
18     SmtpMail.Send(msgMail);
19 }
```

In Listing 7-10, you can see how an instance of the **MailMessage** class (msgMail) is created (Line 2) and prepared by setting the **From**, **To**, **Body**, and **Subject** properties (Lines 5 through 8). On Lines 12 through 14, I use different ways of specifying which SMTP server to use for sending the message. As you can see, I have provided you with three different ways of specifying the SMTP server, but you can also choose not to set the **SmtpServer** property, in which case the **SmtpMail** class assumes that you want to use the local SMTP server.

The example code shown will only work on Windows 2000, Windows XP, or a Windows .NET Server, but you don't need to have an Exchange Server. The mentioned platforms all have a built-in SMTP service that you can use for sending messages. You need to make sure this service is running and correctly set up. You can set up the service from your IIS. Please see the documentation for more information.

Line 18 sends the prepared message using the **Send** method. Please note that the **SmtpMail** class is static; therefore, you can use it without creating an instance of it.

Using the Microsoft OLE DB Exchange Server Provider

The Microsoft OLE DB Exchange Server Provider (ExOLEDB) is intended for use only on the machine that hosts the Microsoft Exchange Server 2000. This means that it is a server-side–only provider, and you can only use it for accessing a local Exchange Server. If you need to access Exchange Server 2000 from a client, look into using the OLE DB Provider for Internet Publishing. See the "Using the Microsoft OLE DB Provider for Internet Publishing" section later in this chapter.

The ExOLEDB provider ships with Exchange Server 2000 and *not* any of the MDACs available for download. (See the "Data Providers" section in Chapter 3A for more information on MDAC.) I guess this makes sense because it can only be run from the local Exchange Server anyway. However, the real problem with the ExOLEDB provider is that it is OLE DB 2.5 compliant, which means that you can't use it with the OLE DB .NET Data Provider that requires a later version. At the time of this writing, Exchange Server Service Pack (SP) 2 is out, but it only features a version 2.5–compliant OLE DB provider. Rumor has it that Microsoft will ship either an add-on or an SP that will let you access your Exchange Server using truly managed code. This add-on or SP is supposed to ship in the first quarter of 2002. If that doesn't happen, I'm sure you'll find plenty of support for the .NET Framework in the next version of Exchange Server.

Now, I won't leave you empty-handed with regard to the OLE DB Exchange Server Provider, because you can always use good old ADO through COM Interop. See the "COM Interop" section in Chapter 3B for more information. Listing 7-11 is a very simple example that shows you how to retrieve all the contacts for the UserMan user.

Listing 7-11. Retrieving Contacts for the UserMan User from Exchange Server 2000

```
1 public void RetrieveContactsUsingExOLEDB() {
2    ADODB.Connection cnnExchange = new ADODB.Connection();
3    ADODB.RecordsetClass rstExchange = new ADODB.RecordsetClass();
4    string strFile = "file://./backofficestorage/userman.dk/mbx/userman";
5
6    cnnExchange.Provider = "ExOLEDB.DataSource";
7
8    try {
9        // Open the connection, keeping in mind that
10       // the ExOLEDB provider doesn't authenticate
11       // the passed user id and password arguments
12       cnnExchange.Open(strFile, null, null, -1);
13       // Open the recordset
```

```
14      rstExchange.Open("SELECT \"DAV:displayname\" AS Name " +
15          "FROM SCOPE('shallow traversal of \"Contacts\"')", cnnExchange,
16          CursorTypeEnum.adOpenForwardOnly, LockTypeEnum.adLockReadOnly, 0);
17      // Loop through all the returned rows (contacts)
18      while (! rstExchange.EOF) {
19          // Display Contact name
20          MessageBox.Show(rstExchange.Fields["Name"].Value.ToString());
21          // Move to the next row
22          rstExchange.MoveNext();
23      }
24  }
25  catch (Exception objE) {
26      MessageBox.Show(objE.Message);
27  }
28 }
```

Listing 7-11 shows you how to open a connection to an Exchange Server 2000 using the OLE DB Exchange Server Provider and COM-based ADO for retrieving all contacts for the UserMan user.

Using the Microsoft OLE DB Provider for Internet Publishing

The Microsoft OLE DB Provider for Internet Publishing (MSDAIPP) is a client-side–only provider, which means that you cannot use it for accessing Exchange Server 2000 from the machine that hosts your local Exchange Server 2000. If you need to access Exchange Server 2000 from the machine that hosts Exchange Server 2000, look into using the OLE DB Exchange Server Provider. See the "Using the Microsoft OLE DB Exchange Server Provider" section earlier in this chapter.

The MSDAIPP provider is, as the full name suggests, used for accessing documents located in Internet Information Server (IIS) virtual directories, but it can also be used for accessing data in an Exchange Server 2000 Web store remotely. MSDAIPP uses the WebDAV protocol.

One final point to note about this provider is that it uses the Hypertext Transfer Protocol (HTTP) for the transport, which means that the Data Source value in the connection string must be specified using a URL. In Listing 7-12, you can see how the MSDAIPP provider can be used to retrieve all items in a particular folder.

Listing 7-12. Retrieving the Content of an Exchange Server 2000 Folder

```
1 public void MSDAIPPShowFolderProperties() {
2     OleDbConnection cnnExchange = new OleDbConnection();
3     OleDbCommand cmmExchange = new OleDbCommand();
4     OleDbDataReader drdExchange;
5     string strFolder;
6
7     // Set up connection string to bind to the userman folder
8     cnnExchange.ConnectionString = "Provider=MSDAIPP.dso;Data Source=" +
9         "http://exchangeserver/exchange/userman;User ID='Administrator'; +
10        "Password=adminpwd;";
11
12    // Open the connection
13    cnnExchange.Open();
14    // Initialize the command
15    cmmExchange.Connection = cnnExchange;
16    cmmExchange.CommandType = CommandType.TableDirect;
17    // Return all rows
18    drdExchange = cmmExchange.ExecuteReader();
19
20    // Loop through all the returned rows (folders)
21    while (drdExchange.Read()) {
22        // Initialize folder string
23        strFolder = "";
24        // Loop through all the columns (properties)
25        for (int intColumn = 0; intColumn < drdExchange.FieldCount -1;
26            intColumn++) {
27            // Read folder property name and value
28            strFolder += drdExchange.GetName(intColumn).ToString()  + "=" +
29                drdExchange[intColumn].ToString() + "\n";
30            }
31        // Display folder properties
32        MessageBox.Show(strFolder);
33    }
34 }
```

In Listing 7-12, you can see how the property names and values for all items in a particular folder are returned in a data reader object. Please note that all items are returned, including hidden ones. Run the code to see the various properties that are returned. Here's a quick rundown of the code:

- Lines 8 through 10 set up the connection string for the **OleDbConnection** object, with the MSDAIPP specified as `Provider=MSDAIPP.dso`. The name of the data source, which in this case is an Exchange Server, is specified using `Data Source=http://exchangeserver`. You obviously need to change this to the name or IP address of your Exchange Server, and don't forget to add the port number (for example, `http://exchangeserver:86`) if the Web server on the machine that hosts your Exchange Server accepts HTTP requests on a different port, such as 86. After the server name you must specify `/exchange`, because this is the name of the Exchange Server's virtual directory, and then you need to specify the mailbox you want to access (`/userman`). This needs to be changed so it matches a mailbox on your system. Finally, you need to supply the user ID and password of a user on your system that has access rights to the specified mailbox. Change the User ID and Password values accordingly.

- Line 13 opens the connection.

- Line 15 sets the **Connection** property of the **OleDbCommand** object equal to the open connection.

- Line 16 sets the **CommandType** property to the **TableDirect** member of the **CommandType** enum. This way, all rows from the folder specified will be returned.

- Line 18 returns all rows in the specified folder in an **OleDbDataReader** object.

- Lines 21 through 33 loop through all elements in the specified folder and display all properties for each element.

In the example code in Listing 7-12, all elements, meaning all folders, are retrieved from the userman folder/mailbox. You can just as easily add `/Inbox` to the Data Source value in the connection string specified in Line 9 to retrieve all items/messages in the Inbox folder. If you add `/Contacts` to the Data Source value, you retrieve all contacts for the specified mailbox. Basically, you can specify any existing folder from the specified mailbox folder.

Accessing Exchange Server As a Linked Server from SQL Server

If your Exchange Server 2000 is located on the same machine as your SQL Server, you can use SQL Server for linking to your Exchange Server and this way create views on the Exchange Server Web store that can be queried like any regular table in your database.

> **NOTE** *Because the OLE DB Exchange Server Provider (ExOLEDB) is only intended for use on the machine that hosts the Microsoft Exchange Server 2000, your SQL Server also needs to be located on the Exchange Server machine.*

The first thing you need to do is set up the Exchange Server as a linked server from your SQL Server. Then you can create views that access the linked server. See the following sections for more information.

Setting Up Exchange Server As a Linked Server

You can set up a linked server by executing the **sp_addlinkedserver** system stored procedure. Basically, this system stored procedure is used for setting up linked servers so you can create distributed queries, meaning queries that you can run on databases on more than one server at a time. You just need a linked Exchange Server, and you can link to it by executing the T-SQL statement in Listing 7-13.

Listing 7-13. Adding a Linked Exchange Server with T-SQL

```
1 EXEC sp_addlinkedserver 'ExchangeServer',
2 '@srvproduct = 'Microsoft Exchange OLE DB Provider',
3 '@provider = ''ExOLEDB.DataSource'',
4  @datasrc = ''file://./backofficestorage/userman.dk/mbx/UserMan'
5 @provstr = 'User Id=userman@userman.dk;Password=userman;'
```

The T-SQL example code, shown in Listing 7-13, will add ExchangeServer as a linked server to your SQL Server (Line 1). You can give it any name you want as long as it doesn't conflict with a different linked server, or even the name of your SQL Server.

On Line 3, I specify that I want to use the ExOLEDB provider, and on Line 4, I specify the data source, meaning the full path to the mailbox I want to access, which is UserMan in this case. Visit `http://msdn.microsoft.com/library/default.asp?url=/library/en-us/wss/wss/_exch2k_the_file_url_scheme.asp` to see how to construct your Exchange Server file paths.

Line 5 of Listing 7-13 is the OLE DB Provider string, and this one is important if you don't want to get a 7304 error message when you try to access the linked

server. You pass the user ID in the format *mailbox@domainname* and the password for the mailbox or Windows login.

NOTE *The Exchange Server mailbox you're accessing not only must be created from the Active Directory Users and Computers MMC snap-in, but you also need to log onto the mailbox at least once for the mailbox to be*

physically created on your system. You can use Microsoft Outlook to log onto the mailbox.

You can find more information about the system stored procedure **sp_addlinkedserver** in SQL Server Books Online, which comes with your SQL Server. Instead of executing the T-SQL statement shown earlier, you can create a linked server from Enterprise Manager. Here's how you create the same linked server you did with the T-SQL script earlier, but this time using the Enterprise Manager:

1.   Open Enterprise Manager.

2.   Expand the Security node below your database server.

3.   Right-click the Linked Servers node and select New Linked Server from the pop-up menu.

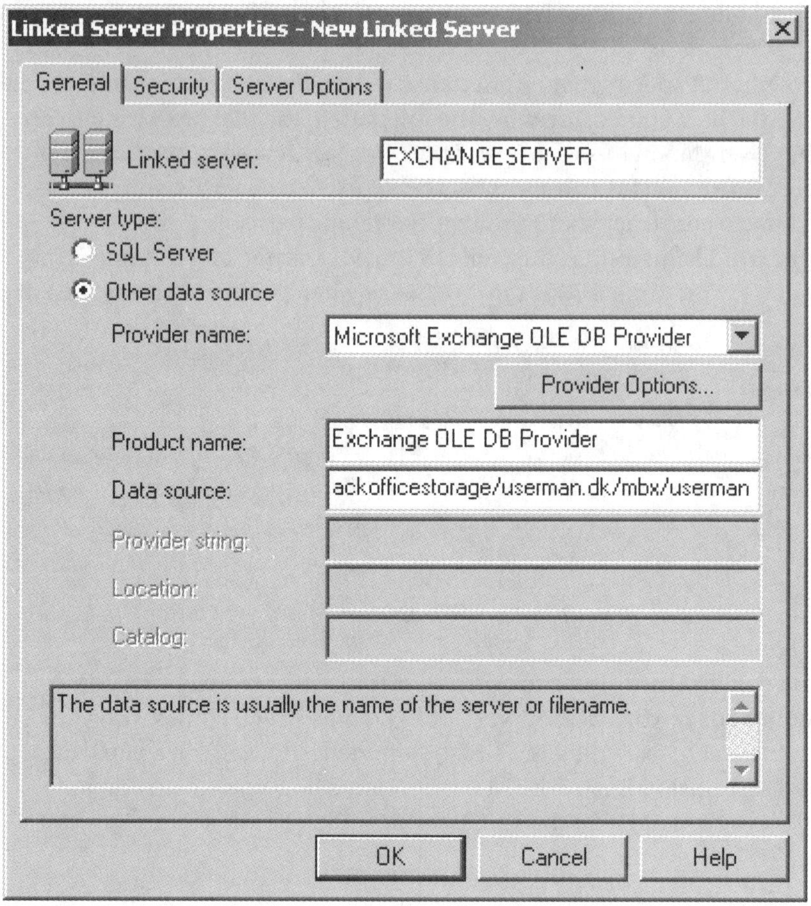

Figure 7-3. Linked Server Properties dialog box

This brings up the Linked Server Properties dialog box shown in Figure 7-3.
Figure 7-3 shows the General tab of the Linked Server Properties dialog box with the Provider name, Product name, and Data source options already filled in. However, as you can see in Figure 7-3, you can't fill in the provider string as you did with the T-SQL statement. Don't worry, there's a way around this. You can

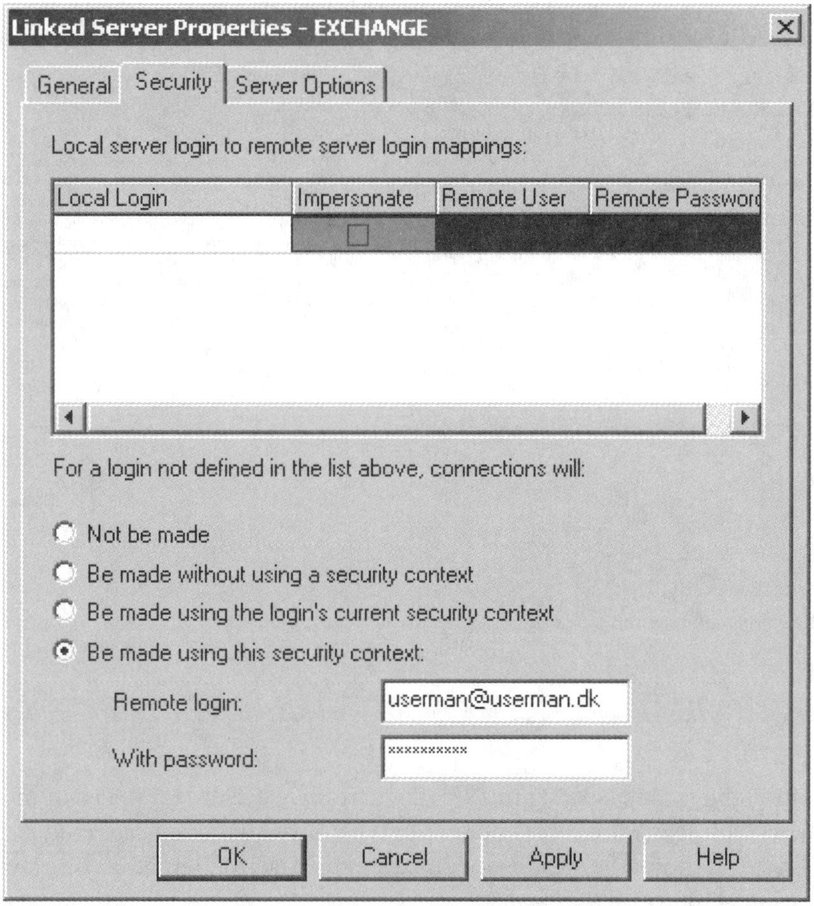

Figure 7-4. Security tab of the Linked Server Properties dialog box

select the Security tab, which is shown in Figure 7-4, and give the same user credentials as you did with the T-SQL statement in Listing 7-13.

Figure 7-4 shows the Security tab of the Linked Server Properties dialog box with the "Be made using this security context" option selected and the Remote login and With password text boxes filled in with the correct user credentials.

Once you click the OK button after having supplied the correct information, you can see the folders in the mailbox you connect to, in the details pane, if you

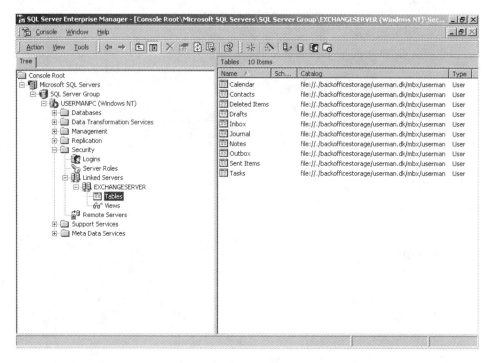

Figure 7-5. Exchange Server mailbox folders shown as tables in Entrprise Manager

select the Tables node (see Figure 7-5). If you receive a 7304 or 7309 error message when you select the Tables node, you have entered invalid user credentials.

Figure 7-5 shows the various mailboxes in the UserMan mailbox displayed as tables in the Enterprise Manager.

Dropping a Linked Exchange Server

You can drop the linked server by executing this T-SQL statement:

```
EXEC sp_dropserver 'ExchangeServer'
```

You can find more information about the **sp_dropserver** system stored procedure in SQL Server Books Online.

You can also drop a linked server from the Enterprise Manager by selecting it under the Linked Server's node and selecting Delete from the pop-up menu. You're required to confirm this irreversable action.

Creating Views on the Linked Exchange Server

Once you've set up your Exchange Server as a linked server from your SQL Server, you can create views on the folders in the catalog you've connected to. If you create a view, or a stored procedure for that matter, you take the pain out of querying the information stored in your Exchange Server. When I say "pain," I mean that for someone who's used to dealing with standard ANSI SQL-92 queries, it can be quite a task to create and set up queries that extract information from Exchange Server. Basically, you can set up a number of queries that will provide your users with all the information they need from the Exchange Server, and this way they'll never have to worry about how an Exchange Server query is constructed. Listing 7-14 shows you a view that extracts information from the Contacts folder in the UserMan mailbox on the Exchange Server.

Listing 7-14. SQL Server View Extracting Information from the Exchange Server 2000 Mailbox

```
1 CREATE VIEW viwUserManContacts AS
2 SELECT CONVERT(nvarchar(30), "urn:schemas:contacts:givenname") AS FirstName,
3        CONVERT(nvarchar(30), "urn:schemas:contacts:sn") AS LastName,
4        CONVERT(nvarchar(50), "urn:schemas:contacts:email1") AS Email
5 FROM OpenQuery(EXCHANGE, 'SELECT
6        "urn:schemas:contacts:givenname",
7        "urn:schemas:contacts:sn",
8        "urn:schemas:contacts:email1"
9   FROM SCOPE(''shallow traversal of "./Contacts"'')')
```

In Listing 7-14, you can see how the view extracts information (first name, last name, and e-mail address) from the Contacts folder. Listing 7-14 doesn't show you that it's from the UserMan mailbox, but that was specified in the "Setting Up Exchange Server As a Linked Server" section earlier in this chapter.

See Chapter 4 for more information on how to create views on SQL Server. If you want to know more about the way you specify the columns to retrieve in your views, please consult the Microsoft Exchange Server documentation.

Now that you've created a view, you can access the information from the view using any standard SQL query, such as SELECT * FROM viwUserManContacts, which will return all the rows/contacts from the UserMan mailbox on the linked Exchange Server. The columns returned are FirstName, LastName, and Email.

Summary

This chapter contains a very brief technology background on LDAP and Active Directory and how they are used in conjunction. I discussed the **System.DirectoryServices** namespace and the classes it encompasses, specifically showing you the **DirectoryEntry** class and its properties and methods.

I also explained how to establish a connection programmatically using the classes in the **System.DirectoryServices** namespace and using the OLE DB .NET Data Provider.

Finally, I described how to access the mailbox folder contents on a Microsoft Exchange Server 2000 using various protocols. I showed you how to add Exchange Server as a linked server to an SQL Server, creating views on the mailbox content and thus making it possible to execute standard SQL queries on the linked server.

I can conclude by saying that although Active Directory is a unique way of storing some of your data, it will not replace your relational database. Active Directory is for storing data objects long term and only objects that are changed infrequently.

The next chapter is about message queues and how you can use them for connectionless programming.

CHAPTER 8

Message Queues

Using Message Queues for Connectionless Programming

MESSAGE QUEUES ARE GREAT whenever you don't have a permanent connection or are working in loosely coupled situations. They're also handy when you simply want to dump your input and return to your application without waiting for the output from whatever application or server will be processing your input. You can make message queues the basis of a fail-safe application that uses them whenever your regular database fails. This can help ensure that no data is lost and you have very little or no downtime at all, if you use transactional queues. Obviously not all applications can use message queues to such advantage, but for storing or accepting customer input it can be a great solution. One example springs to mind that wouldn't benefit from using message queues, and that is a banking transaction that needs to be processed in real time.

Microsoft's messaging technology is called *Message Queuing*. Mind you, in line with other traditional Microsoft marketing stunts, this technology has had other names before Windows 2000 was shipped. However, the release that ships with Windows 2000 is built on a previous version of the technology and includes the Active Directory (AD) integration. AD integration is good because it's now easier to locate public message queues across your domain and it ensures easy Enterprise-wide backup.

Is MSMQ Dead?

Microsoft Message Queue Server (MSMQ) is the name Microsoft gave version 1.0 of its message queuing technology. It was originally included with the Enterprise Edition of Windows NT 4. With version 2.0 it became an add-on to any server version of Windows NT 4, and it was part of the Windows NT Option Pack. The Windows NT Option Pack could be freely downloaded from the Microsoft Web site. Since then the message queuing technology has been integrated into the OS, as is the case with Windows 2000 and Windows XP, and the upcoming Windows .NET. Not only has MSMQ been integrated into the OS, it has changed its name to Message Queuing and been extended in numerous ways. One extension is the integration with Active Directory instead of being SQL Server based.

So to the question, "Is MSMQ Dead?" the answer is yes and no. Yes, because it's no longer a stand-alone product, and no because the features of the original MSMQ have been incorporated into the OS as a service called Message Queuing.

Connectionless Programming

Connectionless programming involves using a queue to hold your input to another application or server. Connectionless in this context means you don't have a permanent connection to the application or server. Instead, you log your input in a queue and the other application or server then takes it from the queue, processes it, and sometimes puts it back in the same or a different queue.

The opposite of connectionless is *connection oriented,* and basically any standard database system these days falls into this category. You've probably heard these two terms in relation to TCP/IP (Transmission Control Protocol/Internet Protocol). The UDP (User Datagram Protocol) part of the protocol is connectionless, and the TCP part is connection oriented. However, a major difference exists between message queuing and the UDP protocol. Whereas the UDP protocol does not guarantee delivery, and a packet sent over the network using the UDP transport protocol can be lost, the message queue doesn't lose any packets. The reason why a message queue is said to be connectionless is that your client doesn't "speak" directly with your server. There is no direct connection, as there is with a standard database.

Now that you have an understanding of connectionless programming in this context, let's move on to an overview of the **MessageQueue** class.

Taking a Quick Look at the MessageQueue Class

The **MessageQueue** class is part of the **System.Messaging** namespace. That namespace also holds the **Message** class, which is used in conjunction with the **MessageQueue** class. The **System.Messaging** namespace holds a number of classes that are exclusively used for accessing and manipulating message queues.

The **MessageQueue** class is a wrapper around **Message Queuing**, which is an optional component of Windows 2000 and Windows NT. With Windows NT it's part of the Option Pack. At any rate, you need to make sure you've installed Message Queuing on a server on your network before you can try the examples in this chapter.

When to Use a Message Queue

Use a message queue in your application if you need to perform any of these tasks:

- *Storing less-important information in a message queue while your DBMS is busy serving customers during the day:* The information in the message queue is then batch-processed when the DBMS is less busy. This is ideal for processing all real-time requests and storing all other requests in a message queue for later processing.

- *Queuing data for later processing, because of the nature of the data at the time of entry:* Some data can't be processed by your system at the time of data entry, because other data necessary for processing the entered data simply doesn't exist at this time and would thus mean that the processing would fail. However, later on, like at the end of the day, the data required to do the processing is available and you can process the entered data. One example of this is when you request an interaccount transfer, and the funds aren't available when the request is made, but they will be at the end of the day.

- *Connecting to a DBMS over a WAN, such as the Internet, and the connection isn't always available for whatever reason:* You can do two things when you design your application. You can set up your application to access the DBMS the usual way, and if you get a time-out or another connection failure, you store the request in a message queue. You then start a component that checks for when the DBMS is available, and when it is, it will forward the requests that are stored in the message queue and return a possible result to your application. At this point your application can resume normal operation and shut down the message queue component. The other possibility is to design your application as an offline one, meaning that all DBMS requests are stored in a local message queue and forwarded by your message queue component to the DBMS.

- *Exchanging data with a mainframe system, like SAP:* You can use a message queue to hold SAP IDocs. These are then sent to and received from the SAP system by the queue manager/component. Anyone who ever worked with SAP will know that real-time communication with SAP is often a problem, because the server is frequently overloaded at specific intervals during the day. So basically you use the message queue for storing and forwarding requests to and from the SAP system. Recall that SAP is originally a mainframe system, but these days SAP is often found running on midsize computers or PCs, and the five most popular platforms for R/3 are Windows NT, Sun Solaris, HP-UX, AS/400, and AIX.

I am sure you can come up with a few applications yourself that would bene-fit from message queuing based on your current or previous work experience.

Why Use a Message Queue and Not a Database Table?

A message queue can be of good use in many situations, but what makes it different from using a database table? When you call a DBMS, it's normally done synchronously, but with a message queue it's done asynchronously. This means it's generally faster to access a message queue than to access a database table. With synchronous access the client application has to wait for the server to respond, whereas with asynchronous access a query or the like is sent to the server, and the client application then continues its normal duties. When the server has finished processing the query, it'll notify you and pass you the result.

When you use a database table, you must comply with a fairly strict format for adding data. There are certain fields that must be supplied, and you don't really have the ability to add extra information. Although the same can be said about message queues, when it comes to supplying certain fields, it's much easier to supply extra information that you have a hard time storing in a database table. Even if the data stored in the message queue eventually hits a database table, which it does in most cases, you have an application that takes care of processing the data, and then storing the data in a database. However, when you do the processing, you can have your processing logic validate whatever extra information you have in the messages held in the message queue and store the data in the messages based on the extra information. This can be the time of entry or other constraints that dictate which table the data is stored in.

This approach is valid for Windows Forms and Web Forms, though it depends on the *application type*. Distributed applications, client-server applications on a local network, and stand-alone applications constitute some of the different application types. If your application isn't distributed and you're accessing a standard DBMS on a local server or on your client, there's probably no reason for using a message queue. However, one such reason might just be that your DBMS is busy during the day, and hence you store your requests and messages in a message queue for batch processing when the DBMS is less busy.

In short, application infrastructure and business requirements in general determine whether you should use message queuing. Having said this, I realize that sometimes it's a good idea to work with a tool for a while so that you can get to know the situations in which you should use it. So if you're new to message queuing, make sure you try the example code that follows later on in this chapter.

A message queue works using the *First In, First Out* (FIFO) principle, which means that the first message in the queue is the message you'll retrieve if you use the **Receive** or **Peek** method of the **MessageQueue** class. See the "Retrieving a Message" and "Peeking at Messages" sections later in this chapter for more information on these methods.

Now, FIFO is the principle applied to how the messages are placed in the queue, but the priority takes precedence over the arrival time, so it's possible to place a message at the top of the message queue even if other messages are already in the queue. If I were to make up a SELECT statement that describes how the messages are inserted into a queue and returned to you, it would look something like this:

```
SELECT * FROM MessageQueue ORDER BY Priority, ArrivalTime
```

Obviously this statement is just an example, but it does show you how the messages are ordered, first by priority and then by arrival time. Priority isn't normally something you would set, so most messages would have the same priority, but there may be times when it's necessary to "jump" the queue. See "Prioritizing Messages" later in this chapter for more information on how to prioritize your messages.

How to Use a Message Queue

Of course, you need to set up the message queue before you can use it in your application. Even if you already have a queue to connect to, it's a good idea to know how to set one up, so first I'll show you how. Please note that you can't view or manage public queues if you're in a workgroup environment. Public queues only exist in a domain environment. See your Windows NT, Windows 2000, or Windows XP documentation for installing Message Queuing. If you're running in workgroup mode, you can't use Server Explorer to view a queue, not even private ones. I'll get to private and public queues in the next section.

Private Queues vs. Public Queues

You need to know a distinction between the two types of queues, private and public queues, you can create before continuing. Table 8-1 compares some of the features of both types of message queues.

Table 8-1. Private vs. Public Message Queues

PRIVATE MESSAGE QUEUE	PUBLIC MESSAGE QUEUE
Not published in the Message Queue Information Service (MQIS) database	Published in the Message Queue Information Service (MQIS) database
Can only be created on the local machine	Must be registered with the Directory Service
Can be created and deleted offline, meaning not connected to Active Directory	Must be created and deleted while you're online, meaning connected to Active Directory
Can't be located by other message queuing applications, unless they are provided the full path of the message queue	Can be located by other message queuing applications through the Message Queue Information Service (MQIS) database
Is persistent, but backup, although possible, isn't an easy task	Is persistent and can be backed up on an Enterprise level with the Active Directory

Creating the Queue Programmatically

Chapter 4 covers how to create a message queue from the Server Explorer, but if you want to do it programmatically, please read on.

It's easy to create a message queue programmatically. Listings 8-1 and 8-2 show you two different ways of creating a private queue on the local machine, USERMANPC.

Listing 8-1. Creating a Private Message Queue Using the Machine Name

```
1 public void CreatePrivateQueueWithName() {
2     MessageQueue.Create("USERMANPC\\Private$\\UserMan");
3 }
```

Listing 8-2. Creating a Private Message Queue Using the Default Name

```
1 public void CreatePrivateQueue() {
2     MessageQueue.Create(".\\Private$\\UserMan");
3 }
```

In Listing 8-1, I specify the machine as part of the path argument, whereas I simply use a period in Listing 8-2. The period serves as a shortcut for letting the **MessageQueue** object know that you want it created on the local machine. The other thing you should notice is that I prefix the queue with Private$. This must be done to indicate that the queue is private. Exclusion of the prefix indicates you're creating a public queue. The different parts of the path are separated using the backslash, as in a standard DOS file path (well, you need two back slashes, because the backslash character is the escape character in a string):

```
MachineName\\Private$\\QueueName
```

A public queue is created more or less the same way, except you leave out the \Private$ part of the path. You can also use the period to specify that you want it created on the local machine, as shown in Listing 8-3.

Listing 8-3. Creating a Public Message Queue Using the Default Name
```
1 public void CreatePublicQueue() {
2     MessageQueue.Create(".\\UserMan");
3 }
```

As stated, the period could have been substituted with the name of the local machine or indeed the name of a different machine on which you want to create the queue.

> **NOTE** *If you try to create an already existing message queue, a **MessageQueueException** exception is thrown.*

There are two overloaded versions of the **MessageQueue** class's **Create** method, and you've seen the simpler one. The other one takes a second argument, a **bool** value indicating whether the message queue is transactional. I'll go into message queue transactions in the "Making Message Queues Transactional" section later on in this chapter, but for now take a look at Listing 8-4, which shows you how to make the queue transactional.

Listing 8-4. Creating a Transactional Private Message Queue

```
1 public void CreateTransactionalPrivateQueue() {
2    MessageQueue.Create(".\\Private$\\UserMan", true);
3 }
```

In Listing 8-4, a private message queue named UserMan is created on the local machine with transaction support. If you run the example code in Listing 8-4, you may want to remove it afterwards, as it might otherwise have an impact on the rest of the examples in this chapter.

Displaying or Changing the Properties of Your Message Queue

Some of the properties of your message queue can be changed after you've created it. You can do this by using the Computer Management MMC snap-in[1] that's part of the Administrative Tools under Windows 2000 and Windows XP. When you've opened the Computer Management snap-in, do the following:

1. Expand the Services and Applications node.

2. Expand the Message Queuing node.

3. Expand the node with the requested queue and select the queue.

4. Right-click the queue and select Properties from the pop-up menu. This brings up the queue Properties dialog box (see Figure 8-1).

---

1. It's also possible to right-click the queue in Server Explorer and select Properties from the pop-up menu, to see the properties in the Properties window of the VS .NET IDE. However, this window doesn't show as many of the properties as in the Computer Management MMC snap-in.

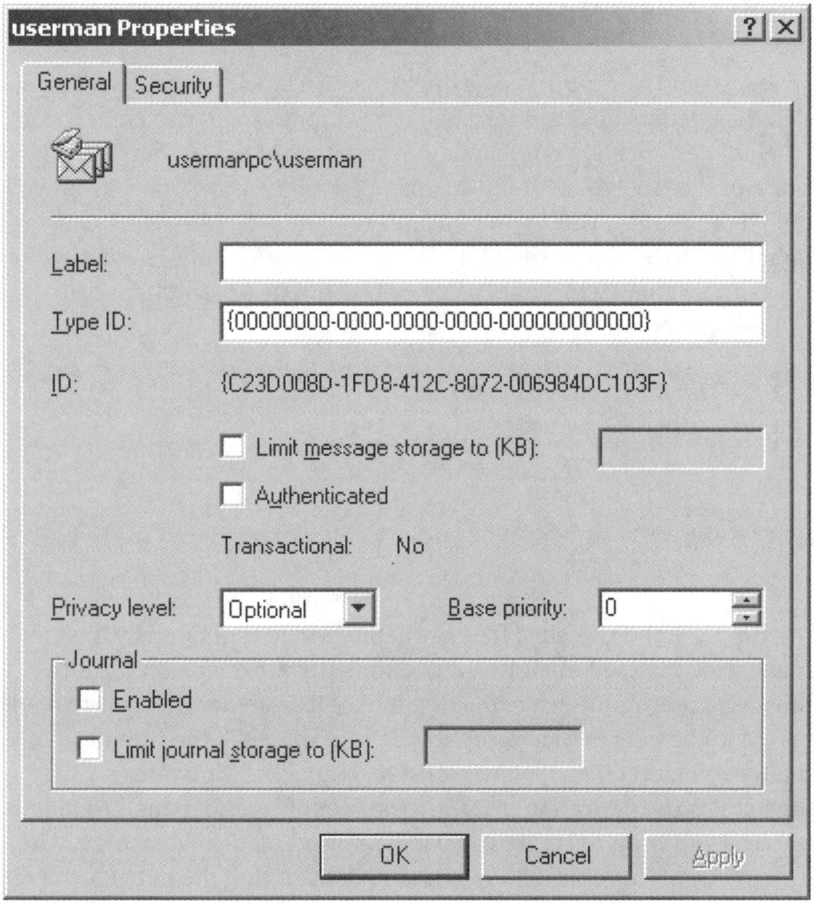

Figure 8-1. The Properties dialog box for the message queue

As you can see from Figure 8-1, one of the options that can't be changed after the queue has been created is whether the queue is transactional or not. This makes it all the more important for you to know if you'll need transaction support before you create the queue.

> **NOTE** *One advantage the Computer Management MMC snap-in has over the Server Explorer when it comes to public message queues is that you can use it when you're not connected to the AD Domain Controller, because it caches the queues. This isn't possible with the Server Explorer.*

Assigning a Label to Your Message Queue

If you want to bind to your message queue using a label, you first need to assign a label to the queue. Looking back at Figure 8-1, notice you can enter the text for your label in the Label text box. One thing you have to remember is that it isn't necessary for the label to be unique across all your message queues, but you are guaranteed problems if you try to bind and send messages to a queue using the same label. So the lesson learned here is make sure your label is unique!

You can also change the label of a message queue programmatically. See Listing 8-5 for some sample code.

Listing 8-5. Changing the Label of an Existing Queue

```
1 public void ChangeQueueLabel() {
2     MessageQueue queUserMan = new MessageQueue(".\\Private$\\UserMan");
3
4     queUserMan.Label = "USERMAN1";
5 }
```

In Listing 8-5, the so-called friendly name, which is defined by the machine and queue name, is used to bind to an existing private queue on the local machine. A friendly name is a name that makes it easier for humans to read and interpret it. In the case of the example code in Listing 8-5, the friendly name tells you that the queue is created on the local machine (.), it's private (Private$), and the name of it is UserMan. You must use the friendly name to bind to the message queue if you want to change the label programmatically! Line 4 is where the actual changing of the label takes place simply by setting the **Label** property.

Retrieving the ID of a Message Queue

If you want to bind to your public message queue using its ID, you can retrieve this using the Computer Management MMC snap-in. See "Displaying or Changing the Properties of Your Message Queue" later in this chapter for more information on how to display message queue properties. If you refer back to Figure 8-1, you can see the ID just below the Type ID text box! Mind you, this ID is only available if you're connected to the AD Domain Controller. If you're not connected, you can't view the properties for a public message queue. If you try to view the ID for a private message queue, this space is simply blank.

You can also retrieve the ID of a message queue programmatically, as shown in Listing 8-6.

Listing 8-6. Retrieving the ID of an Existing Queue

```
1 public void RetrieveQueueId() {
2    MessageQueue queUserMan = new MessageQueue(".\\UserMan");
3    Guid uidMessageQueue;
4
5    uidMessageQueue = queUserMan.Id;
6 }
```

As you can see from Listing 8-6, the ID is a GUID, so you need to declare your variable to be data type **Guid** if you want to store the ID. You must be connected to the AD Domain Controller in order to retrieve the ID of a message queue, otherwise an exception is thrown. If you try to retrieve the ID of a private message queue, an "empty" GUID is returned: 00000000-0000-0000-0000-000000000000. You can display a GUID using the **ToString** method of the **Guid** class.

Binding to an Existing Message Queue

Once you've created a message queue or if you want to access an existing queue, you can bind to it, as described in the following sections.

Binding Using the Friendly Name

Listing 8-7 shows you three different ways of binding to an existing queue, using the **new** constructor, a so-called friendly name (.\Private$\UserMan), or the path of the queue and the name assigned to the queue when it was created.

Listing 8-7. Binding to an Existing Queue

```
1 public void BindToExistingQueue() {
2    MessageQueue queUserManNoArguments = new MessageQueue();
3    MessageQueue queUserManPath = new MessageQueue(".\\Private$\\UserMan");
4    MessageQueue queUserManPathAndAccess = new
5        MessageQueue(".\\Private$\\UserMan", true);
6
7    // Initialize the queue
8    queUserManNoArguments.Path = ".\\Private$\\UserMan";
9 }
```

Line 2 is the simplest way, but it requires an extra line of code because you haven't actually told the message queue object what queue to bind to. Line 8 takes care of specifying the queue using the **Path** property. On Lines 4 and 5,

I have specified the queue as well as the read-access restrictions. When the second argument is set to **true**, as is the case with the example in Listing 8-7, exclusive read access is granted to the first application that accesses the queue. This means that no other instance of the **MessageQueue** class can read from the queue, so be careful when you use this option.

Binding Using the Format Name

Since you can't create or bind to a message queue on a machine in Workgroup mode, you need to access a queue on a machine that is part of Active Directory. However, this creates a problem when the message queue server you want to access can't access the primary domain controller. Because Active Directory is used for resolving the path, you won't be able to use the syntax shown in Listing 8-7 to bind to a message queue.

Thankfully, there's a way around this. Instead of using the friendly name syntax as in the previous listings, you can use the format name or the label for this purpose. Listing 8-8 shows you how to bind to existing queues using the format name.

Listing 8-8. Binding to an Existing Queue Using the Format Name

```
1 public void BindToExistingQueueUsingFormat() {
2     MessageQueue queUserManFormatTCP = new
3         MessageQueue("FormatName:DIRECT=TCP:10.8.1.15\\Private$\\UserMan");
4     MessageQueue queUserManFormatOS = new
5         MessageQueue("FormatName:DIRECT=OS:USERMANPC\\UserMan");
6     MessageQueue queUserManFormatPublic =
7         new MessageQueue(
8         "FormatName:Public=AB6B9EF6-B167-43A4-8116-5B72D5C1F81C");
9 }
```

In Listing 8-8, I bind to the private queue named UserMan on the machine with the IP address 10.8.1.15 using the TCP protocol, as shown is on Lines 2 and 3. On Lines 4 and 5, I bind the public queue named UserMan on the machine with the name USERMANPC. There is also an option of binding using the SPX protocol. If you want to use the SPX network protocol, you must use the following syntax: `FormatName:DIRECT=SPX:NetworkNumber;HostNumber\QueueName`. The last format name shown in Listing 8-8 is on Lines 6 and 7, where I use the ID of the message queue as the queue identifier.

You can connect to both public and private queues with all format name options, so in the sample code in Listing 8-8, you could swap the public and private queue binding among the three different format names. The ID used in the example code is fictive and it will look different on your network. The ID, which is a GUID, is generated at creation time by the MQIS. See "Retrieving the ID of a Message Queue" for more information on how to get the ID of your message queue.

Binding Using the Label

One last way to bind to an existing message queue is to use the label syntax. This syntax can't be used when you're offline, only when connected to the Active Directory Domain Controller. Listing 8-9 shows you how to connect to the message queue with the UserMan label. See "Assigning a Label to Your Message Queue" earlier in this chapter for more information on how to set the label of a message queue.

Listing 8-9. Binding to an Existing Queue Using the Label

```
1 public void BindToExistingQueueUsingLabel() {
2     MessageQueue queUserManLabel = new MessageQueue("Label:Userman");
3 }
```

That rounds up how to bind to a message queue. Now it gets interesting, because next I'll show you how to send, retrieve, and otherwise deal with messages.

Sending a Message

Sending a message is obviously one of the most important aspects of a message queue. If you can't send a message, why have a message queue? Let's take a look at the simplest form of sending a message to a message queue. The **Send** method of the **MessageQueue** class is used for this purpose, as demonstrated in Listing 8-10.

Listing 8-10. Sending a Simple Message to a Message Queue

```
1 public void SendSimpleMessage() {
2     MessageQueue queUserMan = new MessageQueue(".\\Private$\\UserMan");
3
4     // Send simple message to queue
5     queUserMan.Send("Test");
6 }
```

After binding to the private UserMan queue on the local machine, I send a **string** object containing the text "Test" to the queue. Obviously this isn't exactly useful, but you can apply this example to testing whether something is actually

461

sent to the queue. As you've probably guessed, the **Send** method is overloaded, and I've used the version that only takes one argument and that is an object.

If you execute the code in Listing 8-10, you can see the resulting message using the Server Explorer or the Computer Management MMC snap-in. Expand the private UserMan message queue and select the Queue Messages node. Now the Computer Management snap-in should look like what is shown in Figure 8-2; if you're using the Server Explorer, it should resemble Figure 8-3. Please note that in Server Explorer, you need to expand the Queue Messages node to see the messages in the queue, as done in Figure 8-3.

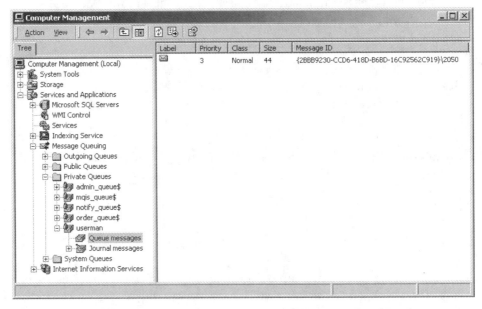

Figure 8-2. Computer Management with Queue Messages node selected

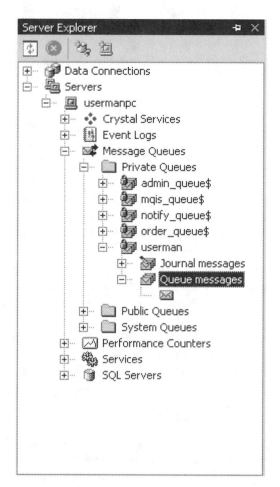

Figure 8-3. Server Explorer with Queue Messages node selected

Retrieving a Message

Obviously it's a very good idea to be able to retrieve the messages that have been posted to a message queue. Otherwise the messages simply stack up in your message queue server and do absolutely no good to anyone. There are actually a number of ways you can retrieve a message from a message queue, so let's start out with retrieving the message sent in Listing 8-10. See Listing 8-11 for the code that retrieves the first message from the message queue.

Listing 8-11. Retrieving the First Message from a Message Queue

```
1 public void RetrieveSimpleMessage() {
2     MessageQueue queUserMan = new MessageQueue(".\\Private$\\UserMan");
3     System.Messaging.Message msgUserMan;
4
5     // Retrieve first message from queue
6     msgUserMan = queUserMan.Receive();
7 }
```

In Listing 8-11, I bind to the private UserMan message queue and retrieve the first message from the queue. When the message is retrieved from the message queue, it's also removed from the queue. If you need to read a message from the queue without removing it, you should take a look at "Peeking at Messages" later in this chapter for more information.

Although the example code in Listing 8-11 will retrieve the first message from the message queue, there isn't a lot you can do with it. If you try to access any of the properties of the msgUserMan message, an exception is thrown because you haven't set up a so-called formatter that can read the message. A message can take on a variety of different forms, so it's a must that you set up a formatter before you retrieve a message from the queue. See the next section, "Setting Up a Message Formatter," for more information on how to do this.

Receive and Peek

The **Receive** and **Peek** methods of the **MessageQueue** class are synchronous, meaning that they will block all other activity in your application or thread until the method has been executed. If there are no messages in the message queue, the **Receive** and **Peek** methods will wait until a message arrives in the queue. If you need asynchronous access you must use the **BeginReceive** method instead. Actually, you can specify a time-out value when you call the **Receive** or **Peek** methods to make sure you don't wait indefinitely. Both of these overloaded methods have a version that takes a **TimeSpan** argument. This means the method will return if a message is found in the queue or when the time specified in the **TimeSpan** argument has elapsed. An exception is thrown if the time elapses.

Setting Up a Message Formatter

Recall that you need to set up a formatter in order to be able to read the messages that you retrieve from your message queue. This is a fairly easy yet important task. A message formatter is employed for serializing and deserializing objects that are used as the body of a message.

The **Formatter** property of the **MessageQueue** class is used for this very purpose. When you instantiate an instance of the **MessageQueue** class, a default formatter is created for you, but this formatter can't be used to read from the queue, only write or send to the queue. This means you have to either change the default formatter or set up a new formatter.

See Listing 8-12 for example code that can retrieve and read the message sent in Listing 8-10. Mind you, if you've already retrieved that message from the queue, the queue is now empty, and you need to send another message before you try to receive again. If the message queue is empty, the **Receive** method will await the arrival of a new message in the queue, or time out if a time-out period has been specified.

Listing 8-12. Setting Up a New Formatter and Retrieving the First Message from a Queue

```
1  public void RetrieveMessage() {
2      MessageQueue queUserMan = new MessageQueue(".\\Private$\\UserMan");
3      System.Messaging.Message msgUserMan;
4      string strBody;
5
6      // Set up the formatter
7      queUserMan.Formatter =  new
8          XmlMessageFormatter(new Type[] {Type.GetType("System.String")}) ;
9
10     // Retrieve first message from queue
11     msgUserMan = queUserMan.Receive();
12     // Save the message body
13     strBody = msgUserMan.Body.ToString();
14 }
```

In Listing 8-12, I specify that the formatter should be of type **XmlMessageFormatter**. This is the default formatter for a message queue, and it's used for serializing and deserializing the message body using XML format. I have also specified that the message formatter should accept message bodies of data type **string**. This is done on Lines 7 and 8. If I hadn't done this, I wouldn't be able to access the message body.

Generally you should use the same formatter for sending and receiving, but because this is a very simple example, the formatter isn't needed for sending to the message queue. Now, let's see in which situations the **Formatter** property is really useful. In Listing 8-13, I set up the formatter so it will be able to read to different types of message bodies: a body of data type **string** and of data type **Int32**. This is done by adding both data types to the **Type** array as the only argument to the **XmlMessageFormatter** constructor.

Listing 8-13. Sending and Retrieving Different Messages from One Message Queue

```
1  public void SendDifferentMessages() {
2      MessageQueue queUserMan = new MessageQueue(".\\Private$\\UserMan");
3      System.Messaging.Message msgUserMan = new System.Messaging.Message();
4
5      // Set up the formatter
6      queUserMan.Formatter =  new
7          XmlMessageFormatter(new Type[] {Type.GetType("System.String"),
8          Type.GetType("System.Int32")}) ;
9
10     // Create body as a text message
11     msgUserMan.Body = "Test";
12     // Send message to queue
13     queUserMan.Send(msgUserMan);
14     // Create body as an integer
15     msgUserMan.Body = 12;
16     // Send message to queue
17     queUserMan.Send(msgUserMan);
18 }
19
20 public void RetrieveDifferentMessages() {
21     MessageQueue queUserMan = new MessageQueue(".\\Private$\\UserMan");
22     System.Messaging.Message msgUserMan;
23     string strBody;
24     Int32 intBody;
25
26     // Set up the formatter
27     queUserMan.Formatter =  new
28         XmlMessageFormatter(new Type[] {Type.GetType("System.String"),
29         Type.GetType("System.Int32")}) ;
30
31     // Retrieve first message from queue
32     msgUserMan = queUserMan.Receive();
33     // Save the message body
34     strBody = msgUserMan.Body.ToString();
35     // Retrieve next message from queue
36     msgUserMan = queUserMan.Receive();
37     // Save the message body
38     intBody = (Int32) msgUserMan.Body;
39 }
```

In Listing 8-13, I use the SendDifferentMessages procedure to send to two messages to the queue: one with a body of data type **string** and one with a body of data type **Int32**. In the RetrieveDifferentMessages procedure, I retrieve these two messages in the same order they were sent to the message queue. The fact that you can send messages with a different body is what makes a message queue even more suitable than a database table for data exchange situations in which the data exchanged has very different structures.

In the example code in Listing 8-13, I have used data types **string** and **Int32** as the body formats that can be deserialized when the messages are read from the queue, but you can in fact use any base data type as well as structures and managed objects. If you need to pass older COM/ActiveX objects, you should use the **ActiveXMessageFormatter** class instead. You can also use the **BinaryMessageFormatter** class for serializing and deserializing messages using binary format, as opposed to the XML format used by the **XmlMessageFormatter** class.

Peeking at Messages

Sometimes it isn't desirable to remove a message from the queue after you've had a look at the contents, as will happen when you use the **Receive** method of the **MessageQueue** class. However, there is another way: use the **Peek** method instead. This method accomplishes exactly the same thing as the **Receive** method except for removing the message from the queue. In addition, repeated calls to the **Peek** method will return the same message, unless a new message with a higher priority is inserted into the queue. See "Prioritizing Messages" later in this chapter for more information on that topic.

Listing 8-14 is actually a nearly complete copy of Listing 8-12 except for the call to the **Peek** method on Line 11. So if you want to look at the first message in the queue, the **Peek** and **Receive** methods work exactly the same, except for the removal of the message. See "Clearing Messages from the Queue" for details about removing messages.

Listing 8-14. Peeking at a Message in the Queue

```
1 public void PeekMessage() {
2     MessageQueue queUserMan = new MessageQueue(".\\Private$\\UserMan");
3     System.Messaging.Message msgUserMan;
4     string strBody;
5
6     // Set up the formatter
7     queUserMan.Formatter =  new
8         XmlMessageFormatter(new Type[] {Type.GetType("System.String")});
9
10    // Peek first message from queue
11    msgUserMan = queUserMan.Peek();
12    // Save the message body
13    strBody = msgUserMan.Body.ToString();
14 }
```

Picking Specific Messages from a Queue

A message queue is designed with a stack-like structure in mind. It doesn't have any search facilities as such, meaning that messages are retrieved from the top of the stack, or rather the top of the message queue. However, it's possible to pick specific messages from your queue. To do so, use the **ReceiveById** method, which takes a message ID as its only argument. The message ID is generated by Message Queuing and it's assigned to an instance of the **Message class** when it's sent to the queue. Listing 8-15 shows you how to retrieve the ID from a message and later use that ID to retrieve this message, even though it isn't at the top of the message queue.

Listing 8-15. Retrieving a Message from the Queue by Message ID

```
 1 public void RetrieveMessageById() {
 2     MessageQueue queUserMan = new MessageQueue(".\\Private$\\UserMan");
 3     System.Messaging.Message msgUserMan = new System.Messaging.Message();
 4     string strId;
 5
 6     // Set up the formatter
 7     queUserMan.Formatter =
 8         new XmlMessageFormatter(new Type[] {Type.GetType("System.String")});
 9
10     // Create body as a text message
11     msgUserMan.Body = "Test 1";
12     // Send message to queue
13     queUserMan.Send(msgUserMan);
14
15     // Create body as a text message
16     msgUserMan.Body = "Test 2";
17     // Send message to queue
18     queUserMan.Send(msgUserMan);
19     strId = msgUserMan.Id;
20
21     // Create body as a text message
22     msgUserMan.Body = "Test 3";
23     // Send message to queue
24     queUserMan.Send(msgUserMan);
25
26     msgUserMan = queUserMan.ReceiveById(strId);
27     MessageBox.Show("Saved Id=" + strId + "\nRetrieved Id=" + msgUserMan.Id);
28 }
```

In Listing 8-15, I bind to the existing private UserMan queue, set up the formatter to accept data type **string**, create three messages, and send them to the queue. Just after the second message is sent to the queue, the message ID is saved, and then this ID is used to retrieve the associated message. This message is second in the message queue. On Line 27, I simply display the saved message ID and the retrieved message to show that they are the same.

If you use the **ReceiveById** or indeed the **PeekById** method, you must be aware that an **InvalidOperationException** exception is thrown if the message does not exist in the queue. So, whenever you employ one of these methods, you should use a structured error handler, as demonstrated in Listing 8-16.

Listing 8-16. Retrieving a Message by Message ID in a Safe Manner

```
1 public System.Messaging.Message RetrieveMessageByIdSafe(string strId) {
2     MessageQueue queUserMan = new MessageQueue(".\\Private$\\UserMan");
3     System.Messaging.Message msgUserMan = new System.Messaging.Message();
4
5     // Set up the formatter
6     queUserMan.Formatter = new
7         XmlMessageFormatter(new Type[] {Type.GetType("System.String")});
8
9     try {
10        msgUserMan = queUserMan.ReceiveById(strId);
11    }
12    catch {
13        // Message not found, return a null value
14        return null;
15    }
16
17    // Return message
18    return msgUserMan;
19 }
```

Listing 8-16 catches an attempt to locate a nonexisting message by ID and simply returns a **null** value to the caller. If the passed message ID can be found in the queue, the retrieved message is returned to the caller.

The ID of a message is of data type **string**, but it's internally a GUID as you can see from Listing 8-15. At any rate, the **Id** property of a message is read-only, so you can't assign your own IDs to your messages. I guess this is one way of ensuring all messages are unique. Your only option is to save the ID of a particular message and then later use this ID to retrieve the message.

> **NOTE** *The **PeekById** method works the same as the **ReceiveById** method, except that the message isn't removed from the message queue.*

Retrieving All Messages in a Queue

Instead of retrieving the messages in a queue individually, you can also use the **GetAllMessages** method to retrieve all the messages in the queue as an array of **strings**. The messages in the array are ordered the way they appear in the queue, meaning the first element in the array is the top or first message in the queue. The **GetAllMessages** method is called like this:

```
object[] arrstrMessages = queUserMan.GetAllMessages();
```

This returns all messages in the queUserMan queue in the arrstrMessages array. However, unlike the other **Receive** methods, this method doesn't remove the messages from the queue, nor does it return message objects that you can manipulate. The **GetAllMessages** method can only be used to retrieve a snapshot of the message queue at any given time. The snapshot is, as the word suggests, static and won't reflect changes made to the queue after calling the **GetAllMessages** method.

Sending and Retrieving Messages Asynchronously

Sometimes it's desirable to be able to send and receive your messages in asynchronous fashion. This makes sure your application isn't held up until delivery or retrieval has been completed. In order to use asynchronous communication with a message queue, you need to set up an event handler that deals with the result of the asynchronous operation. This can be done as shown on Lines 22 and 23 in Listing 8-17.

*Listing 8-17. Receive a Message Asynchronously Using **AddHandler***

```
1  public void MessageReceiveCompleteEvent(Object objSource,
2      ReceiveCompletedEventArgs objEventArgs) {
3      System.Messaging.Message msgUserMan = new System.Messaging.Message();
4      MessageQueue queUserMan = new MessageQueue();
5
6      // Make sure we bind to the right message queue
7      queUserMan = (MessageQueue) objSource;
8
9      // End async receive
```

```
10      msgUserMan = queUserMan.EndReceive(objEventArgs.AsyncResult);
11 }
12
13 public void RetrieveMessagesAsync() {
14      MessageQueue queUserMan = new MessageQueue(".\\Private$\\UserMan");
15      System.Messaging.Message msgUserMan = new System.Messaging.Message();
16
17      // Set up the formatter
18      queUserMan.Formatter = new
19         XmlMessageFormatter(new Type[] {Type.GetType("System.String")});
20
21      // Add an event handler
22      queUserMan.ReceiveCompleted +=
23         new ReceiveCompletedEventHandler(MessageReceiveCompleteEvent);
24
25      queUserMan.BeginReceive(new TimeSpan(0, 0, 10));
26 }
```

In Listing 8-17, I have first set up the procedure that will receive the
ReceiveComplete event. This procedure takes care of binding to the passed
queue, which is the queue used to begin the retrieval, and then the asynchronous
retrieval is ended by calling the **EndReceive** method. This method also returns
the message from the queue.

In the RetrieveMessagesAsync procedure, I set up the message queue, and on
Lines 22 and 23, I add the event handler that calls the
MessageReceiveCompleteEvent procedure on completion of the message retrieval.
Finally the asynchronous message retrieval is started by calling the **BeginReceive**
method on Line 25. I have specified that the call should time-out after 10 seconds
using a new instance of the **TimeSpan** class.

Listing 8-17 makes use of the **BeginReceive** and **EndReceive** methods, but
you can use the example code with only very few modifications if you want to
peek instead of receive the messages from the queue (see Listing 8-18).

*Listing 8-18. Peeking Asynchronously Using **AddHandler***

```
1 public void MessagePeekCompleteEvent(object objSource,
2      PeekCompletedEventArgs objEventArgs) {
3      System.Messaging.Message msgUserMan = new System.Messaging.Message();
4      MessageQueue queUserMan = new MessageQueue();
5
6      // Make sure we bind to the right message queue
7      queUserMan = (MessageQueue) objSource;
8
9      // End async peek
```

```
10      msgUserMan = queUserMan.EndPeek(objEventArgs.AsyncResult);
11 }
12
13 public void PeekMessagesAsync() {
14      MessageQueue queUserMan = new MessageQueue(".\\Private$\\UserMan");
15      System.Messaging.Message msgUserMan = new System.Messaging.Message();
16
17      // Set up the formatter
18      queUserMan.Formatter = new
19          XmlMessageFormatter(new Type[] {Type.GetType("System.String")});
20
21      // Add an event handler
22      queUserMan.PeekCompleted +=
23          new PeekCompletedEventHandler(MessagePeekCompleteEvent);
24
25      queUserMan.BeginPeek(new TimeSpan(0, 0, 10));
26 }
```

Clearing Messages from the Queue

Messages can be removed from a message queue in two ways: you can remove them one by one, or you can clear the whole queue in one go.

Removing a Single Message from the Queue

Removing a single message from the queue can only be done programmatically, not by using either Server Explorer or Computer Management.

You can use the **Receive** method to remove messages from the queue. Although this method is generally used to retrieve messages from the queue, it also removes the message. See "Retrieving a Message" earlier in this chapter for more information.

The **ReceiveById** method also removes a message. Alternatively, you can use the **PeekById** method to find a specific message and then use **ReceiveById** to remove it. See "Picking Specific Messages from a Queue" earlier in this chapter for more information on how to use the **ReceiveById** and **PeekById** methods.

Removing All Messages from the Queue

Removing all messages from the queue can be done either manually using Server Explorer or Computer Management, or programmatically.

> **CAUTION** *Clearing all messages from a queue is an irreversible action, and once you confirm the deletion, the messages are permanently lost. So be careful when you perform this action!*

Removing All Messages Manually

If you want to manually remove all messages from a queue, you can use either the Server Explorer or Computer Management. Select the Queue Messages node (refer back to Figures 8-3 and 8-4), right-click this node, and select All Tasks/Purge (Computer Management) or Clear Messages (Server Explorer) from the pop-up menu. Then click Yes or OK in the confirmation dialog box to clear all messages from the queue.

Removing All Messages Programmatically

If you want to clear all messages from a queue programmatically, you can use the **Purge** method for this purpose. Listing 8-19 shows you how to bind to a message queue and clear all messages from it.

Listing 8-19. Clearing All Messages from a Queue

```
1 public void ClearMessageQueue() {
2     MessageQueue queUserMan = new MessageQueue(".\\Private$\\UserMan");
3
4     // Clear all messages from queue
5     queUserMan.Purge();
6 }
```

In Listing 8-19, I have used the **Purge** method of the **MessageQueue** class to clear all messages from the queue. This method works with any number of messages in the queue, meaning no exception is raised if the queue is empty when you call this method.

Prioritizing Messages

Every now and then it's important that a particular message is read ASAP. Normally when you send a message, it ends up at the end of the message queue, because messages are sorted by arrival time. However, because messages are first and foremost sorted by priority, you can specify a higher priority to make sure that this message is added to the top of the message queue.

> **NOTE** *Setting the priority of a message doesn't work with transactional message queues.*

You can set the priority of a message using the **Priority** method of the **Message** class. See Listing 8-20 for a code example that sends two messages to the queue, one with normal priority and one with highest priority.

Listing 8-20. Sending Messages with Different Priority

```
1 public void SendPriorityMessages() {
2     MessageQueue queUserMan = new MessageQueue(".\\Private$\\UserMan");
3     System.Messaging.Message msgFirst = new System.Messaging.Message();
4     System.Messaging.Message msgSecond = new System.Messaging.Message();
5
6     // Set up the formatter
7     queUserMan.Formatter = new
8         XmlMessageFormatter(new Type[] {Type.GetType("System.String")});
9
10    // Create first body
11    msgFirst.Body = "First Message";
12    // Send message to queue
13    queUserMan.Send(msgFirst);
14
15    // Create second body
16    msgSecond.Body = "Second Message";
17    // Set priority to highest
18    msgSecond.Priority = MessagePriority.Highest;
19    // Send message to queue
20    queUserMan.Send(msgSecond);
21 }
22
23 // Listing 8-20-2
24 public void RetrievePriorityMessage() {
25    MessageQueue queUserMan = new MessageQueue(".\\Private$\\UserMan");
26    System.Messaging.Message msgUserMan;
27
28    // Set up the formatter
29    queUserMan.Formatter = new
30        XmlMessageFormatter(new Type[] {Type.GetType("System.String")});
31
32    // Retrieve first message from queue
33    msgUserMan = queUserMan.Receive();
```

```
34    // Display the message body
35    MessageBox.Show(msgUserMan.Body.ToString());
36 }
```

If you run the code in Listing 8-20, you'll see that setting the priority of the second message to highest makes sure that it goes to the top of the message queue. The message box will display the text "Second Message". If your message queue isn't transactional, the text displayed will be "First Message".

The priority of the second message is set on Line 18. When you set the **Priority** property of a **Message** object, it must be set to a member of the **MessagePriority** enum. The default is **Normal**.

Locating a Message Queue

Sometime you don't know the path to a particular queue or you just need to verify that a specific queue still exists. Let's start with the easy task, how to check if a particular queue exists (see Listing 8-21).

Listing 8-21. Checking If a Message Queue Exists
```
1 public bool CheckQueueExists(string strPath) {
2    return MessageQueue.Exists(strPath);
3 }
```

In Listing 8-21, I use the **Exists** method of the **MessageQueue** class. Because this is a public static function, you don't actually have to instantiate a message queue object in order to use this method.

The CheckQueueExists procedure will return **true** or **false** depending on whether the passed strPath argument matches an existing message queue.

Now this is pretty simple, because you already know the path. However, sometimes you don't know the path, just the name of the machine where message queuing is installed. See Listing 8-22 for an example of how to retrieve a list of all the private queues on a specific machine.

Listing 8-22. Retrieving All Private Queues on a Machine
```
1 public void BrowsePrivateQueues() {
2    MessageQueue[] arrquePrivate =
3       MessageQueue.GetPrivateQueuesByMachine("USERMANPC");
4
5    // Display the name of all the private queues on the machine
6    foreach(MessageQueue queUserMan in arrquePrivate) {
7       MessageBox.Show(queUserMan.Label);
8    }
9 }
```

In Listing 8-22, I retrieve all the message queues on the USERMANPC machine and display their labels. As you can see from Line 2, all the queues are saved in an array of **MessageQueue** class instances. If you need the public queues instead, simply replace the **GetPrivateQueuesByMachine** method call with a call to the **GetPublicQueuesByMachine** method.

The public queues can also be located on the whole network instead of just one machine. There are three different methods that can be used to locate public queues network-wide:

- **GetPublicQueues**

- **GetPublicQueuesByCategory**

- **GetPublicQueuesByLabel**

See Listings 8-23, 8-24, and 8-25 for code that shows you how to use these methods.

Listing 8-23. Retrieving All Public Queues on a Network

```
1 public void BrowsePublicQueuesNetworkWide() {
2    MessageQueue[] arrquePublic =
3        MessageQueue.GetPublicQueues();
4
5    // Display the name of all the public queues on the network
6    foreach(MessageQueue queUserMan in arrquePublic) {
7        MessageBox.Show(queUserMan.Label);
8    }
9 }
```

Listing 8-23 uses the **GetPublicQueues** method to retrieve all public queues on the network and then displays the name of each queue.

Listing 8-24 retrieves all public queues on a network by category using the **GetPublicQueuesByCategory** method. For each returned message queue in the 00000000-0000-0000-0000-000000000001 category, I display the queue name. The category being referred to is the same as the Type ID in Figure 8-1 and the **Category** property of the **MessageQueue** class. This is a way for you to group your message queues, particularly for administrative purposes.

Listing 8-24. Retrieving All Public Queues on a Network by Category

```
 1 public void BrowsePublicQueuesByCategoryNetworkWide() {
 2     MessageQueue[] arrquePublic =
 3         MessageQueue.GetPublicQueuesByCategory(new
 4         Guid("00000000-0000-0000-0000-000000000001"));
 5
 6     // Display the name of all the public queues
 7     // on the network within a specific category
 8     foreach(MessageQueue queUserMan in arrquePublic) {
 9         MessageBox.Show(queUserMan.Label);
10     }
11 }
```

Listing 8-25 shows you how to find all the public queues on the network that have the "userman" label. The name of the machine where each queue is located is then displayed one by one.

Listing 8-25. Retrieving All Public Queues on a Network by Label

```
 1 public void BrowsePublicQueuesByLabelNetworkWide() {
 2     MessageQueue[] arrquePublic =
 3         MessageQueue.GetPublicQueuesByLabel("userman");
 4
 5     // Display the machine name for all the public queues
 6     // on the network with a specific label
 7     foreach(MessageQueue queUserMan in arrquePublic) {
 8         MessageBox.Show(queUserMan.Label);
 9     }
10 }
```

Removing a Message Queue

Now and then you might need to remove a message queue from a machine, and for this purpose you have several options. A message queue can be deleted either manually using Server Explorer or Computer Management or programmatically.

> **CAUTION** *Clearing a message queue is an irreversible action, and once you confirm the deletion, the queue and all its messages are permanently lost!*

Removing a Message Queue Manually

If you want to manually remove a queue, you can use either the Server Explorer or Computer Management. Select the queue node (see Figure 8-4), right-click this node, and select Delete from the pop-up menu. Then click Yes in the confirmation dialog box to remove the message queue and all its messages.

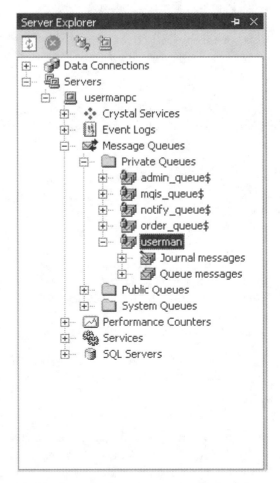

Figure 8-4. The Server Explorer with message queue selected

Removing a Message Queue Programmatically

If you want to clear all messages from a queue programmatically, you can use the **Purge** method for this purpose. Listing 8-26 shows you how to bind to a message queue and clear all messages from it.

Listing 8-26. Removing a Message Queue

```
1 public void RemoveMessageQueue(string strPath) {
2     MessageQueue.Delete(strPath);
3 }
```

In Listing 8-26, I have used the **Delete** method of the **MessageQueue** class to remove the queue with the strPath path. Keep in mind that if the queue doesn't exist, an exception is thrown, so I can only recommend that you don't use the example code in Listing 8-26 without being sure the queue actually exists. See how to use the **Exists** method in the section "Locating a Message Queue" earlier in this chapter. Alternatively, you can set up a structured error handler like the one in Listing 8-27.

Listing 8-27. Removing a Message Queue in a Safe Manner

```
1 public void RemoveMessageQueueSafely(string strPath) {
2     try {
3         MessageQueue.Delete(strPath);
4     }
5     catch (Exception objE) {
6         MessageBox.Show(objE.Message);
7     }
8 }
```

In Listing 8-27, I catch any exception being thrown when I try to remove the message queue specified using the strPath argument. I am only displaying the error message, but I am sure you can take it from there.

Controlling Message Queue Storage Size

Depending on how soon messages are retrieved from your message queue after they've been sent there, the queue can take up a lot of storage.

Generally, you shouldn't be clearing your queues, because you might destroy messages that need to be processed by a client. However, you can solve this by specifying a maximum limit in kilobytes. If you look at Figure 8-1, you can see the General tab of the Message Queue Properties dialog box. Check the Limit message storage to (KB) check box and type the size in the text box to the right of the check box.

Programmatically you can do this using the **MaximumQueueSize** property of the **MessageQueue** class, as follows:

```
queUserMan.MaximumQueueSize = 15;
```

When you set the storage limit, all messages that are sent to a message queue where the limit has been reached are rejected, and a negative acknowledgment message is sent to the administration queue on the client that sends the message.

Making Message Queues Transactional

As with normal database access, it's possible to make your message queues transactional. This means you can send several messages as a single transaction, and then act on the result of the transmission of these messages by determining if you should commit or roll back the messages. Whether a message queue is transactional or not is determined at creation time. You can't change this after the queue has been created.

There are two types of transactions when it comes to message queues: internal and external. Please see the following sections for a brief description of each.

Internal Transactions

The term *internal transactions* refers to transactions that you manage manually or explicitly and only involve messages sent between a client and a message queue. This means that no other resources, such as database manipulation, can be part of an internal transaction and that you must explicitly begin and then commit or roll back a transaction. The Message Queuing's Transaction Coordinator handles internal transactions.

Internal transactions are faster than external transactions, which are discussed next.

External Transactions

External transactions are exactly what the name suggests: external. Resources other than message queue resources are part of external transactions. These can be database access, Active Directory access, and so on. Furthermore, external transactions are NOT handled by the Message Queuing's Transaction Coordinator, but by a coordinator such as the Microsoft Distributed Transaction Coordinator (MS DTC), and external transactions are implicit or automatic.

External transactions are slower than internal transactions. In this chapter, I'll only cover internal transactions, because external transactions fall outside the scope of this book, and could indeed by themselves be the subject of an entire book.

Creating a Transactional Message Queue

If you're creating your queue programmatically, see Listing 8-4 for an example of how to make it transactional. If you want to create your transactional message queue using Server Explorer, Chapter 4 gives you the details. Of course it's also possible to use the Computer Management MMC snap-in. Open the snap-in and follow these steps:

1. Expand the Services and Applications node.

2. Expand the Message Queuing node.

3. Select either the Public Queues or the Private Queues node.

4. Right-click the node and select New/Public Queue or New/Private Queue from the pop-up menu. This brings up the Queue Name dialog box.

5. Give the message queue a name by typing one in the Name text box, and make sure you check the Transactional check box before you click OK to create the message queue.

Starting a Transaction

Because internal transactions are explicit or manual, you must begin a transaction from code before you start sending and retrieving messages that are to be part of the transaction. Actually, the very first thing you should check is whether your message queue is transactional. This can be done using the **Transactional** property, which returns a **bool** value indicating if the queue is transactional or not:

```
if (queUserMan.Transactional) {}
```

The next thing you need to do is to create an instance of the **MessageQueueTransaction** class. The constructor for this class isn't overloaded, so it's created like this:

```
MessageQueueTransaction qtrUserMan = new MessageQueueTransaction();
```

Now it's time to start the transaction, and this is done using the **Begin** method of the **MessageQueueTransaction** class, as follows:

```
qtrUserMan.Begin();
```

You may be wondering how you can reference this transaction object from the message queue object. I understand if you're confused, but it's really not that difficult. You simply pass the transaction object when you send or retrieve a message, like this:

```
msgUserMan = queUserMan.Receive(qtrUserMan);
```

or

```
queUserMan.Send(msgUserMan, qtrUserMan);
```

As you can see from these short examples, you do as you normally would when you write your code without transactions, with the exception that you pass the transaction object when you perform an operation that needs to be part of the transaction. Mind you, the transaction object can only be used with one message queue, meaning that you can't use the same transaction object with two different message queues.

Ending a Transaction

When you've started a transaction, you must also end it. That's pretty logical if you ask me. However, how the transaction should be ended isn't quite so direct. If you don't run into any problems during the operations that are part of the transaction, you'll normally commit the transaction or apply the changes to the message queue(s). If you do run into a problem with any of the transactional operations, you'll normally abort the transaction as soon as the problem occurs. When I refer to problems, I'm not only talking about exceptions that are thrown by the **MessageQueue** object, but also other operations external to the message queue operations that can make you abort the transaction. For example, say you're sending messages to a queue as a result of processing rows from a database, and you come across unexpected data. In this situation, you may want to abort all of the messages you've already sent.

Committing a Transaction

Committing a transaction is straightforward, and it's done using the **Commit** method of the **MessageQueue** class, as follows:

```
qtrUserMan.Commit();
```

The **Commit** method isn't overloaded and it doesn't take any parameters. However, an **InvalidOperationException** exception is thrown if you try to commit a transaction that hasn't been started (**Begin** method).

Aborting a Transaction

In situations where you have to abort a transaction, you can use the **Abort** method of the **MessageQueue** class, like this:

```
qtrUserMan.Abort();
```

The **Abort** method isn't overloaded and it doesn't take any parameters. However, like the **Commit** method, an **InvalidOperationException** exception is thrown if you try to abort a transaction that hasn't been started (**Begin** method).

Using the MessageQueueTransaction Class

I have just gone over all the methods that are important to managing a transaction, but there is one property that I haven't mentioned, and that is the **Status** property. This read-only property returns a member of the **MessageQueueTransactionStatus** enum that tells you the status of the transaction. The **Status** property can be read from the time you create your instance of the **MessageQueueTransaction** class until the object has been destroyed. You can see the **MessageQueueTransactionStatus** enum members in Table 8-2.

*Table 8-2. Members of the **MessageQueueTransactionStatus** Enum*

MEMBER NAME	DESCRIPTION
Aborted	The transaction has been aborted. This can be done by the user with the **Abort** method.
Committed	The transaction has been committed. This is done using the **Commit** method.
Initialized	The transaction object has been instantiated, but no transaction has yet been started. In this state, you should not pass the transaction object to the message queue methods.
Pending	The transaction has been started and is now pending an **Abort** or **Commit**. When the transaction is pending, you can pass the transaction object to the message queue methods.

See Listing 8-28 for an example of how to use transactions combined with a structured exception handler. The example code can only be run if you've created a private, transactional message queue named UserMan on the local machine.

Listing 8-28. Using Message Queue Transactions

```
1  public void UseMQTransactions() {
2      MessageQueueTransaction qtrUserMan = new MessageQueueTransaction();
3      MessageQueue queUserMan = new MessageQueue(".\\Private$\\UserMan");
4      System.Messaging.Message msgUserMan = new System.Messaging.Message();
5
6      // Set up the queue formatter
7      queUserMan.Formatter = new
8          XmlMessageFormatter(new Type[] {Type.GetType("System.String")});
9
10     // Clear the message queue
11     queUserMan.Purge();
12     // Start the transaction
13     qtrUserMan.Begin();
14
15     try {
16         // Create message body
17         msgUserMan.Body = "First Message";
18         // Send message to queue
19         queUserMan.Send(msgUserMan, qtrUserMan);
20
21         // Create message body
22         msgUserMan.Body = "Second Message";
23         // Send message to queue
24         queUserMan.Send(msgUserMan, qtrUserMan);
25
26         // Retrieve message from queue
27         //msgUserMan = queUserMan.Receive(qtrUserMan);
28         // Display message body
29         //MessageBox.Show(msgUserMan.Body.ToString());
30
31         // Commit transaction
32         qtrUserMan.Commit();
33
34         // Retrieve message from queue
35         msgUserMan = queUserMan.Receive(qtrUserMan);
36         // Display message body
37         MessageBox.Show(msgUserMan.Body.ToString());
```

```
38
39        // Retrieve message from queue
40        msgUserMan = queUserMan.Receive();
41        // Display message body
42        MessageBox.Show(msgUserMan.Body.ToString());
43      }
44    catch {
45        // Abort the transaction
46        qtrUserMan.Abort();
47      }
48 }
```

In Listing 8-28, I have demonstrated how you can send transactional messages to a message queue. When you run the code, you'll see two message boxes displaying "First Message" and "Second Message". After sending the messages to the queue (Lines 19 and 24), I commit the transaction, which means the messages are actually placed in the queue. If you notice, I have wrapped the sending and receiving part in a structured exception handler, just in case something goes wrong. If this is the case, the **catch** block (Lines 44 through 47) will abort the transaction. The Lines 27 and 29 have been commented out, but if you were to uncomment these lines and run the example code, your application will stop responding and await the arrival of a message in the queue; they haven't been placed in the queue yet, because you haven't actually committed the transaction at this point.

Looking at System-Generated Queues

So far, I have only been looking at user-created queues, but there's another group of queues that needs attention: the system-generated queues. **Message Queuing** maintains these queues. The following queues are system queues:

- Dead-letter messages

- Journal messages

- Transactional dead-letter messages

The two dead-letter message queues, seen in the Server Explorer in Figure 8-5 on the System Queues node, are used for storing messages that can't be delivered. One queue holds the nontransactional messages and the other one holds the transactional ones. See the next section for an explanation of the Journal message queues.

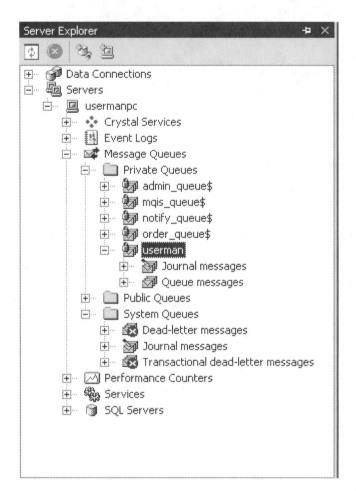

Figure 8-5. The system and journal queues

Using Journal Storage

Journal storage is a great facility for keeping copies of messages that are sent to
or removed from a message queue. It can be very helpful if for some reason
you need to resend a message. The message delivery might have failed, and you
receive a negative acknowledgment. Because an acknowledgment does not contain the message body, you can't use this message to resend the original message.
However, you can use it to find a copy of the original message in the Journal messages queue.

Every message queuing client (machine) has a global journal queue called
the *system journal*. The system journal stores copies of all messages sent *from* the
remote message queuing client, if journaling is enabled on the message being

sent (see "Enabling Journaling on a Message" later in this chapter). This is true whether the message is delivered or not, but only if you send the message from a remote client. Messages sent to a local queue, whether it's a private or public message queue and whether journaling has been enabled on the messages being sent, are *not* stored in the system journal. This is one reason developers prefer working with a remote queue, even if all the messages are handled on the local machine.

Besides the system journal, all message queues have their own journal queue. The journal queue associated with each message queue stores copies of all messages removed, or rather taken from the message queue, but only if journaling is enabled on the message queue. See "Enabling Journaling on a Message Queue" for more information on how to enable journaling on a message queue.

Enabling Journaling on a Message Queue

Journaling can be enabled on a message queue either manually or programmatically. If you want to do it manually, you can from the Computer Management MMC snap-in. In Figure 8-1, you can see the Properties dialog box for an existing queue or a queue that is about to be created. If you want to enable journaling, you should check the Enabled check box in the Journal group and click Apply.

You can also programmatically enable journaling on an existing queue by setting the **UseJournalQueue** property of an existing message queue to **true**, like this:

```
MessageQueue queUserMan = new MessageQueue("USERMANPC\\UserMan");
queUserMan.UseJournalQueue = true;
```

Once you've enabled journaling on a message queue, all messages that are removed, or rather taken from the message queue, are copied to the message queue journal. In Listing 8-29, you can see how message queue journaling can be used.

Enabling Journaling on a Message

It's also possible to use journaling on a per-message basis instead of on the message queue, and this is done programmatically, by setting the **UseJournalQueue** property of an existing message to **true** before sending it to the queue, like this:

```
msgUserMan.UseJournalQueue = true;
```

In Listing 8-29, you can see how message journaling can be used, but please be aware that the example code shown only works if the message queue isn't transactional.

Listing 8-29. Explaining Message Journaling

```
 1 public void ShowMessageJournaling() {
 2   MessageQueue queUserMan = new MessageQueue("USERMANPC\\UserMan");
 3   MessageQueue queUserManJournal = new
 4     MessageQueue("USERMANPC\\UserMan\\Journal$");
 5   MessageQueue queSystemJournal = new MessageQueue(".\\Journal$");
 6   System.Messaging.Message msgUserMan = new System.Messaging.Message();
 7
 8   // Enable journaling on message queue
 9   queUserMan.UseJournalQueue = true;
10
11   // Set up the formatter
12   queUserMan.Formatter = new
13     XmlMessageFormatter(new Type[] {Type.GetType("System.String")});
14
15   // Create message body
16   msgUserMan.Body = "Message";
17   // Enable message journaling
18   msgUserMan.UseJournalQueue = true;
19   // Send message to remote UserMan queue
20   queUserMan.Send(msgUserMan);
21   // Retrieve message from remote UserMan queue
22   msgUserMan = queUserMan.Receive();
23
24   // Retrieve message from local system journal
25   msgUserMan = queSystemJournal.Receive();
26   // Retrieve message from remote UserMan journal
27   msgUserMan = queUserManJournal.Receive();
28 }
```

On Lines 2 through 5 in Listing 8-29, I bind to three different message queues:

- The public UserMan queue on the remote USERMANPC machine (Line 2)

- The journal queue for the public UserMan queue on the remote USERMANPC machine (Lines 3 and 4)

- The system journal queue on the local machine (Line 5)

After binding to the message queues, I set up the message formatter (Lines 12 and 13), create the first message body (Line 16), and enable message journaling on the message (Line 18). The message is then sent to the public UserMan queue on USERMANPC (Line 20) and because it's sent to a remote message queue , and because journaling is enabled on the queue (Line 9), a copy of the message is saved in the local system journal.

On Line 22, I retrieve the message sent to the UserMan queue on USERMANPC, and because journaling is enabled on this queue, a copy of the message is saved in the UserMan journal queue. On Lines 25 and 27, I retrieve the two copies of the message that have been saved to the local system journal and the remote UserMan journal.

> **NOTE** *The **UseJournalQueue** property works differently on the **Message** class than on the **MessageQueue** class. On the **Message** class, setting this property to **true** ensures that a copy of the message is saved to the local system journal, while setting this property to **true** on the **MessageQueue** class ensures that a copy of the message is saved to the system journal on the remote machine that the **MessageQueue** object binds to.*

Retrieving a Message from Journal Storage

Now, enabling journaling is easy enough, but how do you actually retrieve the messages from the journal when needed? Well, you can access these journal queues and other system queues by specifying the correct path to the queue. For example, the following code accesses the journal storage for the private message queue UserMan on the local machine:

```
MessageQueue queUserMan = MessageQueue(".\\Journal$");
```

See Listing 8-29 earlier in this chapter for a more detailed example of how this works.

Controlling Journal Storage Size

Messages that are sent to either of the types of journals, system journal or queue journal, stay in the journal queue until you remove them. Well, this is true for messages in all message queues, but the point is that you're likely to retrieve messages from a standard message queue yourself, whereas messages in the journal queue are left there.

Generally, you should clear out the journal queues you use at a regular interval depending on how long you want to be able to go back in time to retrieve an old message. However, you can still run into problems with space in your journal, and you can solve this by specifying a maximum limit in kilobytes. If you look at Figure 8-1, you can see the Journal frame on the General tab of the Message Queue Properties dialog box. If you check the Enabled check box, you can also specify a maximum storage size in kilobytes if you check the Limit journal storage to (KB) check box and type the desired size in the text box to the right of the check box.

Programmatically you can specify a maximum storage size using the **MaximumJournalSize** property of the **MessageQueue** class, like this:

```
queUserMan.MaximumJournalSize = 15;
```

You obviously need to enable journaling in order to limit the storage size of the journal.

Securing Your Message Queuing

So far in this chapter, you've been shown how to create private and public queues, both transactional and nontransactional ones, and you've seen how you send and receive messages to and from a queue, including peeking at messages without removing them from the queue. However, I've yet to mention Message Queuing security, which is what I am going to cover in this section.

Message Queuing uses built-in features of the Windows OS for securing messaging. This includes the following:

- Authentication

- Encryption

- Access control

- Auditing

Using Authentication

Authentication is the process by which a message's integrity is ensured and the sender of a message can be verified. This can be achieved by setting the message queue's **Authenticate** property to **true**. The default value for this property is **false**, meaning no authentication is required. When this property is set to **true**, the queue will only accept authenticated messages—nonauthenticated messages are rejected. In other words, the message queue on the server requires messages to be authenticated, not just the message queue object you use to set the **Authenticate** property. Basically this means that when you set the property, you affect all other message queue objects that are working on the same message queue. You can programmatically enable authentication as it's done in Listing 8-30.

Listing 8-30. Enable Authentication on a Message Queue

```
1 public void EnableQueueAuthentication() {
2    MessageQueue queUserMan = new MessageQueue("USERMANPC \\UserMan");
3    System.Messaging.Message msgUserMan = new System.Messaging.Message();
4
5    // Enable queue authentication
6    queUserMan.Authenticate = true;
7 }
```

You can also request authentication by setting this property from the Computer Management MMC snap-in. See Figure 8-1 and the section "Displaying or Changing the Properties of Your Message Queue" for more information on how to set the properties of an existing message queue. In Figure 8-1, you can see the Authenticated check box, which you need to enable before clicking OK to request that messages on this queue are authenticated.

If a message isn't authenticated, it's rejected and therefore lost. However, you can specify that the rejected message be placed in the dead-letter queue, as shown in Listing 8-31.

Listing 8-31. Rejecting a Nonauthenticated Message

```
1 public void RejectNonAuthenticatedMessage() {
2    MessageQueue queUserMan = new MessageQueue(".\\Private$\\UserMan");
3    System.Messaging.Message msgUserMan = new System.Messaging.Message();
4
5    // Enable queue authentication
6    queUserMan.Authenticate = true;
7    // Set up the queue formatter
8    queUserMan.Formatter = new
9        XmlMessageFormatter(new Type[] {Type.GetType("System.String")});
10
11   // Create message body
12   msgUserMan.Body = "Message Body";
13   // Make sure a rejected message is placed in the dead-letter queue
14   msgUserMan.UseDeadLetterQueue = true;
15
16   // Send message to queue
17   queUserMan.Send(msgUserMan);
18 }
```

In Listing 8-31, the **UseDeadLetterQueue** property is set to **true**, meaning that if the message is rejected for whatever reason, it's placed in the dead-letter queue (see Figure 8-6).

> **NOTE** *When you set the **UseDeadLetterQueue** property of the **Message** class, the message ends up in the Dead Letter queue if it's rejected by the message queue itself, but this also happens if you delete the message from the queue.*

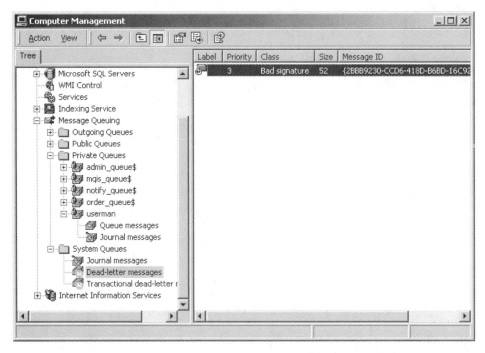

Figure 8-6. A rejected nonauthenticated message in the dead-letter queue

In Figure 8-6, you can see that the message in the dead-letter queue has been rejected because of a bad signature. You can also specify a specific time interval that the message is allowed to stay in the queue for retrieval. When the specified time expires, the message is moved to the dead letter queue as demonstrated in Listing 8-32.

Listing 8-32. Removing a Message from a Queue If Specified Time Elapses

```
1  public void SendDeadLetterMessage() {
2      MessageQueue queUserMan = new MessageQueue(".\\Private$\\UserMan");
3      System.Messaging.Message msgUserMan = new System.Messaging.Message();
4
5      // Set up the formatter
6      queUserMan.Formatter = new
7          XmlMessageFormatter(new Type[] {Type.GetType("System.String")});
8
9      // Create message body
10     msgUserMan.Body = "Message";
11     // Set max time to be in queue
12     msgUserMan.TimeToBeReceived = new TimeSpan(0, 1, 0);
13     // Make sure that a dead-letter ends up in dead-letter queue
14     msgUserMan.UseDeadLetterQueue = true;
15     // Send message to queue
16     queUserMan.Send(msgUserMan);
17 }
```

In Listing 8-32, the message must be picked up from the queue no later than one minute after being placed there (Line 12). Otherwise it's automatically moved to the dead-letter queue.

Another way of dealing with rejected messages is to request notification of the message rejection. Setting the **AcknowledgeType** and **AdministrationQueue** properties does this (see Listing 8-33).

Listing 8-33. Receiving Rejection Notification in the Admin Queue

```
1  public void PlaceNonAuthenticatedMessageInAdminQueue() {
2      MessageQueue queUserManAdmin = new
3          MessageQueue(".\\Private$\\UserManAdmin");
4      MessageQueue queUserMan = new MessageQueue(".\\Private$\\UserMan");
5      System.Messaging.Message msgUserMan = new System.Messaging.Message();
6
7      // Enable queue authentication
8      queUserMan.Authenticate = true;
9      // Set up the queue formatter
10     queUserMan.Formatter = new
11         XmlMessageFormatter(new Type[] {Type.GetType("System.String")});
12
13     // Create message body
14     msgUserMan.Body = "Message Body";
15     // Make sure a rejected message is placed in the admin queue
16     msgUserMan.AdministrationQueue = queUserManAdmin;
```

```
17    // These types of rejected messages
18    msgUserMan.AcknowledgeType = AcknowledgeTypes.NotAcknowledgeReachQueue;
19
20    // Send message to queue
21    queUserMan.Send(msgUserMan);
22 }
```

In Listing 8-33, I have set up the private queue UserManAdmin to receive notification of rejection. Please note that you need to have created this message queue as a nontransactional queue before you run the example code.

As is the case with the code in Listing 8-31, the code in Listing 8-33 rejects the messages that you send. That seems okay, because you requested that all messages should be authenticated, but you "forgot" to authenticate your message.

Setting the **AttachSenderId** property to **true** does this, because it results in Message Queuing setting the **SenderId** property. However, this isn't enough, because you also need to set the **UseAuthentication** property to **true**. This ensures the message is digitally signed before it's sent to the queue. Likewise, the digital signature that Message Queuing has assigned is used for authenticating the message when it's received. Listing 8-34 shows you how to send an authenticated message.

Listing 8-34. Sending an Authenticated Message

```
1 public void AcceptAuthenticatedMessage() {
2    MessageQueue queUserMan = new MessageQueue(".\\Private$\\UserMan");
3    System.Messaging.Message msgUserMan = new System.Messaging.Message();
4
5    // Enable queue authentication
6    queUserMan.Authenticate = true;
7    // Set up the queue formatter
8    queUserMan.Formatter = new
9        XmlMessageFormatter(new Type[] {Type.GetType("System.String")});
10
```

```
11      // Make sure a rejected message is placed in the dead-letter queue
12      msgUserMan.UseDeadLetterQueue = true;
13      // Make sure that message queuing attaches the sender id and
14      // is digitally signed before it is sent
15      msgUserMan.UseAuthentication = true;
16      msgUserMan.AttachSenderId = true;
17      // Create message body
18      msgUserMan.Body = "Message Body";
19
20      // Send message to queue
21      queUserMan.Send(msgUserMan);
22 }
```

In Listing 8-34, I set the **UseAuthentication** and **AttachSenderId** properties of the **Message** object to **true** in order to ensure that the message is digitally signed and can be authenticated by Message Queuing. In this situation, the message queue, unlike in the examples in Listings 8-31 and 8-33, won't reject the message, even if it only accepts authenticated messages. If authentication has already been set up on the message queue, you can leave out Lines 5 and 6.

Now it's obviously good to know if a message has been authenticated or not, but you don't actually have to check anything to find out. If you've set up authentication on the message queue, all messages in the queue will have been authenticated when they arrived in the queue, meaning you can trust any message you receive from the queue.

Using Encryption

Encryption is another way of securing messages sent between message queuing computers. With encryption, anyone trying to spy on the traffic on the network between the message queuing computers will receive encrypted messages. Now, while someone might be able to decrypt your messages, encryption certainly makes it harder to obtain sensitive information.

Some overhead is involved when you encrypt your messages at the sending end and decrypt them at the receiving end, but if your network is public and you're sending sensitive information, you should definitely consider using encrypted messages. Table 8-3 shows you the properties that can be set in order to use encryption with your message queues and messages.

Table 8-3. Encryption Properties

CLASS	PROPERTY	DESCRIPTION
Message	**EncryptionAlgorithm**	This property is used to specify the encryption algorithm for encrypting the message. The property can only be set to one of the **EncryptionAlgorithm** enum members, with **Rc2** being the default value and the most secure option.
Message	**UseEncryption**	You must set this property to **true** if you want to encrypt your message, or **false** (default) to specify a nonencrypted message. If the **EncryptionRequired** property on the message queue has been set to **Body**, you must set this property to **true**; otherwise the message will be rejected.
MessageQueue	**EncryptionRequired**	This property must be set to a member of the **EncryptionRequired** enum. This enum has three members:
		Body, which makes sure that all messages sent to the queue are encrypted. If you send a nonencrypted message to a queue with encryption enabled, the message is rejected.
		None (default), which makes sure that all messages sent to the queue aren't encrypted. If you send an encrypted message to a queue with encryption disabled, the message is rejected.
		Optional, which means the queue will accept both encrypted and nonencrypted messages.

As is the case with authentication, encryption requirements can be applied to the queue, meaning that all nonencrypted messages will be rejected by the queue. Setting the **EncryptionRequired** property of the **MessageQueue** object to **EncryptionRequired.Body**, as in Listing 8-35, does this.

Listing 8-35. Ensuring Nonencrypted Messages Are Rejected by the Queue

```
1 public void EnableRequireBodyEncryption() {
2    MessageQueue queUserMan = new MessageQueue(".\\Private$\\UserMan");
3    System.Messaging.Message msgUserMan = new System.Messaging.Message();
4
5    // Enable body encryption requirement
6    queUserMan.EncryptionRequired = EncryptionRequired.Body;
7 }
```

In Listing 8-35, I set the **EncryptionRequired** property of the **MessageQueue** object to **EncryptionRequired.Body**. As a result, the body of any message sent to the queue must be encrypted; otherwise it's rejected. Instead of setting the encryption property of the message queue programmatically, you can also set it from the Computer Management MMC snap-in (see Figure 8-7), or by selecting the queue in Server Explorer, right-clicking, and selecting Properties from the pop-up menu.

> **NOTE** *Message Queue encryption is also called* privacy, *meaning a private message, not to be confused with a private message queue.*

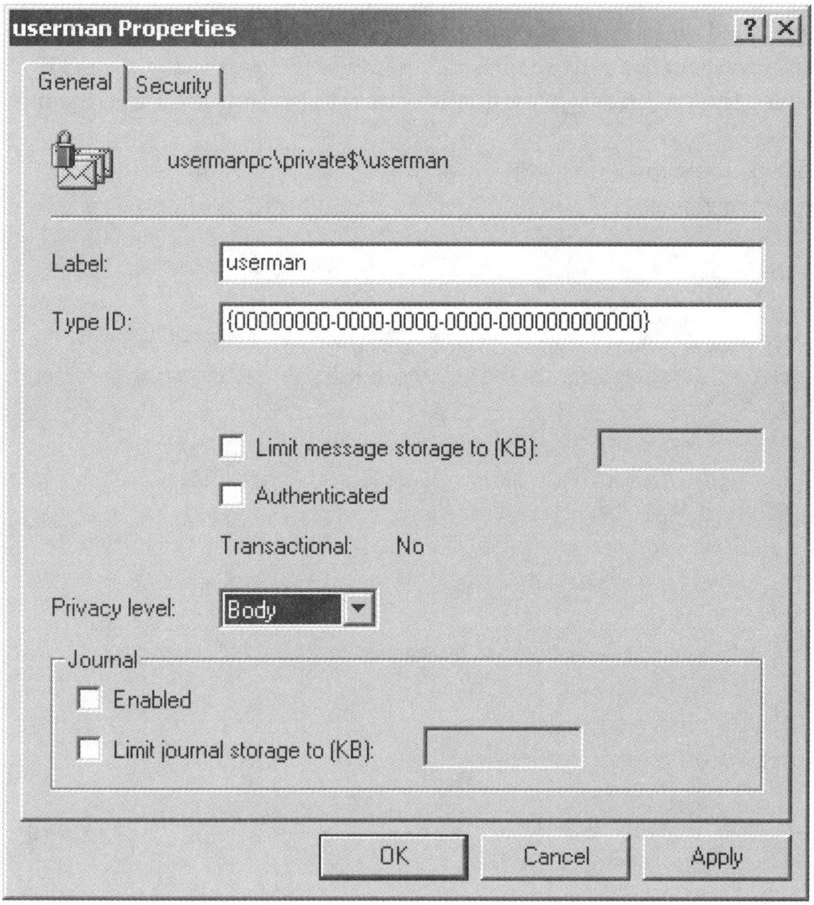

Figure 8-7. The privacy level set to Body

In Figure 8-7, Body has been selected from the Privacy level drop-down list, which has the same results as running the example code in Listing 8-35. Please note that I've unchecked the Authentication check box in this example. This doesn't mean that you can't use encryption and authentication at the same time; I have simply done so to simplify the code in the following listings.

Unlike with authentication, it's possible to use encryption even if the message queue doesn't require it, but only if the privacy level is set to Optional. This can be done from the Computer Management MMC snap-in or programmatically, as follows:

```
// Set message body encryption to optional
queUserMan.EncryptionRequired = EncryptionRequired.Optional;
```

If you specify Optional as the privacy level, you can send encrypted and nonencrypted messages to the message queue. However, if you set the privacy level to None, you can only send nonencrypted messages to the queue. If you send an encrypted message to a queue with a privacy level of None, the message is rejected.

The example in Listing 8-36 shows you how to send and receive an encrypted message.

Listing 8-36. Sending and Receiving Encrypted Messages

```
 1 public void SendAndReceiveEncryptedMessage() {
 2     MessageQueue queUserMan = new MessageQueue(".\\Private$\\UserMan");
 3     System.Messaging.Message msgUserMan = new System.Messaging.Message();
 4
 5     // Require message body encryption
 6     queUserMan.EncryptionRequired = EncryptionRequired.Body;
 7     // Set up the queue formatter
 8     queUserMan.Formatter = new
 9         XmlMessageFormatter(new Type[] {Type.GetType("System.String")});
10
11     // Make sure that message is encrypted before it is sent
12     msgUserMan.UseEncryption = true;
13     // Create message body
14     msgUserMan.Body = "Message Body";
15
16     // Send message to queue
17     queUserMan.Send(msgUserMan);
18
19     // Retrieve message from queue
20     msgUserMan = queUserMan.Receive();
21     // Show decrypted message body
22     MessageBox.Show(msgUserMan.Body.ToString());
23 }
```

In Listing 8-36, I encrypt a message, send it to the queue, and receive it from the queue. During the transport to and from the queue, the message body is encrypted, but the message is automatically decrypted by the receiving **MessageQueue** object. This means decryption of an encrypted message is always performed automatically when the message is received.

Using Access Control

Controlling access to the message queue is probably the best way to secure your messages. As with most other Windows operations, such as creating new users, the reading and writing of messages can be access controlled. Access control happens when a user tries to perform an operation, such as reading a message from a queue. Each user under Windows NT, Windows 2000, and Windows XP Professional has an Access Control List (ACL), which contains all the operations the user can perform. The ACL is checked when the user tries to read a message. If the user has read access, the user can read the message from the queue. However, if the user isn't allowed to read from the queue, the read is disallowed.

Access control can be applied at the message queue level or even at the message level, but it can also be applied at the Message Queuing level, meaning that all message queues in the Active Directory will abide by the permissions you set. Take a look at Figure 8-8, where you can see the Access Control List for the UserMan user of the UserMan domain. The permissions shown are for the UserMan private message queue.

You can bring up the ACL by opening the Computer Management MMC snap-in, selecting the private UserMan queue, right-clicking the queue, and selecting Properties from the pop-up menu. This brings up the Properties dialog box, in which you must select the Security tab to get to the ACL (see Figure 8-8).

Figure 8-8. The User Properties dialog box with Security tab selected

As you can see from the ACL in Figure 8-8, there are permissions for just about anything you can do with the message queue, such as write, read, and peek at messages. Next to the operation there are two check boxes, one for allowing the operation and one for denying the operation. All you have to do is select the user or group you want to set the permissions for in the listbox in the top part of the dialog box. If the user or group isn't listed, you can add it by clicking the Add button. If you need to remove a user or group, you can click the Delete button.

You need to be careful when you set the permissions for groups especially, because as always with ACLs in Windows, the more restrictive permission takes precedence. For instance, if you set the Delete operation to Allow for the UserMan user and then set the same permission for the Everyone group to Deny, the UserMan user is denied the right to delete the message queue. All users in the domain are part of the Everyone group, so you need to be especially careful with this option. Setting group and user permissions is really outside the scope of this book, so if you need more information on how ACLs work and permissions are set with respect to users and groups, you should look in the documentation that comes with your Windows OS.

Using the SetPermissions Method

Instead of setting the user permissions from Computer Management, you can also perform this task programmatically using the **SetPermissions** method of your **MessageQueue** object. Listing 8-37 shows you how to do it.

Listing 8-37. Setting User Permissions Programmatically

```
1 public void SetUserPermissions() {
2     MessageQueue queUserMan = new MessageQueue(".\\Private$\\UserMan");
3     System.Messaging.Message msgUserMan = new System.Messaging.Message();
4     AccessControlList aclUserMan = new AccessControlList();
5
6     // Give UserMan user full control over private UserMan queue
7     queUserMan.SetPermissions("UserMan",
8         MessageQueueAccessRights.FullControl);
9     // Give UserMan user full control over private UserMan queue
10    queUserMan.SetPermissions(new
11        MessageQueueAccessControlEntry(new Trustee("UserMan"),
12        MessageQueueAccessRights.FullControl));
13    // Deny UserMan deleting the private UserMan queue
14    queUserMan.SetPermissions("UserMan", MessageQueueAccessRights.DeleteQueue,
15        AccessControlEntryType.Deny);
16    // Deny UserMan all access rights on the private UserMan queue
17    aclUserMan.Add(new AccessControlEntry(new Trustee("UserMan"),
18        GenericAccessRights.All, StandardAccessRights.All,
19        AccessControlEntryType.Deny));
20    queUserMan.SetPermissions(aclUserMan);
21 }
```

In Listing 8-37, I've used all four overloads of the **SetPermissions** method. The first two (Lines 7 and 8 and 10 through 12) take the name of the user or group and the rights to assign to this user or group. They're basically the same and can only be used to assign rights to a user or group, not revoke rights. Lines 7 and 8 show how to use a member of the **MessageQueueAccessRights** enum to specify the rights that are to be granted to the UserMan user, whereas Lines 10 through 12 show how to use a **MessageQueueAccessControlEntry** object. The next over-loaded version of the method (Line 14) can be used to allow, deny, revoke, or set a specific permission for a particular user or group. The last version of the method (Lines 17 through 19) can be used to allow, deny, revoke, or set generic and standard access rights for a user or group. Actually, the last overloads can be used for changing permissions for several users and/or groups in one go. You simply need to add as many Access Control Entries (ACE) as necessary to the ACL (Line 17) before you set the permission using the ACL (Line 20).

I have constructed the example code in Listing 8-36 only so you can see how all four of the overloaded versions of the **SetPermissions** method can be used. You shouldn't use them at the same time. If a conflict occurs between the rights you assign or revoke, only the last rights assigned or revoked will count, unless preceded by a complementary Deny rights setting.

Using Auditing

In the context of this chapter, auditing is used for logging access to a message queue. This allows you to check the Event Log to see who has been accessing it, or even better, who has been trying to access it and denied the access. Auditing really falls beyond the scope of this book, as it's a generic tool used for logging access to any kind of service or object in the Windows OS, so I'll only touch on it briefly here.

You can set up auditing from the Computer Management MMC snap-in. Select the message queue you want to audit, or indeed all of Message Queuing by selecting the node by this name. Right-click the selected node and select Properties from the pop-up menu. This brings up the Properties dialog box, in which you should select the Security tab. On the Security tab, click the Advanced button. This brings up the Access Control Settings dialog box. Select the Auditing tab to bring up the dialog box shown in Figure 8-9. Normally there are no auditing entries on the list, but in Figure 8-9, I have added an entry that logs when any user (Everyone group) fails to write a message to the message queue.

There are two types of audits: Success and Failure. Try playing around with these audits and don't forget to check the entries added to Event Log (the Application Log). You can view the Event Log using the Event Viewer.

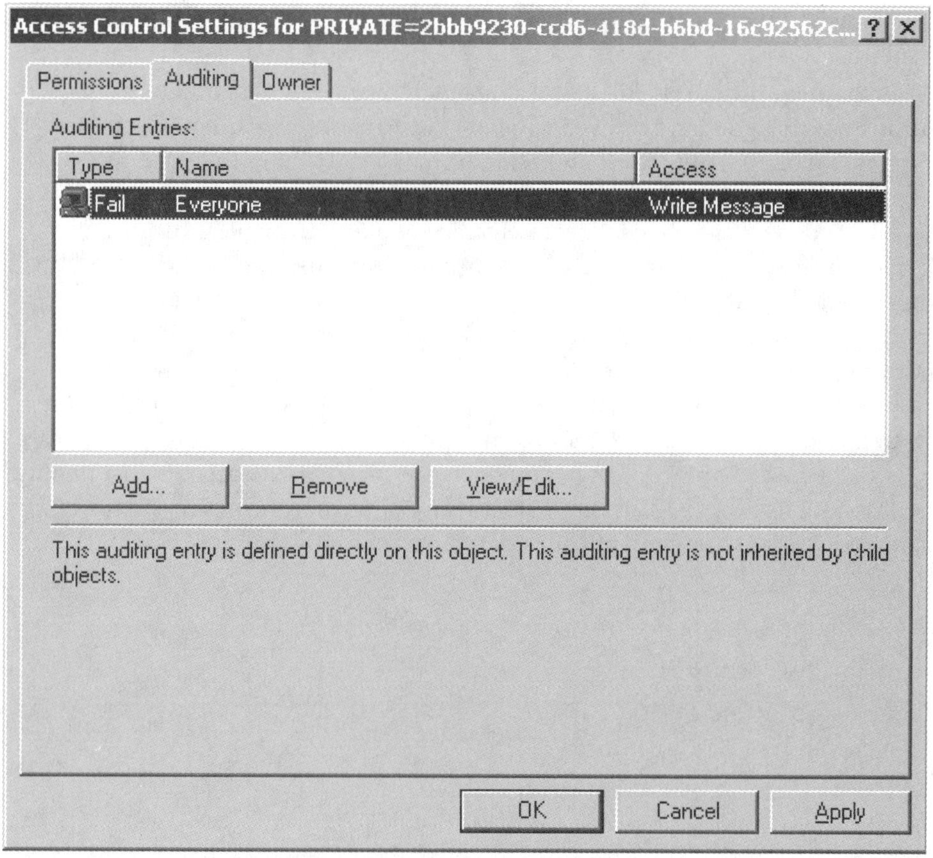

Figure 8-9. The Access Control Settings dialog box

If you want further information about auditing or Message Queuing security in general, I suggest you read the documentation for your Windows OS.

Summary

This chapter introduced you to the concept of connectionless programming using message queues. I showed you how to create message queues from the Server Explorer and the Computer Management MMC snap-in, and how to do it programmatically.

I discussed how you can locate message queues on the network; how message queues work with transactions; why you should use a message queue and not a database table; how the messages are ordered or sorted in a queue; and how you work with the various properties and methods of both the **MessageQueue** and **Message** classes.

In the last sections of this chapter, I introduced you to how you can secure your messaging.

In the next chapter, I'll show you how to wrap your data access functionality in classes. I'll cover OOP fundamentals such as polymorphism very briefly and show you how to use them in your UserMan application.

CHAPTER 9

Data Wrappers

Creating Classes (Wrappers) for Your Data Access

IN THIS CHAPTER, I WILL GO OVER how to wrap, or encapsulate, your data access in classes and components. You will see example code that covers some of the principles of Object Oriented Programming (OOP). *Wrapper* is generally a term used by programmers for the more proper term *class*. In the context of this book, a wrapper is a class. This chapter contains important information that I will use in Chapter 11 to finish the UserMan example application. You'll also find hands-on exercises in this chapter that will take you through creating a database project, and adding scripts, queries, and command files.

Why Use Data Wrappers?

There are a number of reasons for using data wrappers and classes or components in general. Wrapping your data access in a class can prevent direct access to your data. You can set up permissions on the data so that it can be accessed only by an administrator or by your component. This gives you much better control over how the data is accessed and helps prevent potential tampering with your data.

Wrapping the data access in a component allows you to place the component where it is most appropriate in your network. By most appropriate, I mean the place on the network where the component is easy to access for the clients, easy for you to update, and the workload resulting from clients using the component is proficiently handled. This obviously involves how you are distributing your application and what kind of application model you are using—client-server, n-tier, and so on.

Looking at Object Oriented Programming

In this section, I will cover some of the basic principles of OOP. This is only a short introduction, and if you are completely new to OOP, I suggest you do some reading in order to fully exploit the potential of C#. Suggested reading includes the following titles:

- *A Programmer's Introduction to C#, Second Edition*, by Eric Gunnerson. Published by Apress, June 2001. ISBN: 1893115623.

- *C# and the .NET Platform*, by Andrew Troelsen. Published by Apress, June 2001. ISBN: 1893115593.

- *Programming C#*, by Gary Cornell. Apress, anticipated publication date is April 2002. ISBN: 1590590007. Chapters 3 through 5 in this book discuss OOP.

I will compare OOP to general programming guidelines and show you how you can apply OOP to the UserMan example application. This chapter is therefore a brief OOP introduction and in preparation for Chapter 11; the principles discussed in this chapter will be applied to the completion of the example application.

Okay, so let's have a look at the basic principles in OOP: polymorphism, inheritance, and encapsulation.

Polymorphism

Polymorphism, which is also called *many forms,* is the ability to call a particular method on an object instantiated from any class that is derived from a base class, without knowing which class the object was instantiated from.

Let me illustrate this using the standard **Object** class that is part of the Framework base classes. All other classes in the Framework are derived from this class, and they all expose the **ToString** method. This method simply returns a **String** representation of the instantiated object. The idea is that you can always call the **ToString** method on an object to get the **String** representation without really knowing what subclass your object is derived from.

This means classes that inherit from another class should expose the same properties and methods as the base class, which makes it easy for a programmer to use standard methods and properties on any of your objects.

You can extend the inherited methods and properties if they can be overridden, which means that you don't have to expose the functionality of the base class. (Inheritance is discussed in the next section.)

My explanation is very simply put, but essentially this is what polymorphism is. See the section "C# Keywords Related to OOP" later in this chapter for more information on how polymorphism is implemented in C#.

Inheritance

Inheritance is the ability for a class to be derived from another class, or as the name inheritance suggests, inherit the characteristics of another class. You will encounter words such as *superclass* or *base class* to describe the class that is inherited from, and *subclass* or *derived class* for the class that inherits from another class.

There is support for two types of inheritance in C#: *interface inheritance* and *implementation inheritance*.

Interface and Implementation Inheritance

Interface inheritance is also called *Has a . . .* inheritance, whereas implementation inheritance is often called *Is a . . .* inheritance.

Interface Inheritance

An *interface* is a set of related public methods, properties, events, and indexers that the inheriting class must implement. An interface is a contract, so if you choose to implement an interface in your class, you are bound by the contract offered by the interface. This means you must implement all the methods and such specified in the interface. Please note that a class can implement any number of interfaces.

An interface doesn't include any implementation, which means that you cannot directly instantiate an interface. Instead, an interface must be implemented by a class, and it is this class you can instantiate. An interface is an abstract data type, and it provides for a very loose coupling between the interface and the classes that implement it. See Listing 9-1 for an example of how to implement interface inheritance.

> **NOTE** *It might be easier for you to see all the class files in the various projects in this chapter, and the classes and interfaces they contain, if you switch to Class View in Solution Explorer. To do so, press Ctrl+Shift+C or select the View ➤ Class View menu command.*

Listing 9-1. Creating and Implementing an Interface

```
1 public interface IUserMan {
2     string TestProperty{
3        get;
4        set;
5     }
6
7     void TestMethod();
8 }
9
10 public class CUserMan : IUserMan {
11
12    private string prstrUserName;
13
14    // This is where the TestProperty method
15    // of the IUserMan interface is being
16    // defined as an explicit member
17    // implementation (UserName)
18    string IUserMan.TestProperty {
19       get {
20          return UserName;
21       }
22       set {
23          UserName= value;
24       }
25    }
26
27    // This is the explicit interface
28    // member implementation of TestProperty
29    public string UserName {
30       get {
31          return prstrUserName;
32       }
33       set {
34          prstrUserName = value;
35       }
36    }
37
38    // This is where the TestMethod method
39    // of the IUserMan interface is being
40    // defined as an explicit member
41    // implementation (CalculateOnTime)
42    void IUserMan.TestMethod() {
```

```
43       CalculateOnTime();
44     }
45
46     // This is the explicit interface
47     // member implementation of TestMethod
48     public void CalculateOnTime() {
49     }
50 }
51 public void CreateUserManObject() {
52     CUserMan objUserMan = new CUserMan();
53 }
```

In Listing 9-1, I have created the IUserMan interface, which defines the TestProperty property and the TestMethod method. In the CUserMan class (Lines 10 through 50), I have implemented the IUserMan interface (using the colon [:] on Line 10). As you can see from the code, it is necessary to implement public signatures (methods, properties, events, and indexers) in the class that implements the interface, but you are not required to keep the names of the signatures. See Lines 20, 23, and 43, where I specify what signature in the interface is being implemented by the property and method.

I, then, create a procedure that creates an instance of the class that implements the interface (Lines 51 through 53). This is the *only* way to instantiate an interface, so to speak.

Implementation Inheritance

Implementation inheritance should be used when you can use the *Is a . . .* phrase to refer to a subclass or derived class. By this, I mean the subclass is a superclass or that the subclass is of the same type as the superclass. For example, say you have a superclass called CBird and subclasses called CHawk and CPigeon. It's obvious that the hawk and the pigeon are of type bird. That's what the *Is a . . .* phrase indicates.

Implementation inheritance is especially great when a lot of functionality can be put into the base class, which in turn allows the derived classes to inherit this functionality without extending it. Not that you can't extend the code in the base class, but if you find you're extending most of the code from the base class, is implementation inheritance really what you need? Would interface inheritance not be better? Actually, it's not always so easy to make this choice. Keep the *Is a . . .* phrase in mind when considering implementation inheritance. It might just make your decision a little bit easier.

The obvious advantage implementation inheritance has over interface inheritance is that you avoid potential duplication of code by placing all your standard code in the superclass.

Implementation inheritance results in tight coupling between the superclass and the subclass. See Listings 9-4 and 9-5 later in this chapter for examples of how implementation inheritance can be used.

Encapsulation

The term *encapsulation* has been used and abused over the years. You might get many different definitions if you ask different people about this OOP term. I will try to give you a brief explanation of encapsulation and how it is implemented and used in C#.

Encapsulation, also called *information hiding*, is the ability to hide your code or implementation from the user of your class. This means that when you create your classes, you expose some public properties and methods, but your code decides how your private variables and such are manipulated. If you look at Listing 9-5 later in the chapter, you will see I have declared the private **string** variable prstrTest on Line 2; because this variable is declared private, it cannot be accessed directly from a user of your class. Instead, I have created the Test property, which provides access to the variable. I haven't actually implemented any checking of the value passed when setting the property, but this is generally the idea of encapsulation: no direct access to private members, only through exposed methods or properties for which you can validate the input. See Listing 9-2 for an example that validates the passed argument in the property **Set** procedure.

*Listing 9-2. Validating the Argument of a Property **Set** Procedure*

```
1 set {
2     // Check if the string contains any invalid chars
3     if ((value.IndexOf("@") == -1)) {
4         prstrTest = value;
5     }
6 }
```

C# Keywords Related to OOP

In C#, a few keywords are related to OOP, either directly or indirectly. These keywords are as follows:

- *abstract*: Any class that is marked with **abstract** can only act as a base class, and it cannot be instantiated. If you try to instantiate such a class using the **new** operator, a compile-time exception is thrown. **abstract** cannot be used for declaring methods or properties in a class. See Listing 9-3 for an example of how *not* to use this method and Listing 9-4 for an example that shows the right way. A property or method marked with this keyword *must* be overridden in a derived, nonabstract class. If you only want to give the programmer deriving your class the option of overriding the method or property, you must use the **virtual** keyword in your declaration.

- *virtual:* A property or method marked with this keyword can be overridden in a derived class. It does not mean you have to override it, however. If you want to make sure it is overridden in a derived class, you must use the **abstract** keyword in your declaration. See Listing 9-5 for how to override a property in a derived class.

- *sealed:* If you mark a property or method with this keyword, you are explicitly telling the deriving class that the method or property cannot be overridden.

- *override:* The method or property marked with this keyword overrides the method or property in the base class with the same name. See Listing 9-5 for how to override a property in a derived class.

- *interface:* The **interface** keyword is used for specifying an interface. See Listing 9-1 earlier for an example that uses the **interface** keyword.

*Listing 9-3. An **abstract** Class That Can't Be Instantiated*

```
1 public abstract class CAbstract {
2     private string prstrTest;
3
4     public string Test {
5         get {
6             return prstrTest;
7         }
8
9         set {
10             prstrTest = value;
11         }
12     }
13 }
14
15 public void InstantiateAbstractClass() {
16   CAbstract objAbstract = new CAbstract();
17 }
```

In Listing 9-3, the CAbstract class has been declared with the **abstract** key-word, which means that an instance of the class can only be instantiated if it's inherited by another class. This means Line 16 will throw an exception at compile time because the syntax is wrong. However, if you do as in Listing 9-4, where I have wrapped the CAbstract class in the CWrapper class, you can inherit from and instantiate the CWrapper class as shown on Line 7.

*Listing 9-4. An **abstract** Class That Can Be Instantiated*

```
1 public class CWrapper : CAbstract {
2    // Place your other code here
3 }
4
5 public void InstantiateAbstractClassWrapper() {
6    CWrapper objAbstract = new CWrapper();
7 }
```

In Listing 9-5, two classes have been declared: CVirtual and CWrapper. CVirtual is the base class from which CWrapper inherits.

Listing 9-5. Overriding a Property in a Derived Class

```
1 public class CVirtual {
2    private string prstrTest;
3
4    public virtual string Test {
5       get {
6          return prstrTest;
7       }
8
9       set {
10          prstrTest = value;
11       }
12    }
13 }
14 public class CWrapper : CVirtual {
15
16    private string prstrTest;
17
18    public override string Test {
19       get {
20          return prstrTest + "Overridden";
21       }
22
23       set {
```

```
24          prstrTest = value;
25      }
26   }
27 }
```

On Line 4, the Test property is declared as virtual (can be overridden), and in the derived class on Line 18 this property has indeed been overridden using the **override** keyword. The **override** keyword is always necessary when you're overriding a method or property—it doesn't matter if the property or method is declared using either the **abstract** or **virtual** keyword.

Wrapping a Database

Now that some of the initial details are out of the way, let's take a look at what to wrap and how in a database. If you've familiarized yourself with the database concepts in Chapter 2, you will be well off when I enter the analysis and design stage. Basically, wrapping your database access is like grouping your data in related tables. Actually, since you've already broken down your data into tables, you've more or less found a way of defining your classes and wrappers.

Having a class for each table in your database is often the most satisfying solution from a maintenance viewpoint and in regard to the users of your classes and/or components. Now that I mention components, I also have to add that one class doesn't necessarily constitute one component. Quite often you'll have more than one class in your component, but that depends on how you decide to distribute your business and data services.

Okay, so what needs to happen here? Classes and possibly components that hold the classes first need to be created. Because this book is strictly about data manipulation, I won't cover business services, only data services. If you look at the schema for the UserMan database (see Figure 2-10 in Chapter 2), you'll see the following tables: tblLog, tblRights, tblUser, and tblUserRights.

To follow my own advice, I need to create a class for each of these tables; for the purpose of showing you the what and how, I'm just going to create the CUser class.

Creating the CUser Class

The tblUser table has the following columns: Id, ADName, ADSID, FirstName, LastName, LoginName, and Password.

What I need to do now is find out what columns I'll have to expose from the class, and if the column is exposed, whether it will be read-write, read-only, or write-only access. See Table 9-1 for a list of columns, data types, and access types.

Table 9-1. The tblUser Columns

COLUMN NAME	DATA TYPE	NULLABLE	ACCESS TYPE	DESCRIPTION
Id	int	No	Read-only	This is the ID used for looking up values in related tables. This is an IDENTITY column, so you'll never have to set the value for it.
ADName	varchar	Yes	Read-write	This is the Active Directory name for the user, if he or she is a member of the Active Directory.
ADSID	varchar	Yes	Read-write	This is the Active Directory security identifier (SID) for the user, if he or she is a member of the Active Directory.
FirstName	varchar	Yes	Read-write	This is the user's first, or given, name.
LastName	varchar	Yes	Read-write	This is the user's last name, or surname.
LoginName	varchar	No	Read-write	This is the user's login name, which he or she must use in conjunction with the password when logging onto the system.
Password	varchar	No	Read-write	This is the user's password, which he or she must use in conjunction with the login name when logging onto the system.

Now, if you look at Table 9-1, there are a couple of columns for which the access type can be discussed in further detail. ADName and ADSID can change depending on the AD connected, but why do I want the user of the class to be able to do this? First of all, I need to make sure that it's possible to set these values. Who's allowed to do it will be taken care of from the application.

Next, a new Class Library project needs to be created and a new class added to it that holds the methods, properties, and so on of the CUser class.

EXERCISE

Create a new Class Library project called UserMan and rename the existing class (Class1) CUser. Open the CUser class and change the class name to CUser as well.

It's time to add private variables, methods, and properties that can handle access to the database table. For all the columns, it's best to create properties, because all they do is read or write a value. Before creating the properties, it's a good idea to create private variables that hold the values in order to avoid having to access the database every time a variable is read. See Listing 9-6 for some example code that creates private variables to hold the user values from the database table.

Add a private variable to the CUser class for every column in the tblUser table. See Listing 9-6 for an example.

Listing 9-6. Creating Private Variables to Hold the User Values

```
1 private long prlngId;
2 private string prstrADName;
3 private string prstrADSID;
4 private string prstrFirstName;
5 private string prstrLastName;
6 private string prstrLoginName;
7 private string prstrPassword;
```

Listing 9-6 is simply a list of private variables that correspond directly to the columns in the tblUser table. Now properties need to be added to set and retrieve the values from the variables. See Listing 9-7 for an example of the **Id** property.

*Listing 9-7. The Read-Only **Id** Property*

```
public long Id {
    get {
        return prlngId;
    }
}
```

Add properties for all the columns in the tblUser table to the CUser class. See Listings 9-7 and 9-8 for examples.

*Listing 9-8. The Read-Write **ADName** Property*

```
1 public string ADName {
2    get {
3        return prstrADName;
4    }
5    set {
6        prstrADName = value;
7    }
8 }
```

Listing 9-8 shows you how the ADName column in the database table can be accessed using a property. This is not quite true, because only a private variable is being accessed. However, the code for accessing the database table and Active Directory will be added in Chapter 11.

All the properties of data type **string** can be set to a maximum length in the database, so it's a good idea to add a check if the passed string is shorter than or equal to this length. This also means that you need to hold the maximum length values in private variables, as in Listing 9-9.

EXERCISE

Add a private variable to the CUser class for every column in the tblUser table that has a maximum length. See Listing 9-9 for an example.

Listing 9-9. Creating Private Variables to Hold the Maximum Length of Table Columns

```
1 // User table column max lengths
2 private int printADNameMaxLen;
3 private int printADSIDMaxLen;
4 private int printFirstNameMaxLen;
5 private int printLastNameMaxLen;
6 private int printLoginNameMaxLen;
7 private int printPasswordMaxLen;
```

I now need to create the length check for the property **set** procedures. This can be done as shown in Listing 9-10.

Add a check of the length of the passed argument in the property **set** procedures. Keep in mind only those procedures set a variable that corresponds to a column in the database table with a maximum length. See Listing 9-10 for example code.

*Listing 9-10. Creating Maximum Length Checks of Property **set** Arguments*

```
 1 public string ADName {
 2    get {
 3        return prstrADName;
 4    }
 5    set {
 6        if (value.Length <= printADNameMaxLen) {
 7            prstrADName = value;
 8        }
 9        else {
10            prstrADName = value.Substring(0, printADNameMaxLen);
11        }
12    }
13 }
```

In Listing 9-10, I check if the length of the passed argument is shorter than or equal to the maximum length of the table column by comparing the length with the value of the private variable `printADNameMaxLen`. If it is shorter, the value is stored, and if not, the first `printADNameMaxLen` number of characters from the `vstrADName` string are stored. I suppose you could throw an exception here, but is it really that bad to pass a string with too many characters? The reason I need to perform this check is that if I try to pass a string that is too long to the database, an exception will be thrown. All right, this check can certainly be done in different ways, and I'm sure you know one or two other ways you might normally use, but this is merely to demonstrate how you can build up your properties.

Add a check on the `LoginName` property to make sure that the login name doesn't contain any spaces. See Listing 9-11 for example code.

Listing 9-11. Checking for Spaces When Setting LoginName

```
1 public string LoginName {
2    get {
3        return prstrLoginName;
4    }
5    set {
6        // Check if the string contains any spaces
7        if ((value.IndexOf(" ") == -1)) {
8            if (value.Length <= printLoginNameMaxLen) {
9                prstrLoginName = value;
10           }
11           else {
12               prstrLoginName = value.Substring(0, printLoginNameMaxLen);
13           }
14       }
15   }
16 }
```

In Listing 9-11, I use the **IndexOf** method of the **string** class to check the passed value for spaces in the LoginName property. You can choose to ignore it when the LoginName does contain spaces, but that just isn't a very elegant solution. See the "Adding Events" section later in this chapter for ideas on how to handle cases where the LoginName does contain spaces.

Adding a Constructor and a Destructor

You need a constructor and a destructor in any class you create to instantiate and destroy your class. However, when you base your class on the standard **object** class, which ultimately all classes created with the .NET Framework do, you don't have to create the procedures yourself; it's all done for you behind the scenes. If you look at the CUser class that you created earlier, the constructor is already part of your code. Listing 9-12 presents the default class constructor.

Listing 9-12. The Default Class Constructor

```
1 public CUser() {
2    //
4    // TODO: Add constructor logic here
5    //
6 }
```

Listing 9-12 shows you the default constructor that is created for you when you create a new class. In C#, the constructor has the same name as the class—CUser in this case. The destructor isn't automatically created for you in your code, but you can create one yourself. Listing 9-13 shows how simple a default destructor looks.

Listing 9-13. The Default Class Destructor

```
1 ~CUser() {
2 }
```

Listing 9-13 shows you the default class destructor and as is the case with the constructor, it has the same name as your class. You put a tilde (~) character in front of the class name and you have a class destructor. You can't change the accessibility of the destructor and put the **public** keyword in front of it as with the constructor.

The example code in Listings 9-12 and 9-13 doesn't really do anything, but don't let that fool you. The constructor and destructor of the **object** base class are actually called even if it hasn't been specified. The only reason for adding code to the constructor and destructors of your class is if you need to create objects that must be kept alive for the duration of your class. One such object can be a connection to your database. I'm not telling you to implement it this way, but I'm trying to give you an idea of what you can use the constructors and destructors for. Another purpose is to read some initialization values from a file or perhaps the Windows Registry, or when you want to pass one or more values to the class for initialization (see from Line 14 in Listing 9-14). I'm sure you get the idea: put code in the constructor that needs to run before an instance of your class is fully instantiated and make sure you close and destroy any files and/or objects references you've been using in the destructor. One purpose is to close or destroy a connection to your database, if you're not doing this elsewhere, because you need to explicitly close an open connection in order for it to be returned to the connection pool, and to make sure the connection isn't kept alive and thus run the risk of causing memory leaks. The connection might be kept alive because the garbage collector doesn't destroy it, even if there are no references to it! See the "Pooling Connections" section in Chapter 3A for more information.

Adding Events

Sometimes it's preferable to use events rather than to raise exceptions for minor errors in your classes. Events are messages sent to an instance of a class in response to certain action(s). In Listing 9-11, you check the value passed to the LoginName property **set**, but you don't do anything if the value contains spaces.

You can choose to ignore it, but that's really no good. You can also raise an exception using the **throw** statement, perhaps even your custom exception. See the "Creating Your Own Exception" and "Throwing an Exception" sections in Chapter 5 for more information on creating exception classes and throwing exceptions.

Your third option is to create and raise events in your class, as follows:

1. Create an event class that defines the data for the event (see Listing 9-14).

2. Declare an event delegate (see Listing 9-15).

3. Declare an event and a method that raises the event (see Listing 9-16).

Well, you don't have to follow every step in these instructions, because you don't really have to create an event class, but see the documentation if you need more information on events and delegates, or even better, check out the books I mentioned at the beginning of this chapter.

Listing 9-14. An Error Event Class

```
1  public class CErrorEventArgs : EventArgs {
2     public enum ErrorStatusEnum : int {
3        NoError = 0,
4        ServerDown = 1,
5        TimeOut = 2,
6        InvalidLoginName = 3
7     }
8
9     private ErrorStatusEnum printErrorStatus = ErrorStatusEnum.NoError;
10    private string prstrErrorMessage;
11
12    // Class constructor
13    public CErrorEvent(ErrorStatusEnum enuErrorStatus) {
14       // Save the error status
15       printErrorStatus = enuErrorStatus;
16       // Set the error message
17       switch (printErrorStatus) {
18          case ErrorStatusEnum.NoError :
19             prstrErrorMessage = "No error";
20             break;
21          case ErrorStatusEnum.InvalidLoginName :
22             prstrErrorMessage =
23               "There are invalid characters in the LoginName!";
24             break;
```

```
25              case ErrorStatusEnum.ServerDown :
26                  prstrErrorMessage =
27                   "The database server is currently unavailable!";
28                  break;
29              case ErrorStatusEnum.TimeOut :
30                  prstrErrorMessage =
31                   "A timeout connecting to the server has occurred!";
32                  break;
33              default :
34                  prstrErrorMessage = "Unknown Error!";
35                  break;
36          }
37      }
38
39      // Returns the error status
40      public ErrorStatusEnum Status {
41          get {
42              return printErrorStatus;
43          }
44      }
45
46      // Returns the error message
47      public string Message {
48          get {
49              return prstrErrorMessage;
50          }
51      }
52 }
```

In Listing 9-14, I've created the CErrorEventArgs class that is used for defining event data, or rather error data in this case. First, I created a public enum (ErrorStatusEnum) on Lines 2 through 7, which is used for instantiating the class. This enum's purpose is to hold all the possible error numbers you can think of, but I've supplied a few for you to see. The InvalidLoginName member is the one I will show in detail. I've also created two private variables, printErrorStatus and prstrErrorMessage, on Lines 9 and 10 that hold the internal values for the two read-only properties Status (Lines 40 through 44) and Message (Lines 47 through 51). The constructor (Lines 13 through 37) takes one argument, a member of the ErrorStatusEnum enum. In the constructor, the passed value is saved and the message text is determined from the error status in the switch construct on Lines 17 through 36.

> **NOTE** *It's generally a good idea to use enums for passing arguments to methods and properties if possible. You can only use integer values in enums and enums are really only good in situations where you know a variable or the like can only hold a certain subrange of values, such as 1 to 25. Using enums helps you eliminate possible errors in passed argument values because when an argument is specified as of type enum (Line 13) you can only pass a member of that enum.*

In Listing 9-15, I declare the `ErrorEventHandler` delegate, which is to be used for hooking up error events in the `CUser` class. This declaration can't be made within a class, but must be made in a namespace. In the `CUser` class, you now need to declare the event and a method that raises the event, as in Listing 9-16.

Listing 9-15. Declaring an Event Delegate
```
1 // Declare delegate for hooking up error notifications
2 public delegate void ErrorEventHandler(object sender, CErrorEventArgs e);
```

Listing 9-16. Declaring the Event and the Method Raising the Event
```
1 public event ErrorEventHandler Error;
2
3 protected virtual void OnError(CErrorEventArgs e) {
4     // Check if the event has been delegated
5     if (Error != null) {
6         // Invoke the delegate
7         Error(this, e);
8     }
9 }
```

In Listing 9-16, I've declared the event `Error` as of delegate type `ErrorEventHandler` created in Listing 9-15. Lines 3 through 9 of Listing 9-16 are the actual method that raises the event. This method must have the same name as the declared event (`Error`) prefixed with `On`, making the method name `OnError` in this case. On Line 5, there's a check to see if the event has been delegated, and if it has it's invoked, meaning the event is triggered.

All you need to do now is to hook the event with a method with the same signature as the event delegate shown in Listing 9-15. Listing 9-17 shows you a very simple method that displays the value of the **Message** property in a message box.

Listing 9-17. Method That Receives the Event

```
1 public void ErrorEvent(object sender, CErrorEventArgs e) {
2    MessageBox.Show(e.Message);
3 }
```

Listing 9-17 shows the ErrorEvent procedure or method that has the same signature as the event delegate. Now you need to hook the Error event of the CUser class with the ErrorEvent procedure in Listing 9-17. You can see how in Listing 9-18.

Listing 9-18. Hook the Event Receiver with the Event

```
1 // Declare user object
2 CUser objUser = new CUser();
3
4 // Hook the event with a method
5 objUser.Error += new ErrorEventHandler(Error);
6
7 // Set the LoginName
8 objUser.LoginName = "dfhg ljlkj";
```

In Listing 9-18, I declare the objUser object as of type CUser, and I then hook the Error event of the CUser class with the ErrorEvent procedure/method shown in Listing 9-17. Line 8 is where I want to trigger the event by setting the LoginName property to an invalid value.

Great, now your CUser class can throw errors using the protected OnError method shown in Listing 9-16. I show you the modification to the LoginName **set** property in Listing 9-19.

Listing 9-19. Trigger the Invalid LoginName Error Event

```
11      else {
12          // Instantiates the event source
13          CErrorEventArgs objErrorEvent = new CErrorEventArgs(
14              CErrorEventArgs.ErrorStatusEnum.InvalidLoginName);
15          // Triggers the error event
16          OnError(objErrorEvent);
17      }
```

In Listing 9-19, you can see how you can modify the LoginName **set** property procedure of the CUser class when checking for invalid characters in the passed LoginName value. First you create an instance of the CErrorEventArgs class with the error event you want to trigger (ErrorStatusEnum.InvalidLoginName), and then you trigger the event by calling the protected OnError method with your instance of the CErrorEventArgs class. I'm sure you can see how the error event can easily be used in other parts of the user class. Check out the accompanying example code to see the full event example shown in the previous listings.

The CUser class isn't finished yet—a lot more code needs to be added to it, such as data-aware classes (for example, connections and commands), but I'm sure you get the idea of how to create wrappers for all your data access. I'll give you more ideas and hints in Chapter 11, when I finish the UserMan example application.

Summary

This chapter took you on a short journey through OOP and how to apply OOP to your data access code. The three main concepts of OOP were discussed: polymorphism, inheritance, and encapsulation. With regards to inheritance, I briefly outlined the differences between interface and implementation inheritance.

I also went over how to wrap your data access code in classes in the context of creating a class for accessing the tblUser database table in the UserMan example application, including constructor, destructor, events, and delegates. This work will be finished in Chapter 11.

The next chapter covers creating and using data-bound controls in Web Forms and Windows Forms.

CHAPTER 10

Data-Bound Controls

Creating and Working
with Data-Bound Controls

IN THIS CHAPTER, I'LL DISCUSS data-bound controls and why they're so popular with some developers and extremely unpopular with others. I'll explore how to use some of the data-bound controls that come with Visual Studio .NET. I'll also show you how to create your own data-bound controls. Keep an eye out for the hands-on exercises that appear throughout this chapter.

Data-Bound Controls vs. Manual Data Hooking

A *data-bound control,* such as a list box, a grid, or a text box, is a control that's hooked up to a data source. This means the developer doesn't have to take care of updating the control when the underlying data changes or updating the data source when user input has changed the data in the control. Data-bound controls are there to make your life as a developer easier.

Manual data hooking is an alternative to data-bound controls that has always been around. *Manual data hooking* describes the process by which you as a developer retrieve values from a data source and display them in one or more UI controls. However, when Visual Basic[1] started shipping with controls that were data bound, the developer community suddenly had an extra tool to use for displaying and manipulating data.

I think that data-bound controls are a great idea, because they save you from having to develop lots of code that otherwise takes care of the manual data hooking. With manual data hooking you have full control over how the data is handled, whereas data-bound controls often severely limit your ability to intervene and manipulate the data before it's displayed or written back to the data source. This has been an annoying extra "feature" of data-bound

---

1. Visual Basic 3.0 was the first major programming language to introduce data-bound controls.

controls for a long time, and I bet you know someone who tells you *not* to use data-bound controls because of this drawback. I've been using data-bound controls mainly for display purposes or read-only data, because I then don't have to worry about problems with updating the data source once the user changes the displayed data.

Traditionally, all data-bound controls were bound to a single data control that took care of the binding to the data source, as shown in Figure 10-1.

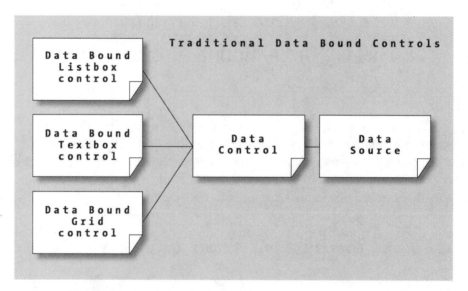

Figure 10-1. Traditional data-bound controls

In Figure 10-1, you can see how the data control takes care of the communication between the data source and the data-bound controls. This effectively means that you as a programmer don't have control over the way data is transferred from the data source to the bound controls and back again. The data control encapsulates all this for you, but it leaves you with very few options regarding how the data source is updated.

Different Controls for Different UIs

Visual Studio .NET supports several UIs, and they each require different controls. The Web and Windows are two of the UIs that VS .NET supports. For example, if you look at the Toolbox in the IDE, you can see different tabs of controls for different purposes. If you display the Toolbox in your IDE and look at the Windows Forms tab and the Web Forms tab, many of the controls are named the same.

This doesn't mean they're the same controls—on the contrary, they aren't. However, they do serve a similar purpose. Read on to find out more about the important distinctions.

Using Data-Bound Controls with Windows Forms

Data binding in Windows forms requires a data provider and a data consumer. The data provider is not just a so-called traditional data source, such as a database table. In fact, data binding on Windows forms can be much more than that. It can involve a collection or an array and any of the data structures from ADO.NET. These data structures include the DataReader and **DataSet** classes. I'll cover data binding with the ADO.NET data structures in this section.

> **CROSS-REFERENCE**   *See Chapters 3A and 3B for more information on the DataReader and **DataSet** data structures.*

All Windows forms have a **BindingContext** object. When you bind a control on a Windows form to a data structure, this control will have an associated **CurrencyManager** object. The **CurrencyManager** object handles the communication with the data structure and is responsible for keeping the data-bound controls synchronized. All controls bound to a currency manager display data from the same row at the same time, and one Windows form can have more than one currency manager. This happens when the Windows form has more than one data source, because the form maintains one currency manager for each data source associated with the form.

Another important aspect of the currency manager is its ability to know the current position in the data source. You can read the position using the **Position** property of the **CurrencyManager** class. This is especially useful with ADO.NET data structures, such as the **DataTable** class, because they don't provide cursor functionality—that is, you can't retrieve a cursor or pointer to the current row. However, this can be achieved with the currency manager. You'll see how the **CurrencyManager** object is used in the section "Looking at the Code Created by the Data Form Wizard" later in this chapter.

Examining the Binding Context

The *binding context* keeps track of all the currency managers on a Windows form. Even if there aren't any currency managers and data sources, your Windows form will always have a **BindingContext** object associated with it. As a matter of fact, this is true for all classes derived from the **Control** class, which is also part of the **System.Windows.Forms** namespace.

It's the binding context with which the data-bound control communicates. The binding context talks to the currency manager, which in turn talks to the data source, as shown in Figure 10-2. I'll show you how the **BindingContext** object is used in code in the section "Looking at the Code Created by the Data Form Wizard" later in this chapter.

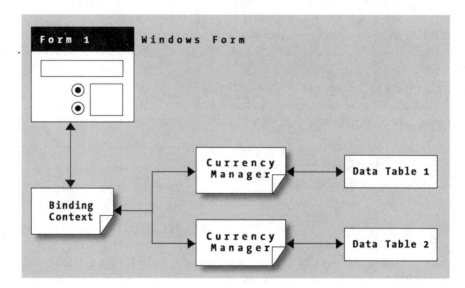

Figure 10-2. How data-bound controls communicate with the data source

Creating a Form Using the Data Form Wizard

Instead of doing all the hard work yourself, you can let the Data Form Wizard create your form with one or more data-bound controls. I'll take you through this process because it will help you understand how controls are bound to data in Windows forms. Here's how to create a new form:

1. Add a new item to your project and make sure you select the Data Form Wizard template.

2. Give the new form a name. This brings up the Data Form Wizard. Click Next.

3. The "Choose the dataset you want to use" dialog box appears (see Figure 10-3). Select the "Create a new dataset named" option if you want to create a new data set, and type the name of the data set in the text box. Or select the "Use the following dataset" option and choose an existing data set from the drop-down list box. (This option is only available if you already have a data set in your project.) Click Next.

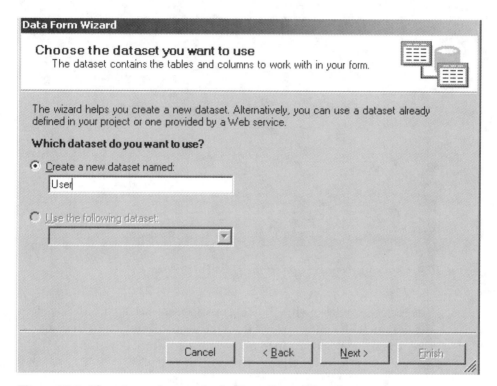

Figure 10-3. Choosing a data set in the Data Form Wizard

4. The "Choose a data connection" dialog box appears (see Figure 10-4). Select the desired database connection in the "Which connection should the wizard use?" drop-down list box. Click Next. You might be prompted for a password depending on how the connection has been set up.

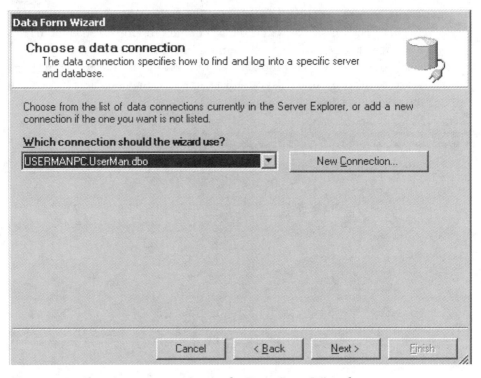

Figure 10-4. Choosing a connection in the Data Form Wizard

5. The "Choose tables or views" dialog box appears (see Figure 10-5). Select the desired tables and/or views from the Available item(s) tree view. Click the right arrow button to make your selections. Click Next.

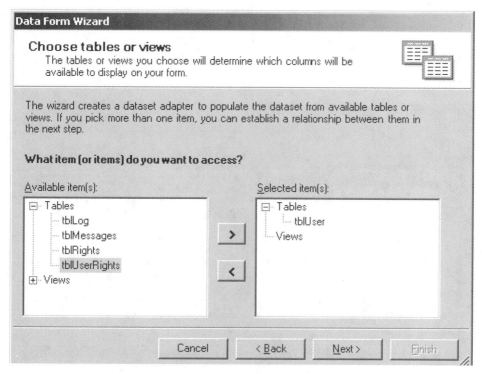

Figure 10-5. Choosing tables and views in the Data Form Wizard

6. The "Choose tables and columns to display on the form" dialog box appears (see Figure 10-6). Select a table from the "Master or single table" drop-down list box. If you only want data from one table in your form, this is all you need to do. If you want to create a master detail form, you must also select a table in the Detail table drop-down list box.

7. Check the columns you want displayed on your form in the Columns list boxes. (The right-hand Columns list box will be activated only if you selected a table from the Detail table drop-down list.) Click Next.

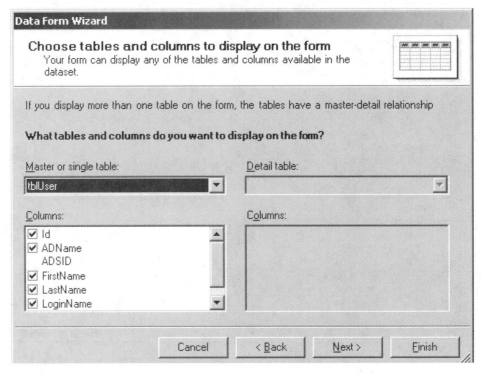

Figure 10-6. Choosing tables and columns in the Data Form Wizard

8. The "Choose the display style" dialog box appears (see Figure 10-7). Select the "All records in a grid" option if you want your data displayed in a grid. Select the "Single record in individual controls" option if you want to be able to navigate and manipulate the data. Check or uncheck the Cancel All check box depending on whether or not you want the form generated with a button to cancel all changes made.

9. Click Finish.

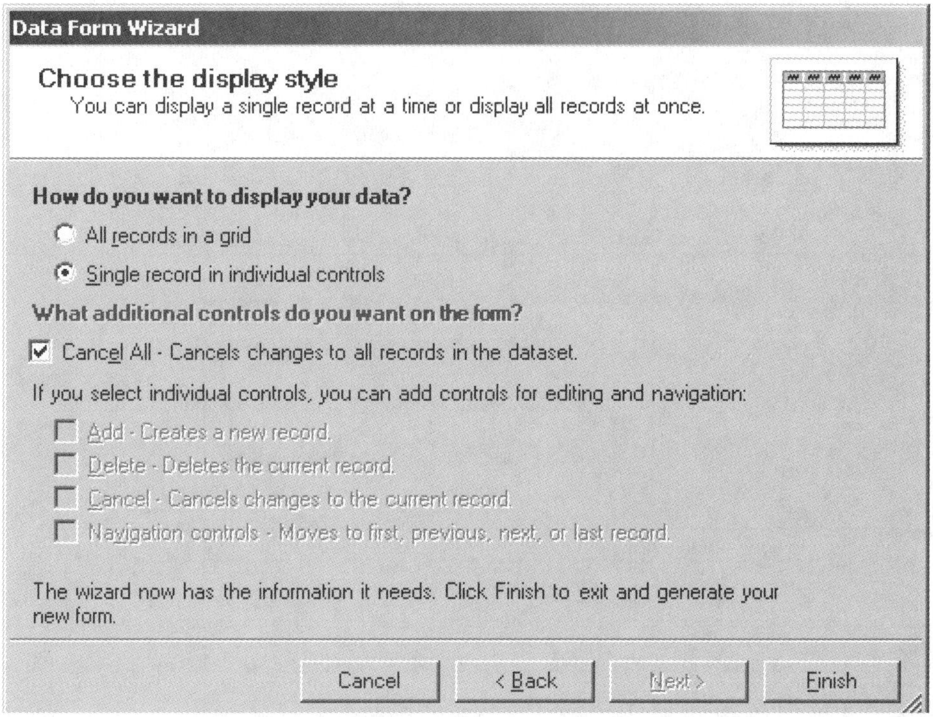

Figure 10-7. Choosing how to display the data in the Data Form Wizard

The data form will now be created and shown in the IDE. If you followed the figures when creating your form, you'll see at the bottom of Figure 10-8 that the wizard creates the objUser data set, the OleDbConnection1 connection, and the OleDbDataAdapter1 data adapter. These objects are only for use by the new form. If you open the code behind file (.cs), you will see how all the code is at your mercy. You can change it to your liking, because it's all there. This is definitely different from the way it was done in versions of Visual Basic[2] prior to VB .NET. You can see how the wizard has created all the OLE DB .NET Data Provider data objects, such as the insert, update, delete, and select commands, the data adapter, and connection objects.

CROSS-REFERENCE   *See Chapter 3A for a discussion of data adapters.*

---

2. I keep referring to previous versions of VB because many Windows developers have used VB either professionally or as a prototyping tool, where data-bound controls have been used extensively.

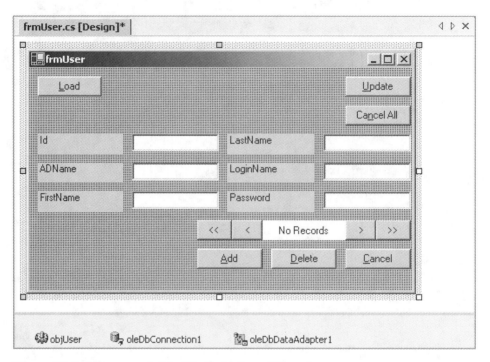

Figure 10-8. A form created by the Data Form Wizard

The wizard also creates a strongly typed XML data set file (.xsd). Another file it creates that is not normally shown in the Solution Explorer is the class file, which encapsulates or wraps the data access. This file has the same name as the data set file (.xsd), but with a .cs extension. You can see this file in the folder you've selected to save your project in, or you can click the Show All Files button in the Solution Explorer. This button is located at the very top of the Solution Explorer window, as shown in Figure 10-9.

Figure 10-9. The Show All Files button in the Solution Explorer window

EXERCISE

1) Create a new connection to the UserMan database from the Server Explorer if you don't already have one.

2) Add a new form using the Data Form Wizard and name the form frmUser.

3) Create a new dataset called User in the wizard dialog box.

4) Select the UserMan database connection and add the tblUser table.

5) Display the data as a single record in individual controls.

The new form should look like the form shown in Figure 10-8.

One thing you might have noticed is that the wizard always uses the OLE DB .NET Data Provider. This is also true when you connect to a SQL Server, which is obviously not ideal. However, this can be fixed using the search and replace functionality of the IDE.

Looking at the Code Created by the Data Form Wizard

I'll now go through the code created by the Data Form Wizard, and if you want to follow along, I suggest you open the project in which you created the frmUser form from the previous exercise. If you didn't perform the exercise, now would be a good time to do so, as I'll cover how the **CurrencyManager** and **BindingContext** objects are used in code.

If you open the frmUser form in the Code Editor, not in Design view, you'll see several hundred lines of code. Just think about that for a minute—how long do you think it will take you to type this in yourself? What I'm getting at here is that even if the code generated by the Data Form Wizard often needs to be adjusted slightly, it will save you a lot of time compared to typing it all in yourself.

If you're following along, scroll down the code until you reach the constructor and the **Dispose** method. To get a better look at the code in the Code Editor, expand the Windows Forms Designer generated code region by clicking the plus sign (+) next to the line number (approximately Line 76) where you see the text "Windows Forms Designer generated code." This is similar to what you would do in Windows Explorer when you go file hunting. If the code region is already expanded, a minus sign (–) is shown, and you'll see the text "#region Windows Form Designer generated code."

Notice that just after constructor and **Dispose** methods, the wizard has put the declaration of all the objects used by the form. This includes the data objects, such as the data adapter, connection, and command objects, as well as all the buttons and labels shown on the form. All these objects and controls are declared so that the objects are only accessible to the form class itself and other classes and so on within the same project.

One declaration I want you to look closer at is the objUser object. This object is of type <*ProjectName*>.User, where *ProjectName* is the name of your project and User is the class. Can't recall creating this class? Don't worry, that's because the wizard did. Right-click the class and select Go To Definition from the pop-up menu. This brings up the User class in the Code Editor window. This class is derived from the **DataSet** class in the **System.Data** namespace, which basically means this class is the disconnected part of the data source you will be binding to. The User class is located in the User.cs file, which also holds the following classes:

- *tblUserDataTable:* Derived from **System.Data.DataTable**. Implements public properties such as **Count** and the indexer. The class also holds procedures such as an enumerator, and procedures for manipulating rows in the table.

- *tblUserRow:* Derived from **System.Data.DataRow**. Implements properties for getting and setting column values in rows in the tblUser table, a constructor, **bool** functions to check for **null** values in columns, and functions to set the column values to **null**.

- *tblUserRowChangeEvent:* Derived from **System.EventArgs**. This class is the base class for event data, which means this class is used for controlling events in connection with data manipulation in the tblUser table through the User class.

Okay, now back in the frmUser.cs file: in the **InitializeComponent** procedure, all the objects are instantiated and initialized. Please take a look at the **ConnectionString** property of the connection—it includes a hard-coded Workstation ID. Do feel free to take it out if it bothers you.

Outside the Windows Forms Designer generated code region, you have all the private procedures for the **Click** events of the buttons on the form; a procedure for updating the current row position label; **Sub** procedures for updating, loading, or filling the **DataSet**; and finally, a procedure for updating the data source.

You should really take a long and close look at these files and classes because they contain loads of information. If you do a search in the frmUser.cs file for the **BindingContext** object, you'll see what operations it actually performs with regard to manipulating the data.

Binding a Windows Form Control to a Data Source

Any Windows form control that is derived from the **Control** class, which is a member of the **System.Windows.Forms** namespace, can be bound to any property of an object and thus a data source. If you go back to the code generated by the Data Form Wizard earlier in this chapter, you can search the code and find how the **DataBindings** property of all the buttons on the form is being used to bind to the objUser object mentioned in the previous section. The **DataBindings** property returns a **ControlBindingsCollection**, and this collection has an **Add** method, which you can see used in the generated code to add a **Binding** object. This **Binding** object is the real trick of the data binding. It is created by the **Add** method of the **ControlBindingsCollection**, and it specifies how a certain control property is bound to a certain member of a data source. The following example code is taken from the code generated by the Data Form Wizard:

```
this.editId.DataBindings.Add(
  new System.Windows.Forms.Binding("Text", this.objUser, "tblUser.Id"));
```

The editId item is a **TextBox** control, but as stated previously, you can bind data to any control derived from the **Control** class. In the example, the text box is bound to the Id column of the tblUser table (data member) from the objUser object (data source). The first argument, which reads "Text", specifies that it is the **Text** property of the editId **TextBox** control bound to the Id column.

Using the BindingContext Object

The **BindingContext** object can be associated with a Windows form and when it is, it's a global object, meaning you don't have to instantiate it. If you do a search, you'll see many instances of **this.BindingContext** in the code, which indicates the **BindingContext** object is indeed associated with, or rather a part of, the current Windows form object. The noninherited, public property and method of the **BindingContext** class are shown in Table 10-1.

*Table 10-1. Public Property and Method of the **BindingContext** Class*

NAME	PROPERTY/METHOD	DESCRIPTION
IsReadOnly	Property	This read-only property returns a **bool** value indicating if the **BindingContext** is read-only.
Contains()	Method	This overloaded method returns a **bool** value indicating whether the **BindingContext** object contains the specified **BindingManagerBase**.

As you can see from Table 10-1, there just aren't that many public properties and methods to use, but this isn't really a problem. Remember that the **BindingContext** object holds a **CurrencyManager** object for each data source on the form. This means you don't really have to manipulate the **BindingContext** object at all, but you have to use this object's indexer to get to the **CurrencyManager** objects and/or the **Contains** method to check if a specific **CurrencyManager** exists. Does this make sense to you? It probably would have if I hadn't used two terms for virtually the same thing: **CurrencyManager** and **BindingManagerBase**.

The **BindingManagerBase** class is abstract, meaning it must be derived or inherited before you can use it. Yes, you guessed it: the **CurrencyManager** class does indeed inherit from the **BindingManagerBase** class. So for the purpose of discussing data-bound controls on Windows forms, these two classes are more or less the same.

Okay, so before continuing on with the **CurrencyManager** class, let me explain how to get to it using the **BindingContext** object. In the case of the source code created by the Data Form Wizard, I'll use **this.BindingContext** to refer to the **BindingContext** object of the frmUser form. Listings 10-1 and 10-2 show you two different ways of accessing the currency manager.

Listing 10-1. Saving a Reference to the Currency Manager

```
CurrencyManager objCurrencyManager;
objCurrencyManager = this.BindingContext[objUser, "tblUser"];
```

*Listing 10-2. Accessing the **Count** Property of the Currency Manager Through the Binding Context*

```
this.BindingContext[objUser, "tblUser"].Count;
```

As you can see from Listings 10-1 and 10-2, you can choose to either reference the currency manager through the **BindingContext** object (as shown in Listing 10-2) or save a reference to it and use it directly (as shown in Listing 10-1). Which method you choose doesn't really make a difference—it's a matter of preference. One thing to notice about the **CurrencyManager** class is that it doesn't have a constructor, so you can only instantiate an object of data type **CurrencyManager** using the indexer of a **BindingContext** object.

Using the CurrencyManager Object

Now look at the **CurrencyManager** class, because that's the juicy one—the one with all the properties and methods you'll be using extensively in your code when you create data-bound controls. Table 10-2 lists all the noninherited, public properties of the currency manager, and Table 10-3 shows you all the noninherited, public methods.

*Table 10-2. Properties of the **CurrencyManager** Class*

PROPERTY NAME	DESCRIPTION
Bindings	This read-only property returns a **BindingsCollection** object that holds all the **Bindings** objects being managed by the **CurrencyManager**.
Count	The **Count** property, which is read-only, returns an **int** value that indicates the number of rows managed by the **CurrencyManager**.
Current	This property returns the current object. Because the returned object is of data type **Object**, you need to cast it to the same data type as the data type contained by the data source before you can use it.
List	This property returns the list for the **CurrencyManager** and the data type is an **IList** object. Basically, this means that you can cast it to any data type that implements the **IList** interface.
Position	The **Position** property retrieves or sets the current position in the data source or rather underlying list. The value is zero based and of data type **int**.

*Table 10-3. Important Methods of the **CurrencyManager** Class*

METHOD NAME	DESCRIPTION	EXAMPLE

AddNew()	The **AddNew** method adds a new item to the underlying list. In the case of a **DataTable**, the new item is a **DataRow**.	`this.BindingContext[objUser,`
		`"tblUser"].AddNew();`
		(taken from the code generated by the Data Form Wizard)

CancelCurrentEdit()	This method cancels the current edit operation. The data is *not* saved in its current condition. Data is reverted back to the condition it was in when you started the edit operation. If you need to end the edit operation and save any changes, you should use the **EndCurrentEdit** method for this purpose instead.	`this.BindingContext[objUser,`
		`"tblUser"].CancelCurrentEdit();`
		(taken from the code generated by the Data Form Wizard)

EndCurrentEdit()	The **EndCurrentEdit** method is used for ending the current edit operation. The data is saved in its current condition, so this does *not* cancel the edits. Use the **CancelCurrentEdit** method for this purpose instead.	`this.BindingContext[objUser,`
		` "tblUser"].EndCurrentEdit();`
		(taken from the code generated by the Data Form Wizard)

(continued)

*Table 10-3. Important Methods of the **CurrencyManager** Class (continued)*

METHOD NAME	DESCRIPTION	EXAMPLE
Refresh()	The **Refresh** method refreshes, or rather repopulates, the bound controls. This method is for use with data sources that do not support change notification, such as an array. Data sets and data tables do support change notification, meaning this method is not needed with objects of these data types.	`this.BindingContext[objUser, "tblUser"].Refresh();`
RemoveAt(int intIndex)	This method deletes the item at the specified index position.	`this.BindingContext[objUser, "tblUser"].RemoveAt(0);`
ResumeBinding()	This method and the **SuspendBinding** method are used for temporarily suspending the data binding. You should use these two methods if you want to let a user perform several edits without validating these edits until binding is resumed. This method resumes suspended binding.	`this.BindingContext[objUser, "tblUser"].ResumeBinding();`
SuspendBinding()	This method and the **ResumeBinding** method are used for temporarily suspending the data binding. You should use these two methods if you want to let a user perform several edits without validating these edits until binding is resumed. This method suspends binding.	`this.BindingContext[objUser, "tblUser"].SuspendBinding();`

As you can see from Tables 10-2 and 10-3, the **CurrencyManager** class has methods and properties for performing just about any action on the data source.

Retrieving the Number of Rows in the Data Source

Occasionally it is desirable to retrieve the number of rows in the data source to which the controls are bound for display purposes, such as to show that the current row is number *n* of the actual number of rows. This can be easily achieved using the **Count** property of the **CurrencyManager** class, as follows:

```
MesssageBox.Show("This is row number " + (this.BindingContext[objUser,
    "tblUser"].Position + 1).ToString() + " of " + this.BindingContext[objUser,
    "tblUser"].Count.ToString() + " rows.");
```

This code obviously uses both the **Position** and **Count** properties to display the current row position and the number of rows. Because the **Position** property is zero based, I've added the value 1 to this property at display time. This is done to make sure that the current position is 1 based as it is with the **Count** property.

Retrieving the Current Row of a Data Source

Sometimes you need to manipulate the content of the current row in the data source. You can do this using the **Current** property of the **CurrencyManager** class. However, this property returns a value of data **Object**, which means you have to cast this value to the same data type used by the data source. When the data source is accessed through a **DataSet**, **DataTable**, or **DataViewManager** object, you're actually binding to a **DataView** object. In this situation, you have to cast the returned object to a **DataRowView** object.

```
DataRowView drwCurrent = (DataRowView)
    this.BindingContext[objUser, "tblUser"].Current;
```

In the example code, drwCurrent now holds the current row in the data source.

Retrieving and Setting the Current Position in a Data Source

You can retrieve and set the current position in the data source using the **Position** property of the **CurrencyManager** class. See the section "Retrieving the Number of Rows in the Data Source" earlier in this chapter for example code of how to read the **Position** property.

However, retrieving the current position in the data source is not the only thing you can do with the **Position** property—you can also set the position. That's right, you can use the **Position** property to move around the data source. Best of all, it's extremely easy to do so, as this example demonstrates:

```
this.BindingContext[objUser, "tblUser"].Position = 3;
```

This code makes the fourth row the current one (the **Position** property is zero based). Table 10-4 shows you how to make specific rows current.

Table 10-4. Navigating to Specific Rows in the Data Source in a Bound Control

POSITION	EXAMPLE
First row	`this.BindingContext[objUser, "tblUser"].Position = 0;`
Last row	`this.BindingContext[objUser, "tblUser"].Position =` `this.BindingContext[objUser, "tblUser"].Count - 1;`
Next row	`this.BindingContext[objUser, "tblUser"].Position += 1;`
Previous row	`this.BindingContext[objUser, "tblUser"].Position -= 1;`

In connection with moving around the data source, it's necessary to check the validity of the move before you actually perform it. This is not necessary with moving to the first or last row, because that is always valid, but moving to the previous or next row can throw an exception if there is no such row.

So, if you want to move to the previous row, make sure you are not at position 0, which is the first row. Check it like this:

```
if (this.BindingContext[objUser, "tblUser"].Position != 0) {}
```

If you want to move to the next row, check if you're currently at the last row, as follows:

```
if (this.BindingContext[objUser, "tblUser"].Position !=
    this.BindingContext[objUser, "tblUser"].Count - 1) {}
```

Controlling Validation of Edit Operations

When you edit the data in the data source, the **CurrentChanged** and **ItemChanged** events are triggered. This is good, because you can respond to these events and perform whatever actions you need to in your application. However, sometimes it is *not* desirable to have events fired. If you're doing a bulk update, it's better to respond to these events after the update has been applied. You can do this using the **SuspendBinding** and the **ResumeBinding** methods. These methods are used for temporarily suspending the data binding. See Listing 10-3 for an example of how to suspend and resume data binding.

Listing 10-3. Suspend and Resume Data Binding

```
1 // Suspend data binding
2 this.BindingContext[objUser, "tblUser"].SuspendBinding();
3 // Perform bulk edits
4 ...
5 // Resume data binding
6 this.BindingContext[objUser, "tblUser"].ResumeBinding();
```

Listing 10-3 shows you how to first suspend the data binding before performing your bulk edits and then finally resume the data binding. No events are
triggered between Lines 2 and 6.

Creating Your Own Data-Bound Windows Form Control

As I've already shown, it's fairly easy to create a data-bound Windows form control. I suggest you always use the Data Form Wizard for this purpose if you're
creating control with a formlike UI. Even if it means you have to change some
of the wizard-generated code afterward, it will nearly always be quicker and
easier to use this approach.

Obviously, when you're using a formlike approach, you'll be creating a component with a UI and that won't do in some cases, such as when you really just need
a control for your existing forms. This is when you need to create a Windows user
control. You can do so in any Windows project by following these simple steps:

1. Add a new item to the project. When the Add New Item dialog box
   appears, select the User Control template, give the user control a name,
   and click OK.

2. Drag the required Windows form controls from the Toolbox onto the
   Windows user control when it's in design mode.

3. Create a class like the objUser class in the wizard-generated code that is
   the data source.

4. Bind one or more properties of each of the Windows form controls that
   you have placed on the Windows user control to a property of the data
   source class.

That's all there is to it!

EXERCISE

Create a new user control and name it UserManId. Add a **TextBox** control to the user control and bind it to the Id column of the tblUser table. You can find an example of how to do this in the accompanying example code for this chapter.

Using Data-Bound Controls with Web Forms

Data binding your Web controls is quite different behind the scenes than with Windows forms. It's especially different because the data-binding architecture for Web forms doesn't support automatic updates. This doesn't mean that it isn't possible to update your data source with changes from your Web UI, but it does take a little more work.

If you want to create Web forms with updateable data,[3] it ultimately comes down to how you maintain the state of your data when the Web form is refreshed, causing a server roundtrip. See the "Maintaining State" section later in this chapter. Another decision you need to make is how the underlying data is kept, meaning where it's stored. Is the data in a **DataSet** or a DataReader? Please see the "Choosing the Right Data Storage" section later in this chapter for more information on what data storage you should choose.

Binding ASP.NET Server Controls to a Data Source

All controls inherited from the **Control** class in the **System.Web.UI** namespace have a **DataBind** method that can bind the control to a data source when called. In order for the data binding to work in single-value server controls,[4] you must set one or more properties of the control. Basically, any property of the control can be set, although most of the time it will probably be the **Text** property, which is the property that generally gets displayed. If you have a **TextBox** control on a Web form and you want to set the property at design time, you need to select the control on the Web form in Design view and open the Properties window (press F4) if it's not already open. Then you need to click the button with the ellipsis (. . .) in the (DataBindings) field in the Properties window, as indicated by the mouse cursor in Figure 10-10.

---

3. If you just want read-only data, you don't really have a problem, because data is retrieved every time the Web form is refreshed.
4. Nonsingle value controls such as the **DataGrid**, which is covered in the next section, require a special form of data binding.

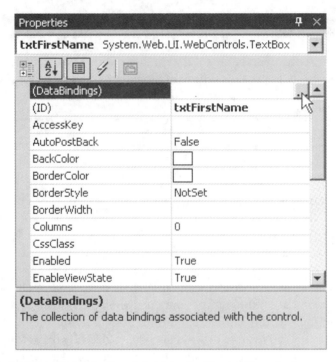

Figure 10-10. The (DataBindings) field in the Properties window

If you click the button indicated in Figure 10-10, the DataBindings dialog box appears. In this dialog box, you must select the property you want to bind from the Bindable Properties list, and select either the Simple binding or Custom binding expression option button. Figure 10-11 shows you how I've opted for setting the **Text** property of the txtFirstName **TextBox** control. You can also see from Figure 10-11 that I've chosen the Simple binding option and selected to bind to the FirstName column of the objdstUser typed **DataSet**. The Simple binding tree view lists as all typed **DataSet**s in your project as well as any data controls you've dragged onto the Web form in Design view, such as Connection, DataAdapter, and **DataView** objects. Another thing you can see from Figure 10-11 is that I'm binding to the FirstName column of the first row (0) of the **DataView** (accessed through the **DefaultView** property) of the **DataTable** (accessed through the **Tables** collection property) of the objdstUser **DataSet**. This isn't necessarily the way you'd normally access a value in a column in a **DataTable** in your **DataSet**, because quite often you would use the **DataTable** directly and not the **DefaultView** property. Anyway, this was just to show you that you're actually binding to the column values of the **DataTable**, even if it's not done directly.

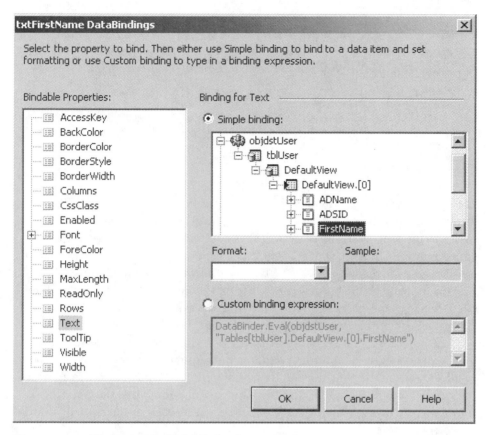

Figure 10-11. The DataBindings dialog box

As I'm sure you've noticed, there's no **DataBinding** property of the **Control** class or any classes derived from it, which is why you can freely choose any other property to be bound to the data source. All there is to do now is to call the **DataBind** method of the **TextBox** control and the control is data bound. You decide if you want to place that call in the **Page_Load** event procedure or any procedure for that matter, as long as it's called after the Web form page initialization (**OnInit** procedure).

> **NOTE** *The **DataBind** method of the **Control** class also calls the method of the same name on all child controls. This means that if you call this method on the Web form itself (accessed through the **this** object), the **DataBind** method will also be called on all controls on the Web form derived from the **Control** class.*

Maintaining State

The problem with any data binding in ASP.NET is maintaining the state. Web forms, and ultimately the ASP.NET page framework, communicate with the client, such as a browser, using the Hypertext Transfer Protocol (HTTP). The problem concerning data binding with HTTP is that it is stateless. This means information is lost every time the page or your Web form is refreshed, including the data to which your controls are bound. The Web form is refreshed when the user of the client requests new or more information from the server, such as when a user clicks the Send button in a browser after filling in his or her personal details.

The problem in this scenario is that the user might have entered some invalid data or even left out some required data. Your Web form would then need to inform the user about the error and at the same time redisplay the form with the entered information.[5] Because the information is lost when the Web form is refreshed, you need to handle this yourself, meaning you have to save the information elsewhere.

How to save this information is not exactly difficult, but choosing the right way of doing so can be a tricky task, because there are several options available to you:

- You can save the information in the Web form's **ViewState** property. This means storing the information on the client.

- You can store information in the **Session** and **Application** objects. These objects are probably familiar to you if you've been developing Web sites using Visual InterDev. I don't cover these objects in this book, but you can find plenty of information about them in the Visual Studio .NET MSDN Library. This means storing the information on the server.

---

5. In many cases you can use some of the server validation controls, which will save you the Web server roundtrip because they're output as client-side script. As such, simple validation, such as required fields, won't need a Web server roundtrip to be validated. However, there are other cases where some or all of the Web form input needs to be checked against your business rules and this must be done dynamically, meaning it must be tested against the current content of your DBMS, and that requires a Web server roundtrip.

The option you should choose really depends on your circumstances. I can make one simple recommendation: try out the different options if and when performance is an issue. "Testing" is the key word here.

Recall that a Web form loses its state when it's being refreshed, but this isn't too difficult to handle, because the current properties of the page (Web form), the page itself, and the base properties of the server controls and their state are automatically saved between roundtrips. All you need to worry about is when you have information that is *not* part of the mentioned controls and/or properties, such as private variables and contents of standard HTML elements.

Choosing the Right Data Storage

When you set out to design your Web forms with data-bound controls, you need to decide where to store your data and, ultimately, how the data is retrieved from your data source. In terms of ADO.NET, which is what this book is about, there are two options:

1. DataReader, Command, and Connection objects

2. **DataSet**, DataAdapter, Command, and Connection objects

The Connection, Command, DataReader, and the DataAdapter classes are explained in detail in Chapter 3A, and the **DataSet** class is explained in Chapter 3B.

Option 1, which is a connected scenario,[6] is hardly ever the right choice for a Web application, because keeping a connection from your Web forms to your data source alive isn't very scalable and certainly requires a lot of resources, and the more resources, the more pages (Web forms) your application serves concurrently. Another issue is that the DataReader class is read-only, meaning you can't really use it for updateable data Web forms.[7]

Option 2 uses the DataAdapter, Connection, and Command classes for retrieving data from and updating the data in the data source, and the DataSet as a local cache of the data in the data source. This is the approach the Data Form Wizard uses when you create your data-bound Web forms with it. See the

---

6. The Connection object must be kept open for as long as you read from the DataReader, effectively ruling out the use of this data class combination. You can, of course, loop through all the rows in the DataReader and add them to a **DataGrid** or a different set of controls, but isn't that just manual data hooking, as discussed in the "Data-Bound Controls vs. Manual Data Hooking" section earlier in this chapter?
7. You can, of course, create your own workaround, effectively overcoming the read-only disadvantage of the DataReader class, but why bother when there are other, easier options, such as using the **DataSet** class?

"Creating a Form Using the Data Form Wizard" section later in this chapter for more information on how to use the Data Form Wizard and learn from the code generated by it.

My recommendation is that if you want updateable, data-bound Web forms, go with Option 2.

Data Storage State

If you've decided to go for working with a **DataSet** object as the data storage in your updateable, data-bound Web form, you'll also need to decide on how to save state of the **DataSet** between server roundtrips, if at all. As I see it, you have two options:

1. Recreate the **DataSet** every time the Web form is loaded.

2. Save the state using one of the options discussed in the "Maintaining State" section earlier in this chapter.

If you decide to go with Option 1, you need to make sure that any changes to the **DataSet** are propagated back to the data source every time the Web form is unloaded. This might involve a lot of data traveling across the network, because you have the data coming from the data source every time the Web form is created, and then you possibly have data traveling the other way when the Web form is unloaded (if any data has been changed). This will require more processing from your data source as well.

The previously mentioned issues might not be problematic at all depending on your setup. How much data is sent from the server/data source for every Web form creation, how loaded is your data source, and how many concurrent users do you expect?

Option 2 doesn't require as much data to travel across the network as frequently as Option 1, but now you need to consider where to store the data between roundtrips: on the server or on the client? If you store it on the server, you'll still need for the data to travel across the network every time the Web form is created, but you won't be burdening your data source. However, you risk the data in the **DataSet** being outdated and you'll have to solve potential problems when you try to update the data source. If you store it on the client, you'll also avoid having the data travel across the network every time the Web form is created, but this requires saving your data in the Web form's view state or a hidden field.[8] This means that it becomes part of the HTML that the client browser needs to parse, and if it's a large amount of data, the Web form might take quite a while to load.

Whichever option you choose, make sure you've considered everything carefully and you understand the implications your choice will have for your application and the client using it. Another thing to do is try out more than one option and perform some benchmarking on network load, Web form loading time, data source load, and so on.

Creating a Form Using the Data Form Wizard

Instead of doing all the hard work yourself (doing the data binding manually), let the Data Form Wizard create your Web form with one or more data-bound controls for you as you would with a Windows form. This wizard does more or less the same thing, but it will only let you create read-only Web forms. This means you have to take care of creating updateable pages yourself. I suggest you try running the Data Form Wizard in a Web application project and perform the same steps as you did with the wizard for the Windows form (see the "Creating a Form Using the Data Form Wizard" section earlier in this chapter). Mind you, you'll have to skip Step 8 because it doesn't apply to Web forms. In addition to restricting your Web forms to read-only, another drawback of the Data Form Wizard is it allows only a data grid as a control on your Web form.

Anyway, try running the wizard and run the project after the wizard finishes to see how nicely it displays your data as read-only in a data grid. You'll see that a typed **DataSet** has been generated and referenced from code. There are two **public** procedures that the Data Form Wizard creates: the FillDataSet and LoadDataSet procedures. I won't show them here, as you can simply take a look at the code in the WebFormsDataBoundControls project or have the Data Form Wizard create a new data-bound Web form for you. The **LoadDataSet** procedure, which calls the **FillDataSet** procedure, is being called from the buttonLoad_Click event procedure. This also means that the Web form, as it has been generated by the Data Form Wizard, doesn't display any data when it loads. You need to click the Load button on the Web form and then the "magic" starts.

---

8. View state is actually implemented as a hidden field as well.

Making the Web Form Updateable

Now that you have your data-bound Web form, it would be nice if it were update-able as well, don't you think? Well, I had to decide whether or not I wanted to recreate the **DataSet** every time the Web form loads or if I wanted to save the state of the **DataSet** between roundtrips, and I decided that with the amount of data that I'm transferring across the network and the number of expected users (no more than 100), I'd go with the notion of recreating the **DataSet** every time the Web form loads. This also means that I need to make sure that any changes to the data on the client are propagated back to the data source every time the Web form is unloaded, or every time a row is updated, or simply when the user clicks an Update button.

Here's what I need to do:

- *Make the **DataGrid** control updateable.* This can be done by selecting the grid on the Web form in Design view, right-clicking, and selecting the Property builder command from the pop-up menu. This brings up the Properties dialog box. Click the Columns button on the left; expand the Button Column node in the Available columns tree view; select the Edit, Update, Cancel node; and click the Add (>) button next to the tree view as shown in Figure 10-12. This adds the Edit, Update, and Cancel buttons (or rather, links) to the **DataGrid**. Click OK.

- *Add code to the Edit, Update, and Cancel events of the **DataGrid**.* You can do this by selecting the grid on the Web form in Design view and opening the Properties window, if not already shown, by pressing F4. Click the Events button in the Properties window (its icon is a yellow lightning bolt). Double-click the **CancelCommand**, **EditCommand**, and **UpdateCommand** properties on the list, as this will create the event handler procedures and all the necessary delegates in your code file. You can see the code in Listings 10-4, 10-5, and 10-6.

- *Remove the Load button from the Web form and move the associated code to the Page_Load procedure.* This way the data is automatically retrieved and displayed when the Web form is loaded. The **Page_Load** event procedure should then look like Listing 10-7.

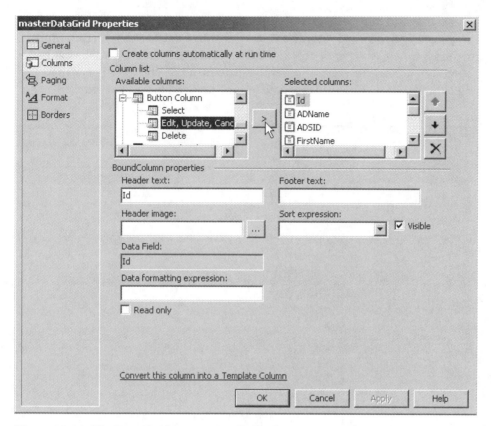

*Figure 10-12. The **DataGrid** Properties dialog box*

In Figure 10-12, you can see how you can use the **DataGrid** Properties dialog box to add Edit, Update, and Cancel buttons or links to a **DataGrid** control. In Listing 10-4, you can see the code needed to start editing a row in the **DataGrid** control.

*Listing 10-4. **DataGrid EditCommand** Event Procedure*

```
1 private void masterDataGrid_EditCommand(object source,
2     System.Web.UI.WebControls.DataGridCommandEventArgs e) {
3     masterDataGrid.EditItemIndex = e.Item.ItemIndex;
4     masterDataGrid.DataBind();
5 }
```

On Line 3 in Listing 10-4, the **EditItemIndex** property is set to the value of the row you clicked the Edit link on (see Figure 10-13), and on Line 4 the **DataBind** method is called, which means that the **DataGrid** control rebinds to the data source and notices the new value of the **EditItemIndex**. This also means that when the Web form has been reloaded in the browser it looks like Figure 10-14.

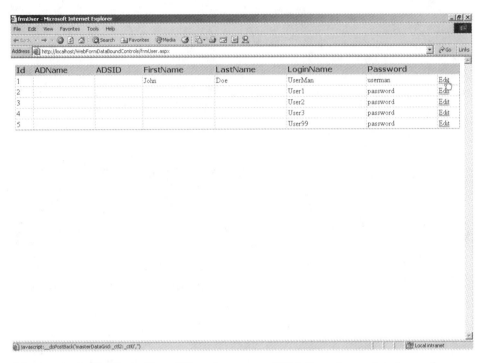

Figure 10-13. The Data Form Wizard generated Web form in read-only mode

In Figure 10-13, you can see the Edit link has been added to the **DataGrid**, making it possible to enter edit mode.

In Listing 10-5, you can see how edit mode is canceled by setting the **EditItemIndex** property to –1 and rebinding to the data source. Edit mode can be canceled by the user clicking the Cancel link, as shown in Figure 10-14.

*Listing 10-5. **DataGrid CancelCommand** Event Procedure*

```
1 private void masterDataGrid_CancelCommand(object source,
2    System.Web.UI.WebControls.DataGridCommandEventArgs e) {
3    masterDataGrid.EditItemIndex = -1;
4    masterDataGrid.DataBind();
5 }
```

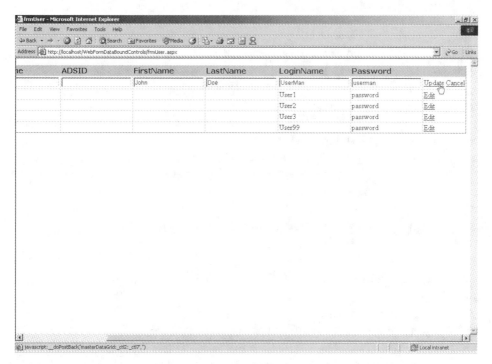

Figure 10-14. The Data Form Wizard generated Web Form in edit mode

In Figure 10-14, the Web form is in edit mode, meaning the Cancel and Update links have been added to the row that is currently being edited.

In Listing 10-6, you can see the code needed to update the data source with the new values in the row being edited. The **UpdateCommand** procedure is invoked by clicking the Update link, which is displayed when the Web form is in edit mode, as shown in Figure 10-14.

*Listing 10-6. **DataGrid UpdateCommand** Event Procedure*

```
1 private void masterDataGrid_UpdateCommand(object source,
2     System.Web.UI.WebControls.DataGridCommandEventArgs e) {
3     dstUser.tblUserRow drwUser;
4     TextBox txtEdit;
5     int intKey;
6
7     // Save the key field of edited row
8     intKey = int.Parse(masterDataGrid.DataKeys[e.Item.ItemIndex].ToString());
9
10    // Locate the row in the the dataset that has been edited
11    // by using the saved key as an argument for the FindById
12    // procedure
```

```
13    drwUser = objdstUser.tblUser.FindById(intKey);
14
15    // Update the DataSet with the changed values, through
16    // the located data row
17    txtEdit = (TextBox) (e.Item.Cells[1].Controls[0]);
18    drwUser.ADName = txtEdit.Text;
19    txtEdit = (TextBox) (e.Item.Cells[2].Controls[0]);
20    drwUser.ADSID = txtEdit.Text;
21    txtEdit = (TextBox) (e.Item.Cells[3].Controls[0]);
22    drwUser.FirstName = txtEdit.Text;
23    txtEdit = (TextBox) (e.Item.Cells[4].Controls[0]);
24    drwUser.LastName = txtEdit.Text;
25    txtEdit = (TextBox) (e.Item.Cells[5].Controls[0]);
26    drwUser.LoginName = txtEdit.Text;
27    txtEdit = (TextBox) (e.Item.Cells[6].Controls[0]);
28    drwUser.Password = txtEdit.Text;
29
30    // Update the data source
31    oleDbDataAdapter1.Update(objdstUser);
32
33    // Take the DataGrid out of editing mode and rebind
34    masterDataGrid.EditItemIndex = -1;
35    masterDataGrid.DataBind();
36 }
  }
```

Listing 10-6 has a lot of "manual" code for updating the data source, but that's the way it works.

In Listing 10-7, you can see the code the Data Form Wizard generated and placed in the **Click** event procedure of the Load button has been moved to the **Page_Load** event procedure. This means that the **DataGrid** control is populated when the form loads instead of when the Load button is clicked.

*Listing 10-7. Web Form **Page_Load** Event Procedure*

```
1 private void Page_Load(object sender, System.EventArgs e) {
2    try {
3        LoadDataSet();
4        // Check if the page is being refreshed
5        if (!IsPostBack) {
6            masterDataGrid.SelectedIndex = -1;
```

```
 7           masterDataGrid.DataBind();
 8       }
 9   }
10   catch (System.Exception eLoad) {
11       Response.Write(eLoad.Message);
12   }
13 }
```

The WebFormDataBoundControls project, which you can find in the accompanying example code, has been created using the Data Form Wizard and then customized according to the previous list.

Creating Your Own Data-Bound Web Form Control

Because the Data Form Wizard for Web forms always creates read-only forms with a **DataGrid** control, it can be a lot of work making it updateable and/or using separate controls instead of the data grid. However, the initial code to build on is there and it's easier to extend the wizard-generated code than to do it all by hand.

When you're using a formlike approach as suggested in the preceding section, you'll be creating a page UI, and that won't do in some cases. Sometimes you need a control that can be dragged from the Toolbox onto a Web form. In those instances, you need to create a Web user control. You can create a Web user control in any Web project by adding a new item to your project. When the Add New Item dialog box appears, you select the Web User Control template, give the user control a name, and click OK. You also need to do the following:

1. Drag the required Web form controls from the Toolbox onto the Web user control when it's in design mode.

2. Create a data set for binding the controls to. To do so, drag the table you want as your data set from the Server Explorer onto the Web user control. This creates a new connection and a new data adapter object, as shown in Figure 10-15. These objects are set to point at the data source you dragged from the Server Explorer, meaning you don't have to initialize them.

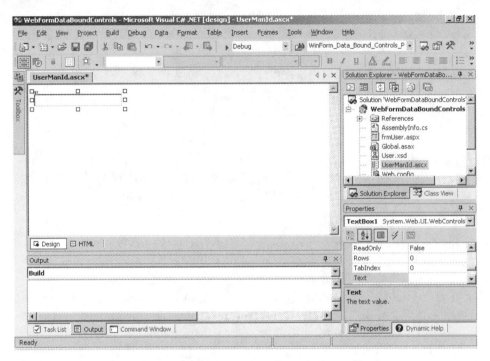

Figure 10-15. A Web user control in design mode with data objects

3. Create a data set from the data adapter object. Select the SqlDataAdapter1 object and right-click it. Then select Generate Dataset from the pop-up menu.

4. In the Generate Dataset dialog box (shown in Figure 10-16), specify that you want to create a new data set by selecting New and then giving the data set a name in the text field next to the New option. Click OK.

5. The data set, User1 in this example, is now visually added to the data design view next to the data adapter object.

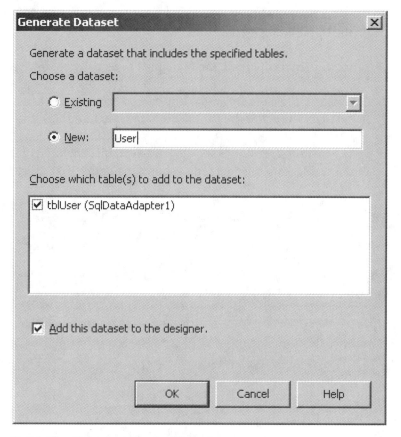

Figure 10-16. The Generate Dataset dialog box

6. Bind one or more properties of each of the Web form controls you have
    placed on the Web user control to a property of the data source class. Do
    so by following these steps:

    a. Select the Web user control in design mode.

    b. Select the Properties window and place the cursor in the
        DataBindings text box.

c. Click the button with the ellipsis (. . .) next to the text box. This brings up the DataBindings dialog box.

d. Select the **Text** property in the Bindable Properties tree view.

e. Check the Simple binding radio button and expand the User1 data set in the tree view below the Simple binding radio button.

f. Keep expanding the nodes so you can select the Id column of the tblUser table from the data set, as shown in Figure 10-17. Click OK.

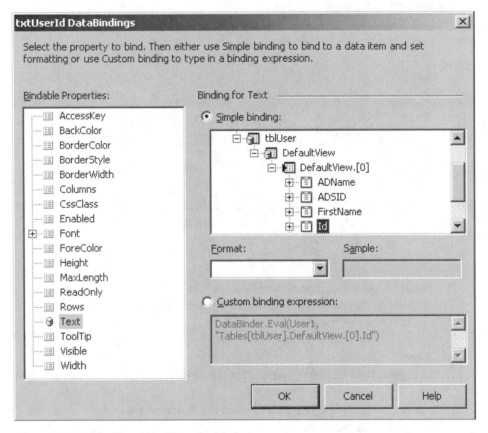

Figure 10-17. The DataBindings dialog box

7. Place the code from Listing 10-8 in the Page_Load subprocedure in the code for the Web user control.

Listing 10-8. Finishing the Data Binding in a Web User Control

```
// Open connection
SqlConnection1.Open();
// Fill data set
SqlDataAdapter1.Fill(User1, "tblUser");
// Bind controls to data source
txtUserId.DataBind();
```

The example in Listing 10-8 is pretty simple, but this really is all you need if you perform the other steps. You now have a data-bound user control you can use on any Web page.

The question is if you really want to do it this way. You may have other considerations: do you really want to open a connection for just one control, what about closing the connection, and so forth. You know the drill—the example code is simply to show how easily it can be done. How you finish the user control is entirely up to you.

EXERCISE

Create a new user control and name it UserManId. Add a **TextBox** control to the user control and bind it to the Id column of the tblUser table. You can find an example of how this is done in the accompanying example code.

Summary

In this chapter, I explained what data-bound controls are and how you use them in Windows forms and Web forms. I showed you the **CurrencyManager** and **BindingContext** classes in regard to data binding in Windows forms and demonstrated how they're used for data binding. I also discussed the **DataBindings** property of the Windows form control derived from the **Control** class and showed you how to manually bind a Windows form control to a data source.

You also saw how data binding works in Web forms, including state management, and how you can create your own Web custom control.

In the next chapter, I'll finish the UserMan example application that I've been referring to throughout the book, and I'll give you some ideas and tips on how to take the example further if you want build your own application based on the UserMan application.

Part Three

Example Applications

CHAPTER 11

UserMan

Finishing the Example Application

IN THIS CHAPTER, I FINISH THE USERMAN example application that you've built upon throughout this book, assuming you've followed the exercises along the way. I also give you some ideas as to how to take it further, if you feel the application can be the building block that you need for your very own .NET application.

The example application created throughout the book is all about implementing a user administration system that works with user information extracted from Active Directory, the directory system in Windows 2000 and later versions.

Identifying the UserMan Information

Let me state all the particulars about what the UserMan application should do, how it should do it, and so on. UserMan is a user management system that performs the following tasks:

- Logging on and off from the system (checking the tblUser table)

- Adding, editing, and deleting a user (tblUser table)

- Updating and checking a user's permissions (tblUserRights table)

- Logging all user activity (tblLog table)

- Adding, updating, and deleting user rights or permissions (tblRights table)

These are the duties of the UserMan application as I've written it, but obviously it needs more than this to be considered for any sort of deployment in an organization.

Discovering the Objects

This section covers the items in the UserMan application that you can identify as actual objects.

Database Objects

The database has already been written and it consists of the following tables:

- tblUser

- tblUserRights

- tblRights

- tblLog

You can see the database schema in the last part of Chapter 2 (Figure 2-10). Keeping the guidelines from Chapter 9 in mind, your next step in developing this application is figuring out how to wrap the access to these tables in one or more classes. Actually, this is fairly easy, because it almost always makes sense to wrap each table in a class. I've had to wrap more than one table in the same class for other applications, but in most cases I've wrapped one table per class. The tables in the UserMan database are clearly defined and although they're related, they should be accessed individually for adding, updating, and deleting rows. So you need four classes for the relational database:

- CUser

- CUserRights

- CRights

- CLog

Finishing the CUser Class

You started creating the CUser class in Chapter 9; so let's finish this particular class now. The rest of the classes look quite alike, and they can be found in the Downloads section of the Apress site (http://www.apress.com) or at the UserMan site[1] (http://www.userman.dk). First, you need to add some database connectivity. Listing 11-1 shows you the private constants and variables needed.

Listing 11-1. Private Database Constants and Variables for the CUser Class

```
 1 // Database constants
 2 private const string PR_STR_CONNECTION = "Data Source=USERMANPC;" +
 3    "User ID=UserMan;Password=userman;Initial Catalog=UserMan";
 4
 5 private const string PR_STR_SQL_FIELD_ID_NAME = "Id";
 6 private const string PR_STR_SQL_FIELD_FIRST_NAME = "FirstName";
 7 private const string PR_STR_SQL_FIELD_LAST_NAME = "LastName";
 8 private const string PR_STR_SQL_FIELD_LOGIN_NAME = "LoginName";
 9 private const string PR_STR_SQL_FIELD_PASSWORD_NAME = "Password";
10 private const string PR_STR_SQL_FIELD_ADSID_NAME = "ADSID";
11 private const string PR_STR_SQL_FIELD_ADNAME_NAME = "ADName";
12
13 private const string PR_STR_SQL_USER_SELECT = "SELECT * FROM " +
14    PR_STR_SQL_TABLE_NAME;
15 private const string PR_STR_SQL_USER_DELETE = "DELETE FROM " +
16    PR_STR_SQL_TABLE_NAME +" WHERE " + PR_STR_SQL_FIELD_ID_NAME + "=@" +
17    PR_STR_SQL_FIELD_ID_NAME;
18 private const string PR_STR_SQL_USER_INSERT = "INSERT INTO " +
19    PR_STR_SQL_TABLE_NAME + "(" + PR_STR_SQL_FIELD_FIRST_NAME + ", " +
20    PR_STR_SQL_FIELD_LAST_NAME + ", " + PR_STR_SQL_FIELD_LOGIN_NAME + ", " +
21    PR_STR_SQL_FIELD_PASSWORD_NAME + ") VALUES(@" +
22    PR_STR_SQL_FIELD_FIRST_NAME + ", @" + PR_STR_SQL_FIELD_LAST_NAME + ", @" +
23    PR_STR_SQL_FIELD_LOGIN_NAME + ", @" + PR_STR_SQL_FIELD_PASSWORD_NAME +
24    ")";
25 private const string PR_STR_SQL_USER_UPDATE = "UPDATE " +
26    PR_STR_SQL_TABLE_NAME + " SET " + PR_STR_SQL_FIELD_FIRST_NAME + "=@" +
27    PR_STR_SQL_FIELD_FIRST_NAME + ", " + PR_STR_SQL_FIELD_LAST_NAME + "=@" +
```

---

1. Don't forget to have the book by your side when you log on to the UserMan site because you're required to enter a word from a page in the book to gain access.

```
28    PR_STR_SQL_FIELD_LAST_NAME + ", " + PR_STR_SQL_FIELD_LOGIN_NAME + "=@" +
29    PR_STR_SQL_FIELD_LOGIN_NAME + ", " + PR_STR_SQL_FIELD_PASSWORD_NAME +
30    "=@" + PR_STR_SQL_FIELD_PASSWORD_NAME + " WHERE " +
31    PR_STR_SQL_FIELD_ID_NAME + "=@" + PR_STR_SQL_FIELD_ID_NAME;
32 private const string PR_STR_SQL_TABLE_USER_FIELD_ID = "Id";
33
34 // Database variables
35 private static SqlConnection prshcnnUserMan;
36 private SqlDataAdapter prdadUserMan;
37 private DataSet prdstUserMan;
38
39 // For direct user table manipulation
40 private SqlCommand prcmmUser;
41 // The command objects for the dataset manipulation
42 private SqlCommand prcmmUserSelect, prcmmUserDelete, prcmmUserInsert,
43    prcmmUserUpdate;
44 // Parameter objects for the data set manipulation
45 private SqlParameter prprmSQLDelete, prprmSQLUpdate, prprmSQLInsert;
46
47 // User table column values
48 private long prlngId = 0;
49 private string prstrADName;
50 private string prstrADSID;
51 private string prstrFirstName;
52 private string prstrLastName;
53 private string prstrLoginName;
54 private string prstrPassword;
55
56 // User table column max lengths
57 private int printFirstNameMaxLen;
58 private int printLastNameMaxLen;
59 private int printLoginNameMaxLen;
60 private int printPasswordMaxLen;
61
62 // For logging user activity
63 private CLog probjLog = new CLog();
```

Listing 11-1 includes a few private constants, one for the connection string (PR_STR_CONNECTION), one for the table name (PR_STR_SQL_TABLE_NAME), some for the field names in the table, and the command strings for selecting, inserting, updating, and deleting rows from the user table (PR_STR_SQL_USER_ . . .). There are also a few database objects, such as the connection (prshcnnUserMan), the data adapter (prdadUserMan), the data set (prdstUserMan), and so on. I'm sure you've already taken a closer look at the way I create my constants and you either hate it or like it. The fact is that it has taken me a while to get used to this approach, but it does save me a lot hassle when I change various names, such as table or column names, because I only have make updates in one place. Feel free to think what you like.

> **CROSS-REFERENCE** *If you need more information on any of these objects, I suggest you read Chapters 3A and 3B.*

I have also added the private variables from Chapter 9 for storing the table column values and the maximum column lengths. Regarding the column length variables, well, you need to set them, and that's what is shown in Listing 11-2.

Listing 11-2. Setting the Maximum Column Length Variables

```
1 private void prSetColumnMaxLength() {
2     const string STR_COLUMN_SIZE = "ColumnSize";
3
4     SqlDataReader drdSchema;
5     DataTable dtbSchema;
6     SqlCommand cmmUserSchema = new SqlCommand();
7
8     cmmUserSchema.CommandType = CommandType.Text;
9     cmmUserSchema.Connection = prshcnnUserMan;
10     cmmUserSchema.CommandText = "SELECT * FROM " + PR_STR_SQL_TABLE_NAME;
11
12     // Return data reader
13     drdSchema = cmmUserSchema.ExecuteReader();
14
15     // Read schema from source table
16     dtbSchema = drdSchema.GetSchemaTable();
17
18     // Save the maxlength values
19     printFirstNameMaxLen = (int) dtbSchema.Rows[3][STR_COLUMN_SIZE];
20     printLastNameMaxLen = (int) dtbSchema.Rows[4][STR_COLUMN_SIZE];
21     printLoginNameMaxLen = (int) dtbSchema.Rows[5][STR_COLUMN_SIZE];
22     printPasswordMaxLen = (int) dtbSchema.Rows[6][STR_COLUMN_SIZE];
23
24     // Close datareader
25     drdSchema.Close();
26 }
```

In Listing 11-2, I use the **GetSchemaTable** method of the DataReader class to retrieve information about all the columns from the tblUser table in a **DataTable** object. Once this method has been called (Line 16), you can save the maximum column length for those columns it applies to[2] by retrieving the value of the **ColumnSize** column (Lines 19 through 22). When you use the **GetSchemaTable** method, each column of a row in the DataReader object is returned as one row with information about the column. This means that Rows[3] (Line 19) refers to the fourth column of the tblUser table, which is the FirstName column (you can see the database schema in the last part of Chapter 2, Figure 2-10).

Making the Connection Object Shared

If you look at the connection object on Line 35 in Listing 11-1, you will see that I have declared it using the **static** access modifier. I have done this so the connection object will be shared amongst all instances of the CUser class—that is, they will all use the same single connection. Also, this keeps the connection object alive until the last instance of the class has been destroyed. Is this good or bad? Well, you be the judge. Just make sure you think about such issues as scalability, performance, and the overall number of users when you decide to change the declaration or leave it.

> **NOTE** *Programming is an art on its own, and it's up to you to make the most of your application. What is good for one application might be extremely bad for another. This book has given you some things to consider when you design and implement your application, if nothing else.*

If you've been adding these private variables and constants to your CUser class, I am sure you've found out that **SqlConnection**, **SqlCommand**, and other such data types aren't being recognized. To rectify this, you need to import the **System.Data.SqlClient** namespace by adding the following as the very first line of code in your CUser class:

```
using System.Data.SqlClient;
```

Opening the Database Connection

If you've added all the database variables needed for accessing the UserMan database, the next step is to set up the code shown in Listing 11-3, which establishes the database connection.

---

2. This is generally columns of any string data type, such as varchar in SQL Server.

Listing 11-3. Connecting to the Database

```
1 private void prOpenDatabaseConnection() {
2     try {
3         // Check if the connection has already been instantiated
4         if (prshcnnUserMan == null) {
5             // Instantiate the connection
6             prshcnnUserMan = new SqlConnection(PR_STR_CONNECTION);
7             // Check if the connection is closed
8             if ((bool) (prshcnnUserMan.State == ConnectionState.Closed)) {
9                 // Open the connection
10                prshcnnUserMan.Open();
11                // Log activity if the user has already been logged on
12                if (prlngId > 0) {
13                    probjLog.Logged = DateTime.Now;
14                    probjLog.Description = "Database connection opened.";
15                    probjLog.UserId = prlngId;
16                    probjLog.AddLogEntry();
17                }
18            }
19        }
20    }
21    catch (SqlException objSqlException) {
22        // A Connection low-level exception was thrown.
23        // Add a description and re-throw
24        // the exception to the caller of this class
25        throw new Exception("The connection to the UserMan database could " +
26            "not be established, due to a connection low-level error",
27            objSqlException);
28    }
29    catch (Exception objE) {
30        // Any other exception thrown is handled here
31        throw new Exception("The connection to the UserMan database could " +
32            "not be established.", objE);
33    }
34 }
```

In Listing 11-3, I open the connection in the private prOpenDatabaseConnection procedure. I have chosen to make the procedure private because clients don't need to perform this operation. It should be handled when you instantiate the class (see Listing 11-4 in the next section). I make sure that the connection hasn't been instantiated before I do so, and that it's closed before I try to open it. If it isn't closed when I open it, an exception is thrown. If an exception occurs, I throw a new exception with a message detailing what went on, and then I add the current exception to the **InnerException** property of the new exception. This way the caller of this class can see the original exception thrown and my error message as well.

Instantiating Your Class

Any initialization of variables and such that isn't handled by an initializer should be placed in the constructor, as shown in Listing 11-4.

Listing 11-4. Open Database Connection at Class Instantiation

```
1 public CUser() {
2     prOpenDatabaseConnection();
3 }
```

Listing 11-4 shows you how to make sure that the database connection is open and ready for use after the client has instantiated the class. Placing a call to the custom prOpenDatabaseConnection procedure in the constructor does this.

Closing the Database Connection

Just as you need to open your database connection, it must also be closed again to preserve connection resources, and ensure that no memory leaks occur. Listing 11-5 shows you how to do this.

Listing 11-5. Closing the Database Connection

```
 1 private void prCloseDatabaseConnection() {
 2     try {
 3         // Close the connection
 4         prshcnnUserMan.Close();
 5         // Log activity if the user has already been logged on
 6         if (prlngId > 0) {
 7             probjLog.Logged = DateTime.Now;
 8             probjLog.Description = "Database connection closed.";
 9             probjLog.UserId = prlngId;
10             probjLog.AddLogEntry();
11         }
12     }
13     catch (Exception objE) {
14         throw new Exception("The connection to the UserMan database could " +
15             "not be closed properly.", objE);
16     }
17 }
```

Listing 11-5 closes the database connection using the **Close** method of the connection class. This method isn't really known for throwing that many exceptions, so the exception handler might be overkill. You be the judge, and take it out if it bothers you.

As you can see, I have also chosen to make this procedure private, as is the case with the prOpenDatabaseConnection procedure. I have done this for the same reason: the client shouldn't be able to call this method—it should be done automatically by your code when the class is disposed of.

Disposing of Your Class

When your class is disposed of, you must make sure that your connection is closed. Placing a call to a procedure that performs the closing of the connection in the class' destructor does this (see Listing 11-6).

Listing 11-6. Disposing of a Class

```
1 ~CUser() {
2     prCloseDatabaseConnection();
3 }
```

In Listing 11-6, I close the database connection from within the class destructor. You need to close the database connection explicitly; otherwise it will stay open and not be returned to the pool.

> **CROSS-REFERENCE** *Chapter 3A tells you more about connections and connection pools.*

Instantiating the Command Objects

The command objects used by the data adapter for manipulating the data source and the generic command object need to be instantiated, as demonstrated in Listing 11-7.

Listing 11-7. Instantiating the Command Objects

```
1 private void prInstantiateCommands() {
2     // Instantiate the data set command objects
3     prcmmUserSelect = new SqlCommand(PR_STR_SQL_USER_SELECT, prshcnnUserMan);
4     prcmmUserDelete = new SqlCommand(PR_STR_SQL_USER_DELETE, prshcnnUserMan);
5     prcmmUserInsert = new SqlCommand(PR_STR_SQL_USER_INSERT, prshcnnUserMan);
6     prcmmUserUpdate = new SqlCommand(PR_STR_SQL_USER_UPDATE, prshcnnUserMan);
7     // Instantiate and initialize generic command object
```

```
 8     prcmmUser = new SqlCommand();
 9     prcmmUser.Connection = prshcnnUserMan;
10 }
```

In Listing 11-7, I instantiate the command objects used by the data adapter for selecting, adding, updating, and deleting rows in the data source. I, then, instantiate the generic command object that can be used directly on the data source so that, for example, I can retrieve only certain columns from a table in a data reader using the command object's **ExecuteReader** method. I haven't specified any command text as this can be done when the command is executed, but I do specify the shared connection as the command's connection, because this is the connection I will use for all queries through this command. The prInstantiateCommands procedure should be added to the constructor in Listing 11-4 after the call to open the database connection.

Instantiating the DataSet Object

In line with most other objects, **DataSet** objects need to be instantiated as well before you can use them. Listing 11-8 shows you how to do this.

Listing 11-8. Instantiating the Data Set
```
1 private sub InstantiateDataSet() {
2     prdstUserMan = new DataSet();
3 }
```

As you can see from Listing 11-8, there isn't much code in the prInstantiateDataSet procedure. You don't really need any more code and as such you can consider taking the single line of code out of the procedure and placing it where you would normally place a call to the procedure. In any case, the instantiation code should be placed in the class constructor.

Instantiating and Initializing the Data Adapter

I just showed you to instantiate the data set, but the data set needs to be popu-lated from the data source, and this must be done using the data adapter. So, let's go ahead and instantiate and initialize the data adapter as shown in Listing 11-9.

Listing 11-9. Instantiating and Initializing the Data Adapter
```
1 private void prInstantiateAndInitializeDataAdapter() {
2     prdadUserMan = new SqlDataAdapter();
3     prdadUserMan.SelectCommand = prcmmUserSelect;
4     prdadUserMan.InsertCommand = prcmmUserInsert;
5     prdadUserMan.DeleteCommand = prcmmUserDelete;
6     prdadUserMan.UpdateCommand = prcmmUserUpdate;
7 }
```

In Listing 11-9, I instantiate the data adapter and initialize the command properties by setting them to the already instantiated command objects. You should add a call to the `prInstantiateAndInitializeDataAdapter` procedure to the class constructor.

Adding Command Object Parameters

Chapters 3A and 3B show you how to add parameters to your command objects so that the data adapter knows exactly how to query your data source. Listing 11-10 shows you how to perform this task for UserMan.

Listing 11-10. Adding Command Object Parameters

```
1 private void prAddCommandObjectParameters() {
2     // Add delete command parameters
3     prprmSQLDelete = prdadUserMan.DeleteCommand.Parameters.Add("@" +
5        PR_STR_SQL_FIELD_ID_NAME, SqlDbType.Int, 0, PR_STR_SQL_FIELD_ID_NAME);
6     prprmSQLDelete.Direction = ParameterDirection.Input;
7     prprmSQLDelete.SourceVersion = DataRowVersion.Original;
8
9     // Add update command parameters
10    prcmmUserUpdate.Parameters.Add("@" + PR_STR_SQL_FIELD_FIRST_NAME,
11       SqlDbType.VarChar, 50, PR_STR_SQL_FIELD_FIRST_NAME);
12    prcmmUserUpdate.Parameters.Add("@" + PR_STR_SQL_FIELD_LAST_NAME,
13       SqlDbType.VarChar, 50, PR_STR_SQL_FIELD_LAST_NAME);
14    prcmmUserUpdate.Parameters.Add("@" + PR_STR_SQL_FIELD_LOGIN_NAME,
15       SqlDbType.VarChar, 50, PR_STR_SQL_FIELD_LOGIN_NAME);
16    prcmmUserUpdate.Parameters.Add("@" + PR_STR_SQL_FIELD_PASSWORD_NAME,
17       SqlDbType.VarChar, 50, PR_STR_SQL_FIELD_PASSWORD_NAME);
18    prprmSQLUpdate = prdadUserMan.UpdateCommand.Parameters.Add("@" +
19       PR_STR_SQL_FIELD_ID_NAME, SqlDbType.Int, 0, PR_STR_SQL_FIELD_ID_NAME);
20    prprmSQLUpdate.Direction = ParameterDirection.Input;
21    prprmSQLUpdate.SourceVersion = DataRowVersion.Original;
22
23    // Add insert command parameters
24    prcmmUserInsert.Parameters.Add(PR_STR_SQL_FIELD_FIRST_NAME,
25       SqlDbType.VarChar, 50, PR_STR_SQL_FIELD_FIRST_NAME);
26    prcmmUserInsert.Parameters.Add("@" + PR_STR_SQL_FIELD_LAST_NAME,
27       SqlDbType.VarChar, 50, PR_STR_SQL_FIELD_LAST_NAME);
28    prcmmUserInsert.Parameters.Add("@" + PR_STR_SQL_FIELD_LOGIN_NAME,
29       SqlDbType.VarChar, 50, PR_STR_SQL_FIELD_LOGIN_NAME);
30    prcmmUserInsert.Parameters.Add("@" + PR_STR_SQL_FIELD_PASSWORD_NAME,
31       SqlDbType.VarChar, 50, PR_STR_SQL_FIELD_PASSWORD_NAME);
32 }
```

In Listing 11-10, I add the parameters needed by the data adapter for manipulating the data source to the command objects. The call to the `prAddCommandObjectParameters` procedure should be added to the class constructor in Listing 11-4.

Filling the Data Set

Now that everything has been set up, all you need to do is fill the data set with data from the data source. See Listing 11-11 for example code that accomplishes this task.

Listing 11-11. Populating the Data Set with Data from the Data Source

```
1 private void prPopulateDataSet() {
2     try {
3         prdadUserMan.Fill(prdstUserMan, PR_STR_SQL_TABLE_NAME);
4     }
5     catch (SystemException objSystemException) {
6         throw new Exception("The dataset could not be populated, " +
7             "because the source table was invalid.", objSystemException);
8     }
9     catch (Exception objE) {
10         throw new Exception("The dataset could not be populated.", objE);
11     }
12 }
```

Listing 11-11 is pretty simple—I try to fill the data set with data from the tblUser table in the data source. If an exception is thrown, I rethrow it with the original exception. This method should also be added to the class constructor.

Hooking Up the Public Properties to the Data Set

Now that the data set has been populated, the public properties can now be hooked up to the data set. All the properties read and set private variables, so you need to read the values from the populated data set and save them in the corresponding private variables, as demonstrated in Listing 11-12.

Listing 11-12. Saving the Data Set Values

```
1 private void prSaveDataSetValues() {
2     // Save user id
3     prlngId = (long)
4         prdstUserMan.Tables[PR_STR_SQL_TABLE_NAME].Rows[0]
5         [PR_STR_SQL_FIELD_ID_NAME];
6     // Check if ADName is Null
```

```
7    if (prdstUserMan.Tables[PR_STR_SQL_TABLE_NAME].Rows[0].
8       IsNull(PR_STR_SQL_FIELD_ADNAME_NAME)) {
9       prstrADName = "";
10   }
11   else {
12       prstrADName = prdstUserMan.Tables[PR_STR_SQL_TABLE_NAME].Rows[0]
13          [PR_STR_SQL_FIELD_ADNAME_NAME].ToString();
14   }
15   // Check if ADSID is Null
16   if (prdstUserMan.Tables[PR_STR_SQL_TABLE_NAME].Rows[0].
17       IsNull(PR_STR_SQL_FIELD_ADSID_NAME)) {
18       prstrADSID = "";
19   }
20   else {
21       prstrADSID = prdstUserMan.Tables[PR_STR_SQL_TABLE_NAME].Rows[0]
22          [PR_STR_SQL_FIELD_ADSID_NAME].ToString();
23   }
24   // Check if first name is Null
25   if (prdstUserMan.Tables[PR_STR_SQL_TABLE_NAME].Rows[0].
26       IsNull(PR_STR_SQL_FIELD_FIRST_NAME)) {
27       prstrFirstName = "";
28   }
29   else {
30       prstrFirstName = prdstUserMan.Tables[PR_STR_SQL_TABLE_NAME].Rows[0]
31          [PR_STR_SQL_FIELD_FIRST_NAME].ToString();
32   }
33   // Check if last name is Null
34   if (prdstUserMan.Tables[PR_STR_SQL_TABLE_NAME].Rows[0].
35       IsNull(PR_STR_SQL_FIELD_LAST_NAME)) {
36       prstrLastName = "";
37   }
38   else {
39       prstrLastName = prdstUserMan.Tables[PR_STR_SQL_TABLE_NAME].Rows[0]
40          [PR_STR_SQL_FIELD_LAST_NAME].ToString();
41   }
42   // Check if login name is Null
43   if (prdstUserMan.Tables[PR_STR_SQL_TABLE_NAME].Rows[0].
44       IsNull(PR_STR_SQL_FIELD_LOGIN_NAME)) {
45       prstrLoginName = "";
46
47   }
48   else {
49       prstrLoginName = prdstUserMan.Tables[PR_STR_SQL_TABLE_NAME].Rows[0]
```

```
50              [PR_STR_SQL_FIELD_LOGIN_NAME].ToString();
51      }
52      // Check if password is Null
53      if (prdstUserMan.Tables[PR_STR_SQL_TABLE_NAME].Rows[0].
54          IsNull(PR_STR_SQL_FIELD_PASSWORD_NAME)) {
55          prstrPassword = "";
56      }
57      else {
58          prstrPassword = prdstUserMan.Tables[PR_STR_SQL_TABLE_NAME].Rows[0]
59              [PR_STR_SQL_FIELD_PASSWORD_NAME].ToString();
60      }
61 }
```

In Listing 11-12, I simply read the values from the data set and save them in the corresponding private variables. Please note that I read from the very first row in the data set. I do this in order to facilitate sorting and filtering, which can be added later on. I have added a check for null values for the columns in the database that allow this.

Specifying the Parent Class

I don't know if you are wondering about what class your CUser class is derived from. If you've followed along with the example, you haven't actually told the compiler to inherit from another class. For the purposes of the UserMan application, you don't have to, because you want to inherit from the **object** class, which is done implicitly. This means you don't have to add the : object statement to your class declaration. However, if there is a different class you want to inherit from, you need to add the statement right after the class declaration, like this:

```
public class CUser : object {
```

CROSS-REFERENCE   *I discuss these issues in Chapter 9, where you started creating the* CUser *class.*

What Else Is Needed?

Obviously the CUser class isn't finished yet, although you've added a lot of code to it. What you need now is to add code to allow filtering and sorting of the rows in the data set, and, more importantly, code for updating the data source.

> **NOTE** *I have already added this code and a few other procedures to the* CUser *class, which can be found in the Downloads section on the Apress Web site (*http://www.apress.com*).*

Active Directory Object

You need an object for reading the values for the ADSID and ADName columns in the tblUser table. Listing 11-13 shows example code for this purpose.

Listing 11-13. The Active Directory Class

```
1 using System;
2 using System.Data.OleDb;
3 using System.Runtime.InteropServices;
4
5 namespace UserMan {
6     /// <summary>
7     /// Summary description for CActiveDirectory.
8     /// </summary>
9     public class CActiveDirectory {
10        private const string PR_STR_CONNECTION_STRING =
11            "Provider=ADsDSOObject;User Id=UserMan;Password=userman";
12        private string prstrADName;
13        private string prstrADSID;
14        private string prstrUserName;
15
16        public CActiveDirectory(string strUserName) {
17            prstrUserName = strUserName;
18            prOpenConnection();
19        }
20
21        ~ CActiveDirectory() {
22            prCloseConnection();
23        }
24
25        // Database objects
26        private OleDbConnection prcnnAD;
27        private OleDbCommand prcmmAD;
28        private OleDbDataReader prdrdAD;
29
30        private void prOpenConnection() {
```

```
31          // Instantiate and open connection
32          prcnnAD = new OleDbConnection(PR_STR_CONNECTION_STRING);
33          prcnnAD.Open();
34          prRetrieveUserInformation();
35      }
36
37      private void prCloseConnection() {
38          // Close connection
39          prcnnAD.Close();
40      }
41
42      private void prRetrieveUserInformation() {
43          try {
44              // Instantiate command
45              prcmmAD = new OleDbCommand("SELECT objectSid, samAccountName " +
46                  "FROM 'LDAP://userman.dk' WHERE objectCategory='person' " +
47                  "AND objectClass='user' AND cn='" + prstrUserName + "'",
48                  prcnnAD);
49              // Retrieve user info in data reader
50              prdrdAD = prcmmAD.ExecuteReader();
51              // Move to the first row
52              if (prdrdAD.Read()) {
53                  // Save SAM account name (pre-Windows 2000)
54                  prstrADName = prdrdAD["samAccountName"].ToString();
55                  // Save human readable SID
56                  prstrADSID = prConvertSID2SDDL((byte[]) prdrdAD["objectSid"]);
57              }
58          }
59          catch (Exception objE) {
60              throw new Exception("An error occurred trying to retrieve " +
61                  "the user information from Active Directory.", objE);
62          }
63      }
64
65      public string ADName {
66          get {
67              return prstrADName;
68          }
69      }
70
71      public string ADSID {
72          get {
```

```
73              return prstrADSID;
74          }
75      }
76   }
77 }
```

As you can see from Listing 11-13, I have used the OLE DB .NET Data Provider for retrieving the user information from AD. This provider is read-only when used with Active Directory, but this is okay because I only want to retrieve information.

> **CROSS-REFERENCE** *You can find more information about Active Directory access in Chapter 7.*

> **NOTE** *A finished* CActiveDirectory *class can be found in the Downloads section on the Apress Web site (*http://www.apress.com*) or at the UserMan site[3] (*http://www.userman.dk*).*

The constructor (Lines 16 through 19) for the CActiveDirectory class takes the login name of a user as the only argument, and this name is used for searching Active Directory for the samAccountName and the SID. This means that the CActiveDirectory class can be called from any client, such as the CUser class shown in Listing 11-14.

Listing 11-14. Calling the Active Directory Class

```
1 public void GetADUserInfo() {
2    probjActiveDirectory = new CActiveDirectory(prstrLoginName);
3    prstrADName = probjActiveDirectory.ADName;
4    prstrADSID = probjActiveDirectory.ADSID;
5 }
```

Other Objects

You need to create more classes than the ones you've already created, because you haven't finished wrapping all your data access. Here are some suggestions:

---

3. Don't forget to have the book by your side when you log on to the UserMan site because you're required to enter a word from a page in the book to gain access.

- Message queuing

- Data-bound controls

You will find implementations of these classes in the Downloads section on the Apress Web site (`http://www.apress.com`).

Wrapping Classes as Components

When you are done creating all your classes, you need to decide if one or more of them needs to be wrapped as a component for deployment on a server. It's really beyond the scope of this book to cover component building, but for your pleasure, I have included all the table classes wrapped in one component for deployment to be found in the Downloads section on the Apress Web site (`http://www.apress.com`). In most cases, it's a matter of which architecture your application has that determines if a class is wrapped in a component.

Creating the Client

At this point, the database has been put together and I have shown you how to create wrapper classes for some of the data-related access that I have covered in this book. So, now I need to show you how to create the client application. I have decided to show you how to create both a Windows client based on a Windows Form and a Web client based on a Web Form because these are the UIs I have covered in this book.

Creating a Windows Client

There isn't much in creating the Windows client that has anything to do with accessing the data in the UserMan application. I have therefore decided to leave out any sample code from the Windows client in this chapter. However, you can find a finished sample of the UserMan Windows client in the Downloads section on the Apress Web site (`http://www.apress.com`) or at the UserMan site[4] (`http://www.userman.dk`). The code holds plenty of comments that make it easier for you to read.

---

4. Don't forget to have the book by your side when you log on to the UserMan site because you're required to enter a word from a page in the book to gain access.

Creating a Web Client

As is the case with the Windows client, I haven't found any potential in showing you example code from the Web client here in this chapter, but you can find a finished version of the UserMan Web client in the Downloads section on the Apress Web site (http://www.apress.com) or at the UserMan site (http://www.userman.dk). The code is fairly well documented through the use of comments.

Tips and Ideas

In this section, I give you some tips and ideas for further developing the UserMan application so that you can perhaps use it for your own purposes. I have grouped the suggestions so that they are easier for you to go through.

Database Suggestions

In this section, you will find all the suggestions that are related to database improvements and/or enhancements.

Password Column in User Table

As you've probably noticed, the Password column in the tblUser table is a varchar(50) column that anyone with read access to the table can read. This means the password of any user, including the administrator's (UserMan), can be read by a user with read access. This is obviously not the way it should be. Several third-party vendors produce encryption components, but at the time of this writing, I haven't seen any for the .NET Framework. However, when you read this there probably will be one, or you could use a COM component though COM Interop (COM Interop is covered in Chapter 3B).

Another option is to create your own password encryption scheme. If you feel access to your network is fairly secure, a handy little routine of your own might be all that's needed.

Logging to the Event Log

Instead of logging to the tblLog table in the UserMan database, you could log events in the Windows NT Event Log. This will make your events available to all users able to read the Event Log on your network. Check out the **EventLog** class in the **System.Diagnostics** namespace for more information on how to read from and write to the Event Log.

Passing the Connection Object to the Various Classes

Instead of having a connection in each of your classes, you should consider passing an open connection to them for their use. This way you can share a connection between the classes. Again, this depends on how you've created your application, how it's been deployed, and the amount of traffic you expect on a single connection.

One last thing to consider if you want to implement this enhancement is whether any data reader you include will use the connection exclusively while it's open. So with data readers this is obviously not an option, unless you choose to have a general connection for your **DataSet** objects and one or more others for your DataReader objects.

Create Stored Procedures for Accessing Your Database Tables

As the classes are currently implemented, they access the data directly. However, you can change the implementation of the classes to use stored procedures instead. You might not want to do this until you see how performance is and determine whether it could be improved by using stored procedures instead. One of the really good things about using classes for database access in your application is you can change the implementation of your classes as long as you leave the interface intact, and the client applications won't detect that anything has changed.

Set Up Triggers to Enforce Business Rules

In Chapter 6, I showed you how to implement simple triggers, such as enforcing the inclusion of both a first name and a last name for a user, if you supply either. This is just one of many simple tasks that you can let a trigger handle for you instead of placing this functionality in your classes or, even worse, in your client code.

Setting up Database Security

I haven't done anything to implement security on the database level, meaning that more or less anyone with access to your network and DBMS can access your

UserMan database. I suggest one of the first things you do is add some sort of security if you haven't already done so. Ask your system administrator or read the documentation that comes with your DBMS for more information on how to implement security at the database level.

Use Constants for Table and Column Names

Replace all hard-coded table and column names such as tblUser and Id with constants as shown in Listing 11-1. It makes your code easier to update and maintain, and I personally think it makes your code easier to read, although you should feel free to disagree on this one.

Use Local Transactions

It's always a good thing to use transactions with any operations that write to a database. This hasn't been implemented in the classes for UserMan, and I strongly suggest you consider adding local transaction support.

> **CROSS-REFERENCE**   *Chapter 3A discusses local transactions, which are transactions that are explicitly started and ended using the connection object.*

General Suggestions

This section contains ideas and suggestions that don't really fit in elsewhere.

Let Active Directory Validate Users

Instead of having your own validation routine, why not let Active Directory perform one for you? This of course means that all users of your application need to be stored in Active Directory. Simply extend the Active Directory class to allow writing as well as reading.

Use Web Services to Expose Some Functionality

You could expose some of the application functionality from one or more Web Services. I won't be going into detail about Web Services in this book, but basically you use Web Services as methods of a Web Server to expose certain functionality across the Internet, intranet, or indeed any network using Simple Object Access Protocol (SOAP) over HTTP. This guarantees that you can use this functionality through a firewall.

> **NOTE**   *I am currently writing a book on basic Web Services, called* Building Web Services with Visual Basic .NET *(ISBN: 1590590074), to be published by Apress, and it will be available June 2002.*

Exception Handling

The two client applications have very little exception handling, and this is obviously not good. Go through the code and place exception handlers where you feel it's necessary. Looking over the various classes for places to add exception handling is probably not a bad idea either!

Use Automatic Transactions

All .NET Framework classes can be part of an automatic transaction. This means you can roll back or commit changes made in classes just as you can with database operations. All you have to do is make your class transactional. See the documentation for more information on how to do this.

Summary

This chapter finished the example application that the rest of the chapters in this book have been built upon. I showed you how to use some of the data-related tools and/or methods, such as Active Directory access and SQL Server access, introduced in earlier chapters, to build and finish the sample application.

I went on to give you some ideas and tips on how to take the sample application further and customize it for your own use.

Here we are at the end of the last chapter of this book. I sincerely hope you've enjoyed reading it as much as I have enjoyed writing it. I would love to hear from you if you have any queries and/or suggestions regarding this book. You can reach me at carstent@dotnetservices.biz. I am also interested in hearing from you if you have any improvements to the example application that you want to share with other readers. If so, please take a look here: http://www.userman.dk.

Using XML with SQL Server 2000

IN THIS APPENDIX, YOU'LL LEARN SOME ASPECTS of using XML with SQL Server 2000, and you'll be introduced to the SQLXML 2.0 plug-in, which you can use to access SQL Server databases using HTTP[1] once it's configured in IIS, and manipulate SQL Server data using the SQLXML Managed Classes, such as the **SqlXmlAdapter** class.

Microsoft started adding built-in XML capabilities with the release of SQL Server 2000. Now you can have result sets returned as XML documents and access data in an SQL Server database using HTTP. I've already mentioned one of the new XML capabilities in Chapter 3A, Listing 3A-25, where I showed you how the FOR XML clause can be used in a SELECT statement to make sure that the result set is formatted using XML. A few more keywords you can use in connection with the SELECT statement are shown in Table A-1. Please note that the SELECT . . . FOR XML construct must always be used with any of the shown keywords.

> **NOTE** *Because I feel it's important to understand some of the XML basics, you won't get to the actual C# listings until later in this appendix. If you feel that you know about using XML with SQL Server, you might want to go straight to the "Inspecting the SQLXML 2.0 Managed Classes" section later in this chapter.*

---

1. I'm using Internet Explorer 6.0 for the browser tests in this chapter, and I can't guarantee you'll get the same results with other browsers.

Table A-1. SELECT . . . FOR XML Statement Keywords

SELECT...FOR STATEMENT KEYWORD	DESCRIPTION	EXAMPLE	EXAMPLE OUTPUT
AUTO	This XML mode keyword is used for returning the result set as a nested XML tree. Each table that is referenced in the SELECT statement and returns at least one column as part of the result set is included in the XML output.	`SELECT * FROM tblUser FOR XML AUTO`	See Listing A-1.
BINARY BASE64	This is the default format for binary data when AUTO is specified; thus, it is not needed. However, you need to specify this mode when you retrieve binary data using either EXPLICIT or RAW. This mode means that the binary data is encoded using the Base-64 format.	`SELECT * FROM tblUser FOR XML RAW, BINARY BASE64`	
ELEMENTS	When you use the ELEMENTS keyword, the result set is returned as an XML document, like using just FOR XML AUTO. However, when ELEMENTS is also specified in the query, all the column values are also returned as elements, or rather as subelements of their respective table elements.	`SELECT * FROM tblUser FOR XML AUTO, ELEMENTS`	See Listing A-1.
EXPLICIT	The EXPLICIT keyword is used for letting the query writer (you, in most cases) control how the returned XML document should be shaped. I don't cover this topic in this chapter and I refer you to the SQLXML or SQL Server documentation.		

(continued)

Table A-1. SELECT . . . FOR XML Statement Keywords (continued)

SELECT...FOR STATEMENT KEYWORD	DESCRIPTION	EXAMPLE	EXAMPLE OUTPUT
RAW	The RAW XML mode keyword is used for transforming each row in the result set into an XML element. This means that each row is output as an element with name "row."	`SELECT * FROM tblUser FOR XML RAW`	See Listing A-2.
XMLDATA	The XMLDATA keyword option makes sure that an XML document schema is returned, but without a root element. The result set is then appended to the schema within the same namespace.	`SELECT * FROM tblUser FOR XML AUTO, XMLDATA`	See Listing A-3.

Listing A-1. SELECT . . . FOR XML AUTO, ELEMENTS Output

```
<?xml version="1.0" encoding="utf-8" ?>
- <UserMan>
  - <tblUser>
      <Id>1</Id>
      <FirstName>John</FirstName>
      <LastName>Doe</LastName>
      <LoginName>UserMan</LoginName>
      <Password>userman</Password>
    </tblUser>
  - <tblUser>
      <Id>2</Id>
      <FirstName>Carsten</FirstName>
      <LastName>Thomsen</LastName>
      <LoginName>User1</LoginName>
      <Password>password</Password>
    </tblUser>
  - <tblUser>
      <Id>3</Id>
      <ADName />
      <ADSID />
      <FirstName />
      <LastName />
      <LoginName>User2</LoginName>
```

```
            <Password>User2</Password>
        </tblUser>
    - <tblUser>
            <Id>4</Id>
            <ADName />
            <ADSID />
            <FirstName>FirstName</FirstName>
            <LastName>LastName</LastName>
            <LoginName>User3</LoginName>
            <Password>User3</Password>
        </tblUser>
    </UserMan>
```

Listing A-1 shows you the output of the SELECT * FROM tblUser FOR XML AUTO, ELEMENTS query. Notice how all the columns are subelements of the table element, which are repeated for each row, and not attributes, as you can see in Listing A-2.

Listing A-2. SELECT . . . FOR XML RAW Output

```
<?xml version="1.0" encoding="utf-8" ?>
- <UserMan>
        <row Id="1" FirstName="John" LastName="Doe" LoginName="UserMan"
            Password="userman" />
        <row Id="2" FirstName="Carsten" LastName="Thomsen" LoginName="User1"
            Password="password" />
        <row Id="3" ADName="" ADSID="" FirstName="" LastName="" LoginName="User2"
            Password="User2" />
        <row Id="4" ADName="" ADSID="" FirstName="FirstName" LastName="LastName"
            LoginName="User3" Password="User3" />
    </UserMan>
```

In Listing A-2, you can see how specifying the RAW mode creates elements for each row with the name of row, instead of tblUser, as browser output in Figure A-9. Please note that the row elements are too long to fit on one line. Listing A-3 shows you how the output from an XMLDATA query looks.

Listing A-3. SELECT . . . FOR XML AUTO, XMLDATA Output

```
    <?xml version="1.0" encoding="utf-8" ?>
- <UserMan>
    - <Schema name="Schema1" xmlns="urn:schemas-microsoft-com:xml-data"
        xmlns:dt="urn:schemas-microsoft-com:datatypes">
      - <ElementType name="tblUser" content="empty" model="closed">
            <AttributeType name="Id" dt:type="i4" />
            <AttributeType name="ADName" dt:type="string" />
```

```
        <AttributeType name="ADSID" dt:type="string" />
        <AttributeType name="FirstName" dt:type="string" />
        <AttributeType name="LastName" dt:type="string" />
        <AttributeType name="LoginName" dt:type="string" />
        <AttributeType name="Password" dt:type="string" />
        <attribute type="Id" />
        <attribute type="ADName" />
        <attribute type="ADSID" />
        <attribute type="FirstName" />
        <attribute type="LastName" />
        <attribute type="LoginName" />
        <attribute type="Password" />
    </ElementType>
  </Schema>
  <tblUser xmlns="x-schema:#Schema1" Id="1" FirstName="John" LastName="Doe"
    LoginName="UserMan" Password="userman" />
  <tblUser xmlns="x-schema:#Schema1" Id="2" FirstName="Carsten"
    LastName="Thomsen" LoginName="User1" Password="password" />
  <tblUser xmlns="x-schema:#Schema1" Id="3" ADName="" ADSID="" FirstName=""
    LastName="" LoginName="User2" Password="User2" />
  <tblUser xmlns="x-schema:#Schema1" Id="4" ADName="" ADSID=""
    FirstName="FirstName" LastName="LastName" LoginName="User3"
    Password="User3" />
</UserMan>
```

Listing A-3 shows you the output of the SELECT * FROM tblUser FOR XML AUTO, XMLDATA query. First you see the schema enclosed in the Schema tags, and after the schema you see the data in the result set, where each row is an element of the named schema.

There is certainly more to know about XML than this book can cover. If you need more information about XML, visit http://www.msdn.microsoft.com/library/default.asp?url=/nhp/Default.asp?contentid=28000438. You can also buy the XML book recommended in the "Installing SQLXML 2.0" section later in this chapter.

Using SQLXML 2.0

SQLXML 2.0 is a new plug-in for SQL Server that can be used to extend the XML capabilities in SQL Server 2000. As the version number 2.0 suggests, this is indeed a second release following the Web Release 1. I won't go into detail about what was included in the first version, but I will tell you about the features in SQLXML 2.0 that are related to the .NET Framework and HTTP support.

Installing SQLXML 2.0

You need to install the SQLXML 2.0 plug-in on a machine with at least the SQL Server client tools installed. In the scenario that I'm going to go through with you, I'm installing it on a machine with SQL Server 2000 installed and on my development machine, but as stated, you can choose to install it on just your development machine, as long as it has the SQL Server client tools installed. See your SQL Server documentation if you need to install the client tools. Basically, you're required to run the SQL Server Setup and choose what you want to install.

Another thing you need to have installed if you want to install HTTP support is IIS. This is the default on Windows 2000 Server versions, but if you're installing on a workstation such as Windows 2000 Professional or Windows XP, you need to make sure that you have IIS installed.

Anyway, you can download the SQLXML 2.0 plug-in from the MSDN Web site at this address: `http://msdn.microsoft.com/downloads/default.asp?url=/code/sample.asp?url=/MSDN-FILES/027/001/602/msdncompositedoc.xml&frame=true`.

Once you've downloaded the plug-in, you need to install it, which you do by running the sqlxml.msi file, a Windows Installer Package. Double-click the file to start the setup. A complete installation doesn't take up that much space (a few hundred megabytes), so I chose to do a complete installation on both machines. A complete installation includes the following:

- ISAPI Extension and Configuration for SQLXML (HTTP support)

- SQLXML Bulk Load (COM object for loading XML data into SQL Server tables)

- SQLXML Managed Classes for the .NET Framework (that's us . . .)

- SQLXML SDK

- Microsoft XML Parser 4.0

You can obviously choose to install any combination of the items in the preceding list, but you need to install the SQLXML Managed Classes and the XML Parser. This is the minimum requirement if you want to work with SQLXML from the .NET Framework. The ISAPI extension is for accessing SQL Server databases from a browser using HTTP, and it's necessary to reproduce the examples in this book. I don't cover the XML Parser or the Bulk Load feature in this chapter, but I can refer you to this book for more information:

- *XML Programming Using the Microsoft XML Parser,* by Soo Mee Foo and Wei Meng Lee. Published by Apress, February 2002. ISBN: 1893115429.

Configuring the ISAPI Extension

You need to configure the ISAPI extension using the IIS Virtual Directory Management for SQLXML 2.0 MMC snap-in (see Figure A-1) to gain access to data in your SQL Server databases using HTTP.

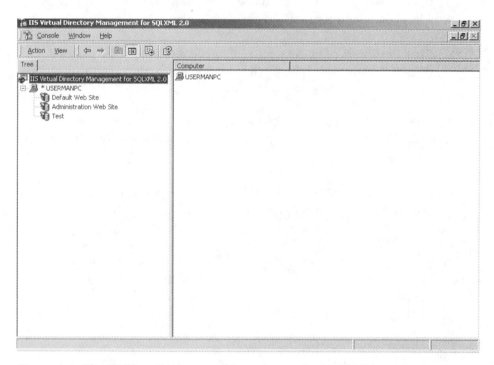

Figure A-1. The IIS Virtual Directory Management for SQLXML 2.0 MMC snap-in

In Figure A-1, you can see the IIS Virtual Directory Management for SQLXML 2.0 MMC snap-in opened on the machine I've also installed SQL Server on. If you install it on a machine, such as your development machine, where only the SQL Server client tools are installed, your MMC snap-in will look different. However, you'll have the Default Web Site node. You can use the Configure IIS Support menu shortcut in the SQLXML 2.0 menu that SQLXML 2.0 Setup creates. Actually, there's a similar shortcut in the Microsoft SQL Server menu on the machine that hosts your SQL Server installation, but this is the one that shipped with SQL Server, meaning it's an older version. Here's what you need to do:

1. Expand the node for the machine on which you have installed SQLXML.

2. Select the Default Web Site node, right-click the node, and select New/Virtual Directory.

3. On the General tab, give the virtual directory a name (as in Figure A-2), which also explains how the name is used from a browser. Then assign a local path for the virtual directory (as in Figure A-2).

4. Click the Security tab. Please note that you must create the path if it doesn't already exist. Here you'll enter the user credentials you want to connect to SQL Server with (see Figure A-3).

5. Click the Data Source tab to indicate which SQL Server to access. You can also select which default database to use on the specified server (see Figure A-4).

6. On the Settings tab, you'll need to change one default setting (Figure A-5): Check the Allow sql= . . . or template= . . . URL queries check box.

In Figure A-2, you can see General tab of the New Virtual Directory Properties dialog box. You need to give the virtual directory a name that can be used from an HTTP-capable application (a browser, for example) to access the content of the virtual directory. You also need to assign a local path where file content is stored.

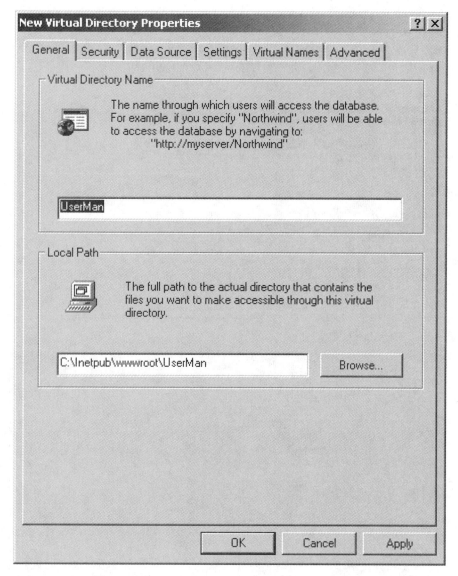

Figure A-2. The General tab of the New Virtual Directory Properties dialog box

In the Security tab of the New Virtual Directory Properties dialog box, shown in Figure A-3, type in the user credentials you want to connect to SQL Server with. You can use Windows Integrated Authentication, which means you need to log on as an existing user in Windows network; Basic Authentication, which means that the user needs to fill in a user name and password (typically done in an HTTP form) that is sent as clear text (nonencrypted) to SQL Server for validation as an SQL Server login; or you can choose to always use the same login, either Windows or SQL Server. The option you choose really depends on your setup, but I have chosen to always use the UserMan SQL Server login, as shown in Figure A-3.

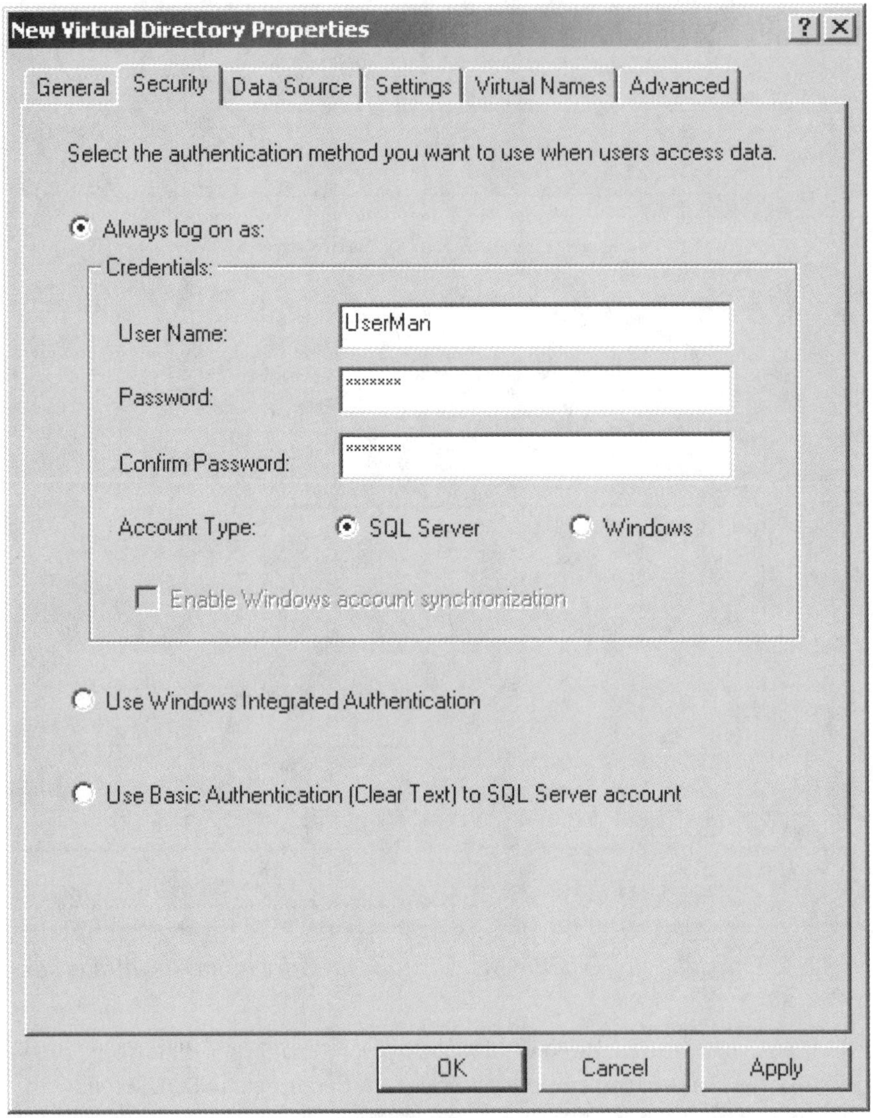

Figure A-3. The Security tab of the New Virtual Directory Properties dialog box

Figure A-4 shows the Data Source tab of the New Virtual Directory Properties dialog box. This is where you specify which SQL Server to access and, optionally, which default database to use on the specified server. You'll need to type in the

SQL Server you want to use for your virtual directory. You can also browse by clicking the Browse button next to the text box in the SQL Server frame. I've used (local), as shown in Figure A-4, because I installed SQLXML on the machine with the SQL Server. You can also select a different default database if the supplied credentials on the Security tab give you a "wrong" default database. I recommend you use the Browse button for this purpose, because this way you ensure that the connection, security settings, database name, and so on are confirmed. The default database is the database that is used when you log on—don't change it. I have chosen the UserMan database as my default database.

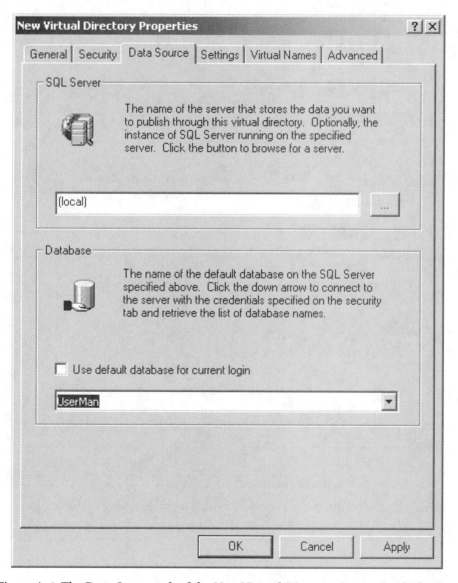

Figure A-4. The Data Source tab of the New Virtual Directory Properties dialog box

There are other options that you can set, but the ones already shown are the only ones that aren't optional. However, for the purpose of the exercises later in this chapter, you need to set change one default setting on the Settings tab, as shown in Figure A-5. On the Settings tab, check the "Allow sql= . . . or template= . . . URL queries" check box for some of the queries later in this chapter.

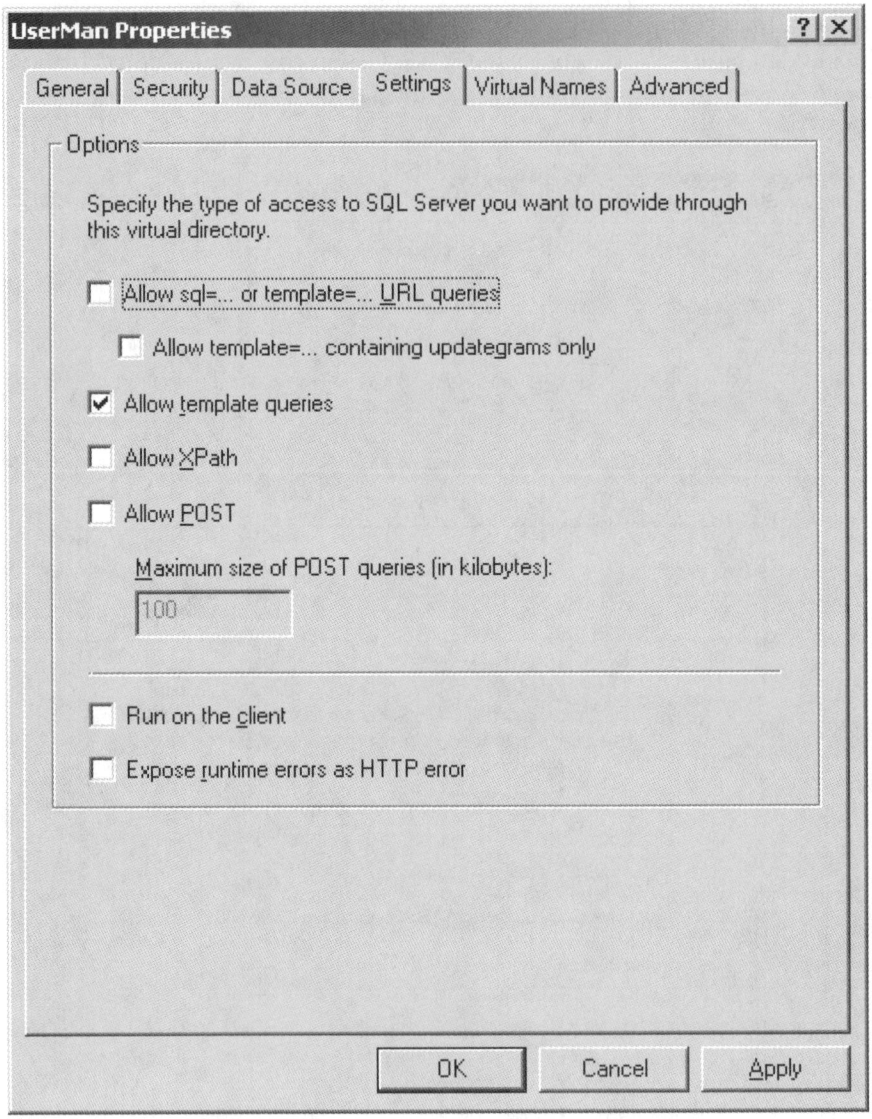

Figure A-5. The Settings tab of the New Virtual Directory Properties dialog box

Testing the ISAPI Extension

Once you've configured the ISAPI extension, you can test it using your browser. My first idea was to browse to the URL I specified during the ISAPI configuration, which is `http://localhost/userman`. Figure A-6 shows the result.

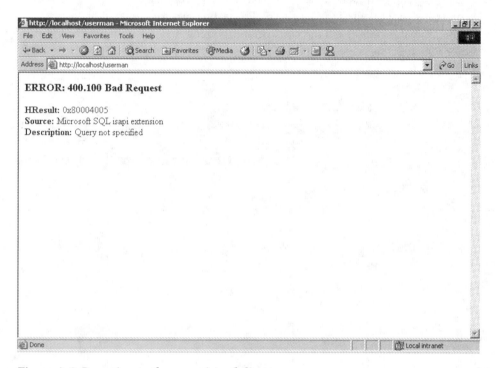

Figure A-6. Browsing to the new virtual directory

In Figure A-6, you can see from the error description on the page that I didn't specify a query to execute, which is really what this is all about. Mind you, if you were to try to access the same virtual directory from a remote client and not the machine you configured the ISAPI extension on, you would get a standard HTTP 400 Bad Request error: "The page cannot be found."

Restarting the Virtual Directory Application

When you've made changes to your virtual directory, it's always a good idea to restart it to make sure that your changes are applied immediately. You can restart the virtual directory application by right-clicking the virtual directory in the IIS Virtual Directory Management for SQLXML 2.0 MMC snap-in. You can see the virtual directory selected in Figure A-7. From the pop-up menu, click Restart Application and click Yes in the confirmation dialog box. Now a dialog box with either a success message or an error message is displayed. Click OK to close the message box.

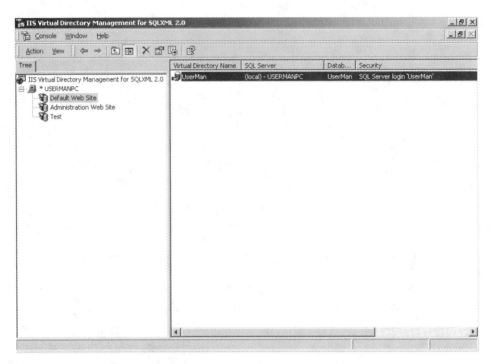

Figure A-7. Virtual directory selected in the IIS Virtual Directory Management for SQLXML 2.0 MMC snap-in

When you restart the virtual directory application this way, the application is unloaded from memory and actually not restarted until the next time it's accessed. Not that it really matters—just thought you'd like to know.

Besides restarting your virtual directory application, you should close any browser windows you've been using to query your SQL Server database using SQLXML 2.0.

Executing a Direct Query from the Browser

Now let's see if you can actually execute a query directly from your browser. "Directly" in this case means without a template—just a simple query expressed directly in the address bar of your browser. The basic syntax is as follows:

```
http://servername/virtualdirectory?sql=
```

where `servername` is the name of the server you've installed SQLXML on, which is localhost in my case. `virtualdirectory` is the name you gave your virtual directory when you set up the virtual directory. (See Figure A-2 earlier in this chapter.)

The `?sql=` bit is where the fun starts, because this is the actual query. Try this in your browser (don't worry about the lack of URL formatting—IIS and the ISAPI extension take care of it for you):

```
http:/servername/virtualdirectory?sql=SELECT * FROM tblUser FOR XML AUTO
```

If you've done as suggested when setting up the virtual directory, you should now have a browser window that looks similar to the one shown in Figure A-8.

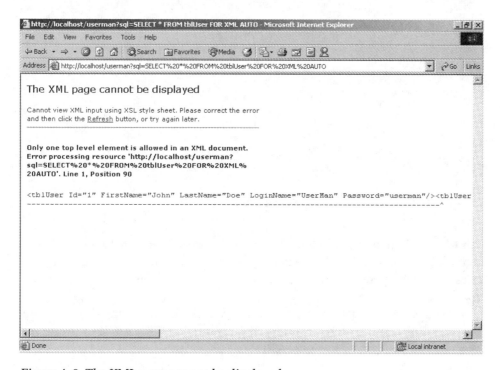

Figure A-8. The XML page cannot be displayed.

Figure A-8 shows you what your browser window looks like when executing the query after making sure that URL queries are allowed. The problem here is obviously that the returned XML has several root elements (tblUser). One way of fixing this is to execute this query:

```
www.servername/virtualdirectory?sql=SELECT * FROM tblUser FOR XML AUTO&root=root
```

Now your browser window should look similar to Figure A-9.

The query used for producing the results shown in Figure A-9 is shown just before the figure. Basically, it makes sure that you have a root tag/node, or

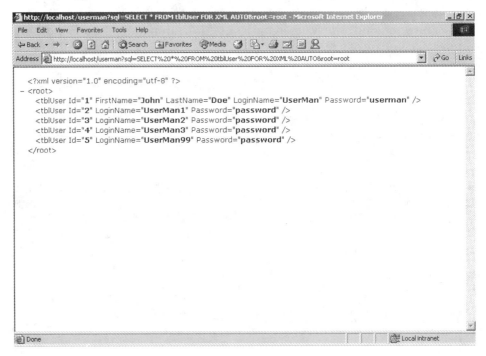

Figure A-9. The tblUser table displayed as XML in a browser

top-level element as it is called in Figure A-8. Instead of root=root you can use root=UserMan, or any other name than UserMan for that matter, as long as it doesn't contain spaces or special characters. It adds a root element by the name you specify.

You can also specify a template directly in the URL. The template in this case is a valid XML document that contains SQL statement(s). You can see the output of such a template query in Figure A-10.

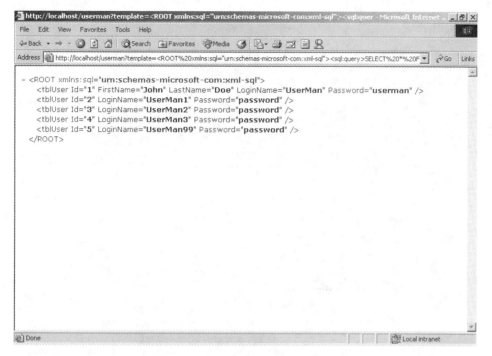

Figure A-10. The tblUser table displayed as XML using a template directly in the URL

In Figure A-10, you can see that the output from the template query is almost identical to the output shown in Figure A-9. The full template statement used in Figure A-10 looks like the one shown in Listing A-4.

Listing A-4. Template Query

```
<ROOT xmlns:sql="urn:schemas-microsoft-com:xml-sql">
   <sql:query>
      SELECT * FROM tblUser
      FOR XML AUTO
   </sql:query>
</ROOT>
```

The full template statement shown in Listing A-4 has obviously been formatted to make it more readable. In your browser's address bar, it needs to be input as one line, with no carriage return or line feed characters.

Another way of querying the tables in your database is using XPath by first creating the dbobject virtual name. You do this by opening the IIS Virtual Directory Management for SQLXML 2.0 MMC snap-in and double-clicking your virtual directory. This brings up the properties dialog box for the virtual directory. Click the Virtual Names tab in the dialog box. The Virtual Names tab is shown in Figure A-11.

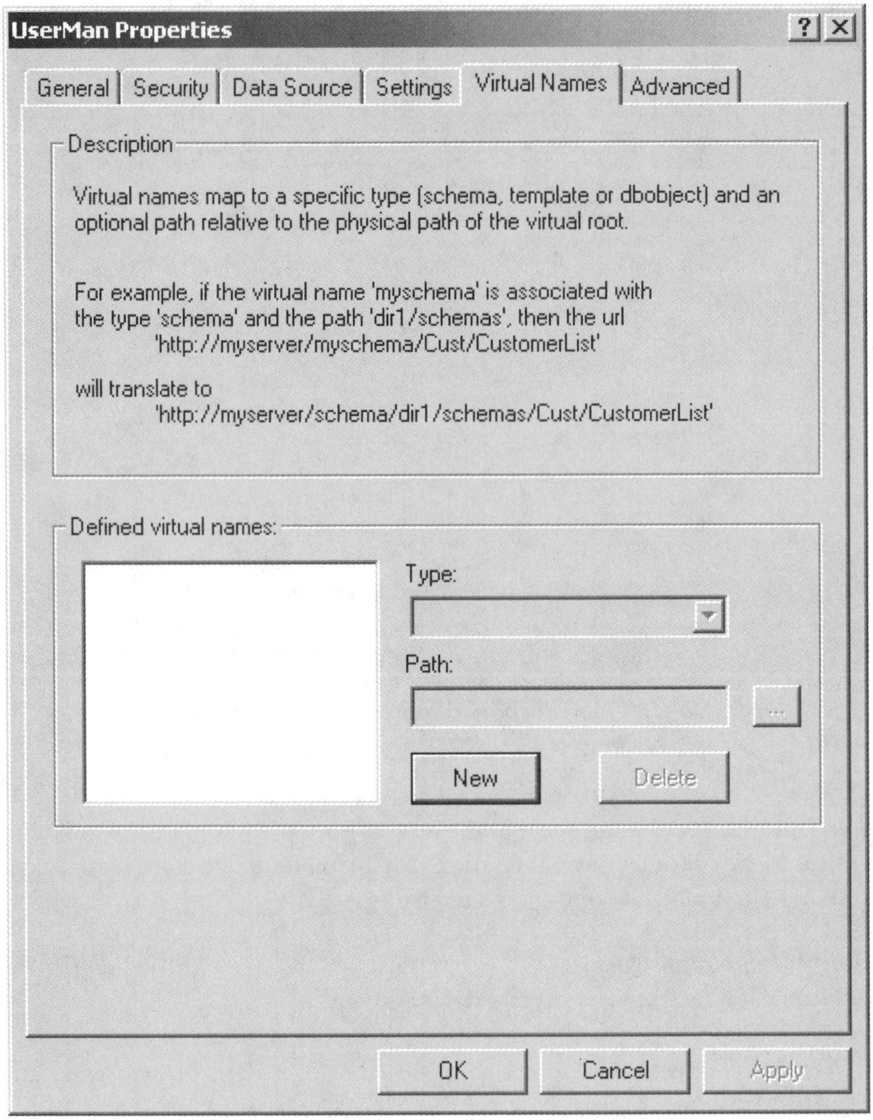

Figure A-11. The Virtual Names tab of the virtual directory properties dialog box

On the Virtual Names tab, you need to create a virtual name for the dbobject type. You do this by clicking the New button and typing in the name of your new dbobject type in the Virtual Name text box of the Virtual Name Configuration dialog box (see Figure A-12).

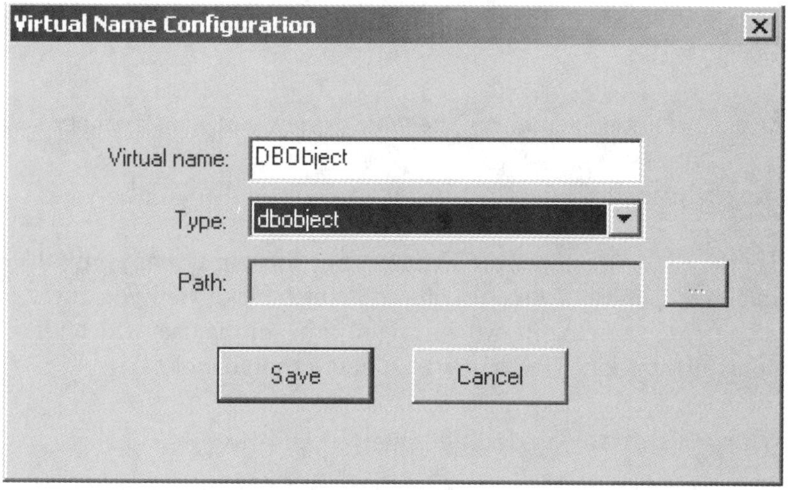

Figure A-12. The Virtual Name Configuration dialog box

In Figure A-12, you can see that you need to select the dbobject item from the Type list. Click OK once you've done this. You also need to make sure that XPath queries are allowed by checking the Allow XPath check box on the Settings tab of the properties dialog box. Close the properties dialog box. Now you can try this direct database object query from your browser:

```
http://localhost/userman/DBObject/tblUsers/@LoginName
```

> **NOTE** *You can find a detailed description of XPath at* http://www.w3.org/TR/xpath.

If your browser doesn't display any output, you might have to restart the virtual directory application for the changes to be applied immediately. See the "Restarting the Virtual Directory Application" section earlier in this chapter. Otherwise, all the values from the LoginName column of the tblUser table are shown in your browser window as one long line of text without spaces to separate the various values. Actually, only non-null values are displayed. You can use the DBObject virtual name for querying objects in your database, such as tables and views. Let's take a look at the previous query:

- localhost: This is the name of the Web server.

- userman: This is the name of your virtual directory.

- DBObject: This is virtual name used for querying table objects directly using XPath.

- tblUser: This is the name of the table or view you want to query.

- @LoginName: This is the column name you want displayed.

All of the elements shown are required, but you can actually limit the output by specifying a valid value for any column in the table or view you query. For example, say you want to retrieve the LoginName for the user with an ID of 1 from the tblUser table. This is how your query should look:

```
http://localhost/userman/DBObject/tblUsers[@Id=1]/@LoginName
```

The optional predicate, which must be enclosed in brackets as shown, should be used when you only want a single value returned, because when you specify the predicate all values except for the first one are ignored.

Security Concern with Direct URL Queries

One problem with the direct query or template query approach is that it is a security concern: basically, anyone can execute queries on your SQL Server, including action queries or non–row-returning queries. A better approach is to use templates directly, so for your own sake, please uncheck the "Allow sql= . . . or template= . . . URL queries" check box on the Settings tab of the Virtual Directory Properties dialog box and click OK. You might have to restart the virtual directory application for the changes to be applied immediately. See the "Restarting the Virtual Directory Application" section earlier in this chapter.

Executing a Query from the Browser Using File-Based Templates

Instead of executing queries and templates directly from a URL, it's much safer to provide some templates that users can execute. This way, you know exactly what kind of queries will be executed, because you can manage the templates. Before moving on, you need to make sure that the Allow template queries check box shown in Figure A-5 is checked. Otherwise, you won't be allowed to execute file-based queries. You also need to define a virtual name for a template folder before you can execute any template from the folder. You do this by opening the IIS Virtual Directory Management for SQLXML 2.0 MMC snap-in and double-clicking your virtual directory. This brings up the properties dialog box for the virtual directory. Click the Virtual Names tab in the dialog box. (The Virtual Names tab is shown in Figure A-11.)

On the Virtual Names tab, you need to create a virtual name for the template folder. However, I recommend creating a subfolder for holding your templates first, because you can't create a new folder from this dialog box. Open Windows Explorer and create a subfolder in the UserMan folder with the name Templates. Basically, what you need to do is associate a virtual name with the new physical subfolder. You do this on the Virtual Names tab, where you click the New button and type in the name of your new subfolder, Templates, in the Virtual Name text box of the Virtual Name Configuration dialog box. You can see this dialog box in Figure A-13.

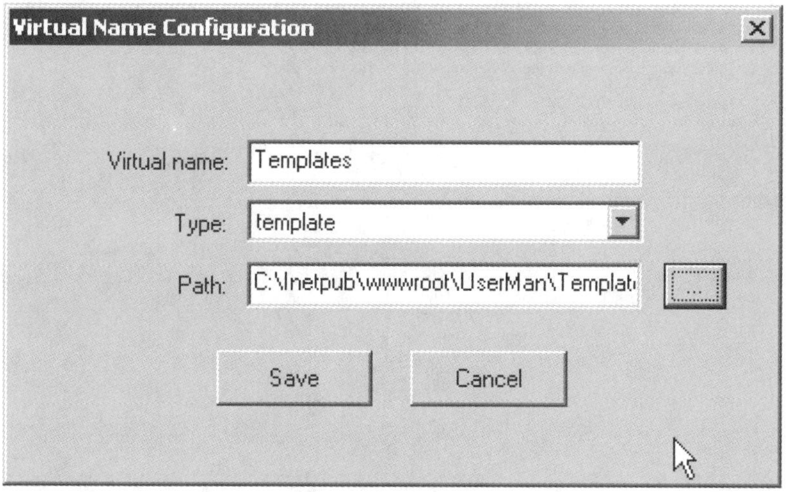

Figure A-13. The Virtual Name Configuration dialog box

In Figure A-13, you can see that you also need to select the Template item on the Type list and type in or browse to the new subfolder. Click OK once you've done this and close the properties dialog box. Now try out the file-based template functionality. You can type in the template shown in Listing A-4 into any text editor, such as Notepad, or even an XML editor, and save it as the file AllUsers.xml in the physical folder that maps to your Templates virtual directory. Then you can test it from your browser, as shown in Figure A-14. Well, you might need to change the URL slightly so it reads

```
http://localhost/userman/templates/allusers.xml
```

This URL consists of the server name (`localhost`), the virtual directory (`userman`), the virtual name (`templates`), and the name of a template (`allusers.xml`).

Does your browser window look like the one shown in Figure A-14? If not, you might have to restart the virtual directory application. See the "Restarting the Virtual Directory Application" section earlier in this chapter.

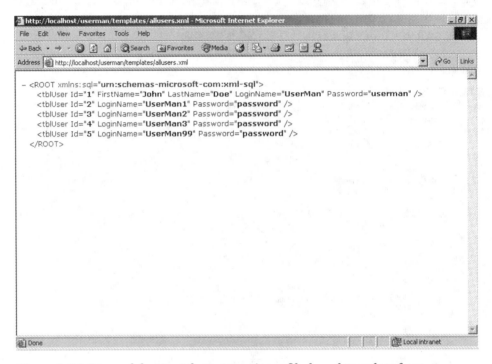

Figure A-14. Successful output from executing a file-based template from a browser

As you can see from Figure A-14, you simply need to add an XML document template, such as the AllUsers.xml one created earlier, and stick it in the Templates folder. Then your users can run the templates against your SQL Server data source.

Now, the template created earlier is fairly simple, but you can also create query templates that accept parameters, as shown in Listing A-5.

Listing A-5. Template Query with Parameters

```
<ROOT xmlns:sql="urn:schemas-microsoft-com:xml-sql">
  <sql:header>
    <sql:param name='LName'></sql:param>
  </sql:header>
  <sql:query>
```

```
    SELECT *
    FROM tblUser
    WHERE LastName = @LName
    FOR XML AUTO
  </sql:query>
</ROOT>
```

In Listing A-5, I've created a query that accepts one parameter, LName. Parameters must be defined in the sql:header section of the template using an sql:param tag for each parameter. You can't specify the data type, and as such, all parameters are strings. SQL Server takes care of converting the pass parameter if it doesn't match the data type in the column being compared with the parameter. An XML error message is returned if the parameter is of a wrong data type.

Save the query in Listing A-5 to a text file named Users.xml in the Templates folder, and run the following query from your browser:

```
http://localhost/userman/templates/users.xml?LName=Doe
```

Does your browser window now look like the one shown in Figure A-15?

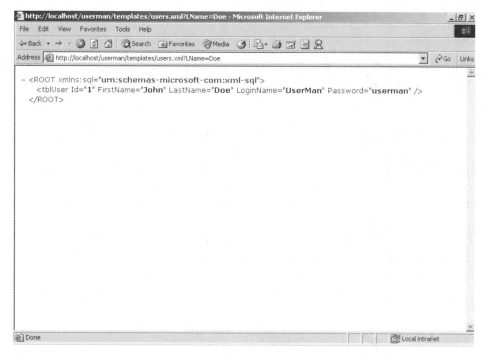

Figure A-15. Successful browser output from a template with parameters

This is all very simple because you specified that you want all users with a last name of Doe to be returned and that's that. What happens when you don't specify a value for LName? Run the query without specifying it, and now your browser should look like Figure A-16.

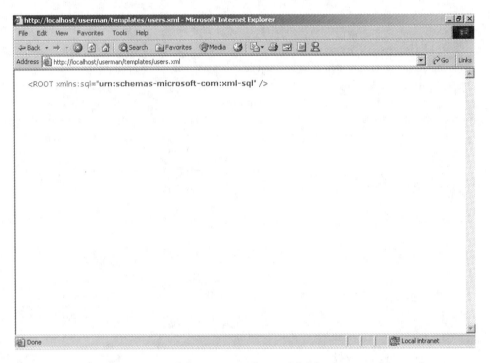

Figure A-16. No rows returned from a template with blank parameter values

It's pretty evident what happens in Figure A-16, isn't it? None of the rows in the tblUser table has a LastName of "" (empty string). If you were to add one row to the table with an empty string, you would have one row returned. However, you can specify a default value if the user running the template doesn't specify one. If you look at Line 3 in Listing A-5, you'll notice that nothing has been typed in between the opening and closing sql:param tags. You can add a value here, such as Doe, which means that if the user doesn't specify a value in the URL, all users with a last name of Doe are returned.

Inspecting the SQLXML 2.0 Managed Classes

The SQLXML 2.0 plug-in comes with a set of managed classes that you can use from within the .NET Framework just like any other managed classes. The managed classes can be used to manipulate XML data on an SQL Server. You should look at these managed classes as an extra option for manipulating data in SQL Server using XML and not as an alternative to the SQL Server .NET Data Provider. You should use the SQL Server .NET Data Provider, which is discussed in detail in Chapters 3A and 3B, when you want to manipulate your SQL Server data using standard relational SQL queries. You should use the SQLXML 2.0 Managed Classes when you want to manipulate your SQL Server data using XML DiffGrams and UpdateGrams.

Basically, the difference between the SQLXML Managed Classes and the SQL Server .NET Data Provider is that the SQLXML Managed Classes can be used to manipulate nonrelational data, whereas the SQL Server .NET Data Provider can't. You can use the SQL Server .NET Data Provider with the XML FOR clause in your SELECT statement to extract data, but you can't execute XPath queries and templates as you can with the SQLXML Managed Classes.

The SQLXML 2.0 Managed Classes use the SQL Server OLE DB Provider (SQLOLEDB) for connecting to SQL Server 2000. See the "Data Providers and Drivers" section in Chapter 3A for more information. In order to use the SQLXML Managed Classes, you need to reference the **Microsoft.Data.SqlXml** namespace from your project. Needless to say, you need to install the SQLXML 2.0 plug-in first (see the "Installing SQLXML 2.0" section earlier in this chapter).

The SQLXML Managed Classes include the following classes:

- **SqlXmlParameter**

- **SqlXmlAdapter**

- **SqlXmlCommand**

As you can see by comparing these three classes with the number of classes in the SQL Server .NET Data Provider, SQLXML 2.0 has substantially fewer classes. However, the three classes in SQLXML 2.0 can perform most of the functionality in the SQL Server .NET Data Provider classes. You'll be introduced to the three SQLXML Managed Classes in the following sections. I make references to the equivalent SQL Server .NET Data Provider classes, and you can find detailed descriptions of these classes in Chapter 3A.

Looking at the SqlXmlParameter Class

The **SqlXmlParameter** class is a rather simple class that is used for specifying parameters with your SQL statements. Basically, this class can only be used in conjunction with the **SqlXmlCommand** class (discussed later in this chapter). An object of type **SqlXmlParameter** is instantiated using the **CreateParameter** method of the **SqlXmlCommand** class, like this:

```
SqlXmlParameter prmLastName = cmdUserMan.CreateParameter();
```

This class has no methods, but it does have two properties, as shown in Table A-2.

*Table A-2. **SqlParameter** Class Properties*

NAME	DESCRIPTION	EXAMPLE
Name	This is the name of the property, which must equal the column name you're supplying a value for. Actually, this is only true when you're using named parameters. If you specify your parameters with a question mark (?), you don't have to give your parameters a name, but instead you must make sure that you add the parameters by calling the **CreateParameter** method in the order the parameters appear in the query (counting from left to right).	`prmLastName.Name = "LastName"`
Value	This mandatory value is what you want to pass as the parameter. You don't have to specify the single quotes when the column you're querying is a string column; the parameter class takes care of it for you.	`prmLastName.Value = "Doe"` `prmLastName.Value = "'Doe'"`

Refer to Listings A-16 and A-17 in the "Looking at the SqlXmlCommand Class" section later in this chapter for some example code that shows you how to use the **SqlXmlParameter** class.

Looking at the SqlXmlAdapter Class

The **SqlXmlAdapter** class serves the same purpose as the **SqlDataAdapter** class, but it has no properties and only two noninherited methods. The two methods are **Fill** and **Update**, which I'm sure you recognize from the **SqlDataAdapter** class. See the "Retrieving SQL Server Data Using the SqlXmlAdapter Class" and "Updating SQL Server Data Using the SqlXmlAdapter Class" sections later in this chapter. The **SqlXmlAdapter** class can only work with the **DataSet** class for retrieving and updating data in your data source.

Another difference between the **SqlDataAdapter** and **SqlXmlAdapter** classes is the constructors for the class, as you'll see in the next section.

Instantiating an SqlXmlAdapter Object

The **SqlXmlAdapter** class can be instantiated in three different ways:

- Using an **SqlXmlCommand** class as the only argument. You must make sure that the **SqlXmlCommand** object (cmdUserMan) has been instantiated before you execute any of the methods of the **SqlXmlAdapter** class.

```
SqlXmlAdapter dadUserMan = new SqlXmlAdapter(cmdUserMan);
```

- Using a command text string (strCommandText), an **SqlXmlCommandType** enum member, and a connection string (strConnectionString).

```
SqlXmlAdapter dadUserMan = new SqlXmlAdapter(strCommandText,
    SqlXmlCommandType.Sql, strConnectionString);
```

- Using a command stream (stmCommand), an **SqlXmlCommandType** enum member, and a connection string (strConnectionString).

```
SqlXmlAdapter dadUserMan = new SqlXmlAdapter(stmCommand,
    SqlXmlCommandType.Sql, strConnectionString);
```

It's beyond the scope of this book to work with streams, so I won't cover how to use a stream to instantiate an **SqlXmlAdapter** object, but besides that, here is a list of the various arguments:

- *cmdUserMan:* This must be an instantiated and initialized **SqlXmlCommand** object. See the "Looking at the SqlXmlCommand Class" section later in this chapter.

- *SqlXmlCommandType enum:* Use DiffGram, Sql (default), Template, TemplateFile, UpdateGram, or XPath. You'll see how to use these enum members later in this chapter.

- *strConnectionString:* Well, this one is pretty obvious as it's really an OLE DB provider connection string. Please see the "ConnectionString Property" section in Chapter 3A for more information. Listing A-6 shows you the one I use for the example code in the SQLXML 2.0 section.

Listing A-6. An SQLXML 2.0 Connection String

```
1 private const string PR_STR_CONNECTION_STRING =
2     "Provider=SQLOLEDB;Data Source=USERMANPC;User Id=UserMan;" +
3     "Password=userman;Initial Catalog=UserMan";
```

In Listing A-6, you can see how I've set up the connection string to be used with the SQLXML 2.0 Managed Classes. Basically, it's just another OLE DB connection string.

Retrieving SQL Server Data Using the SqlXmlAdapter Class

There are two ways to retrieve data from your SQL Server and into your **DataSet** object: with or without a command object. Listing A-7 shows you how to do it both ways.

*Listing A-7. Populating a DataSet Using the **SqlXmlAdapter***

```
1 public void PopulateDataSetUsingSql() {
2     // Declare SELECT statement
3     string strSQL = "SELECT * FROM tblUser FOR XML AUTO, ELEMENTS";
4     // Declare and instantiate DataSet
5     DataSet dstUserMan = new DataSet("UserMan");
6     // Declare, instantiate and initialize command
7     SqlXmlCommand cmdUser =
8         new SqlXmlCommand(PR_STR_CONNECTION_STRING);
9     cmdUser.CommandText = strSQL;
10
11     // Declare and instantiate adapters
12     SqlXmlAdapter dadUserMan1 =
13         new SqlXmlAdapter(cmdUser);
14     SqlXmlAdapter dadUserMan2 =
15         new SqlXmlAdapter(strSQL, SqlXmlCommandType.Sql,
16         PR_STR_CONNECTION_STRING);
17
18     // Fill DataSet. Uncomment one of the lines below
19     // and comment out the other to test either
20     dadUserMan1.Fill(dstUserMan);
21     //dadUserMan2.Fill(dstUserMan);
22 }
```

In Listing A-7, you can see how the two **SqlXmlAdapter**s, dadUserMan1 and dadUserMan2, are used to populate the dstUserMan **DataSet** object. If you notice the SELECT statement saved in the strSQL variable on Line 3, you'll see that I have specified the `,ELEMENTS` keyword as the last part of the SELECT statement. I've done this because otherwise the adapter will complain about too many root elements in the returned XML document. See Table A-1 for an explanation of the ELEMENT keyword. Remove the `,ELEMENTS` part of the statement and run the code to see an exception being thrown. Basically, what happens is that now all the rows returned are returned as elements, or rather subelements of the table element, which is then the root element.

If you leave out the ELEMENTS keyword in the SELECT statement, you can't use the dadUserMan2 adapter (Line 21) for populating your **DataSet**, because there's no way of getting around the "missing" root element. However, when you use the dadUserMan1 adapter that is instantiated using an **SqlXmlCommand** object, you can actually set the **RootTag** property of the command object and thus specify a root element to be used in the returned XML document. See Listing A-8 for an example of this.

*Listing A-8. Populating a DataSet Using the **SqlXmlAdapter** and **SqlXmlCommand** Classes*

```
1 public void PopulateDataSetUsingSql2() {
2     // Declare SELECT statement
3     string strSQL = "SELECT * FROM tblUser FOR XML AUTO";
4     // Declare and instantiate DataSet
5     DataSet dstUserMan = new DataSet("UserMan");
6     // Declare, instantiate and initialize command
7     SqlXmlCommand cmdUser =
8         new SqlXmlCommand(PR_STR_CONNECTION_STRING);
9     cmdUser.CommandText = strSQL;
10    // You need to set the RootTag property, because
11     // otherwise there is no root tag and an exception
12     // is thrown
13    cmdUser.RootTag = "UserMan";
14
15    // Declare and instantiate adapter
16    SqlXmlAdapter dadUserMan1 =
17        new SqlXmlAdapter(cmdUser);
18
19    // Fill DataSet
20    dadUserMan1.Fill(dstUserMan);
21 }
```

In Listing A-8, which is almost the same as the example code for the dadUserMan1 adapter in Listing A-7, I've used a SELECT statement (Line 3) without the ELEMENTS keyword, but instead used the **RootTag** property (Line 13) of the **SqlXmlCommand** class to specify the root element of the returned XML document.

So far, you've seen how to use a straightforward SELECT statement with the XML-specific SQL Server 2000 keywords appended (FOR XML . . .). However, you have other options. One option is to use a template string instead of an SQL query string, as Listing A-9 shows.

*Listing A-9. Populating a **DataSet** Using the **SqlXmlAdapter** and a Template String*

```
1 public void PopulateDataSetUsingTemplate() {
2     // Declare template
3     string strTemplate =
4         "<ROOT xmlns:sql='urn:schemas-microsoft-com:xml-sql'>" +
5         "<sql:query>" + "SELECT * FROM tblUser FOR XML AUTO" + "</sql:query>" +
6         "</ROOT>";
7     // Declare and instantiate DataSet
8     DataSet dstUserMan = new DataSet("UserMan");
9
10    // Declare and instantiate adapter
11    SqlXmlAdapter dadUserMan =
12        new SqlXmlAdapter(strTemplate, SqlXmlCommandType.Template,
13        PR_STR_CONNECTION_STRING);
14
15    // Fill DataSet
16    dadUserMan.Fill(dstUserMan);
17 }
```

In Listing A-9, the **SqlXmlAdapter** is instantiated with a template string (strTemplate) and the **Template** member of the **SqlXmlCommandType** enum (Line 12), which means that you execute an XML template in the form of a template string containing an SQL query instead of an SQL query.

If you look closer at the content of the strTemplate variable, you'll find that it's actually the same as the template query specified in Listing A-4. The template in Listing A-4 was used for executing from your browser's address bar, whereas Listing A-9 shows you how to do the exact same thing using the SQLXML 2.0 Managed Classes. The output from Listing A-4 is shown in Figure A-9, and if you add the code in Listing A-10 as Line 17 in Listing A-9 and open the C:\ReturnedDocument.xml XML document, you can verify that it is the same output.

Listing A-10. Writing an XML Document to Disk
```
dstUserMan.WriteXml("C:\\ReturnedDocument.xml");
```

One thing you have to be careful about with the template string method is that the content of the `strTemplate` variable isn't checked, meaning you can have all sorts of invalid characters and so on in the string. The problem—or maybe it isn't a problem to you—is that no exception is thrown, so you have to spot this in a different way. One very simple way is to check the number of tables in the **DataSet** after you've executed the **Fill** method, like this:

```
MessageBox.Show(dstUserMan.Tables.Count.ToString());
```

If the message box shows 0, then there's probably something wrong with your query template string, and if it shows 1, then it's probably working. I know this is simple, but it gives you an idea as to how to find out about possible problems: you check the content of your **DataSet**.

So far, so good, but you can also execute the same query (Listing A-4) using a file-based template, just as you did from the browser (see Figure A-14). Listing A-11 shows you how to execute the file-based XML template from your code.

Listing A-11. Executing a File-Based XML Template from Code
```
 1 public void PopulateDataSetUsingTemplateFile() {
 2     // Declare template file
 3     string strTemplateFile = "C:\\AllUsers.xml";
 4     // Declare output file
 5     string strOutputFile = "C:\\ReturnedDocument.xml";
 6     // Declare and instantiate DataSet
 7     DataSet dstUserMan = new DataSet("UserMan");
 8
 9     // Declare and instantiate adapter
10     SqlXmlAdapter dadUserMan =
11         new SqlXmlAdapter(strTemplateFile, SqlXmlCommandType.TemplateFile,
12         PR_STR_CONNECTION_STRING);
13
14     // Fill DataSet
15     dadUserMan.Fill(dstUserMan);
16     // Write xml document to disk
17     //dstUserMan.WriteXml(strOutputFile);
18 }
```

If you compare Listings A-9 and A-11, you'll find that the only real difference between them is that the very same XML template is input as either a string or a file, but the output is the same. If the template file you specify doesn't exist, a **FileNotFoundException** exception is thrown.

The template that you executed in Listing A-11 doesn't take any arguments, but you can execute the XML template shown in Listing A-5 and get the same result as in Figure A-15. However, if you replace the filename in Listing A-11 with the name of the XML template with an argument (Users.xml), you'll have an empty XML document returned. It's empty, or rather, it doesn't have any elements but the ROOT one, because you didn't specify the LName argument (see Lines 3 and 8 of Listing A-5). The problem is that you can't specify any arguments or parameters with the **SqlXmlAdapter** class. You need to use the **SqlXmlCommand** class for this.

> **NOTE**   *Arguments or parameters can't be used with the **SqlXmlAdapter** class; they can only be used with the **SqlXmlCommand** class.*

Updating SQL Server Data Using the SqlXmlAdapter Class

If you think back to the **SqlDataAdapter** class introduced in Chapter 3A, you'll remember that it's fairly easy to update your data source with changes from your **DataSet**. All you need to do is call the **Update** method of the **SqlDataAdapter** class, so this should be possible with the **SqlXmlAdapter** as well (see Listing A-12).

*Listing A-12. Updating the Data Source from a **DataSet***

```
1  public void UpdateDataSourceFromDataSet() {
2      // Declare template file
3      string strTemplateFile = "C:\\AllUsers.xml";
4      // Declare and instantiate DataSet
5      DataSet dstUserMan = new DataSet("UserMan");
6
7      // Declare and instantiate adapter
8      SqlXmlAdapter dadUserMan =
9          new SqlXmlAdapter(strTemplateFile, SqlXmlCommandType.TemplateFile,
10         PR_STR_CONNECTION_STRING);
11
12     // Fill DataSet
13     dadUserMan.Fill(dstUserMan);
14     // Update DataSet
15     dstUserMan.Tables["tblUser"].Rows[0]["FirstName"] = "Johnny";
16
17     if (dstUserMan.HasChanges()) {
```

```
18          // Indicate to the user that the dataset has changes
19          MessageBox.Show("The DataSet has been modified");
20          // Update data source
21          dadUserMan.Update(dstUserMan);
22     }
23 }
```

Basically, the example code in Listing A-12 is the same as in Listing A-11, except for Lines 14 through 22, where the **DataSet** is updated (the first row in the tblUser table has the FirstName column value set to "Johnny") and the changes are propagated back to the data source. In Listing A-12, I've used a file-based XML template to extract the data from the data source, but you can just as well use a SELECT command, as in Listing A-7, or a string-based XML template, as in Listing A-9, when you want to update your data source.

> **NOTE** *If you want to use DiffGrams or UpdateGrams with the SQLXML 2.0 Managed Classes, you must use the **SqlXmlCommand** class because the **SqlXmlAdapter** class doesn't support this.*

Looking at the SqlXmlCommand Class

The **SqlXmlCommand** class is the richest of the three SQLXML 2.0 Managed Classes because it exposes a number of methods and properties. I won't show you all of the methods and properties, but I will show you how to use most of them. Many of them will be used in various combinations in the example code listed in the following sections.

You can execute a simple row-returning query using the **SqlXmlCommand** class for populating a **DataSet** just as you can using the **SqlXmlAdapter** class (see Listings A-7 and A-8). However, the command class can do much more than the adapter class when it comes to executing queries. See the following sections for more information.

Instantiating an SqlXmlCommand Object

The **SqlXmlCommand** class is instantiated as follows:

```
cmdUser = new SqlXmlCommand(PR_STR_CONNECTION_STRING);
```

This is the only way to instantiate an **SqlXmlCommand** object. You can see an example of this in Listings A-7 and A-8.

Executing an SQL Query

A row-returning query executed by the **SqlXmlCommand** class obviously needs to save the result of the query somewhere. You can see how you can use the command class in conjunction with the **SqlXmlAdapter** class to save the return result to a **DataSet** in Listings A-7 and A-8, but you can also save it to an **XmlReader** class, as it Listing A-13.

*Listing A-13. Retrieving a Result Set in **XmlReader***

```
1 public void PopulateXmlReader() {
2     // Declare XmlReader
3     XmlReader xrdUser;
4     // Declare SELECT statement
5     string strSQL = "SELECT * FROM tblUser FOR XML AUTO";
6     // Declare, instantiate and initialize command
7     SqlXmlCommand cmdUser =
8         new SqlXmlCommand(PR_STR_CONNECTION_STRING);
9     cmdUser.CommandText = strSQL;
10    // Retrieve result set in Xml Reader
11    xrdUser = cmdUser.ExecuteXmlReader();
12 }
```

In Listing A-13, you can see how the SQL query declared on Line 5 is used for retrieving a result set from your data source by setting the **CommandText** property of the **SqlXmlCommand** class to the declared query string (Line 9). You don't have to specify the **CommandType** property, because the **SqlXmlCommandType.Sql** enum member is the default. Check out the "XmlReader" section in Chapter 3A for more information about the **XmlReader** class.

Besides saving the result set in an **XmlReader** class, you can save it to a stream (see Listing A-14). A *stream* is an abstraction of a sequence of bytes, where the abstraction can be a file or any other means of sequential data storage. There are two methods for saving to a stream: one for creating a new stream (**ExecuteStream**) and one for appending the results to an existing stream (**ExecuteToStream**).

Listing A-14. Saving a Result Set to a Stream

```
1 public void SaveCommandResultToStream() {
2     Stream stmUser;
3     StreamWriter smwUser;
4     // Declare SELECT statement
5     string strSQL = "SELECT * FROM tblUser FOR XML AUTO";
6     // Declare, instantiate and initialize command
```

```
 7    SqlXmlCommand cmdUser =
 8        new SqlXmlCommand(PR_STR_CONNECTION_STRING);
 9    cmdUser.CommandText = strSQL;
10    // You need to set the RootTag property, because
11    // otherwise there is no root tag
12    cmdUser.RootTag = "UserMan";
13
14    // Execute command and save result set in stream
15    stmUser = cmdUser.ExecuteStream();
16    // Read content of stream into stream reader
17    StreamReader smrUser = new StreamReader(stmUser);
18
19    // Create new file to hold the result stream
20    smwUser = new StreamWriter("C:\\Users.xml");
21    // Write the result set to disk
22    smwUser.Write(smrUser.ReadToEnd());
23    // Flush and close the stream writer
24    smwUser.Flush();
25    smwUser.Close();
26 }
```

In Listing A-14, I'm using the **ExecuteStream** method of the **SqlXmlCommand** class to save the result set to a stream. The stream is in memory, so I have also set up the example code so that the result set is read from the **Stream** object by a **StreamReader** object (Line 17) and finally written to disk by a **StreamWriter** object (Line 22). The output file, Users.xml, will look like Listing A-2. You can also use the **Console** class to output the result set to the console, like this:

```
Console.WriteLine(smrUser.ReadToEnd());
```

You can obviously choose not to write the content to disk, but I have done this so that you can actually see the result set. Using streams and readers, it is possible to manipulate, display, and exchange your XML data in many different ways.

In cases where you have an existing stream of XML data, you might want to append another result set to the existing data. Listing A-15 shows how to do this.

Listing A-15. Appending a Result Set to a Stream
```
1 public void AppendCommandResultToStream() {
2    Stream stmUser;
3    StreamWriter smwUser;
4    // Declare SELECT statement
```

```
5    string strSQL = "SELECT * FROM tblUser FOR XML AUTO";
6    // Declare, instantiate and initialize command
7    SqlXmlCommand cmdUser =
8        new SqlXmlCommand(PR_STR_CONNECTION_STRING);
9    cmdUser.CommandText = strSQL;
10   // You need to set the RootTag property, because
11   // otherwise there is no root element for the XML
12   // document
13   cmdUser.RootTag = "UserMan";
14
15   // Execute command and save result set in stream
16   stmUser = cmdUser.ExecuteStream();
17   // Append new result set to existing stream
18   cmdUser.ExecuteToStream(stmUser);
19   // Read content of stream into stream reader
20   StreamReader smrUser = new StreamReader(stmUser);
21
22   // Create new file to hold the result stream
23   smwUser = new StreamWriter("C:\\Users.xml");
24   // Set the stream position to 0
25   stmUser.Position = 0;
26   // Write the result set to disk
27   smwUser.Write(smrUser.ReadToEnd());
28   // Flush and close the stream writer
29   smwUser.Flush();
30   smwUser.Close();
31 }
```

In Listing A-15, I reuse the example code from Listing A-14 and add the call
to the **ExecuteToStream** method on Line 18. On Line 25, I make sure that the
Position property of the **Stream** object (stmUser) is set to 0, because the
ReadToEnd method reads from the current position in the stream. Basically, if
you don't reposition the stream, you'll end up with an empty XML document
(Users.xml), because the **ExecuteToStream** method positions the stream at the
very end of the stream. As you can see from Listing A-15, it's the same query
I execute on Lines 16 and 18, which also means it's the same result set I add to the
stream. If you run Listing A-15 and open the resulting Users.xml XML document,
you'll see that only one result set has been added to the stream and then written
to disk. Actually, this isn't quite true, because if you add a row to the tblUser table
in the UserMan database in between the two calls, this row will also be added to
the stream. This means that because the Id attribute of the tblUser element must

be unique, the rows that already exist in the stream are rejected. If you look at Figure A-17, you can see what I mean.

You can see that Figure A-17 differs from Figure A-9 by having one extra element—the element with an Id attribute of 6. This row was added to the tblUser table in between the calls to the **ExecuteStream** (Line 16) and the **ExecuteToStream** methods (Line 18).

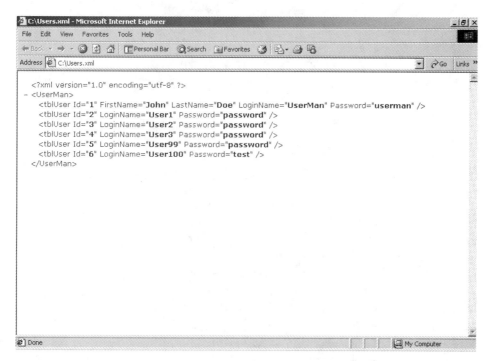

Figure A-17. Output from Listing A-15 with an extra row added between method calls

In this section, you saw how to execute standard SQL queries that don't take arguments or parameters. However, quite often you'll need to execute queries that do take parameters. Please see the following two sections, "Executing an SQL Query with Named Parameters" and "Executing an SQL Query with Positional Parameters," for more information on how to do this.

Executing an SQL Query with Named Parameters

SQL Server supports *named* parameters, meaning parameters that are referred to by name and not position. Listing A-16 shows you an example of the code from Listing A-14, where a named parameter has been added to the query.

Listing A-16. Executing a Query with Named Parameters

```
1 public void ExecuteNamedParameterCommand() {
2      Stream stmUser;
3      StreamWriter smwUser;
4      SqlXmlParameter prmLastName;
5      // Declare SELECT statement
6      string strSQL = "SELECT * FROM tblUser WHERE " +
7          "LastName=LastName FOR XML AUTO";
8      // Declare, instantiate and initialize command
9      SqlXmlCommand cmdUser =
10         new SqlXmlCommand(PR_STR_CONNECTION_STRING);
11     cmdUser.CommandText = strSQL;
12     // You need to set the RootTag property, because
13     // otherwise there is no root element for the XML
14     // document
15     cmdUser.RootTag = "UserMan";
16     // Add named parameter and set properties
17     prmLastName = cmdUser.CreateParameter();
18     prmLastName.Name = "LastName";
19     prmLastName.Value = "Doe";
20     // Execute command and save result set in stream
21     stmUser = cmdUser.ExecuteStream();
22     // Read content of stream into stream reader
23     StreamReader smrUser = new StreamReader(stmUser);
24
25     // Create new file to hold the result stream
26     smwUser = new StreamWriter("C:\\Users.xml");
27     // Write the result set to disk
28     smwUser.Write(smrUser.ReadToEnd());
29     // Flush and close the stream writer
30     smwUser.Flush();
31     smwUser.Close();
32 }
```

In Listing A-16, you can see how the query has been set up to accept a named parameter (Lines 6 and 7) and a named parameter is added to the **SqlXmlCommand** object using the **CreateParameter** method (Line 17). On Line 18, I set the name of the parameter, which must equal the name of the column you're using the parameter on, and on Line 19, I tell the parameter to only retrieve rows where the LastName column equals 'Doe'. The simple example in Listing A-16 is the same as executing this query:

```
SELECT * FROM tblUser WHERE LastName='Doe' FOR XML AUTO"
```

> **NOTE**   *It doesn't matter if you add single quotes to the **Value** property of the **SqlXmlParameter** class when the parameter is a string column, because the parameter class takes care of this.*

Figure A-18 shows you the resulting XML document from Listing A-16 in a browser.

Figure A-18. Output from Listing A-16

> **NOTE**   *If you don't supply a parameter—for example, if you comment out Lines 17 through 19 in Listing A-16—all rows from the tblUser table will be returned. This is also true if you have more than one parameter and you only supply some of the parameters. The fact that all rows are returned when one or more parameter values are missing is in contrast to working with positional parameters (see Listing A-17), where an exception is thrown if you don't supply the parameters.*

Executing an SQL Query with Positional Parameters

Instead of using named parameters when executing a query, you can use *positional* parameters, meaning that the order in which they're added to the command object must match the order in which they occur in the query, counting from left to right. For example, consider the following query:

```
SELECT * FROM tblUser
WHERE LastName=LastName AND FirstName=FirstName FOR XML AUTO"
```

In this query, you must first add a parameter for the LastName column and then the FirstName column. If you do it the other way around, you won't find any matching rows (unless you reverse the parameter values as well). Anyway, Listing A-17 shows you how to execute a query with positional parameters.

Listing A-17. Executing a Query with Positional Parameters

```
1 public void ExecutePositionalParameterCommand() {
2     Stream stmUser;
3     StreamWriter smwUser;
4     SqlXmlParameter prmLastName, prmFirstName;
5     // Declare SELECT statement
6     string strSQL = "SELECT * FROM tblUser WHERE LastName=? " +
7         "AND FirstName=? FOR XML AUTO";
8     // Declare, instantiate and initialize command
9     SqlXmlCommand cmdUser =
10        new SqlXmlCommand(PR_STR_CONNECTION_STRING);
11    cmdUser.CommandText = strSQL;
12    // You need to set the RootTag property, because
13    // otherwise there is no root element for the XML
14    // document
15    cmdUser.RootTag = "UserMan";
16    // Add positional parameters and set value properties
17    prmLastName = cmdUser.CreateParameter();
18    prmLastName.Value = "Doe";
19    prmFirstName = cmdUser.CreateParameter();
20    prmFirstName.Value = "John";
21    // Execute command and save result set in stream
22    stmUser = cmdUser.ExecuteStream();
23    // Read content of stream into stream reader
24    StreamReader smrUser = new StreamReader(stmUser);
25
26    // Create new file to hold the result stream
27    smwUser = new StreamWriter("C:\\Users.xml");
28    // Write the result set to disk
29    smwUser.Write(smrUser.ReadToEnd());
30    // Flush and close the stream writer
31    smwUser.Flush();
32    smwUser.Close();
33 }
```

In Listing A-17, which produces the same output as Listing A-16 (see Figure A-18), I use positional parameters to specify the rows I want returned. I add the LastName parameter first and then the FirstName parameter, because they're specified in that particular order in the query (Lines 6 and 7). I then set only the **Value** property of the two parameter objects, prmLastName and prmFirstName. Actually, it makes no difference whether or not you specify the **Name** property of the parameter objects, as it's done on Line 18 in Listing A-16. You can even give the parameter a completely different name than that of the column you're querying; it's simply ignored when you use the question mark (?) to specify a parameter in the query. Personally, I prefer the named parameters approach because I find that it makes the code easier to read and, more important, it saves you the potential problem of an incorrect parameter sequence when your code is later changed.

> **NOTE** *If you don't supply the parameters specified—for example, if you comment out Lines 17 through 20 in Listing A-17—a* **COMException** *exception is thrown. This isn't so when you work with named parameters (see Listing A-16).*

Executing XPath Queries

You can execute XPath queries in one of two ways: using a simple XPath query or against a mapping schema. I'll show you both ways.

A simple XPath query is executed as shown in Listing A-18.

Listing A-18. Executing a Simple XPath Query

```
 1 public void ExecuteXPathQuery() {
 2     Stream stmUser;
 3     StreamWriter smwUser;
 4     // Declare, instantiate and initialize command
 5     SqlXmlCommand cmdUser =
 6         new SqlXmlCommand(PR_STR_CONNECTION_STRING);
 7     cmdUser.CommandText = "tblUser/@LoginName";
 8     cmdUser.CommandType = SqlXmlCommandType.XPath;
 9     // You need to set the RootTag property, otherwise
10     // there is no root element to form a valid XML
11     // document
12     cmdUser.RootTag = "UserMan";
13     // Execute command and save result set in stream
14     stmUser = cmdUser.ExecuteStream();
15     // Read content of stream into stream reader
16     StreamReader smrUser = new StreamReader(stmUser);
17
18     // Create new file to hold the result stream
19     smwUser = new StreamWriter("C:\\Users.xml");
20     // Write the result set to disk
21     smwUser.Write(smrUser.ReadToEnd());
22     // Flush and close the stream writer
23     smwUser.Flush();
24     smwUser.Close();
25 }
```

In Listing A-18, you can see how the **CommandType** property of the command object is set to the **XPath** member of the **SqlXmlCommandType** enum (Line 8). Besides this, you need to set the **CommandText** property to the XPath query as is done in Line 7. The XPath query specified (`tblUser/@LoginName`) returns the non-null values from the LoginName column in the tblUser table. If this looks familiar to you, it's probably because you've read the paragraphs following Listing A-4 in which I discussed executing XPath queries from a browser. The way you construct your simple XPath to be executed from code or the browser query is exactly the same.

Anyway, the output from Listing A-18, which is the Users.xml XML document, can be displayed in a browser (see Figure A-19).

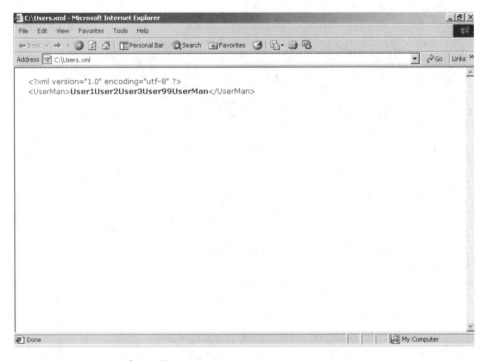

Figure A-19. Output from Listing A-18

In Figure A-19, you can see the content of the Users.xml document, which is created when running the example code in Listing A-18. There is no formatting of the XPath query output; as you can see from Figure A-19, all column values are displayed as one long string, without spaces between the column values, within the UserMan root element.

If you need formatting of the returned XML document or values from more than one column returned, you must use a mapping schema, such as the one shown in Listing A-19.

Listing A-19. Mapping Schema for an XPath Query

```
 1 <xsd:schema xmlns:xsd="http://www.w3.org/2001/XMLSchema"
 2     xmlns:sql="urn:schemas-microsoft-com:mapping-schema">
 3     <xsd:element name="Users" sql:relation="tblUser" >
 4         <xsd:complexType>
 5             <xsd:sequence>
 6                 <xsd:element name="FName"
 7                     sql:field="FirstName"
 8                     type="xsd:string" />
 9                 <xsd:element name="LName"
10                     sql:field="LastName"
11                     type="xsd:string" />
12                 <xsd:element name="LogName"
13                     sql:field="LoginName"
14                     type="xsd:string" />
15                 <xsd:element name="Pwd"
16                     sql:field="Password"
17                     type="xsd:string" />
18             </xsd:sequence>
19             <xsd:attribute name="Id" type="xsd:integer" />
20         </xsd:complexType>
21     </xsd:element>
22 </xsd:schema>
```

The mapping schema shown in Listing A-19 defines an element named Users (Line 3) that you can query using XPath. This element has a relation to the tblUser table in the database. Then you have the definition of a complex type with the FirstName, LastName, LoginName, and Password columns in sequence. The columns, or rather elements, as they are in the XML document, will be returned in the XML document that is the output from an XPath query. Finally, you see the attribute definition on Line 19, which means that the value of the Id column in the table is added to each Users element as an attribute. This way, you have unique Users elements returned (see Figure A-20). Listing A-20 shows you how to output all the columns from the tblUser table, using the mapping schema shown in Listing A-19, which has been saved to the file C:\Users.xsd.

Listing A-20. Executing an XPath Query Against a Mapping Schema

```
1 public void ExecuteXPathQueryUsingMappingSchema() {
2      Stream stmUser;
3      StreamWriter smwUser;
4      // Declare, instantiate and initialize command
5      SqlXmlCommand cmdUser =
6          new SqlXmlCommand(PR_STR_CONNECTION_STRING);
7      cmdUser.CommandText = "Users";
8      cmdUser.CommandType = SqlXmlCommandType.XPath;
9      cmdUser.SchemaPath = "C:\\Users.xsd";
10     // You need to set the RootTag property, otherwise
11     // there is no root element to form a valid XML
12     // document
13     cmdUser.RootTag = "UserMan";
14     // Execute command and save result set in stream
15     stmUser = cmdUser.ExecuteStream();
16     // Read content of stream into stream reader
17     StreamReader smrUser = new StreamReader(stmUser);
18
19     // Create new file to hold the result stream
20     smwUser = new StreamWriter("C:\\Users.xml");
21     // Write the result set to disk
22     smwUser.Write(smrUser.ReadToEnd());
23     // Flush and close the stream writer
24     smwUser.Flush();
25     smwUser.Close();
26 }
```

The only differences between Listings A-18 and A-20 are in Line 7, where I have specified an XPath query (Listing A-18) or an element that's mapped to an SQL Server table in a mapping schema (Listing A-20), and the **SchemaPath** property, which has been set to the mapping schema file shown in Listing A-19. You can see the output from running the example code in Listing A-20 in Figure A-20.

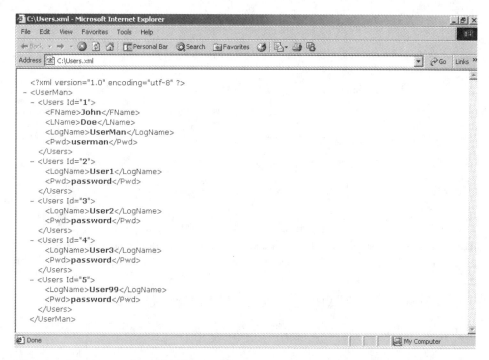

Figure A-20. Output from Listing A-20

Updating the Data Source Using the SqlXmlCommand Class

So far, you've seen how you can use the **SqlXmlCommand** class for querying the data source in various ways, but you can also use it to update the data source. There are a few different ways of doing this:

- Using the **ExecuteNonQuery** method

- Using a DiffGram

- Using an UpdateGram

The **ExecuteNonQuery** method is pretty straightforward. It works exactly like the method of the same name of the **SqlCommand** class, which you can find more information about in Chapter 3A. Listing A-21 shows you how to execute an action query or non–row-returning statement, such as an SQL DELETE, INSERT, or UPDATE statement.

Listing A-21. Executing a Non–Row-Returning SQL Statement

```
1 public void ExecuteNonQuery() {
2    // Declare, instantiate and initialize command
3    SqlXmlCommand cmdUser =
4       new SqlXmlCommand(PR_STR_CONNECTION_STRING);
5    cmdUser.CommandText = "UPDATE tblUser " +
6       "SET FirstName='FirstName' WHERE FirstName IS NULL";
7    // Execute non query
8    cmdUser.ExecuteNonQuery();
9 }
```

Listing A-21 updates the FirstName column of all rows in the tblUser table where the FirstName column holds a null value to the string 'FirstName'. There isn't much magic to this as it's a simple SQL statement. However, the **ExecuteNonQuery** method can also be used to execute XML string templates and file-based XML templates.

Listing A-22 shows you an XML template for updating your data source.

Listing A-22. XML Template for Updating the Data Source

```
1 <ROOT xmlns:sql="urn:schemas-microsoft-com:xml-sql">
2    <sql:query>
3       UPDATE tblUser
4       SET FirstName='FirstName'
5       WHERE FirstName IS NULL
6    </sql:query>
7 </ROOT>
```

The template in Listing A-22 does the same thing as the SQL statement in Listing A-22: it updates the tblUser table. Listing A-23 shows you how to execute the template as a string template.

Listing A-23. Executing a Non–Row-Returning String Template

```
1 public void ExecuteNonQueryStringTemplate() {
2    // Declare, instantiate and initialize command
3    SqlXmlCommand cmdUser =
4       new SqlXmlCommand(PR_STR_CONNECTION_STRING);
5    cmdUser.CommandText =
6       "<ROOT xmlns:sql='urn:schemas-microsoft-com:xml-sql'>" +
7       "<sql:query>" +
8       "UPDATE tblUser " +
9       "SET FirstName='FirstName' WHERE FirstName IS NULL" +
10      "</sql:query>" +
11      "</ROOT>";
```

```
12    cmdUser.CommandType = SqlXmlCommandType.Template;
13    // Execute non query
14    cmdUser.ExecuteNonQuery();
15 }
```

Listing A-23 uses a string template for updating the data source, but you can also use a file-based template as in Listing A-24, where the template shown in Listing A-22 has been saved as a file named UpdateUsers.xml to C:\.

Listing A-24. Executing a Non–Row-Returning Template
```
1 public void ExecuteNonQueryTemplate() {
2     // Declare, instantiate and initialize command
3     SqlXmlCommand cmdUser =
4         new SqlXmlCommand(PR_STR_CONNECTION_STRING);
5     cmdUser.CommandText = "C:\\UpdateUsers.xml";
6     cmdUser.CommandType = SqlXmlCommandType.TemplateFile;
7     // Execute non query
8     cmdUser.ExecuteNonQuery();
9 }
```

Listings A-23 and A-24 are both used for executing a template that updates the data source. However, as stated earlier, you have two more options when you want to do this: DiffGrams and UpdateGrams.

DiffGrams were introduced with the .NET Framework for serializing **DataSet** objects for transporting over any network where the **DataSet** can be reconstructed from the information in the DiffGram. This means that DiffGrams are *not* specifically for use with SQL Server, although the coverage here is all about SQL Server usage. You can find more detailed information about DiffGrams at http://msdn.microsoft.com/library/default.asp?url=/library/en-us/cpguide/html/cpcondiffgrams.asp.

In Listing A-25, I show you how to create a DiffGram from a populated **DataSet** and then update your data source using the DiffGram.

Listing A-25. Generating and Executing a DiffGram
```
1 public void ExecuteDiffGram() {
2     // Declare template file
3     string strTemplate = "C:\\AllUsers.xml";
4     // Declare and instantiate DataSet
5     DataSet dstUserMan = new DataSet("UserMan");
6
7     // Declare and instantiate adapter
8     SqlXmlAdapter dadUserMan =
9         new SqlXmlAdapter(strTemplate, SqlXmlCommandType.TemplateFile,
```

```
10          PR_STR_CONNECTION_STRING);
11
12     // Fill DataSet
13     dadUserMan.Fill(dstUserMan);
14     // Update DataSet
15     dstUserMan.Tables["tblUser"].Rows[0]["FirstName"] = "Johnny"; // Update
16     dstUserMan.Tables["tblUser"].Rows[3].Delete();                    // Delete
17     dstUserMan.Tables["tblUser"].Rows.Add(new object[5] {null,
18        null, null, "NewLogin", "password"});                        // Insert
19     // Save dataset as diffgram
20     dstUserMan.WriteXml("C:\\Users-DiffGram.xml", XmlWriteMode.DiffGram);
21
22     // Declare, instantiate and initialize command
23     SqlXmlCommand cmdUser =
24        new SqlXmlCommand(PR_STR_CONNECTION_STRING);
25     cmdUser.CommandText = "C:\\Users-DiffGram.xml";
26     cmdUser.CommandType = SqlXmlCommandType.TemplateFile;
27     // Execute diffgram
28     cmdUser.ExecuteNonQuery();
29 }
```

In Listing A-25, I populate the dstUserMan DataSet (Line 13) with the
dadUserMan **SqlXmlAdapter** that uses the AllUsers.xml XML template file from
Listing A-4 saved to C:\. I then update, delete, and insert a row in the
DataSet (Lines 15 through 17) and save the **DataSet** as a DiffGram in the file
C:\Users-DiffGram.xml. Finally, the DiffGram file is used as a template for updat-
ing the data source (Lines 23 through 28). The DiffGram looks like Figure A-21.

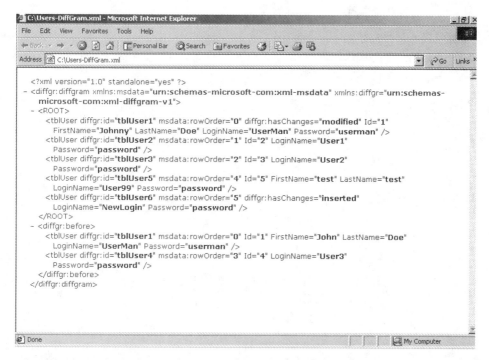

Figure A-21. The DiffGram created in Listing A-25

In Listing A-25, I use the **DataSet** class to create a DiffGram, but you can just as well create a DiffGram manually instead of programmatically. You can use a DiffGram for any kind of update to the data in your data source, and it's XML, meaning it's in plain text format. This is very handy for communicating over the "wire" or the Internet, and especially through firewalls that generally don't allow binary objects to pass through.

A DiffGram is really a subset of an UpdateGram, which was introduced with the XML for Microsoft SQL Server 2000 Web Release 1, the previous version of SQLXML 2.0. I won't cover UpdateGrams in this appendix.

Summary

This appendix showed you how to use the SQLXML 2.0 plug-in for accessing SQL Server databases using HTTP (typically in a browser), including configuring and testing the ISAPI extension. You also saw how to use the three SQLXML Managed Classes (**SqlXmlAdapter**, **SqlXmlCommand**, and **SqlXmlParameter**) from within the .NET Framework to manipulate data in SQL Server databases as XML.

Index

using Connection class events with, 85–86

using Connection class methods with, 80–84

using Connection class properties with, 76–80

using DataReader class with, 146

using **Equals** method in, 87–88

using members of **ConnectionState** Enum with, 89

ADO.NET disconnected layer
introduction to, 193

role of data source locking in, 265–276

using classic ADO and COM Interop with, 276–278

using cursors in, 261–265

using **DataColumn** class in, 249–252

using **DataRelation** class in, 252–261

using **DataRow** class in, 245–249

using **DataSet** class with, 193–194

using **DataTable** class with, 218–223

using **DataView** class in, 238–245

using XML with **DataSet** class in, 195–196

ADSID column in tblUser column for CUser class, details of, 514

adsPath, retrieving from Active Directory with OLE DB .NET data providers, 432

AFTER triggers, functionality of, 406

aggregated data, using views for, 398

Alias grid pane column in Query Designer, 326

AllowDBNull DataColumn class property, description of, 250

AllowDelete DataView class property, description of, 239

AllowEdit DataView class property, description of, 239

AllowNew DataView class property, description of, 239

Alt+F11 keyboard shortcut, accessing Macros IDE with, 22

anomalies in normal forms, explanation of, 46

Antechinus C# Programming Editor, Web site for, 15

Append grid pane column in Query Designer, 326

Application Name **ConnectionString** property value, details of, 66–67

ApplicationException class, explanation of, 356

ApplyDefaultSort DataView class property, description of, 239

Apress Web site
accessing, 57

downloading UserMan classes from, 567

ArgumentException exception, 351
handling for DataReader, 160

throwing, 113

thrown by **CommandTimeout** property, 143

thrown by **CommandType** property, 144

thrown by **UpdatedRowSource** property, 145–146

ArgumentNullException exception, 351, 353

ArgumentOutOfRangeException exception, 170, 351, 354

arguments
advisory about usage with **SqlXmlAdapter** and **SqlXmlCommand** classes, 617

creating stored procedures with, 382–384

using stored procedures with, 384–385

arguments and return values, running stored procedures with, 385–387

ASP (Active Server Pages), evolution of, 5

ASP.NET data binding, maintaining state in, 548–549

ASP.NET, explanation of, 5

ASP.NET server controls, binding to data sources, 545–548

assemblies
functionality of, 9–11

interaction of namespaces with, 13

assembly attributes, customizing, 11

Assert Debug class method, 363

assertions
definition of, 360

using with **Debug** class, 362–364

asterisks (*), advisory about, 434

AttachDBFilename **ConnectionString** property value, details of, 66–67

AttributeCount XmlReader class property, 162

auditing, securing message queuing with, 502

authenticated messages, sending, 494–495

authentication, securing message queuing with, 490–495

AuthenticationType property of
  DirectoryEntry class,
  description of, 417
AUTO SELECT . . . FOR XML statement
  keyword, description of, 588
AutoIncrement DataColumn class
  property, description of, 250
AutoIncrementSeed DataColumn class
  property, description of, 250
AutoIncrementStep DataColumn class
  property, description of, 250
automatic garbage collection, role in
  .NET Framework, 8
automatic transactions
  explanation of, 110
  use of, 586

B

backslash (\) in Active Directory hierar-
  chies, 420
BaseURI XmlReader class property, 162
BEFORE triggers, functionality of, 406
Begin method of Transaction class,
  description of, 109
BeginEdit DataRow class property,
  description of, 246
BeginLoadData DataTable class
  method, description of, 221
BeginTransaction method
  exception handling, 111–112
  of **OdbcConnection** class, 83, 101
  of **OleDbConnection** class, 81
  of **SqlConnection** class, 80, 100–101
BINARY BASE64 SELECT . . . FOR XML
  statement keyword,
  description of, 588
binding context, examining for Windows
  forms, 527–528
BindingContext object, role in Windows
  forms, 527–528, 538–539
Bindings property of **CurrencyManager**
  class, description of, 540
Body setting for message queue encryption, explanation of, 497–498
BOF (Beginning-Of-File), moving cursors to, 263–264
Broken member of **ConnectionState**
  Enum, description of, 89
broken ownership chain, explanation of,
  376
browsers
  appearance after restarting virtual
    directory in SQLXML 2.0, 602
  troubleshooting in SQLXML 2.0,
    609–610
browsing scope, definition of, 19

Bulk Load feature of SQLXML 2.0,
  resource for, 593

C

*.cmd extension, explanation of, 303
C (country) moniker, role in LDAP syntax, 421
C# keywords related to OOP, list of,
  510–511
Cancel Command class method,
  description of, 138
CancelCurrentEdit CurrencyManager
  class method, description of,
  540
CancelEdit DataRow class property,
  description of, 246
CanResolveEntity XmlReader class
  property, 162
Caption DataColumn class property,
  description of, 250
cascades, role in referential integrity, 44
CaseSensitive property
  of **DataSet** class, 197
  of **DataTable** class, 219
catch blocks
  role in exception handling, 344,
    348–349
  role in filtering exceptions, 355
ChangeDatabase method
  of **OleDbConnection** class, 81, 83
  of **SqlConnection** class, 80
  throws exception, 114
Chaos member of **IsolationLevel** Enum,
  description of, 102
child tables
  explanation of, 39
  and referential integrity, 44–45
ChildColumns DataRelation class
  property, description of, 254
ChildKeyConstraint DataRelation
  class property, description of,
  254
ChildRelations DataTable class property, description of, 219
Children property of **DirectoryEntry**
  class, description of, 417
ChildTable DataRelation class property,
  description of, 254
Class View in Solution Explorer, switch-
  ing to, 507
classes, wrapping as components, 582
clear **DataSet**, explanation of, 209
clear **DataTable**, explanation of, 227
Clear method
  of **DataSet** class, 199
  of **DataTable** class, 221

644

.NET Framework class library, contents
of, 13–14
Net or Network Library
ConnectionString property
value, details of, 72–73
Network Address **ConnectionString**
property value, details of,
72–73
network directory services, explanation
of, 413
network resources, performance
resources optimization of, 369
New Project dialog box, displaying, 296
New Value grid pane column in Query
Designer, 326
NewRow DataTable class method,
description of, 222
NextResult method of DataReader class,
159
nodes, separating in Active Directory
hierarchy, 420
NodeType XmlReader class property,
163
non-row returning SQL statements, executing, 632
non-row-returning string templates,
executing, 632–633
non-row-returning templates, executing, 633
normal forms, explanation of, 46–51
normalization in databases, explanation
of, 46
not equal to (<>) column comparison
symbol, role in Query
Designer join types, 323
NotSupportedException exception,
handling for DataReader, 160
null values
advisory when using
CommandBuilder class, 190
checking in columns, 149–150
in databases, definition of, 36
role in databases, 36
NullReferenceException exception,
explanation of, 350, 352

O

O (organization) moniker, role in LDAP
syntax, 421
Object Browser, role in VS .NET IDE,
19–20
object property values, manipulating
with Active Directory, 426–429
objects
binding to in Active Directory,
421–422

checking structural integrity with
DBCC, 371–372
determining for databases, 37
querying with DBObject virtual
name, 605–606
searching in Active Directory,
422–425
objectSid retrieving from Active
Directory with OLE DB .NET
data providers, 432
objUser object declaration, examining
in Data Form Wizard,
536–537
ODBC connection pooling, disabling,
94–96
ODBC connection strings, setting up,
61–62
ODBC object pooling, clearing, 96
ODBC (Open Data Base Connectivity),
Web site for, 96
ODBC (Open Data Base Connectivity)
data sources, accessing in
ADO, 59
ODBC standard escape sequences, Web
sites for, 137
OdbcCommand class
instantiating, 126–127
properties of, 79, 135–137
usage of, 124
OdbcConnection class,
BeginTransaction method of,
101
OdbcConnection data type, pooling
connections of, 94–96
OdbcConnection exceptions, handling,
119–123
OdbcConnection managed connection,
explanation of, 63–64
OdbcDataAdapter class, setting com-
mand properties in, 182–184
OdbcDataReader class, use of, 147
OdbcError class, examining, 119–120
OdbcException class, examining,
121–123
ODBC .NET data provider, downloading,
58
OdbcTransaction classes, nesting trans-
actions with, 106
OLE DB connection pooling, disabling,
93
OLE DB drivers
in ADO.NET connected layer, 59
specifying when connecting, 61–62
OLE DB .NET data provider, accessing
Active Directory with,
429–436

Apress Titles

ISBN	PRICE	AUTHOR	TITLE
1-893115-73-9	$34.95	Abbott	Voice Enabling Web Applications: VoiceXML and Beyond
1-893115-01-1	$39.95	Appleman	Dan Appleman's Win32 API Puzzle Book and Tutorial for Visual Basic Programmers
1-893115-23-2	$29.95	Appleman	How Computer Programming Works
1-893115-97-6	$39.95	Appleman	Moving to VB. NET: Strategies, Concepts, and Code
1-59059-023-6	$39.95	Baker	Adobe Acrobat 5: The Professional User's Guide
1-893115-09-7	$29.95	Baum	Dave Baum's Definitive Guide to LEGO MINDSTORMS
1-893115-84-4	$29.95	Baum, Gasperi, Hempel, and Villa	Extreme MINDSTORMS: An Advanced Guide to LEGO MINDSTORMS
1-893115-82-8	$59.95	Ben-Gan/Moreau	Advanced Transact-SQL for SQL Server 2000
1-893115-91-7	$39.95	Birmingham/Perry	Software Development on a Leash
1-893115-48-8	$29.95	Bischof	The .NET Languages: A Quick Translation Guide
1-893115-67-4	$49.95	Borge	Managing Enterprise Systems with the Windows Script Host
1-893115-28-3	$44.95	Challa/Laksberg	Essential Guide to Managed Extensions for C++
1-893115-39-9	$44.95	Chand	A Programmer's Guide to ADO.NET in C#
1-893115-44-5	$29.95	Cook	Robot Building for Beginners
1-893115-99-2	$39.95	Cornell/Morrison	Programming VB .NET: A Guide for Experienced Programmers
1-893115-72-0	$39.95	Curtin	Developing Trust: Online Privacy and Security
1-59059-008-2	$29.95	Duncan	The Career Programmer: Guerilla Tactics for an Imperfect World
1-893115-71-2	$39.95	Ferguson	Mobile .NET
1-893115-90-9	$49.95	Finsel	The Handbook for Reluctant Database Administrators
1-59059-024-4	$49.95	Fraser	Real World ASP.NET: Building a Content Management System
1-893115-42-9	$44.95	Foo/Lee	XML Programming Using the Microsoft XML Parser
1-893115-55-0	$34.95	Frenz	Visual Basic and Visual Basic .NET for Scientists and Engineers
1-893115-85-2	$34.95	Gilmore	A Programmer's Introduction to PHP 4.0
1-893115-36-4	$34.95	Goodwill	Apache Jakarta-Tomcat
1-893115-17-8	$59.95	Gross	A Programmer's Introduction to Windows DNA
1-893115-62-3	$39.95	Gunnerson	A Programmer's Introduction to C#, Second Edition
1-59059-009-0	$39.95	Harris/Macdonald	Moving to ASP.NET: Web Development with VB .NET
1-893115-30-5	$49.95	Harkins/Reid	SQL: Access to SQL Server
1-893115-10-0	$34.95	Holub	Taming Java Threads
1-893115-04-6	$34.95	Hyman/Vaddadi	Mike and Phani's Essential C++ Techniques
1-893115-96-8	$59.95	Jorelid	J2EE FrontEnd Technologies: A Programmer's Guide to Servlets, JavaServer Pages, and Enterprise JavaBeans
1-893115-49-6	$39.95	Kilburn	Palm Programming in Basic
1-893115-50-X	$34.95	Knudsen	Wireless Java: Developing with Java 2, Micro Edition
1-893115-79-8	$49.95	Kofler	Definitive Guide to Excel VBA
1-893115-57-7	$39.95	Kofler	MySQL
1-893115-87-9	$39.95	Kurata	Doing Web Development: Client-Side Techniques
1-893115-75-5	$44.95	Kurniawan	Internet Programming with VB

ISBN	PRICE	AUTHOR	TITLE
1-893115-38-0	$24.95	Lafler	Power AOL: A Survival Guide
1-893115-46-1	$36.95	Lathrop	Linux in Small Business: A Practical User's Guide
1-893115-19-4	$49.95	Macdonald	Serious ADO: Universal Data Access with Visual Basic
1-893115-06-2	$39.95	Marquis/Smith	A Visual Basic 6.0 Programmer's Toolkit
1-893115-22-4	$27.95	McCarter	David McCarter's VB Tips and Techniques
1-893115-76-3	$49.95	Morrison	C++ For VB Programmers
1-893115-80-1	$39.95	Newmarch	A Programmer's Guide to Jini Technology
1-893115-58-5	$49.95	Oellermann	Architecting Web Services
1-893115-81-X	$39.95	Pike	SQL Server: Common Problems, Tested Solutions
1-59059-017-1	$34.95	Rainwater	Herding Cats: A Primer for Programmers Who Lead Programmers
1-59059-025-2	$49.95	Rammer	Advanced .NET Remoting
1-893115-20-8	$34.95	Rischpater	Wireless Web Development
1-893115-93-3	$34.95	Rischpater	Wireless Web Development with PHP and WAP
1-893115-89-5	$59.95	Shemitz	Kylix: The Professional Developer's Guide and Reference
1-893115-40-2	$39.95	Sill	The qmail Handbook
1-893115-24-0	$49.95	Sinclair	From Access to SQL Server
1-893115-94-1	$29.95	Spolsky	User Interface Design for Programmers
1-893115-53-4	$44.95	Sweeney	Visual Basic for Testers
1-59059-002-3	$44.95	Symmonds	Internationalization and Localization Using Microsoft .NET
1-893115-29-1	$44.95	Thomsen	Database Programming with Visual Basic .NET
1-59059-010-4	$54.95	Thomsen	Database Programming with C#
1-893115-65-8	$39.95	Tiffany	Pocket PC Database Development with eMbedded Visual Basic
1-893115-59-3	$59.95	Troelsen	C# and the .NET Platform
1-893115-26-7	$59.95	Troelsen	Visual Basic .NET and the .NET Platform
1-59059-011-2	$39.95	Troelsen	COM and .NET Interoperability
1-893115-54-2	$49.95	Trueblood/Lovett	Data Mining and Statistical Analysis Using SQL
1-893115-16-X	$49.95	Vaughn	ADO Examples and Best Practices
1-893115-68-2	$49.95	Vaughn	ADO.NET and ADO Examples and Best Practices for VB Programmers, Second Edition
1-59059-012-0	$49.95	Vaughn/Blackburn	ADO.NET Examples and Best Practices for C# Programmers
1-893115-83-6	$44.95	Wells	Code Centric: T-SQL Programming with Stored Procedures and Triggers
1-893115-95-X	$49.95	Welschenbach	Cryptography in C and C++
1-893115-05-4	$39.95	Williamson	Writing Cross-Browser Dynamic HTML
1-893115-78-X	$49.95	Zukowski	Definitive Guide to Swing for Java 2, Second Edition
1-893115-92-5	$49.95	Zukowski	Java Collections
1-893115-98-4	$54.95	Zukowski	Learn Java with JBuilder 6

Available at bookstores nationwide or from Springer Verlag New York, Inc. at 1-800-777-4643; fax 1-212-533-3503. Contact us for more information at sales@apress.com.

Apress Titles Publishing SOON!

ISBN	AUTHOR	TITLE
1-59059-022-8	Alapati	Expert Oracle 9i Database Administration
1-59059-015-5	Clark	An Introduction to Object Oriented Programming with Visual Basic .NET
1-59059-000-7	Cornell	Programming C#
1-59059-014-7	Drol	Object-Oriented Flash MX
1-59059-033-3	Fraser	Managed C++ and .NET Development
1-59059-038-4	Gibbons	Java Development to .NET Development
1-59059-030-9	Habibi/Camerlengo/ Patterson	Java 1.4 and the Sun Certified Developer Exam
1-59059-006-6	Hetland	Practical Python
1-59059-003-1	Nakhimovsky/Meyers	XML Programming: Web Applications and Web Services with JSP and ASP
1-59059-001-5	McMahon	Serious ASP.NET
1-59059-021-X	Moore	Karl Moore's Visual Basic .NET: The Tutorials
1-893115-27-5	Morrill	Tuning and Customizing a Linux System
1-59059-020-1	Patzer	JSP Examples and Best Practices
1-59059-028-7	Rischpater	Wireless Web Development, 2nd Edition
1-59059-026-0	Smith	Writing Add-Ins for .NET
1-893115-43-7	Stephenson	Standard VB: An Enterprise Developer's Reference for VB 6 and VB .NET
1-59059-032-5	Thomsen	Database Programming with Visual Basic .NET, 2nd Edition
1-59059-007-4	Thomsen	Building Web Services with VB .NET
1-59059-027-9	Torkelson/Petersen/ Torkelson	Programming the Web with Visual Basic .NET
1-59059-004-X	Valiaveedu	SQL Server 2000 and Business Intelligence in an XML/.NET World

Available at bookstores nationwide or from Springer Verlag New York, Inc. at 1-800-777-4643; fax 1-212-533-3503. Contact us for more information at sales@apress.com.

***books for professionals by professionals*™**

apress™

About Apress

Apress, located in Berkeley, CA, is a fast-growing, innovative publishing company devoted to meeting the needs of existing and potential programming professionals. Simply put, the "A" in Apress stands for *"The Author's Press*™*"* and its books have *"The Expert's Voice*™*".* Apress' unique approach to publishing grew out of conversations between its founders Gary Cornell and Dan Appleman, authors of numerous best-selling, highly regarded books for programming professionals. In 1998 they set out to create a publishing company that emphasized quality above all else. Gary and Dan's vision has resulted in the publication of over 50 titles by leading software professionals, all of which have *The Expert's Voice*™.

Do You Have What It Takes to Write for Apress?

Apress is rapidly expanding its publishing program. If you can write and refuse to compromise on the quality of your work, if you believe in doing more than rehashing existing documentation, and if you're looking for opportunities and rewards that go far beyond those offered by traditional publishing houses, we want to hear from you!

Consider these innovations that we offer all of our authors:

- **Top royalties with *no* hidden switch statements**
  Authors typically only receive half of their normal royalty rate on foreign sales. In contrast, Apress' royalty rate remains the same for both foreign and domestic sales.

- **A mechanism for authors to obtain equity in Apress**
  Unlike the software industry, where stock options are essential to motivate and retain software professionals, the publishing industry has adhered to an outdated compensation model based on royalties alone. In the spirit of most software companies, Apress reserves a significant portion of its equity for authors.

- **Serious treatment of the technical review process**
  Each Apress book has a technical reviewing team whose remuneration depends in part on the success of the book since they too receive royalties.

Moreover, through a partnership with Springer-Verlag, New York, Inc., one of the world's major publishing houses, Apress has significant venture capital behind it. Thus, we have the resources to produce the highest quality books *and* market them aggressively.

If you fit the model of the Apress author who can write a book that gives the "professional what he or she needs to know™," then please contact one of our Editorial Directors, Gary Cornell (gary_cornell@apress.com), Dan Appleman (dan_appleman@apress.com), Peter Blackburn (peter_blackburn@apress.com), Jason Gilmore (jason_gilmore@apress.com), Karen Watterson (karen_watterson@apress.com), or John Zukowski (john_zukowski@apress.com) for more information.

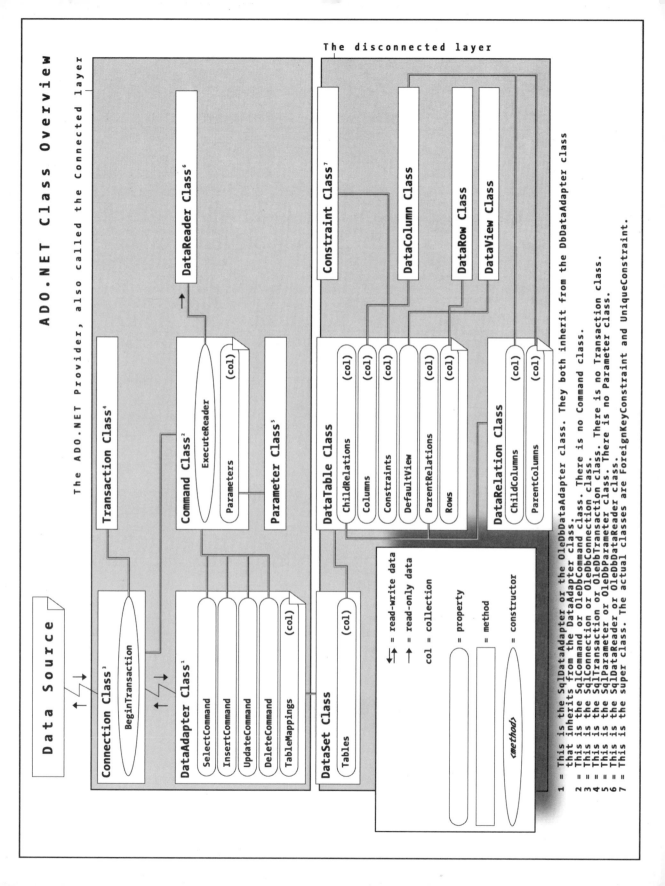

ADO.NET Class Overview

The ADO.NET Provider, also called the Connected layer

The disconnected layer

Data Source

Connection Class [3]
- BeginTransaction

DataAdapter Class [1]
- SelectCommand
- InsertCommand
- UpdateCommand
- DeleteCommand
- TableMappings (col)

DataSet Class
- Tables (col)

Transaction Class [4]

Command Class [2]
- ExecuteReader
- Parameters
- (col)

Parameter Class [5]

DataReader Class [6]

DataTable Class
- ChildRelations (col)
- Columns (col)
- Constraints (col)
- DefaultView
- ParentRelations (col)
- Rows (col)

DataRelation Class
- ChildColumns (col)
- ParentColumns (col)

Constraint Class [7]

DataColumn Class

DataRow Class

DataView Class

Legend:
- ⇄ = read-write data
- → = read-only data
- col = collection
- (oval) = property
- [rectangle] = method
- <method> (oval) = constructor

1 = This is the SqlDataAdapter or the OleDbDataAdapter class. They both inherit from the DbDataAdapter class that inherits from the DataAdapter class.
2 = This is the SqlCommand or OleDbCommand class. There is no Command class.
3 = This is the SqlConnection or OleDbConnection class.
4 = This is the SqlTransaction or OleDbTransaction class. There is no Transaction class.
5 = This is the SqlParameter or OleDbParameter class. There is no Parameter class.
6 = This is the SqlDataReader or OleDbDataReader class.
7 = This is the super class. The actual classes are ForeignKeyConstraint and UniqueConstraint.

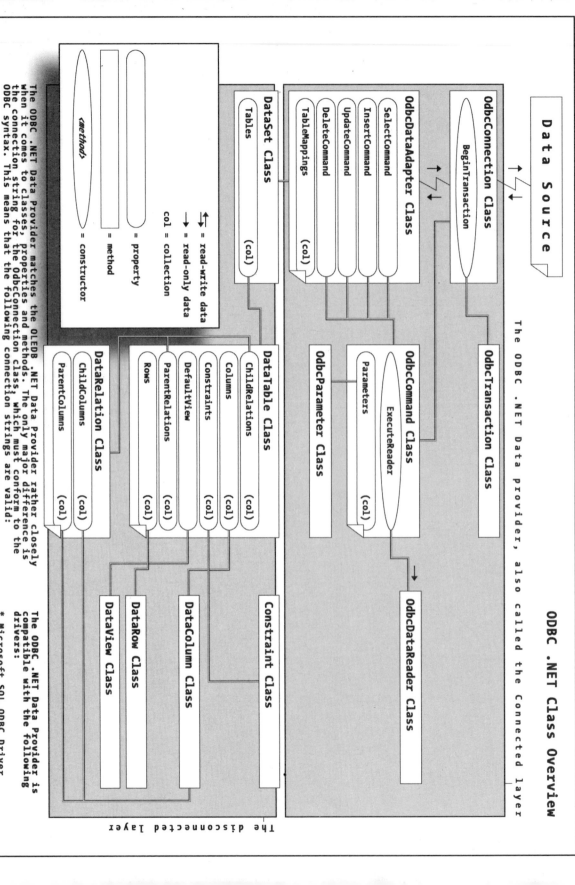